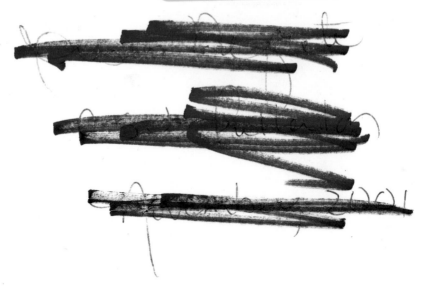

CHRISTMAS IN JULY

Christmas in July

The Life and Art of Preston Sturges

Diane Jacobs

UNIVERSITY OF CALIFORNIA PRESS
Berkeley   *Los Angeles*   *Oxford*

University of California Press
Berkeley and Los Angeles, California

University of California Press
Oxford, England

Copyright © 1992 by The Regents of the University of California

Library of Congress Cataloging-in-Publication Data

Jacobs, Diane.
    Christmas in July : the life and art of Preston Sturges / Diane
Jacobs.
        p.   cm.
    Includes bibliographical references and index.
    ISBN 0-520-07926-4
    1. Sturges, Preston.   2. Motion picture producers and directors—
United States—Biography.   3. Screenwriters—United States—
Biography.   I. Title.
    PN1998.3.S78J3   1992
812'.52—dc20
[B]   92-19690
                                                          CIP

Printed in the United States of America

1 2 3 4 5 6 7 8 9

For Gerry and Masha

That's the wise thrush; he sings each song twice over,
Lest you should think he never could recapture
The first fine careless rapture!

Robert Browning

CONTENTS

ACKNOWLEDGMENTS

My thanks go first and foremost to Sandy Sturges, for her great generosity in granting me access to Preston Sturges's letters, diaries, scripts, and photographs; for countless indispensable discussions, frequently cross-country; and for her warm support throughout the long gestation of this book. Preston and Sandy Sturges's sons, Preston and Tom Sturges, were similarly encouraging; and I am grateful to Louise Sturges for the two long afternoons she spent dredging up often painful memories from the past. During a luncheon in Paris and a long phone conversation, Eleanor Close Barzin and Frances Ramsden, respectively, also vividly recreated for me their years with Sturges.

Special thanks go to the gallant staff at the UCLA Special Collections Library, who were unfailingly helpful during my long tenure, and to Eleanor Tanin at the UCLA Film Archives, who screened for me Sturges's home movies and a beauty pageant at which he officiated as well as many of the thirties films based on Sturges's scripts. At the Museum of Modern Art, Charles Silver, Steve Harvey, and Ron Magliozzi cheerfully granted me multiple screenings of Sturges's movies, while two earlier Sturges chroniclers, Jim Curtis and Jim Harvey, plied me with tapes, shooting scripts, and other treasures of their research. Elizabeth Shaw at Universal and Herbert Nusbaum at MGM made an exception so that I could borrow drafts of Sturges's screenplays, which proved invaluable for my chapters on the thirties and fifties. Thanks also go to Selise Eisman at the Directors Guild, who helped me locate Sturges's former colleagues.

Unless otherwise stipulated, all the photographs come from Sandy Sturges's private collection—yet another kindness on her part. I am grateful too for the stunning portrait of herself which Frances Ramsden sent me, and for Nina Laemmle's photographs of young Gilletti going off to war and of Sturges poring over a script in his study. The lucid reproductions are all the work of

ACKNOWLEDGEMENTS

Vincent Tcholakian at Diana Custom Photographic Laboratories. He is an artist, indeed.

Hoping that I've done some justice to their stories, I offer thanks to the many people who spoke and wrote to me about Sturges: Muriel Angelus, Dr. Shepard G. Aronson, Eddie Bracken, Alida Carey, Cecil E. "Teet" Carle, Claudette Colbert, Ron Durling, Mel Epstein, Judy Feiffer, Edwin Gillette, Irene Haiman, John Huston, Paul Kohner, Robert Kreis, Nina Laemmle, Richard Leacock, Robert Lescher, Joel McCrea, Colleen Moore, Holly Morse, Mary Orr, Budd Schulberg, Herb Sterne, Billy Wilder, Priscilla Woolfan, Tally Wyler, and Rudy Vallee. Special mention must be made of "Teet" Carle who went way beyond the call of duty, writing me letter after informative letter filled with his amazingly vivid recollections of Paramount in the Sturges era.

A grant from the National Endowment for the Humanities allowed me to research this project; a grant from the Camargo Foundation (under the kind stewardship of Michael Pretina) gave me three joyful months to work, like the older Sturges, in French exile, and with a view of the Mediterranean besides. I am grateful to many people who assisted in the preparation of this manuscript: to my agent Howard Morhaim; my forbearing editor Chick Callenback; and also to Beryl Abrams, Betsy Lindley Bird, Lance Bird, Freddy Bush and Dave Gilbert, Joan Cohen, Tom Goldstein, Ann Powell, Rose Schacht, and Judy and Michael Stern, many of whom lent me their Los Angeles houses as well as their expertise. I was touched by the diligence of Al LaValley, who read my final draft three times and whose suggestions proved invaluable. But, more than usual, my greatest indebtedness is to Gerry Rabkin, my most assiduous editor, most demanding critic, greatest supporter, and best friend.

Like so many writers of his generation, Preston Sturges went west in the early thirties to Hollywood. He was in love with the idea of success in America— the promise of romance and fortune and fame—though he had little film experience and no particular attraction to the movies. Nor was he a writer or even an American in any conventional sense. Born in Chicago, he'd spent much of his childhood in Paris with his mother and her best friend, Isadora Duncan; and at thirty-four he was very much a bohemian, with no fixed home or goal in life. He'd been a stage manager, a flier in the Air Service, a songwriter, the manager of his mother's cosmetics firm, and the inventor of a kiss-proof lipstick and a vertical rising airplane—as well as a promising playwright. But while his 1929 *Strictly Dishonorable*—about a girl who exchanges her boring American fiancé for a poetic Italian—was a Broadway hit, his last three plays had failed. His mother had recently died in New York, and his second wife was leaving him. So when Universal Studios offered Sturges $1,000 a week to come to California and write screenplays, he accepted immediately, but with no commitment to stay on.

He did, though, and between 1939 and 1943 at Paramount Pictures he wrote and directed seven of the wittiest and most distinctive comedies Hollywood ever sent out to the world: *The Great McGinty, Christmas in July, The Lady Eve, Sullivan's Travels, The Palm Beach Story, The Miracle of Morgan's Creek,* and *Hail the Conquering Hero.* They were films about wild success which also made Sturges wildly successful. A mid-forties article in *Vogue* observed: "Lubitsch and Hitchcock, each with the stamp of a great personality on his work, are names not half as familiar to the American public [as Preston Sturges]." The familiarity was short-lived. Quarrels with the studios soon followed, then an ill-fated partnership with Howard Hughes, and finally expatriation to France in the early fifties. When he died in New York's Algonquin

Hotel at the end of that decade, Sturges, once the third best-paid man in America, was poor, and remembered mainly by ardent cineasts.

During the ensuing years, Sturges's films have reemerged to an increasingly wider public. This past decade has seen numerous revivals not only of the classic Hollywood comedies, but of the later, no less original *The Sin of Harold Diddlebock* (1946) and *Unfaithfully Yours* (1948). Narratively audacious, his films range from the tale of a scandalously pregnant girl who becomes a celebrity when she gives birth to sextuplets on Christmas (*The Miracle of Morgan's Creek*), to the black ruminations of a famous conductor who grows suspicious of his adored young wife (*Unfaithfully Yours*). And whether set on a luxury liner, on Manhattan's Lower East Side, or in a Midwestern hamlet, they're unmistakably the product of a formidable intelligence—frantically paced, elliptical, formally self-conscious, spewing voluptuous, geographically unrooted language, filled with slapstick and brilliant repartee. For the French theorist André Bazin, they reflected "the deepest moral and social beliefs of American life." [1]

But, true to Sturges's loathing of artistic pretension, they also despise solemnity. "Nothing like a deep-dish movie to drive you out in the open," quips one of Sturges's characters. And while Sturges's movies boast more than their share of wise one-liners, his genius was always for dialogue—for conversation rather than pronouncement. Nor can his protagonists, played by stars like Henry Fonda and Rex Harrison, be disentangled from the flagrant misfits who surround them: a bilious juror (William Demarest) insisting on his democratic prerogatives in *Christmas in July*; a judge (Jimmy Conlin) squeaking an appeal for selflessness in *Hail the Conquering Hero*; a dastardly private eye (Edgar Kennedy) who lives for beautiful music in *Unfaithfully Yours*. Evoked by what came to be known as Sturges's stock company, these eccentrics suggest a society that all but overwhelms the main characters, that seems condemned to remain always in a state of unrelieved agitation though the protagonists move on. However grudgingly (he would have died before embracing *any* artistic movement!), Sturges heeded the modernist admonition, "Make it strange!" The world of his films was never merely mimetic. Yet, if it was not realistically American, it was American, all right, in its plurality, and in its loosing of so many clamorous individual wills.

Influenced by everything from cubism to the Keystone Kops, Sturges's films were, on one level, very much of their time and genres, sharing both Ernst Lubitsch's worldly sophistication and Frank Capra's populist fascination with the American Dream. Yet, Sturges's films were also utterly different. Take their attitude toward money, for instance. While most Depression and wartime comedies went out of their way to portray the "have nots" as no less happy—probably happier—than the "haves," a butler in *Sullivan's Travels* speaks for Sturges when he calls poverty "a virulent plague." And what an unlikely lot the winners are in Sturges's great success stories: a (bad) slogan-writing clerk in *Christmas in July*, an allergy-besieged draft reject in *The Miracle of Morgan's Creek*. They're virtuous, to be sure. Yet, it's always fantastic luck rather than hard work and good deeds which brings Sturges's heroes their penthouses and brides and circuses.

From the start, Sturges's films have perplexed their most fervent admirers. Writing in the forties, James Agee in one breath called Sturges "the most gifted American working in films" and in the next accused him of "a radical lack of love" and a failure to "fully commit" his emotions and intelligence.[2] Similarly, Manny Farber, while deeming Sturges "probably the most spectacular manipulator of sheer humor since Mark Twain," despaired of "a certain thinness in his work."[3] And when they attempted to make sense of an *oeuvre* at once conservative and radical, erudite and anti-intellectual, satiric and sentimental, Agee and Farber inevitably turned to Sturges's tales of his schizophrenic childhood: an "art happy" mother who dragged him through "every goddam museum in Europe" when all he wanted was to be a solid businessman like his Chicago dad.

Biographical criticism runs the risk of reducing art to psychology. And, for me, Agee's and Farber's often brilliant essays on Sturges are diminished not only by a caricatural view of the filmmaker's parents (encouraged by Sturges himself, the deft mythographer) but by a too narrow vision of the relationship between life and art. Yet in approaching Preston Sturges, I was also impelled to go beyond criticism, as well as the strictly expository format followed in the two existing Sturges biographies. I chose to write a critical biography, because I was confident that the man would shed light on the works, and vice versa. Each did, though never in predictable ways.

Fiercely intelligent, given to extremes in love and anger, and passionately alive to experience, Sturges was more vivid than any of the characters he created. Yet, unlike Sir Alfred in *Unfaithfully Yours*, he was not the man to expiate his personal demons through his art. Nor, except in the rare instance, were his narratives explicitly autobiographical. The rich story of Sturges's life is revealed obliquely in his films—in the odd, almost foreigner's view of America, in the violent plot swings and scorn for political solutions, and, most conspicuously, in the many powerful, ebullient, free-spirited women protagonists, who bear little debt to Sturges's own wives and lovers but much to his mother and that other (purported) great nemesis of his youth, Isadora Duncan. Indeed, it is my contention that these two complex women, far more than the upstanding Solomon Sturges, on whom Preston consciously tried to model himself, were the crucial influences on Sturges, the artist *and* the man.

On this point as well as on many others I diverge from the earlier biographers. My canvas is also broader, focusing not only on the famous movies but on the plays and unproduced screenplays and stories. From these lesser-known works I discovered, among other things, that even in the late fifties, when he was poor and drinking heavily, Sturges was still capable of creating at the height of his talent, and that he had every right to view himself as a melodramatist as well as a *farceur*. I have made a point of never putting words in Sturges's mouth, so all the quotes are his. But the conjectures—always presented as such—are my own, for while I was determined to avoid facile psychoanalyzing, I was eager to understand and convey Sturges's state of mind whenever I authentically felt I could. My impression of Sturges has been enhanced by hundreds of conversations with the wonderfully patient Sandy Sturges and generous interviews with two of Sturges's former wives and numerous friends and colleagues. But the one who "spoke" loudest and longest to me was Preston Sturges, through the thousands of letters he wrote to most anyone who ever meant anything to him, from the early twenties until just days before his death. (And this in the telephone era—another sign of his connection to the Old World.) What's more, he saved his correspondence. These fascinating letters—by turns funny, seductive, bitter, euphoric, righteous, and teasing, but always lucid—show his ascent and decline as a public figure, his many fallings in and out of love, his reactions to becoming a husband, a celebrity, a parent. (That Sturges evaded other subjects—notably, every large political question of his time—is in itself revealing.) But, for all the intriguing changes in Sturges's remarkable forty-year adult life, what most strikes the reader is the constancies—a persistence in certain fundamental attitudes and desires and values.

In a discarded prologue for his film *The Great Moment*, Sturges wrote: "Of all things in nature, great men alone reverse the laws of perspective and grow smaller as one approaches them." This is not true in his own case. The closer I came to Sturges through both his life and his *oeuvre*, the larger, if more contradictory, he grew.

Sentimental Education

*The end of the American artist's pilgrimage to Europe
is the discovery of America. That this discovery is un-
intended hardly matters; ever since Columbus it has
been normal to discover America by mistake.*
Leslie Fiedler, *An End to Innocence*

*The real American is not a gold chaser or money lover,
as the legend classes him, but an idealist and a mystic.*
Isadora Duncan, *My Life*

C H A P T E R 1

To the common eye, they could not have seemed a promising pair, this mother and child confronting the cold realities of American life at the turn of the century. The child, a boy, was not yet three years old. The mother was twenty-nine, poor, Irish Catholic, and had just run away from her husband, a boozing debt collector and the father of the boy. Chicago was all she knew of the world. And while she'd been told she had a pretty voice, she had no practical skills or wealthy relatives to fall back on. Two decades before, *her* mother, also around thirty and without a man, had hired herself out as a housekeeper. But Mary decided instead to go to France.

Somehow, she gathered money for the boat and arrived at a railroad hotel in Paris one bitter winter's day. Everything was damp and uninviting. The baby was shivering from his bath. She climbed with him into bed and may even have momentarily wondered at her own audacity. Then, friends from the boat turned up and, overpaying the chambermaid to watch the baby, spirited her off to the Grand Opera ball. What a glorious sight this was, and how in her element she felt. "Oh, la belle Américaine," cried the Frenchmen, vying to dance with her. It was four A.M. before she could drag herself off. The next morning, the baby was feverish, but she pushed on. Looking for permanent rooms, she met a Mrs. Duncan, who rushed her to a studio on avenue de Villiers to meet her daughter Isadora, who was just now captivating Paris with her radical notions about dance. "Had I been ushered into Paradise and given over to my guardian angel, I could not have been more uplifted," she would recall.[1]

This woman was Mary Desti, or d'Este as she was calling herself at the time, insisting on a kinship with Italian aristocrats. Her given name, Dempsey, seemed not to suit who she *really* was. Her actual heritage was also somewhat dreary, so she frequently improved upon it in tales in which the facts are difficult to decipher. Her parents were Dominic and Catherine Dempsey, Irish Catholics who settled in Quebec and bore six children. Mary arrived in the world with part of the amniotic sac still clinging to her head. "Caul" is the name for this shroud on a newborn. Irish folklore considers the caul a portent of great good luck, and Mary, claiming that it extended to the next generation as well, would invoke the caul to explain her son's blessings and triumphs. It also, she felt, explained the difference between herself and the rest of the Dempsey clan—Dominic, a drunk and womanizer, who died of consumption at thirty-six; and Catherine, the long-suffering wife and mother, who moved her brood to Chicago and took a job as a housekeeper in a church to support the family. Pious and good-hearted, Catherine was very much a person of her class and times—as were Mary's sisters, brothers, and cousins, all of whom wound up, perfectly satisfied, in convents or conventional Midwestern marriages, while Mary roamed the world and "was never contented with anyone."[2] Mary told a story about how early on she renounced Catholicism. As a child, she said, she discovered her beloved mother reduced to washing church floors and blamed the diocese, giving up religion then and there. Like so many of her tales, this is true at least in spirit—for Mary was never a practicing Catholic. She was, however, enduringly fascinated by faith in every form and deeply superstitious.

It may have been in her teens that Mary conceived of aligning herself with the romantic-sounding d'Estes. She clung to their name until 1912 when the Italians discovered she was calling her new Paris cosmetics firm the Maison d'Este and threatened to sue. Though no doubt piqued, Mary at this point changed both the firm's name and her own to Desti—a more fitting signature, anyhow, for it was exclusively hers.

And whatever one thought of Mary Desti, she was original. Many described her as beautiful. "La belle Américaine," the Frenchmen called her, at the Grand Opera ball. She would continue to enchant people of all nationalities over the next thirty years, though her physical attributes were not extraordinary—curly black hair, a full, pretty face, a body forever struggling with plumpness. Dark, penetrating eyes were her most striking asset, and she had an air of intelligence; but what—by all accounts—distinguished her was charm. She had the mysterious capacity to attract ardent love and friendship, and she loved deeply in return, though she was also restless and fickle and selfish.

That first morning in Paris, for instance, Mary raced off to meet Isadora, though her child was growing increasingly sick. All his short life Preston had been prone to respiratory disease. Now pneumonia settled in his lungs. His

Mary Desti.

temperature rose. Doctors were consulted, but to no avail. Mary was beside herself with fear when Isadora Duncan's mother arrived with a bottle of champagne and proceeded to feed the delirious child the sparkling wine by the spoonful. Thus, claims Mary in her book about life with Isadora, *The Untold Story*, Preston was saved.

But, champagne notwithstanding, Preston from the start had reason to resent the Duncans, who were forever distracting his mother's attention away from him. Indeed, no sooner was he well than Preston was trundled off with Mrs. Duncan to the nearby village of Giverny so that Mary could spend more time with her fascinating new friend. It was the height of the "belle époque" in Paris, and Isadora Duncan, performing at salons and in her own Montparnasse studio, was making a name among the French avant-garde. Roger Shattuck, the chronicler of the art of the "banquet years," writes of its childish gaiety, scorn of convention, its infatuation with popular culture and its "full aliveness to the present moment."[3] Isadora's lyrical dance particularly embodied this "aliveness." Like Oscar Wilde, she also cast her life as a work of art. She scorned thrift and lived recklessly.

Mary, still chafing from domesticity in Chicago, must have been deeply impressed by this impulsive creature who spoke of fidelity to the classic spirit while creating a dance of the future, who despised mechanical exercise, yet was committed to rigorous technique. Mary had no doubt that Isadora was a genius. And, though she said she had come to Europe to study voice and pursue a career in singing, it's doubtful she ever viewed Isadora as a personal model. It was her son she hoped would follow in the great artist's footsteps. Mary's own relationship with Isadora was a girlish one, replete with wild spending sprees and giggling about lovers. If Mary was drawn to Isadora's dedication and rebelliousness, Isadora was no less charmed by Mary's mischievousness, wit, and style. Theirs was an equal relationship, and they became instant best friends.

And, with Preston off in Giverny, Mary was free to enjoy the expatriate life: to wander the streets of Paris, sit in the cafés, go to balls and theatres, and flirt with handsome foreigners. In her *The Untold Story*, she speaks of immersing herself in acting and singing classes. But more persuasive are her accounts of meeting interesting and famous people at Isadora's recitals: the actor Monet-Sully, the painter Eugène Carrière. Some Sundays, Carrière would invite her to join his children on tours through the Louvre, where he spoke eloquently about the works of the great masters and afterwards brought her home to lunch. Other times, on weekends, she and Isadora visited Giverny where they stayed at a beautiful small inn, socialized with the great painter Claude Monet, and basked in the local pleasures. For Mary, eating was a particularly sensual experience. Thus she describes a typical breakfast at the inn: "Steaming hot chocolate in bowls, not cups, with great slices of peasant bread and a big pot of homemade jam. How we loved it and how happy we were!"[4]

Mary also speaks of an "allowance" of $150 (no mean sum in those days) which arrived on the first of every month for nearly a year, at which point she and Isadora would move from the dancer's Montparnasse studio to "the Hotel Marguerite or some other hotel and feast for as many days as our money lasted," then scrounge until the next check arrived. Planning for the future was not their forte; in truth, they looked down on savings accounts and insurance policies as the needs of lesser souls. Isadora got some of her ideas from reading Nietzsche; Mary, though not much of a reader, also knew she was among the world's elite; other people's rules simply did not apply to her. She was entitled to do as she pleased.

Still, this allowance is puzzling. Money, as a force in the world and as a foil for character, would become important in Preston's work, so it's a shame his mother never mentions the name of her benefactor. It's hard to imagine that anyone in Mary's Chicago world could have afforded such an endowment. And what was the motive? All Mary says is that her trip to Paris was cut short because "my mother called me home." So perhaps workaday Mrs. Dempsey was the first to indulge and then grow weary of her daughter's destiny.

Once home in Chicago, Mary Desti married a man who, but for her, might never have heard the name Isadora Duncan. She and Solomon Sturges eloped in Memphis, Tennessee on October 2, 1901. "A childhood sweetheart," Mary calls Solomon, though it's hard to imagine where their childhoods would have crossed. The story of their courtship is sketchy, but their rush to marry suggests—on the groom's part at least—behavior as passionately aberrant as Harold Lloyd's in *The Sin of Harold Diddlebock*. Preston suspected that the Sturgeses saw it as a tawdry affair, with "Solomon disappearing from Chicago for a week and coming back with a wife and child."[5] For Mary, intoxicated with Paris and the bohemian life, this marriage may well have been a compromise. Solomon was thirty-seven at the time and a confirmed Midwesterner, she was thirty and nothing of the sort. Four months after their marriage, Solomon, who was childless, officially adopted Preston. Now, there were three branches in Preston's family tree.

Preston's biological father, after whom he was named—Edmund Preston Biden—was Edmund C. Biden. "A disastrous runaway marriage"[6] is how Mary describes their relationship. Though the "runaway" part is doubtful, the marriage—probably not her first—was unhappy and brief. Preston's birth, on August 29, 1898, was its high point. At that time, Biden, who frequently changed jobs, was working for a collection agency. At home, he was a short fuse. There were "rousing fights that brought all the neighbors in."[7] Biden kept a gun. Once he fired a bullet at the ceiling of their Chicago apartment, and it soared through the toes of a man brushing his teeth on the floor above.

Or so Preston heard the tale from Mary. Preston's own recollections of Biden were that he was feckless and mean spirited. He stood five foot seven, with his hair parted in the middle, and had a knack for playing the banjo. Biden claimed he saved Preston's life, the year he was born, by overriding Mary's objections and paying $500 for a throat operation. After he and Mary separated, Biden kidnapped Preston—maybe out of love, or maybe just to torment his wife. Whichever, he returned Preston the same night and seems to have made no protest when Solomon Sturges asked to adopt him.

Preston and Biden met, acrimoniously, for the last time in their lives in 1914, after which the father made no attempt to contact his son until Preston was thirty-one and wrote *Strictly Dishonorable*. Then, Biden wrote to Preston asking for money, and Preston turned him down. Biden wrote a letter Preston described as "sadistically imaginative," expressing joy at Mary Desti's death.[8] When he read of his son's engagement to the heiress Eleanor Hutton, Biden threatened to reveal Preston's "true" identity. Preston, for whom it was a point of honor never to make a secret of his origins, advised his father to go right ahead.

Preston told his third wife Louise that he considered Solomon Sturges his father, "partly by adoption and completely by love and devotion."[9] And this was true, though it is also true that he believed deeply in the importance of heredity. He would be a devoted nephew to his father's brother, Sidney Biden, who was a *lieder* singer in Berlin during Preston's childhood; and, late in life, Preston would take a great interest in his half-brother, Edmund Biden's son by another wife (and also named Edmund Biden!). So Preston's ties to the Bidens were significant. As with the Dempseys, he knew little of his Biden forbears, who were either German or English and had settled for a while in Rochester before moving west. They were patriots with a flair for battle; and their marriages were turbulent as well, the men being overly fond of drink, women, and music. Preston remembers his grandmother Biden as a wonderful cook and "confirmed grouser." She was a boisterous, capable woman who sent her husband packing because he drank too much and who managed to get a teaching degree while raising two small boys on her own. When Preston was a child, Grandmother Biden brought him lovely presents. Grandfather Biden, a scalawag, once sold Mary acres of Oregon apple lands for his grandson on which, it turned out, there was no fruit.

What the Bidens and Dempseys shared, with each other and with the many matriarchies in Preston's films, were committedly domestic women making the best of limited means. Their men were shiftless if often charming, perfectly fine fellows by their own lights. Edmund Biden excepted, there wasn't a villain among them, but they scarcely reflected the male virtues Preston held most admirable: honor, wealth, superior intelligence, power in the world. These traits Preston associated with his adopted father's family. And, unlike the Bidens and Dempseys, the Sturgeses left behind an oral history describing their accomplishments in detail.[10] Thus, Preston could boast that his father's ancestors were blue-blooded Anglo-Saxons, among the first settlers of Fairfield, Connecticut, whose motto was "Esse Quam Videri" (To be, not to seem to be). This, said Preston, fit them "like a glove"; and Solomon was a favorite name.

The entrepreneurial spirit was strong in the Sturges men. They were patriotic, intelligent, and temperamental, while their women were fertile and, like the Dempseys and Bidens, resourceful and energetic.[11] A picture of Preston's great grandfather shows a fierce-looking man with a long, stern face, pinched jaw, and small, fiery eyes: someone to be reckoned with. He too was named Solomon, and he married Lucy Hale and moved west from Fairfield, first to Putnam, Ohio and then to Chicago. Here Solomon bought an entire half block of the city's finest land and made a fortune storing grain for the Illinois Central Railroad. Not trusting Midwestern banks, Solomon founded his own and, at the outbreak of the Civil War, he raised his private troop of union volunteers, called, of all things, "The Sturges Rifles."[12]

"The country has had few men of greater financial ability than Mr. Sturges," the elder Solomon was eulogized in a local newspaper. "Eminently was he the architect of his own fortune. . . . If in any case there was a spice of romance in his plans, the instances were few considering his quick and excitable temperament, and may be pardoned for the lofty ideal which floated in his imagination."[13] In this depiction of his great grandfather lies a key to Preston's powerful attraction to the Sturges ethos. To be the architect of one's fortune— what a triumph this must have seemed to Mary Desti's son, ever at the whim of his mother's moods, superstitions, and equivocal social position. And if the means to such a "lofty ideal" was business, well, so be it. But it's also worth noting that even great grandfather Solomon had his romantic schemes and eccentricities. The Sturgeses were distinguished, but not predictable.

Albert, Preston's grandfather, also was a gifted businessman. With his brother Buckingham, Albert founded a banking house and then the Leavenworth, Lawrence, and Galveston Railroad. Trains were in the Sturges blood. But Albert, too, had an eccentric side. Late in life he abandoned Chicago to develop a mine in Sonora, Mexico. He stayed away for years at a time, returning only "to visit" his wife and fifteen children. The seventh of these, Preston's father Solomon, was considerably more conservative and less prolific. Solo-

Solomon Sturges.

mon went east to MIT and then returned to Chicago where he entered a comfortable and decidedly unglamorous stock brokerage career from which he never deviated.

Preston used words like tall, honorable, strong, straightforward, and "popular with men" to describe Solomon's attributes. He was a bicycle champion of

Illinois and played football in his youth. He was very gentle, a point Preston stressed, and when Preston was young Solomon brought him a new present nightly; Preston would try to remember to do the same for his youngest sons. Solomon's head was bald on top, it was wonderful to kiss him there, and his scent was a delicious mixture of maleness and the best Havana cigars.[14] In a rare surviving picture, Solomon's aging face is considerably less angular and more ironic than his grandfather Solomon's. Still, he must have inherited a streak of the old man's impetuousness, for, whatever else it was and would become, his marriage to Mary Desti was an imaginative leap.

Was it also, at the start, happy? This is more difficult to discern. Most of Preston's romantic comedies stop at the altar, and the memorable parents in his films—J. B. Ball in *Easy Living*, Colonel Harrington in *The Lady Eve*, Constable Kockenlocker in *The Miracle of Morgan's Creek*, Mrs. Truesmith in *Hail the Conquering Hero*—are temporarily or permanently without spouses. Nor does Mary write about the years between her wedding in 1901 and her Berlin reunion with Isadora in 1904. She calls Solomon "the kindest, truest friend a woman ever had," but these are the words of an ex-wife, not a wife. Preston, writing half a century later and with his own experience of domesticity, would remember his mother as somewhat disgruntled by her life with Solomon.

There was, for instance, the time when Mary complained to Solomon that, in Chicago, "if Mrs. Potter Palmer, the acknowledged queen of society, started the season off with Duck Bigarde . . . you never got anything but Duck Bigarde wherever you went for the rest of the whole goddam season. . . ."[15] And there was the night when his mother emerged from a fashionable party, suspecting the hostess had been "a little cool" toward her. "You mean Mrs. Van Ingen?" inquired her husband, and Mary said she supposed that was her name. "I can't imagine," said Solomon, "unless it was because you called her Mrs. Finnegan during the whole evening."[16] So in their son's memory, Solomon is the bemused and tolerant Chicago gentleman, Mary the cosmopolitan stuck in the provinces. Preston insists that Mary was good-hearted and never hurt anyone *intentionally*, and, as with Isadora, this seems to be true. Certainly, too, she enjoyed the trappings of wealth, the jaunts *en luxe* to the opera and the respect that her husband's position—as partner first with the firm of Alfred L. Baker and then with Noyes & Jackson—won her with the jewelers and the dressmakers—albeit of Chicago.

Doubtless, she was less enamored of the family occasions Preston describes: visits by Grandmother Biden with her endless presents; Sunday outings to the old wooden house of Solomon's cousin Kate and her father, Ebenezer Buckingham, who was then blind and wore green eyeshades. A frustration of his childhood, Preston recalls, was Aunt Kate's never coming through on her promise to dance the jig. And a signal event was a 1903 visit to his parents' friends the Morrises in Green Lake, Wisconsin. There in a large tent, at a birthday party for one of the Morris children, Preston saw *The Great Train Robbery*—his first movie.[17]

Mary Desti's opinions notwithstanding, turn of the century Chicago was in many respects an exciting place. By 1890, it spread over 181 square miles and was geographically the largest city in the country. Crucially located, with a large railroad and booming port, it was a natural center of industry, and its population was second only to New York's.[18] In *Newspaper Days*, Theodore Dreiser describes the Chicago of his youth as "a city which had no traditions but was making them." Three decades after the great fire, the skyscrapers of Louis Sullivan and the prairie houses of Frank Lloyd Wright were establishing Chicago as the seat of modern architecture; its newspapers (and later Margaret Anderson's *Little Review*) were developing the Midwestern voices of Dreiser himself, Ben Hecht, and Sherwood Anderson. Flat and intemperate and graced by a Great Lake, Chicago was a city of contrasts and excesses. It was home to the nation's yellowest journalism, most graft-riddled politics, most egregiously corrupt meat-packing industry; and also to a fervid anarchist movement and the burgeoning IWW. It had hosted a splendid World's Fair, which celebrated its authority as gateway to both the west's possibility and the east's culture. For the generation before Hemingway and Dos Passos and Hollywood, it was frequently an imaginative end in itself.

Just as he both treasured *and* never felt altogether deserving of his father's name because "'Sturges' was not mine by rights but had been *given* to me,"[19] so Preston's feelings for Chicago were more and less than that of the native son. Chicago was where he lived on and off for seven years in a comfortable house in fashionable Glencoe, where he attended Dr. Coulter's Harvard School, ate club sandwiches, and rode the retired polo pony his sportsman father bought him. But it was also "the city of my dreams," embodying "the magical attributes of wealth, security, gaiety and good food."[20] It was to Chicago (and his father) that Preston would flee when his first wife declared she no longer loved him; it was in Chicago that he would write his first and only hit play; and in the late forties, it was a Chicago—rather than a New York or Boston—specialist whom Preston would turn to when his lung was diagnosed as cancerous by a Los Angeles physician.

In 1958, guilty and fearful about his eldest son's future, Preston wrote the boy: "I wish to God old Solomon Sturges were alive—because there was a port to go to in a storm—*there* was a man one could depend on *never* to let you down."[21] Mary Desti, who throughout her life relied on both Solomon's affection and his financial support, would surely have agreed with her son. But Solomon seems to have inspired a similar confidence in far more distant relations. Preston's ex-wives, Estelle and Eleanor, also sought his advice; the normally reticent Estelle imploring Solomon : "God bless you and please keep on loving me, it is the one dependable thing in my life which gives me a sense of security."[22]

Mary took off for her second trip to Europe in 1904, buoyed by the sense of security Solomon had inspired. How composed she must have seemed in contrast to the impetuous divorcée of three years earlier! Now she was dressed in Chicago's finest, sailing first class, waving her curly black head and her six-year-old son's hand at a distinguished young man who was both her husband and a bastion of Chicago society. Yet, like Mary in *Easy Living*, Mary Desti was fundamentally unchanged by her good fortune. "There's nothing the matter with one that a little money won't cure," she would frequently quip to Preston. But she also, and more meaningfully, told him that there were intangibles which were of far greater value than material wealth.[23] Nor is there reason to suspect that Mary's leaving for Europe three years after her marriage to Solomon Sturges was precipitated by anything more dramatic than *her* perpetual yearning to be abroad and *his* ability to understand and underwrite such a voyage.

Probably, Solomon accompanied Mary and Preston as far as New York on the Twentieth Century. Some of Preston's fondest childhood memories are of this train—its stately porters crooning out the stops, the dining car waiters balancing their trays, the dark green curtains wrapped around the berths. Preston was always permitted the upper berth, and he would peek over the top of the curtain or swing down it to pay his parents a visit. Most of all, he loved sitting out on the observation platform, watching the wheels of the train click against the rails, disappearing behind. In New York, the Sturgeses stayed at the Wolcott Hotel and, before or after *one* of their trips, Preston remembers being taken by Solomon to see Buffalo Bill and his Wonderful Wild West Show at the old Madison Square Garden.

This time Mary headed straight for Berlin. Here Isadora, by now a famous dancer, was performing to great acclaim. Isadora was also recovering from a first serious love affair and contemplating founding a school to train young dancers in her theory of movement. She was not a person to do things by halves or to slavishly follow a single goal. In words very like those Preston would use to defend his own life choices, Isadora wrote in her autobiography,

"I was never able to understand . . . why if one wanted to do a thing one should not do it. For I have never waited to do as I wished. This has frequently brought me to disaster and calamity, but at least I have had the satisfaction of getting my own way." [24]

Though delighted to see Mary, Isadora was just now preparing to leave for the Wagner summer festival at Bayreuth; Cosima Wagner had commissioned her to dance the first Grace in the Bacchanal of *Tannhäuser*. Isadora invited Mary to accompany her, and also to abandon her "bourgeois" attire for the flowing Greek robes, gold sandals, and ribboned coiffure that were Isadora's trademark. To both requests Mary happily acceded, and a contemporary journal describes the two inseparable American women parading about town, classically coiffed and in their tunics, as a "peculiar feature" of Bayreuth 1904.[25] Isadora's biographer, Fredrika Blair, interprets Mary's readiness to follow Isadora's sartorial lead as the sign of an impressionable nature.[26] Perhaps, but it must also be noted that—having survived the influence of two strong husbands—Mary Desti was *selectively* impressionable.

At Bayreuth, Mary shared a cottage with Isadora and sent Preston to a nearby inn with a governess and Isadora's niece, Temple.[27] This separation was equally satisfactory to mother and son, for while Mary basked vicariously in Isadora's romantic conquests, Preston got to spend all the time he wanted with Temple Duncan, "a few months older than I and my first and desperate sweetheart."[28] Preston was a strikingly handsome boy, tall for his age, with wavy dark hair and his mother's penetrating eyes. He would spend that summer, and many years after, courting pretty Temple with perfumed soaps. Even at six, Preston's love was ardent and romantic, for that was his nature, and Temple was wise to demand her perfumed soaps because he never enjoyed an easy conquest. Both children wore small Duncan-style tunics, Preston's dark and Temple's white. Doubtless they attended several performances of *Tannhäuser*, which Preston, ever at odds with his mother's cultural agenda, must have loudly regretted at the time. He would choose *Tannhäuser*'s Overture for the forgiving sequence in *Unfaithfully Yours* some forty years later. The children were trotted out to meet visiting musical and literary celebrities and also given free run of the grounds. One day, while Preston and Temple played in the ruins of a Roman theatre, Richard Wagner's grandson snuck up and struck Preston a blow from behind. Temple swiftly felled and then sat on top of the future august music producer, tugging his long yellow hair while five-year-old Preston beat him up.[29]

It was during their summer at Bayreuth, Mary claims in *The Untold Story*, that Isadora threw the fit of jealousy that put an end to Mary's own theatrical aspirations. Isadora, wanting some distance on the *Tannhäuser* production, had asked Mary to dance her role in rehearsal. Mary gladly agreed and, when she finished dancing the Grace, had the satisfaction of overhearing Cosima Wagner exclaim, "But how she resembles you!" to Isadora. This did not please the great dancer, who leapt on stage and accused Mary of deliberately mocking her, then demanded that her friend vow never to perform again. Though Isadora quickly forgot her pique, Mary held to her promise—friendship, presumably, being more important than career. The incident may well have occurred, for Isadora, while essentially generous, was known to resent the success of her followers. Still, Mary, with her high standards for achievement, lacked discipline and, possibly, even talent. This clash with Isadora may have proved just the excuse she needed to pass the torch on to her son.

For it must have been around this time that Mary decided that her son should become an artist, and not just any sort of artist, but a genius, like Isadora Duncan and Gordon Craig. Gordon Craig, soon to become Isadora's lover, was the illegitimate son of the actress Ellen Terry and a passionate theatre rebel, best known for his radical stage designs. Like Isadora with dance, Craig wanted nothing less than a revolutionary transformation of theatre. More than Isadora, Craig was an obsessive who, often penniless and constantly in and out of love, flaunted his scorn for the bourgeois code. From Preston's earliest memories, this man, who abandoned wives and sired illegitimate children, was held up as someone for him to emulate. But Preston recoiled, both from Craig personally and from the romantic idea that genius excuses everything. At Bayreuth, for instance, Preston must have longed for his trustworthy father—these artists were so involved with themselves. A child could never really feel safe with them.

Indeed, at the end of his summer at Bayreuth, by *both* Isadora's and Mary's account, Preston for the second time had a brush with death. On a holiday from Bayreuth, Mary, traveling with Isadora and her then lover Oscar Beregi, deposited Preston, Temple, and their governess in a "flimsy" hotel on a tiny bathing island off the coast of Helgoland in northern Germany. Promising to be back soon, the adults proceeded on to Helgoland and a gay farewell dinner for Beregi. After dinner, a great storm came up. The children were in grave danger because, Mary and Isadora were informed, their hotel and indeed the entire tiny island was unlikely to withstand such wind and waves. Fishermen, declaring, "No one could live in such a sea," refused to boat them to the children. But lifeguards were prevailed upon, and, not a moment too soon, Preston, Temple, and the governess were plucked from the lurching island and delivered, with fanfare, to Helgoland. Here they were fed hot tea and dollops of whisky and—good luck and maternal ardor once again trium-phant—ushered safely off to bed.

From Germany, the entourage traveled on to Venice. Here, waiting for Solomon Sturges to join them, Preston, with his delicate respiratory system, caught what would become a yearly bronchial infection. Mary, in Italy for the first time, was predictably captivated by her surroundings. Solomon Sturges, we can presume, was less so because no sooner had he arrived and put Isadora on a train for Berlin than he was anxious to be off to Paris. In *The Big Pond*, Preston's first screenplay, a wealthy American couple violently disagrees on the subject of Venice, she extolling its every clichéd virtue, he assuring her it's a "swamp." Caricatures allowing, these were surely the opinions of the re-spective Sturgeses. Solomon was surprised to find his son and wife in tunics, and Mary insisted she'd never wear anything else, even in Chicago in the winter. But her resolution did not last long, for "my dear kind husband told me I had 'carte blanche' in Paris to buy what I liked if I would only be good enough to confine my Grecian clothes and sandals to the house," she wrote.[30] The tunics went.

One of Sturges's most quotable lines is the bit of wisdom Barbara Stanwyck tosses Henry Fonda in *The Lady Eve*: "You know, good girls aren't half as good as you think, and bad girls aren't as bad, not half as bad." The homage is unmistakenly to Preston's unconventional mother. Yet, Mary was not altogether the renegade. It was she, after all, who informed Preston that "women are absolutely stymied without a man . . . they can't go *anywhere* or do *anything*."[1] Marriage was the necessary, if not the ideal state for Mary, who was rarely out of it for long. And though her spirit was free, her code was always the bourgeois code. She never left the fold.

In this she was as Victorian as was Solomon Sturges, and surely they had hopes their marriage of strong opposite temperaments would endure. Mary writes that, after the Bayreuth summer, she did not see Isadora for "several years."[2] So she made an effort to limit her travels, while Solomon came to a larger understanding of domestic life. His wife, he must have seen, was never going to bear him children or be the hostess his background and position demanded. He made his peace with that and even encouraged her in his fashion. Preston remembers Solomon's backing a Chicago production of Mary's play *The Law*.[3] The quality of the play, Preston would coyly observe, was not for him to judge, but the event was splendid. Solomon gallantly pledged the ticket sales to Chicago's Women's And Children's Convalescent Home. The noted impresario Donald Richardson was brought in to direct, and the opening was scheduled for a summer's night in Ravinia Park. Just before curtain time, Preston disappeared. He was found out front opening carriage doors and bowing from the waist like a little German prince, while he inquired, "How do you do! You have probably come to see my mother's play. . . . I hope you will enjoy it!"[4]

But despite its happier moments and deep affection on both sides, the marriage would not endure. Years later, Solomon wrote his son: "Right here I want to tell you, Preston, that when a wife wants to get away from you the best thing for all concerned is to let her have her way. She will never be happy living with you, as you will always suspect her, and it will affect your mind and render you useless. I cannot tell you how badly I felt for years about your mother leaving me because I was foolish enough to feel I had done nothing to deserve it."[5]

Preston's recollection of his parents' break-up is that one night in 1907, Mary and Solomon wandered out into their garden, and here a "terrible row" ensued. The issue was Mary's traveling—she and Preston were just back from some too long trip, and Solomon was fed up. Mary must have countered that she also was fed up—with Chicago and the omnipresent Duck Bigarde. And, presently, they went upstairs and woke their son to inform him that they'd decided to separate. Solomon was weaving from his cocktails; Mary very sweetly inquired, "Mother is going to live in Paris, darling, and Father is going to stay here in Chicago. What do you want to do?" Without hesitating, Preston replied that he wanted to stay with his father, and to this Solomon replied, "I am not your father."

"I looked at him in stupefaction for a moment, then at my mother to see if he was joking, then back at Father. Then I started to cry. . . . I cried . . . long enough to sober Father up, wake up the servants . . . and get [Mother] crying too. . . . Father went downstairs to a glass case he had, and one by one, trying to get me to stop, gave me all the trophies, medals, cups and everything else he had ever won. . . . The one I liked the best was a high bicycle made of gold with a sapphire in the hub of the big wheel and a diamond in the little wheel in back. This was an idiotic thing to give a small boy. . . . I naturally lost it a few days later . . . but I think that night he thought I was going to die of grief."[6]

This story Preston told in various forms to scores of show business reporters over the years. Its literal truth is impossible to determine, and even its poetic truth is suspect. For what father who hopes to win custody of his child reveals that he is *not* the child's father at a moment like this? And offers athletic medals rather than promises of undying love? Preston's protests notwithstanding, Solomon emerges as somewhat less than a perfectly devoted father. And yet Solomon's behavior is not really the point of Preston's tale. The crucial point for Preston is not what Solomon did or did not do, but that Solomon *was* not his father and thus was powerless to keep him from Mary and Paris. His fate was sealed.

There's an irony to this, for literal parentage is not something Preston Sturges's films set great store by. In every major Sturges work the protagonist's same sex parent is either dead or, as in his own case, out of the picture, with no noticeable harm to anyone. Frequently, as in *The Miracle of Morgan's Creek*, a surrogate parent is shown to be by far the better bet. "Of course," Preston concludes, "[Solomon] became my father very soon again. More accurately, he had never ceased being my father. Pagnol expressed it better than anyone in *Fanny*. . . . The father, he said, is not the one who gives life . . . dogs give life. . . . The father is the one who gives love."

Indeed, Preston might well have wished that Solomon, rather than showering him with athletic medals, had made him a speech like Marcel Pagnol's, but Solomon did not. He said, I am not your father. And furthermore, with money as no obstacle, he neither visited Preston in Europe nor called him back to Chicago in the crucial adolescent years ahead. In Solomon's defense, it must be said that he was in the process of losing his wife, and though a reasonable man, he was not reasonable about her. "I did not see my father for many years," writes Preston, "but we never stopped loving each other." This is undoubtedly true. But theirs was a romantic devotion, defined by long absences. Just as Isadora was, in Mary's mind, all that Chicago was not, Solomon was Preston's alternative to Mary, Isadora, and Paris. And it might be that Preston's much-vaunted ambition to grow up and become a businessman like his father was no less a matter of perverse and quixotic yearnings than was his mother's determination that he should not.

There's some question as to exactly when Mary and Preston landed in Paris. They arrived at the Wolcott Hotel in New York only to learn that Solomon, in their absence, had been thrown forty feet in the air and rendered unconscious in an automobile accident. Mary hurried back to Chicago, and the move was postponed so she could nurse Solomon back to health. Preston's account of this incident shows Mary far more loyal and scrupulous than the Sturges family ever imagined her,[7] while Solomon emerges as the victim rather than the perpetrator of emotional confusion. "It was about this time," Preston writes, "that [Father] began to get sad things and funny things mixed up. . . . When finally he was well enough to go for a walk, he took me with him into Lincoln Park. . . . Suddenly something made him laugh very hard. . . and then he threw his very heavy ivory handled cane at me. . . . It just missed my head and I was terribly frightened because I loved him so much and was so sure of his love for me . . . and I am sure he didn't mean me any harm. . . . He had a very bad concussion and fracture of the skull and his emotions still got badly mixed up for two or three years and slightly mixed up for the rest of his life."[8]

By 1908, Mary and Preston were verifiably settled in Paris at 10 rue Octave

10 rue Octave Feuillet, Mary Desti's first apartment house in Paris. (Author's photograph)

Feuillet. Irma Duncan,[9] one of the pupils in Isadora's dancing school, remembers spending a night in their "tiny, three-room apartment" at that time. Isadora was then on tour in America and concerned about the well-being of her dancing school. So Mary drove forty miles from Paris to Montparnasse to inspect it. Mary brought a photographer with her, and they clumped the school's dozen girl students, in their matching Polish coats and pillbox hats, around her spanking 1908 limousine. The idea was to have a cheerful picture for Isadora, but the photograph—with Preston barely discernible in the back seat—is a triumph of Mary's personal mythmaking as well. It displays a world of order and amusement, and the childrens' sandals, jutting out from under white wool coats, add a touch of piquancy, as does Mary's beautiful automobile. Mary's car, Irma Duncan wryly comments, had "more polished brass trim than room to sit in." She had a similar opinion of its owner: "A gay rather frivolous woman who liked to laugh at everything and was constitutionally unable to take anything seriously."[10] Irma's verdict (echoed in many accounts of the era) is severely one-sided. Yet, there *was* about Mary a willful frivolousness that made her unpredictable and difficult to rely on. The photograph of the girls against the car, for instance, was arranged for the "serious" purpose of reassuring Isadora that her pupils were happy and well. But they were not. They were neglected and abysmally fed, living not in a chateau, as Isadora supposed, but in the mice-ridden grooms' quarters of a stable.[11] That Mary chose the white lie of a pretty picture over alarming Isadora or troubling to improve matters herself speaks volumes on the nature of Preston's childhood and the strengths he must have summoned to survive it—and Mary.

Preston's European childhood began in 1908 on the rue Octave Feuillet in the sixteenth arrondissement and ended, on the eve of the First World War, in a Swiss boarding school. This short time saw the arrival of Stravinsky, Cubism, and cinema for the masses. For Preston, there were many changes in personal fortune and situation as well: His mother married once and switched "suitors" often. She opened a business, traveled constantly, though not extensively, and frequently changed apartments, being careful always to remain in the thick of the city because a central location, preferably with a room at the top, was something she believed in. She also, of course, believed in the arts, and Preston chafed at being sent to nap, rather than to play, in the afternoon so he would be fresh for the Odéon or the Opéra at night. Mary believed in pleasure, she *and* Preston took the Frenchman's pleasure in food at every level. Among their favorite spots were La Rue's, Foyot's, La Coupole, Prunier's for shellfish, Le Clou for its shadow plays. Mary believed in formal education to a point, and Preston was exposed to a number of very different schools, none of which made much of an impression on him.

The first was La Petite École, the lower school of Paris's Lycée Janson de Sailly, which he described as "this huge, grim academy, with its thousands of pupils." Presumably, Mary Desti wanted her privacy that year because Preston was registered as a boarding student. He quickly established an aversion to the violin and was so indifferent to his studies that he needed special tutoring to pass into the next grade. He won a first prize in drawing, however. And the following year, when Mary moved to the avenue Elisée Reclus with "a handsome young French actor," Jacques Gretillat, Preston was allowed to live at home with them. Jacques Gretillat was fourteen years younger than Mary and—even she had to admit—not especially talented, but a sweet-natured man who enjoyed good food and liked her plucky, worldly little boy. The worldliness, he must have seen, was mostly bluff, was mostly a manner Preston had picked up spending so much time with adults. Mary was in love with Jacques, and when in love Mary was monogamous.[12] So for a time the avenue Elisée Reclus felt like family to Preston. Now, as in Chicago, he biked to school—from the Champ de Mars, through the Eiffel Tower, across the Seine, up many steps to the old Trocadero, past a graveyard and down the avenue Henri Martin.[13] Weekends he played with the Duncan dancers. One girl would remember him as "the boy who used to sit on the bed with Irma, Theresa, Anna, and me, eating ice creams and talking of Isadora."[14]

This was in 1909, the year Isadora became pregnant with Paris Singer's child Patrick. Singer and Isadora invited Mary and Preston to accompany them on a trip down the Nile that winter, but Mary said no and went briefly to the Plaza Hotel in New York instead.[15] The purpose of this visit is unknown. It may be that she was trying to sell an operetta she had co-written called "The Vendor of Dreams,"[16] it may be she had business to discuss with Solomon Sturges, who was apparently still supporting her. Preston was sorely disappointed about the Egyptian trip, for he was a curious boy and would have liked to see the pyramids. Temple was going, and so was Singer, whom Preston called Uncle Mun. Solomon Sturges's nickname was "Mon," and during Preston's adolescence, Paris Singer in many ways took his father's place. "Paris Singer," Preston would tell his wife Louise, "had vastly more to do with shaping my character than Mother had; although Mother made innumerable sacrifices for me, and Paris Singer made none. *I wanted to be like him.*"[17]

Paris Singer, who stood an imperious six foot six and was heir to the sewing machine millions, certainly made a powerful impression on eleven-year-old Preston. A few years younger than Solomon, Singer was a distinguished-looking man, with blonde curly hair and beard and an unshakable sense of his own importance, which had nothing to do with accomplishment in the arts.

Raised and educated in England, he was as firmly entrenched in British and continental society as Solomon was in Chicago. And he was given to gestures rather grander than Solomon's: for instance, he once set out to buy Madison Square Garden so Isadora would have a place to work. Singer himself never had to work, and his bursts of intense energy were often followed by bouts of depression and lethargy, though he professed great faith in the American work ethic. In her memoirs, Isadora recalls an occasion when she was reading Whitman's "Song of The Open Road" aloud. Suddenly Singer's face contorted with anger, and he exclaimed, "'What rot! . . . That man could never have earned his living!'"[18]—a sentiment one can well imagine Solomon Sturges applauding. Solomon would not, however, have had much use for Singer's rash enthusiasms. And Singer could be cruel and capricious; his lavish gifts to Isadora were predicated upon her fidelity and obedience. She took malicious pleasure in denying him both.[19]

Still, Singer was a man even Isadora could not manipulate, and this must have impressed Mary's son. Preston was now eleven, a tall, outgoing, and—his school records notwithstanding—precocious boy. That he preferred Singer to the various men in his mother's life is not surprising. Singer had considerably more stature than a bad French actor or a portly American judge. And while the men who pursued Mary tended to be either creative and poor or rich and tedious, Singer managed to be fabulously wealthy and fun at the same time. He lived in a magnificent mansion at Place des Vosges. And while the Jacques Gretillats would come and go with Mary's passions, Singer, whatever the status of his volatile relationship with Isadora, remained a constant friend to Mary and Preston. Mary he took at her own measure and would describe, even in her fifties, as beautiful and mysterious.[20] For Preston, who was around the age of his own son Cecil, Singer developed a special fondness. And if Singer made no great sacrifices on Preston's account, a certain responsibility was assumed. For instance, years later, when Isadora's tragic accident made international headlines, it was Singer who thought to immediately cable Preston that his mother was safe.[21]

Singer, Preston, Temple, and Mary were with Isadora in Beaulieu for the birth of Patrick, her second child, on May 1, 1910. This was a happy period in all their lives. Isadora, who had suffered with her daughter Deirdre, had an easy delivery this time. Preston and Temple played on the rocks by the water, and Mary must have thoroughly enjoyed herself at the celebration Singer threw later that summer at the Palace Hotel in Versailles. As usual, Singer spared no expense—the gardens were wreathed with multicolored lights, a huge tent was erected, and the Cologne Orchestra accompanied Isadora who, in fine form, danced Schumann and Beethoven for fifty-odd distinguished dinner guests. Among these were Nijinsky and Diaghilev; their *Sheherazade*, choreographed by Fokine, was currently the sensation in Paris.[22]

It's almost certain that Preston was taken to see *Sheherazade* that year, for Fokine was a great admirer of Isadora's. Preston may also, in 1910, have seen Mary Garden in *Salomé* and Lucien Guitry—a neighbor on the avenue Elisée Reclus—in Edmund Rostand's much-acclaimed *Chantecler*, a parable of French idealism which was neither wholly patriotic nor satirical. Picasso and Braque staged their first exposition of Cubist art that year, Halley's Comet could be seen in broad daylight in the streets of Paris, and, in the cinema, Louis Feuillade's *Bébé* series and Max Linder's short comic films were attracting an ever-wider audience. Linder's persona, Max, is often compared to Chaplin's—though Max is suaver, less graceful, and not at all sweet; there's something of Max in Sturges's supercilious businessmen and oily lawyers. And in all of Sturges's work, there's a good deal of the boulevard theatre which, more than cinema, flourished in 1910 Paris. Bataille's *La Verge Folle* opened that year, and Feydeau's *On Purge Bébé*, the tale of a chamber pot salesman and a constipated baby, was both a masterpiece and a box office hit. Whether or not Preston actually saw *On Purge Bébé* in 1910 or the more conventional *Occupe-toi d'Amélie* in 1908, Feydeau and the tradition of intricate French farce he perfected, would—more than any lycée and perhaps even more than Molière—be an education for the future playwright.

In the fall of 1910, the always tenuous routine of Preston's life was again disrupted when Mary broke with Jacques Gretillat and moved across the Champ de Mars to another small apartment on the avenue Charles Floquet. Mary's heart could not have been terribly broken because she also managed to change Preston's school at this time. His new school was "a very swell Anglophile school," École des Roches in the Normandy countryside. Here Greek, French, and American students were routinely commanded to sing "Rule Britannia." Here Preston learned to play soccer and drew a caricature of his drawing professor which got printed in the school paper. He made no lasting friends here. How could he? He was never given the time. Nor would he remember what—if anything—he read during this period in his life. Preston would, however, remember the annual productions of Molière's *Le Malade Imaginaire* or *Le Bourgeois Gentilhomme*, "my old friends, both considered excruciatingly funny and quite possibly so if played by a cast other than the one scraped up in my school."[23] He would vividly recall the day his mother appeared on the cricket fields of École des Roches with a "large Turkish gentleman" she introduced as Vely Bey—they had just been married.

The avenue Charles Floquet. Mary and Preston moved here after Mary broke with Jacques Gretillat.
(Author's photograph)

Vely Bey and Preston disliked each other on the spot. Bey, a man with no apparent profession, considered Mary Desti's son "wild," by which he probably meant outspoken, while Preston found his new stepfather temperamental and meddling. It was Bey, Preston suspected, who got him transferred from the genteel École des Roches to "a sort of cramming establishment" back in Paris. Worse, the arrival of Bey put a decisive end to Mary's marriage to Solomon. Probably, Solomon reduced his payments to Mary at this time, while Bey contributed little to the household finances. But Bey did give Mary and Preston something of enduring value. Or, more precisely, Bey's father, the physician Elias Pasha, gave them this.

Shortly after Preston's return to the avenue Charles Floquet, the Pashas arrived from Constantinople. "I remember your sweet mother Grandmère," Preston would write Bey years later, "and how nice she was to me and the big diamonds she wore and the *kohl* she wore on the edges of her eyes between the eyelashes and the eyeballs which she put on with a little orange stick and which she told me was very healthy for the eyes. I remember the rugs and the hangings with little pieces of mirror sewed on them and the bonbonnières encrusted with big yellow diamonds, which she and Grandpère Elias Pasha brought to Paris, and I remember his little pointed beard and his long pointed lemon-yellow shoes." [24]

When Mary developed a face rash, Elias Pasha concocted a "purple lotion with a white deposit on it," which in no time cleared the rash and would also, he informed her, remove wrinkles. It had been a great success in the Turkish harems. As Preston tells the story, Mary quickly conceived commercial possibilities for her father-in-law's elixir. No sooner had she coaxed him to divulge his secret formula than she set about manufacturing "Secret of the Harem" and looking for a shop where she could sell it. Thus, the Maison Desti (Maison D'Este until the famous Italian family protested) was born.

Between the lines, we can read Vely Bey's insufficiency as a provider, for Mary had never before shown much enthusiasm for business. Nor had she the American zeal for accumulating money; she liked to spend it fast and recklessly. Vely Bey would later claim it was lack of money which doomed his marriage to Mary. And though they were never less than comfortable, this is probably true. Just as Mary Biden did not fear poverty, Mary Sturges was loathe to part with her smart cars, lavish holidays, and the queenly freedom *not* to think about money. What was a silly extravagance for someone else was an assurance of well-being and also a mark of favor for her. Mary's priorities are nicely captured by Gerry in *The Palm Beach Story*, who walks out on a husband she still loves *not* because they are poor but because she has the imagination to prefer luxury.

Yet, if the Maison Desti was conceived as a means of redressing the balance between marriage to a Sturges and marriage to a Bey, it was also an elaborate enterprise from the start. It was located on an entresol, or mezzanine floor, in a lovely old house at 4 rue de la Paix, between the Place Vendôme and the Opéra—as smart an address as any in Paris. Isadora's friend, the noted designer Paul Poiret, was brought in to decorate; Mary proclaimed the results "fantastic." And Mary, who had a passion for detail and a way of making people *want* to do her favors, proved a gifted conceiver and packager of cosmetics. Soon the Maison Desti was offering, as well as Elias Pasha's ointment, its own line of creams and rouges and special face powders. To the standard colors of the times, Mary added ocher, lavender, and "sunburn" tints. Mary hired a famous manicurist named Mrs. Kantor and a hairdresser and a chemist. Two Chinese chiropodists were brought in, jars were ordered from Baccarat and Lalique. And when the perfume firm of L.T. Piver made her a present of one of their scents, Mary called it Beatrice D'Este and had special perfume bottles—with a picture of Beatrice burned into the glass—blown in Venice.[25]

Isadora was chagrined that Mary, "an artist," should be sullying herself in business, and one day she suggested that the two of them stand at the window of the Maison Desti and throw all the perfume bottles into the street. "That," she said, "would be a great ending and show your disdain for business."[26] Mary did not warm to this suggestion. But, since none of her friends were business people, she did, rather shrewdly, play down the commercial angle of her shop. The Maison Desti, she would say, was an "amusing" salon sort of place where famous beauties and even the King of Spain and the Crown Prince Rupert of Bavaria felt comfortable turning up on an afternoon.

It was also, initially, a modest financial success. Preston was proud of it and spent many happy hours in his mother's shop. Here he discovered how good he was with his hands and how, particularly when it came to solving practical conundrums, his mind was so much more agile than most people's. They only perceived the obvious, he could see around a problem. He designed boxes to fit his mother's special needs and, winner of drawing awards that he was, made posters as well. One he was especially proud of showed a pretty Mexican girl with a big sombrero and lovely skin—ocher, of course, for Mary's ocher powder.[27]

Vely Bey, very much the traditional Turk, took little interest in his wife's entrepreneurial venture. What greater affluence it brought them came too late, and at too high a cost to his pride. Bey's disposition grew increasingly splenetic; the break with Mary was inevitable. But the *coup de grâce*, as Preston tells the story, came the night Mary, Bey, and fifteen-year-old Preston went to see Sacha Guitry's *La Prise de Berg-Op-Zoom*:

4 rue de la Paix—the "europe tourisme" office, on the entresol, is the site of the former Maison Desti.
(Author's photograph)

This howlingly funny play by Sacha Guitry was being played by Mr. Guitry himself and his charming first wife: Charlotte Lyses. I howled along with everybody else, naturally, until my strident boyish voice so grated on my stepfather's ears, that after telling me to pipe down a couple of times, he suddenly hauled off and slapped me in the face. Completely unaccustomed to this form of treatment, I immediately riposted with a right to the nose, which fortunately drew blood. After this, to the stupefaction of Mr. Guitry, his pretty wife, the other actors on the stage, about a thousand roaring spectators and the prompter who stuck his head out of his shell like a turtle, we went to it. We were immediately thrown out, of course.[28]

On the cab ride home, the fight grew increasingly violent until Mary felt compelled to intercede:

Mother screamed and the cabdriver pulled over to the sidewalk where a couple of French policemen were conversing, and suggested that they take a gander inside his cab, as what he was hearing didn't sound good. The instant the door started to open, with a tremendous effort, Vely regained a semblance of composure and started brushing off . . . the whole matter as "a little family dispute." "By all means," said the policeman starting to close the door, "please excuse me." At this moment, Mother who was really afraid for my life . . . said, in ringing tones: "That is a dirty lie, Monsieur L'Agent, I have never seen this man before in my life!" "Ah hah," said the policeman, "this is then an entirely different pair of detachable cuffs!" with which he reached into the cab, grabbed Vely by the back of his collar, and yanked him out onto the sidewalk. Mother immediately opened the door on the other, or traffic side, of the cab, took my hand and said: "Come on! Let us go while the going is good."[29]

What a wish fulfillment this story is—the stepfather revealed as violent and foolish, while the child is exonerated; and how satisfying that the mother never questions where her commitment lies: "Let us go while the going is good." To make matters even neater, what is the humorist-to-be defending but his right to laugh? And at the theatre no less! Still, whatever the facts, there's certainly much emotional truth to Preston's version of events. Vely Bey didn't like Preston, and Preston, whose charm rarely failed to please adults in particular, must have been puzzled and tremendously threatened by that. He may have thought about Vely Bey years later when he wrote one of his most effective dramatic scenes, between Lee and her mother in *Remember the Night*. The mother, a strict disciplinarian with a narrow code of ethics, has never forgiven her daughter an early transgression. Now their reunion is bitter; it's no coincidence that the unforgiven child grew up a criminal in earnest. Preston was doubtless remembering the pain his stepfather's disapproval caused him when, at the height of his Hollywood fame, he took the trouble to caution his former stepfather, "So you see, my dear Vely, that my memories of you are not exactly hazy and although I may not have been a very good scholar as a small boy, there was nothing the matter with my thinking apparatus. Think back on that and don't be too severe with your eldest son who does not agree with you exactly in everything." [30]

Vely Bey and Mary did not officially divorce, and for all the apparent tumult of their marriage, they would soon meet again as friends. This was a pattern of Mary's life. Though she was no more inclined to work at a marriage than to work at a smile, she was also not one to confuse disappointment in love with bitterness toward an ex-lover. The truly irrevocable event that year, 1913, for both herself and Preston, had nothing to do with Mary's marital affairs. One day in early spring Isadora brought her two children to lunch with Singer in Paris. Deirdre was six and Patrick not quite three. This was the first time Isadora and Singer had met since a violent argument that fall; the lunch went well, and all parted in high spirits—Isadora going off to rehearsal and the children, with their nurse and a chauffeur, home to Versailles. On the way to Versailles, the car stalled. The chauffeur forgot to put on his safety break when he got out to crank the motor; and, while he stood helpless in front of it, the automobile lunged backwards and into the Seine. By the time they were brought to the surface, the nurse and two children were dead. Isadora would never recover from the loss of her children, and Mary, who so intimately identified with her, for once could not overstate her grief. Preston was fourteen at the time. He had been at Beaulieu for Patrick's birth, and all the Duncans were, in a sense, his extended family. The funeral was his second funeral (the first was his Uncle Tom's in Chicago) but, in his eventful young life, it was the first real tragedy.

That year Preston's bronchitis dragged on longer than usual. When he was still coughing after a month in Trouville, Mary consulted a lung specialist who discovered a very mild tuberculosis. No great fuss was made, but the Swiss mountains seemed a good idea. And as a new school was also now in order, Preston was sent to his final *école*, La Villa, in Lausanne. Preston was now five foot eleven. He weighed a hundred and seventy pounds and, except for the small spot on his lung, was a healthy boy. No one took the tuberculosis very seriously. He played all the sports La Villa was known for—rowing, soccer, tennis, skiing in the winter—and made many friends among the mostly American and Canadian students. Though scholarship was, once again, not his school's strong point, La Villa's math teacher, Preston would observe in his autobiography, "did very well." By this, Preston did not mean to imply that the man was brilliant but rather that his teaching—notably a trick for multiplying large numbers—had practical application. Like Ben Franklin, whom he revered and may have first studied in Switzerland, Preston, even as an adolescent, was not impressed by the merely theoretical. An idea had to be lucidly expressed and have a practical application to please him. Preston's greatest thrill that year came when someone sent him a copy of the French arts periodical *l'Oeuvre* from Paris. He opened it to find his own caricature of Isadora's eccentric brother, Raymond Duncan, printed inside.

At the end of spring term 1914, Preston traveled to the fashionable resort town of Deauville where his mother thought him sufficiently mature at fifteen to oversee a new branch of the Maison Desti. This was his first experience of work, and he did no worse a job for thoroughly enjoying everything about Deauville—from the bankers and barons and gigolos who flocked to the posh gambling casino, to the international beauties who half-believed him when he claimed to be nineteen, to the cuisine at the world-renowned Ciro's Restaurant. Mary arranged for Preston to have a room above Ciro's, with meals thrown in for free, and he would later attribute his "easy familiarity with a large number of rare and sometimes precious dishes" to his culinary experiences that summer. He would also learn the advantage of putting on an elegant front. Since the Maison Desti could not afford a night porter, Preston had to fill the bill—but he didn't have to admit to it. While the town slept, he would rise at five-thirty A.M. and in his old clothes dust, sweep, polish the brass, and wash the windows of the Maison Desti, then go back to bed. When he returned to the shop at a more civilized ten thirty, he was "wondrously decked out in white flannel trousers with brown and white shoes, a tan gabardine jacket with belt in the back, and a carnation in my button hole. Having assured myself, by running a suspicious finger along the shelves, that the night porter had done his work efficiently, I would retire to Ciro's for an exotic breakfast."

The Deauville season ended abruptly that year. War broke out in late July, and in a matter of days the casino was emptied of its billionaires and prepared to receive the wounded. Mary, driving north with Isadora, quickly volunteered her services. She can be seen, in a picture of the casino during that era, looking pretty and shrewd in a white nurse's wimple, surrounded by sickbeds with candelabras dangling above. Preston, however, did not stay on in Deauville. Mary sent him home to America—perhaps, as he supposed, because she feared he would enlist, or maybe out of some vague feeling of patriotism, for Mary was always *malgré tout* an American at heart. And Preston was no longer her little boy; he was tall and sophisticated and, with no vocation but much resourcefulness, ready to strike out on his own. The end of an era in Europe also marked the end of Preston's childhood and his expatriation.

3

Preston arrived in New York with as many Desti perfume bottles and cosmetics as he could squeeze into his trunk and went immediately to 347 Fifth Avenue where Daisy Andrews awaited him. Daisy, "a remarkably stout lady who lived on nothing but gin," had established an American branch of the Desti business. The business, she informed Preston, was not doing especially well. She couldn't imagine what use he'd be to her there; he'd might as well go to Chicago.

So Preston boarded the Twentieth Century for the first time in seven years. "Father," wrote Preston,

hadn't seen me since I was a little boy and had no idea of what I looked like, so when he went to meet me at the Union Station where the Twentieth Century came in, he stopped at the head of the platform, abreast of the locomotive, and took off his hat . . . hoping that I would remember what *he* looked like. Suddenly out of the stream of strangers appeared a young man about six feet tall who seized him fondly in his arms and then making joyful sounds, kissed him, European style, on both cheeks. This amused my father very much, and the next time I came to Chicago, having learned the American style of *not* kissing your father, he grabbed me in *his* arms, kissed *me* on both cheeks and said: "I've been saving that for you."[1]

Solomon must have been pleased at Preston's health and good looks and bewildered at cultural changes more profound than his manner of greeting. Preston, with the image of Paris Singer fresh in his mind, was surely touched and maybe a little awed by Solomon's homelier dignity and reserve. In the years since they'd last met, Solomon had moved from his house on the golf course in Glencoe to his city apartment at 20 Goethe Street, near the lake. Though he showed no intention of remarrying (and indeed would not take a second wife until after Mary's death), he'd resumed an active social life. Often now, when Preston visited, the house was full, and Solomon put him up in a "wonderful" room and bath at the University Club on Monroe Street. Always, charge accounts miraculously appeared—for the best restaurants, for Solomon's own tailor, even for shoes that Solomon insisted on buying Preston at fifty dollars a pair at Moberg Brothers when perfectly good ones could be had for five dollars elsewhere. Solomon brought Preston along to parties and reintroduced him to old friends. Among these was the bon vivant stock broker and speculator Sidney Love, a "wonderfully handsome and energetic man, with the aquiline nose of a Barbary pirate,"[2] who would end his days a night porter in Preston's Players Restaurant. Solomon was as eager to spoil Preston as Preston was to be spoiled.

But this was a trip, not a homecoming. When the question of education arose, "I don't know whether Father felt there was some bitterness toward me in the Sturges family, but for some reason or other it was decided to send me to school in New York." Thus, the Irving Preparatory School on Central Park West has the distinction of being Preston's last. Preston found Irving no more inspiring than its predecessors, and as he was unmoved by Molière at École Des Roches, Preston claims to have "loathed" Shakespeare class at Irving: "If there had been a contest to guess which boy in that class was least apt to become a playwright, I would certainly have won hands down."[3]

The anti-intellectual pose notwithstanding, Preston was reading on his own at this time—probably Nietzsche, whom he frequently quoted in Hollywood, and certainly the *Smart Set*, where H. L. Mencken and George Jean Nathan had just been made co-editors. The small room Preston rented in a brownstone on 129th and Fifth had only a single light in the middle of the ceiling. One of his first inventions was a candle stuck to a round piece of cardboard and suspended by strings from the ceiling by which he contrived to read in bed.[4]

Daisy Andrews had found Preston a grander apartment in the east thirties, but he let it go when the Desti business began seriously to flounder. He could live on the allowance of fifteen dollars a week Solomon Sturges was sending, but at sixteen Preston liked the idea of supporting himself. And the Maison Desti, where he'd invested his energy and talents, began to signify his own as well as his mother's independence. In the fall of 1914, the rue de la Paix store closed. Preston writes that a mob of patriotic Parisians learned of Mary's marriage to Bey and stormed her shop when Turkey allied with Germany. But Mary's absence in Deauville must also have taken its toll. Now the war made it nearly impossible to ship the Desti line to America. Daisy Andrews's reports from New York grew so dire that in November Mary arrived to appraise the crisis. She was glad to see Preston but fought with Daisy Andrews, who walked out, and a lawyer now encouraged Mary to make a clean sweep of things and declare bankruptcy. "Mother took his advice," comments Preston in his autobiography, "and regretted it the rest of her life."[5] Not, one senses, because the advice was unsound but because bankruptcy was shameful. As a Sturges, Preston must have felt it doubly so, and the shame was personal as well as financial; you cannot, Preston believed, separate your business from yourself.[6]

Still, the bright side of Mary's bankruptcy was that Preston got to leave the Irving School and help his mother move the remnants of their Fifth Avenue store to another small but pretty shop two steps down in a smart renovated brick townhouse at 23 East Ninth Street. Preston suspects that Mary chose the area for its French flavor—the Café Lafayette was just across the street, the old Hotel Brevoort around the corner. The Café Lafayette has made way for a fashionable high rise, but Mary's shop, now an animal hospital, still stands on the old, tree-lined block just off University Place. While Mary was fixing it up, six of Isadora's best pupils arrived in town, followed by Isadora herself, and for a few months life was much as it had been in Paris. Isadora hung her old blue drapes and spread low divans around a Gramercy Park studio, and painters, poets, set designers, journalists, musicians, and photographers began congregating. The photographers—Edward Steichen and Alfred Stieglitz—particularly impressed Preston, who began experimenting with a camera.

Isadora, feuding with Singer, was, as usual, desperate for money. Though her early performances received only mixed reviews and she made a point of antagonizing potential supporters (mocking the American rich for their indifference to the arts), she soon found a patron in millionaire Otto Kahn, who gave her free run of the Century Theatre. Here, to considerable acclaim, she staged her version of three Greek pieces including *Oedipus Rex*, starring her brother Augustin. Isadora thought the Century's orchestra seats too close to the stage and had no qualms about plucking out the first ten rows and replacing them with tubs of shrubbery suggestive of ancient Greece. "I happened to be out front the afternoon Otto Kahn, that patron of the arts, came to see how things were getting along," observed Preston. "His face, when he took a good look at what had been done to his expensive theater . . . was, as they say, a poem."[7]

It was at the Century that Preston made his theatrical debut as "assistant stage manager, call boy and backstage elevator operator" for *Oedipus Rex*. One of his jobs was to signal thunder, with a red flashlight, and lightning, with a green, for a storm scene when Oedipus is cast from Thebes. Sometimes Preston confused his signals, and thunder drowned out the opening lines of Oedipus's crucial monologue, earning him the wrath of Gus Duncan. "The fourth or fifth time the cue went wrong . . . I felt that apologies were superfluous, so I just went down into the big dimmer room and waited until everyone had gone home. Thus ended my first job in the theatre. I was sixteen and a half and did not come back to it until I was twenty-nine." [8]

It was now the spring of 1915. Mary, hard at work at the ninth street Maison Desti, moved Preston to a nearby hotel, off Washington Square. Together, they revived the Desti line—the ocher and sunburn and lavender powders, the Aurore Rouge and the Secret of the Harem cream, which, in light of Turkey's current alliances, was now simply Youth Lotion. Importing was still out of the question, so they had to make do with American boxes and bottles and oils and alcohol for perfume, which were not up to French standards. Still, orders began—slowly—coming in. One day Vely Bey showed up with an idea for "paperless" cigarettes, which seemed a good idea, and Mary, a nonsmoker, devised a scented tobacco called Desti's Ambre Cigarettes, which was very popular with the ladies.

While Mary seemed determined to make a go of the Maison Desti, Isadora was anxious to be off for Europe. Her Century audiences were not what she'd hoped, and with her equally passionate commitments to ideal performance conditions and low ticket prices, she'd run quickly into debt. Besides, though very much an American abroad, she was never really at home in America. In the beginning of May Isadora made a public appeal for funds and was delighted when admirers came through with enough money to book passage for herself and her pupils on the May 6 crossing of the *Dante Alighieri*. She was delighted, but not, it must be said, especially surprised or overly grateful; she possessed a mystical faith in her art and her luck. She was used to anxieties and to getting her way in the end.

A large group of well-wishers turned up to see Isadora off: among them were Mary and Billy Roberts of the *Literary Digest*, the photographer Arnold Genthe, the sculptress Sara Greene, the publisher and art gallery owner Mitchell Kennerly. Mary and Preston were there, of course. When the departure whistles blew, Preston followed the other guests down the gangplank, but Mary stayed aboard. By Mary's account, Isadora "begged me to go with her"; Isadora would have it Mary's idea. [9] Whichever, Mary sailed—without baggage or passport, tearfully entrusting the New York Maison Desti to Preston, who would remember this transaction. Preston would also remember Mary and Isadora collapsed in giggles, Mary having just revealed that she hadn't a cent on her . . . and Mitchell Kennerly gallantly throwing an envelope with passage money from the pier. [10]

Departing for Europe on a moment's notice was impulsive even for Mary, but it's doubtful Preston was tremendously surprised. She'd *seemed* committed to the Maison Desti, but then she'd also *seemed* committed to acting in her twenties and to playwriting for a while in Chicago and to her marriages. As for her financial plight, Mary was capable of worrying intensely but never very deeply. Like Isadora, she had faith in her luck, and if she had no art to justify the bounty of a rich gentleman like Mitchell Kennerly, well, hadn't her life always been a sort of art—beautiful and unpredictable? For his part, Preston may have congratulated himself on being sixteen years old, waving at Mary from dry land and no longer at her shirttails. She'd left him in charge of the store; very well, he'd make a success of it.

To save money, Preston now moved to a three-dollars-a-week, bug-infested room across the street from the Maison Desti. Louise and William, Mary's young employees, continued to help him out for what little money he could pay them, and Preston's classmates Eric Dressler and Rodney Combes from the Irving School also lent a hand from time to time. Where the rue de la Paix store had depended on retail customers, the New York branch had from the start courted department store orders. Now, Bonwit Teller, B. Altman, and Chicago's Marshall Field had sold out their Desti products and were writing for replenishments. "Everyone would help fill the powder or rouge boxes through a round hole in the bottom," Preston recalled, "packing the . . . powder or Aurora Rouge in tightly with a soup spoon, after which a piece of green calendered paper would be glued over the bottom to hide the hole, then the shade would be marked on with a rubber stamp. After this I would cover each box with a new product which had been invented in Belgium. . . . It was called cellophane and I always thought it would have a big future, but I hadn't the sort of mind which would make me try to share in this future."[11]

Preston would compare running the Maison Desti to watching a roulette wheel. Orders generally arrived—or did not arrive—in the morning mail, and after these were dutifully packed and posted, the day was spent wondering if customers would turn up. Ben Franklin's autobiography, one of Preston's bibles, cautions that for the successful businessman the appearance is almost as important as the fact of industry; but Preston, far more the European in this respect, never felt compelled to flaunt his diligence. He figured he could dash from the Café Lafayette to the Maison Desti in "six seconds flat." So, by taking a window seat within view of his business, Preston was able to spend long hours at the café and—in principal at least—never miss a customer. The customers, when they came, might simply wander down the street or, like one very wealthy black beauty enamored of the ocher powder, be driven to the door in a long Pierce Arrow by chauffeur in full livery. Preston, never one to sentimentalize the humble, thought his better known customers—Evelyn Nesbitt, Polish opera singer Ganna Walska, Peggy Guggenheim, bridge player Hal Simms, politician Hamilton Fish—were also his nicest. Mae Marsh was his most recognizable client; her latest film, D. W. Griffith's *The Birth of A Nation*, was being hailed and excoriated and selling out at top prices at the Liberty Theatre.[12] Lillian Russell, whom Preston found remarkably amiable, came just once to the Maison Desti, but Preston could see her limpidly in his mind's eye two decades later when he wrote *Diamond Jim* for Universal. In the 1935 film, "the part of Lillian Russell was played by the exceptionally pretty Binnie Barnes. Exceptionally pretty . . . but not *quite* up to the original."[13]

Preston's nearly three years in New York before America joined the war were a fine education for a future commercial playwright. The Maison Desti gave him something to do, and with erratic support from Mary—again established in Europe—and Solomon Sturges to fall back on, Preston never lost sleep worrying about profits. With evenings to himself, he did what he'd always done—he went out, now to clubs rather than operas. Of those in his price range, he favored the "Beaux Arts" club on Fourteenth Street and the "Domino Club" above Columbus Circle where he once had the memorable experience of watching "fat and vulgar" Diamond Jim Brady dine with *both* Dolly sisters. Preston was always welcome at Chez Fysher, a cabaret-restaurant run by Daisy Andrews, who had not only resurfaced but was now in partnership with, of all people, Vely Bey. When Paris Singer came to town, life picked up considerably. Now Preston could go anywhere he pleased—the Biltmore Roof, Sherry's, Delmonico's. His favorite club of all was the Knickerbocker Grill on Broadway and Forty-second Street where "Arthur Kraus and his orchestra would play the 'Tishomingo Blues' for me, and the great Maître d'Hôtel, Ernst Cerutti, who was privately persuaded that I was Paris Singer's illegitimate son, always treated me like a young prince." It was at a table at the Knickerbocker that Preston got his first glimpse of the great film pioneer D. W. Griffith, though at the moment Preston hadn't the slightest interest in filmmaking.

Besides spending time with Paris Singer and his mother's friends, Preston made contacts of his own during this period. Through a former French classmate, he met Georges Renevant, an aspiring actor with a wonderful sense of humor, who—the opposite of Preston—had been raised in America, by French parents. Preston and Georges began seeing each other regularly. Georges was already married, and Preston, with sophistication beyond his years, was starting to take well-bred girls dancing and to dinner. At seventeen,

Preston as a young man in New York.

and with another sort of girl, Preston's sexual life began. In his autobiography Preston describes a first affair with a former London chorus girl named Doris, who, he says, betrayed him when he went off for a weekend with Paris Singer in Canada. Doris may be apocryphal, but the dumb broad, vaguely foreign and with no dreams of social acceptance, is a familiar character in Preston's plays and scripts. Preston's double standard was also real and obdurate, and even in his teens he had a horror of betrayal by anyone.

In his teens too Preston got his first taste of the prewar American theatre, with its formula farces, melodramas, and romances. Theatre historian Joseph Wood Krutch laments it as "the last refuge for attitudes and sentiments not only long demoded in serious fiction but the subject of satiric comment in intellectual circles";[14] and for the most part so it was, and Preston loved it. Jack Welch, Temple Duncan's uncle, was general manager for George M. Cohan's production firm. Welch liked Preston, and, seeing he was short on money, offered him a free ticket for any show in town. Preston took him up on his offer and saw all the 1915 and 1916 seasons, which, as well as the routine fare, included Rachel Crothers's *Good Gracious* and the American premiere of George Bernard Shaw's *Getting Married.*

In the fall of 1916 Preston could well have dropped in at 137 MacDougal Street where The Provincetown Players, who the year before opened the Wharf Theatre on Cape Cod, were making a New York debut. Or he may have avoided them because, though champions of a nascent American drama, they were as arrogantly artistic and experimental as Isadora and Gordon Craig. Eugene O'Neill's *Bound East for Cardiff* was on their first bill. Two years later Preston would open his *Smart Set* and read that George Jean Nathan considered O'Neill America's "first really important dramatist." But for now Preston was not especially interested in serious drama. What intrigued him were the comic sketches of this era. He loved the annual Cohan and Harris revues, send-ups of the previous Broadway season, which were, he felt, often cleverer than the material they mocked. He so liked Richard Carle's performance in one of these sketches that he still remembered it twenty years later and brought Carle to Hollywood to play the head of the reform party in *The Great McGinty.*

Despite the war, Mary summoned Preston across the Atlantic in the summer of 1916. She had recently opened a branch of the Maison Desti over a tobacconist's shop on Old Bond Street in London. Though she'd added many new selections to her line, the business was struggling. Which was not to say that she hadn't managed to get a lovely apartment by Trafalgar Square and to rent a cottage in Uxbridge. Preston saw a zeppelin in the London skies that summer, he ate roast beef at Simpsons, and had a full dress and dinner jacket tailor-made. When he got back to New York in the fall, he'd passed his eighteenth birthday and suddenly wanted no more to do with the Maison Desti. Perhaps Mary had reminded him of his greater destiny; perhaps he was merely fed up minding the shop. When his helper Louise agreed to take his place for the time being, Preston flirted with the idea of a career in photography. He bought what he describes as a primitive version of the Polaroid camera, but then couldn't quite see snapping people's pictures for a living. Soon he was reminding Solomon Sturges that what he'd always wanted to be was a stockbroker. Skeptical at first, Solomon soon telephoned the New York correspondents of his Chicago firm, and Preston was engaged as a runner for seven dollars a week by F. B. Keech & Co. This was his only foray into his father's world, and his account of Wall Street life begins like a Harold Lloyd two-reeler:

> I thought a "runner" was supposed to run, as a result of which, in practically no time I wore out all the expensive shoes Father had paid . . . for in Chicago. When I returned to the office in a heavy sweat having run all the way to make my comparisons and deliveries, I imagined that somebody would notice this like they did in those Horatio Alger novels and say: "Keep your eye on Sturges!" or "Do you realize that Sturges went to twenty-four places this afternoon in the time the other boys went to eight?" All this ever did for me was to cause me to soak my feet at night in a little chowder made with ten cents worth of Allen's Foot Powder or, as I think it was called: Foot-Ease. Nobody in the office gave a damn about how fast I ran because they were all busy doing something else.[15]

The something else was feeding their family and friends hot investment tips so they could get rich fast, and beyond Preston's disapproval of this sort of chicanery, we can read his fundamental indifference to success in business. He may well have longed to be steady and secure like his father, but his father's métier was a bewilderment to him. It was neither noble nor amusing, and as with school, there were so many small-minded people to account to. Preston would make a delirious playground of Wall Street in *Easy Living*, but the clock-punching offices of *Christmas in July* and *The Sin of Harold Diddlebock* come closer to his own experience of the business world.

Preston had been at F. B. Keech & Co. for less than half a year when America entered World War I and, like the Eddie Bracken characters in *The Miracle of Morgan's Creek* and *Hail the Conquering Hero*, he quickly volunteered to serve his country—and was turned down. Where Woodrow, in *Hail the Conquering Hero*, wants to be a marine and gets rejected for hay fever, Preston

Preston at the School of Military Aeronautics in Austin, Texas, 1918.

wanted to be a flier in the U.S. Signal Corps and was sent away because he had a larger than normal blind spot in one eye. This was a keen disappointment, for he was eager to fight. When the United States turned him down, Preston got himself appointed to Canada's Royal Flying Corps. This enraged Mary, who, determined that her son should serve only his own country, crossed the Atlantic and began pulling strings. Influence, she assured her son, was the key to success. She got a letter of introduction from a Chicago general and in her best grande dame manner escorted Preston to a second physical where "everything went like a buttered eagle." Preston emerged a cadet in the Aviation section of the U.S. Signal Corps, 57th Squadron.[16]

He reported for duty in May 1918 and was sent first to Camp Dick near Dallas and then on to the school of Military Aeronautics in Austin where the education was, for once, practical, and he excelled in most of his courses. In Austin, a cadet two bunks down from Preston's was said to own a movie theatre. His name was Spyros Skouras, and they would see a lot of each other in Hollywood. Preston flew his first plane at Park Field in Millington, Tennessee and, while training for combat, was asked to contribute a weekly cartoon for the camp's newspaper. "I obliged with the gruesome adventures of a flying cadet and his instructor called: TOOT AND HIS LOOT," he remembered forty years later. "I refer to it as gruesome because it was supposed to be funny. I may add that all of my days became gruesome from this moment on while I tried to think up my weekly boffo. It is my remembrance of these horrible days of anxiety that has prevented me from accepting humorous television series even today."[17]

Preston would deeply regret that the war had ended before his training and, like the protagonists of *The Miracle of Morgan's Creek* and *Hail the Conquering Hero*, would feel somehow cheated and unmanly because he never got to fight. But the war was a turning point for him, and it is significant that he ended it not as an ambulance driver in France or Italy, but as a member of the U.S. Air Service in Tennessee. While Dos Passos and Hemingway, middle Americans to the core, had rushed to serve Europe in whatever capacity, Preston had been sent home from France and insisted on flying for America. And the end of the war notwithstanding, Preston stayed on to graduate his Air Service training with honors and to win the wings and the title of officer which were the first official achievements of his manhood. Then, with no other options on the horizon, he took off for New York and the Maison Desti.

When Preston came back to his mother's business in 1919, he was out of step not only with his upbringing but with his generation. The war had not been a crucible for him, as it had been for so many of his contemporaries. And now the Jazz Age, with its rejection of American Puritanism, was not his party. Nor was he the least inclined to follow the lost generation to Paris. Paris was where he had come from. And if, as Leslie Fiedler claims, "the end of the American artist's pilgrimage to Europe is the discovery of America,"[1] then his pilgrimage was over, and America was found. But, of course in Preston's case, the pilgrimage had been Mary Desti's idea, and he was not and never could be altogether an American. "Writers have to have two countries," wrote Gertrude Stein,[2] "the one where they belong and the one in which they live really." The country where Preston *belonged*, where he would write his plays and films and conceive his comic vision, was no single place, or as he would years later tell his French friend Marcel Pagnol: "At best my efforts have been a French point of humor filtered through an American vocabulary."[3]

Not that he now had any thoughts of becoming a writer, though he loved language and had begun reading with an eye for style. It was a great era for that. Disrupted continuity, compression of past and present, characters splintered and elided in the mischief of chance: what was familiar in painting was new to writing, especially American writing. Speed, the machine age transposed to literature, fascinated Gertrude Stein and Hart Crane, but also the more mainstream Hemingway and Dos Passos and Fitzgerald. Preston, who loved a lucid and virile prose, must have felt a keen affinity to Hemingway, while Fitzgerald's tales of flappers and college boys—so remote from his own experience of America—may have attracted him because of their vision of the very rich.

An author Preston read eagerly now, in the *Smart Set* and then the *Mer-*

cury, and over and over for the rest of his life was H. L. Mencken. Walter Lippmann called Mencken the most powerful influence on a whole generation of educated Americans,[4] and for Preston, Mencken's appeal was enduring and intensely personal. Like himself, Mencken was the son of a prosperous businessman. Like himself, Mencken was wary of artistic pretense and as ready to dismiss a bad book as to praise a good one. Ideas fascinated Mencken, who had published a study of Nietzsche, but he also liked the sound of his own prose and the sport of ridiculing: democracy, reform, women, the "Bible Belt." Mencken's wit lent distinction to so much Preston already believed—that it was a man's world, that honor was important but ideals were mostly foolish, that we are not born equal. Mencken's satire struck a chord. One essay that must have particularly attracted Preston was a 1921 *Smart Set* piece called "The Archangel Woodrow." Here Mencken went to town analyzing Woodrow Wilson's appeal to the emotion-driven American populace. The people, or "boobery," in Mencken's view, were a mindless mass, without the slightest interest in learning the truth or grappling with political complexities. The secret of Woodrow Wilson's success, claimed Mencken, was that he "managed to arrest and enchant the boobery with words that were simply words, and nothing else. The vulgar like and respect that sort of balderdash. A discourse packed with valid ideas, accurately expressed, is quite incomprehensible to them."[5]

Preston would remember Mencken's image of Wilson and his credulous American electorate. Preston would call the "hero" of *Hail the Conquering Hero* Woodrow and, in the forties, would still be laughing with Mencken at the mindlessness of political rhetoric and the vulgarity of the common man. But his films would also dispute much of Mencken's easy cynicism. For Sturges could never see just one side of any issue.

More than any prose writer but Mencken, the theatre attracted Preston in the early twenties. It was the beginning of Broadway's golden age. A hundred and fifty-seven new plays opened in the 1920–21 season—among them were Shaw's *Heartbreak House*, Eugene O'Neill's *The Emperor Jones*, and *Dulcy* and *Ladies First* by the new team of Marc Connelly and George S. Kaufman. Most of the openings were comedies, more adventurous than in the prewar years. Morals were looser now, money was easy. Broadway, until recently just one stop on the national circuit, was now the undisputed capital of American theatre. Here you came to prove your salt; here, George S. Kaufman's famous quip to the contrary, even satire did not have to close on Saturday night. For look at the success of Kaufman's own plays! And look at what he, and others like George Kelly, were mocking—American provincialism, middle class morality. Even materialism was fair game, though—as in the *Smart Set*—you attacked its surface folly, not its capitalist roots. Capitalists were your audience, after all, and for the most part what they wanted was the thrill of the dig—like a swig of Prohibition whiskey or a quip by Dorothy Parker—not sustained thought, certainly not ideology. Nor had all the predictable farces and melodramas suddenly disappeared. It was just that something was being born beside them. You didn't have to love Eugene O'Neill—and Preston for one did not—to see that playwriting could be an art like any other, and that America could produce and support it.

One night in August, 1920, Preston was eating dinner with Daisy Andrews at Rogers Restaurant on Sixth Avenue. As they finished their meal, Daisy suggested that they wander into the second act of a popular new show, *Enter Madame*. Written by Gilda Varesi and Dolly Byrne, it told the story of a volatile diva married for twenty years to a man who is finally fed up with her absences and her unpredictable nature. What he wants are his creature comforts and a solicitous mate, or so he believes, until his wife makes him see romance is more important than all that, more important, in fact, than anything. Though a conventional romantic comedy, *Enter Madame* was knowing and well-observed, and the fact that the lovers who are destined for each other are already married made a nice twist on the formula. The performance Preston and Daisy caught the end of was a final preview; the curtain brought wild applause and cries for the producer. "After some urging," Preston would remember, "a rather vinegary-looking, bald-headed man sidled out of the wings, riveted his eyes firmly upon his shoes, and in the warm accents of East Kansas froze the audience to its seat by informing it that this hollering . . . was all very nice but that the real story would be told the next night at the box office. . . . The play, of course, was a smash hit." [6]

The vinegary-looking producer was Brock Pemberton, a former newspaperman making his Broadway debut. In a few years, Pemberton would play a crucial role in Preston's career. For now Preston, twenty-two years old, had no career to speak of, though it's hard to believe, as he so often claimed, that he had no thoughts of career. Raised to a calling, Preston had, like Prince Hal, rebelled but could scarcely have forgotten what was expected of him. More than in the prewar years, he knew what he didn't want—business with its niggling rules and injustices, nor photography: he was not, he could see, cut out to be a journeyman picture snapper or a journeyman anything. He had a strong streak of laziness and the sense to look for discipline elsewhere. His return to the Maison Desti after the war shows less a failure of the imagination than a conscious rejection of alternatives and a refusal to be rushed into new commitments. He was young, after all, and very much his mother's son, unafraid of risk and eager for love and experience.

While Preston was in the Air Service, Mary had moved the Maison Desti from Ninth Street to 4 West Fifty-seventh and turned it into a sort of beauty salon. The "perfumed warm atmosphere" did not suit Preston, who now spent most of his time out of the shop selling Desti products. John Huston, Preston's good friend in Hollywood, remembers that Preston had an ability to persuade people through his sheer, irresistible enthusiasm.[7] He was also perceptive. "I . . . visited all the stores and hairdressers and beauty parlors I could find in New York and also went on selling tours down Long Islandway," he wrote of his efforts for the Maison Desti. "Everybody was very nice to me and I was so innocent of any selling technique whatsoever that the customers used to help me. They would say, 'You shouldn't put it that way, Preston! You should say something like this!' After which they sold themselves a bill of goods. Presently, a sort of commercial callowness became my technique."[8] Preston produced one of his first and most commercial inventions at this time: Desti's Red Red Rouge, a lip rouge that stayed on day and night and purported to defy kissing as Youth Lotion defied age.

Not long after Preston returned to New York, Mary went back to Paris and in the summer of 1921 saw Isadora off on her famous trip to Russia. After many frustrations, Isadora would have the satisfaction of running a school exactly as she wanted, and both women (Mary, the elder, was nearly fifty) would marry much younger men in the coming year. With Mary gone, Preston had no more qualms about closing the retail end of the business than she'd had about bringing in manicurists and makeup artists while he was off in the Air Service. If his mother saw the Maison Desti as a salon, for Preston it was a small cosmetic manufacturing and packaging business. He may have consulted Mary on the change, but it's more likely he did not, for both were strong-minded, possessive individuals; since Mary first dressed Preston in a tunic, power had been an issue between them. Now, Preston bade a fond good-bye to the Desti staff, one of whom, Peggy Sage, would later approach him as a celebrity in her own right. To save money, he left Fifty-seventh Street for the considerably less glamorous Williamsburg section of Brooklyn, where he continued filling orders and pursuing new customers.

Around this time, Preston's French actor friend Georges Renevant moved with his wife and mother-in-law into a small house in Douglaston, Long Island. Why, Renevant wondered, didn't Preston come fix up their chicken coop and live there rent-free for the winter? "I am a fairly good carpenter," wrote Preston in his autobiography, "and it was mostly the prospect of doing some pleasant carpentering that sucked me in to this deal." It was also his love of a lark and of makeshift families—photographers in the basement, wrestlers in the garage, would always appeal to him—and, even then, an aversion to being alone. The chicken coop arrangement did not last long, but the friendship with Renevant grew.

Paris Singer's son Cecil showed up in New York after the war, and Preston also saw a lot of Cecil at this time. Cecil was Preston's own age, thoroughly good-natured and more placid than his father. One night Preston invited Cecil to the Biltmore Roof with himself and Laura Grove, a "sweet and lovely girl" Preston often took dancing. Soon Cecil and Laura were married, and Preston had lost a dancing partner. There was no bitterness here because Laura, though a lover, was not a fiancée. Preston got great pleasure from introducing friends. And he was not the sort of man who had trouble finding girls to go out with. Everyone who remembers Preston speaks of his appeal to women, and Sandy Sturges, Preston's fourth wife and widow, adds that, from his teens on, Preston, "like his mother, was almost always in love with *someone.*" [9]

He was also, like his father, happy in a crowd of men, at a bar or club, or holding forth in his own apartment; and he was given to Paris Singer's rash but revocable enthusiasms. For instance, one day a photographer showed up at the Maison Desti, and Preston, liking the look of him and his photographs, took the man in and gave him a studio and darkroom of his own—which Preston just as quickly rescinded when the man's business tactics displeased him.

Preston did not begin saving his correspondence until the late twenties, and his autobiography and Mary's *The Untold Story* are both extremely vague about dates between Isadora's departure for Russia in the summer of 1921 and Preston's marriage in December 1923. Little too is known about Mary's last husband, except that he was a thirty-year-old Englishman named Howard Perch whose friends called him "Punch." He believed that Mary, with her black hair and youthful spirit, was also young in years until he set eyes on her grown son. Perch was obviously no breadwinner since Mary was still short on cash. In London, she'd begun writing a weekly beauty column for the London *Daily Sketch* and opened a fashionable supper and dancing club for elegant society and people in the arts called Desti's Club. Its patrons included John Galsworthy, Ellen Terry, and the Prince of Monaco; it had been respectfully reviewed, but did not deter Mary from returning to Paris.[10] Now she and Perch were living in her customary style, on the rue St. Honoré, and she had begun writing Preston letters very much like Isadora's dire notes to her. Here is a typical reproach from Isadora: "Dear Mary—It is a whole year since I have had a word from you! I have sent you *five* letters and four telegrams without answer." She did not stoop to explanations, merely remarking: "I have found myself in a truly terrible position." [11]

Mary's cables were usually more to the point—"CABLE MONEY CAN'T WAIT DAY DESPEROTA [sic] MOTHER"—and, though addressed to Preston, were calculated to win his father's sympathy. [12] Both women were effective criers of wolf because a real, if fleeting fear did grip them, and just as they were always, ultimately there for each other, Paris Singer and Solomon Sturges could not deny them for long.

In the summer of 1922, Paris Singer made plans to sail with his wife Joan and his son and daughter-in-law for Europe. Preston, eager to meet Perch, arranged to accompany them. The weekend before they were to leave, Cecil and Laura Singer insisted that Preston also come with them to the home of their friends the Godfreys in Fairfield, Connecticut. Preston thought the Godfreys sounded dull and wasn't much surprised when Mr. Godfrey turned out to be "a white-haired gentleman of sixty-four with a very white moustache . . . [who] struck me immediately as new-rich, uneasy and pretentious." Then Preston got his first glimpse of *Mrs.* Godfrey:

> I found myself alone in the front hall . . . when a very well-bred quiet voice behind me said, "How do you do." I spun around and saw, up two or three steps . . . a very handsome very young and, as the French say, very well-rolled young person of the opposite sex. Her hair was parted in the middle and coiled flatly over her ears. She had bangs. She was five foot three. She was three years younger than I. I said, "Who are you?" She said, "I am your hostess. How do you do, Mr. Sturges." I said, pointing weakly to the car outside and obviously looking thunderstruck, "You mean Mrs. Uh Uh Uh. . . . " She laughed and said: "That's right . . . Mrs. Godfrey." [13]

Mrs. Godfrey's maiden name was Estelle Mudge, and her cloistered Rhode Island childhood had been nearly as bizarre for the times as Preston's European youth. Estelle's father was dead, and her mother, crippled at an early age, took drugs, which made home life so difficult that Estelle at eighteen married a man in his sixties principally to get out of the house. Preston would not be the first to take the marriage to Godfrey less than seriously. "When I married Mr. G.," Estelle wrote, "[another] man asked me if I would marry him—when Mr. G. died!" [14]

Her history notwithstanding, Estelle was more than extremely handsome, she was spirited and levelheaded. She was daring. Like a girl in a Fitzgerald story, she drove the car very fast, and she rode horses. On that first weekend visit, Preston was told by her golf instructor that she had the makings of a champion. Preston, drawer of posters and caricatures, made a colored wash portrait of Estelle, which pleased her. On both Friday and Saturday night, they drank a lot and danced very close and met in the kitchen for scrambled eggs. Preston, who hadn't yet packed for Paris, took a train home early Sunday morning. Estelle drove him to the station, and "as the train pulled out, I said, so that she could just hear it: 'I love you.'" [15]

Preston spent a few months in Paris, in a painter's studio Mary found and furnished with couches and a long peasant sideboard known as a "bahut." Preston, who inherited his mother's eye for both quality and a deal, remarked, "If there was a good piece of furniture in the neighborhood, it would come out by itself and follow Mother down the street." [16] He had brought over his Red Red Rouge and a new formula for the ocher powder, but found Parisians less responsive to mail orders than New Yorkers. He and Perch must have gotten along because they soon set up a firm called Sturges, Perch & Company, Importers and Exporters. Though the business never took off, the sequence of names on their letterhead is telling; clearly, Preston was determined no longer to play second fiddle, either to Mary or to her spouse.

Evenings, Preston regularly stopped in at the storm cellar below the New York Bar where the pianist Les Copeland played "Tishomingo Blues" and "Yellow Dog Blues" and "Ain't We Got Fun." Copeland was soon a friend. Another friend was the "Russian wildcat" singer Preston also visited nightly, and then there was "the girl" of eighteen he fell for on the tennis courts of Deauville. What about Estelle Godfrey in Fairfield? "All I can tell you," wrote Preston, "is that I loved them all." [17] At the end of Preston's Paris visit, an incident occurred that is revealing of his relationship with Singer. In Preston's own words:

A few days after I got back to Paris [from Deauville], Paris Singer showed up and scolded me for wasting my time in Europe when I should be in New York developing my business. I told him the ticket was beyond my means at the moment and he said, "Aha! I should have kept my mouth shut!" then laughed, then became serious again and told me he wouldn't pay my fare back to New York because he didn't wish to contribute to my becoming a bum. He said, however, that if he could discover some useful service I could render him, he would then be very glad to have me accompany them. About three minutes later he said: "Why couldn't you be my secretary?" I said I would be delighted but I was not sure that I had the qualifications necessary. "What," I asked, "would I have to do?" "Well," he said, "you would have to call up the restaurants and reserve tables for us for dinner, and you would have to arrange for theatre tickets, to which you would naturally come, and also the railroad and steamship tickets to get us back to America. Do you think you could do all these things?" I said I felt I could discharge these duties with ease, so very pleased with himself he congratulated me upon my new appointment as his secretary and then said he supposed I could use a little money in advance. I said he was not wrong in this assumption and he pressed the equivalent of fifty dollars into my eager hands. . . . He then told me that my secretarial duties were to start at nine sharp the next morning, at which hour I was to report to his house.[18]

Preston celebrated the end of modest living with a spectacular night on the town and woke up in the "Russian wildcat's" hotel room, dimly aware that he had some duty to perform. When he staggered into Uncle Mun's at nine o'clock exactly, he was unshaven and in evening clothes. Joan Singer assured Preston that since Paris, no early riser, was still asleep, there'd be plenty of time for Preston to bathe and change. However:

I suppose we had been whispering louder than we thought, because just as I tiptoed past [his] door, it suddenly opened wide, revealing Uncle Mun, magnificent in his six foot three and a Japanese dressing gown. Fixing me with an accusing finger, he said, simply: "You are fired."[19]

This incident Preston and Singer would soon laugh about—though Singer meant what he said, and Preston had to appeal to his father for a boat ticket home. The story shows Paris, with Preston as with Isadora, capricious and jealous of his position; but it says something too about Preston, who knew his Uncle Mun's temperament and provoked him nonetheless. The perspective Preston the writer takes on his younger self confronting Singer—"magnificent" in his robe—shows, more than nodding self-effacement, an abiding fascination with power.

Soon after Preston returned to his business in Brooklyn, an invitation arrived from Estelle Godfrey. Would he join her for tea at the Ritz? Embarrassed now at his impulsive avowal of love, Preston dreaded a recriminatory scene or worse. Which he didn't get because Estelle was anything but naïve, and in the end it was he who asked her for a second meeting, later that week. From here on the desire to be together was mutual.

Preston made a point that, as Americans, he and Estelle handled their love affair very differently than Europeans in similar circumstances. They were "clean and honorable," if rather old-fashioned. For she, soon after they began meeting regularly, left the Fairfield house and joined her father's sister in Boston. He took a room in the Hotel Breslin in New York. The letters they exchanged during this period are the first Preston saved and show the intelligence as well as the consuming nature of their passion.

Americans or not, it's doubtful they were chaste for long. In an early letter, Estelle wrote Preston:

> I have been told you couldn't love or respect me after what I have done—but it does not seem reasonable. I love you all the more and I hoped you would me. I felt that you were big enough to understand and love and respect me still and (even in the midst of my doubts) I cannot believe that you are not. Anyway—if you are not (big enough) I don't want you anyway.[20]

The "what I've done" may refer to some infidelity during her marriage, or perhaps to her leaving Godfrey without consulting Preston. Estelle's is the first of many letters, from men *and* women, which accuse Preston of stuffiness and a double standard, but also speak to his humor and good sense. The wording here is affectionate and carefully nonconfrontational. Like two of the three other women Preston would marry, Estelle was Catholic and far from a crusader for women's rights. Like the others too, she had a mind of her own. Some time after receiving Estelle's letter, Preston, in an equable mood, wrote her:

> I don't want to hear about whatever you did that was foolish. I hope you weren't untrue to your marriage vows, but if you were it can't be helped and it doesn't matter and I shall love you much too much to give you time to think of anyone else.
>
> Besides, if you tell me what you did, I shall have to tell you all the things I have done, and then you won't marry me.
>
> Who am I to judge anyone?[21]

They were warm and playful with each other—"Darlin, how could you fall in love with such a mutt?" asked Preston in one note, and he drew her a funny picture of himself "at the age of five." They both exclaimed that they loved babies, and when she confessed that she sometimes feared insanity, he told her, "I believe that most people with brains have that feeling occasionally. When you begin to think that people around you are going insane, *then* is the time to worry. If you tell me *I'm* insane, I shall have you locked up."[22] Not altogether in jest, Preston speculated about marriage: "I know that you will be a darling little wife but I wonder what kind of husband I'll be. Awful probably though I shall try hard not to be."[23] He informed Estelle sweetly, but firmly of his feelings on religion:

> Though I believe in God I don't believe in religion for everybody. Some people who are a little weak and don't want to shoulder any responsibility need Catholicism. For people at the other extreme there is Christian

Science. . . . I think a powerful conscience is worth all the religions put
together.

I must tell you one thing and I hope, Darlin, that it will neither shock nor
hurt you. I do not believe Christ was the son of God anymore than I am his
son or you are his daughter. . . . All of this will make it clear why I get hor-
ribly bored in Church and am not ashamed of it.[24]

He added, "You shall be my religion, darling!" He also warned her, "I have
the terrible temper of calm people," and intimated that self-discipline was not
his strength. Sometimes, he said, it was hard for him to make fifty dollars a
week, but if she would "promise to make me get out and on the job," he would
do better. He wanted her to know everything he did and thought. "Pep" was
a catchword of the times, and Preston wrote Estelle about his idea for bottling
concentrated clam broth as a cocktail drink and calling it "Pepoclam." Ideas
for making money came readily to him now. Estelle, he hoped, would help
him weed and coddle them. "Pepoclam," and most of Preston's twenties'
schemes, never materialized, but this did not daunt him. "I always was and
always will be optimistic," he wrote at sixty, and, irrefutably, this is true.[25]

By Preston's account, it was not until Estelle announced that she was leaving her husband that he did the "honorable" thing and proposed marriage: if
so, he took a passive role wholly inconsistent with his nature. It was, in any
case, some time after they'd decided to marry that Estelle told Preston she
had an income in trust of $11,000 a year, from her father's estate. While the
news would not have fazed Mary Desti, Preston—probably thinking of the
Sturges code of honor—was sincerely troubled.[26] "I will tell you something—I
don't know whether it will make you happy or not," he wrote her, "but here
it is: If I had known that you had that money I should never have dared propose to you. I really wouldn't have. It's all very strange the way it has worked
out, because I have always loathed young men who married girls with money.
And I should certainly never knowingly have done the same thing. Anyway
that's that, and I am very glad, and don't you let me borrow any when I get
hard up."[27]

Estelle did not sue for divorce immediately. She bought herself a Stutz car
and rented a country house with a pool in New Jersey. When Godfrey belat-
edly began threatening them, Estelle and Preston drove off in the Stutz for
Chicago. Here Solomon Sturges was happy to help out and doubtless also
delighted to be part of the action. The lovers returned to New York, ready to
negotiate with Godfrey and set the legal process in motion.

The divorce itself was filed for and waited out in Paris, because Preston
wanted Estelle to spend time with his mother. Mary met them at the train

station in the summer of 1923: "To my masculine eye," observed Preston, "the two ladies in my life appeared to love each other at first sight. So much for my masculine eye." [28]

The reason Mary and Estelle did not love each other on the spot may have been, simply, that they were rivals for Preston's affection. Mary, after all, had often been cruel about Preston's girlfriends in the past. [29] She had never relished the idea of sharing him, for just as she was the only constant in Preston's youth, he was the one tangible accomplishment of her adult years. And as she grew older, she increasingly pinned her hopes on him. Mary may also have wondered why Preston, always in love, had now decided to marry, and why this woman? He had not proposed to the "Russian wildcat," who was lusty and clever, he had not proposed to "the girl" on the Deauville tennis courts, who was beautiful and rich. With Estelle, there was, of course, the matter of the divorce and her reputation, but Mary knew Preston too well to suppose he'd marry for honor alone. Preston's mother probably found his wife-to-be somewhat subdued in the face of Europe, the arts—and herself. Certainly, Estelle was a very different sort of person from Mary Desti. Preston's tribute to his mother would be the women in his work, not the women he married. His wives were smart and spunky, but far from free spirits and certainly less impetuous and domineering than Mary. As for Estelle's feelings about Mary, surely these were colored by Preston's stories about the Greek robes and his pain at being separated from Solomon. Still, it is doubtful that Estelle truly disliked Mary, even at the outset, and she would grow increasingly impressed with her gallant and unpredictable mother-in-law in the coming years.

Mary was not at her best, however, the morning she met Preston and Estelle at the Paris train station. Indeed, she'd barely managed to meet them at all. She'd had to leave Isadora alone in Germany; or rather, she'd left Isadora with her husband, the young Russian poet Sergei Esenin. Esenin was, by Mary's account, a deeply disturbed man who, when he drank, routinely destroyed hotel rooms and verbally and physically abused his wife. Mary had spent the last few weeks traveling with them as a kind of chaperone for Isadora—which did not endear her to Esenin. Nor was Esenin the only culprit, for Isadora was not above responding to his assaults in kind. Mary's seemingly boundless sympathy for the creative temperament palled, and she was exasperated with them both by the time she left for Paris. Then, they turned up in Paris as well. Isadora stayed on during and beyond the summer of Estelle's divorce. Preston remembers lunching with her and Esenin, whom he dismissed as yet another outrageous artiste. When Estelle's divorce came through, she and Preston returned to New York; they would marry as soon as her papers allowed. Isadora also left for Russia with Esenin, but not before exacting a promise from Mary that she would join them. And while Mary could not obtain a visa and stayed behind in the end, the whole experience took its toll. She wound up in a Paris hospital, in her words, "a complete wreck."[30] With Isadora in Russia, Preston in New York, and Perch apparently out of the picture, she was also very much alone.

Preston, however, was experiencing one of the most harmonious periods of his life. He and Estelle married on December 23, 1923 and threw themselves into hard work and domesticity. Preston, who had enjoyed being the ardent lover, now took the role of bread-earning husband in stride. With the help of Estelle's inheritance, he hired a chemist, bought some grinding and sifting machinery, and prepared to make the Maison Desti a first-rate cosmetics factory. They found larger working quarters, also in Brooklyn, and when the sweatshop upstairs became vacant, Preston asked Estelle if she would mind doing like the French and living thriftily above their shop. She said she wouldn't mind at all. She said she also wouldn't mind learning to cook and sew. Preston's description of the early days of their marriage sounds like a chapter from *David Copperfield*, and not coincidentally, because Preston had a Dickenslike image of the way marital love should be. The ideal marriage, for him, was not exotic, like his mother's to Vely Bey, or experimental, like so many of his peers' marriages in the twenties. It was less like the marriages of the protagonists in his films than like those of their parents: pure, devoted, and monogamous. If the complexities of his nature, and of life, never permitted Preston to sustain such simple bliss, this was what he imagined he wanted. His marriage to Estelle, he later wrote, was "a complete and true marriage" in that "I never looked at another woman . . . I mean admiringly. . . . Also . . . it embarrassed me to dance with other women and feel their bodies against me. That all this was highly ridiculous and probably some form of arrested development, I am the first to admit, but that's how it was."[31]

The beginning of Preston's marriage was also a happy time for the Maison Desti. While Preston's ambitions up to now had been lofty and vague, Estelle's goals were conventional and pragmatic: she wanted her husband to be a success in his chosen field. Encouraged by Estelle, Preston worked hard; the business grew. One day two perfume distributors from the Lionel Trading Company turned up in Brooklyn. In exchange for exclusive distribution rights, they offered to buy the "enormous amount" of $1,000 worth of Desti products a month. "I became dizzy with joy," Preston later recalled, "and felt that at last the business I had been in since my boyhood and that my mother had given me on her departure from America in 1915 was finally going to become successful and bear rich fruit. Within sixty days Mother returned from Europe and asked for her business back." [32]

Preston made a point of his technical rights to the Maison Desti—Mary having entrusted it to him when she sailed off with Isadora on the *Dante Alighieri*. But it was really his *droit moral* he spoke of: the fact that this business he had worked in since childhood was as much a part of him as it was of his mother. It was also the only business he knew, and he was so recently married. He pleaded his case, but Mary was for once wholly obdurate, she would have the business back and to herself. Of all Mary's abrogations, this is the one Preston never forgave. She was, he must have perceived, lonely and ill and not altogether herself; but she also acted out of jealousy, which was unworthy. And when his marriage broke up some two-and-a-half years later, with Estelle accusing him of "laziness," [33] Preston would on some level hold Mary Desti to blame.

How long Preston could have enjoyed the life of a businessman and devoted husband, had Mary not intervened, is impossible to determine. Restlessness and uncertainty were in his future. Some thirty-odd years later, Preston would write, "I go through life accumulating possessions. . . . I've always done it . . . and then every once in a while a sort of tidal wave comes along and washes them all away." [34]

Still, in 1924, all this was ahead of him. Just twenty-six, he must have chafed as he watched his mother cast about for a pretty new shop while he dismantled his factory and saw the deal with Lionel Trading Company come to nothing. He and Estelle moved back to Manhattan, to a "very lovely studio" on East 39th Street. Then, Estelle sold property in Rhode Island and, using the profits, they bought a country estate in upper Westchester County, between Yorkstown Heights and Peekskill.

Preston was captivated by the estate, which had "a lovely millpond, a dam, some small white Bossert houses, and an old buckwheat flourmill." [35] Here Preston and Estelle spent the better part of two years, moving to their New York apartment only during the cold winter months. Here too, Preston writes, "I . . . became exposed to the dangerous charm of the life of a country gentleman whose wife has a little money." [36] He spent most of his time lazing about, fishing and swimming, or so Estelle perceived it, and he eventually came to accept her judgment. But he was also inventing—an intaglio photo-etching process for which he actually received a U.S. patent, a design for a vertical rising airplane and for a lightweight automobile, and more as well. He may have worked on these fitfully, but he worked nonetheless, and during this era he must have seen himself less as a country gentleman than as a contemporary Ben Franklin. For Franklin too, as soon as his financial situation allowed, gave up business to pursue the practical sciences. The difference was, of course, that Franklin's inventions were successful, while Preston's, though often ingenious-sounding, never achieved recognition. Still, he fought for them, he wrote letter after letter to the patent office, and would continue to do so—and to conceive of instruments to make life easier and more interesting—all his life. Indeed, it was as an inventor rather than a writer that he liked to identify himself. Dialogue, he once said, was a matter of inventing two lines that match.[37]

Preston's twenties were not as different from his later years as he would claim they'd been. If he was often indolent in 1925 and 1926, he could also be lazy during his heyday in Hollywood. And he was always sociable and a great collector of stories. In Westchester, he had long conversations with a neighbor named Andrew J. McCreery, a former Brooklyn lawyer who told him about Tammany politics, and how bosses got the vote out in bad weather, and how "repeaters" used the names of the dead or sick. McCreery's irreverent tales, like Mencken's articles, fell on sympathetic ears.

In the winter of 1927 Preston came up with a business scheme that involved a trip to Paris. "I told Estelle we would probably have to pay our own fares," he wrote in his autobiography,

> that there was a gambling element to the whole set-up which might quite possibly not pay off, but that on the other hand the chances might turn out to have been pretty good; then asked her how she felt about going to Paris. She looked at me strangely and said, "Why don't you go alone?" This does not sound like a particularly startling remark today . . . but at the time I felt as if she had slashed me across the face. . . . I said, "What do you mean? How can you say such a thing?" and then she took a long breath and said, "Because really I don't love you anymore." Then . . . I said that under the circumstances it would be very immoral of her to continue to frequent my bed, after which I cried like a ninny. . . . I then left for Chicago . . . dragging my high principles after me.[38]

Certainly, this is a simplification—for Estelle must have been unhappy for some time and for specific reasons that doubtless Preston on one level realized. The laziness she spoke of surely signified more than Preston's swimming and fishing. Perhaps, he was the "awful" husband he had feared he'd be, or more likely a distracted and inattentive spouse. Passionate as his mother, he was no more than she inclined to work at sustaining romance, and, for all Estelle's and Preston's enthusing about babies during their courtship, there was as yet no sign of a child. Preston longed for a son, so this may have been a frustration. Besides, once the first ecstasy passed, lovers were prey to Preston's irascibility, which may well have escalated to physical violence, as Mary's had with Edmund Biden and Vely Bey. What models, after all, had Preston of domesticity? And with his "terrible temper" and need for power in relationships, Preston could not have been an easy man to live with; nor would Estelle—demanding, outspoken, and experienced in infelicity—have kept her growing dissatisfaction to herself.

And yet on some deep level, Preston may have been caught completely unawares by Estelle's announcement that she no longer loved him. How momentous that remark, particularly to a man of Preston's pride and vulnerabilities, and how unanswerable. Whether it was true or merely calculated to wound scarcely matters, and Estelle must have known that, must have known that with Preston's sense of honor he had no choice but to leave. Skeptical as Preston was about organized religion, he was a believer in destiny.[39] The end of this first marriage, so often reworked in his art, would over time come to seem not an event in which he played an active role, but an existential loss he suffered. And also—like his mother's appropriating the Maison Desti—a stroke of equivocal fortune, which marked the end of his connubial bliss and spurred him toward a career he would not otherwise have sought.

PART II

Child of
Manhattan

*It was an age of miracles, it was an age of art, it was
an age of excess, and it was an age of satire.*
F. Scott Fitzgerald, *Echoes of the Jazz Age*

CHAPTER 5

Preston would say that he was so anguished by Estelle's rejection that, while staying with his father in Chicago, he seriously contemplated suicide. The city of his dreams now held no charms for him. Solomon's worldly assurances that Preston would soon be himself were comfortless—what was the use of living without Estelle? One day he decided to jump in the lake and be done with his suffering. But no sooner had he conceived this plan than he heard a piercing scream; a mason who'd been working on an adjacent building swung by Sturges's window as he plunged sixteen floors to his death. So horrified was Preston that he was forever cured of the desire to kill himself. As difficult as it is to fully credit this story, given Preston's profound optimism, there is no doubt his grief over Estelle was devastating.

Preston stayed just a few days with his father in Chicago and then cabled Estelle that he was coming home. When he got back to their Thirty-ninth Street apartment and found her gone without a trace, "the three most terrible weeks" of his life began.[1] Estelle, meanwhile, fearing Preston's mood, had also fled to Solomon Sturges, who—an unusual father-in-law—took her in and agreed not to notify his son. When Estelle finally arrived in New York, Solomon in tow, it was to announce that the marriage was finished. Preston remembers her laughing at his request for a period of adjustment: "I learned for the first time how completely through with a man a woman is . . . when she is through with a man."[2]

Grieving over the loss of Estelle, Preston felt, gave him the heart, if not the craft, of a playwright. He also observed something about laughter at this time:

I was walking down Fifth Avenue with my mother . . . and my expression was so sour and despondent that my mother was actually embarrassed by it. Presently she said, "When you feel cheerful, you smile, don't you?" I growled this was probably the case, then she said, "Well, I'll tell you a funny thing: try smiling and you'll find that cheerful thoughts come into your head automatically . . . because the two always go together." Very reluctantly I tried a smile and felt so stupid about it that I burst out laughing, and while laughing had only the most cheerful thoughts in my head.[3]

Mary's remedy for sorrow, so characteristic of her impatience with other people's problems, is in very crude form the moral of *Sullivan's Travels*.

Though Preston would always hold Mary in part responsible for the breakup of his marriage, neither he nor Estelle stayed angry with her for long. Estelle now struck up a friendship with her mother-in-law. And Preston too, once he came to terms with his separation, began dropping in on Mary's 603 Fifth Avenue apartment and the pretty shop where, in her haphazard fashion, she was currently selling batik scarves as well as perfumes and cosmetics. Tired of New York, Mary was now more than willing to give Preston the run of the Maison Desti, if money could be found for a trip to Paris. Solomon Sturges said he'd provide that and also at least half a year's rent and would send Preston a "salary" of $150 a month. Preston would work hard to upgrade the business and forward what he could of the profits on to Paris.[4] Mary set sail for Europe on April 23 and was soon reunited with the widowed Isadora.

On May 29, Preston wrote his father:

> Thank you very much indeed for sending the money to mother so quickly. In the flush of excitement at getting back to Paris she apparently spent her money a little too freely and I received a desperate cable for funds. By now she is installed in a little apartment and her living expenses will be much less than a hotel.

Preston said he hadn't written before because he wanted to report "serious progress," which now he could: A firm that distributed Conti's Castile soap also wanted to handle the Desti products. Red Red Rouge was the leader of the Desti line, though "the quality of our merchandise had slumped terribly since I last manufactured it and I have been busy with the chemist getting it up to standard again." By the way, Preston wondered if Solomon could send him $750 or, even better $1,000? If not he'd get along fine just the same.[5]

In the spring of 1927 Mary confided in Paris Singer that she believed Estelle was still "madly" in love with Preston and "only acted as she did for [Preston's] own dear sake."[6] But there's no evidence this is so, and the former sweethearts were soon conspiring about what the best sort of divorce would be, and where they should get it, in a warm and ironic correspondence that continued until Estelle's death, ten years before Preston's own.

For now, Preston was brokenhearted, to be sure, but he was also beginning to enjoy life as a bachelor in New York. As always, there was the theatre. George Abbott's *Broadway*, with its jazzy nightclub setting and physical action was the hit of the season. Joseph Wood Krutch observed that *Broadway's* greatest achievement, "technically," was "the discovery, or rather the rediscovery of the theatrical value of mere speed";[7] and Preston, so attuned to French farce, may have noted that the achievement was more than technical and that speed was anything but "mere." Robert Sherwood's *The Road to Rome*, a fanciful satire about the Romans and Hannibal, would become one of Preston's favorite works; he chose to produce it at his theatre in Hollywood and may have borne it in mind while adapting *If I Were King*.

But theatre for Preston was no longer just the plays he saw, it was equally the world he moved in. More than ever, evenings were spent with Georges Renevant and his struggling actor and playwright friends—often at Pirolle's Restaurant. Here, Preston remembers, his credit was "excellent because my French was." Furthermore, Pirolle's owner was the former headwaiter of the Ritz, Monsieur Pillet: "That nobleman of restauration, that patron of the arts, that man who fed talent where he thought he saw it."[8] Another favorite theatre haunt was Tony's and yet another was Tomaso's speakeasy at 336 West Forty-fifth Street. Mary Desti's friend the actress Jeanne Eagels first brought Preston to Tomaso's, which fascinated him not so much for its celebrities flouting Prohibition as for the truculent bartenders and inscrutable regulars with languages—and stories—all their own. The proprietor, Tomaso Gandolphi, was "a great character," and there was distinction too to the brash look of the place, with its heavy drapes, banquette, wall telephone, slot machine, portable phonograph, and, of course, the bar.[9]

Preston set an undated story he wrote around this time at a speakeasy very like Tomaso's. The name of the bar is Tom's, and the characters are a gang of aging hopefuls who while their nights away, moaning about their children and lovers and contemplating "what was wrong with a theatre that had no need for five inspired men like ourselves." "Mr. Trotter's Two Children" and the more predictable "Dust in the Sunlight" are the only two stories Preston saved from this period; they may indeed be his only attempts at the short story form. Neither was published; and both manuscripts, scrupulously typed and corrected, have pages missing. Still, what remains refutes Preston's suspicion that his gift was for dialogue-writing only.[10] Though first efforts, very much in O. Henry's voice, they reveal a flair for the rhythm and subterfuges of narrative. Here, for instance, the young Sturges achieves a nice bit of indirect characterization:

Then one night I came in and found Jerry weeping on Mr. Trotter's shoulder. He was good and drunk because that was the day the Court allowed him to see his little boy and he always got soused afterwards. Spending the afternoon with a little boy is enough to drive any man to drink, but Jerry thinks it reminds him of his broken heart and what might have been and what a beautiful girl Marie was and all like that although I saw the lady once, not to mention the little boy who looked like a snake with spectacles, and I think the man who broke up Jerry's home was a public benefactor who will find his reward in Heaven, for having missed it so completely on this earth.

"Dust in the Sunlight" engages one of Preston's most enduring concerns—ambition. An unmarried working woman of forty has come to terms with her solitude. Then, she finds love for the first time, blossoms and—fatally—is for the first time duped. Her story is framed by that of the policeman, Officer Mulligan, who is summoned to handle her suicide. If the narrator of "Mr. Trotter's Two Children" is a little like the too-smart-for-their-stations protagonists of *The Palm Beach Story* and *The Sin of Harold Diddlebock*, Officer Mulligan is a forebear of the manager Mr. Waterbury in *Christmas in July*: "At twenty [Officer Mulligan] had hoped to become a police captain. At forty he had hoped to become a sergeant. At fifty-five he realized it was best to be a patrolman." The "best" in this last sentence initially read "better": Preston's revision emboldens the language and works a curious psychological shift.

Around the time he began writing stories, Preston, who loved music and especially jazz, answered an ad in *Popular Mechanics* for a correspondence course with Piano Bill. Piano Bill's gimmick was he'd get you playing tunes without having to read a note of music or fathom the scheme of the keyboard. The attraction here, as with Preston's Swiss math professor's tricks for multiplication, was speed. Soon Preston was not only playing, but composing songs and, always careful to see the business angle, trying to sell them. His efforts were not unfruitful because, though it was some time before he sold a song, he soon met music publisher and popular songwriter Ted Snyder.

Snyder was, like so many, charmed by Preston's mixture of worldliness and boyish enthusiasm. He informed Preston, "You don't know a goddamned thing about lyric writing, but you can write a short sentence." Snyder then proceeded to teach Preston all about songwriting: "How superfluous words, there just for the rhyme, are absolutely forbidden . . . how the accented syllable of the word must jibe precisely with the accented beat of the music . . . how a short word phrase must have a short music phrase."[11] Together they composed "My Cradle of Dreams," one verse of which read:

There's a nest
Not so far away,
Where I rest
At the end of day
Heaven-blessed,
It's my cradle of dreams,
Small and white
Little treasure chest
of delight,
All I love the best
Waits tonight
In my cradle of dreams.[12]

On the evidence of this and his libretto for *The Well of Romance*, music brought out Preston's coyness and sentimentality. But Snyder's kindness was whole-hearted and would soon be repaid in style.

On the eighth of July Isadora Duncan gave the last performance of her life, at the Mogador Theatre in Paris. Her selection of pieces included the Overture to *Tannhäuser*; the audience was "hushed, then weeping, wildly applauding."[13] Mary wrote Preston that the concert was a "marvelous success."[14] A week later Mary wrote again, observing that Isadora was "penniless," but she failed to mention that Isadora's by now compulsive extravagance had accounted for so many of the "Desperato Mother" cables that spring and summer. It was wise of Mary to omit this information, because neither Preston nor Solomon would have been happy to learn that she was sharing their money, Robin Hood-style, with her friend. Mary and Isadora left for Nice shortly after the Paris concert, and a month of feverish spending, most of it by Isadora against Mary's credit. In the beginning of September 1927, having run through Solomon Sturges's allowance, Mary went on Isadora's part to ask Paris Singer, literally, for lunch money. Singer, seeing no end to Isadora's indulgence, turned Mary down at the time but two days later showed up in Nice, offering to underwrite not only Isadora's living expenses but her preparations for a new production. It was now that Isadora arranged for the handsome driver of a Bugatti sports car to take her for a ride. He came to pick her up on the evening of September 14. Throwing a Maison Desti red silk batik scarf around her neck, Isadora waved to Mary, stepped into the car, and seconds later the fringe of the scarf caught in the spoke of a wheel, and she was dead.

Paris Singer radiogrammed Preston on September 15: "Mary Was Not In Auto With Isadora And Is Well Love Uncle Mun." The next day, Mary, in the midst of funeral preparations, thought to send Preston a birthday card with no mention of the tragedy: "Darlin—This for your birthday to tell you it was and always is the happiest day of my life. You are my ONE treasure in all the great big world. . . . God bless you and keep you—Mother."[15] Preston, writing about Isadora's death in his autobiography, commented: "My mother died three-and-a-half years later of myelogenous leukemia. Nobody knows anything about it, or what brings it on, it might be shock."[16]

Preston himself suffered what he would come to perceive as a cathartic brush with death later that year. As he tells the story, he was low on funds and equally lacking in purpose. Business was terrible. With Christmas a week away, he set off for Chicago wearing a "horrifyingly old" suit, which served its purpose, prompting Solomon Sturges to propose a visit to his tailor the following day. But the next morning Preston woke up with a pain in the lower right side of his abdomen: appendicitis, he recognized. Badly wanting a new suit, he dragged himself to the fitting nonetheless and then upon returning home, doubled up in pain by now, called his father, who accused him of exaggerating. The doctor, finding no fever, concurred with Solomon and prescribed bicarbonate of soda. It was not, Preston claims, until Christmas Eve that he was taken seriously and rushed to the Presbyterian Hospital of Chicago, where a long and delicate appendectomy saved his life.

Preston's image of himself, sipping bicarbonate of soda at death's door, is doubtless embellished a bit, and—with the doubting father who almost gets his comeuppance—Freudian to boot. Still, Preston's illness was certainly grave because Mary was alerted. Recently back from a pilgrimage to Isadora's school in Moscow, she wired from Paris on January 6: "CABLE NEWS TONIGHT DISTRACTED WILL SAIL IMMEDIATELY."

Preston told countless friends and interviewers over the years that it was this brush with death that turned him into a productive human being. He had "wasted" his first twenty-nine years; from now on he would create. The implication that if Preston had never gotten appendicitis he would never have written a play is, like his assumptions about the break-up with Estelle, a bit romantic. Preston was, after all, writing songs and stories some time before his attack, and he had produced many, albeit unpatented, inventions in Westchester. Still, there was a greater sense of purpose to Preston's choices in the early months of 1929. During his six weeks of convalescence, he set about writing a musical farce. Based on Irvin S. Cobb's 1915 comic essay, "Speaking of Operations," the play disappointed him finally, and he discarded it even before it was done. But in the meantime he'd begun to conceive of himself as a playwright; he'd also picked up the only book he would ever credit with influencing his work in theatre and film—Brander Matthews's *A Study of the Drama*.

Preston's attraction to Brander Matthews is not as uncharacteristic as it at first appears. A Columbia University professor, Matthews was very much a theatre scholar and prolific critic; he was also—in the midst of an era giddy with drama's possibilities as art—concrete in his advice and matter-of-fact in his assumptions. The playwright's talents, Matthews declares, are "instinctive"; his most important decision is the selection of subject matter. He should follow the strategy of the elder Dumas and make "the first act clear, the last act short, and all the acts interesting." His play should aim to "please the people for whom it is composed; and if, for any reason it is unable to do this, then it has missed its mark, the final verdict has been rendered; and there is no hope of moving for a new trial." Preston was especially fond of thrusting this last proclamation in the face of the Gordon Craigs of the world; though, Matthews's vision of the artist—as "born," as ineffably bound to his audience—is not fundamentally at odds with Isadora's. Nor, for the most part, are his pragmatic-sounding instructions any less vague than hers. For instance, what in the world do Dumas, Matthews, and Sturges mean by, "make all the acts interesting?" Still, Matthews's cocksure tone and endorsement of the commercial standard must in their context have seemed provocative. Preston may have given some thought to what Matthews had to say about genres:

> In high comedy (the comedy of manners) . . . we perceive that the plot is made by the characters, that the characters dominate the plot, and that the plot is what it is solely because the characters are what they are. But in farce, and again in melodrama the reverse is seen to be the case; the plot, the situation, the incidents are the controlling factors, and the characters are only what the plot allows them to be or forces them to be.[17]

While oversimplifying, Matthews presents the classic view of comedy and farce, as divided by a vision of character. In farce, with its antisocial message, the characters are volatile and powerless; in comedy, they are stable and strong. Some ten years later, Sturges's films would begin challenging these distinctions.

For now, though, Preston's concern was to assimilate a pleasing formula and follow it through, for as he would later advise a friend, "About the only difference between amateur and professional playwrights is that the latter always complete their plays."[18] Subject matter, Preston agreed with Matthews, was crucial, though what actually triggered the writing of *The Guinea Pig* is a matter of conjecture. Preston told one 1929 interviewer that his play avenged "a warm friend" who was used as "a subject of love analysis" by a cold and cunning woman. Since the interview goes on to characterize Preston as "too modest to be in show business," it can be taken for what it's worth; as can another piece from the time which, describing Preston as "one of America's gold-spooned lads," cites his motive for writing a play as ennui. Tired of lolling about the club, Preston announced, "If I can't find real situations that interest me in real life then I'll go and write them in play form."[19] Here Preston's depiction of reality as something that might not exist in "real life" is intriguing. However, the story he most often told in later years was that he was himself used as a guinea pig by a well-known stage actress. In the midst of an argument, this woman revealed that she was writing a play and dated him merely to observe "how dull a human being could actually be."[20]

Given Preston's pride and luck in love, this explanation is only slightly more credible than the others. Besides, like the others—and like the message of *The Guinea Pig* itself—it says more about what Preston presumed people wanted to hear about art's indebtedness to life than it does about his own creative impulse.

The Guinea Pig's plot revolves around three characters—Small, a furrier turned Broadway producer, Catherine Howard, a novelist turned playwright, and Wil Smith, a young author. Act I opens in Small's office where Wil has come for a verdict on his first play. Set in a fantasy kingdom, requiring a chorus of ninety and expensive sets and uniforms, this opus is definitely not for Small, who nonetheless counsels Wil to persevere. Playwriting isn't easy. Why, look at young Catherine Howard, who's currently adapting her "hot" bestselling novel for the stage, and can't seem to make the love scenes play.

Catherine now arrives with dreary love scenes, indeed. Her problem, Small discerns, is that while a novel leaves much to the reader's imagination, "You got to write [plays] from personal experience. . . . You can change it a little bit maybe, but it's got to be something you know just the same." Since Catherine, widowed by an older man, has never known passionate love, it's no wonder she can't convey it. Catherine appeals to Wil for dialogue tips and then invites him home for dinner. The next morning, and Act II, finds them lovers. He's blissfully asleep, she's frantically scribbling dialogue.

What's more, when Wil declares his love, Catherine reveals she's exploited him for copy: "I never had any romance in my life. . . or any love. . . . I didn't know how sweet a young man could be. . . . I was . . . I was like a scientist, making an experiment." Time passes, Wil appears at Catherine's opening night, and she urges Small to invite him to her party. Here both Catherine and Wil have confessions to make. She tells him she's loved him all along:

> I mean . . . you remember you said that . . . women were very . . . noble . . . and . . . primitive or something . . . huh? You said they couldn't . . . ah . . . ah . . . unless they were in love . . . you remember you said that . . . you were right, Wil.

He too loves her but, no less than she, has profited from their affair. His extravaganza forgotten, he's got a new play in the works—the tentative title is "The Spider and the Fly," the subject is themselves.

The Guinea Pig is derivative, calculating, filled with caricatures—but also tight, good-natured, and plucky. Though Wil and Catherine are somewhat listless prototypes, Small, the lovable heavy, has a number of lively moments. In a typical one, while lecturing Catherine Howard on theatre versus the fur business, Small "absentmindedly picks up her fur piece," and tugs and strokes until it stands on end. This scene, like so much of Preston's writing, seems headed for the conclusion that business is much saner than art. Says Small of his career switch: "I didn't know when I was well off, the raw fur business, there *is* a business." But he goes on, "You buy 'em, you scrape 'em, you soften 'em, you sweat blood over 'em and then . . . you put 'em in the storehouse to add to the other monuments to your dumbness." So, even in this first work, Preston shows business and art as uneasy opposites, morals as slippery, and— through Catherine's deception of herself as well as Wil—actions as rarely what they seem.

He also shows a nice woman unable to make love without being *in* love and art as an evocation of real experience. Or does he? For Sturges's gift, emerging even here, is to question every value judgment, to search not for a single truth but for a dialogue, or, as he would phrase it, "two lines which match." The theatre producer advocating passionate experience may seem to speak for Preston, who despised abstraction and, quoting Tolstoy, called art "a medium for the transmission of emotion."[21] But then the theatre producer's name is Small, as is his understanding, and his broken English is played for laughs. By putting his own ideas in the mouth of a crass former furrier Preston in effect challenges those ideas. And so too Catherine Howard's "women are noble" apology is belied by the fact that, woman or not, she's the most forceful character in the play. Wil, his name notwithstanding, is a passive sort, and has as little in common with Preston as does intellectual Catherine Howard with Estelle Godfrey (although, through Catherine's bloodless husband, Preston does get in his dig at Godfrey).

Still, too much should not be made of *The Guinea Pig*, which is a slight tale, high comic by Matthews's definition, and thoroughly sentimental. Small's none too nuanced pseudo-Yiddish excepted, the language is textured and natural. A subtle pleasure is its closely observed Broadway ambience, and there are some engagingly cheeky self-references. Small, for instance, avers: "A one minute wait to an audience is like one minute to a man standing on a tack." Thus, for all its seeming modesty, *The Guinea Pig* declares itself equipped to deliver what an audience wants—scarcely the presumptions of a man too modest for show business!

Preston sent *The Guinea Pig* to the theatre in Provincetown that had given Eugene O'Neill his first production. On June 10, Mary Bickwell, president of the Wharf Players, wrote back: "I have read your play with great pleasure and amusement and am sending it at once to the Director." The director, Louis Leon Hall, must have liked it as well, for arrangements were quickly made for a one-week run, beginning July 13, 1928.

The Wharf Theatre, constructed out of an old Cape Cod fish house, was now more than a decade old. Committed to the voice of the new American playwright, it offered unknowns a faithful production of their work, but no money. Indeed, Preston remembers having to borrow twenty-six dollars to buy his train ticket from New York to Provincetown. For now the Maison Desti was in its last gasps. Mary was still in Paris, and Solomon Sturges, who had lived through Preston's passions for photography, songwriting, stockbroking, and entrepreneurship must have been skeptical about supporting this latest enthusiasm. Skeptical but, with his predilection for the long view, probably not discouraging. A dialogue in Preston's (unproduced) screenplay *Great Love* may reflect *both* of Solomon's opinions about his son at this crucial time. Speaking of an inventor past thirty who still hasn't made his mark, one character quips: "At his age Alexander had conquered the world"; to which another character replies, "It was a very SMALL world. You just don't recognize talent when you see it. . . . People with talent are forever groping around in all directions."

On the night of July 13, sitting among a crowded and appreciative audience, Preston may well have felt his own groping was over. It was his first opening night, and though he had qualms about the production (the local actor playing Small was, he feared, a little hammy)[22] the experience was overwhelmingly gratifying. While Preston had always been ambivalent about "art" *per se*, from his earliest experience of Paris Singer's wit and Sacha Guitry's "howlingly funny" performances, he'd had nothing but respect for humor. And now an audience was laughing because of his imagination and his skill. As Preston would have Sullivan conclude at the end of *Sullivan's Travels*: "There's a lot to be said for making people laugh." And furthermore, how satisfying to be recognized for it! "The more you stand in the limelight the more scarred you will become and the more you will love the limelight," Preston would write years later. "It is shameful but that is how it is."[23]

Still, it is hard to discern anything shameful about Preston's long-awaited pride of accomplishment in Provincetown. A July 1928 review in the *Wharf Notes* observes that "the author of *The Guinea Pig* shows a knack for clever characterization, smart dialogue, and the manipulation of comedy scenes which should carry him far in writing for the stage." So he was now an author, a figure of news, someone to be predicted about.

Back in New York, he was also penniless and without a job. He strolled into Pirolle's restaurant, and while enjoying Monsieur Pillet's sixty-five-cent lunch "on the cuff," learned that Georges Renevant was rehearsing a new play called *Goin' Home*. It was a melodrama about miscegenation, and one of the directors was the cantankerous Kansan Preston had seen seven years earlier on the stage of *Enter Madame*—Brock Pemberton. Pemberton's partner, Antoinette Perry, was a friend of Renevant's. Renevant assured Preston that Perry would find him some work.

Perry was as good as Renevant promised, and though Pemberton, Preston remembers, "looked longingly at his shoes and then balefully at me," they hired Preston as assistant stage manager for the run of the show.[24] The stage manager was Jack Gilchrist, another aspiring author who would become a close friend. Tony Perry too was friendly to Preston. Perry was a shrewd judge of talent and every bit Pemberton's equal, but she was a woman; and for Preston—so long under Mary Desti's control—women would always be problematic as figures of power. Pemberton, Preston could see, was the boss he would have to please.

Brock Pemberton—gruff, decent, perspicacious, instinctively commercial—may, with Solomon Sturges, be the model for the businessmen fathers in *Easy Living* and *The Lady Eve*. Certainly, his bantering, irascible relationship with Preston suggests that of *Easy Living*'s Wall Street tycoon Ball and his gifted, but insubordinate heir. When Jack Gilchrist was unavailable for the next Pemberton-Perry production, Preston was hired to stage manage and also play a bit part. The play was *Hotbed*, a campus comedy, and Preston, as obstreperous Lawrence Binnings, got to bash the French window of the

Dean's office with a baseball bat. He was paid eighty-five dollars a week. Pemberton, writing a somewhat tongue-in-cheek account of their association at this time, remembers Preston forever enthusing about his accomplishments and one day showing up with his script for *The Guinea Pig*. Antoinette Perry thought the play was good but needed work, as did the Pemberton reader Clarence Taylor, but Preston, says Pemberton, insisted that the play needed no work whatsoever.[25]

It's easy to imagine Preston, having been produced and well-reviewed in Provincetown, bristling at a mere reader's objections to his play. Still, though proud and stubborn, Preston was anxious to see his work on Broadway and would scarcely have turned down a concrete offer, on any reasonable terms. For perhaps the first time in his life, he badly wanted not just success, but a very specific success and, wanting it, was coming to an understanding of how patience and shrewdness, as much as talent and intelligence, would be needed to realize his ambitions. "A friend of mine once told me that the hardest thing about directing a picture was finding somebody who would give you a picture to direct," he observed a decade later. "I think that holds true of most professions, and it seems to me that most young people spend a great deal more time learning how to fulfill the duties of a job than they do in learning how to get the job. Getting it seems to be the trick and requires a rarer talent than doing it."[26]

With the goal of getting the job of Broadway playwright, Preston and Jack Gilchrist formed the Broken-Down Stage Managers Club, which met nightly at Child's cafeteria, in the basement of the new Paramount Films building on Broadway. Like Tony's and Tomaso's, Child's was a favorite theatre haunt, and here the two men talked plays from midnight sometimes until dawn with producers, manuscript readers, actors, anyone who cared to join them. George Renevant and Dick Hale, Temple Duncan's actor husband, often turned up. Here too Preston met a man who would become his friend and professional ally for life.

Charles Abramson was tall and dapper. Formerly a lawyer, he came from a religious Jewish family who never adjusted to his passion for show business.[27] Though he called himself a producer, Charley seems to have been more of an agent for creative talent. His great joy in life was camaraderie, he was enormously generous and had an unusual capacity for identifying with the success of others. Twenty-five years of correspondence also reveal an endearingly eccentric spirit, kindred to many of Sturges's film characters. Typical of Charley's letters to Preston is one which, with no irony intended, read, "As for me I am still doing business at the same old stand and the same unprofitable customers. But I have never felt better or more hopeful. . . . . Really, while nothing seems to be any good and conditions are terrible, I for one am convinced the trend is up and all will be well." [28] Abramson told a mutual friend that Preston "has fortified me in my ideal of friendship"; [29] and Abramson was himself the ideal friend. If he was drawn to Preston the Byronic young playwright—"his striking physical appearance, his succinct expression and forceful voice, his executive ability and creative talent" [30]—Abramson would remain similarly devoted three decades later.

Charley Abramson read *The Guinea Pig* the night Preston gave it to him. [31] The following night, at Child's, Preston asked Charley what he thought, and Charley replied that the play showed talent, but needed work. In any case, Abramson had no interest in producing *The Guinea Pig*. Preston said he'd been contemplating producing the play himself, and wondered, what was the absolute minimum sum he'd need for a Broadway opening? Charley calculated $15,000 but added that a producer who knew the ropes might get by with $2,500. Preston must have thought of the contributions from friends that enabled Mary to set up her first Maison Desti at 4 rue de la Paix. He began mentioning the $2,500 figure wherever he went. One night at a dinner party, he no sooner mentioned the figure than his hostess wrote him a check. Preston immediately brought the money to Abramson, who, though still unwilling to produce, agreed to help out where he could. [32]

For a theatre, Abramson suggested the three-hundred seat Tottem on Forty-eighth Street and—since it was known for a long string of failures—convinced the owners to rename it The President and charge an extremely reasonable $300 a week. [33] Charley also showed Preston how to avoid putting money up front by promising shares of his profits, enabling Sturges to approach popular comic Alexander Carr for the crucial role of Sam Small. Carr, a notorious spendthrift, was a virtual prisoner in the Hotel Manger when they found him. Besides guaranteeing him 10 percent of the gross, they had to pay $750 in back bills to "ransom" their star from his room. Scenery was procured by offering a set builder 25 percent of the show, and when only $43 were left for Catherine's costumes, Preston professed to see no alternative but Klein's Bargain Basement. At the threat of such an indignity, his actress shopped at Milgrims on her own money: to be repaid, when and if. . . . [34] Bending rules was, of course, a familiar strategy for Mary Desti's son.

Hotbed closed, after only nineteen performances, at the end of November, and Mary was back in New York when *The Guinea Pig* began rehearsals two weeks later. She quickly struck up a friendship with Mary Carroll (whom she somewhat resembled). Mary Carroll and John Ferguson were cast as Catherine and Wil after two sets of ingenues had defected. Jack Gilchrist was stage manager, Walter Greenough—a fellow actor in *Hotbed*—directed, and Preston got his first taste of the ranging creativity, power, and abundance of sheer detail work that is the lot of the producer.

The temptation is great for a first-time playwright, insecure of his position, to stanch criticism from the cast. But Preston, though never one to suffer fools or sacrifice authority, was less self-conscious than eager to learn. He had noticed, for instance, how so much playwriting was static because characters discoursed with one idea only; when that was exhausted, the dialogue collapsed. The answer, he felt, was a "hook system," whereby, as in verse, a word or idea in one speech triggers a response that meanwhile sets up a new thought, and so on.[35] Sturges was proud of the fluidity of *The Guinea Pig*, but not so smug as to ignore Alexander Carr's resistance to the beat of many of his comic lines. Sturges's problem, Carr told him, was a tendency to lead with the punch. In Act I, for instance, Catherine observes of her passionless husband, "I admired his writings. Isn't it silly? He had a brilliant mind." Small originally replied, "No, dearie. He was a damn fool. Excuse me to contradict you." At Carr's suggestion, Small's line was reversed: "Excuse me to contradict you . . . but he was a damn fool."[36] So for all the complaints about Sturges's egoistic obstinacy in Hollywood, he started out and, for the most part, remained too much a perfectionist to ignore a good idea from *anyone*.

Preston was fond of telling how his mother, during the war, opened a French bank account on a friend's guarantee of $10,000 in francs. Mary immediately withdrew the entire guarantee which, the franc being then worth twenty cents, came to 50,000 francs. It took a very special mind to perceive that when the franc devalued after the war, $10,000 was worth not 50,000 but *280,000* francs, and that Mary had 230,000 coming to her: which she demanded and furthermore received. The story reveals much about the peculiar resourcefulness of Mary Desti. And Preston showed similar ingenuity when, having no money to open *The Guinea Pig* out of town, he remembered a summer theatre on the Frank A. Vanderlip estate in Westchester. Wouldn't it be novel for the estate to host a winter preview? He convinced them that indeed it would be and commercial as well and thus got the Beachwood Theatre for thirty dollars a night, with the gardeners thrown in as stagehands.[37] The event was a success and, most important for Preston, his work could now be fine-tuned on the advice of the only critic he thoroughly trusted: a general public.

The Guinea Pig opened at The President on January 7. Preston described the event as an evening of delightful torture. All of us young all of us poor; clammy-handed and ashen-faced, hoping for the best: the chance in a thousand, but fearing the worst: ridicule and failure. The pretty little house, packed downstairs and dear Charley Abramson wringing his hands in the empty balcony. My mother sitting proudly in the third row, laughing gaily with trembling lips. The great George Kaufman sitting in the worst seat in the house . . . he was kind to the play. The pale Bide Dudley sitting in the best seat . . . he was most severe. Which proves nothing. The asbestos curtain sticking four feet up from the stage, and Charley Abramson busting his suspenders in the balcony trying to push it up with will power. The man who walked up to the box-office and actually bought a pair of seats.[38]

Next morning's reviews, while not effusive, were mostly favorable. The *New York Sun* called it "a charming little comedy," the *New York Telegram* hailed it "1929's first new comedy success in this humble person's humble opinion." And though the *Evening Post* complained that "a generous allowance for the fact [that *The Guinea Pig* is Mr. Sturges's first play] leaves it still hopelessly amateurish," George S. Kaufman, then second-string critic for the *Times*, was more typical in finding *The Guinea Pig* "an uncertain little comedy miles from sure about where it is going and how it is going to get there, but with quite a little simple and entertaining humor."

Preston's producer's salary of fifty dollars a week earned him less than had his stage-managing and bit part in *Hotbed*. His author's contract called for 5 percent returns on the first $4,000 of profits, 7.5 percent on the next $2,000, and 10 percent after that: but it's doubtful *The Guinea Pig*'s sixteen-week run brought the playwright a penny, for the box office was never strong. Preston suspected his play's title hindered it and at one point ran a newspaper contest for a replacement.[39] (Also a good publicity stunt.) The title he chose was *Passion Preferred*, and with its new name, Preston took his production for a final run in Philadelphia.

Preston was disappointed at *The Guinea Pig*'s closing, but sixteen weeks on Broadway is hardly a disgrace, and the new author must have been cheered by his reviews, which—bad as well as good—he pasted neatly in a scrapbook. On May 23, Preston signed an Actors' Equity contract with A. H. Wood for a road company version of *Frankie and Johnnie*. There's no mention of what role he played; as with *Hotbed*, some stage managing seems to have been involved, and he was to be paid eighty-five dollars a week for his efforts. Preston told critic/theatre historian Ward Morehouse that he was "fired" from *Frankie and Johnnie* "because I insisted on getting the eighty-five dollars a week I had been promised rather than sixty-five dollars and a quick shuffle. . . . As it was a bad time to try for a job and there was plenty of food in my father's apartment I decided to knock off a play before leaving."[40] In fact, *Frankie and Johnnie* gave closing notice the first week in June in Chicago, and there's no indication Preston was either fired or underpaid before then. He did, however, wind up at his father's apartment, where on June 15 he embarked on *Strictly Dishonorable*.

Embarked is the word because, just as he had Wil write *The Spider and the Fly* to punish a lover, Preston now perceived his own playwriting as a campaign against thirty years of anonymity, as a financial coup, a test of personal discipline: anything but a reckoning with the muse. Or rather, whatever his surely conflicting feelings, it was fruitful for Preston to think of writing as a business requiring, like most others, craft, enterprise, luck, and what his era vaguely termed "pep."

A diary he kept during this time reveals as much by what it doesn't say as by what it does:

Friday June 14
Beginning work on "Strictly Dishonorable." Promise myself to do five pages every day. . . . Had breakfast with Father at 7:45.
The play should be finished inside of a month.
5 1/2 pages finished 11 P.M.

June 15
No work today.

June 16
Or today either.
Midday dinner with the Bentons.

Monday, June 17
Did 11 pages today.
Pretty good . . .
Finished 3 A.M.

June 18
Worked very hard—not really as the play is beginning to move at last—it's like getting a regiment out of the marsh. . . . I've done 30 3/4 [pages]. Finished 3 A.M.

June 19
Wonderful progress today—Finished first act, 37 pages, and did six full pages of Act II. . . . Mr. Schoolcraft came to dinner. We had a long discussion about philosophy, history, the Papacy and many other things. . . . How little I know.

June 20
. . . Finished Act II. Got through at 7 A.M.

Friday June 21
slept 1—6 P.M. worked all day and till 5 A.M. . . . 83 [pages]

June 22
No work today. Am resting for strong finish.

June 23
. . . Strictly Dishonorable finished 5:40 this afternoon. Will polish tonight.
Did so and drew set plans. Wrote to Pemberton.

Pemberton immediately replied, instructing Preston to send his play along
when it was finished. Preston mailed *Strictly Dishonorable* on June 26 and
boasted to his father that Pemberton would read the play and cable his congratulations the following Saturday. Solomon, though skeptical, stayed home
for the occasion, but rather than the telegram, Preston's manuscript arrived:
returned for insufficient postage.[41] Preston reposted it Special Delivery on
June 28 and on the same day wrote Pemberton:

> Thank you for your nice note and your kind invitation to forward the
> script.
> By now, of course, you have received it, read it, laughed the wrong way and
> thrown it into the spittoon. At least that's what I'm supposed to say, giggling
> with False Modesty and hoping for the best.
> HAHA! But I don't. . . . Because I know that what I sent you is a good
> sound comedy, Clarence or no Clarence. It's far from a great play, but it has
> plenty of laughs, a little pathos, and above all I think the interest is sustained. I
> suspect that it is underwritten in a couple of places but that is easily remedied.

So far Preston, borrowing terms from Brander Matthews, gives a judicious
appraisal of *Strictly Dishonorable*'s structure and dialogue. What follows is the
intriguing part. For here, in pointed suggestions about cast, set, and crew, is
revealed Sturges's instinct for all aspects of a dramatic production. "If you
want to see what Tom looks like," Preston's letter to Pemberton continues,
"go to dinner at 336 West 45th street, Tomaso Gandolphi, Prop." *Strictly Dishonorable*'s set, Preston felt, should also evoke Tomaso's, and Leo Bugakov,
who for *The Sea Gull* produced "some of the finest lighting effects I've ever
seen in my life," had to handle the lights. The only man who could play the
role of the Judge, in Preston's opinion, was Carl Anthony from *Hotbed*; Preston had written the role for him. Preston did not, as he would later claim,
write Count di Ruvo for his friend Georges Renevant, but did ask Pemberton,
"Could Georges Renevant do it? He's too good a friend of mine for me to
judge." And of Temple Duncan's husband, "Is Dick Hale sexy enough? I'm
afraid. . . ."

On July 2, Pemberton cabled Preston: "CONGRATULATIONS IF YOU ARE WILLING TO DO A LITTLE WORK THINK YOU HAVE FINE COMMERCIAL PROPERTY FIRST ACT HUNDRED PER CENT SECOND AND THIRD SKIMPY NEED DEVELOPING PLAY TEN MINUTES TOO SHORT BUT CONTAINS WORLDS SWELL MATERIAL CAN YOU COME FOR CONFERENCE AND WHEN WOULD LIKE TO TRY FOR AUGUST PRODUCTION BROCK PEMBERTON."

But Preston was not so grateful as one might expect. He had confided in his diary on June 30: "Diary-prepare for a surprise. Today, beginning 9 A.M., I planned the sets and then did 18 pages of the first act of *Recapture*. . . . I think it's going to be a *fine* play so far ahead of *Strictly Dishonorable* it makes me ashamed of it." So on July 2, Preston cabled Pemberton in New York, and after thanking him for his "charming telegram," announced: "JUST FINISHED ACT II OF RECAPTURE, YOUR SECOND SUCCESS THIS SEASON AND WOULD LIKE TO STAY HERE WEEK LONGER. . . . DON'T WORRY ABOUT REWRITING GO AHEAD AND LINE UP YOUR CAST."

He was wrong, on the whole, about *Recapture*, but right about himself. A fresh challenge, psychological intensity, and the will to succeed were, more than aesthetic, purgative, or moral compulsions what would fire his talent from now on.

C H A P T E R **6**

The mounting of *Strictly Dishonorable* involved Preston with two creative personalities no less stubborn than himself. When Pemberton cabled his congratulations in early July, he had expressed wholehearted enthusiasm for the play's first act, but complained that the second and third acts were "skimpy" and needed developing.[1] Preston replied that he knew precisely what Pemberton meant and would by all means flesh out Act II, pages eleven and twenty-one, and Act III, pages ten and twenty-three.[2] This was scarcely the revision Pemberton had in mind, as he informed his playwright—probably in no uncertain terms, for by mid-July, Preston was writing, "Thank you for your letter of July 13th. Its tone and its viewpoint reassure me as to the state of your health. Lately you had become so amiable I was afraid you were going to die or something."[3]

They settled into friendly contention, with Pemberton explaining, "Practically all the ideas I have had are expansions to clarify or bolster. You have some quick transitions and you have underwritten in spots so the full effect is lost. But if you have done this much without apparent effort you can do the rest. I do think you have most of a commercial property and that getting the balance will be a comparatively simple matter."[4] Preston received a $500 advance on July 17 and soon after finished *Recapture* and set off for New York. He arrived, according to Pemberton, wholly absorbed with his new drama, but "by offering an immediate production if he would do some more work on the comedy, a few more scenes were forthcoming, and then by threatening postponement if further scenes were not written, a tentative first draft was reached."[5]

Pemberton, Tony Perry (who was directing the play), and Preston all had good eyes for talent, and casting began casually, in an air of mutual trust. Since

Preston wrote the role of the Judge for Carl Anthony, Carl Anthony, they agreed, would play the Judge; just as Louis Greene, whom Preston admired in *Frankie and Johnnie*, would play Henry. It was Perry who thought of William Ricciardi for Tom; Irish character actor Edward McNamara seemed a natural for the cop; and Tulio Carminati turned up in Pemberton's office the same week as Preston's script. He was immediately cast as Gus. For Isabelle, however, no obvious choice emerged. As Pemberton recalls, agents were rung up and dozens of "the most beautiful choristers" and ingenues called in.

> A few of all these prospects seemed to catch the elusive charm compounded of great naiveté and great sophistication that is Isabelle Parry. Leading this small group by several lengths ran Muriel Kirkland. Unknown to us except for a brief glimpse in a smallish part in "Cock Robin" she came to us from an agent. Her first reading convinced us she was the girl, but in truthfulness I am ashamed to confess we did not accept her immediately because we were too saturated with the idea that she must outglorify all American girls in physical beauty.

Pemberton and Perry were soon persuaded that "beauty of spirit rather than of face or form was what the part cried for,"[6] but Preston was not, or perhaps was not convinced of Muriel Kirkland's beauty of spirit. He fought with all his cunning and temper against casting Kirkland, he threatened there'd be no more revisions from him if she got the role. But Perry in particular was adamant, and Pemberton answered Preston's threats by assembling the cast, all of whom, he announced, would be given a week's pay and dismissed unless the playwright decided to cooperate. Preston relented. As in so many of his dealings with Paris Singer, he'd assailed a man more powerful than himself, and was willing to admit it. There's no reason to presume Preston respected Pemberton any less for their confrontation; but then neither was he gracious in defeat. Grudgingly, he agreed to some rewrites. Not enough, however, to satisfy Pemberton and Perry who—in a preemption commonplace in film but rare to theatre—added dialogue of their own.[7]

The additions were minimal, but they appalled Preston, who heard them first at the Jackson Heights opening. Whether because of these, or Kirkland, or the sheer exhaustion of the past few months, he began predicting his play's failure. His despondence made no impact on Mary Desti, who in the afternoon of September 18 sent two telegrams to the Avon Theatre:

GOD BLESS YOU MAY THIS BE THE FIRST OF MANY HAPPY
SUCCESSES = MOTHER

And ten minutes after that:

I KNEW YOU WOULD MAKE GOOD. HERE'S TO A LONG RUN I
ADORE YOU YOU ARE MY SUCCESS = MOTHER

Later that night, Charley Abramson joined a long list of well-wishers, cabling, "NO LONGER HOPE IT'S A FACT A POSITIVE SMASH"; and so it was.

Strictly Dishonorable, wrote Burns Mantle in his roundup of that Broadway year, "practically made new men of the generally depressed reviewers." Brooks Atkinson, in the *New York Times*, called it "a well-nigh perfect comedy," and, while praising Kirkland's performance, devoted most of his review to Sturges. "No one," said Atkinson, "could write such deft, amusing lines and describe characters with such understanding who did not have genuine talent for the theatre. . . . Mr. Sturges has not only an extraordinary gift for character and dialogue, but for the flow and astonishment of situation." The other dailies, if less far-seeing, were equally lavish in their praise. "The cleverest comedy in town," said the *Evening World*, "a gay, deftly written comedy," said the *World*, and the *Herald Tribune* reviewer, among the first to observe Sturges's antirealist impulse, found *Strictly Dishonorable* "a happy combination of fairy tale and sex." Preston's script rather than the Pemberton-Perry production was stressed in most all the reviews. They appeared on Thursday the nineteenth, and the box office immediately sold out, with brokers buying up all the Avon's small orchestra, and much of the balcony as well. That Sunday's *Times* cryptically noted, "Tomorrow night the box office price of the best seats will be raised to $3.85, just as if you could get them there." Some time early in the run a man paid a scalper sixty-six dollars for a pair of seats.

Strictly Dishonorable ran at the Avon for 557 performances, opened almost immediately in Chicago and San Francisco, toured the country and was produced in London, Berlin, and Rome. Carl Laemmle's Universal Pictures paid $125,000 for the screen rights, and the Dramatists Guild gave Preston their $500 Magrue Award, informing him: "Under the terms of the award, the Council of the Dramatists Guild decides each year which play, written by a member and produced in New York City that year has made the audience a little brighter and a little more cheered up when it leaves the theatre than when it came in."[8] Nobly, Preston returned the $500 and told the Guild: "Ever since winning the Magrue Prize I have been wondering how to invest the money. I cannot think of a safer or better way than to send it to you, to be added to the Authors League Fund."[9] It was, by now, the beginning of the

Depression, but Preston was rich. Beyond movie deals and radio spin-offs, his royalty came to $1,500 a week. Mary Desti declared her life validated, and reserved Solomon Sturges announced, "I am elated at your success." [10]

Preston was on the *Nation*'s Honor Roll for 1929. The only other dramatist so honored that year was Elmer Rice, whose *Street Scene*—with its naturalistic style and political subtext—far more than *Strictly Dishonorable* prefigured the trend of American drama in the decade ahead.

Strictly Dishonorable reflected an America which, ten years after rejecting the League of Nations, was only mildly curious about the world at large. Outspoken about money and sex, scornful of provincialism, and indifferent to politics, this play is very much a product of its times. It reveals the awakening of an original American talent, and is a good love story besides.

Strictly Dishonorable is set in Tom's speakeasy, where Henry and Isabelle, an engaged young couple, arrive for a fashionable drink. Isabelle does not love Henry, although, since she's poor, southern, and no great beauty, she figures she's lucky to have him. He is, after all, a businessman with prospects—if a bit provincial. But, emboldened by drink, Isabelle now announces that she doesn't like Henry's plan for living in New Jersey, she likes Manhattan. She also likes the conviviality of the speakeasy and is soon swinging on a bar stool and swapping remarks with Tom, the expansive Italian proprietor, and a besotted regular who calls himself the Judge. Henry, who likes neither of these men, is even less pleased by the entrance of the Count di Ruvo, a famous Italian tenor. The Count di Ruvo, known as Gus, is a handsome womanizer, who flirts with Isabelle and asks her to dance. She accepts, and when Henry flounces off, jealous and confused, Gus apologizes for making trouble. "Trouble?" she says. "You darling—you've saved me from trouble—and a lifetime of boredom." Having escaped what is for Sturges the worst fate imaginable, Isabelle asks Gus, "What are your intentions toward me?"

"Strictly dishonorable," he replies, and tries to seduce her, but falls in love instead; as does she, and some minor obstacles disposed of, the play ends with promise of marriage and progeny.

Clever, engaging, full of deft characterizations, *Strictly Dishonorable* delighted audiences with its mingled wholesomeness and audacity. Here was a count who slept around but was capable of true love and fidelity. Here was a not especially brave girl who could spot a good thing and risk her future on it. Here too was a speakeasy which, as with *Broadway*'s nightclub two seasons earlier, was bad in name only. And while the sex was there for a touch of prurience (a long scene has Gus dressing Isabelle in his pajamas), it was also an issue of the play; also, as Sturges used it, a means of getting not into but *out* of trouble. For it is her strong sexual attraction to Gus that saves Isabelle from Henry and New Jersey. Sex also gives Gus a larger purpose than his music, and if he and Isabelle don't consummate their affair on the spot (this being, after all, mainstream American theatre), the inevitable is only delayed. As Isabelle informs Henry the following morning, "I still have my virginity, if that's what's worrying you . . . though why they make so much fuss about it is more than I can understand. . . . As if it mattered to anybody but me. By the way, I forgot to ask you! Are *you* pure?"

What twenties' audiences found bolder than Isabelle's views on sex was her decision to throw over an American for a foreign mate. The European, in isolationist twenties theatre, was usually romantic but a cad, or romantic but hopelessly impractical, or not half so romantic as he appeared. In a typical mid-twenties comedy, *The Big Pond*, Barbara Billing lures a poetic European home, only to watch him transform into a perfect American businessman, at which point he loses her love. She marries local Ronnie Davis in the end: he may not be extraordinary, but at least he's up front. Sturges's Isabelle, with fewer illusions and much less fuss, declares there's nothing inexorable or even especially safe about marrying an American. Love and the promise of an interesting life are less risky enticements in the end.

There's a fine irony to the fact that Preston, who so loudly complained about his mother's dragging him to the opera, grew up to make his first real hero an opera star. With businessman Henry a quintessential member of the booboisie, art and business are opposed more heavy-handedly than in *The Guinea Pig*. Subtler, though, are the conflicts *within* characters. Gus, for instance, though a dangerous foreigner to Henry and a celebrity to Isabelle, is in his own mind essentially a regular guy. Of his brilliant voice, he half-jokingly observes, "To own a talent like singing is to own maybe a trained bear that dances to make people laugh," drawing a distinction between himself and his gift. Gus's dilemma will be pursued in terms of virtue and success in Sturges's later work. Here, it is wittily reversed in a subplot involving a bibulous Judge and Mulligan, the bribable neighborhood cop. While these two wink at misdemeanors, they're no more corrupt by their own standards than Gus is laudable by his. Essentially, like McGinty to come, they're loyal, honest when it counts, and—unlike upright Henry—secure enough to laugh at themselves. Here, for instance, they make their peace with temperance:

JUDGE (crosses to bar, lower end): Would you like a little drink, Mulligan?
MULLIGAN: Sure, your honor, an' me tongue is like blottin' paper, but I never touch a drop whilst pursuin' a criminal.

JUDGE: And a very good rule too. How about a little ginger ale, out of a non-refillable bottle? That's what I'm having.

MULLIGAN (crosses to top of bar—eyeing the bottle): Oh, ginger ale! With pleasure, your honor.

(The Judge pours two stiff drinks)

Well, here's to Prohibition, sor [sic]: a noble law.

JUDGE: Experiment.

MULLIGAN: Whatever it is.

Strictly Dishonorable's dialogue not only "hooks," but, far more than *The Guinea Pig*'s, evolves out of character, as do the immigrant malapropisms though they're still overdone. Yet, the spirit of Sturges's world is felt throughout: in the classlessness of the barroom, the relished eccentricity of the Judge and cop,[11] and most conspicuously in Isabelle herself. Isabelle's liberated views on sex read like Estelle Godfrey's love letters, but the model for her high spirits and strong will is unmistakably elsewhere. Like Mary Desti, Isabelle emerges out of a large and complacent family. Like Mary, she has a knack for conquest, wisdom beyond her experience, the imagination to perceive and the equanimity to embrace good luck. Also like Mary, she has a passion for Preston's great nemesis: opera. And there's even a wry homage to all those cramped Parisian apartments in Isabelle's yearning to trade a large house in New Jersey for "a tiny little apartment" in New York.

Then too, Isabelle, though in no wider sense rebellious, can't see why *her* life should be constricted by rules. When the Judge warns her not to waste herself on Gus since he'll never marry, she tells him, "Let me be foolish." And when he speaks approvingly of "good" women," she retorts, "Maybe good women are good because . . . because it takes two to be bad."

But there's a darker side to this (as doubtless also to Preston's vision of Mary), for while we know Gus can marry if he pleases, and whomever he pleases, Isabelle has no option but to be *someone's* spouse: Gus's preferably, but her fiancé's if she must. Isabelle acknowledges as much when, with Gus seemingly out of the picture, moments before curtain she accepts Henry back. Gus rushes to the rescue, of course; but rescue it is, for Isabelle's happiness, as we are made to see it, evolves not inevitably from her worth and convictions, but mystically from the good luck of a good man's love. Obliquely, this first of Sturges's success-against-odds endings engages the issue of chance, and our vulnerability to it, which will so profoundly underlie his films. More specifically it comments on Isabelle, as a powerful character who is nonetheless relatively powerless in the world, and as such she is a precursor not only of free-spirited Jean in *The Lady Eve* and Gerry in *The Palm Beach Story*, but of more socially entrenched women in Sturges's art—and life.

By mid-1930, *Strictly Dishonorable* would already be reappraised and found wanting. But in the fall of 1929 Preston's triumph was unspoiled. Lifted up, like many a Sturges hero, from penury to wealth, from anonymity to fame, he set about remaking his life in a manner Great Grandfather Sturges himself could applaud. Determined to be modest, Preston chose a 1922 model Mercedes, bought just a few of the clothes he longed for, and kept an apartment at 603 Fifth Avenue, above his mother's and smaller even than hers. He sent his father $10,000 to invest and declared he would send $90,000 more soon, he was going to be careful, he was going to save for his future.[12] With the stockmarket crisis that fall, most of Preston's $10,000 vanished—and so, biographers have speculated, his determination to save. But to blame Sturges's later extravagance on this traumatic loss is to presume a deep conviction about saving, which nothing in his past or his works suggests. Those truly traumatized by the Crash put their money in bank accounts or safety deposit boxes or under their mattresses—not, like Preston and his characters, into yachts and pipe dream inventions and trips to Palm Beach. Besides, it's doubtful the returner of the Magrue Award was ever really impelled by anything so mundane as caution. Trust in his father, a desire to please and show off a bit, these were his more likely incentives to invest.

Beyond his Broadway triumph, Preston saw his and Ted Snyder's song, "A Cradle of Dreams," finally published that fall. He wrote an original film musical called *After the Rain* and negotiated with Paramount Films to adapt a Broadway play. "When you haven't worked for thirty years you have quite a lot of accumulated energy," Sturges explained to his father.[13] He also, like Isadora Duncan, could not abide delay. "Nothing," he would insist, "is more demoralizing than NOT doing something . . . like NOT going on a trip, or NOT building the playroom on your house, or NOT owning a restaurant. Even the troubles and heartaches that come with positive things seem preferable to [that] futile emptiness."[14] So he was unswayed by the many friends who advised him NOT to proceed with *Recapture*, or not to proceed now. Presenting two plays in a year was unwise, following a comedy with a drama was foolhardy: this seems to have been the argument pursued by Charley Abramson and others.

Pemberton, passing on his option to the play, offered similar admonishments: a bit disingenuously, as he followed comedies with dramas all the time. Perhaps, Pemberton just didn't like *Recapture*, or liked it, but doubted Preston—especially with his new celebrity—would agree to the major rewrites this difficult work required. Perhaps too, Pemberton, tough as he seemed, took the Kirkland conflict, and whatever Preston threatened in his anger, more seriously than did his playwright. For while Preston purported to be well rid

Preston in the late 1920s, photographed by his friend Arnold Shroeder.

of Pemberton and Perry, he would offer them every subsequent play he wrote—and Pemberton would just as regularly turn them down. Once Pemberton agreed to reconsider after a rewrite, always he was gentle. And there was no personal animus, they stayed friends, but—despite the considerable incentive of their past success—Pemberton would never again agree to work with Sturges.[15] He was the first of many sympathetic bosses whose tolerance Preston misjudged.

Pemberton was not, however, indispensable to *Recapture*. With *Strictly Dishonorable* selling out, even after Black Thursday, Sturges soon found a major Broadway producer, A. H. Woods (who'd hired him for *Frankie and Johnnie*), anxious to mount his new show. So anxious, indeed, was Al Woods that he enlarged upon the standard author's contract (5 percent of the first $5,000, 7 percent of the next $2,000, and 10 percent of the weekly gross exceeding $7,000) to promise Sturges a flat 10 percent of the weekly gross up to $15,000 and 20 percent of everything over that. There were advantages too in the fact that Woods, unlike Pemberton, was a showman with no pretense to writing talent. An "old war horse," Preston called him, mass appeal plays like *The Green Hat* and *Up in Mabel's Room* had made him rich. Since he'd never put a cent in the stock market, he could afford a lavish production. Best of all, Woods admired Sturges's play.

Woods was known for his farces and melodramas, and these are precisely the forms that *Recapture* attempts to fuse. It also attempts to turn a broken elevator from a comic gag in the first act to an instrument of death in the last and to reconcile the high comic premise of a man still in love with his ex-wife with the dramatic revelation that she can't return his love. If, ultimately, it fails to live up to its promises, it is an audacious work.

The plot revolves around Pat and Harry, a couple five years divorced, who meet by chance in a hotel in Vichy, France. Neither is alone—Pat has come with British officer Hubert, who's eager to marry her; Harry with a chorus girl, Bunny, who loves him in vain. For Harry still passionately loves Pat. He nearly committed suicide when she left him; he begs her now, just for a few days, to run off with him to the nearby Villa Lune-de-Ville, where they spent their honeymoon: "Maybe, MAYBE we can recapture that thing we used to have." She reluctantly agrees, but while the experiment is wholly successful for him, for Pat, who recalls her former ecstasy, retrieving the past is impossible. She confesses as much to Bunny, who begs her, for Harry's sake, to pretend: surely, he'll kill himself if he loses her again. Pat agrees to leave Vichy with Harry, but then strides into a defunct elevator and plunges to her death.

Its wild mood swings notwithstanding, *Recapture*, like *Strictly Dishonorable*,

abounds in comic prototypes: a weakling porter, a priapic clergyman, a cuck-
olded fiancé, a bribable concierge. And as with booze in the earlier play, there's
a running joke on a busted elevator, which sluices the weakling porter with
soot and compels a laggardly staff to lug baggage up stairs. Here too the main
characters are superior to the others: Harry is wealthy and honorable and
kind, Pat is beautiful and greedy for life. Though Harry could never contemplate marrying Bunny, a social inferior, she is a bit more than a whore with a
heart of gold. Putting Harry's happiness above her own, Bunny informs Pat
of Harry's penchant for suicide and thus sets up the central conflict of the
play: should Pat acquiesce to Harry's love and lose her freedom, or grasp her
freedom and become complicitous in Harry's death? The calamitous resolution is (at least in Preston's draft) ambiguous:[16] maybe an accident, maybe a
suicide through which Pat rejects a passionless fate.

Comparisons to Noel Coward's *Private Lives* (which opened a year later)
are inevitable. But though their premises are similar, Coward's play—for all
the lovers' sardonic badinage—is a comedy of remarriage, while *Recapture* is
not. *Recapture* is not even a comedy, humor is incidental to this fundamentally
dramatic plot. It is an awkward play—the segues are clumsy, the confessions
overwrought. Still, there is a core of emotional truth. If, for Harry, romantic
love is a matter of adoring one person always, for Pat it's something more
troublesome: "I don't want to be contented, like a cow," she says. "I want to
be unhappy and jealous and suspicious. I want to lie awake at night." A man
who's "fine and thoughtful" will only bore her; remarrying Harry will be like
"going to jail."

Biographical references abound—not only to Preston and Estelle, but also
to Solomon Sturges, whose feelings for Mary Desti may well have been those
of Harry for Pat: and vice versa. Pat's heightened language also smacks of
Mary and Isadora, though Pat's justification for breaking with her spouse—"I
can't live with a man I don't love. . . . It'd be immoral"—evokes the break-up
of Estelle and Preston. Brian Henderson, tracing a theme of "recaptured"
love throughout Sturges's work, speculates that "psychologically speaking,
[*Recapture*] . . . fuses the fantasy of recapture with the fantasy of revenge."[17] In
other words, Preston gets Estelle back and gets to kill her too! The theory
(even more applicable to *Unfaithfully Yours*) is intriguing, but limited, since the
closer one looks at *Recapture* the less a purgative impulse makes sense. Preston
was not only smarter and less agreeable than Harry: after five years, he was
wholly out of love with his former spouse. Harry's long-suffering devotion
was foreign to Preston, nor could Sturges bring Harry the character fully to
life. The women characters are more credible. As with Isabelle in *Strictly Dis-*

honorable, it is Pat who determines the course of the play: her large hopes and integrity must compel us, we must be frustrated by her powerlessness, and watch not for Harry's happiness, but Pat's deliverance in the end.

Al Woods spared no expense on Sturges's drama. The cast—Ann Andrews as Pat, Melvyn Douglas as Harry, Glenda Farrell as Bunny—was first-rate, the sets as splendid as money could buy. Especially fine was a real elevator, which lifted, got stuck and, in the spectacular finale, crashed before one's eyes. Don Mullally directed, apparently with no protests from the playwright. The play previewed in Atlantic City, and opened to high expectations at the Eltinge Theatre, on January 29, 1930.

Preston described the following morning's reviews as "the most violently destructive notices I have seen in years. The critics boiled me in oil and then danced a swan song on my corpse." [18] In fairness, while critical of the play—and particularly its structure—reviewers were for the most part respectful of the playwright himself. *The Herald Tribune* noted "moments of amusement, instants less frequent of real feeling and a net effect which, if the author had never been heard of before, one would describe as 'promising,' though queer." The *Times* found "a merry first act" to praise. "Anyway," summed up the *Daily News*, "here is a new piece that proves young Mr. Sturges' sense of the theatre to be a definite gift and puts his lack of experience in the theatre to an expensive test."

It was that, and a setback, but scarcely devastating. Preston told his father, "*Recapture* is not a bad play, but I took some liberties with the dramatic construction which [the critics] might have forgiven O'Neill but which, in me, they considered only impudence." [19] The issue is well-taken. O'Neill plays like *Strange Interlude* are filled with contrivances, and that O'Neill could get away with these while he could not may have troubled Sturges the artist as well as Sturges the figure of news. That Preston cited O'Neill is revealing. Still, his commitment was not to "serious" drama, any more than he was convinced his gifts were for comedy alone. The reviews did not depress him for long. When *Recapture* closed, after twenty-four performances, he still had a play running on Broadway and would soon have a new one in the works. He had, in a little over a year, come a long way from dependence on stage managing and the Maison Desti; no one would ever define him as Mary's child again. Optimistic by nature, he had every reason to be hopeful: he was celebrated, wealthy, full of ideas—and in love.

Eleanor Hutton was the daughter of Post breakfast foods heiress Marjorie Merriweather Post, who—when Eleanor was eleven—married Ed Hutton, a self-made Wall Street financier. Together, Ed and Marjorie founded General Foods. They were a striking couple, smart and flashy—they built a 350-foot yacht, full of gold and marble, they bought estates in Long Island and Palm Beach. Eleanor's real father, Edward Bennett Close, came from a line of prominent Connecticut Yankees; with them, Eleanor shared her unassuming self-possession and quiet strong will. If the rich are different, Eleanor was that to Preston. In 1929, she was also nineteen years old, blonde, beautiful, courted by millionaires and European nobility, but determined to marry whom she wished.

> I met Preston Sturges [Eleanor recalls] at a dinner party on Park Avenue given by Dudley Field Malone, Commissioner of the Port of New York, and a great friend of my mother's. Shortly after that, I came down with bronchitis, and mother sent me to Atlantic City for the air. In Atlantic City, there was this new play being given a tryout—*Recapture*. I went to it because I'd met Preston Sturges, and he saw me in the audience and asked me to come out to dinner.[1]

Around the time Preston met Eleanor at the Park Avenue dinner party, he began talking to a young French composer named H. Maurice Jacquet. Jacquet's musical comedy, *The Silver Swan*—about romantic intrigues in an opera company—had, after just twenty-one performances, closed that fall. Now, in late December, he was eager to try again. Since production costs for musicals were prohibitive, Jacquet proposed to Preston that they salvage the costumes, sets, and score from *The Silver Swan*, then Sturges would write the new lyrics and book. The economy appealed to Preston, as did the prospect of collaborating on a musical. *Recapture* was now in production. Once it opened, Preston promised to get down to work.

Preston had also promised to visit an ailing Paris Singer in Palm Beach and now announced he would like to bring Jacquet along. "WE ALWAYS HAVE ROOM FOR PRESTON, THOUGH VILLA SMALL," replied Singer, "BUT NOT FOR KING PRESTON STURGES AND HIS PALESTINE SUITE OF RETINUE." [2] Preston immediately cabled back, explaining that the idea had been not to miss seeing Singer: "ALL BECAUSE OF A DAMNED CONTRACT AND [I] SUGGESTED HAVING JACQUET JOIN ME SO WE COULD WORK DOWN THERE INSTEAD OF HAVING TO LEAVE YOU TOO SOON."

"I DO NOT HAVE A SWELLED HEAD," he added, and though surely he did—and an increasingly grand manner—his sense of humor was un-harmed. "YOU CAN PAY FOR THIS TELEGRAM WHEN I SEE YOU," [3] Preston teased Singer, who, ego appeased, booked the playwright and the composer a maisonette at his club.

That club was the fashionable Everglades, and, by Preston's recollection (corroborated by Singer's correspondence), his *only* destination in Palm Beach. On the train south with Jacquet,[4] he—by chance—ran into Eleanor Hutton, also heading for Florida. They knew each other, he says, though only slightly. It was, as in *Remember the Night*, along the journey that they fell in love.

Eleanor, however, remembers dates in New York, and after considerable acquaintance, *inviting* Preston to Palm Beach. Once there, both agree, they spent all their time together. Paris and Joan Singer were enlisted as allies. Jacquet was forgotten, Preston never wrote a word.

Preston, in fact, rarely left the Hutton's singular Palm Beach mansion, Mar-A-Lago, though his presence pleased no one but Eleanor. For her, he was dashing, knowledgeable, a man from the arts; for her parents, he was twelve years Eleanor's senior, suspiciously ardent and without a regular job. Even eminent Paris Singer's endorsement made no impact; the Huttons, so-cially ambitious and wary of fortune hunters, immediately set their minds against Preston.

And Preston retaliated by disparaging their nouveau riche life-style and garishly decorated home. As he'd been dismayed to learn of Estelle Mudge's $11,000 annual income before his first marriage, he made it a point that he was attracted to Eleanor *despite* her position, telling her (somewhat defen-sively): "I fell in love with a blonde born Eleanor Close, with straight limbs, a high-bridged nose and a clear forehead. Although brought up in a Shubert revue atmosphere more absurd than anything conceived by Brother Florenz

Eleanor Hutton, 1929.

Ziegfeld . . . or *because of it perhaps*, she [has] a sense of humor and pretty good taste. If she [wears] a pound or so too many jewels in the morning and afternoons, it must be remembered that this is done in certain circles where, as Diamond Jim Brady put it so aptly, 'Them as has 'em, wears 'em.'"⁵

Preston's concession that Eleanor's humor and taste partially resulted from her affluent upbringing shows he's shrewdly considered the impact of wealth on character. Even Eleanor's indifference to millionaire suitors could be in part attributed to her never having wanted for luxuries. And when he could distance himself from their disapproval, how fascinated Preston must have been by these ostentatious Huttons! Unlike discreet Solomon Sturges or frequently indolent Singer, they were—like Singer's father—real American dynasty builders: ruthless in a way, crude certainly, but inventive, philanthropic, fantastically energetic, and among the most powerful people in America. Though he despised being thought a fortune hunter, Preston must initially have hoped his charm, sincerity, and accomplishments would win over at least Marjorie Hutton, who was devoted to her three daughters. Meanwhile, he enjoyed attending beach and yacht parties with Eleanor, for they were head over heels in love.

Preston remained three weeks at Mar-A-Lago, until an irate cable from Jacquet—now back in New York—summoned him home to write their play. By now Preston and Eleanor had secretly planned a June 3 wedding. The rush may have been Preston's idea, since he was the more impetuous, but Eleanor was as eager to be married as he.

Before leaving for New York, Preston told the Huttons of his and Eleanor's intentions, and—as he recalled in a subsequent letter to Eleanor—"consternation and vexation reigned. I was informed that you had no money of your own and replied that it was really none of my business." [6] Then the Huttons, making clear they suspected both Preston's character and his interest in Eleanor, threatened their daughter with disinheritance if she failed to satisfy their demands. (Not that Eleanor would, in any case, have been without money for long, since she came into a sizable inheritance from her grandfather at twenty-one). First, Marjorie Hutton asked that Eleanor wait six months before marrying so they could all be sure she *really* loved Preston. Soon the six months became a year.

And like mean-spirited August who, in *Unfaithfully Yours*, hires sleuths to trail the innocent Daphne, Ed Hutton sent private detectives to follow Preston in New York. Disreputable-looking characters loomed behind Preston on street corners, and one sleuth went so far as to wake Brock Pemberton in the middle of the night, probing for gossip. To make matters worse, Preston's biological father Edmund Biden, after years of silence, now surfaced and wrote Ed Hutton a letter that was by turns unctuous and whiny and filled with what he must have perceived as damning allegations against Mary Desti—claiming, for instance, that she'd deceived him into proposing to her by hiding the fact that she'd been married *three* times before! Biden also claimed he was owed at very least $500 for Preston's 1898 throat operation, and while no one seems to have taken his pathetic revelations seriously, this father could not have enhanced Preston's desirability as a mate.[7]

On a more flattering note, columnists like Walter Winchell were speculating about the unofficial engagement of the brilliant playwright and beautiful heiress, while at home in Palm Beach the Huttons opened Preston's love letters and read them aloud to their socialite friends. "To me," Preston told Eleanor, "it seems silly of your family to be so violent about me and tell you such things that I will never be able to forgive them or be friendly with them. The policy is short-sighted and does not take into consideration the fact that—oh horror of horrors!—I might become your husband. A good general plans his retreat the while he is attacking. The Huttons are burning their bridges behind them." [8]

Preston's letters to Eleanor are as passionate as those he wrote to Estelle eight years earlier; though this time there's less talk of abstract subjects, like religion and insanity, and more moralizing about circumstances. "I am sorry you are being made unhappy, but probably most unhappiness is caused by well-meaning people," [9] Preston wrote Eleanor. And "Please," she told him, "don't worry about all this confusion as the trouble is so superficial—In my true purpose I never vary the slightest." She also told him, "I not only am in love with you but you have my greatest admiration. There are certain things you have great knowledge of that give me great joy and happiness." [10] And because of the twelve-year difference in their ages, but also because of Eleanor's extreme modesty about her education and awe of the arts, Preston sometimes interspersed adoring poems and private jokes with lectures: "You must try in your letters to write the way you talk," he counseled her. "If you speak the lines out in your head, you'll find that it is just like talking to the person you are writing to, and you will be relieved of the peculiar constipation of ideas that most people suffer from when they write." [11]

Other times he was lovelorn. One Tuesday night, "rainy and blue," Preston wrote Eleanor:

> I'm afraid I do love you, and very much too. I wish I were a fortune hunter, it would be so much simpler for both of us. Because the minute I was informed you were to be disinherited I'd lose interest; and when you realized what sort of a bimbo I was, you'd lose interest. And you'd go your way, and I'd go my way, and in a little while you'd fall in love with an overgrown boy-scout and your parents would be delighted and give him a good job as a coffee-taster in [their] Maxwell House Company and you'd be happily married and live on your family's money and your husband could take personality courses by mail to while away the evenings; and while you were producing little coffee-tasters for the further glory of the good old Maxwell House Company I would be

working at my regular business of pursuing heiresses hoping some day to achieve a good catch and achieve the honorable position of a lap dog so that I could give up trying to write plays which don't bring in any money anyway and which I probably never did in the first place anyway, besides.[12]

Preston was now distracted from his work, not only by the ups and downs of his love affair with Eleanor, but also by his parents' health. "Mother got back from Chicago two days ago," Preston wrote Paris Singer, soon after returning from Florida. "Father had his second operation just before she left."[13] Beyond his prostate operation, Solomon, though conservatively invested, had suffered both financially and psychologically from the Crash. Mary, increasingly debilitated by leukemia, made the arduous journey to see him. Perhaps they realized this was the last time they would meet.

Saddened for his parents, and longing to be with Eleanor, Preston, after much importuning by Jacquet, sat down on March 6 to write his play. On March 21, he finished a first draft of *The Well of Romance*: a highly improbable story of love between a princess and a poet king, which—in its only surviving version—is obviously a spoof.

Like Wil's unproducible first play in *The Guinea Pig*, *The Well of Romance* is all costumes and song. The setting is the mythical kingdom of Magnesia, at an inn known for its magic well. Drink the well's foul-tasting water, and you'll fall in love. Or so local wisdom has it. Only a miracle could make beautiful young Princess von und zu Heimer und Spiegelungen fall in love with middle-aged General Krankeit. That's why the General bribes the Grand Chancellor to lure the Princess to the well. Once there, though, the Princess falls not for the aging General but for the feckless young king (disguised as a poet). This poses sticky problems of priority for the ambitious Grand Chancellor—commonly known as Cohen.

This also poses problems for Sturges who has set up and must, for another act, sustain the play's one-note idea: a deflating of formulaic light opera strategies with earthy details and twenties comic types—a surly hero, a marriage-shunning ingenue, a discreetly graying suitor, a garment district Jew. Grand Chancellor Cohen is the politician equivalent to *The Guinea Pig*'s lovably greedy producer and—like him—the play's motivating force. It is he, bankrolled by the General, who gets the Princess to the well in the first place. His ineptitudes keep the Princess and Poet-King separated during most of Act II; then he brings them together for the obligatory happy end.

Characterization of the lovers is, as in *The Guinea Pig*, perfunctory, accents (and now names) are made much of, and the humor is *very* broad. Typical is Cohen's exhorting royalty to marry: "How can we urge the plain pipple to reproduce and begat when instead from showing them an exemple the upper classes loaf on the job?" Or the General's missing his fateful tryst with the innkeeper because he's bursting with "well of romance" water, and must dash off to pee!

While parodying the clichés of light opera, Sturges strikes an off-handed pose. Instructions for a dancing scene at the opening of Act II trail off: "When enough of this sort of thing has gone on, the girls go off, leaving us, God help me! to continue. . . ." And there's no bite to the ironies, for—though always serious about his writing—Sturges has not, in spoofing platitudes, discovered a serious point.

Still, this was a first draft, only of the book. The next step was to coordinate lyrics with Jacquet's music. The final work, Sturges must have reasoned, would depend as much on the composer's contributions as on his.

And the composer—whose music was of precisely the Viennese light opera tradition Sturges's book set out to parody—had strong ideas of his own. Early on, he hired as director the playwright J. Harry Benrimo and, while Preston dallied in Palm Beach, Jacquet began raising money for a prominent musical cast. Though in principle all for comedy, Jacquet in fact had a weakness for elegance and dismissed as "too prosaic" the camper of Sturges's lyrics, in songs like "I'll Never Complain":[14]

> Many people seem to think that money
>   is the only link to happiness.
> Be that as it may I wish to say
>   I do not agree with this or acquiesce.
> Therefore let's not wait,
> Pause or hesitate. Let us rusticate together now
>   because
>
> CHORUS: A loving heart is quite enough
> For us to start the marriage stuff
> Baby, I'll never complain.

Sturges's lyrics here perfectly convey his state of mind in mid-March, 1930: for he was insisting that Eleanor *not* wait the year her mother wanted, but say the hell with the Huttons and their money and marry him right away. "Up to now," he wrote,

I've been pretty much of an outsider in all this. Although my own happiness was at stake, I've sat on the side-lines and hoped for the best. From now on, I'm in the fight, and I'll either win or lose quickly. As a matter of fact, the cards are stacked: I can't lose. If you really love me, I win. If you don't love me, I still win, because nothing could be a worse catastrophe than marrying some day a girl to whom money and her Mama meant more than her husband.[15]

On March 23, Paris Singer's wife Joan cabled Preston: "AM ON SEC-OND SECTION OF MIAMIAN . . . ARRIVE SIX THIRTY MUCH TO SAY FROM ELEANOR." Soon after, Eleanor risked not just financial disin-heritance but a deep rift with her mother and came to New York herself. On Saturday April 12, reporters, looking for a story, found Sturges's apartment suspiciously empty. That Monday the *Times* made Preston and Eleanor's mar-riage front page news: "ELEANOR HUTTON ELOPES WITH PLAY-WRIGHT; WEDS PRESTON STURGES OVER PARENTS' PROTEST." They had been married Saturday by a justice of the peace in Bedford Hills, and had gone on to visit Eleanor's beloved Uncle Harry Close in Cornwall-on-Hudson and then to Mary Desti's country house in Woodstock for the week-end. Now they were planning to visit Solomon Sturges in Chicago.

While the acrimony with the Huttons persisted, Preston became close friends with Eleanor's father's brother, Uncle Harry. And Eleanor immedi-ately warmed to both Preston's parents, who liked her enormously. Indeed, Mary so loved her daughter-in-law she left Eleanor, who scarcely needed en-dowment, a Woodstock house in her will. Not since Isadora's death had Mary felt so close to another woman; and Eleanor remembers being utterly capti-vated by "Madame Desti," who—when not in Woodstock—lived in the apart-ment below theirs at 603 Fifth Avenue and still sold Desti products in a front room, looking out on the street. Eleanor's own mother, furious over the mar-riage, refused to see Preston *or* Eleanor and for months withheld all Eleanor's jewelry. Finally, she returned a diamond wrist watch. Eleanor recalls running to show this favorite possession to Mary, who "looked at it, and she said, 'My dear child, as long as you own *it*, that's fine, but the moment it owns *you* throw it away, give it away, do anything.'"

"And that," says Eleanor, "has marked me for life."

Mary had written *The Untold Story*, about her friendship with Isadora, and got it published the same year *Strictly Dishonorable* came out. She now told Preston she couldn't understand why she'd fought getting old all those years, it was such a relief *not* to have to bother putting on lipstick, to really let yourself go.[16] Solomon still sent her monthly allowances. She was nursed by her cousin Marion Whitely, and by Eleanor, who anyhow loved running down for stories or advice. Mary had a pet monkey. "The monkey pee-peed every-where," says Eleanor. "Preston and I made curtains for Mary's bedroom, and the monkey pee-peed all along the print. I took the monkey and spanked it like a good Connecticut Yankee, and after that the monkey would set up the most awful clamor whenever I came in."

Eleanor recalls another animal incident, involving Preston's preternaturally clever tiger cat, Elmer Thompson. Before their marriage, Preston, an excellent cook, had prepared gourmet dishes for Elmer. Now Preston insisted that Eleanor (who'd never so much as boiled an egg) make all the meals; and she said, "look friend, if I've got to do the cooking here, we're going to get Elmer Thompson on cat food." Elmer Thompson would have none of this and for four days refused to eat. "So I went out, and I bought him a beautiful piece of salmon, and he sat there looking so pleased, because he could smell it, and I put the salmon down beside the cat food, and he looked at me and he went and ate the cat food." This anecdote is revealing for it shows Preston indisputably the master, while Eleanor and Elmer Thompson come to accept their subordinate positions—though not without salvaging pride.

Eleanor's memories of life with Sturges sound like scenes from *You Can't Take it with You*. Eleanor and Preston both loved animals and, as well as Elmer Thompson, soon were housing a goldfish and a bird. All competed for space in the tiny studio apartment, above which Preston had constructed a sun roof—so in hot weather they broiled. Eleanor used to buy a cake of ice and sit in the bathtub. And it was not only animals, but humans Preston brought home—an out-of-work actor was just who they needed to paint the apartment. He had, of course, to eat meals with them while he worked, as did the down-on-his-luck elderly (and alcoholic) sea captain Preston hired to steer their yacht. For Preston had refurbished a burned-out fifty-two-foot cruiser and christened it *The Recapture*. Weekends, he, Eleanor, Elmer Thompson, and the sea captain sailed up the sound.

"All I want to do is bring your brains out of baby ribbons," Preston told Eleanor, and she thanked him for that. She had up to now had such little exposure to literature, art, and even music, though she knew she could sing. Many nights, that first summer of their marriage, Preston would come in after working late with Jacquet, dish up something in the kitchen, and wake Eleanor to perform a song they'd just thought up. She was a wonderful help, he told her. She was the woman he adored. And she thought Preston, with his talent and human concern even for strangers, was a fascinating man, but also—like passion itself—exhausting.

There was never a dull moment. They were out all hours, at Sardis, or Tony's, for Preston loved a crowd and was happy to go to bed at dawn and wake up at noon. The unemployed actor was always painting their floors, so they couldn't walk around, and one day the man took Preston's instructions to paint the bathroom literally. That night, Preston sat down on the john, and screamed. What's the problem? asked Eleanor. I can't get up, called Preston—he was stuck to a newly painted toilet seat. They laughed and laughed at that one. . . .

But other times were less amusing, for Sturges was determined to exercise power: Temple Duncan's husband, Dick Hale, recalls Preston's making a great fuss one night, ordering Eleanor to brew them coffee.[17] And, though he was always sorry immediately afterwards, Preston vented his violent temper on his wife, not only verbally, as the following incident reveals.

Both Eleanor and Preston tended to be chubby (one of Preston's pet names for Eleanor was "Butterball"), but "Preston," Eleanor recalls,

> was quite vain, and one day when he was saying how handsome he was, I said to him, "You look like an apple with two tooth picks as legs." He got perfectly furious and went and got the carving knife, and he chased me. I rushed downstairs into Madame Desti's apartment, and she said, oh lock the door, lock the door; so we locked the door, but he got through that, so we ran into the bathroom. We heard Preston raging around muttering, "I'll get you, I'll get you"; and we stayed in the loo until we heard him go out.

Maybe, Eleanor says, it was all an act, but probably it was both an act and serious, and in any case, scenes like this were not Eleanor's idea of domestic life. Nor, after the excitement wore off, was the small apartment crowded with Preston's friends. Her splendid clothes hung on a makeshift rack by the kitchen. She missed her mother, and Preston fluctuated between inveighing against the Huttons' pretensions and trying to outdo them at their own tricks. He wrote Solomon Sturges, asking for an introduction to someone who could get him into the New York Yacht Club.[18] He went to the pawn shop and bought Eleanor a bracelet of the biggest diamonds she'd ever seen. When Marjorie Hutton finally summoned Eleanor to Long Island, "You wear that diamond bracelet," Preston told her. And she did.[19]

But Marjorie Hutton never condescended to see Preston, and this must have rankled. Eleanor, beautiful and sweet-tempered as she was, could also be irritating. For, though eager to learn, she was as yet far from Sturges's intellectual equal, and she hadn't Estelle's quick tongue to talk back to his arrogance. Nor, besides wishing him success, did she show much interest in Preston's writing.

Preston and Jacquet were not having as easy a time as they'd hoped raising money for *The Well of Romance*. In July they signed G.W. MacGregor on as producer, but, even with *The Silver Swan*'s sets and costumes, they could not mount their increasingly opulent musical on the backing they'd accrued. Faced with an alternative of courting new financiers, Sturges began throwing in thousands of dollars of his own. He must have seen this as an investment in his future. They cast Howard Marsh and Norma Terris, stars of the 1927 hit *Showboat*, as their poet-king and princess. They booked a theatre in Pittsburgh for a September run.

Meanwhile, Eleanor had contracted scarlet fever. All she wanted was to stay in bed, but Preston begged her, "You have to come with me, you're my youth." So, once the fever died, she let him drag her to Pittsburgh. There, the heiress attracted more favorable attention than her husband's play.

A "juvenile attempt at libretto writing," wrote the *Pittsburgh Press* of Sturges's contribution to *The Well of Romance*, while praising Jacquet's score. And reviews were scarcely more enthusiastic when the musical opened November 7, 1930, at the Craig Theatre in New York. Typical was the *World*'s reaction: "When considering *The Well of Romance* our chief difficulty lies in deciding whether it is intended as a glamorous musical romance or a pitiless burlesque of old-fashioned opera. . . . The plot is preposterous enough to suggest a thorough if misguided attempt at satire." But the cast "play it seriously with a zest and bounce that date back to the days when a mythical kingdom was a glorious discovery." So Sturges's first draft broad parody had evolved into an elaborate musical production, caught between tired fable and halfhearted spoof.

"On its arrival in town [*The Well of Romance*] received one of the most unanimous critical lacings any production has had this season," reported the *Evening Post*. When his play closed a week later, Sturges lost, he estimated, $64,000[20] and had a second failure in a year.

"Well, you tried to do too much," Solomon had written his son after *Recapture*. "It is better to go slow and not put out anything unless you know you have a winner. You must not let the critics get down on you for these newspaper people are very powerful and can break anyone if they have the mind."[21]

Mary's advice now was the opposite. "You have a marvelous talent, and I beg you let nothing interfere with it—nothing," she wrote from Woodstock. "Then too, money never meant much to you or to me—we always held other things of far greater value—and if you are worrying about the loss of . . . money throw it out of your mind. If you are worrying about taking care of me, dearest, remember I lived so many years on so little." And she went on to say she would gladly do it again to know he was happy and well and interested in his work.[22]

Early in the morning of December 25, Preston and Eleanor drove out to Woodstock to surprise Mary at Christmas. She hemorrhaged and died on their first wedding anniversary, April 12, 1931. The name on her death records was Perch. She was fifty-nine years old, and wanted her ashes buried with her mother in Chicago.[23] She left Preston and Eleanor each a house in Woodstock, and the Maison Desti went jointly to both.

Condolences poured in from everywhere. "JUST HEARD OF YOUR GREAT BEREAVEMENT DEAR PRESTON WE LOVED HER AND MOURN ALSO,"[24] the Singers cabled from Cap-Ferrat. And mourn Preston did, though his love for Mary was always complex. She was an extraordinary, but not an easy, mother. In his youth, she wrenched him from his father, she thrust him into the arts. Even at death, she did not give all she had to him. Nor did she ask to be forgiven; she lived her life as she wanted. Mary was Preston's point of reference. So many of his stories, in the coming years, would begin, "My mother . . ."

"My mother," wrote Preston, "felt there was no tragedy in dying, but that was because she had lived so much."[25]

With Mary gone, there was no reason for Preston and Eleanor to remain in their small Fifth Avenue apartment. Eleanor, now twenty-one, came into her grandfather's inheritance, and they bought a townhouse at 125 East Fifty-fourth Street. It was a gracious old building on a quiet block, with a garden in back and servants' rooms and—what especially delighted Eleanor—a sunken bathtub. Preston set about decorating their new place regally.[1]

Eleanor, though, had other projects in mind. A year ago she'd told Preston that she'd rather be kept by him than be his wife. Now she declared, throw out the marriage books! What she needed, besides a new apartment, was a trip to Europe and a singing career. Eleanor's yearnings, Preston may have recognized, were very like his mother's when she left Edmund Biden.

Assuring Preston the separation was temporary, Eleanor sailed for Europe on June 5, taking Mary's cousin Marion Whitely as her chaperone. Marion reported that Eleanor was prettier than ever, "though her terrible indigestion never leaves her." And Preston must have at first refused to correspond because Marion chided: "Hope now that you have started to write [Eleanor] you will keep up the good work no matter how busy you are."[2]

Eleanor and Marion stopped in Istanbul, Rome, and Venice before Marion returned to New York and Eleanor settled in Paris, where her father, Edward Close, now lived with his second wife and twin boys. Eleanor quickly found herself a studio apartment with a piano, began singing lessons, and showed no inclination to come home.

"It is so long since I have been nice to you that you may have forgotten that I ever was,"[3] Preston wrote Eleanor. And to his father Preston confided:

I've thought out a lot of things this summer and I'm going to be a much nicer husband than I was before. I used to think of myself as the proprietor . . . very foolish I know . . . but I'm all over that. From now on I ask only to be the Favorite Man . . . a sort of Lover-in-Law. If you figure this out, you'll see it has far-reaching effects. It means that one cannot sit back and rest on one's laurels, but on the contrary [must] continue to put the best foot forward and be at least as gentle and nice to one's wife as one was to one's fiancée.[4]

These are the sentiments and nearly the exact words Sturges would put in the mouth of Sir Alfred, the self-deceiving protagonist of *Unfaithfully Yours*, two decades later.[5] Preston would be wiser about love by then, but also more resigned.

Now, he fervently believed he could change and win Eleanor back. He also believed in his talent and was determined to salvage his career. *Strictly Dishonorable* closed, leaving him no regular income, and his expenses were mounting. (By January he and Eleanor would be $50,000 in debt.)[6] It was time for a new play. People were always warning him to be careful. Very well, he'd proceed scientifically this time. He began *A Cup of Coffee* early in the morning of June 23. "If I think of a good title this will be a fairly successful play," he wrote in a note to himself on the top of the manuscript. "It will be carefully constructed, will appeal to the simplest emotions and be very conscientiously written."

So Sturges was aiming for a solid product. It was two years into the Depression, and though he himself was not hungry or desperate, everywhere he looked, people were. Times Square was lined with the formerly prosperous waiting for hand-outs of coffee and donuts. Professionals were peddling apples; nineteen shoe shiners competed for business on a single block of Forty-third Street alone.[7] There were hunger strikes and acts of frustrated violence. Ordinary people talked of revolution. A will to change was all the fashion. Dos Passos introduced a radical voice to American literature with *The Forty-Second Parallel*; and even Broadway's S. N. Behrman would make committed leftists protagonists in his upcoming comedies of manners.

Such a radical switch from the refulgent twenties must have reminded Preston of the wild swings in his own childhood—and also of his mother's impoverished youth. "I remember once as a boy speaking scornfully of some very poor people and saying, 'At least they could be clean!'" Preston would tell a friend in the fifties, "and my mother who had known the ultimate poverty as a widow's child in Chicago replying: 'That's where you're wrong—there's a point at which you can't do *anything*—you just sit and stare.'"[8] Now Preston saw the emotional pain of friends like actor Joe Roeder, who was forced to take a job as a clerk in a department store, and joined the alcoholic sea captain and the painter at Sturges's at meal time. While, intellectually, Preston ascribed to Mencken's view that existing governments and reform were similarly ridiculous, his befriending of down-and-outs shows a sympathy with despair.

A Cup of Coffee reflected the spirit of the moment. With its emphasis on the Maxwell House coffee business, one of the Huttons' thriving enterprises, it also revealed Preston's continued preoccupation with Eleanor's family. Its setting is the offices of Baxter's Best Coffee, a family operation founded by the once dynamic Ephraim Baxter. Now, though, Ephraim is growing senile, and authority is increasingly appropriated by his sons: Bloodgood, a misanthropic dollar-and-cents type and Oliver, who, though kinder, has no imagination whatsoever. Business is bad for everyone. The staff barely scrape by on their piddling salaries, and Jimmy, the new salesboy, cajoles orders from hard-up grocers by cheering them with news that their competitors are even worse off. Jimmy is an ambitious young man, impatient with his lowly position and the state of the world. Something has to give, he tells the clever office secretary, Tulip:

JIMMY: I mean with things going the way they are now, pretty soon there'll be a sort of general bankruptcy and then the working man will come into his own.

TULIP (Her eyes round): You mean a revolution?

JIMMY: No . . . uh . . . just sort of a readjustment . . . Of course, I haven't got it all figured out yet.

What Jimmy has figured out, and submitted, is a slogan for the Maxwell House Coffee contest: "If you can't sleep at night, it's not the coffee, it's the bunk." Get it? he asks Tulip. Sure, she says, though it's clear she does not. She loves Jimmy, however, and is outraged when irascible Bloodgood Baxter fires him for playing a phonograph. Then a cable arrives informing Jimmy he's won the Maxwell House contest: he'll get $25,000, plus a terrific job.

Now, of course, Bloodgood regrets firing this apparent genius, and the Baxter brothers spend most of Act II scheming to win Jimmy back. Would he like his own office, a large pay increase, a title? They love all his new campaign ideas. He can have a free hand at advertising, they tell him, and Jimmy agrees to stick by Baxters. He proposes to Tulip, buys gifts for the family. After all this, a Maxwell House messenger arrives with the bad news that it's not Jimmy but a guy from Utica with the same name who won the contest. That cable was a mistake.

Why should this change Jimmy's position at Baxters? Perhaps it shouldn't, the Baxter brothers concede, but it will. Bloodgood again clamors to have Jimmy fired, and as for all those great ideas—well, they *seemed* great when

Jimmy *seemed* to have won the contest, but he didn't, so they weren't. Jimmy himself now doubts his value, but Tulip is convinced the man who founded Baxter's will see things her way. "Think of the thousands of boys who have talent, who could make something of their lives if they just had the chance to show it," she implores doting Ephraim Baxter, who momentarily recovers his wits and orders his sons to give Jimmy a break. Not a contract, that's understood, just the opportunity to show what he's got. Jimmy and Tulip soberly embrace, and then once again comes the Maxwell House messenger: "One million, eight hundred and seventy-six thousand answers is a lot of answers," he tells Jimmy. "It wasn't the fellow from Utica. . . . It was YOU. Congratulations!" Curtain.

A Cup of Coffee is Sturges's first attempt to grapple with success in America. Its plot, conventional structure, and many of the characters' names are replicated in his 1941 film, *Christmas in July*. Yet, the play's Jimmy is edgier and more desperate, his company's underdog relationship with Maxwell House more intense. Preston, in one of his lovelorn letters to Eleanor, had fantasized about her marrying some "overgrown boy-scout" the Huttons would employ as coffee-taster at Maxwell House; and indeed, the whole play could be read as a sort of Oedipal drama, with Jimmy, the Sturges character, aiming both to seduce and unseat his in-laws. (The senile Ephraim Baxter, whose part is excised in the movie, could also be an allusion to Eleanor's dynasty-founding grandfather C. W. Post, who was the first American to make his fortune through advertising and whom Preston probably imagined as more tolerant than his heirs). Then too, while the film does not stress its period, *A Cup of Coffee* depicts a very particular world in crisis. Money is scarce, the black office boy Julius worries about his next meal. Jimmy predicts vast social changes, though when asked how they'll come about, he hasn't a clue. Nor, once he's got his boss's ear, does Jimmy waste time pleading the workers' cause.

Rather, in Act II, he launches into a defense of unrestrained capitalism: "I don't care for these namby-pamby methods that they call fair competition . . . every great fortune in this country was founded with methods that the word [unfair] doesn't begin to describe. Big business was a hard game and a man's game. Look at Johnny Rockefeller, the elder Morgan, Hill, Fisk, Vanderbilt, Astor, and the rest of them—what a fine upstanding bunch of pirates those babies were." Ephraim Baxter agrees and boasts of his own unscrupulous rise from rags to riches.

This exchange is Sturges's first allusion to the railroad tycoon Hill and his fellow robber barons. Ruthless they were, but—in Jimmy's mind—also effective and grand, also an alternative to the futility of patiently waiting your chance. And what of starving office boys like Julius, without the wits to be barons? Well, Julius, Jimmy rationalizes, is a lucky man since he can get pleasure just watching the elevated train.[9]

A Cup of Coffee's political messages may be conflicting, often wrongheaded; yet, in a larger sense, this is a deeply political work: appalled at the world's injustice and the powerlessness of man. "You see how unjust it seems to me," Jimmy complains to Tulip, when the Baxters turn against him. "If my ideas were good this afternoon, why aren't they good now?" Why not? Why too aren't diligence and fair play rewarded? Why should robber barons and their querulous offspring rule? These are questions Sturges will rephrase more profoundly in the coming years. He will continue to ask whether boys like Jimmy *really* are gifted, whether talent can ever be isolated from luck. For as with Isabelle in *Strictly Dishonorable*, the happy ending bespeaks not worth rewarded, but gratuitous deliverance.

Preston spent more time on *A Cup of Coffee* than on *Strictly Dishonorable* and *Recapture* combined. He finished July 31 and sent it off to Pemberton, who promptly turned it down: "I think the play has a lot of quaint charm, its form is good and the humor plentiful. I question, however, its story pattern which does not strike me as fresh enough to sell in these tough times."[10] Rather than balking, Preston readily conceded his own reservations about *A Cup of Coffee*, telling Pemberton, "If it served as nothing else it was a very good exercise in writing and, as a result of grinding away on *A Cup of Coffee* for two months, I have practically finished *Consider the Lily* in ten days. With any kind of break, the latter is a smash hit as it is a compound of just those things which go to make smash hits: plenty of humor, plenty of pathos, and some sensational passages."[11]

Preston had not really abandoned *A Cup of Coffee*, which he continued submitting to Broadway and Hollywood producers and finally sold to Universal in 1934. (It would not be produced as a play until 1988, and then by a small New York repertory company.) Still, there's something disturbing about his unprotesting surrender to Pemberton, a hint of vulnerability not unlike Jimmy's in the play. "The funny thing about success," Sturges would observe in the fifties, "is that either everyone wants you or nobody wants you and you yourself never know exactly why."[12] In August of '31, he was bewildered about his talents. Yet, he threw himself into his new play.

One night, Preston, Charley Abramson, and their photographer friend Arnold Shroeder had ventured into a dance hall: "One of those places," as Preston wrote Eleanor, where you dance with the hostess for ten cents a dance. We had a lot of fun, and we went down again the next night and then ten nights thereafter. The hostess I drew for my lot proved to be a charming little creature who looked like a diminutive Helen Morgan, and used such marvelous words as "apperntment" and "berled" eggs and "take your cherce" and "ersters." Although we spoke supposedly the same language, half the time I didn't know what she was saying and three-quarters of the time she didn't understand me. As a result we each found the other very funny. This idea, the attraction to each other of people opposite in education, is the basic idea of *Consider the Lily*.[13]

Charley Abramson gives another view of the episode. Sturges's dance hall escapades were made so much of by gossip columnists, Abramson says, that Preston wrote the play to justify his nights on the town to Eleanor.[14]

Consider the Lily's hero is New York real estate magnate Otto Paul Vanderkill, a widower who wouldn't be caught dead in a dance hall—unless it occupied his land. Learning that one does, he sets out to inspect it, and winds up madly in love with a dime-a-dance beauty named Madeleine. Madeleine is poor and ignorant, but good. She can't be bought for thousand-dollar tips or beautiful clothes or a love nest apartment. She adores Vanderkill and accepts his gifts because she knows how much it pleases him to spoil her. Marriage, she realizes, is out of the question—they're simply too different, and, besides, he's got grown daughters and a reputation to maintain. "I'm in love with you," he tells her. "Absolutely, completely and insanely in love with you. I don't know why it is, and I don't want to know why it is. There's no rhyme or reason to it, and it's . . . grand!"

Their folie à deux lasts until Madeleine gets pregnant. Vanderkill marries her secretly ("I won't never tell a soul honey," she assures him); but then the baby dies. Vanderkill starts coming home late; Madeleine returns to the dance hall, and when Vanderkill follows her, she storms off to Mexico for a divorce. No longer married, they can once again love passionately. "If some time you want to get married, just come and tell me, Paul, and I won't make no trouble, 'cause I love you, and I want you to be happy. But I won't ever let you marry nobody like me," she declares. And in answer to his mild protests, she cajoles: "We'll just be sweethearts," which is happiness enough.

Embarrassingly sexist by today's standards, *Consider the Lily* was awkward even for its time. Formally, it's not melodrama, farce, or happy ending comedy. The play's easy, boulevard morality is undermined by sentimental declarations of love. Its humor, like *The Guinea Pig*'s, hinges on malapropisms and grammatical blunders—Madeleine's "bluepernts" and "dunnos" and "ain'ts." Then too, like Bunny in *Recapture* and the black office boy Julius in *A Cup of Coffee*,

Madeleine is strangely deficient in desire. The fact that she's *really* content with her lot as a rich man's mistress challenges a basic assumption of Depression drama: that class is no barrier to marriage in America.

Consider the Lily was at first glance a far cry from *A Cup of Coffee*, though the two plays are less different than they seem. In both, the answer to powerlessness is money; the way to succeed in an unjust world is to acquire privilege.

Preston wrote his father in early September that *Consider the Lily* had "'stood on his ear' everyone who has read it. Everyone who has seen it has offered to produce it immediately and I have several offers from people who have only heard about it." [15] This was an exaggeration, for Pemberton, with his usual suggestions for rewrites, had turned the play down. But William Harris soon signed on as producer, and rehearsals were set for November 1.

"I've grown awfully fat," Preston told Solomon, "and as soon as this play is on, will occupy myself solely in getting thin again. . . . Incidentally, I've grown a long flowing mustache, which makes me look about fifty years old. So what with my weight and my whiskers, you won't be able to treat me like a little boy any longer. In fact, you wouldn't know me if you saw me." [16]

Preston also wrote Eleanor about this curious new mustache, which beveled over his narrow lips and emphasized the angular lower portion of his face. He assured his wife he was no longer jealous of her singing career, but wished her well. [17] She ought to come home for a visit, he told her. But when she wouldn't he set off on September 23 to visit *her*.

It was nearly ten years since his last trip to France, and the first time he and Eleanor were together in Paris. It was fall. They visited the original Maison Desti on the rue de la Paix, and Mary's Champ de Mars apartments; they went to the elegant Place des Vosges where Paris Singer, though now a very sick man, still held court. Preston wrote Charley Abramson:

Every man in Europe is in love with [Eleanor] and wants her to divorce me and marry him. I can't swing a cat without hitting a rival, and frankly I don't blame them all. Rumors are rife—but they're all horsefeathers. As you know, neither of us can be seen with anyone without a reporter having a hemorrhage—and it means nothing. Eleanor has conducted herself admirably. With every Prince, Lord, millionaire and fortune hunter over here pursuing her, she has been completely fine, dear and honorable—I worship her.

At last, the other night, I found the words to describe her as I think of her. We were in a delightful restaurant. A gypsy orchestra was playing and I said: "A thousand poets dreamed for a thousand years—and then you were born." [18]

Eleanor was studying *Rigoletto* with a distinguished Italian maestro whom Preston was eager to meet. Preston bought himself a big hat and a scarf and strode into Maestro Alberti's studio, announcing, "*I am the lady's husband.*" After listening briefly to Eleanor's practice, Preston informed Alberti that he'd decided to give up playwriting. From now on, he would devote himself to Eleanor's career; he would become her impresario. Of such altruism Eleanor was rightly skeptical, for that same night, she recalls, Preston got mad, hit her and knocked her down the stairs. "Afterwards, he felt terribly badly, of course, he picked me up and carried me back to bed"—not Eleanor's first experience of Preston's violent swings in mood or behavior.[19] She returned to New York with him in late October for an appendectomy, but sailed back to Paris as soon as she was well.

Throughout that winter, Eleanor continued to affirm her commitment to their marriage, and Preston vacillated between trying to believe her and calling her insincere. "[My secretary] showed me your letter to her and you sound very young, very alone, and very blue," he wrote, at one point. "I doubt, however, whether you are any of these, except very young, as I have written long successions of just such letters during my life, generally for a purpose: such as getting sympathy, or a cheque from father, or my allowance increased when I was at school."[20]

Meanwhile, Universal's movie version of *Strictly Dishonorable* opened to mixed notices, and Sturges was embroiled in production disputes with William Harris over his new play. Harris wanted major script changes, which Sturges wouldn't give him, and they parted, with no hard feelings—at least on Preston's part—in mid-November. Sturges now rewrote *Consider the Lily* according to Pemberton's suggestions. Pemberton promptly responded: "I think the idea of the relationship of the two is better in this version but the difference in the second division is not great enough to make me change my mind. . . . I still think [the first half] is one of the slickest acts I have read in a long time. . . . If eventually you want to change the second half I shall be more than happy to see it again."[21]

It is revealing that while Sturges refused to revise *Consider the Lily* for William Harris, he did a rewrite, with no contract whatsoever, hoping to attract Pemberton. Beyond his professional stature, Pemberton was a talismanic figure for Preston. He had produced Sturges's one great hit, he had taken a chance on him as an unknown. He had also written a warm note to Preston after Mary Desti's death and disinterestedly wished Preston success with *Recapture* and *Well of Romance*. As would be true with Y. Frank Freeman at Paramount, Pemberton was family. Family, as Preston knew it, could argue and pull rank; they did not cut you off.

Two months after Pemberton for the second time sent back *Consider the Lily*, former Ziegfeld dancer Peggy Fears bought up rights to the play. Her husband, the millionaire realtor A. C. Blumenthal, would pay for everything, this was her first production, and she was bent on wielding creative control. And control Fears did—either with Sturges's approval or because he'd given up on finding a more malleable collaborator. Fears chose Howard Lindsay to direct and Dorothy Hall and Reginald Owen to star. She spent a fortune on couturier dresses, and on Jonel Jorgulesco's ingenious sets, which dropped from the flies during split-second scene changes—creating a movielike effect. Sturges changed his play's name to *Child of Manhattan*, but, according to actress Mary Orr, took little part in the production fanfare. He did, however, have sufficient power to play a crucial role for her.

In 1932 Mary Orr was a pretty young actress, more than a year out of work, and "about absolutely broke," she recalls. "I was doing my usual rounds of agents' offices, and I walked into one of the big ones, Chamberlain Brown, but Mr. Brown wouldn't have anything to do with me. It was one of those cold February days, so I said to the girl at the desk, do you mind if I just sit here? And she said, 'sit as long as you like, I can't help it.'"

Soon, Chamberlain Brown came out and asked the secretary to send their client Sue Moore over to Preston Sturges, who was casting the minor part of a dance hall girl in *Child of Manhattan*. Mary Orr's ears perked up. She went quietly out, found Sturges's address in the phone book, and took the crosstown bus to Preston's door. "The butler answered the bell, and I said, 'I'm Sue Moore, and I've come from Chamberlain Brown's office to see Mr. Sturges.' Sturges took one look at me, and didn't ask me to read or anything, he said, 'You're perfect for the part, sit down.'"

"I said, 'Oh, isn't that nice I'm perfect for the part, I really need this job, you know,' and he looked at me and said, 'Have you had breakfast?' It was noon, and I said, 'Well, I haven't had anything except a cup of coffee in the automat since seven.' He said, 'Have lunch with me.' And I said, 'Oh, Mr. Sturges, that would be lovely,' and I thought is he going to make a pass at me, but he didn't look the type."

"We'd just about finished our lunch when I heard the bell ring, and up came the butler, and he said, 'Mr. Sturges, there's another Sue Moore downstairs.' And Sturges gave me a kind of quizzical look, and I just looked at him, and he said, 'What's your real name, honey?' And I said, 'Mary Orr.' He said,

'I see.' And he turned around to the butler and said, 'Tell Miss Moore that Mr. Sturges regrets very much but the part is cast.'"[22]

Mary Orr remembers Sturges greeting her unshaven in a silk dressing gown, looking like Noel Coward with black hair. He was very handsome, she thought, and his house was lovely. He loaned her twenty-five dollars toward her first salary check before she left, and she can't recall that they ever spoke again.

Opening night, the Fulton Theatre was packed with celebrity friends of Fears's and Blumenthal's—Mary Pickford, Adolph Zukor, George Gershwin, Irving Berlin, Flo Ziegfeld, the list went on and on. Sturges would later surmise that it was all these famous people, turning to peer at one another, who stole his play's thunder. Though, of course, there were other factors involved, and the morning's reviews show how deeply ingrained in American popular culture was the ideal of sexual equality in love. Madeleine's romance with Vanderkill was despised as tasteless, sophomoric, and improbable. "Tawdry," said Brooks Atkinson in the *Times*, and he added: "Patronizing Madeleine is not Mr. Sturges's intention. On the contrary, he admires her native integrity. But he has insisted so much on her ignorance and made such continuous sport of her pronunciation that he keeps her always in an inferior position." Dorothy Hall's acting was praised, as were odd bits of Sturges's humor. Fears quickly moved her production to the smaller Court Theatre, where it played a respectable eighty-seven performances, but Sturges was crushed.

Child of Manhattan's failure "has been a heavy blow to me,"[23] Preston wrote his father, who replied:

> I am sorry your play was not a success, because I know you worked hard. I think you had better pattern after Barrie next time instead of these racketeer playwrights and I would get a man producer, too, instead of a Follie's beauty.[24]

Eleanor no more perspicaciously advised him to "try along a different line of writing for a change—I feel it is the dialect and the humorous names they get you on—and without these your plays lose nothing and I think gain a lot."[25] Eleanor cabled Preston not to consider coming to Paris as she was planning a trip to New York.

But Preston was not in a mood to be deflected. As usual, low on cash, he borrowed $2,000 from his play's backer, A. C. Blumenthal, agreeing to forfeit his share of *Child of Manhattan*'s movie sale rights if the debt was not repaid within a month. Blumenthal insisted that their agreement be spelled out in a contract. Still, Preston, eager to set off for Paris, apparently never suspected

Blumenthal's motives.[26] So it was a great surprise when, lingering in France a month-and-a-half later, Sturges learned that because he'd not repaid his $2,000 debt, Blumenthal had gone ahead and unilaterally sold the film rights to *Child of Manhattan*—what's more, he'd sold them to himself.[27] Blumenthal had contrived to produce the movie version of Sturges's play without paying the author a cent. "CANNOT BELIEVE SUCH SHYLOCKERY,"[28] Preston cabled home. And he really couldn't believe it and was beside himself with rage: first, because he'd been used, but also because he'd been shabbily used, and by a very wealthy man, which violated his deeply held conviction about the rich. Paris Singer and even the Huttons might be arbitrary and outlandish, but there was a regality to their consorting, they didn't stoop to petty schemes. Later in life, Sturges would be called anti-Semitic, and while this was not true, he would presume the worst of a certain type of Jew. That type was epitomized by Blumenthal, who—though Sturges quickly repaid his debt and rallied the Author's League to defend him—was legally affirmed in his contractual rights. Technically, after all, Sturges *was* wrong, and he might have learned a lesson here about punctiliousness—instead he did what was very rare for him, he carried a grudge. Blumenthal's name would always signify hatefulness to Preston. Now, though, Sturges had more than Blumenthal on his mind.

He had no hopes of capitalizing on a movie sale to Hollywood, and with *Child of Manhattan* playing to increasingly sluggish audiences, there were few royalties waiting in New York. There were bills, however, for beautiful new furniture, two cars, and a household of servants, and Eleanor had an irritating way of counseling him that financial security would come not from writing another play, but from reviving his mother's shop.[29]

Their marriage was finished. Preston later claimed that Eleanor's lawyers, like Hopsie's in *The Lady Eve*, demanded to know how much a divorce would cost her; Preston (like Jean) replied, "It will cost you one courteous request, Madame, and a polite thank-you when it is all over." The story is probably more symbolic than factual. Eleanor insists she never mentioned money, and knowing Preston's pride, it's hard to imagine she would have. She did, however, choose to sue for an annulment (on the grounds that Sturges's first divorce was improperly finalized), rather than divorce, and this deeply hurt Preston, who somehow felt their passion and life together were thus invalidated.[30] Preston told his first wife, Estelle, "I think this has all been done because the Hutton family is afraid I would sue for damages, charging alienation, than which I would rather change my name to Hutton."[31] (The more likely reason is that Eleanor was planning to marry a Catholic Frenchman).

He made a point that Eleanor owed him $90,000—perhaps for investments in what was now her New York townhouse, but that she could pay him back when and if she wanted. He would never ask her for anything, unless he were "ill or desperate." [32] As with his mother's promising him the Maison Desti, Preston would not forget his claim on Eleanor.

"I think it was a very good thing that Eleanor and I parted," Preston, writing Estelle, summed up his second marriage. "We loved each other very sincerely but disliked each other as much because of the dissimilarity of tastes, education, and ideas, that there was no hope for us. I'm quite reconciled to the turn of events and, though my heart is a little sad, my head is shouting 'hooray.'" [33]

PART III

Westward Ho!

*L.A. is silly—much motoring, me rather tired and
vague about it. California is a queer place in a way, it
has turned its back on the world and looks into the void
Pacific. It is absolutely selfish, very empty, but not false,
and at least not full of false effort. I don't want to live
here, but a stay here rather amuses me. It is a sort of
crazy sensible.*

D. H. Lawrence, quoted in *Los Angeles*

CHAPTER 9

Clear-eyed as he could be about life in the abstract, Preston was ever the optimist about his own fate, eager to move on. Friendships would endure, but passion was fleeting, you put it out of your mind, like disaster. "I think the Depression will be over pretty soon," Preston wrote his father in the darkest days of 1932, when Solomon's own business was collapsing. "People have taken their losses now and are pretty well reconciled to the idea. They are treating it as a joke rather than a calamity. Under those circumstances, they will be spending again shortly."[1]

Shortly Preston, in any case, would be leaving his townhouse and the New York theatre for Hollywood. George S. Kaufman, Herman Mankiewicz, the Marx Brothers, Dorothy Parker, Marc Connelly, S. J. Perelman, and hundreds of lesser wits and playwrights had already gone and were spreading horror tales of relentless sun and hokum and cupidity. "Hollywood," declared S. J. Perelman, "is a dreary industrial town controlled by hoodlums of enormous wealth, the ethical sense of a pack of jackals, and taste so degraded that it befoul[s] everything it touch[es]."[2]

Hollywood was also part of Los Angeles, which had in less than a century grown from a cow town to the largest city in the West, splaying forty miles from the Pacific to the desert and boasting architecture by Frank Lloyd Wright and Richard Neutra as well as orange trees and outrageous imitations of Versailles. With the coming of the sound film, it was a place where writers were indispensable. There was a good living to be made in the movies, which were also magical and potentially great. Charles Chaplin had seen this, and so had D. W. Griffith, who had once been a New York playwright himself.

And it was Griffith's former boss, Walter Wanger of Paramount's Astoria Studios, who'd given Sturges his first script assignment in the fall of 1929. Wanger asked Sturges to adapt George Middleton and A. E. Thomas's Broadway play *The Big Pond* for Paramount stars Maurice Chevalier and Claudette Colbert. Sturges changed the play's thrust so the rich Midwestern girl marries her Latin lover instead of a plodding American, and he worked in some Sturges touches—like having the businessman father dismiss Venice as a "swamp." Sturges also made scenic and directorial suggestions, though his credit was for dialogue only. Sturges wrote quickly. Wanger was pleased and paid him $10,000 to adapt another play about wealthy Americans, *The Best People*, released in 1930 as *Fast and Loose*. Preston and Wanger struck up a friendship. Once, when Sturges was vacationing at his father's, Wanger cabled: "THINK YOUR STORY SWELL WHEN ARE YOU COMING BACK LOVE AND KISSES WALTER WANGER."³

Wanger, who had attended Dartmouth, was unusually erudite for a studio boss. He was in his early twenties when Paramount made him head of their East Coast office, where he answered only to production chief Jesse Lasky, who admired his wit and literary tastes. Had these two remained powerful, Sturges might have made a screenwriting career without ever leaving Broadway. But Wanger competed with the equally ambitious B. P. Schulberg, who, also under Lasky, headed Paramount's studio in L.A. Schulberg, in his youth an aspiring author, was well-read, shrewd, and one of the few producers New York writers like Herman Mankiewicz deigned to converse with; but he was also volatile and combative. When the Depression finally struck Hollywood in 1931, Paramount fired Lasky, Schulberg got Wanger ousted, and the Astoria studio closed.

A. C. Blumenthal's scheming for Preston's movie rights must have seemed delicacy itself beside this sort of power jousting. Loyalty in Hollywood could be grand scale and bizarre. Carl Laemmle, founder of Universal, as a twenty-first birthday gift put his son in charge of production, and rumor had it that half their staff were foreign nephews gathered during European jaunts. Universal, one of Hollywood's "little three" studios, had lost money on what were then called quality pictures even during the profitable late twenties; now they made mostly low-budget horror films that Tod Browning or James Whale could direct and in which the mercurial Lon Chaney or Bela Lugosi might star. Still, both Laemmles were pleased with their movie version of *Strictly Dishonorable*, and in the summer of '32 invited Sturges, for $1,000 a week, to come write for them full time.

Sturges, in his 1944 memoir, ascribes his defection from Broadway to legitimate theatre's outdatedness and its erratic rewards. The writer's life, he felt, should be predictable:

I was willing to admit that I was not a second Shakespeare, positive that I was not a second Eugene O'Neill . . . but I still thought I ought to be able to earn my living as a playwright. Not necessarily in that five story mausoleum [theatre], but constantly and sufficiently like a carpenter or a plumber or even a dentist does instead of making an occasional killing like a tin horn sport at Belmont.[4]

Preston must also have been just plain delighted to leave New York, since Eleanor was planning to begin annulment proceedings, and while both tried to be high-minded on the larger issues, they were not above quibbling about who deserved the tray with the bone handles and the pitcher from Mary Desti's house. Preston had spent the past months rewriting yet another play—*Unfaithfully Yours*, a farce about adultery—that no one seemed to want. And Paris Singer, the last link to his European childhood, had died in July.

Yes, Preston told the Laemmles, he'd be glad to come west—and he packed his bags and his mother's bed and portrait, both of which he'd carry with him, out of sentiment and superstition, until his death.[5] Charley Abramson and Jack Gilchrist were installed, with the cat Elmer Thompson,[6] in Preston's old 603 Fifth Avenue apartment, which he'd never given up and would continue paying rent on now. Preston wasn't burning any bridges.

Nor was he leaving for Los Angeles alone. His photographer friend Arnold Shroeder was coming to live with him, as was Bianca, or "Mrs. Gilchrist" as Preston made a point of calling this singular woman. Bianca was officially Preston's secretary. She was also still technically married to his friend Jack Gilchrist, though those two had long gone their separate ways. Bianca had typed, kept accounts, and proved both a fan and an exacting critic for Preston ever since *Strictly Dishonorable*. While Eleanor's love for Preston was not predicated on any particular attraction to his writing, Bianca was as deeply involved with the artist as with the man.

Some time after Eleanor left for Paris, Bianca and Preston became more intimate. She moved into the Fifty-fourth Street townhouse when Preston returned in June from France. But then Charley Abramson (who would long remember his stimulating talks with Preston and Bianca)[7] also moved in at that time. Preston was very discreet about his relationship with Bianca—not a single love letter passed between them—and she was certainly like no woman he'd been involved with before. Years later Preston described her with admiration: "She is and always was smart as a whip, knows what time it is and which way the wind is blowing."[8] She spoke three languages and was dark, Jewish, striking, rather than pretty, passionate, and eager to please. She wore

smashing clothes and struck some as haughty, though in fact Bianca was anything but a snob, and the grand style was mostly a defense, though the flair
was real. She was not to everyone's taste, nor was everyone to hers. But many
who were initially put off by Bianca's brash or superior manner came later to
appreciate her humor, first-rate intelligence, and wide understanding of life.[9]

Arnold Shroeder drove Preston's car cross-country, while Bianca and Pres-
ton took the train to Chicago, where they spent a few days with Solomon
Sturges and then gratified Preston's desire to fly. Of his first airplane voyage,
Preston, lover of trains and boats, wrote Solomon:

> The beginning of our flight from Chicago was delightful, but just before
> reaching Omaha we ran into the godingest thunder-lightning rainstorm I have
> ever seen and as it was impossible to fly around it we had to go right through
> it. Mrs. Gilchrist was petrified and I was speechless. It was really horrifying
> and not an experience I should enjoy reliving. Later in the night and in the
> early dawn we had to fly 10,000 feet to get over the mountains and I had a
> magnificent earache for hours. All in all I think a railroad train is not a bad
> invention although terribly slow compared to flying.[10]

They arrived at the Hotel Roosevelt on September 9, and, with Arnold
Shroeder, immediately began looking for a house. "Every time I see one that
suits my requirements I don't like it,"[11] Preston wrote Charley Abramson; for
he was fussy like his mother, and wanted to be in the hub of things, but hated
pretension on the one hand and common taste on the other. It took him two
weeks to find a small but charming bungalow at 2070 Ivar—which was as
central as you could get in this centerless town; the cost was $110 a month,
and there was a patio, large living room, and two bedrooms. Across the street
was a *very* small house that Preston rented for butler's quarters and Arnold's
workshop. Preston informed Charley Abramson that he'd bought himself and
Bianca "beautiful" Fords for their two-car garage; and Charley, relishing every
detail of this adventure, wrote Bianca: "You must look positively stunning in
your red dresses and green car."[12]

Preston and Bianca had offices in a bungalow on the sprawling Universal
lot, where Sturges was adapting H. G. Wells's *The Invisible Man* for director
James Whale, who'd made a great success the year before with *Frankenstein*.
Sturges found Whale "a very intelligent fellow, witty and talented," and while
Preston had no experience whatsoever with science fiction, and was the ninth
writer assigned to this same project, he was full of enthusiasm. "I'm interested
in my work and doing the very best I can,"[13] he wrote Charley. Carl Laemmle,
Jr., had advised him to have no false reverence for Wells, so he was changing

the book's splenetic phantom to a village idiot, setting the script in Prussia rather than England, and adding romance and revenge.[14]

In one of a series of memos to "My dear Junior," Sturges described his writing strategy: "While creating a story it is my custom to write down the whole thought as it comes to me. This method often results in new twists and fresh material coming to light. For this reason you will see some speeches a very great deal too long, in this continuity. They will be boiled down to the best of their contents."[15]

Sturges worked nearly two months on *The Invisible Man* and received all sorts of encouragement, and a lesson in how the wheels turn in Hollywood. "I am pretty sure I turned in a good continuity," he wrote Charley, "but whether they will shoot it or not is something else again. As far as I can make out, Junior Laemmle and the powers that be want something in the picture which they cannot describe but which they insist upon having. To date there have been eight continuities made but none of them embodied this idea."[16]

However provoked, Sturges was determined to show no signs of temper, but to make a good impression. "Always have everybody liking you,"[17] his father had time and again admonished him, and even when Universal chose *not* to film his script and not even to renew his contract (which compelled a $250 raise), Sturges made a point of staying on three weeks, for no pay, to finish revising a Zazu Pitts/Slim Summerville vehicle: "I hope this bread cast upon the waters will return as ham sandwiches,"[18] he told Charley.

Of Los Angeles, he wrote: "I do nothing but rave about the beauties of this joint, which is really like Bridgeport with palm trees, only Bridgeport is greener and it has Fairfield in its outskirts and it's only two hours from New York. California is all right for the Californians. The people who rave about it are the people who came from somewhere worse."[19]

Preston, in the deepest sense, came no more from New York than from California; like so many in Hollywood, he had lots of places in his past and was anxious to put down roots and make a name for himself, but also was restless and would never be content as *simply* a Hollywood screenwriter, or simply *any* one thing. Much as he loved drama, he could be equally passionate about machines and blueprints and the smell of food cooking and the excitement of a crowd. Now, as he started a new screenplay, he was also perfecting an idea he'd conceived for a nearly vibrationless diesel engine, and was helping Arnold Shroeder—billed as "Dr. Shroeder the Painless Photographer"—experiment with photographs enlarged from motion picture film. Preston was reading so much he'd started getting headaches, and though by no means

121

Three faces of Preston Sturges, from his early days in Hollywood.

the intellectual many in Hollywood supposed him to be, he'd come a long way from a child who hated books. His favorite novelists were H. L. Mencken's friend Joseph Hergesheimer—the naturalist who profoundly influenced Sinclair Lewis—and James Gould Cozzens, whose 1930 S.S. *San Pedro* thrilled Preston so much he often brought it out to read to guests. It was a seafaring tale, with lots of action and male camaraderie, but also an allegory of inevitable failure, dubious about the very codes of honor and loyalty its most laudable characters uphold.

Sturges had strong opinions on writers and, indeed, on most everything; which is why his silence on the upcoming 1932 elections and later the New Deal is conspicuous. His father and Charley Abramson, both troubled conservatives, wrote him at length on the subject. Solomon (whose brokerage firm closed by the late thirties) declared in the fall of 1932 that neither Hoover nor Roosevelt deserved his vote. Then, when business briefly rallied in 1933, Solomon praised the New Deal, but by 1937 he considered Roosevelt "certainly the worst president the U.S. has *ever* had." [20] Preston, throughout the thirties, cajoled his father with New Dealish bromides, like "prosperity is only a feeling," [21] but he never expressed a single opinion in writing for or against Roosevelt. Like Isadora Duncan, he may have considered his ideals too lofty for politics, though it's more likely he took his cue from Mencken, whose attitude was *plus ça change. . . .* Mencken's cynicism was increasingly unpopular in Depression America; perhaps Preston learned from this and was determined to keep his convictions to himself.

Yet Sturges made no bones about his attitude toward the politics of Hollywood, where he intended to succeed or fail by *his* wits alone. He made it clear he had no interest in writers' unions, or at first even agents. "I have services to sell," he wrote a Mr. Geller of William Morris, who wanted to represent him, "but the way I wish to sell them and the terms under which I would like to work can be explained better by myself than by a third person." [22]

When his Universal contract ran out in late November, Sturges did something almost unheard-of in Hollywood—he went home and began a script no one else had conceived or was paying him to write. It involved trains and power, subjects that had fascinated him since childhood, and pursued the ideas he'd begun exploring in *A Cup of Coffee* about robber barons and the American Dream.

Preston wrote Eleanor's Uncle Harry Close that *The Power And The Glory* was "inspired by some incidents Eleanor told me of the life of her grandfather," [23] C. W. Post. His tactics were shrewd, but, unlike Morgan's and Rockefeller's, mostly honest, and he was not inclined to flamboyance, though he spent money freely and encouraged his daughter Marjorie to do the same. There are obvious parallels between the histories of C. W. Post and *The Power and the Glory*'s flawed hero Tom Garner: both rise from undistinguished beginnings, succeed through their resourcefulness and energy, marry young, and become increasingly estranged from domestic wives. In middle age C. W. Post, like Tom Garner, married a much younger woman who purportedly betrayed him with a colleague, and Post too shot himself while still in his prime. But the differences between Sturges's character and C. W. Post are just as conspicuous as the similarities; for Tom Garner hasn't a trace of C. W. Post's crippling tendency toward depression, and while a central point of *The Power and the Glory* is Tom's disgust for his son, C. W. Post found an adoring soul mate in his daughter Marjorie. [24]

So Preston's statement to Uncle Harry (calculated, perhaps, to flatter or just interest him in the screenplay) characteristically overstresses the single autobiographical influence. Preston must also have been intrigued by Solomon Sturges's father, Albert, who, in the nineteenth century founded the Leavenworth, Lawrence, and Galveston Railroad and spent long periods of time away from home. Certainly, too, Preston drew from experiences with powerful men like Ed Hutton and Paris Singer, but also from stories about the train barons Jay Gould and Jim Fisk. Fisk especially would have been well known to Sturges, for there's a famous Chicago ditty praising his generosity during the great fire; and though Fisk was ruthless and despised by many, an awesome number of admirers turned up to mourn his death.

Sturges's script opens at Tom Garner's similarly crowded funeral, then flashes back to probe for an understanding of the great man's rise and fall. We see Tom as an extraordinarily capable and generous, but poor boy who at twenty still hasn't been taught to read and write. Yet, once the local school marm, Sally, takes it upon herself to teach him, he quickly learns and as quickly falls in love. He and Sally marry, and at Sally's instigation Tom pursues higher studies, then gets a job for the railroad while she gets pregnant and produces a son.

Tom's career takes off, so by middle age he's the most powerful railroad owner in America, but he's no longer above bribing and cheating and is increasingly estranged from the devoted Sally and their spoiled and resentful child. "You've built so many miles of railroad," says Sally, "and every mile has taken you further from me."

Now, Eve, a beautiful and ambitious daughter of Tom's competitor, seduces Tom, who falls passionately for her. From here on, both his career and personal life degenerate. When Sally finds out about Eve, she hands her purse to a shoe-shine boy and walks in front of a streetcar. A few months later, Tom marries Eve (who's never loved him), but he's increasingly guilty and beset with troubles at work. When a strike calls Tom off, Eve begins spending time with her husband's handsome son. Eve gives birth to a child Tom believes is his own until he overhears Eve intimate the boy may in fact be his son's. Horrified, Tom shoots himself.

Merely reciting the plot of *The Power and the Glory* does it an injustice, for the script's strength derives from swift flashes back and forward, which undermine all the melodramatic incidents and stress atmosphere and the characters' inner struggles. The tale is told in voice-over by Tom's boyhood friend Henry. "The . . . advantage of a narrator," explained Sturges, "is that, like the author in a novel, he may describe what people do and say and also what they feel and what they think." [25] He can furthermore deepen interpretation by offering a perspective other than the author's and the protagonist's. And though familiar today, the idea of a running narration and disjointed plot, eight years before *Citizen Kane*, was strikingly original.

Typical is a flashback where Tom invites Sally for a Sunday walk because he yearns to ask her to marry him. Once on the road, he loses courage, and on and on they journey to the very peak of a mountain before he gets the nerve to pop the question. She immediately accepts. This is not narratively exceptional. What's ingenious is how Sturges sets the scene up as a silent picture courtship—with Tom and Sally intensely miming their emotions, as Henry, on the soundtrack, speaks their thoughts in flowery prose. The impact is curious. For while summoning the "lost innocence" both of Tom and of cinema, Sturges also stylizes his nostalgia and casts an ironic glance at the past.

The film's railroad scenes are keenly evocative. And Tom, with his fierce desires and calumnies, is a complex character: "You can't judge him by ordinary standards . . . he was too big," observes Henry; and Sturges manages to convey this, as much through reticence as explication. His robber baron, like the sea captain in Cozzens's S.S. *San Pedro*, is a man of few words who feels no compunction to justify his choices; nor—unlike Jimmy in *A Cup of Coffee*—does he moon about waiting for a lucky break. Tom creates his own opportunities, and though the film's a bit overstressed moral is that power, greed, and sex bring misery to upright Americans, its best scenes show Tom relishing his control—sweeping into a boardroom and within minutes converting all the opposition, or cutting a powerful foe down to size by receiving him with his feet up on the desk.

There are a number of mawkish sequences focused on an idealized Sally, and Sturges's glimpses of small-town Americana—the child Tom frolicking with his friend at the water hole, or young husband Tom blissful at Sally's wholesome dinner—are sentimental. Sturges is also unconvincing when he attempts to attribute Tom's enormous ambition to Sally's gentle nudging, or to pin Tom's troubles at work on his lust for Eve.

Yet, whatever its shortcomings, *The Power and the Glory* is bold and formally innovative. "In case it interests you," Preston wrote his father, "I have invented an entirely new method of telling stories. This is the method used in *The Power and the Glory* and it is quite apt to be greatly remarked. It is neither a silent film nor a talking film but rather a combination. It embodies the action of a silent picture, the reality of voice, and the storytelling economy and richness of characterization of a novel. It is called a narrative picture, and I wish to heaven I had been able to patent it." [26]

Some time after he arrived in Hollywood, Preston met a story editor named Hector Turnbull, who arranged for him to relate the plot of *The Power and the Glory* to Jesse Lasky. Lasky, formerly Walter Wanger's boss at Paramount, was now producing films for a smaller studio, Fox. Lasky liked Sturges's ideas and invited him to submit a short treatment, but Preston, to Lasky's surprise, declined. "I will not negotiate with anyone until the job is completed," Preston explained to Charley. "I think that in this way I will be in a better position to get terms than I would be bargaining about something which had not yet been written." [27]

Lasky admired Sturges's spirit, and was so greatly impressed by *The Power and the Glory*, when it was finished, that he granted Sturges privileges truly extraordinary in the movie world. No score of Hollywood writers would be called in for revisions: "We tried to find something in the script to change," Lasky told a reporter,[28] "but could not find a word or a situation." Should the producers later wish changes, these would have to be sanctioned by the author, who—for the first time ever in Hollywood—would receive a percentage of his movie's profits (3.5 percent on the first $500,000 gross, 5 percent on the next $500,000, and 7 percent on anything over a million dollars) as well as a $17,500 advance.

Sturges, in other words, was to be treated like a playwright; and some exulted at his success. "Writers want to write," read an editorial that launched a heated debate about Sturges's contract in the *Hollywood Reporter*. "They want respect for their writing. They do not want their yarns pulled from one end of a conference room to another by eight or ten individuals, thinking along that many different lines." [29]

But B. P. Schulberg, formerly Lasky's subordinate (and Wanger's rival) at

Paramount, predicted only mischief if others followed Preston's example. Schulberg was so dismayed by Sturges's contract that, in a reply to the *Hollywood Reporter* editorial, he made no attempt to disguise his industry's contempt for writers. Successful films, he argued, were written not by individuals, but by teams of two to eight. The reason, he felt, was obvious since "there are very few writers in the world today and still fewer who can or will adapt themselves to studio regime, who can, with equal facility and efficiency, write a great emotional scene and a great comedy scene." Screenwriters should by no means get an inflated view of their own importance—most producers could write just as well.[30]

Sturges must have forgotten his conviction that writing was a craft like plumbing, not to mention his determination to solace everyone, when composing his reply to this Hollywood hard line. Preston's are the last words the *Hollywood Reporter* printed on *The Power and the Glory*, and they stand in angry contrast to his flip denials of artistic intentions later on.

To Schulberg's argument that eight can produce a better screenplay than one, Sturges asked, then why not eighty writers rather than eight, or better still eight thousand? "I for one can think of no surer way of stamping out originality, initiative, pride of achievement, and quality. You can't play football with a thought. The ideal talking picture would result from the alliance of painting, literature, and music."

And to Schulberg's contention that the same writer couldn't produce comedy and sentiment: "Entirely apart from the fact that writers transmit emotions through words and that sad emotions are no more difficult to transmit than funny ones, there is the other fact that without a sense of humor, a writer's sad scenes might easily become ludicrous and, without a sense of pathos, his funny scenes would not be very funny. Writers as double-jointed as all this are: Shakespeare, Tolstoy, Noel Coward, Owen Davis, all of the Authors' League, and the members of the Writer's Club in Hollywood, to name but a few."

Finally, Sturges couldn't resist observing how Schulberg "takes all the [producers] to his bosom, pats them on the back, and tosses off the conviction that they write at least as well as writers, that they are in fact, interchangeable with the latter. Having read his article carefully, I doubt this statement, but I may be mistaken."[31]

This last quip about Schulberg's prose was *ad hominem*, and Sturges would pay for it. But his piece on the whole is honorable and gleefully adept. Cinema is an art, it says, and the writers of cinema are artists. Tolstoys they may not be, but then who's the worse for that? Sturges here is a young man proud both of his business sense and his erudition. His coupling of Shakespeare and the Writers' Club shows no awe for the "high brow," while his "ideal" film sounds almost visionary. Sturges's response to Schulberg—printed the day before *The Power and the Glory* went into production—was his greeting card to Hollywood, an announcement that Mary Desti's son had arrived and did not intend to abide by the rules.

The Power and the Glory began shooting on March 23, with thirty-three-year-old Spencer Tracy and silent screen star Colleen Moore in the lead roles, and the competent William K. Howard directing. The train sequences were shot on location in a desert town, but most of the film was made on the Fox lot. "You will find it difficult to believe, but I have risen with the milkman every morning and arrived at the studio, eight miles away, promptly at eight," [32] Preston wrote his father, in early April. And Colleen Moore, who'd never before seen a writer on the set, vividly remembers both Preston's and Bianca's presence. Preston, she recalls, was full of energy and fascinated by every aspect of filmmaking, [33] but particularly by directing because he'd quickly observed that directors rather than writers were nobility in Hollywood. And Preston must have remembered his breach with Pemberton because there were no temper tantrums now.

When, at an early preview, the audience loved the beginning, but were baffled by the second half of *The Power and the Glory*, Sturges was quick to concede his story "went wrong in several spots," [34] and he worked night and day with Howard and the producers to make it better. He respected Howard and was obviously energized by teamwork, for his letters from this period speak of "we," not "I," and he seemed happy to share credit for his film's success—though it's perhaps not wholly coincidental that Preston's name, on the titles of a preview print, read larger even than the director's. This mysterious error was noted by many, and studio memos went out ordering that it be rectified at once. [35]

Fox executives treated *The Power and the Glory* as a work of art and made it known they expected both critical and commercial triumph. They planned a prestige road show opening at the Gaiety Theatre on Broadway and, during the summer of '33, bombarded journalists with teasers about their spectacular "narratage." When *The Power and the Glory* opened on August 16, some critics, like Charles Parker Hammond of the *Evening Post*, wondered why there'd been so much fuss about a mere flashback and voice-over. But, for the most part, reviews were excellent. The *New York Times* called it "a compelling film, thoroughly human and always believable." The *Sun* predicted that "after all the novelty of its new scenario technique has faded away, *The Power and the*

The Gaiety Theatre, celebrating the opening of The Power and the Glory. *Note the plaque dedicated to Jesse Lasky and all the trumpeting of "narratage."*

Glory will still be a good picture. It has other merits to stand upon, such sure and steady ones as powerful drama, some of the best acting the screen has yet enjoyed and as skillful direction and dialogue as such a film deserves."

The Power and the Glory was also influential in ways perhaps only Sturges could have anticipated. When in 1941 *Citizen Kane* was hailed as a cinema

129

landmark, a few shrewd critics noted Orson Welles's indebtedness to Sturges; as, reputedly, did Welles himself, saying he wore out a print of *The Power and the Glory*, studying its technique.[36]

The *Power and the Glory* played for two highly successful weeks at the Gaiety, where photos of Preston and a framed copy of his script were conspicuously displayed in the lobby.[37] All signs pointed to a long commercial run. But outside New York, the film never found an audience. Some blamed the era, figuring that none wanted to spend precious dimes on a film about a philandering tycoon, even if he does get his comeuppance. Others blamed Sturges's experimental strategies. Solomon Sturges for once was supportive of Preston's artistic goals. Pleased at how Preston had managed to work the name of his Aunt Kate Buckingham's Bald Head Farm into the story, "I am delighted with the reports of your play and its reception," he wrote his son. "I see, however, that there seems to be some doubt as to [its] value as a money producer. This may be true, but . . . artistic success is worth something."[38]

So, Preston might have added, is experience. And, though he immediately went off to write another script on his own time, Preston had learned something vital about the movie business. Years later, he would tell his own son: "When I first went to Hollywood I discovered that the directors were treated as Princes of the Blood, whereas writers worked in teams of six like piano movers. In the beginning I tried to prove that writers were easily as important as directors, then one day I realized that it was easier to become a Prince of the Blood myself than to change a whole social order."[39]

Preston also said that it was while watching Bill Howard, on the set of *The Power and the Glory*, that he conceived a "tremendous yen to direct coupled with the absolutely positive hunch that I could [do it]."[40] At thirty-five, he had found his vocation.

10

In April of 1933, Charley Abramson wrote Bianca Gilchrist in Los Angeles: "I was happy to infer from your letter that all is proceeding happily with Preston and especially your intimation that he may become active directorially. If any man was ever cut to order for this work, that man is Preston. With his striking physical appearance, his succinct expression and forceful voice, his executive ability and creative talent he is fitted to perfection to direct. He will be the Director par excellence. But it is as good as done." [1]

It would in fact take Preston nearly seven years to win his first directing assignment, for there was no rule that good writers were destined to direct in Hollywood—in fact most studio executives presumed the opposite and urged Sturges to hone his single well-paying craft. "Shoemaker stick to your last," was a frequent admonishment. "It has taken me . . . years," he later wrote, "to find the answer to that one, which is show me the man who sticks to his last and I'll show you a shoemaker." [2]

Yet, though Preston chafed at small-minded studio heads' thwarting his ambitions, for the most part he thoroughly enjoyed the thirties in Hollywood. It was the beginning of a golden era that so valued creative talent that, in 1935, Ernst Lubitsch was made head of production at Paramount, and directors like John Ford and Frank Capra were valued nearly as highly as the stars. Lubitsch, with his wide understanding of women and irony about conventional values, and Frank Capra, with his daring to speak for all Americans, were probably the strongest artistic influences on Sturges during this crucial decade. Both Lubitsch and Capra were masters of comic timing, but Lubitsch's sophisticated cynicism was dangerous in a Hollywood increasingly confined by the Production Code; Capra's was clearly the ethos to be reckoned with.

And even before *It Happened One Night* was hailed as the first screwball comedy, Capra's *Ladies of Leisure* had set the model for Depression romance. Like *Child of Manhattan*, this 1930 comic melodrama follows a rich socialite (Ralph Graves) who falls for "party girl" Barbara Stanwyck in her first leading role. Love transforms Stanwyck from a tough-minded adventuress into a demure beauty, but Graves's parents are appalled that he should consider marrying beneath his class, and his mother visits Stanwyck and convinces her she will prove his ruin. Stanwyck, wanting only Graves's happiness, pretends no longer to love him and takes off for Havana so he can marry a more suitable fiancée. But Graves, alerted to her real feelings, cables Stanwyck that she's all he's ever wanted, and after much ado they happily unite.

Although the subject of both is social misalliance, there are disparities between Capra's financially successful film and Sturges's *Child of Manhattan*. For Capra, class differences provide frisson rather than a real obstacle to marriage; and in order for a spirited woman to prove worthy of her mate, she must lose her rough edge. Sturges must have thought hard about *Ladies of Leisure*'s message about romantic love. From the mid-thirties on he too would argue that social differences need not stand in the way of marriage in America; but he would make it a point that his characters don't—indeed, that character does not—change.

Preston's belief in the durability of character came equally from Mary Desti and Solomon Sturges and brought constancy to his often tumultuous life. If he was high-spirited and restless like his mother, he shared both his parents' capacious view of human relationships and their loyalty to the past. He was a man of violent temper, but his rifts with people were rarely violent and almost never irrevocable. Four decades after he fell in love with Temple Duncan at Bayreuth, Preston wrote to her in Florida: "Temple darling, this is in no sense the letter I have owed you for fourteen years. It is merely to tell you that. . . . Although I have never been a very good letter writer, I have never stopped loving you."[3]

And so too with Estelle and Eleanor, who, when he was madly in love, Preston envisioned as goddesses. Afterwards they became wives, privy to all his moods. He was, like H. L. Mencken, philosophically a male supremacist. He could project ugly and patronizing fantasies on the women he loved. Yet, when the marriages were over, when Preston's spouses were no longer adored or reviled and the illusions so necessary for him in a romance had vanished, he continued to care for his ex-wives as friends.

Shortly after Eleanor obtained her annulment from Preston she wrote that she intended to marry a Frenchman: "You always told me the highest compliment a woman could pay her ex- was to directly remarry, so take it for what it is worth."[4] And though Preston grumbled to his father that Eleanor still owed him $90,000, he was soon writing Eleanor news of his success in Hollywood and wondering if she would send him a very special type of stationery you could only find in Paris. And what about some bed sheets?

When Estelle wrote Preston that her third husband had died (in 1930), Preston portentously informed her: "I am glad that you are beginning to think a little on the vagaries of life and ask yourself questions about them, because in answer to these questions will come philosophy or understanding, which is the greatest happiness intelligent people can hope for."[5] To this Estelle lost no time retorting: "Do you really think it is possible to have had the kind of childhood you know I had, to have left one husband because of senility, another because of laziness and to have lost the third by death *and only be just now* beginning to 'think a little on the vagaries of life'?"[6] So they were at it again; and again quickly reconciled. Estelle, to the end of her life, went on confiding in Preston about her husbands, while his tales of the film world moved her to comment, "It is too bad Mary couldn't have lived to have been with you in Hollywood. I think she would have loved it and would have been very popular."

Solomon Sturges also maintained warm ties with Preston's former wives both of whom, throughout the thirties, wrote and visited him. Once, Eleanor, her mother, and governess happened to arrive in Chicago the same weekend as Estelle.[7] And they spent their days calling upon each another. Of Preston's former archenemy, Solomon reported, "I thought Mrs. Hutton very agreeable and pleasant."[8]

About Bianca, Solomon, in his early thirties correspondence, was considerably cooler, merely sending "regards to Mrs. Gilchrist" and cautioning Preston against cohabiting with his friend's wife. "Are you and Mrs. Gilchrist living in that little house you say you have?" he wrote. "If you are you had better look out for her husband. He may object."[9] But in 1937, Solomon, after a long visit to Los Angeles, concluded, "Bianca is a wonder."[10] Though he still found their living arrangements "too nonconventional for the U.S.," Solomon now advised Preston, "If you cannot get along without Bianca—marry her and clear the situation."[11]

Like Vanderkill and Madeleine in *Child of Manhattan*, Preston and Bianca themselves probably never considered marriage. The letters Bianca wrote Preston after their break-up accuse him of other broken promises but say nothing about wedding plans. Hollywood friends say Preston was not in love with Bianca. Still, "*she made him work*," observes a neighbor from that period.

Moreover, Bianca managed to live under the same roof as Preston for longer than *either* of his wives.

Their relationship was anything but tranquil. During one tussle, Preston broke Bianca's nose;[12] during another, she slammed a glass door against his raised arm, sending him to the hospital for two weeks. They regularly appeared at the fights together on Friday evenings, but gave parties infrequently, for Solomon Sturges was right that their relationship was "nonconventional" for small-town California. While Bianca's urbanity endeared her to Preston's more sophisticated friends, many others dismissed her as bizarre. Bianca's response, to even presumed disapproval, was to flaunt her singularity. One night Bianca arrived late for a Hollywood party. She swept into the room, and announced, "Well, good evening everyone, I'm Preston's mistress."[13]

She remained, until the late thirties, his secretary as well, organizing Preston's increasingly chaotic finances and staying up with him sometimes until two or three in the morning when inspiration or terror of a deadline finally impelled him to write. Then, Bianca served as both typist and audience. For Preston's method of composing dialogue was to pace the floor and declaim speeches in the voice and posture of one after the other of his characters. Bianca's laughter or tears were his first indication that a scene would play.

Perhaps most important, Bianca was Preston's loyal companion during the decade in which he established independence from both his parents and made a place for himself in the world. Preston arrived in Hollywood at approximately the same age his mother had been when she moved to Paris; and if he was less infatuated with the West than she with Europe, he was more eager to make his mark. During the thirties, he wrote almost two dozen commissioned scripts, opened a restaurant and an engineering company, got an agent and changed houses twice, but left California only to race his boat to Hawaii. He was settling in. But setting himself apart from those who built Bel Air and Beverly Hills mansions, he chose older Spanish stone or shingled houses, off narrow, twisting roads in the Hollywood hills. Close to the studios and fashionable nightspots, they were distinctly Californian in style. The smell of tamales emanated from Preston's office,[14] and his early appraisal of Los Angeles as merely "Bridgeport with palm trees" gave way to a strong attraction for its Monterey furniture, hundred-year-old Spanish pines, gardens of trellised pears and pink hibiscus, and even a bland climate that could turn terrible, as the earth could shake.[15]

Inspired by his Uncle Sidney Biden, Preston began raising dachshunds. Louise Sturges first knew her future husband as the man up the hill who owned "yapping" puppies, one of whom chewed up Rouben Mamoulian's new suit jacket while Preston gave the Russian director a lesson in pool.[16] Preston called his first two dachshunds Adam and Eve. The female was red and had, Preston informed his uncle, "only about three-quarters of a pedigree, there being a few mollies and Rovers mentioned." But as with her namesake in Sturges's great screwball comedy, "I think the trouble with Eve is only documentary, as she is very beautiful and quite obviously [purebred]."[17]

While he objected to ostentation, Preston relished luxury. He sought out special billiard table covers and custom-made model railroads, hired a series of live-in Filipino houseboys and a cook named Joseph, who specialized in pastries. Like his mother, Preston enjoyed haggling for valuable antiques at bargain prices.[18] He entertained infrequently but with consummate style. "Mine lord of the manor" is how many friends remember Preston. He joined the comic writers' West Side Asthma and Riding Club whose meetings were held at a different member's house each Monday. Everyone vied to prepare the most elegant meal. Preston's evening, recalls a fellow member, Allen Rivkin, put the rest to shame.

Though he would later say he hated groups of any sort, Preston also soon joined a bowling club, the Pacific Writers' Yacht Club, and the Writers Club, which produced one-act plays. One night the Writers Club hosted a dinner honoring Walt Disney, whose films, Preston wrote Solomon, "are really charming—full of imagination and humor." For the occasion, Charlie Chaplin performed "two very funny pantomimes, one of a bull fighter describing a mishap with the bull who eventually caught him in the seat of the pants, and the other a complete French farce in which he played all the parts."[19] Three weeks later Preston had dinner with Chaplin and reported to his father, "we became good friends. He is a most interesting little man, thoroughly intelligent and amusing."[20]

Preston quickly met not just Chaplin, but all the most interesting people in the movie world, for he was an outgoing and charismatic figure. Many who knew Preston only slightly presumed that his mother was a French aristocrat who'd given him a princely education, which accounted for his now being a renaissance man and an intellectual: a suitably Hollywoodish embellishment. Those who knew Preston better appreciated his odd and contradictory nature. "Everyone has individual traits, but people are cut from patterns," said Rouben Mamoulian, who worked with Preston on *We Live Again* in the early thirties. "So when you meet someone like Preston who's cut from a totally different pattern, it's a great joy."[21]

Though he never suffered fools and loved to be the center of attention, Preston also had the gifts of charm, insatiable curiosity, and an almost childlike vulnerability for affection which, while it made him an easy prey for flatterers, was endearing in so strong a man. "You wanted to embrace Preston," recalled his friend John Huston. "He had a style that amounted to a flourish and was a great liver of life. Most egotists wear you down," added Huston (who had some expertise in this matter), "and you can tolerate just so much of them. But in Preston's case, he was certainly an egotist, but one subscribed to it. I liked Preston as well as he liked himself." [22] William Wyler's wife Tally, also noting that Preston was a "terrible listener, he would talk and other people would listen," agrees that Preston was "lovable. You couldn't help but like him. We never had to call on him, but you felt that if you needed anything, he would be a generous friend."

Bianca, writing home, gives an idea of their social life during the shooting of *The Power and the Glory*: "Little by little one meets all the stars," she wrote. "There was an array of them last night at Mr. Lasky's charming house on the beach at Santa Monica: Gloria Swanson (who is getting on a bit in years) . . . and Gary Cooper with his countess, and Loretta Young (gloriously beautiful), and Kay Francis and many, many others. So far we have seen hard-working Hollywood, mildly amusing itself at night—not the crazy, garish place it is reputed to be." [23]

How like Mary Desti Bianca sounds, though unlike Mary, Bianca did not rush to immerse herself in the world of luminaries, nor was Preston especially eager to socialize with celebrities. Edwin Gillette, who replaced Bianca as Sturges's secretary in 1937, feels Preston was deeply insecure and cultivated less distinguished friends because they made him feel important. And it is true that some of Preston's best friends were marginal types like Georges Renevant (now relocated in Los Angeles where he played bit parts in the movies) and character actor William Demarest and Charley Abramson, of course. Surely, Preston was gratified by their dependence and admiration, but surely too they had lovable traits—and how much was Preston really stooping, since he'd until lately led a bohemian life himself?

Besides, it was not only with off-beats that Preston surrounded himself. Among his best friends, from the thirties to the end of his life, were the gifted émigré filmmaker William Wyler and producer Henry Henigson, both of whom Sturges met at Universal. Wyler was born in 1902 in Alsace, came to America as one of Carl Laemmle's "nephews" in the early twenties, and had already directed several Tom Mix films and *A House Divided* when Sturges was assigned to work with him on *The Good Fairy*. Willie to his friends, Wyler was far more athletic than Preston, but both men were ambitious, witty, loyal, and

From left to right, Henry Henigson, Bianca Gilchrist, and Willie Wyler, about 1934.

fun-loving; they'd been raised in Europe and took great pleasure in conversing in French. "Mon vieux," is how Willie and Preston addressed one another. Theirs was "a real friendship," says Tally Wyler, who adds that Sturges actually *listened* to her husband: "They talked back and forth on an absolutely equal basis."

Henry Henigson, an influential producer several years older than Sturges and Wyler, was also every bit Preston's peer. Henigson's intellect and business acumen were widely admired. He was nearly deaf. Once, Tally Wyler recalls, as a practical joke, Willie Wyler and some friends burst into Henigson's office, wildly moving their lips, pretending to speak. Henigson, sure his hearing aid was off, began excitedly turning buttons until he guessed what they were up to and laughed as hard as they. With a large nose, the perennial cigar at his lips, and weighed down by a huge hearing aid in his shirt pocket, Henigson was not physically alluring. "Do not let his frightening exterior rob you of the friendship of a wonderful man," is how Sturges introduced Henigson to Marcel Pagnol. "He pretends to be deaf, but has never failed to hear an appeal for help." [24] This was particularly true where Preston was concerned. During the thirties, Henigson, settled with a family, came increasingly to replace Solomon Sturges as the wise man Preston turned to in moments of crisis.

For, as the decade and the Depression progressed, Solomon Sturges was growing old, increasingly sick with heart trouble, and impecunious: though he never failed to send his famous son twenty-five dollars at birthdays and only once requested money from Preston (which he promptly repaid, with 5 percent interest!).[25] Nearly two years after Mary Desti's death, Solomon, in March of 1933, married his nurse, Marie Agnes Fulton, a woman much younger and less educated than himself. This was no love match, but Marie cared for Solomon during his last days and in the late thirties would move with him to California, so he could be near his son. Then, Preston took great joy reciprocating in his fashion for profound security Solomon had since childhood provided for him. Devotion, friends say, is too weak a word for Preston's feelings for his father: Preston held Solomon in "great awe, reverence." [26] Preston kept his father and Marie in his home during Solomon's long illness, amused Solomon while he recuperated, and never let the proud old man sense a debt.

Yet, if Sturges's generosity to his father was as unselfish as the Wienie King's to Gerry in *The Palm Beach Story*, Preston's attitude toward giving in general was considerably more complex. Those who never depended on Preston remember him as exceedingly magnanimous—always eager to pick up bills for meals, to give lavish gifts and loans at a moment's notice. During the years he knew Bianca, Preston bought her, among other luxuries, a yellow Cadillac and a mink coat, which she everywhere displayed, showing off his munificence. Like Paris Singer, Preston took no less pleasure in pleasing others for needing to have his generosity admired. But also like Singer, the more and the longer he gave, the more Sturges expected in return.

Preston's ambivalence about giving is revealed in his early thirties correspondence with Charley Abramson. Not knowing how long he would remain in Los Angeles, Preston had kept his apartment in New York, installing Charley and Jack Gilchrist as tenants, rent free. Their only responsibility was to watch Elmer Thompson the cat, and at first Preston even went so far as to send stipends for cat food. Charley was blissful. "Preston has fortified me in my ideal of friendship," he wrote Bianca,[27] and Preston was gratified to have helped his friend.

Once he arrived in L.A., however, Preston began thinking up little projects for Charley. First, he needed some scripts airmailed to California. Then he wanted Charley to deal with a New York troublemaker who, claiming debts against Mary Desti, had seized her Studebaker. Charley was only too happy to be useful and wore himself out making calls and writing irate letters, finally retrieving the Studebaker and getting his own father to house Mary Desti's car in his garage. Preston was appreciative, though not overly so; nor did Preston's requests stop. Soon Preston had Charley bargaining over bills for a diesel engine, battling a foreclosure on Mary Desti's Woodstock property, and negotiating about storage of the scenery and costumes from *A Well of Romance*.

Meanwhile, "Any time you want to come out to see me you can drive and bring my Mercedes out to me,"[28] Preston informed Charley—though one wonders when Charley would have found the time. Besides, Preston now had a new project for his friend to execute. "I'm going to have my boat sent around by freight," he wrote Charley, on May 4, 1933, of his plans to ship the *Recapture* to California. "I hope you will take care of the details for me."[29] So Charley dutifully telephoned the railroads and shipyards and began the laborious task of preparing the boat to be moved. "I shall personally supervise the entire assemblage and see that it gets off properly," he assured Preston on May 8,[30] and spent the next three weeks worrying over shipping details while imploring Preston not to be "disappointed" at the many delays. On May 26 Charley could at last cable Preston: "RECAPTURE LEAVES NEXT WEEK EXPLANATORY LETTER FOLLOWS."[31] Only now Preston had news of his own. "HAVE BOUGHT ANOTHER BOAT SO CANCEL ALL ARRANGEMENTS SHIPPING RECAPTURE," he wired Charley, and he had the temerity to add that Charley should "RUSH" to send the Recapture's controls and inboard engine nonetheless.[32]

So, without ever stating it, and probably without consciously conceiving such a trade-off, Preston had, for seventy-five-dollars a month rent, procured both an apartment and a secretary in New York. And also, it should not be underestimated, a loyal friend—for though *even* Charley must at moments have felt exploited, his affection for Preston never wavered.

Preston named his new boat the *Destiny*, "in memory of Mother," he told a friend. "You will remember that her cable address was DESTI, N.Y."[33] The name honored Mary in larger ways besides. Where the *Recapture* alluded specifically to Preston's second play and his retrieving of romance with Eleanor, the *Destiny* spoke to an impersonal future, to chance, to impending challenges and accomplishments.

The *Destiny* was sixty-two feet long, ten feet larger than the *Recapture* and a "seafaring yacht" rather than a power boat. It was only a hull, without sails or rigging, when Preston fell in love with it and bought it for, he proudly informed his father, $3,000 from a sea captain who'd been building it to go around the world, but ran out of money. "I can probably finish it for another $5,000 and then have a ship worth $20,000,"[34] he speculated. Preston liked the idea not only of a good deal, but of constructing a boat according to his own desires. He may have remembered how Marjorie Hutton designed the entire interior of her million dollar 350-foot *Sea Cloud*, and vowed to do the same with *his* boat, with far less money and more taste. He spent months supervising the building of the *Destiny* and would spend years tinkering with it, inventing such conveniences as cups that remained upright however the boat lurched. In 1936, he would race the *Destiny* to Honolulu. Preston also spent many weekends during the thirties cruising with friends around the off-shore island of Catalina, and Louise Sturges remembers some of the happiest days of their marriage on that boat.

When the *Recapture* arrived, thanks to Charley, Preston found a use for it, demonstrating the opposed piston diesel engine he'd conceived years ago and was sure had a market, though few buyers so far. The quality of this engine only an expert could appraise. But certainly Preston made a good case for its usefulness, telling a friend how it ran for thousands of hours "without any signs of wear whatsoever and with a minimum noise and vibration. . . . It starts instantly with an electric starter after days or weeks of idleness, it has never overheated. . . . It is ideal for 'steam' shovels, tractors, marine work, generating plants, etc., in the big size. In the small size it is indicated for generating plants, pumping, and other light uses."[35] Nor was Preston daunted when the engine failed to drum up business immediately; he continued manufacturing and selling what engines he could until the day he left Hollywood.

About the same time he bought the *Destiny*, in July 1933 Preston moved from 2070 Ivar to a "nicer" house, around a steep bend at 6377 Bryn Mawr Drive in the Hollywood hills. This yellowing white stone Spanish-style house, Preston's only Los Angeles residence not demolished by freeways, still stands—the most prominent on the block, with a tower jutting from its left flank like a barn's silo, mosaics over an arched door, and on a ridge across the road, a colonnade of giant poplars. Preston described his new home to Solomon: "It has three bedrooms, a three-car garage, a woodworking shop with electrical equipment in the basement, a lovely patio full of flowers, a huge living room, dining room, breakfast room, kitchen and servants' quarters, a runway for my two puppies, a study next to my bedroom, and an open living room with a fireplace off the patio. . . . My room is furnished with Monterey Spanish furniture and the white walls are furnished with blueprints of the new schooner."³⁶ Bianca now had a suite of her own rooms, which she decorated with antique furniture, and Preston's photographer friend Arnold Shroeder had quarters here too.

Arnold would suffer a trauma that summer. Early one morning in August, while driving home from a night on the town, he fell asleep at the wheel and plunged thirty feet into a canyon. Though he landed clear of the car, the photographer's head struck the ground, and he was unconscious when Preston got to him. Preston called the only doctor he knew, his new landlord, Bertie Woolfan. Bertie rushed to the hospital and saved Arnold's life that day, winning Preston's gratitude and marking the start of two important friendships.³⁷

Bertie and Priscilla Woolfan lived directly behind Preston. Bertie was a respected Hollywood doctor whose many patients included stars like Barbara Stanwyck. People in all walks of life found it easy to confide in Bertie, an unassuming man, who from the start greatly admired and was a little afraid of Sturges. Priscilla, then in her thirties, was breathtakingly pretty—with high cheekbones and rolled light hair. Before marrying Bertie she had been Priscilla Bonner, a silent movie actress. Now she was a devoted wife and would have liked children, but an accident prevented her from conceiving. Since Bertie had lost both of his parents as a child and Preston now had only his father, Priscilla believes they all came together out of a shared need for family.

Though they were the same age, Priscilla played a maternal role for Preston. Like the matriarchs in *Remember the Night* and *Hail the Conquering Hero*, she had a quiet strength that must have appealed to something in his own nature. Priscilla remembers a conversation with Preston where she informed him that while she had known many gifted creative people, he was one of the most complex men she'd ever encountered. And he replied, "But I'm a simple man. I have simple wants." And the strange thing, Priscilla observes, is that this also was true.

The Woolfans, like Charley Abramson, had the rare capacity to uncompetitively identify with Preston's triumphs, and Preston allowed Priscilla in particular to counsel him in his sorrows. Priscilla saw a side of Preston which he exposed only to intimates. "He had a streak of melancholy," she says, and relates how one day Preston called and asked her and Bertie to come over. "Preston opened the door, and we said *hello*, and he said, 'Do you realize that every day you live you're that much closer to death?' And Bertie said, 'Oh, Preston, for Christ's sake.' And Preston laughed then, but he was in a state of melancholy." The Woolfans are among very few people with whom Sturges discussed metaphysical questions. In the late forties, at a low point in his life, Preston, Priscilla, and Bertie would stay up all night on the deck of the *Destiny*,

Priscilla Bonner (later Priscilla Woolfan) as a silent movie actress, in the mid to late 1920s.

Priscilla lying between the two men, who speculated on and on about the existence of God. Neither Sturges nor Bertie could believe in organized religion, but Priscilla remembers their agreeing that, with all the suffering in the world, "there has to be a reason."

Priscilla also vividly remembers Preston's temper. "I have sat and literally shuddered when he (verbally) tore into somebody," recalls Priscilla, who adds that, no matter how angry he became, Preston scorned vulgarities, because he

thought cursing betrayed a limited vocabulary. Theirs was an instantly intimate relationship. When Preston met the Woolfans, he was eager to have
offspring and told Priscilla he wanted "six sons to bear him to his grave."
Meanwhile, he treated his close friends with the possessiveness of a patriarch.
Priscilla remembers how, when Preston bought property in the late thirties,
he wanted her and Bertie to leave their own house and move next door to him.
(They refused.) "Preston," she says, "was like an octopus; when he embraced
you, you belonged to him." [38]

During the summer of 1933, Preston, while moving homes and waiting for
the opening of *The Power and the Glory*, started a second original screenplay.
He explained the premise of his script to his father's friend, Sidney Love:

> I am just completing a new story called "The Vagrant." It has a nice idea.
> There are two men exiled in Mexico. One of them was a banker cashier, hon-
> est all his life except for one crazy minute. He had to get out of the country.
> The other was a crooked politician, dishonest all his life except for one crazy
> minute. He had become the governor of the state. To earn the respect of his
> wife and growing children he tried to turn honest. His party immediately sent
> him to the penitentiary for thievery committed much earlier in his career. He
> also lands in Mexico. [39]

This is such a precise plot summary of *The Great McGinty* that one is
tempted to imagine a finished screenplay ready for shooting, six years before
Preston sold it to Paramount. In fact, *The Vagrant*, which opens with a close-
up of a sleeping dog who is nowhere to be found in the finished picture, is
more sentimental and far more leisurely than the film. For what Preston told
Junior Laemmle about his writing strategy—"It is my custom to write down
the whole thought as it comes to me" and condense afterwards—was true; [40]
as was Preston's later observation to Darryl Zanuck: "Fortunately, I spritz
dialogue like seltzer water. My trouble has never been in inventing it but
rather in throwing three-quarters of it away." [41]

Yet, these statements are perplexing. For, if he really "spritzed dialogue like
seltzer," why was it two or three in the morning before Preston could sit down
to dictate his screenplays? If he willingly concedes that his first drafts were
turgid, why was he so loathe to revise? Certainly, Preston's strong streak of
laziness was part of the answer: while boating and inventing engines were
diversions, writing, however easily it came, was work. And he was erratic, of
course, though perhaps the erratic behavior was not merely instinctive, but
cultivated. For ever since his diary charting the progress of *Strictly Dishonorable*, Preston had studied how best to stimulate his creativity, and—since he'd

perceived the equally unsatisfying outcomes of *Child of Manhattan* (composed in a flurry) and *A Cup of Coffee* (written diligently)—he knew he was neither Byron nor Flaubert. "You are quite right about the effect continuous writing has on a man," Preston told Jack Gilchrist. "It is slightly smothering and very bad for the creative impulse, although I believe very good for the perfection of one's craft."[42] There would come four magic years in the forties when, for Preston, creativity and craft were indistinguishable, when in Yeats's conceit, the dancer and the dance were one. Until then, Preston's method remained much as it had been for *Strictly Dishonorable*—he composed with a vengeance and grudgingly honed his craft.

During the thirties, Sturges would grow from a promising writer of clever entertainments into a mature artist. As well as *The Vagrant*, he wrote early versions of *The Lady Eve* and *Unfaithfully Yours*, which are extraordinarily complex scripts by any standards. And even his less accomplished screenplays show impressive variety and an increasing cinematic facility: adaptations that range from *Diamond Jim*, about the flamboyant Diamond Jim Brady, to *If I Were King*, about the poet Villon, to *We Live Again*, from a late Tolstoy novel; formula melodrama in *Next Time We Love*; screwball comedy in *Easy Living*; and an exuberant mixture of farce and satire in *Song of Joy*.

Sturges was most adept at comedy, but now also showed a flair for drama and romance. His familiar thematic concerns—power, success, money, luck— were deepened, and he began exploring the relationship between morality and love, between the well-being of groups and of individuals. In an era when L. B. Mayer declared movies should reflect the shared values of all Americans, Sturges's characters resist homogeneity. Unlike Capra's superficial eccentrics, they not only seem different, they are. "Right or wrong," says Lee in *Remember the Night*, "is the same for everybody, you see, but the *rights* and the *wrongs* aren't the same. Like in China they eat dogs." And Sturges was courageous not only in his dialogue but in all his creative decisions. For much as he tried personally to ingratiate himself with powerful people, when there was a choice between appeasing a boss and attempting something innovative, Sturges most always did as he pleased.

"I am in the depths of depression," Preston informed Solomon in September of 1933, "as I owe several thousand dollars on my boat and have no money left. Your generosity pulled me through this week. I may have to wire you next week and possibly, God forbid, even the week after. You may be quite sure that I will pay it back promptly, but I hate to have to ask you when your business has been so very bad."[1]

Preston was in such dire straits because, as one after another of his friends attests, he loved spending, but had absolutely no facility with or respect for money. Though he admired his father's Puritan equation of financial well-being with virtue, and certainly enjoyed the prestige of commanding high wages, deep down Preston, like Mary Desti, found something vaguely unsavory about preserving capital. Maybe it was his subconscious identification with the truly rich, like Paris Singer and Eleanor Hutton, or maybe it was the opposite: that he on a certain level despised the world's inequality; that he could never come to terms with some people's having so much while others had nothing at all.[2] Spending was a way of lessening the disparity. And also of testing his luck, for Preston had been raised to expect miracles, not stability. He thrived on calamities averted, the greater the desperation the more balming the relief.

Yet, no more than his mother was Preston capable of outright lying to Solomon Sturges. Preston's anxiety was real. Three studios had turned down *The Vagrant*, which he'd been working on throughout August, and had hoped would support his household in the months ahead. "They say [*The Vagrant*] is beautifully written but they are afraid of the subject matter which contains a fairish amount of politics and which leads them to suppose that the picture would not interest women, who make up the majority of the audiences. Warner Brothers is still interested in the story as a vehicle for Edward G. Robinson."[3]

Warner Brothers may ultimately have also turned down *The Vagrant*, or perhaps Preston rejected Warner Brothers, because they were known for making films on low budgets. And, while Sturges was realistic about his script's commercial drawbacks, he knew it deserved a first-rate production. (In 1935 he would angrily dismiss Universal's proposition that he direct this script on a $100,000 budget because he felt it would be impossible to do justice to his screenplay with such meager financing.)[4] Throughout the thirties Sturges would continue polishing and trying to market various versions of what had now become *The Great McGinty*—at one point submitting it as a story idea to the *Saturday Evening Post.*[5]

For the present, though, his main concern was to find regular work at a studio, because bills were mounting, and he was working himself into a great anxiety over his financial predicament. *The Power and the Glory* was proving difficult to sell at the box office, and the producers Sturges had hoped would be lining up at his doorstep were, on the contrary, avoiding him.

Preston would later cite the events of September 1933 as indicative of his ferociously erratic luck in Hollywood. The William Morris Agency contacted him once again. And though Preston continued to suspect he could do better on his own, in exchange for a $600 loan to pay Arnold Shroeder's hospital bill, he agreed to let William Morris find him work. September 13, Preston signed the contract with Morris and then went to sit with Arnold in the hospital. "When I got home around seven my secretary was waiting out on the front steps for me, nearly insane with anxiety herself. Irving Thalberg had started calling me five minutes after I left and would wait in his office for me until 8. He put me to work at 8:30."[6]

This story conjures a tantalizing image of Bianca totally identified with Preston's precarious fortunes. And Sturges's perspective on the day's events is telling. For while he makes a point that he overcame pride and signed on with William Morris in order to pay Arnold's hospital bill, he also stresses that Morris had nothing to do with his getting the job with Thalberg. Thalberg called *him* at *his* home, Preston won a reprieve from ruin after performing a good deed, but without *anyone's* interceding.

In 1933 Irving Thalberg was considered the ideal producer. Writers vied to join his prestigious unit at MGM. Preston complained that he was paid only $1,000 a week (his former salary at Universal), but was happy with his project, which was to adapt Michael Arlen's bestseller, *The Green Hat* (also the source for Greta Garbo's 1929 *A Woman of Affairs*), into a movie for Thalberg's wife, Norma Shearer. Recently, Katherine Cornell had starred in a play based on Arlen's novel, and Sturges set about conscientiously studying how others had dealt with this material, for though he had every intention of creating something original and distinctly cinematic, he was committed to careful research.[7]

Set in the teens and twenties among the British upper classes, the plot of the *The Green Hat* goes roughly as follows: Iris, kept from marrying the man she loves, Napier, because his father scorns her background, marries her brother's idol, Boy, who "falls" from his hotel room on their wedding night. To preserve Boy's honor (and her brother's illusions), Iris tells friends that Boy died "for purity," implying that she had revealed a secret from her past that had revolted him. In fact, Boy killed himself because he had syphilis and was too weak to acknowledge it. Ten years pass, and Iris still loves Napier, who, once he's learned the truth about Boy, is determined to marry her, whatever the consequences with his family. But he wants Iris to reveal her innocence, though she refuses to sully Boy's name. When Napier insists on disclosing the truth to his father, Iris departs—literally to her death.

Sturges's script leaves her, more ambiguously, just driving off. But either way, *The Green Hat*, full of anguishing over honor and empire, is pure melodrama, scarcely less contrived than *Recapture*. Thalberg, in his long memo of suggestions to Sturges, locates the book's crucial narrative conflict: "It is the ideals of Iris and Napier which clash. She wants him to love her first, no matter what she has done. He can love her under certain circumstances only. He can be swayed by argument, by offenses to tradition. She cannot."[8] And while Sturges's script is faithful to Arlen's dreary sentimentality on this point as elsewhere, the idea of lovers with clashing moral codes and of a man who could be driven mad over some secret revealed on a wedding night must have intrigued him. For he would make comic use of both in *The Lady Eve*.

Sturges wrote a workmanlike script for *The Green Hat*. But because either Thalberg or others at MGM were dissatisfied with it, Preston was dismissed in the middle of November. Now began nearly three years of bouncing from one studio and screenplay to another, which would end only in 1936 with Sturges's Paramount contract. Meanwhile, his letters to his father, like Mary Desti's in the twenties, fluctuate between anxiety and ebullience: he portrays himself on a precarious but noble mission that will end either very badly or in triumph.

Preston, who despised powerlessness under any circumstances, particularly resented working for bullying studio heads like his next boss, the infamously crude and mercenary Harry Cohn, of Columbia Pictures. Columbia, which had the previous February released the film version of *Child of Manhattan*,[9] was where Frank Capra made his movies. It so happens that the week of November 20, 1933, when Sturges began his contract with Columbia, was the week Capra started shooting *It Happened One Night*. It was also Sturges's *last* week at Columbia.

The morning he arrived he was asked to come up with "a rather tragic original story" for the actress Elissa Landi.[10] The long synopsis he quickly devised, and called *Matrix*, was everything *The Vagrant* was not—narrowly focused, concerned with primal emotions, and utterly without irony. Sturges would describe *Matrix*'s subject as "the two different kinds of love that women have . . . and that sometimes conflict: the passionate and the maternal."[11] Its argument is that a woman's maternal love for a weak man, while self-destructive, can be more powerful than her passion for someone who is strong and attractive.

As in *Child of Manhattan*, the female protagonist is named Madeleine and is beautiful and poor, but—in contrast to the dance-hall girl—clever and virginal. The two men competing for Madeleine's love are the rich, smart, and handsome Gerald and the feckless and dependent Tommy. Madeleine loves them both, but marries Tommy out of sympathy, believing she can make him stop drinking and find work. A year passes, and Tommy is still morose and jobless. Madeleine sees no alternative but to get a job herself—as Gerald's secretary. Gerald and Madeleine reaffirm their love, but Madeleine remains guiltily devoted to Tommy.

When Gerald hires Tommy for an important position, Madeleine can finally contemplate leaving her husband for Gerald, and the two lovers go off on a secret holiday. But when Tommy finds them out, Madeleine feels bound to solace her needing husband. Vowing to renounce Gerald, she comes home to Tommy—but discovers him dead, "his outstretched arm clutching a vial."

This tale is neither witty nor emotionally complex, and there's nothing in the characterizations or the texture of the writing which distinguishes *Matrix* from its "weepy" genre. Tommy is maddeningly weak, while Gerald is not only appealing but virtuous, so the only question is whether good sense or the mothering impulse will triumph in Madeleine—an issue Sturges conveniently deflects by having Tommy commit suicide. Like her namesake in *Child of Manhattan*, Madeleine perceives self-sacrifice as a privilege, which binds her to the heroines of French melodrama and sets her distinctly apart from the smart-talking Depression women who were beginning to look out for themselves in Hollywood movies. And whereas the minor characters in *A Cup of Coffee* allow Sturges to engage wider social issues, *Matrix* is virtually without subplots.

So it's tempting to see this story, and the several scripts that would evolve out of it, as pure calculation on Sturges's part. After all, *The Vagrant* had just been widely rejected on grounds that its politics and abstractions would bore women. Shrewd businessmen like Samuel Goldwyn had explained to Preston how it was "only with a woman's story"—for example, a domestic pot-boiler—that you could make money. (The logic being that women see twice as many films as men.) Goldwyn cited *Back Street* to Preston as the exemplary "woman's picture," and *Matrix* shares the weepy predilections of that 1932 hit. Yet, whatever impelled Sturges to write *Matrix*, there's no denying that he *liked* his story. He would continually rework and champion it over the next two decades, and in the late forties sold it to Darryl Zanuck in return for the third largest salary received in America that year.

Sturges always thought well of his most recent work, but his sustained high opinion of *Matrix*—for all its obvious shortcomings—is revealing. Though his comedies would win him fame, riches, and a place in history, he would continue to believe almost equally in his gift for solemn drama. And Sturges's comic vision, to us so rare and brilliant, may have seemed to *him* no truer than pathos, the powerful women of *The Lady Eve* and *The Palm Beach Story* no more emblematic of their sex than his Madeleines.

Sturges was doubly punished for *Matrix* at Columbia, where his synopsis was first dismissed out of hand and then, amazingly, held up as proof that he could not write comedy. "I thought [that] conclusion rather a stupid one, but the executives in this business are often not bright," Preston wrote Solomon. And to Harry Cohn: "I am sorry that you and your masterminds decided that I was not a writer of comedy. Your joint memories must be failing you." [12]

Sturges sent *Matrix* on to Twentieth Century Fox, where he got a more gentle rejection from the story editor, Julian Johnson. "Whoever said *Matrix* was a bad story is crazy," wrote Johnson. "I think it is a swell story but it is not for pictures now. You have a natural tendency toward tragedy and this story is too undeniably tragic to make a popular box-office picture in this day when people have so many troubles of their own." [13]

While there was no work for Preston at Fox, he got a two-week assignment at Universal, working on the script for *Imitation of Life* with John Stahl, who'd directed the film version of *Strictly Dishonorable*. But "unfortunately," Preston wrote his father, "this job lasted exactly two weeks, and I have not worked since," he gloomily reported on the third of January.[14]

Soon, however, he was working for, of all people, B. P. Schulberg, with whom he'd sparred about *The Power and the Glory* in the *Hollywood Reporter*. Now an independent producer, Schulberg hired Sturges to expand upon Clarence Buddington Kelland's magazine story about a commoner who poses as a princess on a U.S. press tour. The film, *Thirty Day Princess*, was to star Sylvia Sidney, Cary Grant, and Edward Arnold. Sturges's script is as competent and mildly amusing as its material. Still, Schulberg felt compelled to bring in another writer, which, predictably, infuriated Preston; and one can't help suspecting Schulberg's *real* purpose in hiring Sturges was to teach him a lesson. "You had one fair love scene," Schulberg informed his irate writer, "one very tender, beautifully written love scene, and one very bad and flat. You will notice, if you read the script, that we have improved your fair love scene, have left intact your good one, and have added another one equally good." [15]

"When and if I am content to hear another man praised for something I created and, above all, when I am willing to accept praise for the work of somebody else, then I will have truly gone Hollywood, will have accepted the system and will no longer be worth my salary," Preston, in high dudgeon about his shared script credit, replied. His concluding fillip was a perspicacious observation about producers: "By the very nature of your occupation you have accepted praise for pictures as generals accept praise for their soldiers." [16] Sturges too yearned for credit, but had no desire to change places with Schulberg, who neither wrote nor directed, but merely exhorted others. If Sturges had his way, he'd do everything himself. And while he couldn't yet manage that, Preston did get his name placed first among the screenplay acknowledgments for *Thirty Day Princess*, which at least improved his status in the industry.

If, in March of 1934, Sturges was losing the battle for writers' power in the studios, he prevailed over Schulberg in the press: the *Hollywood Reporter* awarded the *Power and the Glory* its medal for the year's best original story. The following month Preston finally got a screenwriting assignment worthy of his talents. Samuel Goldwyn was preparing to make the third film adaptation of Tolstoy's *Resurrection*, and hired Rouben Mamoulian to direct it as a vehicle for Anna Sten. The Russian-born actress had appeared in Pudovkin's *Storm Over Asia* before coming to Hollywood in 1933, under the sponsorship of Goldwyn, who hoped to make her as famous as Garbo. Mamoulian recommended Sturges as screenwriter, and, maybe because of Preston's award or his credit on *Thirty Day Princess*, Goldwyn agreed to raise Preston's salary from $500 to $1500 a week. "My new boss, Mr. Goldwyn, was very leery of me but he has just seen the first fifty pages I wrote for him, and I understand that he is now a little easier in his mind," [17] Preston wrote his father. In his autobiography, Sturges more explicitly recalls that Goldwyn "loathed" him and every morning approached Mamoulian, eagerly demanding, "When can we get rid of this fellow Sturgeon?"

Though relations with Goldwyn were tense, Mamoulian, a man of taste and sophistication, recalls that he and Sturges enjoyed a harmonious collaboration.[18] Their assignment was tricky, for *Resurrection* is no *Anna Karenina* or *War and Peace*. Finished when Tolstoy was in his seventies and had dedicated the past twenty years of his life to polemical writing, it spends much of its nearly six hundred pages inveighing against the church, the Russian penal and justice systems, and private ownership of land; and while advocating mystical Christianity and pacifism, some of its most attractive characters are revolutionaries. Worse still, for Hollywood's purposes, the hero winds up not winning the girl but discovering the Gospels!

Nonetheless, at the heart of *Resurrection* is a compelling story, based on the real-life experience of a peasant girl and a Russian aristocrat. In Tolstoy's novel the man is Dmitri, the peasant girl Katusha, adopted and educated by Dmitri's aunts, who employ her as a house servant. Dmitri, a dreamy youth who reads Henry George on tax policy and flirts with theories of land reform, first meets Katusha at his aunts' estate over summer vacation from college. Now their love is innocent. But three years later when Dmitri, who's become a dissolute young officer, comes back to spend Easter with his aunts, he seduces Katusha before returning to his regiment. Katusha becomes pregnant (and refuses to reveal the name of the father), and the aunts dismiss her; her child dies, and she's soon reduced to making her living as a prostitute. Nearly a decade passes before Dmitri again encounters Katusha: now he's a juror in a trial where she is accused of robbery and murder. All the jurors agree Katusha is innocent; however, by mistakenly wording their verdict, they condemn her to hard labor in Siberia. Dmitri, appalled at the part he's played in Katusha's misfortunes, dedicates all his energies to changing her verdict; when that fails, he insists on accompanying her to Siberia and implores her to let him marry her. But Katusha refuses, perceiving that Dmitri is impelled not by love for her personally, but by hunger for his own redemption and social justice.

While very much in his own voice, Sturges's script is true both to the spirit and to the moral subtleties of Tolstoy's novel. Its opening scene, where the peasants welcome lord Dmitri home for the summer, is a model of economical exposition—and, in its comic attention to the myopia of overly zealous welcomers, a precursor of Norval's homecoming in *Hail the Conquering Hero*. Significant too are this scene's ironic comments on generosity. One welcoming peasant offers Dmitri a potato, another makes a great fuss handing him a rooster. Dmitri, of course, has no idea what to do with these gifts, and reciprocates with a high-minded speech about peasants' rights which is similarly baffling to his tenants.

151

No more than Tolstoy does Sturges belabor Dmitri's love for Katusha, which is swiftly established: in one sequence Katusha diligently milks a cow while Dmitri, lazily watching her, extols a system whereby the industrious, rather than the entrenched rich, would prosper. Equally deft is Sturges's portrayal of Dmitri's dissipation, and Sturges must have gone out of his way to study Russian cinema, for he suggests a "stock shot" of "ripe wheat waving in the breeze," noting that "there was a fine one in the Russian film [Eisenstein's] *The Old and the New*."

At other times Sturges revealingly misreads Tolstoy. For instance, when Dmitri, in his remorse over Katusha, decides to give his lands up to the peasants, rather than thanking him, the peasants grumble about their modest rent and wonder who'll now take care of them. The event is the same in the novel and the film. But while Tolstoy mocks Dmitri's vanity at expecting gratitude from people so long exploited, Sturges stresses the greed of the peasants. As in the automat scene in *Easy Living*, the poor are, if anything, more grasping than the rich.

Struges's only remaining draft for *Resurrection*, dated April 27 (1934) and emphatically titled *We Live Again*, finishes with Katusha and Dmitri madly in love and pledged to marry. The sentimental ending was inevitable in a commercial picture. Still, this script's compression of complex material, intelligent shading of character, and balance of worldliness and mysticism was a considerable achievement.

Far less so is the released film, which (though well reviewed at the time) suffers not only from Anna Sten's overeager performance and a surfeit of what Goldwyn must have considered typically Slavic folk music but from script changes that destroy ambiguities and emphasize the obvious. How much Sturges himself revised, and how many of the changes were created by others is uncertain. Mamoulian remembers that, except for one love scene added by Thornton Wilder, Sturges did all the writing. But according to the *Hollywood Reporter*, Maxwell Anderson wrote a draft before, and Leonard Praskins a draft after Sturges.[19] And while Sturges's name appears first on the credits, he dissociated himself from the finished movie. "You will remember [*We Live Again*]," he wrote Solomon, "as the picture from which Mr. Goldwyn fired me with great alacrity."[20]

Whatever the truth here, Sturges's script for *We Live Again* was his first important hired work in Hollywood, and observing Mamoulian, who'd infused genre films like *Applause* and *City Streets* with his own cynical view of the world, must have given Preston ideas about transcending conventional material. More important, Sturges discovered what he *didn't* like about Mamoulian's self-conscious style and indebtedness to the then highly influential school of German expressionism. "My friend Mamoulian told me he could make the audience be interested in whatever *he* showed them," Sturges would recall in the forties, "and I told him he was mistaken. It is true that he can bend my head down and force me to look at a doorknob when my reflex wants to see the face of the girl saying goodbye, but it is also true that it stops my comprehension of the scene, destroys my interest and gives me a pain in the neck." [21]

The most tangible result of *We Live Again* was that Sturges was now in a higher salary bracket, which assured him, if not power over his work, at least the ability to command more prestigious projects. Soon after leaving Goldwyn, he was hired back at Universal and, with his French background and flair for dialects, assigned to adapt the first two films of Marcel Pagnol's *Fanny* trilogy—*Marius* and *Fanny*—into a romance for their new star, Jane Wyatt.

Pagnol's tales of a young Marseilles girl who sends her true love off to sea, discovers she's pregnant, and marries another man for her child's sake had been a hit not only in Paris, but in Tokyo and New York. *Marius* opened in 1931 and *Fanny* the year after. For Sturges, one aspect of the story was particularly moving. The sailor Marius returns two years after leaving Fanny to reclaim her from Panisse, the older man she's married, who is now a doting father to her son. That son, Marius insists, is *his* child. No, says César, Marius's own father. The father is not the one who gives life. Dogs give life—the father is the one who gives love. Perhaps because of this passage, which Sturges cited time and again to explain his wholehearted affection for his own adopted father, the *Fanny* films would remain favorites with Preston always.

Now Sturges was especially gratified to be working on *Fanny* because this was to be a Henry Henigson production, which William Wyler would direct. Preston probably knew both Henigson and Wyler slightly from his earlier work at Universal. He may also have known Wyler's distant cousin Ernst Laemmle, Universal's foreign dialogue supervisor, and Paul Kohner, the head of Universal's European production. Like Wyler, Ernst Laemmle and Kohner were "nephews" recruited by Carl Laemmle, Sr., on his visits to Germany. All were worldly, intelligent men, bemused by Hollywood mores but at the same time eager to do well. (Kohner later became an important agent.) Henigson and Ernst Laemmle naturally gravitated toward Sturges, and Wyler too told his biographer that Preston was the first of his contemporaries to influence him profoundly. [22]

Wyler and Sturges were not having an easy time with *Fanny*, however. There were casting troubles and, more important, threats from the industry's watchdog, the Motion Picture Producers and Distributors Association, commonly known as the Hays Office (after its director Will Hays), which, in 1934, under growing pressure from the Catholic Legion of Decency, was beginning to take its mission to "clean up" movies seriously.[23] The Association had been formed in 1922 to discourage more rigid censorship by the government. But for twelve years Will Hays did little more than sanction what the studios produced. Then came the church uproar over Mae West's blatant sensuality, followed by the bishops' long lists of offensive movies (including *Of Human Bondage* and *It Happened One Night*). "We can be clean without being prudish," replied Carl Laemmle, Sr., to what initially seemed much ado about nothing.[24] But when Church proscriptions began affecting ticket sales, the industry capitulated by conceiving a production code, which was prudish indeed: no double beds, or unpunished sex outside marriage, or insinuating language, and even *animal* sex organs were tabu. (Molly Haskell, in *From Reverence to Rape*, points out how by this logic Cheetah and his baby apes were made to wear body stockings.[25]) What's more, the Hays Office, now headed by Joseph I. Breen, was zealously enforcing its new standards.

Sturges would in time learn ingenious strategies for circumventing the production code. Now, however, he could not convince the Laemmles to proceed with a film about a young girl pregnant out of wedlock, and work on *Fanny* was in July of 1934 indefinitely postponed.[26] Sturges, Wyler, and Henigson were reassigned to adapt another European drama: Ferenc Molnar's *The Good Fairy*, which, ironically enough, also involves an unmarried woman who sleeps where she likes.

She does not, however, get pregnant, which was one advantage. Though recently a success with Helen Hayes on Broadway, the Hungarian play was less well known than *Fanny* and so more easily transformed. Its heroine, Lu, is a young usherette who has a natural desire to bestow favors, and infallible instincts: "I only make mistakes when I think," she says. "When I do something blindly I always hit the mark." Lu, though loved by a handsome waiter, wants to rise in the world by associating with rich married businessmen like her current admirer, Konrad. She has no moral objections to sleeping with Konrad, it's just that the prospect completely repels her. So to defer Konrad's ardor and also improve her status, Lu tells him she's the wife of a respectable lawyer. Konrad decides that the way to win Lu is to award his company's business to her husband. When he asks for this husband's name, Lu—happy to do a good deed, hopefully for someone needy—"blindly" picks a lawyer out of the phone book: Max Sporum. Sporum, as it turns out, *is* poor and idealistic—in Molnar's play he's also the ugly and adored boss of a long-suffering

Willie Wyler (left) and Preston, about 1934.

secretary. How Lu brings all the right people together and herself winds up rich and happily married to neither Konrad, Sporum, nor the waiter is the subject of Molnar's elegantly orchestrated plot.

Sturges and Wyler set about changing that plot, as well as every line of the play's dialogue. In their film, Lu becomes Luisa, an orphan with no experience of men who, when she meets Konrad by chance at a party, mentions her lawyer husband only to fend off this pesky adulterer. Asked to produce her spouse's name, she too pulls Sporum out of the phone book, but now Sporum has no secretary, and once Luisa convinces him to shave off his beard, she and the lawyer fall madly in love. The reason Sturges's script softened the play's cynicism, Wyler explained, was that their heroine would be played by Universal's new star, Margaret Sullavan, who had a natural innocence that belied

155

the amorality of Molnar's Lu. But this seems dubious, as Margaret Sullavan projects intelligence more than innocence, and in fact balked at her character's guilelessness, at one point refusing to exclaim "Oh, isn't this wonderful?," at the sight of a fancy restaurant. "I'm not going to say that one more time," she informed Wyler.[27]

Clearly, it was less Margaret Sullavan's nature than fear of the Hays Office which impelled Sturges to turn *The Good Fairy*'s heroine from a woman of the world who *chooses* her virtues to a naïf who, like Harry Langdon, survives dangers through a kind of idiot's luck. Sturges also adds some silent-comedy-like physical business. In an opening scene at the orphanage, for instance, Luisa pounces too hard on her rope ladder and winds up dangling from a chandelier. Sturges's tone is as giddy as in *The Guinea Pig* and *The Well Of Romance*. Luisa's last name becomes Ginglebusher, while Konrad appears not so much lecherous as playful.

Sturges opens the play up and for the most part broadens its ironies. He also adds an inspired scene in a movie theatre where the audience hilariously interacts with the film characters. On the screen, two lovers named Mitzi and Meredith are in the throes of a histrionic separation. "Go!" Meredith orders Mitzi, while Mitzi pleads, "Go? Oh, you don't mean that Meredith!" "Go!" says Meredith. "Oh, you don't mean 'go' Meredith! Reconsider . . . ," says Mitzi. "Go!" says Meredith. "Meredith," says Mitzi. "Go!" suddenly chimes in a man watching the movie, who Sturges now shows us in looming close-up. And after a few more "gos" from the screen, a family in the audience, whispering among themselves, begin unconsciously repeating the movie dialogue.

This scene, though not the first to play with film's suggestive powers (Buster Keaton had made *Sherlock, Jr.* ten years earlier), shows Sturges's delight at the nature of his medium. And while it's here pursued merely for laughs, the idea that art can infiltrate life will resonate in the great cartoon scene climax of *Sullivan's Travels*. Like *A Cup of Coffee*, *The Good Fairy* is also fascinated by what money enables. "This is one of the most wonderful sensations I've ever experienced!" declares the lawyer Sporum, after buying a motor car. "I feel like a bird." Liberty, Sporum will discover, is expensive.

Though Sturges did his best to avert the wrath of the censors, his first draft of *The Good Fairy*, submitted to the Breen Office in early September, came back filled with orders for cuts. A mere look on the face of the orphanage director at the beginning the film was deemed unacceptable, and a scene where this same Dr. Schultz struggles to discreetly convey the facts of life to Luisa was "definitely and gravely objectionable" and had to go at once. Furthermore, "There should be no divan or any reference to it, anywhere in the script," and on, and on, so Preston had his work cut out for him; and he continued rewriting and submitting new versions of *The Good Fairy* to the censors long after the film went into production. There were times when Sturges got his scene approved no more than a day before Wyler had to shoot it, which made life difficult, but exciting. "I have been working very hard. I'm here at eight in the morning to see the rushes and I rarely go to bed before two through sheer habit," Preston wrote his father.[28]

Sturges and Wyler set their film in Molnar's Hungary, and Universal hired four hundred extras and insisted on authentic detail. The art director spent a month creating an intricate miniature of Budapest, replete even with tiny trolley tracks. A European department store was erected on Universal's largest sound stage, and the dining room where Luisa meets Konrad was elaborately modeled after a famous Hungarian restaurant. Wyler, like Sturges, loved food, so they probably consumed a few fine meals themselves while consulting on the script, which Wyler greatly admired. Sturges was developing an instinct about actors and may have suggested some of the first-rate cast. Herbert Marshall was to play Sporum, opposite Margaret Sullavan's Luisa, and Frank Morgan and Reginald Owen were Konrad and the waiter, respectively. Shooting began early in October, and though everyone involved was a gifted professional, the atmosphere on the set was tense because Wyler and Sullavan squabbled constantly: first over their different interpretations of Luisa, and finally over anything at all. Sullavan, a former stage actress, had starred in *Only Yesterday* and *Little Man, What Now?* and was currently Universal's most flaunted new talent. She must have felt she had every right to assert herself with so young a director as Wyler; and Wyler—who often lied about his age to enhance his authority—grew increasingly determined to exert control.

Then, one day Wyler, watching the rushes, realized that Sullavan's resentment was showing in her performance. He made a concerted effort to be nice to her on the set, and afterwards asked if she'd come out with him to dinner. Margaret Sullavan was surprised, but went. Afterwards, her relationship with Wyler improved noticeably, and some weeks later Wyler came to Preston with a proposition. "What would you say if I got married to Maggie?" he asked.

"Well, she's not marrying you for your money, that's for sure," replied Preston, alluding to Margaret Sullavan's large income, which would become a bone of contention in Wyler's (short) first marriage.[29]

Wyler and Sullavan chartered a plane and eloped to Yuma, Arizona, on Saturday November 25, but proved themselves good professionals by returning the same day so they could be back on the set Monday morning. Shooting continued for a month after that, finishing just before Christmas. On January 31, Carl Laemmle, Sr., received a cable from an executive at the Radio City Music Hall: "FOR THE FIRST TIME IN THE HISTORY OF THE MUSIC HALL WE HAVE BOOKED A PICTURE WITHOUT PREVIEW AND BACKED IT WITH OUR ADVERTISING ON FAITH. I HAVE JUST LEFT OUR PREVIEW ROOM AFTER SEEING THE GOOD FAIRY WHICH OPENS TOMORROW. IT IS ONE OF THE GREATEST COMEDIES I HAVE EVER SEEN." Two days later Wyler and Sullavan, in New York waiting to sail on the Île de France for their honeymoon in Europe, wired Preston and Henry Henigson that their movie was a triumph, both with the public and critically.[30]

The reviews were in fact mixed. After calling *The Good Fairy* "the best screen comedy of this infant year," the *Times* went on to unfavorably compare it to a recent French film, *À Nous la Liberté*, by René Clair; and *Variety*, showing more attention to Sturges than to Wyler or Sullavan, noted: "Preston Sturges has translated Molnar's dainty comedy for the screen, and has turned out a somewhat vociferous paraphrase. . . . It is rather slapsticking a master but it's for the box office and the box office reaction should be robust." The *New York Sun* and the *Post* were more enthusiastic, and the *Herald Tribune* summed up the general opinion saying, "On the whole it is good fun."

It was also a hit, Preston's first in the over five years since *Strictly Dishonorable*. If he was not yet in a league with René Clair, he had at last received sole screenwriting credit on a popular movie, and had a taste of Hollywood success.

Preston told Solomon Sturges that everyone has his area of cheapness, and his own was the telephone—he couldn't bear to make long distance calls. This helps explain the abundance of Sturges's correspondence, though Preston must also have felt frustrated by brief calls and believed he could express himself more expansively in letters, which—unlike dialogue—he composed with painstaking care.[1]

After one unsatisfying phone conversation with Solomon, Preston sensed that his father didn't like *The Good Fairy*; and he wrote him an earnest letter, asking why. "I am sure that you laughed and were entertained. I wonder if it is because the story was so light and improbable." Solomon wrote back, expressing his usual financial reservations: "I did not dislike the film. It was very well acted and very funny but it did not seem to me that it would be a money earner for any great period of time."[2] But what's revealing is that, even for an audience as entertainment-minded as his father, Preston makes a distinction between light and likable comedy, and he's not merely hurt by his father's lack of enthusiasm, but eager for advice. In the same letter, Preston says he is pretty sure Solomon will like the script he is now writing, which is "simple and sincere but also very funny." This was *A Cup of Coffee*. Even before *The Good Fairy*, Universal had bought Preston's unproduced Depression comedy, and they now had him adapting it into a movie, which, Preston proudly informed Charley Abramson, he would also be allowed to direct.[3]

But then Universal asked Preston to postpone his film so he could help out on a favorite project of Carl Laemmle, Jr.'s. While Preston surely resented this deflection, he agreed, on the condition that his salary be raised to $2,500 a week. "I know you will be pleased," Preston wrote Solomon, "as this salary puts me in the top bracket of Hollywood writers."[4]

The script Carl Laemmle, Jr., wanted Preston to work on was *Diamond*

Jim, based on the life of Diamond Jim Brady, the gay nineties bon vivant, whom Preston had seen before the war in New York at the Delmonico Club— an enormous man, decked out in jewels and dining with the Dolly sisters. Brady, like the fictional Tom Garner in *The Power and the Glory*, rose from rags to riches through success in the railroad business, but here comparisons end because Brady was generous to a fault, unlucky in love, and affably amoral. Brady was interested not in power but in making and spending money. He bought the biggest diamonds and showiest suits, ate the grandest meals, sat front row center at the theatre, and refused to apologize for his nouveau riche indulgence. Preston must have been impressed with Brady's candor and how he never disguised his poor Irish origins (or bothered to improve his grammar), for he quoted Diamond Jim approvingly when he was courting Eleanor. Brady, whose great love was show business, sustained a long platonic friendship with Lillian Russell, whom Preston had also met in New York, the one time she came to the Maison Desti. Twenty years later, he remembered her as "a tall and buxom blonde so beautiful and so good-natured she took your breath away."[5]

Carl Laemmle, Jr., had bought the rights to Simon and Schuster's *Diamond Jim* biography the day it was published and then invited the biographer, Parker Morell, to come to Hollywood and write a script in which Edward Arnold, who was born for the part, would star. But Parker Morell, a jeweler whose family had sold Brady many of his diamonds, had little experience with writing, much less moviemaking. He was appalled by endless story conferences and executives curiously indifferent to historical accuracy. His first efforts were rejected, and he was soon teamed up with screenwriters Harry Clork and Doris Malloy. It was when their script too failed to please Carl Laemmle, Jr., that Universal agreed to give Sturges a raise of $1,000 a week for his help. In the two-and-a-half years since Preston was fired from *The Invisible Man*, he'd learned a lot about screenwriting and, what's far trickier, gotten Hollywood to reconceive his worth.

As with *The Invisible Man*, Preston felt no compunction to consult the existing script for *Diamond Jim*, though he stuck to the broad outline of Brady's life as envisioned by Morell. Sturges's screenplay opens with Brady's birth in 1856, the son of a poor saloon keeper; then shows Brady winning his first railroad job, proving himself a consummate salesman, and striking up a partnership with the Englishman Sampson Fox, whose railroad fixture, the "Fox truck," makes both of them rich. No sooner does Brady get the taste of money than he begins custom-ordering gems in the shape of train parts, strutting about with a diamond-encrusted walking stick, and consuming enormous meals, always beginning with at least a dozen oysters and finishing with candy after dessert. Eating is an unequivocal passion for Brady, as is philanthropy and his friendship with Lillian Russell, but Diamond Jim won't touch liquor (he consumes huge pitchers of orange juice) and is ambivalent about romance. After an innocent southern belle rejects his marriage proposal, Brady declares he'll never love again. Then, years later, he falls for a woman of the world— Jane in Sturges's version, Edna McCauley in real life—who uncannily resembles his first love. Jane, though good-hearted and for a time loyal, leaves Brady to elope with Lillian Russell's fiancé. Meanwhile, Brady's eating takes its toll, and doctors at Johns Hopkins Hospital tell him his life depends on sticking to a rigid diet. But Brady returns to his gluttony and dies at sixty-one.

Though Preston would later make a point of deprecating fictionalized biography, he now took considerable poetic license with *Diamond Jim*.[6] Numerous crowd-pleasing scenes were insinuated—such as a chase sequence where Brady and Sampson Fox dive off a moving train to escape vindictive gamblers, and a spectacular train crash, when Jim demonstrates an all-steel railroad car at the World's Fair. More subtly, Sturges hypothesizes about Diamond Jim's emotional make-up, conceiving him as a far from naïve do-gooder, who satisfies his own needs through generosity, but is incapable of real intimacy or of inspiring romantic love. Sturges's final scene, where Diamond Jim, deserted by Jane, prepares to disobey doctor's orders and gorge himself on truffles and guinea hen—in effect to eat himself to death—shows a man who, like Mary Desti, sees no great tragedy in dying, it's better to go out in style than to live timidly.

For the most part, Sturges merely exaggerates Diamond Jim's adventures, but on two points he distorts reality. First, where in real life Jim Brady's mother was an alcoholic and religious fanatic who persecuted Jim for his loose morals (and whom Jim ultimately committed to a mental institution), Sturges makes her a saintly creature who dies when Jim is very young. She has such a lasting impact that, because of a promise to her, Diamond Jim never drinks.

Sturges also twists Brady's attitude toward the stock market. When hard times struck, in 1893, the real Jim Brady quickly liquidated his stocks and sat on his money. But Sturges's Jim, like Mr. Dickson in Capra's 1932 *American Madness*, believes the economy is fundamentally sound and won't submit to panic. Scoffing at his fickle colleagues, Jim declares, "This ain't the time to sell . . . THIS IS THE TIME TO BUY." And he waxes emotional about America: "There ain't nothin' the matter with this country except you fellers. It was built up with guts . . . and more guts. And guts is the one thing you guys don't even know the meaning of."

The adoring mother and the panic-defying financier were, of course, favorite figures of the era. Yet, Sturges's transformations reflect more than mere convention. Throughout his life, Preston revered motherhood. Even in *Hail the Conquering Hero* where he satirizes mother love, mothers themselves are never mocked. The Irish Mrs. Brady marks the first of Sturges's exemplary matriarchs. These can be read as not only wish fulfillment alternatives to the self-interested and volatile Mary Desti, but as oblique paeans to a mother who, however different from the ideal, did unquestionably love her son.

Jim Brady's refusal to retreat from the stock market can also be seen as a filial tribute. For Solomon Sturges had persisted in investing after the Crash, he'd advised Preston to spend the first real earnings of his life on commodities. Later, Solomon became guilty and depressed about his imprudence. Now Preston, through Diamond Jim, could declare that imprudence was not a fault, but a heroic act of faith in America.

While the major studios quickly recovered from the early Depression and thrived during the thirties, Universal was always on the verge of financial disaster; and by the time Sturges finished his Jim Brady script, rumors of imminent takeovers or mergers were commonplace. Carl Laemmle, Sr., spoke openly about selling the studio. Still, his son remained convinced quality films could pull them out of the crisis, and Junior spared no expense on *Diamond Jim*.

Opposite Edward Arnold's Jim Brady, the English actress Binnie Barnes was cast as Lillian Russell, and Jean Arthur was chosen to play both Brady's innocent first love, Emma, and the worldly Jane. Character actor Eric Blore (Sir Alfred in *The Lady Eve*) played Sampson Fox, and William Demarest, whom Preston may have first seen on the *Diamond Jim* set, had a cameo role as restaurateur Harry Hill. Another future Sturges stock-company member, Al Bridge, had a bit part as a poker player. *Diamond Jim*'s producer was the up-and-coming young Edmund Grainier, its director was Edward Sutherland, whose father had been a friend of Brady's. Their $500,000 production abounded in realistic detail: Parker Morell scrupulously copied Brady's gaudy jewelry collection. Set designers reproduced famous turn-of-the-century night spots on the Universal sound stage, where the largest workable kitchen ever displayed in a film was installed. Edward Arnold put on fifteen pounds consuming real gourmand dinners—one morning he had to eat five whole lobsters before Sutherland was satisfied with his scene. Authentic period trains were found or recreated, and, for Brady's World's Fair train crash, a real crash was staged on a narrow gauge railway near San Luis Obispo.[7]

Sturges finished the script in March, and filming began the middle of April, with him on the set, changing and tightening scenes as they shot. Edward Sutherland frequently consulted with Sturges before directing Edward Arnold, so Preston must have been on his best behavior, eager to help but respectful of Sutherland's authority. Still, perhaps because of his high salary, Sturges for the first time since *The Power and the Glory* felt free to fight for his artistic vision. The real Diamond Jim had died of a heart attack exacerbated by a kidney disorder; the script's final scene—where the fat man prepares to eat himself to death—was Sturges's imaginative projection, and a daring one. Edmund Grainger, who'd had few qualms about fictionalizing train crashes, objected to it because it was unfactual, but surely also because it left an unjoyous image of the famous bon vivant. Sturges argued that this macabre, yet triumphant ending was what the whole film moved toward. Sutherland defended Preston, and in the end Grainger gave in.[8]

Carl Laemmle, Jr., chose *Diamond Jim* as Universal's first release of the season; it had a strong opening run at New York's Roxy, but reviews were mixed. Most everyone praised Edward Arnold's performance and the period detail, but many objected to Sturges's screenplay, claiming that since Diamond Jim's real story was sufficiently compelling, there was no need to cheapen it with action scenes and overstressed romance. "*Diamond Jim* suffers both from the fraudulent inventions of its scenario staff and from a certain pious reluctance to tell the whole truth about one of our most authentically American heroes," complained Andre Sennwald in the *Times*. While the *World Telegram* called it "a fine, rousing portrait of a man and an epoch," *Variety*, noting its deviation from Parker Morell's biography, found *Diamond Jim* an "amusing fiction."

A pleasure of *Diamond Jim* is that Sturges creates a psychologically complex protagonist strikingly different from himself. Yet, Preston, who loved food and had once chased Eleanor with a carving knife for insinuating he was chubby, must on at least one level have identified with his 240-pound hero. And Jim Brady's story must have disconcerted him. For Preston himself weighed 204 pounds and, though otherwise healthy, had for years been suffering from stomach troubles. As soon as *Diamond Jim* began shooting, Preston threw himself into the then popular Dr. Hay's diet, lost eight pounds the first week, and eighteen pounds by the end of June. "Next week," Preston wrote his father on June 20, "the doctor starts the galvanizing treatment to dry up the hemorrhoids that have been poisoning my existence for the last eight years. I hope their removal will cure the nervous indigestion and constipation which have also done their bit to make things pleasant."[9] In the same letter Preston managed to boast a bit to the formerly affluent Solomon. "While going over the figures, Bianca horrified me with the information that for the last six years I have averaged a little more than sixty-two thousand dollars a year. It is disgusting to think how little I have managed to hang onto. I hope I will be able to learn, although I don't know what one could put money into safely if one had it." [10]

In the spring of 1935, Preston's New York composer friend Ted Snyder turned up with his whole family in Hollywood. Preston, who still loved popular music and made records of himself and Bianca singing, was happy to see the man who'd taught him everything he knew about songwriting. While Preston recovered from his hemorrhoid treatments, he and Snyder wrote five musical comedy songs, one of which, "Paris In The Evening," Jesse Lasky bought for his upcoming film, *The Gay Deception*.

There was little talk now about *A Cup of Coffee*. Universal, over its head in expensive productions, was more than ever short on money. With Carl Laemmle, Jr., offering rewards even to mail room clerks for tips about economizing, low-budget movies were a priority. Preston believed he could devise a way to create quality films cheaply. Some time after *Diamond Jim*, he approached the Laemmles' new general manager, Fred Meyer, with his scheme for selling Universal original stories at a very low price on the condition that he would be allowed to direct his screenplays. He proposed *The Vagrant*, now retitled *Biography of a Bum*, as a first project, and Meyer seemed very enthusiastic and said he'd get back to Preston with an approval soon. But three weeks passed with Preston pushing for and Meyer evading a commitment. When Meyer finally answered Preston's memos, it was to suggest a meager $100,000 budget for his film.

Preston took this figure as a personal insult, and his reply to Meyer shows both how much he'd counted on support from Universal, and how deeply he longed, not for money, but for the power and prestige of a writer-director. Preston made no effort to repress his annoyance at Hollywood myopia, telling Meyer:

> I feel the courtesy I have shown to you and other producers on the lot in the way of free suggestions, criticisms and whatever help I could give permits me to point out that if you had made any mention of a $100,000 picture three weeks ago in Mr. Laemmle's office you would have saved me the fairly valuable time I have spent waiting for a decision and the bitter disappointment I feel today.
> The story we proposed to make was comparable in every way to a first-line Universal picture costing between three and four hundred thousand dollars.

Comparable in every way, that is, except the cost, which amounted to approximately half. The low cost, instead of delighting your general manager's soul, has led you to suppose that the picture would be low also in quality.

I have never been associated with nor am I at all interested in the making of Class Z pictures. I am, on the other hand, intensely interested in making Class A pictures for a great deal less than is expended on them now.[11]

However personally chagrined Meyer may have been by Preston's lecture, Universal, in early September, sought to placate Sturges's ego by offering him two script assignments simultaneously: *Next Time We Love* for Margaret Sullavan and *Love Before Breakfast* for Carole Lombard. Based on typical stories of the era, both flirt with, then back away from social conflicts. In *Next Time We Love*, about a two-career marriage, the wife is spared having to make the feminist choice of career over spouse, first because she becomes pregnant, then because the husband becomes mortally ill. In *Love Before Breakfast*, a screwball variation on *Matrix*, the girl gets to marry the rich man not because he's rich but because he truly loves her (and couldn't care less about money), while the poor boy she thought she loved turns out to be greedy and a cad. Preston quickly wrote first drafts for both scripts, and even a second one for Carole Lombard, but—though *Love Before Breakfast* uses whole chunks of Sturges's material—he got credit for neither, as other writers were called in soon afterwards.

By then, Sturges probably was not especially concerned, as he'd *finally* been assigned to write an original screenplay. The name, *Song of Joy*, was all he inherited from earlier writers. His project was to conceive a musical comedy suitable for the famous European diva Marta Eggerth, whom Paul Kohner had enticed to Hollywood with a generous Universal contract. Kohner was in charge of Eggerth's first film. Assigning Sturges to the project was probably his idea, and Sturges must have felt particularly inclined to write precisely what he liked, knowing this sophisticated man was his producer.

Though *Easy Living* is really the first true Sturges comedy, *Song of Joy*—while thematically atypical—shows some of Preston's finest wit and nimblest mixture of silliness and satire. His target is Hollywood, where, in an opening scene, Mr. Apex, President of the Apex Film Company, sits "in a fever of activity": manning four phones at once, hollering at agents, wheedling his way out of signing contracts, and scheming to steal talent from the competition. Into his office walks the world-famous young European opera star Lilli Pogany, whom Apex doesn't recognize and hasn't heard of, though once he's been informed she's important, he gallantly welcomes her to California, hissing to his publicist: "Get a picture, get a picture." How long, Apex wonders, will

Lilli be visiting? "Only four weeks. Then I sing at La Scala," replies Lilli, who has some difficulty getting Apex to understand she's here because his studio has hired her, her enormous salary begins tomorrow, and he has only a month to exploit her talents.

First, Apex is furious: which of his dim-witted underlings hired this creature without consulting him? But when he discovers he's signed Lilli's contract himself, Apex moves right on to the current problem—how to get a script by yesterday.

From Apex, to his screenwriter Jasper (whose "face with one single expression reflects all the grievance of the Writers' Guild"), to the pompous foreign director, Vladimir, who brags that he "don't make no pictures vit' accents," all *Song of Joy*'s characters emerge as Hollywood types: absurd but wholly credible. Their common goal is to make a good film fast, but what is a good film? "Something big!" crows Vladimir. Something for "the little tots who don't understand anything," opines Apex, while Lilli merely wants a vehicle for her true love's (inept) songs, and Jasper longs to write a tale about phony producers luring innocent girls to Hollywood. So much for the great collaborative art and—since everyone gets his or her way and winds up happy—reality in the movies.

Hollywood egoism is satirized in endless power struggles, embroiling even such lowly sorts as Lilli's costumer and her wig man—who refuse to be confined either by the story or the era of the clothes! The Apex Film Company's trademark—a roaring lion, sitting on a mountain, holding the world on his paw and circled by an airplane—makes a hilarious collage of all those grandiose studio logos. And the film-within-a-film, featuring Lilli as an all-American girl who can't speak English, sends up small-town musicals, as does Lilli's true love's theme: "Mine is not a song for sale / It's just a noncommercial wail / A low-falutin' lyric to your eyes."

Complete with shots of the extras' dressing rooms, of daily rushes and a production number on the sound stage, *Song of Joy*, for all its outrageousness, is very much a behind-the-scenes film about the process of filmmaking. Clearly, Sturges identifies with beleaguered writer Jasper, and some of *Song of Joy*'s most exuberant spoofs are of Jasper's story conferences with Apex and the increasingly befuddled Vladimir. During a typical one, they all bicker about a dance number:

VLADIMIR: My idea goes like this: The young girl dances wit her aunt in the background.

JASPER: Why does she dance with her aunt?

MR. APEX: Why don't she dance with a young fellow?

A reading of Preston's first draft of Song of Joy. *From left to right, Ernst L. Frank, Preston, Marta Eggerth, Edward Sutherland, and Paul Kohner.* (Photo courtesy of Paul Kohner)

LILLI (smiling): So is better.

VLADIMIR (Yelling a little): She is dancing with her *aunt* in the background.

MR. APEX (with a trace of irritation): Why should she be in the background, she's the star.

LILLI (approvingly): Yes.

VLADIMIR (a little louder): Her *aunt* is in the background . . . she's in front dancing with a young fellow.

MR. APEX: Well why didn't you say so?

VLADIMIR (at the top of his lungs): I did say so and anyway it don't start there. It starts in a cab with her aunt where she's going to her first dance. . . . It's very foggy.

JASPER (sourly): Why?

VLADIMIR (spreading his arms): Because it's Vienna.

JASPER: It's in London they have the fogs.

VLADIMIR (exasperated): All right, make it London . . . or make it snow . . . or make it oatmeal, what do I care? All I'm telling you is she's in a cab with her aunt.

MR. APEX: It could be a sleigh.

VLADIMIR (at the top of his lungs): It could be a gyroscope! Whatever it is, she sits there with her aunt.

MR. APEX: Why does it have to be her aunt? Why can't it be some nice young fellow in a uniform? Give it some class.

VLADIMIR (as loud as he can): Why don't you let me finish? All I'm telling you is: SHE SITS IN SOMETHING SOMEPLACE WIT SOMEBODY!

In another palaver, Jasper tells Apex his story's "all about Hollywood." "Not with *my* money it isn't," retorts Apex. "I wouldn't put a dime in a Hollywood story. . . . What are you trying to do . . . give the industry a black eye?"

Sturges may have anticipated this would be precisely Fred Meyer's response to *Song of Joy* because he waited way past deadline to submit it. "Eggerth must return to Europe and we are all just out of luck unless we have a complete script well in advance of shooting,"[12] Meyer was still pleading with him at the end of October. But when Sturges submitted his work the following week, there was no sigh of relief.

How could there be, really, since, Carl Laemmle, Sr.—desperately needing $750,000 to complete *Sutter's Gold* and *Showboat*—had that very month all but sold his studio for a loan, admitting in so many words that he was, like Apex, extravagant and a bad businessman? Carl Laemmle, Jr., had been replaced as head of production: a great shame to the company. So the fact that Universal executives found *Song of Joy* too close for comfort was not amazing. What surprised Sturges was that Edward Sutherland, his friend from *Diamond Jim*, would so quickly cover his tracks and condemn the story. Sutherland, who had a history of commercial successes for Universal, piously informed his boss, "I am sure that making fun of producers, writers, etc. is not entertainment."[13] Still, Paul Kohner stood by Sturges, and it was also in Preston's favor that Marta Eggerth—just like Lilli!—was due back for an opera engagement in Europe. Universal was currently paying her a fortune to do nothing; it was in everyone's interest to immediately put her to work.

Studio conferences were called, and Preston argued (somewhat disingenuously) that whereas that thorn in the side of the movie industry—Kaufman and Hart's *Once in a Lifetime*—had got laughs out of the "supposed stupidity" of film people, *Song of Joy*'s humor derived from the predicament of "perfectly normal businessmen." "Besides," he more candidly informed Carl Laemmle, Sr., "without fear of permanent, or even temporary damage, professors tell jokes on professors, doctors are most fond of doctors' stories; hardware men laugh about other hardware men. This is healthy. Surely our industry has sufficient background and a sufficient record of achievement to place it on a secure foundation." And he added that his script showed off many facets of Marta Eggerth's talent: "That she is of the same opinion, I mention in passing." [14]

The night of November 13, Sturges and Kohner fought their case into the small hours of the morning, but they failed to persuade Meyer, and the next day Universal abandoned *Song of Joy*. Sturges then immediately submitted it to MGM where Louis B. Mayer, model for so many of the Apex jokes, adored it. He announced MGM was ready to buy Sturges's script, provided they could get Marta Eggerth. Over a friendly lunch, Eggerth's husband informed Mayer that his wife's price was $3,500 a week ($1,600 more than Lilli's). [15] No thanks, said Mayer, and *Song of Joy*, as wickedly meaningful now as in the 1930s, remains unproduced.

In his dealings with the Laemmles, as with Brock Pemberton, Preston displayed a certain obdurate loyalty to those who first took a chance on him. On the one hand a loner—refusing to join writers' unions and only under duress hiring an agent, he was, paradoxically, also most comfortable working within a family-type unit: traveling from one studio to another didn't appeal to him as a way to proceed in the world. But he was no fool, and after *Song of Joy*, he was more than ready to move on. Henry Henigson, who believed in Preston's talent, had after years with the Laemmles this past spring gone over to Paramount, where he was made their executive in charge of seeking new talent.

Four months after *Song of Joy*, Henigson hired Preston to write another vehicle, now for the radio couple George Burns and Gracie Allen. This, Preston knew, was a trial run for something larger, and he was careful not to impose too many of his own ideas on *Hotel Haywire*, which evolved as a broad domestic farce, geared specifically to its stars (who were ultimately unavailable, so their roles had to be recast). The script was slight, but Paramount was satisfied. On September 29, 1936, they gave Sturges what he had never received from Universal, a writers contract that lasted not for a month or a picture but until 1938 and, what's more, was renewable. The best years of his professional life had begun.

C H A P T E R

13

Paramount, which seven years before had given Preston his first script assignment, was a sprawling twenty-six-acre studio in the center of Hollywood, next to RKO at Melrose and Gower.[1] Its famous gates were named for Cecil B. DeMille, the studio darling. DeMille was one of the few men in Hollywood who both directed and produced his own movies. He had a private table in the commissary and complete autonomy on his set. But off the set even DeMille had no real power over Paramount's policies. The creative staff came and went at the whim of the money men. But, nonetheless, an abundance of comic and European talent, a certain stylishness and audacity somehow thrived. Mae West, The Marx Brothers, Josef von Sternberg, and Ernst Lubitsch all made their most distinctive films at Paramount. Here, the year Sturges signed his first contract, former theatre manager Barney Balaban was elected president. For West Coast chief, Balaban chose his colleague, Y. Frank Freeman.

Frank Freeman was a gray-haired, soft-spoken Georgia businessman. Before coming to Paramount, he had managed a chain of Atlanta movie theatres and made no pretense whatsoever to artistic judgment. Deceptively naïve-seeming, with his southern drawl and passion for Coca-Cola, Freeman was a shrewd diplomat. He forged valuable connections with the Hays and Motion Picture Academy offices, established a reputation for absolute fairness with labor, and became one of the few studio figures genuinely admired by his peers. He was not, however, loved by everyone. Producer John Houseman remembers Freeman as "ignorant" and "bigoted."[2] He was prudish and so opposed to liquor on the lot that Paramount publicist Cecil "Teet" Carle had to host press parties at Lucy's, a favorite studio haunt across the street.[3]

Yet, Carle, like so many at Paramount, gladly forgave Freeman his blind spots, because Freeman was such a loyal and unusually accessible boss. He kept his door open at all times and took a genuine interest in many of his employees. Though Freeman was only eight years older than Preston, he called him "Papa Freeman." Freeman treated Preston like a naughty, but brilliant son.

Teet Carle remembers an incident that is revealing of their relationship. In the heyday of Sturges's fame, *Life* Magazine was planning a long article on Veronica Lake. When Sturges was interviewed for the piece, he observed that the source of Lake's sex appeal was the fact that her buttocks were pear-shaped rather than apple-shaped, like most women's. *Life*, amused, printed Sturges's theory and sketches of both sorts of rears. Carle was in the studio commissary the day the *Life* story appeared and saw Freeman stride angrily up to Sturges's table "to issue what can only be described as a scolding." And Preston, for all his pride and instinct to lash back at figures of authority, stopped smiling and "submitted to the kindly bawling-out." [4]

As crucial for Sturges as Frank Freeman's fatherly affection was the support of William LeBaron, who in 1936 replaced Ernst Lubitsch as Paramount's acting head of production. Like Freeman, LeBaron instinctively responded to Preston's charm and enthusiasm. As a former playwright, he appreciated Sturges's talents and how he yearned to progress beyond screenwriting. LeBaron, who had himself directed and produced at RKO before moving to Paramount, must have laughed at all the "rumors" Preston planted in the trades about his imminent assignment to direct one film or another. But, as much as he valued Sturges's talent, LeBaron feared his unpredictable nature, and so would continually put off promoting this gifted writer—trying to placate him with ever-higher salaries, with praise, finally by agreeing he could have what was unheard-of for a screenwriter: a three-room suite with a reception and conference room leading to his office. [5]

The man who won Sturges these accommodations from Le Baron was another important figure for Sturges, his new agent, Frank Orsatti. Orsatti's agency consisted only of himself and his three brothers, and Preston must have found the Orsattis' entrepreneurial spirit far more appealing than the big business approach at William Morris. Orsatti, a former real estate operator who was rumored to have connections with the Mafia, was the sort of man some loved and some hated. Budd Schulberg remembered him as an "agent-pimp . . . with a touch of *Little Caesar*"; [6] but Sturges, who shared Orsatti's feisty individualism, liked him both personally and professionally. It was Orsatti who would give Preston's third wife, Louise, all her favorite gourmet cook books and who, from 1936 until *The Great McGinty*, tirelessly pushed Paramount to let Sturges have a chance to direct.

Sturges's first assignment at Paramount was to write a script based on Vera Caspary's story, "Easy Living," about a facial masseuse so desperate for the appearance of wealth that she steals her client's fur coat. Passing as rich, she finds love and happiness for a while, but then is caught and forced to pay for her hypocrisy. With its theme of social ambition, Caspary's tale was a far cry from a new sort of Hollywood film that focused on high-spirited women indifferent to class and money. These screwball comedies were all the vogue in 1936. So Preston reconceived Caspary's plot, making it more like *It Happened One Night* and *My Man Godfrey*.

In Sturges's *Easy Living*, the poor working girl becomes honest Mary Smith, whose fur coat literally falls on her head while she's riding the top of a double-decker bus down Fifth Avenue. Her benefactor is J. B. Ball, the third biggest banker in America. Ball, thrifty for all his wealth, has thrown the coat off his balcony to deprive his wife of her latest extravagance. "What's the big idea anyway?" bristles Mary, as the sable squashes the feather on her cap. "Kismet," observes an Arab seated behind her, setting the tone for what will follow.

Mary tries to return Ball's sable, but Ball tells her to keep it. They're spotted together, and soon all New York believes they're lovers. This misconception totally transforms Mary's life, though unlike the masseuse in Caspary's tale, Mary herself is unaffected. She remains bemusedly unimpressed as Cartier begs her to sample their jewels, and Rolls Royce sends her a private car with chauffeur. Louis Louis, the owner of an elegant but floundering hotel, invites Mary to live in his Imperial Suite for just seven dollars a week, hoping she'll lure J. B. Ball's friends as customers. Though mystified, Mary moves in and embraces her good luck. Then, dining at the automat, she falls in love with a waiter she presumes is poor, though he's in fact J. B. Ball's renegade son, Johnny.

The plot thickens as a stockbroker begs Mary to tip him off about the future of steel. The price is falling, she informs him, on a whim. And the price falls, sure enough, when this broker spreads the word, for it's not worth but appearances that count at the stockmarket. J. B. Ball alone continues pouring money into steel. His company is on the verge of bankruptcy when Johnny cleverly turns the tide and wins his rightful spot in the family business. It now remains only for J. B. Ball to convince his wife there's never been anything but a fur between Mary and himself. For her part, Mary offers no disclaimers at all. If Johnny loves her, he must accept her on faith: which he does.

With its spirited heroine, tone of salubrious lunacy, and insistence that the world needs shaking up, *Easy Living* at first seems a typical screwball comedy. Yet, while screwball's madcap escapades reflect the protagonist's will, the mania in *Easy Living* is, on the contrary, circumstantial. And much mania there is—from J. B. Ball's kicking and falling slapstick pursuit of his wife up to the roof to grab her sable, to a long sequence in the automat, where the food doors fly open, exposing free meat pies and creating chaos. In its characters' vulnerability to chance and the physical world, *Easy Living* seems farcical rather than comic. Yet, farce, commonly defined as "more bitter, more cruel, more downright unfair"[7] than comedy, is not so full of joy. Nor are farcical characters so complicated.

In *Easy Living*, even the hysterical hotel owner Louis Louis is a believable individual: one of the earliest of Sturges's luminous eccentrics. Gullible, cunning, naïve, manipulative, and unabashedly self-interested, he is nonetheless compelling of some respect since he's forsworn his one indisputable talent, cooking, and dared to tackle the hotel business. "Everybody knows you're the finest cook in the world. . . . Now you get back into that kitchen where you belong, you'll be better off," J. B. Ball (doubtless echoing Sturges's own advisers) lectures him. But adversity only intensifies Louis Louis's resolve to move into new spheres.

And similarly, J. B. Ball and Mary behave for all the world as if their inner lives and wills mattered. Mary insists that Johnny marry her for what she manifestly is, ignoring whatever has been said against her; and Ball too refuses to bow to conventional wisdom. He continues throwing money into steel, though its market price plunges, because he knows it is inherently valuable; he insists Mary keep the sable coat she's caught because he feels sure she deserves it.

Easy Living is the first script where Sturges, imposing a farcical plot on screwball protagonists, discovers a structure to mirror his uneasiness about luck and virtue. The film's ending, where another fur coat lands on the hat of yet another working girl, underscores the very arbitrariness of Mary's and Johnny's story, the capriciousness of their happy union now. But they're happy, nonetheless, for this is, after all, comedy, rejoicing in order restored and the miracle of success. "Let me give you a little piece of advice, young lady!" J. B. Ball lectures Mary, in an early draft of Sturges's screenplay. "Don't be *too* wise! Don't think you know all the answers. Sometimes nice things *happen* to people . . . if they didn't we'd all be bookkeepers and stenographers the rest of our lives."

Alongside this wistfulness, *Easy Living* is filled with broadly comic moments: Ball bellowing insults at his extravagant foreign servants, Mary attacking her boss with a little boy's portrait, the debacle in the automat. Here, when the food doors burst open, New York's poor rush to slobber over free turkey bones, grab each others' trays, and generally show themselves every bit as greedy and selfish as stockbrokers. These are Sturges's answer to Capra's virtuous "little people." With isolationism in full swing, Sturges mocks foreigners as well, creating such preposterous Europeans as a hat salesman who calls a flat hat "recherché" and a chef who grows apoplectic at the prospect of cooking without butter.

Autobiographical resonances abound, beginning with Mary's name. Her nature, even more than Isabelle's in *Strictly Dishonorable*, is both innately aristocratic and worldly wise. When Johnny observes that there's something "awfully funny" about everyone's showering Mary with presents, she pointedly responds, "Are you just beginning to find that out?" And Mary Smith also shares Mary Desti's attitude toward luxuries, which she adores, but will gladly sacrifice rather than endure indebtedness. For his part, J. B. Ball, the blunt, moral banker, recalls many honest businessmen in Preston's experience, particularly Solomon Sturges. While Ball's raucous laugh and bellowing commands clash with Solomon's dignity, Ball's righteous meddling in other people's business is Preston's father to a tee.

Easy Living's producer was Arthur Hornblow, Jr., whom Preston described as "the only man who can strut sitting down,"[8] and Sturges had nothing better to say of its amiable director Mitchell Leisen, formerly Cecil B. DeMille's set designer. Leisen, Sturges grumbled to friends, was merely an "interior decorator."[9] Since Preston would later go out of his way to thank Leisen for his support at Paramount, Sturges probably had nothing against Leisen personally. What rankled was that a man only a year older and (to Preston's mind) so much less gifted than himself should be allowed to direct—his script no less—while Sturges remained a screenwriter. Sturges complained that Leisen overwhelmed his dialogue with ornate sets and physical business. Leisen himself took credit for *Easy Living*'s slapstick, especially in the automat scene; though in fact that sequence's opening image of a bum with a turkey bone "stridently" whistling news of free food was in Sturges's first draft, as were indications that the poor should cause havoc, and detailed depictions of other slapsticking bits.

Paramount, impressed by Sturges's script, gave *Easy Living* a first-rate cast, including Jean Arthur (fresh from her success in *Mr. Deeds Goes To Town*) and Ray Milland as the lovers, and Edward Arnold, with his wide mobile face and jittery corpulence, as J. B. Ball. Paramount character actors Franklin Pangborn and Luis Alberni became the hat seller and Louis Louis, respectively, and Louis Louis's luxury hotel, which Preston based on New York's Waldorf (also initially a failure when it opened during the Depression), became an opulently designed character itself, supporting Preston's contention that Leisen remained at heart a designer. Preston told his father that Leisen's *Easy Living* left him "cool," [10] and indeed Leisen's farcical scenes are at once slower and more shrill than Sturges's would be, his direction of actors like Pangborn and Arnold more mechanical, evoking superficial rather than deep-seated strangeness. Yet, Leisen strikes just the right straightforward tone in the love story. And, on the whole, *Easy Living* deserves its current reputation as both Sturges's first major comic script and a Depression classic.

When he'd finished the first draft of *Easy Living*, in January 1935, Preston answered an ad in the *Hollywood Reporter*, which in bold type read, "Here's Your Man." The man was lanky, fresh-faced Edwin Gillette, a trained engineer in his late twenties who'd been fascinated with motion pictures ever since a stranger pointed a movie camera at him when he was a small child in Chicago. Gillette had read that Andrew Carnegie advised, if you want to get ahead in the world, be a secretary to a big man; so he was now bent on working for an important person in the film business.[11]

Preston wanted a secretary because Bianca, nursing a broken nose, was refusing to work. Though Bianca claimed she broke her nose in a car accident, Gillette figured Preston had busted it during some ferocious fight, because he could see right away they both had fiery tempers. He also could see that Preston, though not yet a big man in Hollywood, would be an amusing boss: "Interesting chap," he jotted in his diary after their first meeting, "with all sorts of hobbies: boats, electric trains, diesel engine." Gillette too was inventive and had patents of his own as well as relatives who knew Solomon Sturges from the Chicago Athletic Club; so the two had much in common, and Gillette was hired at once and remained until he went off to war in the early forties. Though Gillette's relationship with Sturges was friendly from the start, they maintained a certain distance. Gillette felt it was a sign of respect that Preston called him "Gilletti," rather than the more casual Ted or Ed; and Gilletti always addressed his boss as Mr. Sturges.

They spent a lot of time together because Preston, Gilletti soon learned, wanted a companion as well as a private secretary; and Sturges's habits were unusual. Most mornings he'd sleep late and putter around the house until it was time to go over to Paramount, where he'd nap on the couch or serve tea laced with applejack and regale whoever stopped by with stories. Later Preston might work on his boat or diesel engine or read, drinking a lot of coffee all the while, though it was not until evening that he came into his full energy. Then he'd drag Gilletti, Bianca, or maybe Henry Henigson off to the fights, or the Brown Derby, or perhaps he'd just stay home and play pool: anything to put off work as long as possible. ("You had to almost back him into a corner to get him to work," Gilletti recalls.) Then, around midnight, Preston would say, "Well, let's knock off a few pages." "So I'd stagger upstairs to the typewriter," says Gilletti, a day person himself, "and he'd sit down in a chair, and his mind would come alive. He'd start spouting his dialogue" and go on often until three in the morning, while Gilletti took dictation. Usually, Preston wrote only a couple of hours each day. But sometimes he'd have put off writing so long that there'd be no choice but to stay up until dawn and finish a script in a single sitting. Once, Gilletti recalls, the studio resorted to stationing a delegate on Sturges's porch so he couldn't leave the house without delivering his screenplay.

Gilletti always insisted on getting eight hours' sleep. Still, if he left Sturges's at three A.M., he was back at the house by one P.M., performing some new duty, like helping Bianca manage Preston's finances. These were always in disarray—checks bouncing, no money left to pay taxes. "Dearest Baby Boy," Bianca once pleaded with Preston. "The [bank account] balance: $1,628 does *not* take care of Orsatti's check or Frankel or rent or a large month's market bill—so be careful, honey, how you spend it." [12] But it was not in Preston's nature to be careful. Preston, Gilletti felt, did not intentionally squander money, he simply had no respect for it.

Similarly, Preston did not knowingly take advantage of people, but "unknowingly he took great advantage of people," Gilletti included. For Preston was happy to enjoy Gilletti's round-the-clock services, but made no effort to help his capable secretary find a job in the movie business. Still, Preston was "by his own standards an ethical man," and, as Hollywood figures went, he didn't have all that many vices. He wasn't a big drinker, for instance, or a womanizer—during the many years Gilletti knew Sturges, he was aware of just a single affair with a secretary at Paramount. And, for all his large ego and aversion to criticism, Sturges would laugh at a good line, even if he was the target. Gilletti remembers how once, when Preston announced he was going to dive into a pool like an arrow, Gilletti replied, "Yes like a Pierce-Arrow," alluding to the car and how heavy Preston was, and Preston—who'd once chased Eleanor with a carving knife for a similar comment—just laughed, maybe because he was older now, doubtless because Gilletti was a man.

Like Eleanor, Gilletti found life with Sturges exhausting, but constantly exciting: He was "a great talker," a natural self-salesman, and also, despite his yachts and political conservatism, "very bohemian." Once, Gilletti recalls, Preston found some purple brocade material, normally used for covering sofas, and had that made into a coat he proceeded to wear to the studio. It impressed Gilletti that Sturges, rich as he became, never bought a Hollywood show place and that he remained faithful to old friends like Charley Abramson, whom Gilletti also befriended.

By the time Gilletti joined Sturges's household, relations between Preston and Bianca had deteriorated; vicious rows were by now routine. Not surprisingly, since Bianca, brilliant as she was, had no career or friends of her own and must increasingly have depended on Preston for her identity, while Preston may well have wondered why she'd stayed with him so long. Estelle and Eleanor, after all, had left without half so much provocation. Soon after Gilletti began work, there was a particularly dramatic fight, where Bianca, "running for her life" from Preston, slammed a half-glass door behind her, and Preston's outstretched arm burst through the glass. He began bleeding alarmingly. A workman installing venetian blinds in the house at the time had the presence of mind to grab a neck tie and make him a tourniquet. Then they quickly packed Sturges into Gilletti's Ford convertible and raced down Hollywood Boulevard, skipping through lights, horn blasting, to the same doctor who'd treated Bianca's broken nose.[13]

Preston somewhat tidied up the domestic violence when reporting his ordeal to Sidney Love: "I was running after Bianca to return a friendly slap. She closed a door to stop me. The door was ripple glass and my arm went through it, severing three arteries and cutting halfway through the muscle. Fortunately no motor nerves or tendons were cut, but the experience was extremely unpleasant nevertheless. I was in the surgeon's chair without any anesthetic whatsoever for an hour or more. They put fourteen stitches in me, and then I spent two weeks in the hospital."[14] The fact that Preston endured surgery without any painkiller whatsoever is significant, for he would soon grow very excited about the invention of anesthesia and write a first draft of a screenplay entitled *Triumph Over Pain*.

Preston and Bianca managed to keep their tempers in check that March when Solomon Sturges and his wife Marie came to visit. It was after this first trip that Solomon told Preston, "Bianca is a wonder." Ever since Preston had arrived in Los Angeles, Solomon had been urging him to contact relatives in the area, and surely father and son now called on these cousins and aunts. How proud they must have been that Mary Desti's child, of which so much bad had been prophesied, had turned out just as she'd foreseen. Solomon had a wonderful time, and—since his health was fragile and business in Chicago as bad as ever—he began contemplating retirement and moving west.

During the spring of 1936 Preston threw himself into two demanding new projects. Ted Snyder, Preston's songwriter friend, was eager to open a restaurant, and though Henry Henigson warned Preston to "look back to places

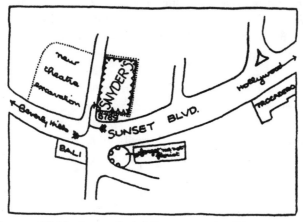

Preston and Ted Snyder open Snyder's Restaurant, spring 1936.

where you have, up to the moment, poured out moneys without proper re-turn,"[15] Preston immediately offered to back him. Sturges felt indebted to Snyder for teaching him songwriting, and the venture must have seemed solid as there were so few places in Los Angeles where one could find good food, much less entertainment: nothing, for instance, like Le Clou, with its shadow plays, in Paris, or even like the dance clubs Preston loved in New York. Be-sides, since he'd grown up with the Maison Desti, Preston liked the idea of a family business. Marcel Pagnol would call Preston's own restaurant, The Players, "une idée poetique,"[16] and Preston probably took the same attitude toward Snyder's—as his friend's restaurant was to be called. The building they chose was an old house on the strip at 8789 Sunset Boulevard. Sturges could feel virtuous that he got a bargain price, because the house was run-down and needed refurbishing;[17] but its location, on a knoll, between the Trocadero nightclub and Beverly Hills, was ideal. Besides food, its neat green and white poster promised "drink, music, pool, chess, checkers, and dominoes."

That spring, Preston also bought the second and last house he would ever own, near Paramount on quiet Ivar Avenue. It was white shingled, deceptively small on the outside, and old by California standards. Lois Weber, one of the first women movie directors, had built the house in the twenties, and Preston was intrigued by that. He also liked the novelty that the garage had a turntable that could swivel your car around and face it outwards. And it must have pleased him that because the front of the house was so unassuming the spacious inside rooms came as a surprise: the reverse of pretension. The property was graciously laid out and amenable to his plans for a large garden filled with hibiscus and fruit blossoms.[18] He discovered cloth in the gables and knew the house was carefully built. But what really sold Preston on 1917 Ivar were the old California trees on the property. "For an enormous amount of money" he immediately hired tree surgeons to cure them of fungus, dry rot, and termites, move them about and intersperse them with Canary Island pines.[19]

"The place is in an uproar, but I think they plan to pour the swimming pool tomorrow," he wrote his father that summer. "The racket of steam shovels, trip-hammers, and concrete mixers, not to mention the carpenters and the dogs barking at them has been lovely for the people on the street including myself. The pool is not of the old rectangular type but is shaped like a mountain lake or, more exactly, a kidney. The Badminton Court, on the other hand, is shaped like a swimming pool, and the barbecue house is shaped like a Badminton Court."[20] Soon Preston brought in carpenters to work on a new kitchen, dining room, pantry, and servants' quarters. He hired a Filipino named Leo Calibo as houseboy and his American wife Edna to cook. Both, according to Gilletti, were extremely likable.

It was fortunate Preston had Snyder's and his new house to distract him that July when *Easy Living* opened to reviews as unimpressive as its box office receipts.[21] Frank S. Nugent in the *Times* praised the film's excellent cast, but found them "frequently overwhelmed by Sennett touches." "Its theme is preposterous and its comic invention is about as subtle as a custard pie," wrote Howard Barnes in the *Herald Tribune*. And while Wanda
News gushed that *Easy Living* was "the maddest, merriest, a
enjoyable comedies Hollywood has turned out in many a da

1917 Ivar. The old trees attracted Preston.

in *Variety* called it "uneven, uninspired and only occasionally funny." Despite Paramount's full support and wide publicity, *Easy Living* attracted little attention in its era. Its reputation would build in the years to come.

Since he'd finished *Easy Living*, Preston had not received any particularly challenging work at Paramount. First, he was assigned to write *The Buccaneer*, about the French pirate Jean Lafitte, for Cecil B. DeMille. Though DeMille was revered at Paramount, Preston found him a thoroughly pedestrian director[22] and refused to pander to DeMille's passion for spectacle. His script's very first scene—where a cackling Napoleon mistakes Lithuania for Louisiana—so appalled DeMille that Preston was fired in less than a month.

He moved on to write another Burns and Allen project, *College Swing*, the tale of a dumb heiress forced to pass exams or hand over her fortune to the

family college. Sturges's by turns silly and pointed spoof of American education is thoroughly engaging. Still, it was for some reason deemed unacceptable, and Sturges receives no credit at all on the finished film. His next project,
to adapt the 1912 play *Never Say Die* for Jack Benny, proved equally thankless.
After he'd worked twenty-six weeks on this *very* slight story (about a hypo-
chondriac whose acidity test is confused with a dog's so his doctor believes
he's dying), Sturges was peremptorily informed that Jack Benny was needed
for a musical. By the time Benny was free, Sturges had been succeeded by two
other writers, who receive credits before his for the script.

Sturges got his first challenging work since *Easy Living* shortly after Christmas 1937 when he was asked to adapt Justin Huntly McCarthy's 1901 play *If
I Were King* for producer-director Frank Lloyd. Lloyd, who'd made *Oliver
Twist* (1922) and *Mutiny on the Bounty* (1935), was one of the few Hollywood
directors Preston truly admired; and though he was put off by McCarthy's
arch style, Preston was intrigued by the play's premise which, like *Road to
Rome*'s, embroiled real historical figures in fantasy relationships. The hero
here was medieval poet François Villon, something of a fifteenth-century Jean
Genet, who spent his life in and out of prisons and wrote his famous "Frères
humains qui après nous vivez" in 1463 after he'd been condemned to hang.
Villon had already been the subject of two silent films, *The Beloved Rogue*
(1927) with John Barrymore and an earlier *If I Were King* (1930), starring
William Farnum. Sturges was determined his script should resemble neither
of these.

And he immediately set about making McCarthy's language more collo-
quial and adding humor to his highly romantic plot. The story is set in Paris
during the reign of Louis XI, with the Burgundians storming the city walls
and the people starving. The plot hinges on a fantasy encounter between the
brave rogue Villon, who claims France would be far better off "if I were king,"
and ineffectual Louis XI, who dares him to prove it. In Sturges's version,
prince and poet meet in a workman's tavern where Louis, disguised in student's cowl, comes looking for traitors, and Villon arrives to share the fruits
of his recent raid on the royal storehouse, Robin Hood-like, with the poor.
While dispensing Louis's provisions to beggars and whores, Villon loudly insults the king ("a child of two" could do a better job ruling) and then kills his
grand chancellor in a sword fight. Since this grand chancellor was a traitor,
Louis now faces a dilemma: how at once to punish and honor Villon? He
decides to appoint him grand chancellor as reward, but secretly plans to hang
him after a week as punishment.

Villon adjusts as quickly as Mary Smith to his rise in the social scheme. He

immediately frees his petty thief friends from prison and orders Louis's laggardly generals to stop pleading for peace and begin fighting off the Burgundians. Villon uses his title to woo the queen's beautiful lady in waiting, Katherine de Vaucelles. It is Katherine who, itching for battle, gives Villon the idea
that the generals' problem is they're overfed; they'd fight, soon enough, if like
the people they too needed food from outside Paris. So Villon swipes the
soldiers' six months' remaining provisions, handing their goods over to the
poor. With the people behind him, Villon sets the enemy packing and wins
the day for the king, who repays him by commuting his death sentence to
mere exile. Villon accepts his fate, though he refuses to ask Katherine to leave
Paris with him. She follows, anyway.

If I Were King is an accomplished work, introducing wit without undermin-
ing romance, balancing credible relationships and motivations with a swash-
buckling plot, and not letting Villon lose a beat, switching from prose to poetry. Its characters are consistent from start to finish. The good poor behave
decently whether their mouths are full or empty. Villon's moral code, which
allows him to steal but not to kill a king's guard who's witnessed his theft, per-
mits him to give away all the king's food but demands that he defend Louis's
honor in the end.

Sturges had great fun reading up on Villon's era and made a point of writing all his own translations of the poems, while adding a few new ones. "Here's
one that Villon didn't write but that I pretend he did," Preston told his father:

> Father Time lay not thy frost
> Upon this budding flower,
> On bitter seas of passion tossed;
> Forgive its tiny hour!
> And thou, Huguette, waste not thy heart
> Upon this juiceless mold
> Ere all thy fragrant youth depart
> And leave thee useless . . . old.[23]

If I Were King was superbly cast: besides Ronald Colman in the lead, there
was Basil Rathbone playing Louis, Frances Dee as Katherine, and a new member of the Paramount stock school, Ellen Drew, as the whore Huguette. With
all the sword fights and battle scenes, the most frequent production injuries
were skinned noses from the slipping of helmet visors. The poor people's costumes were tattered in barrels filled with rocks and rolled along the roof of
the wardrobe building; the period tapestries were painted on burlap, then
soaked in filthy water and left to fade in the sun.

As much as *Easy Living* was ignored, *If I Were King* was celebrated. The
L.A. Times praised the "splendid new accents" of Sturges's adaptation,[24] the

Daily News favorably compared its "slyly satirical, openly romantic quality" to similar effects in *The Prisoner of Zenda*,[25] and *Variety* proclaimed it "the hottest thing at the box office Broadway has seen in some time." [26] Yet, *If I Were King*'s very popularity subjected it to a sort of scrutiny that was now terrifying the studios far more than the Catholic Legion of Decency. With the Depression, the Spanish Civil War, and the rise of Nazism, an unprecedented number of artists and intellectuals had begun joining radical causes, even in Hollywood. So Villon's eagerness to battle the Burgundians was seen by some as a veiled endorsement of the Popular Front which, under Communist auspices, was currently urging America to fight fascism abroad. The parallel was obscure, admittedly, but "with the world acutely conscious of propaganda, and the motives of all men suspect, it is conceivable that the more sensitive of our citizens will profess to see the red light of Moscow shining through the beard of Villon," began an article in *Redbook*, which went on to report that Paramount vociferously denied any such connections, insisting "*If I Were King* was devised solely for entertainment purposes." [27] Paramount's word was generally accepted, and no serious objections to the film were pursued.

Still, it is ironic that anyone could suspect Sturges of advocating revolutionary action. While true radicals like Dashiell Hammett contemplated going off to Spain to fight Franco, while even moderates like Preston's friend Paul Kohner, with Ernst Lubitsch and Salka Viertel, established the European Film Fund to find work for émigrés fleeing Hitler, and while most every important writer in Hollywood was joining either the liberal Screen Writers Guild or the more conservative Screen Playwrights, Preston joined nothing and sided with no one. He continued to evade or personalize his father's persistent attempts at political discourse. For instance, when Solomon contended, in the fall of 1937, that business was "shot to pieces" because of Roosevelt,[28] Preston simply ignored the reference to F. D. R. and noncommittally sympathized: "When the bottom fell out of the market [a few months ago] it also fell out of Snyder's. I don't exactly know why but it did. It is building up now again at Snyder's. I hope the market will do likewise." [29]

Preston avoided political movements as he avoided religions, and for somewhat the same reason: because so much evil was done in their names. But politics in the wider sense was, of course, inescapable. *Not* supporting the screenwriters' attempt to unionize was itself a political statement, as Preston well knew. And, in the late thirties, Sturges did spell out a political philosophy of sorts in a letter to his uncle, Sidney Biden, recently back from years in Berlin:

> Your adventures in Germany sound unpleasant enough and yet the Nazi political machine is interesting, representing as it does the most natural hereditary impulse in Homo Sapiens. As dogs dislike cats, so do Teutons dislike

Latins, Slavs dislike Semites, etc. etc. Only the dislike of one's own kind surpasses in intensity the dislike of foreigners. The Civil War, the bitterness between the Jews and the Arabs, and the dreadful family feuds we see on all sides are fine examples of this. I don't know why I started on this business except to say that hatred seems to be the most natural, the most usual, and the most enthusiastic emotion in man. There is no use denying it and very little hope of changing it. Unborn millions will arrive with a fresh supply. The God of Hate seems infinitely greater than the God of Love and always much nearer and easier to get at. The study of man should start with a true portrait of him in all his stink, unretrieved by sentiment or gentle Christian embellishments. These thoughts could easily entwine themselves into a pretentious book so I call a halt . . . and conclude by saying that if small boys were running Germany they would run it just as it is being run. I suppose the moral is that only men of the highest character and intellect should be allowed to enter the political lists; the populace could decide the winner but never under any circumstances the contestants.[30]

This unblinking indictment of human nature is the most expansive political statement Preston ever put in writing. Its style is derivative of Mencken. Yet, the forthright anger, elitist's mistrust of the masses, and skepticism about change on any level are unmistakably Preston's own. So too is the contention that small boys left to their own devices would behave as abominably as their fathers, that people are who they are from birth. Still, while Preston doubtless meant what he said, he also seems seduced here by his own cynicism. He must have enjoyed impressing his uncle with sweeping statements like, "The God of Hate seems infinitely greater than the God of Love," and his conclusion that "men of the highest character," rather than "the populace" should select political candidates.

While seemingly straightforward, this last statement is every bit as vague as Preston's fatalistic commiserations with his father about business. For who, indeed, is this ignoble "populace"? The rabble in *If I Were King*, perhaps, and the greedy poor in *Easy Living*, but are they also Jimmy in *A Cup of Coffee*, the card sharks in *The Lady Eve*, and those nice laughing prisoners in *Sullivan's Travels*? What of the low-born prickly individualists in all Sturges's best films—are we to believe he "never under any circumstances" wants them to choose their rulers? And, furthermore, what about the people who *ought* to choose? What of those "men of the highest character and intellect"? Who are *they*? Who deems *them* worthy?

André Bazin would call Sturges the "anti-Capra," and it is true that he was in no easy sense a populist; but to perceive him as an antipopulist, to take this letter to Sidney Biden at face value is also wrong. For, politically as elsewhere, Sturges was a contradiction.

Preston boating in his pool at 1917 Ivar.

And he thoroughly enjoyed that in himself. He freely disputed with his friends over moral priorities. Let others agonize about trade unions and Spain. Sturges would concentrate on his own house and restaurant, he'd worry not about the fate of all screenwriters in the long run, but about winning the opportunity to express himself now. So, in the spring of 1938, while building

185

a new kitchen at Ivar Avenue and trying to make ends meet at Snyder's, Preston and his agent Orsatti waged an intense campaign at Paramount.

Preston's contract there ran out in September. Reviewing his accomplishments over the past two years, a Paramount executive named Botsford praised Sturges's talents (*"If I Were King* alone is extraordinary") and recommended that Paramount do whatever was necessary to keep him. Though, at $2,750 a week, Preston's salary was already higher than most any other screenwriter's, Botsford suspected MGM would offer Sturges $3,000 and urged that Paramount match their price.[31] Money, however, was not what Sturges was after. "Sturges and Orsatti have made it known [that Sturges] wants to stay at Paramount providing he can direct," an interoffice memo later that summer reported. "Mr. LeBaron is willing to do this if we can get the right subject, a script written by Sturges, say for example a Ruggles-Boland picture."[32]

LeBaron may have been "willing," but he was certainly not eager to make any more commitments to Preston than were absolutely necessary. And in the end, both sides compromised. Preston agreed to go on writing, for another year, at his present salary, while Paramount made a "good faith stipulation" that within that year Sturges would get a chance to direct his own script. There would be no penalty, however, if he did not.[33]

When, in the summer of 1938, Paramount loaned Sturges to MGM to write *Broadway Melody of 1939* for Don Ameche and Eleanor Powell,[1] his contract stipulated that he could race his boat to Honolulu on July 4. Left behind, Bianca wrote to Preston in Hawaii: "All my love to you. Be bad or good or anything but never tell me—even when I ask you. No broken hearts this time, eh darling?"[2] Bianca's letter implies more than just affairs; it suggests she's become resigned to her less than ideal relationship with Sturges, maybe even that her temper has mellowed. That, however, is unlikely because, around this time, she so angrily berated a contractor Preston had hired to design his garden that the man quit,[3] and soon after Preston got back from Hawaii Bianca began loudly threatening to make travel plans of her own. Preston was never home anymore, Preston took her for granted, Preston thought her chief function in life was to oversee his house improvements: these were a few of the complaints she regularly confided in Priscilla Woolfan. Then some time in August Bianca announced she was going to Mexico; she'd give Preston a taste of what it was like to be left alone.[4]

Bianca could not have intended to be gone for long because Solomon Sturges, who'd retired in June, was planning to visit them in early September. And if Preston was lonely without Bianca, he was also, for the first time in nearly seven years, free. One day, shortly after Bianca's departure, Preston ran into an acquaintance, Gordon Tevis, and invited him and his wife Louise for dinner at Snyder's. Preston had reason to suspect the Tevises' marriage was now merely a friendship. That night, he danced with Louise as he had danced at a Connecticut country club with Estelle Mudge and in Palm Beach with Eleanor Hutton. Before the evening was through, they were madly in love.

Louise Tevis was born Louise Sargent in Ft. Dodge, Iowa. "Of pioneer stock," Preston proudly declared her. He would fashion Mrs. Sargent in *Re-*

member the Night after Louise's mother, who was devotedly maternal and a wonderful cook. Louise, twenty-nine when Preston met her, had seven years before married Gordon Tevis, sixteen years older than she. Though Gordon came from a wealthy San Francisco family, he himself was not rich. Finances were a perennial sore point in their marriage. For while Gordon, a talented amateur chef and magician, had no interest in making money, he insisted on living like his millionaire friends. He was forever accepting lavish invitations (to places like the Hearst castle) he couldn't hope to reciprocate, so in Louise's mind, the Tevises became "professional house guests." Louise grew frustrated that Gordon made little effort to repay his debts. She felt great affection and sympathy for her husband, but he'd lost her respect.[5]

Louise was a tall, remarkably beautiful woman—stylish, wholesome, intelligent though not intellectual, with a wry sense of humor, flowing thick light hair and a squint in one eye that grew pronounced when she was tired and made her, many of her friends felt, more endearingly vulnerable. One good friend from this time remembers Louise as "a complete person—she knew who she was and was at peace with herself."[6] Louise was Catholic like Estelle and, like Eleanor, mild-tempered: needless to say, quite a contrast to Bianca.

The Tevises had lived just down the hill from the house the Woolfans rented Preston. They had mutual friends, and Louise remembers conversations, at various parties, where Preston poured his heart out to her about his second wife and how perplexed he still was that Eleanor wanted to annul their marriage, because annulling a marriage was like saying it didn't exist. Louise vividly recalls the day she first met Preston. It was at her friend Lila Lee's in Catalina. Preston had come down on the Destiny, and Louise was there with Gordon. Consciously, Louise knew only that she'd met a handsome, charming and boyishly self-centered writer, but something deeper, she later figured, must have transpired; because shortly after she spoke with Preston, Louise left the party to go back and pick up something at her own place, and she stumbled on the way and slightly bruised her knee. "And I'm the reverse of prone to tears, I do not cry readily. But I burst into tears and cried, cried all the way home," she recalls. "And I couldn't make up my mind why this was. So he must have put a whammy on me."[7]

As with Estelle Mudge, the fact that Louise was married became a challenge for Preston. But neither Estelle nor Louise was in love with her husband when Preston came along, and he had no casual seduction in mind. From that night at Snyder's, Preston was determined to marry Louise, and after their third dinner together he proposed. Apparently, Preston was attracted to Louise for some time before he invited the Tevises to his restaurant. Yet, until

Louise Sargent.

Bianca left for Mexico, he never so much as asked Louise to dance. Though he demanded power within a relationship, Preston couldn't bear to be the one to call it quits. Out of honor, perhaps, or compassion, or some romantic ideal however ill-suited to his nature, Preston in every important affair of his life waited for the *woman* to leave him.

Now that Bianca was gone, however, Preston wasted no time worrying about her. He was so utterly in love with Louise that fifty years later friends still recall his euphoria and how he doted on her: summoning not just every courtly gesture, but all that was noble, yearning, and imaginative in his being. For Preston at forty it was as if he'd never loved before, or met any woman with a tenth the charm of Louise Tevis; and Louise, normally skeptical, threw off all reticence and wildly loved him back. Both were emboldened by their passion. Louise, raised to believe that divorce was evil, agreed to leave her husband; and Preston, in his best Paris Singer fashion, dressed to the nines and hired a chauffeur to drive him to an appointment with Gordon, where he formally asked Louise's startled, but accommodating husband for her hand.[8]

Preston was not so bold, however, in his dealings with Bianca, who came home to find her housemate out day and night and poor Gilletti, sworn to silence, pleading ignorance about where he was and what in the world had transpired. Solomon and Marie Sturges soon arrived on the scene and met Louise at Snyder's, but while Bianca wore herself out escorting them around town, they too guiltily perpetuated Preston's subterfuge. For weeks, Preston simply declared himself "busy": doubtless, because he dreaded hurting this woman he'd lived with for so long; doubtless too because he was determined to have no unpleasant scenes spoil his ecstasy.

Louise left for Reno at the end of September. "MY VERY PRIVATE NUMBER IS RENO 22392. I'M AWAITING YOUR CALL WITH MORE ABSURD PALPITATIONS,"[9] she cabled Preston, who immediately cabled back "MUCH ABSURD LOVE" and soon joined her. They were married when Louise's divorce was finalized, on November 7. Gilletti, who came along so Preston could claim to be writing, remembers them wholly absorbed in one another, "lovey-dovey" and very sexually attracted. Many times Gilletti offered to "jump out the window" to give the lovers privacy, in their one-room apartment. Louise, Gilletti felt, brought out the best in Preston, and this was a charmed week for them both.

But not, of course, for Bianca, who must have learned the full truth about her situation only just before Sturges took off, and was hurt and righteously indignant. She was also alarmed since Preston was not only the center of her emotional life, but her landlord and provider. "What makes it so hard for me now is that I've lived your life for all these years. I never had to make a decision for myself and now it's as if my arms were useless,"[10] she wrote Preston; though her arms, as it turned out, weren't as useless as she thought. She managed to move to an apartment and, as soon as Preston left for Reno, ordered his servants to transport some 150 possessions—including a Mexican chair, a copy of *The Golden Bough*, and six out of eighteen water goblets—from his home to hers. Preston, predictably irate, wrote Bianca an accusing letter, which she answered with an itemization of what she'd taken, needlingly insisting, "The listed things on these pages were borrowed in good faith."[11]

Preston did not for a moment believe her, but neither was he anxious to confront Bianca face-to-face. He was refusing to acknowledge her even as an ex-mistress. She was a former secretary. What he wanted, Preston told Bertie Woolfan, was to offer Bianca a monthly allowance of $300 for her loyal services. In return, Bianca would have to give back his property. Preston, arguing that he couldn't convey this himself without eliciting tears and recriminations, pleaded with Bertie to speak with Bianca for him. Bertie agreed, but since he too was terrified of Bianca's temper, he insisted on bringing his wife along.

On the appointed night, Priscilla and Bertie arrived at Bianca's apartment and conveyed Preston's wishes as gently as they could. Bianca listened calmly enough. Then, the telephone rang, and Dr. Woolfan was summoned off to treat an ailing actress. With Bertie gone, Bianca's reticence vanished. She began cursing Preston in three languages, smashed some framed hunting prints Preston especially cherished, then most everything breakable in the room. Priscilla, delicate and soft-spoken, literally huddled under a chair, though Bianca never attacked her personally. By the time Bertie reappeared an hour later, Bianca's temper was spent, and she agreed to return what remained of Preston's things.[12]

Vicious tantrums notwithstanding, Bianca soon proved remarkably good-natured about Preston's new relationship. "I wish this wasn't such a stuffy world," she wrote him, two weeks after his marriage. "I'd adore to wish your wife happiness. I remember her as a lovely wistful thing with the . . . oh drat the French name for it [*louche*], you know the thing that Claudette Colbert has in her eye and I would hate for her to think of me as an ogre."[13] She even claimed to pray with him "for the son you've always wanted."[14] Best of all, from Preston's point of view, Bianca refused his generous offer to buy her a house with a pool (which he'd anyhow modified to an apartment without one) and left L.A.

Unlike Estelle and Eleanor, Bianca did not immediately (or ever) remarry, but like Mary Desti, always her model, in August 1939 sailed for France. She went on Preston's urging. He told her to ignore all the rumors about war breaking out imminently, though the Germans indeed invaded Poland just days after her boat docked. True to character, Bianca was undaunted. She disobeyed the embassy's orders to go home and proceeded to dance in Montmartre, "weep" in Sacré Coeur, volunteer in a hotel converted to a soldier's hospital, seek out all Preston's old haunts, have drinks with Paris Singer's widow at the Plaza Athenée, and go "swathed in mink" and "wild with excitement" to her first French fashion show. After the Germans occupied Paris, she one night "ill-advisedly" broke curfew and went to the movies, where "two German giants" grabbed and threatened her; but then, addressing them in their native tongue, she so beguiled these Huns that rather than arresting Bianca they begged her to let them take her to the beach.[15]

This is not to say that when Preston's checks were overdue, Bianca's letters weren't, like Mary Desti's, filled with (usually false) alarm—"Preston, dear, there is something strange in my breast," she once dramatically asserted but never again mentioned; she complained of collapsing in the street and "frightful conditions" that did finally impel her to leave France—for Spain.[16] From here she begged Preston to get her home, and Preston, now directing *Sullivan's Travels*, did everything in his power, including writing the secretary of state, to successfully book her passage on one of the few commercial boats sailing for New York; though by the time her ticket arrived, Bianca had decided not to leave Europe after all. She stayed on to risk her life spying for the allies, and Preston heard nothing from her for three years. Then, in 1945 she cabled him out of the blue, "INDICATIONS EXCELLENT [I CAN] LAND JOB [AS] RESIDENT BUYER PARIS. . . . WILL YOU HELP UNTIL GET STARTED . . . OTHERWISE I SINK."[17] And he replied, "VERY FAMILIAR WITH DESPERATE CABLE TECHNIQUE FROM LIFETIME WITH MOTHER. WRITE AND TELL ME MINIMUM MONTHLY FRANCS YOU CAN LIVE ON AND I MIGHT BE INCLINED TO HELP."[18] He was. She became an extremely successful businesswoman—representing South African diamonds to the fashion houses in Paris—and remained, until the end of Preston's life, an adoring friend.

The first months of Preston's marriage to Louise were among the happiest he would know. "You shall be my religion, darling," Preston had in his twenties promised his first wife, and he began by worshipping Louise as well. Though, like Eleanor, eleven years younger than Preston, Louise was more mature. She'd been away from home for nearly a decade when they met. So, while Louise's father, like the Huttons, disapproved of Sturges, there was no need to lecture Louise about loyalties, and Louise was less preoccupied with

Preston and Louise, about 1939.

wealth and material possessions than Preston himself. It also must have helped that Mary Desti was out of the picture, though, because of all Preston's wives, Louise was least likely to be influenced by her mother-in-law. For she was neither a romantic nor a believer in destiny, and unlike Mary with her explosive passions, Louise fully expected her intense attraction to Preston to mature into conventional married love.

Louise even felt motherly toward her new forty-year-old husband. Preston had told her about his peripatetic childhood and his traumas in New York with A. C. Blumenthal and Eleanor's family, and, like many a new wife, she thought she could heal the wounds of the past. She had little interest in Preston's becoming a great success and, unlike Bianca, no preoccupation with Preston's film work. An excellent sailor, she loved boating on weekends and was as happy to hear Preston describe the principles of his diesel engine as to counsel him on his scripts. In keeping her distance from Preston's work, Louise resembled Eleanor, and like Eleanor too she was both gratified and dismayed by

Preston's romantic ardor. From the start she could sense he wanted to possess her, and tried with subtle gestures—like insisting (over his protests) that she retain S. from her maiden name as a middle initial—to convince him he could not. She was herself verbally agile, and Gilletti remembers how in the nicest way possible Louise used her dry humor to bring Preston down to earth or criticize him when he was displeasing her; though they could read each others' minds and, in the early days of their marriage, seemed united in most every wish.[19]

One of their first joint projects was creating a hospitable space in the Ivar house where they could relax and give parties. A large thirty-by-sixty-foot back room seemed the obvious spot, and Louise, with her keen sense of style, thought to remodel it like the den of a "spectacular roué" she knew in Carmel. While the dining room was dark, with heavy sideboards and a long mahogany table, they made the game room airy and playful. There was a billiards table at the entrance. Unattached ceiling-high bookcases led to a great expanse of windows and screened French doors, which opened onto the terraced yard with its ancient trees, pool, and badminton court. The walls were painted green and white. Two benches from one of Rouben Mamoulian's movie sets, covered in pink velveteen, served as couches, and a brick inglenook fireplace stood at the far wall. The room's most spectacular unit, up from the entrance and set off by a wrought iron balustrade, was the bar, upholstered in green leather, and complete with an authentic copper-topped nightclub bar table[20] and untippable bar stools Preston had invented himself.[21]

Their first year together Preston and Louise often stayed home alone or socialized with just one other couple, maybe William Wyler and his new wife, Tally, who had married around the same time they had and were extremely fond of Louise. Once Preston said to Louise, "Isn't it a good thing? We have a good life and we have also the great boon of privacy," but she sensed even then that their intimacy would not satisfy him for long. Soon, they began entertaining regularly in their game room. Just as Ernst Lubitsch gave Sunday luncheons, Preston and Louise threw large Sunday night parties where Louise, an increasingly fine cook, bought and prepared all the food and had great fun tending bar.

There was some sadness too during the first weeks of Preston's marriage. In early November, Solomon Sturges, now seventy-three years old, had a severe heart attack. Then, he seemed to recover, and since Solomon was constantly asking for his son, Marie got him on the Santa Fe Chief, going west. Along the way, he became delirious, imagining a great flood, and tried to leap from the train car.[22] When Preston met his adored father at the Los Angeles

Preston and Louise with Solomon Sturges (bottom left) and his second wife, Marie (bottom right), about 1939.

depot in the middle of January, Solomon was a sorry sight. Yet, settled at the Sturges's with two round-the-clock nurses, he was soon well enough to walk about and finally to move with his wife to a house they'd bought in Santa Monica, where Preston often visited. He invited Solomon's family and friends to congregate at his Ivar Avenue home. Solomon could not have asked for

195

more filial treatment. "[My father] has lived well but not wisely,"[23] Preston wrote a friend of his father's illness, and Bertie Woolfan, who treated Solomon at the end, remembers he suffered not only from heart trouble, but from syphilis. His physical strength and acumen degenerated precipitously, but Solomon would live to see his son direct a film.

Amazingly, Preston's writing did not suffer from all the excitement in his real life. Working with one of Paramount's wittiest and most astute producers, Al Lewin, between August and December he wrote a first draft of his great comedy *The Lady Eve*. Lewin's reactions to this script would in a few years prove invaluable for Sturges. Now, though, Lewin encouraged Sturges to put his comedy aside and concentrate on an original dramatic project, also about a woman crook.

This, *Remember the Night*, was a courtroom love story. The screenplay opens just before Christmas as Jack Sargent, one of the New York District Attorney's most gifted deputies, is forced to delay his trip to his mother's home in Indiana in order to prosecute a pretty young woman, Lee, for stealing jewels. Lee is obviously guilty. But since jurors are notoriously compassionate to defendants before holidays, Jack contrives to delay the case until January 3. Then, feeling sorry because he's condemned someone to a prison cell over Christmas, he arranges Lee's bail. Lee, though, is not especially grateful; with no money where could she go? Learning that, like himself, Lee has a widowed mother in Indiana, Jack offers to drive her home.

Their trip, filled with wrong turns and adventures with small-town justice, brings the couple closer. Lee confesses she hasn't been back to the Midwest in years, and when they arrive at her mother's, it is obvious she has not been missed. "Never doing what she's told till she winds up stealing like I always said she would," complains the embittered old woman, evoking a long-ago incident where Lee took—or in her own mind borrowed—her mother's pin money. In response, her mother drove her out of town because she refused to forgive her. Sargent, appalled at this maternal obduracy, ushers Lee off to *his* mother's home and the American Christmas of her dreams, complete with popovers, singing around the piano, a barn dance, and family warmth to spare. Lee and Jack fall in love at the Sargents' house over the holidays, and though Mrs. Sargent also likes Lee, she begs her not to marry Jack and spoil his future. Back in New York, Jack tries to throw the case by badgering Lee under cross-examination (a sure way to antagonize the jury), but she senses what he's up to and pleads guilty to save *him*. Both affirm their love in a tearful final scene at Lee's prison cell, where Jack vows to wait and marry Lee when she's released.

Since *Remember the Night* is the last film Preston wrote before he began directing comedies, it's tempting to read into it some path not taken, a sign that Sturges could have gone on to make masterful serious films. As indeed, his best thirties dramas—*The Power and the Glory, Resurrection, Diamond Jim, If I Were King*—suggest he might have. And certainly, *Remember the Night* shows no dearth of storytelling talent, though it's an oddly conventional work, filled with pop psychological assumptions. Like *The Power and the Glory*'s Tom Garner, whose success undermines his virtue, Lee is one of the few Sturges protagonists susceptible to change. Mrs. Sargent speaks *Remember the Night*'s message when she tells Jack it was his happy home life that made him a law-abiding citizen. By implication, Lee's background, as opposed to her nature, made her a criminal, and the film's journey is toward Lee's redemption and reform through love. What a contrast to Diamond Jim who'd die rather than change his diet, not to mention perpetual rogue Villon!

There are insightful moments in *Remember the Night*. Over their first dinner, for instance, Lee asks Jack what he'd do if he were starving and had no money and there were loaves of bread in front of a market and the grocer's back were turned. "Would you swipe one?" "You bet I would!" he vehemently answers, anticipating Lee's reactions. But, "That's because you're honest," says Lee. "You see I'd have a six-course dinner at the table d'hôte across the street and then say I'd forgotten my purse." So much for a universal morality. The scene between Lee and her mother similarly undermines clichés about motherhood. For this woman isn't bluffing, she truly dislikes her child. And though obviously calculated to better show up Mrs. Sargent's fervent welcome, Lee's chilly homecoming, and her frustration at never achieving forgiveness, linger in the mind through all the holiday merriment with its talk of healing love and change.

Still, for the most part, *Remember the Night* is standard melodramatic romance and not, it's interesting to note, because of any pressure from Paramount. After reading an early draft of Sturges's script, Al Lewin wrote William LeBaron an incisive memo urging Sturges to toughen the characterizations and be more audacious with his plot. The whole idea of Jack's career being ruined by Lee was, he felt, "unbearably old-fashioned," the incidents in the Sargent home "a bit trite and corny," and even the Sargents' servant, Lewin suggested, could be "more originally eccentric," and not such a stereotype.[24] Sturges's final draft was narratively sharper and more credible for this memo's prodding, and Preston accepted some of Lewin's individual points, but not the spirit of his critique. In final draft as in first, the Sargent household remains stock characters, though the love story is genuinely affecting.

By the time Sturges completed *Remember the Night* in the summer of 1939, Al Lewin had been replaced as producer by Mitchell Leisen, who was also to direct the film. These developments infuriated Preston, who anticipated that his long scenes would be excised or truncated, as sure enough—and usually for the best—they were. Yet Leisen never rewrote a word of Sturges's dialogue, and as displeased as Preston was by Leisen's pruning, he was heartened when it was announced that Barbara Stanwyck would play Lee. Most everyone who ever worked with Stanwyck admired her talent, good nature, and professionalism, but Preston went further to declare that Stanwyck possessed such a rare inner beauty that she would still be radiant in old age. During the shooting of *Remember the Night*, Sturges told Stanwyck, so often cast in weepies, that he'd one day write her a great comic role. He made no such promises to her co-star Fred MacMurray, who showed neither the nimble wit nor commanding presence Sturges had imagined in his protagonist. What he conveyed was a stolid reserve, which Leisen used well. Beulah Bondi was type-cast as Mrs. Sargent, and Georgia Caine took on the difficult cameo role of Lee's mother.

Shooting for *Remember the Night* went smoothly, with Sturges frequently on the set supervising revisions. This time Paramount's optimism about Sturges-Leisen team work was justified, for the film opened to excellent reviews. The *New York World Telegram* called it "glowing and heartwarming."[25] Frank Nugent in the *Times* found it "memorable . . . blessed with an honest script, good directing and sound performance." "Perhaps," wrote Nugent, "this is a bit too early in the season to be talking of the best pictures of 1940; it is not too early to say that Paramount's nomination is worth considering."[26] With characteristic generosity, Leisen wrote Sturges: "Do you suppose it's possible for you to arrange an extension from my office so you could get in on some of these charming compliments I have been getting on the picture? As you know, I have always said a picture is only as good as the story and in my opinion, honors should be equally divided between us on this one."[27]

But Preston was in no mood to share credit with anyone. When his one-year Paramount contract ended in September, Sturges rebuked LeBaron for failing to come through on his "good faith stipulation" and now threatened he really would quit unless he was immediately allowed to direct—and not just any project, but a script he wrote himself. From the start Sturges conceived of filmmaking as one man's venture. And maybe, as his agent Orsatti supposed, because LeBaron felt Preston was more stable since his marriage, or maybe out of sheer respect for his perseverance, LeBaron finally submitted to Orsatti's highly unusual deal. Sturges would sell Paramount *The Vagrant* for a single dollar and in return be assigned to direct this film.

PART IV

The Power and the Glory

A happy ending represents the successful conclusion of a given segment of time and stands as a metaphor for the success, through all time, of human life and will.
Robert M. Polhemus, *Comic Faith*

A good director can contrive a happy ending that leaves you dissatisfied. You know that something is wrong—it just can't end that way.
Rainer Werner Fassbinder, *Five Interviews with Fassbinder*

In the end, Sturges sold *The Vagrant* for ten dollars because Paramount's legal department was suspicious of a one dollar deal. The script's name was now *Down Went McGinty*, and it had undergone other sea changes since Preston wrote it, the summer after *The Power and the Glory*, with Spencer Tracy in mind for the lead. The screenplay was shorter, more fleshed out visually, and inclined to display rather than discuss ideas. The opening scene in a Caribbean bar, for instance, was now a third as long and made its points as much through physical gesture as dialogue. For, hoping to attract various studios during the thirties, Sturges had pruned his overly explicit first draft as Leisen pruned *Remember the Night* and *Easy Living*. Still, the premise was exactly what it had been.

And *McGinty*, which would make Preston famous, was, of all things, a satire on American politics, truly an audacious venture in December 1939, with Europe at war and fascism very much a reality. Even Frank Capra's benign *Mr. Smith Goes to Washington* had that October enraged senators and congressmen. And *Mr. Smith* said democracy can be saved by one honest person. Sturges's plot suggests quite the contrary.

The script opens as two Americans meet in a dive south of the border and exchange hard luck tales. Clean-cut Tommy boasts that he was a cashier of the First National Bank, respectable all his life until "one crazy moment" when he embezzled from his boss and had to flee town. "Cashier of a bank," scoffs his fellow expatriate, Dan McGinty, who has execrable grammar and a tough guy look. Today McGinty is a bartender. But once, "I was governor of a state."

Flashback to a snowy election night in some big American city (suspiciously like Chicago) during the twenties. Young McGinty, tipped off by a cook on a soup line, learns he can make two bucks by voting for the incumbent mayor. "What do you get for repeatin'?" he asks the recruiting politician, who replies, "Two tickets is four fish."

When McGinty returns with proof he's voted no less than thirty-seven times for Mayor Tillinghast (who wins by a landslide), the party's immigrant boss is so impressed he offers him a job. McGinty's first assignment is extorting "protection" money from unwilling madams and bootleggers. But, because the boss identifies with his forthright style and refusal to be awed by power, McGinty quickly rises in the world of graft. "This is a land of great opportunity," the boss solemnly informs his prodigy. When Tillinghast is suddenly exposed as a dirty trickster, the boss needs some "clean, typical American" to run on his "reform ticket" for mayor.

McGinty strikes the boss as an ideal reform candidate—to win the woman's vote, though, he'll need to find a wife. Catherine, McGinty's secretary, divorced with two children, volunteers to assume the role, demanding no emotional commitments. So McGinty stumbles into marriage as he fell into his career. First, McGinty wins the election. Then he realizes he's in love with Catherine, who has always secretly loved him. Living in a mansion with his wife and adoring toddlers, Dan McGinty is perfectly happy. The rub is that Catherine is a reformer for real.

She sees Dan as a "fine honest man with decent impulses" and begs him to break off from the crooked politicians and do something for the world: change child labor laws, clean up the tenements. And when he protests, "You've got to understand, honey, no man is strong enough to buck the Party," she insists *he'll* be strong enough some day.

Thus, the day McGinty is elected governor, to please his wife, he informs the boss there'll be no more unnecessary dams and bridges, he's going to work *for* the people from now on. "The people? Are you sick or something?" wonders the boss, who threatens, "I'll put you in the jug so long, you'll splash when you come out." By evening, these two cronies occupy adjoining cells in jail. Catherine vows to work for Dan's release, but with his history of extortion and grafting, it seems he'll do years for the "crazy moment" he considered helping the poor. Then the politician, posing as a prison guard, frees McGinty and the boss, and all three flee to a "banana republic"—which is where the film began. And the film's coda slyly reveals that hierarchy has been reestablished, for we see the politician is now a waiter, McGinty the bartender, and the boss is running this two-bit bar.

The flip side of *A Cup of Coffee, The Great McGinty* is the story of an effortless and undeserved success. Its message is well expressed in a forward Sturges omitted from his final shooting script: "Meat is not good for cows, whisky is terrible for gold fish, and I propose to show that honesty is as disastrous for a crook as is knavery for the cashier of a bank."

Sturges said he based his script both on his knowledge of Chicago politics and on the horror tales about Tammany Hall that his lawyer neighbor, Andrew J. McCreery, regaled him with during those lazy days when he was living with Estelle in Westchester; and *The Great McGinty* contains some of the most biting satire ever written on the democratic process. In the scene where the boss selects McGinty as the "reform" candidate, for instance, Sturges skewers the myth of competing parties:

McGINTY: What do you got to do with the reform party?

BOSS: I am the reform party. What do you think?

McGINTY: Since when?

BOSS: Since always. In this town, I'm all parties. You think I'm going to starve every time they change administrations?

Yet, the script is never smug. And at its best, Sturges's dialogue reflects a true authorial ambivalence—as in this conversation, over the heads of sleeping children, between McGinty and his new wife:

CATHERINE: I just mean that to have all the power and the opportunities you have to do things for people, and never to do anything except to shake them down a little, seems like a waste of something, doesn't balance. You understand?

McGINTY: What are you trying to do, reform me?

CATHERINE: Oh, I was just being dull. I guess I went to one lunch too many this week. I heard so much about sweat shops and child labor and fire traps the poor people live in. I . . .

McGINTY: I couldn't do anything about those things if I wanted to, honey. . . . They're the people that put me in. You've got to understand how those things work.

CATHERINE: You mean you would do something if you could?

McGINTY: What?

CATHERINE: Something about the tenements, maybe?

McGINTY: Why? You got some relatives living down there?

CATHERINE: Oh, you know I haven't.

McGINTY: Oh. You just like that stuff, huh? Don't you know those people just want to be let alone. They want to be dirty. They don't like people fooling around with them. Give them a bathtub, they keep coal in it. You've got to understand, honey, no man is strong enough to buck the party. No matter how much he wants to make his wife happy.

CATHERINE: You'll be strong enough someday, Dan . . .

Although this is a quarrel between a man of the world and a well-meaning but hopelessly naïve woman, it's also about one person wanting to change another, and since the whole film speaks to the danger of defying your nature, Sturges certainly has no sympathy for Catherine here. Yet, he won't dismiss her point of view either. For while McGinty can dispute Catherine's larger social agenda (arguing that the poor are as opposed to reform as he is), there's no denying her premise: that it's a shame "never to do anything except to shake [the people] down."

That a leopard can't change his spots; that politics is ruthless and corrupting—these are familiar ideas for Sturges. What's more revelatory about *The Great McGinty* is its wholly personal style, dramatic sureness, and economy. Like *The Power and the Glory*, it employs a narrator's voice and, leaping between McGinty's political past and "banana republic" present, skews chronology. Like *Easy Living*, it meshes comedy and farce and drastically truncates exposition. Except that (like Mary Desti) McGinty once worked in a candy factory, the hero's past is a mystery. So, Sturges implies, it should be. And he further mocks fashionable Freudianism in a scene where the boss attempts to relate the sad tale of his impoverished childhood to McGinty who, needing no clues from the past to understand this blusterer, squirms in his seat. Sturges conveys McGinty's rise from mayor to governor in a single montage of opposing campaign speeches. He is wise about human nature. Unlike the corrupt officials in a Capra film, Sturges's boss and politician are neither villainized nor conveniently redeemed by remorse. They are who they are and proud of it. They're also, like Louis Louis in *Easy Living*, at once prototypes and wondrously strange.

To capture that strangeness Sturges needed to cast just the right actors, and since his film had a budget of only $400,000, they would have to be found at Paramount. For the boss, Sturges chose Russian-born, Moscow Art Theatre veteran Akim Tamiroff, who conveyed a kind of fervid giddiness as well as gutter imperialism. William Demarest, with his scrappiness and bull dog integrity, became the politician; he would work on all Sturges's Paramount films. As would so many of the character actors Preston now painstakingly selected—Harry Rosenthal, Arthur Hoyt, Frank Moran, Jimmy Conlin, Vic Potel, Robert Warwick. Jimmy Conlin, achingly frail and always in a tailspin, and Robert Warwick, dripping with sarcasm, were particularly distinctive in roles which, while small in themselves, were vital to the view of the world Sturges was creating.

Spencer Tracy, whom Sturges had imagined as McGinty, was not available. So Preston exercised his keen gift for seeing what eluded most people and cast Brian Donlevy, the perennial villain in gangster, adventure films, and westerns

Brian Donlevy and Preston saluting each other. Taken three years after The Great McGinty.

up until then. Preston saw a vulnerability in Donlevy's muscular all-American looks that had yet to be exploited. That Donlevy was thirty-nine was, from Preston's point of view, another asset. For Preston believed there was truth to George Jean Nathan's point about Mae West's success: audiences, bored by a decade of adolescent stars, were glad to see an adult on the screen.[1]

Louis Jean Heyt, who'd ten years before played the prissy fiancé in *Strictly Dishonorable*, was cast as the embezzler Tommy, and Muriel Angelus, the English former stage actress and singer, brought worldliness to the small but crucial role of Catherine.

Muriel Angelus recalls her first meeting with Sturges. "I'd been brought out to Hollywood as a singer, but had never sung a note and was very unhappy. I wanted to get back to the theatre. Then, I got a call from Sturges, and he asked if he could come over to see me. He arrived at my house and said, this is the script of the movie I'm going to make, and I very much want you to play Mrs. McGinty. He said, 'I don't want anyone else for the part.'" Sturges, she remembers, had "all the graciousness of a European," Edwardian gentlemanliness and great flair. "He had a thick mop of curly hair, which during the day would stand on end, and he'd wear a sweater on the set. But in my mind's eye I always pictured that if he went out in the evening he wore a cape—he was that sort of person." Yet, there was nothing phony about him. Unlike so many Hollywood directors, he was utterly himself. He had a rare sense of timing and was rigorous about details. For instance, the film was set in the twenties. Muriel Angelus wanted to look glamorous by late thirties standards, but Sturges was adamant that she wear old-fashioned clothes and a period hair style.[2]

While assistant directors are often mere gofers, for *The Great McGinty*, Paramount wanted an "A. D." who would watch Preston carefully at all times and report any odd behavior back to the studio. They picked George "Dink" Templeton, a former football player with a strong personality and blunt style. Preston constantly lectured Dink about braying obscenities, but he respected Dink's candor, and when Dink saw Sturges in just two days and nights dictate an entire shooting script, he declared his boss a genius.[3] Everyone respected producer Paul Jones, who was physically the opposite of Dink Templeton—small and unassuming. Jones, whom Preston had met on *Never Say Die*, would go on to produce most of Bob Hope's films and become a powerful man in the industry. What made him the ideal producer for Sturges was that, smart as he was, Jones displayed no ego and was happy to be thought just a sweet, funny little guy. He whispered his valuable suggestions and let Preston take the credit. "Somehow he gave Sturges what he wanted," is a typical comment from those who knew Jones only slightly, while those who knew him well saw how, never drawing attention to himself, he curbed Preston's tendency to overwrite and take jokes too far. At the same time, because he believed in Preston, Jones used his influence to win this newcomer unheard-of freedoms from the front office.[4]

How did Preston feel when, after seven years of waiting, he arrived, the eleventh of December 1939, on his film set? Later, when *McGinty* was a great success, he told reporters he'd been scared to death, which surely was true, but he was also bursting with ideas and confidence. At forty-one, slimmer since his marriage and with his dark, piercing eyes and commanding presence, Preston looked very much the director *par excellence* Charley Abramson had deemed him years earlier. And Charley and Dink Templeton were not alone in divining Preston's brilliance. Muriel Angelus saw it right away, and one day William Wyler's mother came on the set and, after watching Preston direct for a while, whacked Louise Sturges on the knee and declared, "The boy's a genius."[5] Preston thoroughly agreed and took some glee informing colleagues, "My mother brought me up to be a genius, and she was the most successful woman I've ever known."[6]

Which is not to suggest that Sturges's first day directing wasn't an enormous challenge, for he was determined not only to get his points across and shoot the scenes as he'd imagined them but to charm everyone and have the cast and crew like as well as respect him, because that was the only way he could work. He'd spent the weeks before meeting with the actors, instructing them to memorize their roles exactly as written. Determined to be in top physical shape, he'd cut down on liquor and the small cigars he so loved, had daily massages,[7] and bought himself a thick belt to support his back because he knew directing was very physical work.

When Preston arrived on the set his first morning, he was distressed to find Brian Donlevy sporting the clipped mustache he'd worn in his villain roles. Preston knew the mustache would have to go. But he couldn't decide how best to approach Donlevy and took a walk around the Paramount lot before returning to confront his star.

"I was wondering about that mustache," said Sturges.

"Don't you like it?" asked Donlevy.

"I certainly do not," said Sturges.

"Off it comes," Donlevy replied.[8]

It's interesting to note that Donlevy's mustache gave him the same slightly raffish look that Preston himself had and that by making him shave it, Sturges asserted his singularity as well as his right to give commands.

Sturges's next problem came when he picked up the viewfinder and saw nothing. Naturally, since he was looking from the wrong end! Preston laughed along with the others, showing he could take a joke, though he just as quickly displayed his prowess. There's an early scene where McGinty signs up to vote under an assumed name, and the suspicious lady poll clerk, squinting at him around her glasses, watches his every move. Sturges told Donlevy and the woman to keep their noses down, then slowly raise them at the same moment. The effect was a piece of Chaplinesque silent comedy. "Boy, you're going to be tops," Donlevy declared.[9] (Typically, this scene Donlevy so liked satirizes democracy on more than one level. For a master shot reveals that the poll booth where McGinty casts his false vote is in the corner of a busy barber shop—entrepreneurship prevailing everywhere.)

From the start, directing was a family affair for Preston, who created a mood of fun and was equally respectful of character actors and stars. Preston wanted Louise with him on the set at all times and, while Mitchell Leisen stationed a guard at his projection room booth to keep anyone not on the picture from seeing the rushes, Preston strolled through the Paramount lot picking up as many as a hundred pals to appraise his day's work.[10] Then, while he laughed at the jokes louder than anyone, he also listened for signs of restlessness. Gilletti and Ernst Laemmle, Sturges's story editor (formerly a colleague at Universal), were critics he particularly trusted, but, like the Chinese poet who declaims his new verse to the first person he encounters, Sturges also needed the response of the man in the street.

Though Sturges used no improvisation and rehearsed thoroughly before shooting each sequence, he allowed for spontaneity. "He was a 'find' director," recalled Bill Demarest. "He'd give you no direction and then see things he wanted in a scene."[11] Muriel Angelus says some scenes Preston wrote were "like music, you couldn't change them because the rhythm was just perfect. But other scenes we'd go over and discuss, and then if he thought a change would be better not just for the script but for [the particular actor or actress] he was always open to that." She believes his humor came across so well because he had the actors play even the most outrageous scenes seriously."[12]

Despite his problem with the viewfinder, Sturges's camera work was also sophisticated. From an opening shot, where bar doors swing back, creating the illusion of a stage space, McGinty is, as Louise Sturges described it, "fresh and passionate," assured both in its scope and in specific details. At last, Sturges had the chance to implement all his cinematic schemes and concepts, and the visual ironies are particularly trenchant. Shots of McGinty alone, walking through spacious government mansions, are juxtaposed against massive torchlight parades and montages of politicians on soapboxes unctuously beseeching the crowds. These twin images of the American leader—as rugged individualist and cog in a system—collide in the memorable scene in which McGinty, arriving for his first morning as governor, strides like a western hero through his marble office, only to discover that the boss is seated in his chair. And Sturges discovers cinematically inventive ways of conveying action. We learn the crucial fact that, though married and living in the same house, Catherine and McGinty have never made love when McGinty opens the wrong door, looking for her room. Later, McGinty's prison escape is conveyed in a famous close-up shot of creeping silhouettes.

Physical business is as carefully planned as dialogue. McGinty and the boss come to friendly blows at a first meeting, and their repeated brawls—in the back seats of cars, over the governor's desk, at the bar in the Caribbean—punctuate the film and foil the sophistry of words: the endless campaign promises, the sloganeering. Talk itself is spoofed in a scene in which Catherine goes on and on about how her marriage to McGinty will be purely a business arrangement, while the camera pans, with McGinty's eyes, to appraise her legs. Towards the end of the film, McGinty's impulsive fist fights with the boss are increasingly contrasted with his more arduous squabbles about morality with Catherine: male camaraderie being so much simpler than romantic love. Although, as always in Sturges's work, dialogue *is* vital—"the bright things you would like to have said except that you didn't think of them in time"[13] is how Preston described his best lines—a distinctive visual imagination is clearly emerging.

Outside of some chiaroscuro effects when Catherine and McGinty, pointing a candle, wander through the darkened governor's mansion, Sturges's lighting rarely draws attention to itself; he used few close-ups and liked classic middle distance shots. Preston explained his preference for inconspicuous cinematography to a colleague at Paramount: "Quite a few years ago . . . when I was new in the theatre . . . I used to watch the audience through a peephole in the [curtain]. The thing that astonished me was that all the spectators in the theatre seemed to have their heads attached together so that they all moved in unison. . . . When I got into the movies . . . I noticed that in some films I was conscious of cutting and in some films I was not. And then I began to understand that there is a law of natural cutting and that this is what an audience in a legitimate theatre does for itself. . . . If the camera moves from one person to another at the exact moment that you in the legitimate theatre would have turned your head you will not be conscious of a cut."[14] Of course, when it suited him he dispensed with the "invisible" camera technique: a shot of McGinty's legs marching through his governor's office, for instance, is as self-conscious as Lubitsch's close-up on a door. Yet, Sturges did strive to capture the excitement he'd experienced in the New York theatre. Muriel Angelus says she often had the feeling she was playing not to the camera but to an audience, and after her love scene with Donlevy the cast and crew broke into applause.

Significantly, that love scene was not pieced together, as was and still is customary, from a master shot and various cut-aways, but filmed whole in a single take. What Sturges considered theatrical was also filmically innovative. His preference for single-take shots frequently got him into arguments with his strong-minded cameraman, William Mellor. Muriel Angelus remembers some "terrific set-tos" over a scene in which Catherine's sopping wet dog (played by one of Preston's beloved dachshunds) runs down a long corridor to descend in her suitor's lap. "Preston said he wanted that in one shot, but the cameraman said it was impossible, it couldn't be done. And Preston said it could and had them rig up this [special dolly], I think it was one of the first times anything like that was done, and it worked. He got his way in the end." [15] (While dolly shots had been long routine, the duration of Sturges's scene and the amount of space covered made his shot unusual.)

Sturges was always the first on his set in the morning and the last to leave. Sometimes he shot a scene several times because he wasn't sure what he wanted, but he learned to work quickly. At the beginning of his second week, he was a half-day ahead of schedule. He was just beginning to feel comfortable with every aspect of directing when, on December 22, for the first time since his bout in the Paris hotel room, Preston came down with pneumonia.

What a truly Sturgesesque coincidence, his succumbing at this crucial point to such an incapacitating illness. Since there was a clause in Preston's contract that said Paramount could replace him if he was "unable to render [his] services," Preston must have felt very like Jimmy in *A Cup of Coffee*—receiving his heart's desire only to have it whisked away. Now his fever hit 104, and he lay helplessly in a hospital bed: not, as when he was felled with appendicitis that Christmas in Chicago, conceiving a play, but cursing his destiny. Yet, his eleven days of rushes had impressed Frank Freeman and William LeBaron, who sent word they intended to hold *McGinty* for Preston's return, no matter if it took three weeks. His temperature went down and, with a scarf at his throat and nurse in attendance, he was back on the set the first day of the new year.

Because of Christmas and New Year's, Preston had missed only four working days and now shot straight through to the twenty-fifth of January. A nurse hovered over him, encouraging him to sit down, but he still worked with tremendous verve. [16] "*McGinty* came in $1,000 under budget, three days ahead of schedule," Preston proudly informed Jack Gilchrist. [17] That February, in a mood of tentative optimism, postproduction began. The title was changed from *Down Went McGinty* to *The Great McGinty*, and some of the crowd scenes were cut (apparently because the studio couldn't discern their satirical intent). [18] Preston insisted that his credit read "Written and Directed By Preston Sturges"; this was the first such billing ever in Hollywood.

Before the July 19 preview, Preston and Gilletti devised their own system for evaluating comic effectiveness. "Sturges was interested in what got laughs and what didn't," Gilletti recalls. "So I invented for him what we called the laugh meter. In other words, I'd sit in the theatre and whenever I'd hear a laugh, I'd jot down the line and make a judgment whether it deserved one, two, three, or four decibels." [19] The system allowed Sturges to fine tune his humor, and the many four-decibel laughs for *McGinty* surely heartened him, though he must have been distressed by Paramount's publicity campaign.

For, obviously baffled and somewhat terrified by the film, Paramount was promoting it on the one hand as "Romance and Comedy" and on the other— equally falsely—as "Controversy and Headlines." The romantic ads waxed silly over McGinty's sex appeal, the serious approach, comparing *McGinty* to *Mr. Smith Goes to Washington*, missed the point that this film was an original. From opening day, August 14, 1940, it was hailed by critics and audiences alike.

McGinty (running with a Cab Calloway stage show) made $44,560 its first week at New York's Paramount and was more resoundingly a hit even than Sturges's play *Strictly Dishonorable*. A review in the *Hollywood Reporter* called it "the answer to any exhibitor's prayer," and the *Times*'s new film critic, Bosley Crowther, was quick to jump on the bandwagon, praising *McGinty*'s "coarse and racy wit, a superior acceleration of action and a flavor as pungent and infectious as the fumes of a red-fire torch." Crowther called Donlevy "masterful" and joined others in finding "shrewdly chosen 'bit' players" crucial to the film's richness.[20] Nor was he in the least put off by Sturges's antirealist tendencies. (Realism, Preston had told a *Times* reporter, "got played out because it was so one-sided. The realists forget the elements of absurdity and fantasy in [reality], and so achieve pseudo-truth and boredom.")[21]

While many left-wing critics (including historian Siegfried Kracauer) read a call to political change in Sturges's satire, *McGinty* was just as appealing to more conservative reviewers, and no one accused Paramount of veiled Communist sympathies. Though the film's message is on the surface cynical, Sturges's joyous energy, his passion both for life and for filmmaking shine through every frame. A subtext of *McGinty* is, I got to make a film, and I made it my way! What particularly attracted critics was *McGinty*'s pacing: the cutting was sharp, the characters possessed a pent-up intensity, which erupted not only when they clobbered each other but even when they spoke. Alva Johnston, writing a two-part profile of Sturges in the *Saturday Evening Post*, called *McGinty* a "landmark," "the nearest thing to a one-man show since the silent days." He added, "The picture has a speed which has seldom been equaled since Mack Sennett used to achieve velocity by loosing herds of lions at the actors,"[22] a point later vividly expanded upon by film scholar Manny Farber (with W. S. Poster): "Basically a Sturges film is executed to give one the delighted sensation of a person moving on a smoothly traveling vehicle going at high speed through fields, towns, homes, and even through other vehicles. The vehicle in which the spectator is traveling never stops but seems

Preston in his office, soon after the opening of The Great McGinty. *Note the photo of Mary Desti displayed on the mantle.*

to be moving in a circle, making its journey again and again in an ascending, narrowing spiral until it diminishes into nothingness." [23]

There's truth to this, but it is also true that *McGinty* is about the American Dream constantly rebuked by American reality. About the inexorableness of character, the dire consequences of romantic love, the inadequacy of justice, and the unresolvable quarrel between free will and destiny. The pulsing forward drive of the film not only satirizes change but with a full heart summons it, as *McGinty's* cacophonous voices celebrate the disharmonious world in all its confusions. And the little people of this world—the boss's driver, the cook—with their flagrancies and private woes, their bursting in and out of the plot, their essential, quirky humanity suggest a strange obduracy to American life that has little to do with change or even democracy.

On the strength of *McGinty* Sturges became an instant celebrity. "Probably never before has a first picture made its director so well known," said Alva Johnston, who astutely added that had a star like Spencer Tracy rather than Brian Donlevy appeared in the main role, *McGinty* would have drawn less attention to Sturges. Sturges would take Johnston's point to heart when casting in the future. Now, though, as *McGinty* turned up on many of the year's Ten Best Films lists and he was nominated for the Academy's first Best Original Screenplay award, Preston was simply overjoyed.

Writing about the night he got his Oscar, Preston would recall wearing a rented tuxedo and cherishing so little hope of winning—against Ben Hecht, John Huston, Charles Bennett, and Charlie Chaplin—that only at the last minute did he think to prepare a few lines. When he was announced as the winner, "I marched up and delivered my joke, which was the following:

"I said, 'Mr. Sturges was so overcome by the mere possibility of winning an Oscar that he was unable to come here tonight and asked me to accept in his stead.' Forgetting that nobody knew what I looked like . . . all the applause ceased and I walked dismally back to my table, missing one of the great moments of my life." [24]

Doubtless he exaggerates his anonymity, for many powerful people in Hollywood knew very well what Preston Sturges looked like—and those who did not soon would.

C H A P T E R

16

Beyond the awards and reviews, *McGinty* brought Preston many personal satisfactions. Reading that his friend was at long last directing a film, Charley Abramson wrote, "My inquiries about you from coast visitors elicit the fact that you are still your handsome self and that time and you are strangers," and he wished fervently for *McGinty's* success. (Since no letter remains, one can only imagine Charley's joy when he saw the finished movie.)[1] Professor Robert Gessner of New York University announced that *McGinty* had been "selected as 'the perfect motion picture script of the season' and will be used for class study."[2] So Preston was to be taught on the same curriculum as those great bores Shakespeare and Molière! Spyros Skouras, now head of a chain of movie theatres, remembered bunking with Preston during World War I and wrote Paramount a letter warmly praising his Air Service comrade's accomplishments. Even reserved Henry Henigson said, "I do want to add my congratulations to the showing that you have made and, without trying to stretch, I am pretty certain that within a very short time you will be aligned as one of the three top directors in this business."[3]

One voice was missing. Solomon Sturges had died April 3, 1940, after Preston finished shooting his film, but before it opened. The previous December Solomon wrote a will, saying, "I leave and bequeath unto my adopted son, PRESTON STURGES, the sum of Five Dollars. I desire to here make mention of my deep affection for my said adopted son and my full appreciation of the sterling qualities in his character and the talents displayed by him in his chosen work, but because of his ample financial circumstances and great earning power I am making no provision for him except as set forth."[4] All else he left to his wife Marie, who needed the money, as Preston understood, but still bequests are symbolic. His mother, after all, had left Eleanor Hutton a house! Surely, Preston would have liked more substantive testimony of Solomon's devotion, for Preston had always made a point that the name Sturges was not his birthright, but an honor he had to prove he deserved. Where now was the acknowledgment that he'd succeeded? That he was the heir to carry on his father's line? After Solomon's death, when Marie asked Preston to help transfer Solomon's stocks into her own name, Preston refused, and son and stepmother soon gave up all pretense of cordiality.[5]

Nine years later, having heard that Marie was dead, Preston tried to locate shares of Solomon's stocks—wanting something tangible of his father's to give to his own son, Solomon's namesake.[6] Little Mon never got those stocks. Yet, it may have given him some comfort that his grandfather chose to be buried not among the formidable Sturgeses in Chicago, where he was born and grew old, but in California, where at the end of his life he had followed Preston.

Before *McGinty* opened, Sturges had already begun shooting his second film and launched a new restaurant. For he was not, like McGinty or Jimmy MacDonald in *A Cup of Coffee*, the ordinary man blessed with opportunity but, like Fitzgerald's rich, *different*: more physically energetic, more imaginative, possessed of the burning desire to live a life as bulging in all directions, as fragmented and surprising as his films. Like Isadora Duncan, Preston was capaciously endowed and extravagant with his whole being. And though it makes him more human that his wives and secretaries complain of his laziness, how he lolled about the house and avoided work to the last minute, the fact is that, between 1940 and 1944, Preston not only wrote and directed eight films, but hosted a highly visible restaurant, oversaw an engineering firm, invented household tools, exercise machines, and motion picture devices, had a son, entertained large groups every Sunday at dinner, and began making plans for his own production company. Andrew Sarris would call Sturges's early forties films "one of the most brilliant and bizarre bursts of creation in the history of cinema," and his life could be similarly astonishing.

The restaurant Preston opened, on the fourth of July, 1940, was called The Players, after a famous actors' club in New York. Two years before, he'd disbanded Snyder's, which lost over $10,000 in its last year and embroiled Preston in exasperating consultations with the songwriter and his family. This venture, which had begun with so much magnanimity on Preston's part, had, like the New York apartment experience with Charley Abramson, left him wanting more for his money. After all, there was nothing extraordinary about backing someone else's place—film magnates did it all the time, and even writers Dorothy Parker and Robert Benchley had partnerships in their friend Mike Romanoff's restaurant. Preston, rich from his film work, now wanted his own enterprise.

To survive, it would have to be distinctive because Los Angeles was far from the gourmet's wasteland it had been even a decade before. The Brown Derby, Romanoff's, and Musso And Frank's all served first-rate, if not especially adventurous food; La Rue's had excellent French cuisine, and a newcomer, Chasen's, had superb garlic bread and steaks. The glamorous Trocadero nightclub and Schwab's Drugstore were popular cynosures for the stars. As with his filmmaking, Preston contrived to outdo the restaurant competition not through radical innovation but by ingeniously combining familiar elements.

Three stories high, The Players could offer something for everyone: on the bottom level a drive-in where beautiful young girls brought inexpensive food to your car door; on the second floor, middle-range prices and casual décor; on the roof, haute cuisine with old world charm and live music. Here tie and jacket were required at all times, and Preston's favorite French food was highlighted. Patrons pronounced The Players's bouillabaisse outstanding, and there were offerings as exotic as tripe à la mode de Caen—perhaps one of those "rare" and "precious" dishes Preston discovered the summer of 1914 at Ciro's in Deauville. Preston made Harry Rosenthal orchestra leader and installed a revolving bandstand, based on the principle of his Ivar Avenue garage, so two musical groups could, without missing a beat, switch places. He created a wall that drew back to expand the room, a gadget that lifted the booth tables so you could easily slide out, and even applied for a permit to land helicopters on The Players's property. (The County of L.A. said, unequivocally, no to that idea.)

While he was pondering whom he could get to manage all this, Preston received, after many years, a letter from Monsieur Pillet, the owner of Pirolle's, who'd fed him and Georges Renevant in those hungry days before *Strictly Dishonorable*. Recently, Pillet had run into financial troubles of his own and, explaining that Pirolle's was losing customers to the World's Fair, asked Preston for a loan of $1,000.[7] Preston replied, "Why throw good money after bad?" He invited this former head waiter of the New York Ritz to come oversee his prodigious experiment.[8]

And prodigious it was. Much larger than Snyder's, and even better-located: on a hill at 8225 Sunset Boulevard, on the corner of Marmont Lane, across from the Chateau Marmont and the Garden of Allah. The original building was a Spanish mission style bungalow, once owned by the actor William Morris, though more recently a catering parlor. Since there was no way the bungalow could be turned into the drive-in Preston envisioned for his first floor, the logical approach would have been to level it and rebuild. Yet, true both to his odd frugality and his respect for beautiful structures, Preston chose not to

Preston holding court at The Players.

destroy the old mansion, but rather to turn it into an elegant top floor and, at
an enormous cost, build the lower two stories *under* it.

Marcel Pagnol thought The Players was a poetic idea, which in a sense it
was, though it was also a business, reminiscent less of Solomon Sturges's cautious investments than of Paris Singer's flamboyant Everglades Club or his

217

scheme to present Isadora with Madison Square Garden. Whether Preston expected to make money on The Players is another matter. In a letter to his father's friend, Sidney Love, Preston confessed in the late thirties that he'd "never made a dime" on Snyder's or his diesel engine, "but I am hardened to that as I have never succeeded in anything outside of writing."[9] So, for all the fuss he made about preferring solid business to flighty art, Preston early on recognized that for him business was the riskier proposition.

And while he posed as the businessman manqué in countless profiles during this era, Preston confided to intimates that he'd inherited his mother's lack of business ability. While their motives were seemingly opposite, Preston's approach to his restaurant was uncannily like Mary's to her shop. For just as she, seeking to hide her commercial ambitions, ran her first Maison Desti like a salon, Preston, though wanting to seem the solid businessman, treated The Players like a private club. And as the Maison Desti attracted the King of Spain and the Crown Prince Rupert of Bavaria, The Players became a Hollywood "in" spot, whose regulars ranged from Ernst Lubitsch and Billy Wilder, to ex-boxers Preston dragged home from the fights, to stragglers, many of them émigrés without jobs, who followed him worshipfully around Paramount. With its vaguely European ambience and heterogeneous clientele, The Players's bar (nicknamed Bar Sinister, for its dim lighting) recaptured the classlessness of Tomaso's; and as Monsieur Pillet, in his Pirolle days, had fed struggling playwrights just because they spoke French, Preston loved to indulge his customers. After your meal, Billy Wilder recalls, Preston would insist on buying you a green or yellow chartreuse, his favorite liqueur, and if someone was short on cash, Preston was more than happy to extend credit. Indeed, from the start, The Players's profits were drastically undermined by unpaid bills and such a plethora of exits that the staff regularly walked off with whole sides of beef under their arms. Yet, Preston preferred to take the loss rather than address the problem.

For where Sturges the filmmaker knew human shortcomings all too well, it grieved Sturges the restaurateur to so much as contemplate that employees or customers might exploit him. Partly this was pride, partly a very deep conviction about hospitality. Besides, if filmmaking was Preston's vocation, the restaurant was his restorative. After a day on the set, he had no patience for counting sides of beef or closing off exits. He just wanted to play the genial host; to have a round table of his own where he could hold forth to twelve or fourteen friends, often until three or four in the morning. Mel Epstein, Sturges's assistant director on *The Lady Eve*, describes a typical evening for Preston at this time as a few hours at the fights, followed by dinner at The

Louise (back left) and Preston relaxing on the Destiny with Ronald Colman (front right) and a friend.

Players, where he'd remain until it closed, then home to start writing. "He'd write until the sun came up. And I would go by his house about a quarter to nine, on my way to the studio, and stop at the side door where the butler would hand me his pages." [10]

Louise quickly adapted to Preston's routine and came to love these late nights at The Players, where Preston's friends became her friends; though, as with Eleanor, Preston was tremendously possessive, and it took little to excite his jealousy. Once, Louise recalls, Preston was standing behind her when a man from across the room called, "You and your card tricks!" Louise's first husband, Gordon Tevis, was a master of legerdemain, and—while there was no physical resemblance between Gordon and Preston—Louise's blood froze because she realized that, in the semidarkness, this person had mistaken her second husband for her first. "Though he had no reason whatever to be jealous, Preston was so upset he barely spoke the rest of the evening." [11]

Still, for the most part, "Preston was in a state of euphoria for his first two pictures," Louise recalls, [12] and being at the same time very much in love, he

219

wanted to share his success and have Louise's opinion on everything. On books, for instance. For she was a great reader, while he read nothing at all during this period; nor did he go to other people's movies, reasoning that if they were very good they'd make him apprehensive about his own work, and if they were bad they'd bore him. About his own gadgets and inventions, though, Preston remained as excited as ever. Louise remembers listening intently for hours while Preston explained the workings of his vibrationless diesel engine (which in the early forties was finally beginning to attract customers), and daily he conceived new projects: a rowing machine for indoor exercise, forty years before its time; a saw with four times the cutting speed of a jigsaw; and all sorts of ideas for motion pictures, from a facsimile of today's laughtrack to a way of achieving variable speed on rear projection and getting 35mm quality sound on 16mm film.[13]

Filmmaking, of course, was his chief passion. William LeBaron was sufficiently impressed with the rushes for *McGinty* to offer Preston his choice of a next project before he'd finished his first. For his second script, Preston returned to *A Cup of Coffee*—the play he'd lavished so much time on ten years earlier, then dismissed as not much good after Brock Pemberton rejected it, and then felt validated when Universal bought it in the early thirties. Significantly, the play's theme is the contingency of talent, how you aren't really good until others recognize you—and how brutally that recognition can be withdrawn. Its happy ending notwithstanding, this is the most cautionary of Preston's success-against-odds tales, and it is revealing that, when he was finally achieving success himself, it is the story Preston picked to film.

Paramount bought *A Cup of Coffee* from Universal for $6,000, and Preston set to work revising and adapting his play for the screen: opening it up, multiplying the cast, complicating the plot and reconceiving characters. The working title was *The New Yorkers*. The film that emerged, retitled *Christmas in July*, would differ in many details from Sturges's Depression play. Baxter's Coffee, for instance, is run not by an aging founder and his two scions, but by an amalgam of the two sons in the person of middle-aged Mr. Baxter, and Jimmy mistakenly believes he's won the coffee contest not because of a misaddressed telegram but because of a prank played by cronies at work. Where the play's hero is a loner, the film's Jimmy MacDonald lives with a widowed mother, among garrulous Lower East Side neighbors; and Tulip, his feisty girlfriend in the play, has become an adoring finacée, Betty.

The narrative, though, is almost identical. Jimmy, a lowly worker at Baxter's Coffee, yearns to win the $25,000 Maxford House Coffee new slogan contest. So he submits a slogan: "If you can't sleep at night, it's not the coffee it's the bunk." Even his fiancée finds this awkward and flying in the face of reason ("Coffee keeps you awake Jimmy, it's a well-known fact"), but then Betty's pipe dreams are of a domestic sort: she wants to convince Jimmy that two can live as cheaply as one.

"Who wants to live cheaply? . . . Everything that means happiness costs money," scowls Jimmy, in the opening scene, where he and Betty spend a hot summer's night on the roof, waiting to hear the radio broadcast results of the Maxford House contest. What they hear is that Maxford's jury is deadlocked. One man refuses to accept a slogan the others have picked and is holding out for his own favorite.

The next morning at work Jimmy calls for the results of the—still unresolved—contest, and three fellow workers, overhearing him, fabricate a telegram telling Jimmy he's won the prize. Jimmy explodes with delight, and things happen so fast the contrite pranksters haven't a chance to confess before their boss, Mr. Baxter, joins the celebration, praises Jimmy's "wonderful" slogan, and, as in the play, offers him a promotion, an office of his own, a raise.

Also as in the play, Jimmy goes off to spend much of his fortune on gifts (including an engagement ring for Betty), now in a lovingly detailed buying spree at kindly Mr. Schindel's store. When he learns Jimmy did not win the contest, Mr. Schindel about-faces and tries to grab back the loot, while Mr. Baxter begins doubting Jimmy's talent. Jimmy is similarly dubious. "You see I used to think maybe I had good ideas and was going to get somewhere in the world, but now [that I've won the contest] I know it," he'd said earlier. Now, Jimmy is again unsure of his slogans, while Betty—like Tulip in the play—eloquently defends her fiancé's right to try writing ads for Baxter's. Reluctantly, Mr. Baxter agrees, though it's understood Jimmy will work at his old salary of twenty-two dollars a week and "for a *very* short time." Meanwhile, across town at Maxford Brothers, the dissenting juror has worn down the eleven others and breathlessly alerts the president, Dr. Maxford, they've got a winner at last: "Listen to this will you? Is this good?" Good or not, the winning slogan is indisputably Jimmy's.

The film deletes the play's explicit political lines about revolution and robber barons, but adds two memorable new characters. The one is stolid Mr. Waterbury, Baxter's office manager, who in an opening scene pulls Jimmy aside to lecture him about success and failure in America:

> I used to think about twenty-five thousand dollars too—and what I'd do with it, that I'd be a failure if I didn't get a hold of it. And then one day I realized I was never going to have twenty-five thousand dollars, Mr. MacDonald. And then another day, a little bit later, considerably later, I realized

something else, something I'm imparting to you now, Mr. MacDonald. I'm not a failure. I'm a success. You see, ambition is all right if it works, but no system could be right where only one half of one percent were successes and all the rest were failures, that wouldn't be right. I'm not a failure, I'm a success, and so are you if you earn your own living and pay your bills, look the world in the eye.

Like Officer Mulligan in Preston's twenties short story "Dust in the Sunlight" (who, "at twenty had hoped to become a police captain. At forty he had hoped to become a sergeant. At fifty-five he realized it was best to be a patrolman"), Mr. Waterbury has come to terms both with the unfairness of life and with his own limitations—and this hasn't made him spiteful or embittered. On the contrary, he seems truly happy for Jimmy when the telegram arrives and even goes out on a limb advising Mr. Baxter to take an interest in the contest winner's future. Proudly drab and unpretentious, Mr. Waterbury is the backbone of free enterprise, the salt of the earth, utterly American.

Then there's the juror Bildocker: grouchy head of Maxford House's shipping department, with his bow tie and racy arm garters, his manner of an affronted tramp: every inch the crackpot and also thoroughly American. He's as expert as a Capra hero on the democratic process, informing his boss, Dr. Maxford, "I'm a member of this jury, and I'm going to vote the way I think is right if it takes ten years. You can fire me out of the shipping department but you aren't going to fire me off this jury because I don't work for you on this jury." Moreover, Bildocker is far from the conventional common man, since he's the sole character in the film who can recognize that Jimmy's slogan is a pun and, as love is in the eyes of the beholder, be tickled pink over it.

Though their paths never cross, the values of Mr. Waterbury and Bildocker war with each other throughout *Christmas in July*. Hard work and resignation seem ahead at one minute, gall and caprice at the next. The ending ostensibly favors audacity. Yet, Jimmy's is such an outlandish victory that one is in almost equal measure cheered by his success and discomfited by its suddenness and improbability.

And the film's style, with its mixture of comic realism in the long scenes between Jimmy and Betty, pie-slinging farce when outraged Mr. Schindel arrives to reclaim Jimmy's purchases, and surrealism in the screaming matches between Dr. Maxford and Bildocker, is similarly unsettling. As are the many odd images: Venetian blinds casting slanting shadows across Mr. Waterbury's office, four ingratiating Schindel Brothers' salesmen looming over Jimmy and Betty, seeming to smother them with good will. Then too, while *McGinty* argues that a man's fate is predestined by his character, *Christmas in July*, like

Easy Living, is obsessed with the tension between luck and virtue. The deserving characters are themselves preternaturally superstitious, and not, we are made to feel, without reason, for a black cat prowls everywhere: tripping Betty in a first scene, still slinking across the screen in the last. "Is it good luck or bad when a black cat crosses your path?" Betty asks the office janitor. "That all depends on what happens afterwards," he replies. Like Sturges, he is hedging his bets and defying single truths.

Though more sentimental than *The Great McGinty*, *Christmas in July* is stylistically brash and awesomely economical. Take the film's opening. Into a shot of the New York skyline, Jimmy and Betty rise like jack-in-the boxes, sitting on a rooftop and arguing about a tiny apartment she's heard of where one room can transform into four. Betty wants to move in immediately, Jimmy is quick to dismiss her scheme. So, within seconds we know they're poor lovers, the woman more eager to marry than the man. Now, "Shut up a minute," he—long-suffering—tells her, and as she touches wood, Sturges cuts to a skyscraper with the neon image of a hand raising a coffee cup plastered across its facade. On the soundtrack a bleating voice announces: "And now, ladies and gentlemen, the moment we all have been waiting for, we are about to give you the result of the fifty-thousand-dollar Maxford House new slogan contest, with a first prize of twenty-five thousand dollars." Cut to a montage of hopeful listeners, then to Dr. Maxford strolling forward to read the winner's name. Then, whispered news that the jury is deadlocked. Dr. Maxford huffs downstairs to berate them ("I've seen far better heads on umbrellas"), then up again to inform the brow-mopping announcer there's still no verdict. The announcer, wiping ever larger regions of his corpus, improvises: "I wish I could have given you the news that you were so anxious to hear, but since I could not, I will conclude with what the prisoner said when the hangman couldn't find the rope: no noose is good noose." Cut back to Jimmy on the roof telling Betty: "How do you like that? They build you up to a big finish and then leave you there hanging on the meathook."

So what Sturges effects, in under six minutes, is breathtakingly terse exposition, nonstop up-and-down motion and glimpses of worlds so radically different in scale the effect is almost visceral. Also characters so formally diverse their very coexistence disconcerts—and at the same time satisfies, like the prospect that anything can happen.

For the part of Jimmy MacDonald, Sturges had chosen Dick Powell, who'd recently made a big fuss at Paramount, complaining that he always got typecast as the crooner and insisting that his new contract entitle him to non-

223

singing roles. Sturges used Powell's restlessness and even his slight archness as an actor, in evoking Jimmy's mixture of bumptious dissatisfaction with his lot in life and uneasiness about his real worth. Sturges chose Ellen Drew, from *If I Were King*, for the rather thankless role of loyal Betty and Georgia Caine (from *Remember the Night*) for Jimmy's mother. He then went to town casting his character parts: William Demarest for Bildocker; Raymond Walburn for Dr. Maxford; Harry Hayden for Mr. Waterbury; Ernest Truex for Mr. Baxter; Franklin Pangborn (Louis Louis in *Easy Living*) for the Maxford House radio announcer; Al Bridge, Torben Meyer, and Vic Potel for salesmen at Schindel Brothers, and Alexander Carr, whom Preston and Charley Abramson had years before ransomed from his hotel room to play Small in *The Guinea Pig*, for Schindel himself. Sturges gave a walk-on part of "sign painter" to his old friend Georges Renevant and made Harry Rosenthal, The Players's orchestra leader, one of the three practical jesters.

Sturges now wrote parts for particular character actors, some of whom had thought their careers were through with silent pictures; others, though they worked regularly, had never before received the attention Sturges lavished on them: laboring over their every gesture, caring not only about the immediate laugh but about the lingering impression of irascibleness or punctured pride or, most often, some sort of hysterical discomfiture. Franklin Pangborn (as the radio announcer) dabbing at his sweating flesh like a bursting water main; Al Bridge (as the Schindel Brothers salesman) so drawing out his vowels he seems to snicker at the customers; William Demarest and Raymond Walburn hurling soliloquies at each other. Together, these oddballs were as important to Sturges's vision of the world as the protagonists themselves.

While, for *McGinty*, Sturges had been tightly budgeted and forced to use Paramount contract actors exclusively, he now was granted slightly more freedom and could even insist on importing Alexander Carr from New York. Sturges also got marginally more elaborate sets, including a studio reproduction of Hester and Essex Streets, which were essentially the same as they had been at the turn of the century. Paul Jones and Dink Templeton were rehired, while the stubborn cameraman William Mellors was replaced by a more peaceable Victor Milner, and shooting began on June 3 and went smoothly. Sturges, always with an eye for publicity, went out of his way welcoming reporters on the set, where he and William Demarest had everyone laughing between takes, and there was always a contagious air of fun, though never any doubts about who was boss.

Beyond his reputation for nonconformity, Sturges, who wore a straw hat to work one day, a high silk hat the next, was cultivating power, both on and

Preston during the production of Christmas in July.

off the set. Though he would offer a fifty-cent piece to anyone who came to him with a suggestion for his movie, woe to the naïf who announced an idea within earshot of others, for Preston had to seem always in command, always the most brilliant person in the room. Which usually he was, but this made him no more tolerant of brilliance or ego in others. Eating at Paramount's commissary, for instance, Sturges was chagrined every day to pass Cecil B. DeMille seated at his private table, surrounded by cast and crew. Everyone on a DeMille set was required to dine with their director, and this put a

225

financial strain on some because the same ham sandwich which cost one dollar at the commissary counter cost two dollars and fifty cents in the dining area. Sturges, determined to one-up DeMille, also established a private table with attendance required, but the difference was that Sturges always picked up the tab—and if you had a friend visiting, he'd pick up his tab too. As at The Players, though Preston did most of the talking, there was an air of openness and liberality at these luncheons. But Preston was not above petty calculating. A Paramount colleague remembers Sturges asking a "special henchman" to go measure the exact dimensions of Cecil B. DeMille's chair—then ordering that his own chair be made grander still. A joke? Certainly, says the colleague, but also a "serious joke," [14] for Sturges was not content simply to make the best films, he had to be the largest presence at Paramount.

And he was on his way to becoming just that in July 1940 when, after twenty-seven days, he brought his second film in on time and well within budget. Indeed, this July was a Christmas for Preston Sturges: with *McGinty* hailed by preview audiences, The Players's opening, his new film already generating excitement. It was exactly nine years since the summer when, Eleanor having left him for Europe, Sturges sat down to write *A Cup of Coffee* in his Fifty-fourth Street garden. Now, life must have seemed altogether different and better, an embarrassment of riches. Preston was no longer one man fighting for recognition. After *McGinty*, William LeBaron and Frank Freeman became as supportive a professional family as anyone could desire. Paramount waged an all-out publicity campaign for *Christmas in July*, suggesting tie-in "Christmas in July" sales for local merchants, touting the up-and-coming stars, and promoting the director as an eccentric, but affable genius. Much was made of Sturges's colorful inventions and background. One release made a point of describing his office, where maps of international cities covered the walls, and there were pictures of his beautiful wife and mother alongside the drawing of "an odd-looking youngster titled 'Typical American Boy.'" [15] After a September screening in Kansas City, Frank Freeman cabled Preston: "ALL PARAMOUNT EXCHANGE MEN ASSEMBLED HERE HAVE JUST SCREENED XMAS IN JULY AND WITHOUT EXCEPTION THEY AUTHORIZE ME TO WIRE YOU AND EXPRESS THEIR APPRECIATION FOR A TRULY GREAT PICTURE. I ALSO ADD MINE." [16] The film opened at the Rivoli in New York on November 5 to almost unanimously favorable reviews, with the emphasis again on Sturges's prodigious talents.

"If Preston Sturges would only act he could undoubtedly put on a one-man screen show," wrote Howard Barnes in the *Herald Tribune*. "In 'Christmas in July' as in 'The Great McGinty' he has written and staged a film which has his signature stamped all over it." [17] Archer Winsten in the *Post* called it "so entirely the creation of Preston Sturges that you feel his humor, flair for situation, and sense of character pulsing through every bit of the film. . . . To put it plainly, Preston Sturges represents a new force in American pictures, the more powerful because in his . . . capacity of . . . writer-director he reinforces rather than interferes with himself." [18] And in the *Times*, Bosley Crowther, affirmed in his early enthusiasm, exclaimed: "As a creator of rich and human comedy Mr. Sturges is closing fast on the heels of Frank Capra." [19] Most of the reviewers acknowledged that *Christmas in July*'s plot was less ingenious than *McGinty*'s. But they also perceived that plot wasn't really the issue, while perhaps the superb acting *was*. "Raymond Walburn," wrote Bosley Crowther, "plays a big coffee merchant as though he were almost ripe for the nut-house. Almost but not quite—that's the secret." [20] Crowther also perceived that Sturges was an evolving talent—*Christmas in July* was a "joyous occasion," there would be more in the years to come.

Preston no sooner finished shooting *A Cup of Coffee* than he began planning his next film, also from an old property, *Two Bad Hats*, which he'd begun writing for producer Al Lewin during the fall of 1938. As with *Easy Living*, the idea for *Two Bad Hats* came from a story, this time an intricately plotted nineteen-page caper by Monckton Hoffe. It follows the fun-loving Kitty, who enrages her distinguished British family by running off to America and marrying a horse dealer. They have twins, Salome and Sheba. The husband and Sheba soon die, but Kitty finds it expedient to pretend Sheba is still alive, since her parents (though still furious at her) send checks to each of their grandchildren.

Salome grows up good-hearted and raunchy like her mother. And as the labyrinthine plot continues, together they return to England where they support themselves running an illegal card game. When Kitty's family learns about this mother-daughter racket, they threaten to stop their checks altogether; so Kitty hits upon the idea of having Salome go alone to her grandparents, posing as her "good" sister Sheba. The subterfuge is even more successful than they'd hoped. For while thoroughly charming her grandparents, "Sheba" meets a handsome young man from an excellent family, Geoffrey, whom she falls in love with, as he does with her.

They marry, but she continues posing as Sheba. For a while, both spouses are very happy. Soon, though, Geoffrey, more raffish than he'd seemed, leaves his virtuous wife for an adventuress, and "Sheba" returns to her mother and her racier identity as Salome. When they meet again at a London dance club, "Sheba" presents herself to Geoffrey as his wife's "bad" twin sister, Salome. And Geoffrey is so totally smitten with her that he soon forgets the adventuress and sets off for America with Salome, the love of his life, and her like-minded mother. Now Salome is tempted to tell her lover the truth, but Kitty advises her to retain their secret—and the possibility of assuming another identity, should the necessity arise.

Monckton Hoffe's *Two Bad Hats* obviously intrigued Preston more than Vera Caspary's *Easy Living*. For though Sturges discards most of Hoffe's plot, he maintains the crucial idea of a woman capable of projecting two very different identities. He also uses Hoffe's genteel vice of illegal card-playing, and in early scripts of *Two Bad Hats*, Sturges keeps Hoffe's British setting and sustains his contrast between stodgy England and the liberating New World.

Unlike Sturges's other major screenplays, *Two Bad Hats* went through important conceptual changes between its original version and the shooting script for *The Lady Eve*. With Europe at war, the opening was changed from England to the Amazon, and the hero's parents from fond British eccentrics to American millionaires, variations on *Easy Living*'s Mr. and Mrs. Ball. Revisions in the script's initial third are particularly revealing. The 1938 screenplay begins as Charles, the naïve ophiologist (snake scientist) son of a wealthy British family, is dispatched to America to dissuade his brother from marrying a chorus girl. He brings his pet reptile, Emma, along for company. On his transatlantic crossing, Charles meets the beautiful Eve, who seduces him into playing bridge with her cardsharp father, who's posing as an oil millionaire. Charles falls head over heels in love with Eve, who to her great surprise loves him back—so much that she begs her father not to cheat him in cards and determines to "go straight," though not to reveal her true identity. As they fall more deeply in love, Charles is alerted to Eve's notoriety by the ship's purser, but he goes on courting her as if nothing is wrong. Only the next morning does he inform Eve that he's been on to her scam since yesterday; he knows she's a fraud and wants nothing more to do with her. Charles is satisfied that he's assuaged his pride, though he feels miserable. She's the woman scorned, and the second half of the film depicts her revenge.

Responding with what he banteringly called "unalloyed brutality" to Sturges's screenplay, Al Lewin was especially critical of this initial third:

> The whole opening of the story is concerned with the necessity of saving the hero's brother from making a misalliance in America, as a result of which Charles reluctantly takes the boat. All this hasn't anything to do with the story. . . . Nothing whatsoever is subsequently made of the brother and his inappropriate wife. This is not only uneconomical writing but it is leading the audience down a blind alley and if I know my audiences, which I admit is open to question, they don't like blind alleys.

229

As for the hero's profession:

> You introduce your hero as an ophiologist for what seems to me inadequate reasons. It is taking an unfair advantage to have your hero inordinately fond of snakes only for the sake of an introductory gag, no matter how good that gag may be. . . . Now it seems to me that the first principles of economy in writing require you to use gags which expose the character of the hero as well as entertain the audience. . . . Whatever Charles . . . does in the first sequence should reveal the fact that he is a very superior young man who is regrettably aware of his superiority. Unless his passion for reptiles can be made to accomplish this purpose it has no place in the script and should be ruthlessly excised.

And on the more significant issue of the love affair:

> Once Charles gets on the boat the romance between him and Eve is all too easy, mainly because there is absolutely no character problem between them. They are kept apart merely because she happens to be a crook, a matter, I must insist, of very slight consequence. They should be kept apart because he is the kind of a guy he is and she is the kind of a gal she is. With both of which ophiology and card tricks have only a superficial connection.
>
> Now when Eve is prepared to marry Charles without letting him know that she is a crook and when Charles, in his turn, embraces Eve without revealing to her that he knows she is a crook, I lose all respect for both of them, and I am sure a lot of other people in the audience will feel the same way. In fact, I fear that at least that handful of intelligent people who occupy almost any audience will, at this point of the story, quietly arise and leave the theatre.[1]

This letter from Lewin, one of the few existing critiques of a Sturges work-in-progress, is fascinating both for its acuity and its wrong-headedness. And Sturges's response to it, over the next several drafts of his script, shows an extraordinary ability to sift useful advice from a highly subjective judgment. About the irrelevance of Charles's brother's marriage, for instance, Lewin was obviously right, and Sturges eliminated this narrative ploy immediately. However, Lewin clearly missed the point that Charles was an ophiologist not merely for the sake of a gag, but because the screenplay was incipiently a Garden of Eden parable: ripe for Freudian slips and sexual suffering. Rather than "ruthlessly" excising his hero's profession, Sturges deepened its significance, making Charles's love of snakes, quite literally, his downfall.

The issues of romance and betrayal were trickier. Lewin's first instruction—that lovers should be separated because of their natures rather than circumstance—merely reflected his own point of view; besides, character differences are indeed established through the lovers' opposite attitudes toward events. So, wisely, Sturges ignored Lewin on this point. But the romance's real problem, as Lewin astutely noted, was that the hero and heroine intentionally deceive one another: she's willing to marry him (as Salome did Geoffrey) without revealing her history, he pretends to believe she's innocent, when he in fact has been informed of her guilt. And the issue is not only that their deception is off-putting, but that it leaves them—and Charles in particular—nothing to learn. For if their passion is never pure, if they never idealize and yearn to know absolutely everything about each other, then they can't discover the limitations of knowledge, can't sacrifice perfection to embrace the contradictory and unknown.

Interestingly, Sturges for a long time resisted Lewin's suggestions about the romance and, in the next few drafts of his script, as in Hoffe's story, at least one of the characters consciously deceives the other. Part of the problem was that Sturges needed the man to do something so horrible the woman would be justified in tormenting him. And only in his final draft did Sturges hit upon a scheme where both lovers could be technically honorable, but she would have plenty of cause for revenge. The result was a near perfect comic screenplay.

The Lady Eve opens in the Amazon where innocent Charles Pike leaves an ophiology expedition to take the S.S. *Southern Queen* home to New York. On board the ocean liner are scores of marriageable daughters seeking husbands; and also the beautiful Jean (Eve in the first draft) Harrington and her father "Colonel" Harry, a cardsharp, looking for prey. When they learn Charles is heir to the Pike's Pale Ale millions, the Harringtons see their work cut out for them:

JEAN: I hope he thinks he's a wizard at cards . . .

HARRY: From your lips to the ear of the Almighty.

JEAN: . . . and I hope he's got a big, fat wife so I don't have to dance in the moonlight with him. I don't know why it is, but a sucker always steps on your feet.

HARRY: A mug is a mug in everything.

JEAN: I don't see why *I* have to do all the dirty work . . . there must be plenty of rich old dames just waiting for you to push 'em around . . .

HARRY: Don't be vulgar, Jean . . . let us be crooked but never common.

And, indeed, Jean and Harry, besides being twice as devoted as "proper" families, are the most debonair team on board. While society girls gawkily struggle to beguile even a word from the reclusive millionaire, Jean puts her shapely ankle in his path, trips him, then complains that he's ruined her shoe. "You can just take me right to my cabin for another pair of slippers," she imperiously berates "the sucker," who trundles off to her stateroom, thoroughly hooked. As in the film's first draft, Jean lures Charles into playing bridge with herself and her father; Harry purposely loses, fattening Charles up for the kill. Meanwhile, Charles prepares to propose marriage to Jean, and she also admits her love for Charles to her father: "I'd give a lot to be . . . well, I mean I, I'm going to be . . . exactly the way he thinks I am. . . . And you'll go straight, too, won't you, Harry?"

"Straight to where?" retorts the cardsharp, who ignores his daughter's entreaties and, as soon as she's left the table, trounces Charles at cards, winning thirty-two thousand dollars, and he only pretends to rip up Charles's check when Jean returns and protests. On the boat's moonlit deck Jean and "Hopsie" (Jean's nickname for Charles) agree they wish they were married and on their honeymoon. But the next morning Charles's faithful valet Muggsy, always suspicious about the Harringtons, gets the purser to show Charles photographs that identify them as crooks. Jean, meeting Charles for breakfast, finds her lover crestfallen. When he shows her the pictures, "I was going to tell you when we got to New York," she gently explains. "I would have told you last night only it wouldn't have been fair to Harry . . . I mean you never know how someone's going to take things like that . . . and well, maybe I wanted you to love me a little more too." But Charles can't appreciate her obvious sincerity because his real concern is with salvaging pride. So he lies and says he's known the truth about Jean since yesterday, it was he who played *her* for a fool.

And, though she doesn't really believe him, Jean, prideful as the ophiologist, determines to avenge her broken heart. Learning that her father's friend Pearlie is currently socializing with the Pikes in Bridgefield, Connecticut, she gets Pearlie to present her to them as his upper-class British niece, the Lady Eve. The Pikes give a party in her honor. "It's the same dame," Muggsy warns his master, but though Jean's only disguise is her British accent, Charles— again smitten—falls for the ruse. (Pearlie further averts suspicion by inventing a variation on Hoffe's "good" and "bad" daughter story, involving an elderly earl, "Handsome Harry" the coachman, and daughters by two different marriages who look scandalously like twins.) Within a month he's proposing marriage, which "Eve" gleefully accepts. Then, after they've wed in style and boarded a splendid train carriage for their honeymoon, the scorned woman reaps her revenge. Because Hopsie despised Jean's reticence, "Eve" is determined to leave no lurid tale untold: beginning with an (invented) tawdry saga involving a first marriage to a stable boy named Angus.[2] And when Charles swallows his pride and forgives her for Angus, Eve assaults him with tales of Herman and Vernon and Cecil until, utterly disillusioned, he stumbles off the train.

Now, vindicated, Jean feels inexplicably sad. When Charles's father contacts her about alimony, she asks only for Charles to come speak with her in person. But he hasn't the heart, or the time for that matter—he's scheduled to sail tonight on the S.S. *Southern Queen*.

The film's final scene takes place on shipboard. As her cardsharp self, Jean trips Charles, who, looking up, recognizes and ardently embraces her. (He's even ecstatic to see Harry and insists they must play many games of cards on this trip.) Ardently in love, they race downstairs to Jean's stateroom, as Jean confesses she adores him. "Will you forgive me?" he implores. "The question is, can you forgive *me?*" says Jean. And when Charles wonders what there could possibly be to forgive: "Oh, you still don't understand."

> CHARLES: I don't want to understand . . . I don't want to know . . . Whatever it is, keep it to yourself. All I know is I adore you, I'll never leave you again, and we'll work it out somehow. There's just one thing. I feel it's only fair to tell you. It would never have happened except she looked so exactly like you. And I have no right to be in your cabin . . . Because I'm married.

In reply, Jean, closing the door, murmurs, "But so am I, darling, so am I."

Now Muggsy pries himself out of their stateroom and, looking dead into the camera, declares, "Positively the same dame."

When Preston said a beautiful woman can get anything she wants, he was speaking of his mother, but he could well have been describing Jean: his most captivating heroine. With its wit, style, and wisdom about life, *The Lady Eve* transcends a conventional genre plot to become a statement on human suffering and resilience.

Where *McGinty* says nature determines fate and *Christmas in July* makes everything hinge on luck, *The Lady Eve* allows its protagonists to choose—their mates and, by implication, their destiny. On the S.S. *Southern Queen*, as in the Garden of Eden, knowledge is a mixed blessing. Yet, where Adam discovers evil, Sturges's Charles comes to terms with ambiguity. And where passion proves Adam's downfall, it is Charles's salvation: transforming him from a brooding prig in search of an ideal spouse to a regular guy blissfully hitched to an adventuress.

Jean, however, is thoroughly appealing from the moment we meet her hanging at the boat rail, trading ribaldries with Harry. That she loses her heart to bungling Charles is both a cosmic joke and a miracle.

Even more than *McGinty* and *Christmas in July*, *The Lady Eve* has memorable supporting characters: Charles's father Horace, who bashes the silver plate covers like cymbals when summoning his servants, is wholly inured to class snobbery, yet, like J. B. Ball, he knows quality when he sees it and immediately recognizes Eve, whatever her pedigree, as a swell person. Harry, the cardsharp, is skillfully evoked as both a devoted father, worried for his child's happiness, and a crook committed to sustaining his chosen career. When Jean presumes that since she intends to marry Charles, Harry can't possibly consider cheating him, Harry lectures her, "The trouble with people who reform is they always want to rain on everybody's else's parade too." And though Harry perceptively warns Jean about narrow-minded righteous people, he's not the stereotypical wise patriarch, for he has his own blindspots. "A mug is a mug in everything," he asserts, while it's the film's point that you can't generalize, that people will surprise.

And then there's Muggsy (Bill Demarest), Charles's preternaturally suspicious valet, whose curse it is always to be technically right and to have Charles never take him seriously. On the boat, Muggsy immediately spots the Harringtons as "a gang of sharpies," and he knows from the moment he sets eyes on Eve in Connecticut until the film's hilarious finale that she's "positively the same dame." Still, no more than Harry does Muggsy *really* have the last word. For he sees only the obvious point that Jean is playing tricks on his master; he has no idea that she's precisely what Charles needs.

From the train named "Louise" where Charles is tormented on his wedding night to the Pike's estate in "Bridgefield," Connecticut, *The Lady Eve* is filled with autobiographical references. Preston later claimed that two scenes came directly from his own experience. In one, Jean/Eve, the morning after her reunion with Charles in Connecticut, tells Pearlie that she and Charles didn't recognize each other last night because they're no longer in love: "You see on the boat, we had an awful yen for each other, so I saw him as very tall and very handsome." Now, though, he seems shorter and bonier. And Sturges said he experienced a similar disorientation when, honeymooning with Eleanor at his mother's house in Woodstock, he answered the door to a young woman. "My mother's sleeping," he informed this apparent stranger, who surprised him by inquiring, "And how are *you*, Preston?" She was the former love of his life, Estelle.[3]

The other scene was Jean's telephone conversation with Charles's father, where she says she'll have no alimony and nothing to do with lawyers, all she wants is for Charles to come to her and ask her to be free. Sturges says this was precisely what he communicated to the Huttons' lawyers when Eleanor was divorcing him, and though Eleanor says she never even considered asking if Preston wanted alimony, Preston—knowing that his wife's family believed he'd married for money—may well have *felt* like Jean.

Still, what's most autobiographical about this film is its female protagonist.

With her keen wit, love of adventure, romantic imagination, aristocratic bear-ing, and free spirit, Jean, more than any of his characters to date, resembled Sturges's mother. The opening boat scenes, with their Freudian allusions to water and the subconscious, also suggest Mary's first liberating journey, albeit to the Old rather than the New World. And it could be argued that while the Pike's "Bridgefield" estate honors the Sturges family's Fairfield origins, the S.S. *Southern Queen*, with its elegance, air of unreality and promise of forward motion, pays tribute to Mary's view of life as a glorious quest.

After the success of *McGinty* and *Christmas in July*, Paramount gave Sturges a significantly larger budget, allowing him to be choosier about casting. He took some time settling on *The Lady Eve*'s lead players: first it was Madeleine Carroll and Fred MacMurray (curiously, considering Sturges's disappoint-ment with *Remember the Night*), next Henry Fonda and Paulette Goddard. Fonda, very much a star since John Ford's *Young Mr. Lincoln* and *Grapes of Wrath*, stayed on. But Goddard backed out just as Barbara Stanwyck was forced to relinquish her starring role in William Wellman's *Reaching for the Sun* because of an eye infection. Two years earlier, Sturges had told Stanwyck, always cast in dramas, that he would one day write her a great film comedy. Now, allowing her weeks to recuperate before shooting began, Sturges cast Stanwyck opposite Fonda (also far from the conventional comic type). He cast Charles Coburn and Eugene Pallette as their respective fathers and William Demarest as Muggsy, while the Paramount character actors who were now considered Sturges's stock company filled in as boat stewards and pursers and bar tenders. Harry Rosenthal has a walk-on as a piano tuner, and Al Bridge, in memorable deadpan, evokes the waiter who insists his customers will drink nothing but Hopsie Pike's Pale: "They want the ale that won for Yale . . . rah . . . rah . . . rah." Robert Greig, the perennial dignified butler, displays magnificent restraint as cake gets slapped in his face and Charles's snake gets wound around his lower leg like an anklet. And Vic Potel is unexpectedly sensitive as the purser who shows Charles photographs incriminating the Harringtons.

Shooting began the last week in October, again with Victor Milner as cine-matographer and Paul Jones producing. Mel Epstein replaced Dink Temple-ton as Assistant Director. Like Dink, Mel was a powerful man, who respected but was not intimidated by Sturges. Mel, who has worked with many gifted filmmakers, feels that Sturges had a more interesting approach to writing comedy than anyone he ever knew. This approach, as Sturges explained it, was to write his protagonists into a box, where there seemed no hope for them.

Then, as the goal of his "hook" system was to have one line trigger a response, the purpose of trapping his characters was to extricate them—ingeniously.

While filming *The Lady Eve*, Epstein recalls, Sturges was determined that he alone should wield power. The two men got off to an uneasy start when, their first day on the set, Sturges gave Mel explicit instructions about wiring, which was the assistant director's province. And Mel replied, "I'm not listening, Preston, you tell me what you want to see in front of the camera, and I'll get it there." Preston, Mel remembers, would not relent, but neither did he flaunt his seniority: "He covered up, he said, 'Well, look I taught wire work at Vassar.' And when we got into some discussion about photography, he'd say, 'Wait a second, I taught photography at Vassar.' He was a great guy. Preston could do nearly everything better than anybody else, and he knew it. When he says, 'I taught photography at Vassar,' he's saying don't tell me about it, but he's doing it in a charming way."

Still, in Mel's opinion, Sturges very much needed a discerning producer like Paul Jones because "Preston had thirty ideas a minute and no way of evaluating them." When he hired Mel, Paul Jones had warned him that Preston required "an awful lot of tightening in," and after shooting began, Paul would ask Mel to call him when Preston got to a particular scene. "I'd say, why Paul? And he'd say, 'Well, I've got a feeling he's going to do such and such'—for instance, have somebody fly off his handle for no reason, instead of behaving in character—and sure enough Preston would do just that. And Paul would whisper to him, and he'd stop."

Nonetheless, Mel did not consider Sturges an extravagant director. "At that time they used to have a rule at the studio that in order to take two prints of the same subject you had to get permission from the front office. Well, working with Preston, I used to ignore that rule. Because Preston knew what he wanted every minute; yet he couldn't always communicate it to the players the first time, and I didn't realize what he was after until he got it." Epstein compares Sturges to another Paramount director, Josef von Sternberg, who had no compunctions about unnecessarily ordering retakes. Sturges, however, was responsible—he just cared more about his art than about finances.[4]

Before *The Lady Eve*, Barbara Stanwyck had starred with Gary Cooper in *Meet John Doe*, and she said that where the Capra set was like a "cathedral," *The Lady Eve* was a "carnival."[5] Stanwyck, who always arrived early and was known for her sweetness and good humor, immediately hit it off with Sturges, but then everyone on the *Eve* set got along, and the film's publicist remembers how, between shots, rather than going their own way, the actors would relax in director-type chairs and just chat or maybe run through their lines with

Preston (middle) with Henry Fonda and Barbara Stanwyck on the set of The Lady Eve.

Preston.[6] The morning Preston shot Stanwyck's bedroom scene he wore a bathrobe: to get into the mood, he told the players. And when they shot a scene where Fonda, seated at Stanwyck's feet, grimaces with repressed desire as she caresses his hair, Stanwyck couldn't help bursting out laughing time and again—and Preston used that ebullience, patiently stopping when she laughed and then starting where he'd left off, now from a slightly different camera angle. Later, the film's gifted editor, Stuart Gilmore, pieced Sturges's thirty-odd takes into one of the film's smoothest and most artful sequences.

There were some difficult moments during the filming because Sturges wouldn't use a stuntman, and Fonda had to do all his own falling, which was dangerous and sometimes painful. Playing against his image as the strong, quiet American, Fonda gave a superb comic performance. And the irony was that while he endured the dinner scene debacles without so much as a scratch, on the final day of shooting, he went to answer a telephone and walked off a three-foot platform, fell on his stomach, and sprained his wrist.[7]

Sturges finished *The Lady Eve* in forty-one days, just two days behind schedule and only slightly over budget. To celebrate, he closed The Players to the public for the night and invited the cast, crew, and their spouses for a party. The advance word on Sturges's new film was so good that three weeks before its opening, Edith Head's costumes for Stanwyck and Fonda were deemed worthy of a long newspaper article. After a private screening of *Eve*, Al Lewin wired Sturges, "[I] laughed till I cried."[8] John Huston cabled, "IT'S PER-FECTLY WONDERFUL AND SO ARE YOU";[9] and Darryl Zanuck, who'd lent Henry Fonda to Paramount on the condition that Sturges would in return some day direct a film for him at Fox, began clamoring for Paramount to immediately make good on its promise. Even those who'd most admired Sturges's earlier films were surprised by the complexity of this romance, which many would consider his crowning achievement.

Indeed, with its luminous images of boats and trains, its healthful eroticism and switches in mood from moment to moment, *The Lady Eve* is the quintessential Sturges movie. Furthermore, it's the film where Sturges's comic vision and love of slapstick most perfectly coalesce. From the second he sets eyes on Jean, Charles gets buffeted about like a silent comic: sprawled flat on his face when Jean trips him in the boat dining room; coaxed onto a chair in her stateroom, only to get swatted off and driven wild as she runs her hand through his hair.

The film is filled with images of descending. At the Pike's party for Eve, Charles three times comes down the same staircase: always with dire results. First, distracted by Muggsy's motioning at Eve, Charles stumbles over a sofa, ruining his dress jacket. Then, Muggsy, trying to spare his master another heartbreak, sluices dinner over Charles's second suit. And finally, Charles, af-ter following Eve's order to untangle her dress from a chair leg, gets butted by a passing tray, which—needless to say—topples him, as coffee scalds his last set of clothes.

Charles's most stupendous descent is from the train steps into the mud as he flees Eve's wedding night revelations, but Charles also races down flight after flight of stairs to consummate his passion in the film's exhilarating end. Beyond their metaphorical subtext (man's falling in love, out of grace, off his high horse), Charles's plunges reflect the nature of this particular romance and also Sturges's view of success. "You have the darndest way of bumping a fellow down and then bouncing him up again," Charles tells Jean, the morning after he meets her. "I could imagine life with you being a series of ups and downs . . . lights and shadows . . . sometimes irritation . . . but very much happiness." So the bumping, while painful, is not without satisfactions; not an obstacle to be fought, but an ongoing and necessary part of happiness on earth.

Many historians, looking back on Sturges's career, would claim his importance was as a writer rather than a director, but *The Lady Eve* shows how seamlessly these two roles intersect. Take the early scene in the ship's dining room where Jean dispenses a running commentary on the husband-seekers vying for Charles's attention. While her repartee is smart ("The dropped kerchief! That hasn't been used since Lily Langtry . . . you'll have to pick it up yourself, madam . . . it's a shame, but he doesn't care for the flesh; he'll never see it"), what makes the scene truly original is that we see all the action through Jean's pocket mirror: a frame within a frame and Sturges's reflexive comment not only on voyeurism but on watching as a way of holding life at bay. Or take the wedding, which is announced, arranged, and executed in a wordless montage sequence, punctuated by shots of a spiraling wedding cake, that lasts just a hundred seconds. Or the revenge scene, whose irony is meaningfully intensified by lightning bolts, forays into train tunnels, and torrential rain. Even the title sequence, with an animated snake slithering through the credit names, and Sturges's use of the film's haunting musical theme contribute enormously to *The Lady Eve*'s effectiveness.

The Lady Eve is a love story, about the terrors and bliss of passion. It's also about pride and prejudice, about the confusion of evil and good. "You don't know very much about girls, Hopsie," Jean warns Charles in the beginning; "the best ones aren't as good as you probably think they are, and the bad ones aren't as bad . . . not nearly as bad." Jean too has much to learn about the enigma of identity, about desire and forgiveness, about sacrificing control. So in a sense this is a film about the getting of wisdom, yet it's also very definitely *against* earnestness. Charles's sober marriage proposal to Eve is mercilessly parodied. And then there's the ending, where Jean, coming to Charles, relinquishes her victory and Charles, saying "I don't want to know," dismisses his right or even his ability to judge. This is Sturges's most eloquent paean to capriciousness, to giddy befuddlement, to the mysterious compulsion and mixed motives that, rather than certitude, propel romantic love.

The Lady Eve opened on Ash Wednesday, February 26, 1941 at New York's Paramount and grossed $115,758 in its first three weeks, becoming Sturges's first bona fide commercial triumph. The reviews were such unqualified raves that Preston told Bosley Crowther, they "scared the bejesus out of me and the Lord only knows how the next film will turn out. I feel like making a good safe tragedy." In his *Times* review Crowther claimed Sturges "the most refreshing new force to hit the American motion pictures in the past five years," explaining: "The secret of Mr. Sturges's distinctive style is yet to be analyzed, but mainly it is composed of exceedingly well-turned dialogue, a perfect sense for the ridiculous in the most mundane and simple encounters, and generous but always precise touches of downright slapstick. . . . Mr. Sturges writes with a skimming but penetrating touch," [10] he observed, and where the *Times* had seven years before unfavorably compared *The Good Fairy* to René Clair's *A Nous La Liberté*, Crowther now called Sturges America's René Clair, further stipulating that Clair, Capra, Leo McCarey, "and even Charlie Chaplin at his best have nothing on Mr. Sturges when it comes to command of his art." [11]

Crowther also compared *The Lady Eve* to *It Happened One Night*: interestingly, since in years to come so many of the same film scholars who would declare this Capra film as Hollywood's first screwball comedy would call *The Lady Eve* its last, the end of an era. Indeed, far more than *Easy Living*, *The Lady Eve*, for all its painfulness, does conform to the curious prerequisites of the screwball genre: notably that all the bizarre events should reflect the will of a strong protagonist. And, slapstick notwithstanding, at heart this of all Sturges's films is less farcical than classically, even realistically, comic. For it is his only major work where success is not conferred by luck but evolves naturally from the actions of the characters. When proposing to the Lady Eve, Charles pompously declares that he does not deserve her. And, preparing to torment him, she with high irony replies he does. And so too, having conquered pride, Charles deserves Jean and his happiness. Buried within the worldliness of *The Lady Eve* is an insidiously romantic message: that love is powerful.

Sturges began writing *The Lady Eve* during the autumn of 1938, when he was courting Louise Sargent, and saw it released three years later when she was expecting his first son. He was forty-two years old, Paramount's "fair-haired boy" of the moment, owner of a burgeoning restaurant, on top of the world. If Preston's life were a Sturges comedy, here is where the story would end.

CHAPTER **18**

Louise wanted five children. She'd wanted five children ever since she was five. And Preston, who'd long ago told Estelle Mudge he loved babies, now had his heart set on producing sons. He was as eager to start a family as Louise was. When, months after their marriage, Louise still had not conceived, they grew frustrated. Louise consulted specialists, who had them making love at certain times, in just the right positions. Then she had three minor surgeries—but still no pregnancy. At first, Louise felt awkward about discussing such an intimate problem with their close doctor friend, Bertie Woolfan. But when nearly two years had passed and there was still no progress she, without telling Preston, made an appointment at Bertie's office. He performed a minor procedure to clear her tubes, and soon after she missed her period and got good news at last. Louise and especially Preston felt deeply indebted to Bertie. Once, he'd saved Arnold Shroeder's life. Now, it seemed, he'd made it possible for them to have a baby.

Preston and Louise were both tremendously happy. Preston began building a special nursery; Louise read up on child rearing. Louise's friend Nina Laemmle, Ernst Laemmle's clever British wife, was also pregnant. And while their husbands stayed up until all hours working, they sat up too, listening to rats running through the paneling of the old Ivar Avenue house, laughing and speculating about motherhood.

It was lucky Preston and Louise had their coming child in common, for in many ways their lives and interests were now separate. Preston was so utterly preoccupied with his work that their only vacation, since they'd married, was a long holiday weekend at Catalina on the boat; and even then he'd spent much of the time writing dialogue. At home, they were almost never alone. If it wasn't Preston's colleagues and admirers, then it was the unfortunates he couldn't help inviting in for meals. Some came back for days or weeks running.

And even in their bedroom, Louise and Preston weren't really on their own since the phone rang constantly. Their so-called private number was common knowledge to every jeweler in L.A. Preston, eager to see his beautiful wife decked out in diamonds and furs, was as sought after as Mary in *Easy Living*.

Preston himself needed four sets of clothes, because as well as chain smoking his little cigars, he was now constantly putting on weight and then feverishly dieting. He did not share Louise's passion for an orderly life any more than her matter-of-fact attitude toward his filmmaking. And it became more and more apparent as the months and years passed that though, to please Preston, she'd come to his rushes or visit his set, Louise had no particular interest in the movie business. Like Eleanor with Preston's playwrighting, she thought of filmmaking as what Preston did, not who he was; she'd married the man, not the vocation.

Besides, Louise had a strong will of her own. One incident, a year after their marriage, is indicative of their opposing priorities. The Sturgeses had scheduled a dinner party. When Louise met Preston at the door that night he excitedly exclaimed, "I got it!" He'd at last hit upon a way to show rather than state that McGinty and his wife have never slept together. Motioning and miming, Preston began describing the idea to Louise, who cut him off, asking, "Preston, do you realize we have dinner guests who have been waiting for you for an hour?"[1]

This sort of quarrel must have been routine—yet, scarcely unique to their marriage. And if Preston was obsessive, even romantic about his films, he was also gregarious. How he detested the Gordon Craig-type solitary "genius" living only for his art! Preston proudly identified himself as a social and connubial creature. Two years after his marriage, he still seemed deeply attached to Louise: at least in public. Gilletti, who was with them day and night, thought the Sturgeses as happy a married couple as he'd ever seen. Their ardor so impressed the Filipino houseboy, Leo Calibo, that when he left the Sturges household in late 1942, he wrote "Missus": "[Mister] is in love to you and I know he will be your loving husband for the lifetime."[2] Or perhaps Leo was trying to allay some insecurity about Preston in Louise.

Superficially, the Sturgeses' life was exactly as it had been since Preston began directing. When he was making a film, Preston's days were spent at the studio, his late nights at The Players and—later still—writing new screenplays with Gilletti and Ernst Laemmle into the wee hours. When he wasn't shooting, Preston spent afternoons holding court in his Paramount suite. A friend remembers charcoal sketches of Victorian women framed in funeral wreaths on the walls, the smell of tamales, and always much commotion.[3] At home,

Preston worked at the four-sided desk he'd created out of filing cabinets topped with varnished pine in his Ivar Avenue study. Here the novelty was that Gilletti was ensconced in the hole in the middle of the desk, while Preston sat on the outside, often with his shoe propped on a corner of the desk, never far from the brewing coffee.

Tuesdays and Fridays Preston religiously went to the fights (Louise went with him on Fridays), and Sunday night he and Louise gave their party. This event, involving up to thirty-odd guests for a buffet meal, was Louise's project. Thursday, she confirmed the guest list. Friday, she went to the Farmer's Market for food, then began cooking that afternoon and continued for the better part of the weekend.[4] Louise had between 150 and 175 cookbooks—most of them presents from Preston's agent, Frank Orsatti, and everyone praised her meals. Though she hated being flattered and sometimes tired of trying to keep her standards up week after week, for the most part she loved entertaining.

Winter parties were in the game room, but on warm summer nights the Sturgeses set up tables with umbrellas in the gardens outside. At one party, Tally Wyler recalls, Willie got carried away and dove fully dressed into the swimming pool. At another, José Iturbi sat down to play a duet with his sister Amparo; then, as an entranced audience gathered round, Iturbi just kept on playing.[5] The Sturgeses' parties were casual and gracious, never flashy. Along with the Wylers and Laemmles, certain very close friends showed up most every Sunday—Priscilla and Bertie Woolfan (who lent Preston their agreeable servant, James, for the occasion), Bill Demarest and his wife Lucille, the Paul Joneses, Gilletti, the Dink Templetons and, after *Sullivan's Travels*, the cameraman John Seitz and his wife. John Huston was a frequent guest, as were a growing number of famous émigré filmmakers: René Clair, Max Ophüls, Jean Renoir. Renoir, who called The Players "the center of the Hollywood Resistance Movement" because it was the meeting point of so many bar stool French patriots, soon became a good friend. Sturges, Renoir notes in his memoirs, "closed his eyes to unpaid bills," and his generosity was "proverbial."[6]

Billy Wilder and John Huston were particularly aware of Preston's generosity in the early forties. Both were then writers who longed to move up in the film world, and Preston wholeheartedly encouraged them. After he'd finished *McGinty*, Preston ran into John Huston in the Brown Derby one night and spent two hours exhorting him to insist that Warner Brothers allow him to direct his screenplays. Then, when he learned Huston's first directing assignment was Dashiell Hammett's *The Maltese Falcon*, rather than an original project, Preston was upset: the point, he lectured Huston, was that a film should have a single creator.[7] Nonetheless, Preston arranged a dinner where he plied Huston with diagrams and all sorts of practical advice about filmmaking. One tip of Preston's which Huston particularly valued was that when a man walks out of a frame on the left side, you must be sure to have him come in on the right.[8] Obviously, Preston wanted to spare Huston all the pratfalls he himself had just encountered.

With Billy Wilder, Preston was similarly solicitous. Wilder, who saw *The Power and the Glory* in Germany, had admired Sturges for years and looked him up when he came to Paramount in the mid-thirties. They became friends. Many evenings these two discussed their similar views of writing versus directing: how you have to be born a writer. It's impossible for a director at age thirty-five or forty to learn to write. However, Sturges and Wilder agreed, it's perfectly possible for a forty-year-old writer to learn the craft of directing. It was Preston's success which impelled Paramount to take a chance and let Wilder direct *The Major and the Minor*. Wilder was touched when Preston appeared the first morning on the set. Wilder was wearing a sweater, which Preston lifted up. "All wrong," Preston, shaking his head at Wilder's slim belt, informed the new director. What he'd be doing now was primarily a physical effort, he'd need a strong belt to support his back. "What size are you?" Preston asked. "Thirty-two," said Wilder. And Preston handed him a wide leather belt which, having added a few extra notches, Wilder still wears today.[9]

Of course, Preston was not equally generous with everyone. When his father's friend Sidney Love lost his fortune and in the early forties wrote Preston, desperate for work, Preston coyly replied, "As far as my influence is concerned it has never succeeded in securing a job for anyone." [10] Then, reluctantly, Preston admitted he might find the elderly man some job at The Players. He did—as nightwatchman. And it's true that even when Sidney Love grew too sick to work, Preston continued paying his salary, but this was a mere twenty-five dollars a week. Where Preston's letters to the wealthy Mr. Love had always been deferential, he now betrayed a certain righteous exasperation, as in this reply to Sidney's fears of penury: "My dear Sidney: I thought I had made clear to you in our last conversation that your well-being and comfort meant a great deal to me and that I would do anything within my power for my father's friend. It goes without saying, then, that your salary will continue indefinitely. Don't worry about it." [11]

Then too, Preston, while supportive of Wilder, Huston, Clair and Renoir, did nothing to promote the careers of his own ambitious employees. Gilletti and Ernst Laemmle were devoted and intelligent. Ernst in particular had a keen appreciation of Sturges's artistic goals and was unafraid to give tough criticism. He sat in on all scriptwriting sessions and sometimes contributed bits of dialogue as well as discerning comments. (For instance, Nina Laemmle believes it was Ernst who came up with "Positively the same dame!" for *The Lady Eve*'s finale.) Yet, whereas Preston made $3,250 a week before his bonus, Paramount paid Ernst just $150—and only when Sturges had a film in production. Preston did not offer to enlarge Ernst's salary, nor did he help Ernst and Gilletti find work more suited to their gifts.

For her part, Louise found Preston not so much generous as eager to shower her with what he felt were appropriate presents. She told Preston she liked emeralds and pearls, not diamonds. Still, Preston felt a man in his position should buy his wife diamonds, so he did. They also disagreed about fur coats. Louise believed a well-cut cloth coat made far more sense in California, but Preston was determined that his wife should own furs.[12] Nina Laemmle remembers one Sturges Christmas party where Preston insisted that Louise model the fox coat he'd just bought her. Louise protested, but finally gave in, while the guests felt embarrassed for both of them.[13]

If Preston was erratic in his personal generosity, he consistently resisted Hollywood's communal drives. In November of 1941, producer Arthur Hornblow, Jr., wrote Sturges: "Perhaps you will be interested to hear that the producers' and directors' group has responded with great generosity to our Community Chest appeal. . . . I have been able to account for everyone but yourself." Preston was also, according to a letter from *their* membership, "the only recognized director in the industry" who refused to join the Screen Directors Guild.

"It is only because of my very deep conviction that guilds are principally useful to the lawyers whom they enrich that I must decline the invitation," he excused himself. "It is the mode at the moment for everyone to belong to some union or subdivision of a union. Being so much out of fashion, I must seem very strange to you. Certainly, I failed to make myself clear to my friends Mr. Frank Capra, Mr. Frank Lloyd, or Mr. William Wyler. Certainly also, I failed to make myself clear to my friends of the Screenwriters' Guild during the years in which I was overpowered by my desire not to join their organization. I am probably a little tetched in the haid [sic] but that's how it is."[14]

Two developments in the spring of 1941 would profoundly affect Preston's future. The first was William LeBaron's decision to leave Paramount for Fox and his replacement by Buddy DeSylva.

DeSylva was a brash, expansive man who made his name composing songs for Broadway hits (*Follies*, *Good News*) and over the past decade had written and produced many successful Hollywood musicals. Since Bing Crosby was now Paramount's top-grossing star, Frank Freeman must have liked the idea of a musically inclined production chief. It helped too that DeSylva had an instinct for the broadly comic road pictures Crosby and Bob Hope were making at the time. DeSylva's problem, from Sturges's perspective, was that he had no feeling for satire or farce, nor did he have LeBaron's intellectual flair, and he had little patience for prestige films, much less movies as an art form. He enjoyed wielding power and would not leave even the studio's most trusted directors alone. Rather, he bombarded them with suggestions. DeSylva's gruff charm appealed to many—Louise Sturges thought him a very funny man, and Billy Wilder found him easy to work for. Sturges too initially hit it off with DeSylva.

That first spring, Preston was so eager to accommodate his new boss that he felt impelled to cable DeSylva in New York even about a change in his current film's *costuming*: "WHAT DO YOU THINK OF HAVING LITTLE GIRL LOCKED OUT OF HER HOTEL IN EVENING DRESS INSTEAD OF GOING AWAY OUTFIT FOR HER FIRST MEETING WITH SULLIVAN? SORT OF ALL DRESSED UP AND NO PLACE TO GO. . . . PAUL [JONES] AND I WOULD LIKE TO DO THIS, IF IT MEETS WITH YOUR APPROVAL."[15] But it was not in Preston's nature to sustain an obsequious attitude. Inevitably, these two large egos would conflict.

The movie Sturges was now filming was his fourth film in less than two years, and he had his own daunting track record as well as a new boss to contend with. Louise, meanwhile, was having a difficult pregnancy. After the fourth month, her doctor put her to bed, and miscarriage was a real possibility. It was around this time that Preston began seeing a twenty-one-year-old secretary. While Louise knew nothing at first, it was all the talk at Paramount. Gilletti and Ernst Laemmle were confused because Preston still doted on Louise, and they knew he was not by nature promiscuous. So why was he so unchivalrously betraying his pregnant wife, and why with this person?

Jeannie La Vell was one of several young girls in the secretarial pool at Paramount. When Preston asked her goal in life, she replied that all she wanted was to make enough money to support her mother and herself. This, she felt, "touched something in him." He asked her to dinner, and the next day the head of the secretarial pool fired her for socializing with a Paramount director. Preston doubled her salary and hired her himself, to work with Gilletti.[16] Soon Jeannie and Preston were lovers, seeing each other constantly. One of Louise's friends describes Jeannie as very attractive and chic, but common. Another remembers her as "just a little minx." The image they conjure is of some cross between Bunny in *Recapture* and Madeleine in *Child of Manhattan*, the presumption being that Preston's interest was purely sexual, but this was not in fact true.

Jeannie was intelligent and deeply involved with his writing. She understood what Sturges was after and fought him as an equal when she *didn't* like some dialogue or slapstick routine he dictated to her. Eddie Bracken, who sat in on many of Sturges's writing sessions, believes Jeannie was his most discerning critic ever. "They would have great arguments, but very pleasant ones. She was the only one who could look at Sturges and say, 'That's terrible.' She would be right on target, she knew him like a book. And Sturges listened to her like he listened to nobody else." Jeannie was also a keen judge of character and loyally protected her boss from enemies at the studio.[17] She did not have Louise's aristocratic bearing, but she was far from a dumb broad.

Sturges would later say that his passion for Louise diminished because of all the unspontaneous sex they had, trying for her to get pregnant. Louise would lament that, when she was pregnant, Preston treated her as if she had some "dread disease; he was terrified I would stumble" and abort the baby.[18] Afterwards, Preston was so desperate for her to be the right sort of mother, "it was as if suddenly I got an aura of the saintly about me"; he put her on a pedestal and, try as she would, she could not get off—could not make him see her as a lover.

Sturges would also say he knew his marriage to Louise was over when he came home that night, having figured out how to show McGinty hasn't slept with Catherine, and Louise, thinking only of her dinner guests, couldn't fathom his relief.[19] This makes the affair with Jeannie La Vell more understandable. It also affirms a pattern in Preston's relationships. From Estelle, who, like his mother, expected Preston to make a name for himself, Sturges turned to Eleanor, who had no interest in his career. Then, from Eleanor he went to Bianca, who identified so intensely with his every endeavor, and from Bianca to the more Eleanor-like Louise. Then to Jeannie. But, of course, it was not that simple. Preston was far from through with Louise when he took up with Jeannie. He was still sending his wife flowers and telling her how deeply he loved her. However brazen he seemed, Preston must have been, far more than his friends, confused and saddened by this affair he'd begun during Louise's pregnancy. As much as the arrival of Buddy DeSylva, it would over time affect his career.

But in 1941 Sturges was in his heyday, beloved at Paramount. Both his eagerness to please and his eccentric energy are evident in an incident from this time which assistant director Holly Morse remembers. One day, wandering through the studio, Preston saw the director Charlie Vidor huffing off, enraged at Buddy DeSylva. "Buddy, what's the matter?" Preston asked DeSylva, who told him Vidor's *New York Town*, with Mary Martin and Fred McMurray, was in terrible shape. They had to rewrite and shoot a whole section by Sunday. But Vidor refused to cooperate, saying he wouldn't spend his weekend revising a perfectly good film.

"I'll do it," said Sturges, making a point that he wanted neither credit nor money. DeSylva agreed and introduced him to Holly Morse, who showed Sturges the film. This was Friday. Before heading off for the fights, Sturges assured Morse he'd write the new scenes Saturday morning. But an increasingly anxious Morse watched Preston fritter away the whole day until, at nine at night, Preston suddenly told Gilletti, "Get your book." Then, to Morse's amazement, he dictated seventeen pages straight, never hesitating. Not a single change was required. They shot Preston's scenes exactly as written and brought the film in to DeSylva's satisfaction the following night.[20]

This was May 1941, and by now Sturges was deeply involved in *Sullivan's Travels*. The idea for it may have come to him years before, in the early thirties, when John Huston and Willie Wyler planned to make a film about wild kids on the road and traveled around as bums, doing research. Preston joined them for a couple of nights in L.A., touring the hobo parts of town, staying in a flophouse with a common shower. For all his cynicism about political solutions, Preston was always distressed by the plight of the poor. He was now also disturbed by his friends' tales about the ravaging war in Europe. And he wondered about his own attitude toward misfortune: how does a lucky man confront an unjust world? In *Christmas in July*, Sturges had shown the poor worker yearning for wealth and happiness. In *Sullivan's Travels*, he would show the successful man determined to join the destitute so he can understand suffering. But *Sullivan's Travels* was to be about more than luck and injustice. After *The Lady Eve*, Preston had told Bosley Crowther he felt like making a good, safe tragedy. His point was that comedy is hard and dangerous, and he was about to prove it in a film that consciously experiments with form.

Sullivan's Travels opens with a shot of two men fighting for their lives on the roof of a boxcar. Moments later, "The End" flashes on the screen, lights come up in a projection booth, and we learn we've been watching a film-within-a-film. John S. Sullivan, a hugely successful comic movie director, has screened this boxcar opus for his studio chiefs because he wants to make a film with the same social impact. He's tired of directing comedies. Comedies are irrelevant in dire times like these. So his next project will be a dark and "meaningful" film called *O Brother, Where Art Thou?* In order to write an authentic script, he'll need to live the life of a bum and "won't come back til I know what trouble is."

The studio heads disapprove, but since "Sully" has made them a fortune with films like *Hey, Hey in the Hayloft* and *Ants in Your Pants of 1939*, they reluctantly indulge him. Sully borrows bum clothes from the wardrobe department and, disregarding his butler's reproof, "Poverty is . . . a positive plague . . . to be stayed away from, even for purposes of study," sets out to court misfortune. Not too successfully at first, for the studio sends a land yacht full of solicitous eccentrics to guard him every inch of the way. Then, the first ride Sully hitches winds him right back in Hollywood.

Here he gets his breakfast bought by a beautiful blonde, who's just that morning given up on her ambition to become a movie star. She's going home, she tells Sully, who, try as he may to concentrate on the larger problems of the world, can't help involving himself in her dilemma. So he gets his automobile to give the girl a lift, and the police, believing him a bum, arrest him briefly for car theft. When the girl learns who he *really* is, she's furious he's duped her but admires his mission. He must take her along, she insists, because: "You don't know anything about . . . anything. You don't know how to get a meal; you don't know how to keep a secret . . . you can't even stay out of town. . . . I know fifty times as much about trouble as you ever will."

Unwillingly, Sullivan agrees she can come. Both dress as hoboes and, with studio cameras hot on their trail, they make a great publicity story while also dabbling in penury: eating wretched food, sleeping in flophouses. They fall in love, and after a couple of weeks Sully has had enough hunger and cold and agrees the adventure is over. His final gesture will be passing out a thousand dollars' worth of five-dollar bills that night at the train station.

And while most of the station's needy beam at Sully's generosity, there's one bum who's not content with five bucks. He follows Sully to a dark area of the tracks, slugs him over the head and steals his shoes and the rest of his cash—then shoves Sully into a freight car. When the bum (chasing his dollars) gets killed by an oncoming train, the world presumes he's the missing John L. Sullivan. Sully's studio heads are appropriately distraught. The girl is beside herself, mourning.

Meanwhile, Sully, temporarily amnesiac and looking very much the bum, turns up the next day in a freight yard. When a railroad attendant insults and strikes him, Sully angrily hits back. The next thing he knows he's in court where he's sentenced to six years of hard labor. Now Sully truly suffers: working on a chain gang, getting punished for one small infringement after the next, and kept from making calls or writing letters. No one for a moment believes he's John L. Sullivan—Sullivan's dead, after all. Besides, a friendly guard informs Sully, he looks more like a soda jerk than a picture director.

There is one reprieve in the prisoners' miserable week. Sunday, a black minister invites them to watch movies at his church—and, not just any movies, but Walt Disney cartoons. The prisoners laugh and laugh, and finally even Sully can't help chortling and cheering up. Maybe comedy is not quite as meaningless as he'd figured.

Still, Sully is not anxious to stick around, testing this theory. Since he's forbidden contact with the outside world, the only way to reach his friends, Sully perceives, is to get his picture in the newspaper. So Sully announces he's murdered John L. Sullivan. And when his face appears in the Hollywood journals, his studio chiefs rush to his rescue—with the exuberant girl in tow. She and Sully will marry, of course. Of course, too, the studio executives presume Sully—with all this suffering under his belt—will make a great hit film of *O Brother, Where Art Thou?* But Sully no longer intends to make his "meaningful" picture: first because he's too happy; second, because he hasn't suffered enough, and mostly because he wants to make a comedy. Yes, a comedy: "There's a lot to be said for making people laugh. . . . Did you know that's all some people have? It isn't much . . . but it's better than nothing in this cockeyed caravan."

With its production chiefs, Capra-admiring hero, and its heroine pining for a letter to Lubitsch, *Sullivan's Travels* is very much a film about filmmaking. It can be unabashedly self-referential: when a Hollywood police officer, wondering about Sully's relationship to the girl, gets told, "There's always a girl in the picture. Haven't you ever been to the movies?" Or, when Sully, languishing on the chain gang, observes, "If ever a plot needed a twist this one does." More subtly, *Sullivan's Travels* appropriates every conceivable movie form: gritty realism in the opening film-within-a-film; farce when the studio land yacht careens through overgrown fields; high comic romance at Sully's mansion; pathos in the flophouses; melodrama in the train scene assault; and even a touch of the musical as black parishioners welcome prisoners to their church.

Audaciously, Sturges mixes genres *within* scenes. The sequence where Sully and the girl set out on their hobo journey opens with a comic shot of the fretting butler bidding his master-dressed-as-bum adieu. Then, there's a swift change in mood as Sully and the girl join very real and stolid-looking tramps seated in a junk heap. Next, Sturges cuts, as in an action film, to the train preparing to take off. And as the train pulls toward the junk heap, an overhead shot of tramps scuttling toward passing cars carries the poignancy and symbolic weight Sully so admired in the box car opus. Then the shot narrows to focus on two individual tramps, bounding into an open car, with Sully and the girl struggling to follow. Though he manages to push the girl ahead, Sully for the life of him can't get up: he leaps, he falls, he huffs, he flails. Meanwhile, the two tramps, like vaudeville foils, watch with undisguised superiority. The one chews on a straw. "Amateurs," he observes, in an accent as cultured as Sully's butler's. So we're back to comedy.

And for all its formal complexity, *Sullivan's Travels* is narratively seamless and filled with recurring motifs. There's the train motif, for instance, introduced in the film-within-a-film opening boxcar struggle and recapitulated through the hobo episodes, the assault on Sully by the train tracks, and Sully's own bitter attack on the railroad employee. By this time, the idea of trouble has come full circle: from a concept Sully relishes to a reality he can't impede. Or there's the congregation motif. The first time Sturges shows a group assembled it's at a weepy movie. The audience is distracted—rustling candy papers, trying to make out with the person in the next seat. One boy petulantly blows his whistle. A baby screeches disconsolately throughout the solemn show. Sturges's next "congregation" scene is scarcely happier. Here we're at a revival meeting where the self-absorbed preacher gesticulates wildly from a raised stage, while, below, the motley crowd mostly doze or stare bewilderedly off into space, undeflected from their private woes. But the parishioners in the black church scene are conspicuously different. Their minister literally walks among them, and they obviously glean communal pleasure singing, "Let My People Go," welcoming the prisoners who file in to share their Sunday cartoon movies. Now, as the cartoon characters cavort on screen, there is release, indeed—and also true community. Laughter is infectious and undiscriminating—available to all humanity. The comic experience, as Sturges portrays it, is—like religion for the faithful—a profound, if temporary release from suffering. It won't change the world, but it will make life more tolerable. It's no coincidence that the cartoon scene, the film's emotional climax, takes place in a church.

Nonetheless, *Sullivan's Travels* shows no great love for groups of any sort. Whenever Sully starts contemplating the plight of the unemployed or wars' victims or any species of sufferers in the general sense, you can be sure his eyes will glaze over or he'll do something impossibly naïve—like inquire what the hobo sharing his boxcar thinks of the "labor situation." (The hobo's response is to promptly quit the car.) His views of "the poor" are so quixotic that he exposes himself to the greedy tramp who attacks and might well have

The church scene in Sullivan's Travels. *For the faithful, religion provides a profound, if temporary release from suffering.*

murdered him. Besides, for all Sully's guilt and good intentions, it's hard to believe his heart is really with the masses. He pities them, but has no answer for their despair. Nonetheless, Sully can use his wealth and ingenuity to help a few troubled individuals—the girl, a man he meets on the road who gratuitously feeds them, and ultimately himself. For what Sully learns is that he's not, as it first seemed, impervious to "real life." With little effort he can join the lowliest, know life at its worst. The trick, he sees, is to *avoid* trouble, to embrace joy with compassion and full knowledge of life's miseries. So comedy is not less but more salutary, perhaps even more meaningful than tragedy. And if, like belting a church hymn, laughter brings spontaneous release from suffering, comedy goes further than religion to insist that success and love are possible—even in *this* world.[21]

Sullivan's Travels downplays Hollywood satire. There are no story conferences, no tantrums by tyrannical producers. Nowhere to be seen are the squabbling egomaniacs who peopled *Song of Joy*, and the studio heads' com-

252

mercial concerns are made to seem eminently reasonable. Whatever their opinions on Sully's social ideals, Sully's bosses couldn't be more solicitous of their director's safety. They send a land yacht after him when he first leaves Hollywood and seem personally touched by his apparent death. Sturges had learned just how far he could go, biting the hand that fed him.

Indeed, it's no coincidence that *Sullivan's Travels* frequently deflects attention from the studio itself to a land yacht full of company oddballs, literally adrift from Hollywood. Sturges had written these parts specifically for his stock company: Bill Demarest was cast as a harassed publicity chief, Mr. Jones, Vic Potel as the omnipresent cameraman, and Torben Meyer, the purser who revealed the Harringtons' identities to Charles in *The Lady Eve*, became a doctor, who fusses over Sully. Torben Meyer, one of Sturges's most devoted players, remembers arguing with Preston during rehearsals about bits of business. Always, Meyer wanted to sport a toupee and speak English as if it were his native tongue, while Preston (whom Meyer addressed as "Maître") liked Meyer's bald head exposed and his lilting German accent. In *Sullivan's Travels*, they compromised. The accent remained, but Meyer got to cover his pate with a jaunty British cap—wholly incongruous with his discombobulated demeanor.

After the great success of *The Lady Eve*, Sturges could have cast major stars for the parts of Sully and his girl. Instead, he picked the unassuming Joel McCrea and Veronica Lake, who'd made only three films and was mostly known for her "peek-a-boo" hairstyle.

Sturges had first noticed Veronica Lake in rushes for Mitchell Leisen's *I Wanted Wings*, some months earlier. She was not sophisticated like Stanwyck, but had a cool, sulky charm and, with her skinny frame and languorous gait, a mixture of coltish innocence and sensuality. There was the obvious seductress quality about Veronica but also a porcelain doll mysteriousness that had not yet been tapped; and Sturges made a point of coming to Veronica's table at lunch and telling her in front of everyone that he knew she was going places.[22] Veronica, considered a difficult actress, was greatly buoyed by Sturges's support and—like so many others at Paramount—eager to work with him.

While Veronica was a new face, Sturges had met Joel McCrea long ago, when Joel came to visit Spencer Tracy on the set for *The Power and the Glory*. Joel told Sturges how much he admired his dialogue, and Sturges replied, "Some day I'll direct pictures, and you're going to be in them." Years passed. McCrea made a solid career, specializing as the hero in western and action films, often with William Wyler or Howard Hawks directing. He fell in love with Frances Dee, and they began one of Hollywood's few enduring marriages. Then, one day, shortly after Joel finished making *Union Pacific* with Cecil B. DeMille, Sturges came over to him at the commissary. Preston said he'd written a film about a movie director specifically for Joel, and Joel said, "What do you mean? They don't write scripts for me. They write them for Gary Cooper, and if they can't get him, they take me." But Sturges insisted *Sullivan's Travels* was written only for Joel. Partly, Joel feels, this was because Preston identified with him, but certainly it was also for the opposite reason: because Joel, *unlike* Preston, was modest about his talents, because he conveyed a certain quizzical naïveté and a deep stability. As with Jimmy in *Christmas in July*, it was important that Sully not be a genius in his field. It was important too that Sullivan should long to make *O Brother, Where Art Thou?* not for his own glory but because he truly wished to do good. No more than McGinty or Jimmy MacDonald was Sully to be a surrogate for the author.

From the start, Joel and Preston got along splendidly. "Many actors and actresses have difficulty interpreting directors, but Preston and I thought along the same line," says McCrea, who believes he and Preston were a marriage of people who loved cinema, though "if we hadn't been in pictures, if we'd been in the ice box business together, Preston and I would have gotten along." And this was not, as with Preston and Willie Wyler or Georges Renevant, because they had similar childhoods—like Louise Sargent, Joel was of pioneer stock, there were no divorceés or European sojourners in *his* family. Joel lived on a ranch outside Los Angeles and thought of himself as a cowboy, while Preston, to him, was a cosmopolitan and an artist. As McCrea saw it, Frank Lloyd (*If I Were King*) was a man of character. Sturges was a man of talent—it was a miracle his character was as good as it was, considering his background. But, "he was a lovable man," and also a man who, unlike the formidable John Ford, needed affection from the people he worked with. You couldn't hurt Ford's feelings, but you could hurt Preston's because he was very emotional.

Joel often had trouble remembering dialogue, but when Preston wrote lines he could remember them—because, he felt, they were so natural. McCrea also admired the way Preston extemporized. For instance, Joel had a cold when they began shooting *Sullivan's Travels* and, rather than covering that up, Sturges worked his sneezes and coughs into the script, making Sully more vulnerable.[23]

What Sturges did have to cover up was Veronica Lake's belly. Though she'd said nothing during casting, Veronica was pregnant. Her costumer, Edith Head, was the first to detect her condition and insisted that Veronica immediately inform Preston, but Veronica was scared and sought out his wife instead. Louise, pregnant, was on the set with another pregnant friend Mary Martin. "The stork club," Preston called them. "Don't tell Preston, but I'm pregnant too," Veronica whispered to Louise. And Louise, in her wry way, responded, "I certainly will not tell him, but I'll give you a two-minute running start to tell him yourself." [24]

At first, Preston was furious. Yet—as when Mary Orr tricked him into interviewing her for *Child of Manhattan*—he was not recriminatory. Preston could understand wanting something so badly you'd even lie to get it: especially if it was a part in *his* film. Still, the movie he'd planned was physically arduous. Because Veronica was nearly six months pregnant when they began shooting, on her doctor's advice, the hobo scenes had to be radically restructured, and a double, the former Rose Bowl Queen, Cheryl Walker, was used for difficult leaps and jumps off trains cars. As for her clothes—besides the girl's hobo outfit, which was naturally baggy, Edith Head skillfully designed empire waist robes and specially cut coats and dresses which, viewed from certain angles, hid Veronica's expanding belly.

After work, Veronica lived up to her reputation for causing trouble. Assistant director Holly Morse remembers her cursing every other word, and, pregnancy notwithstanding, she was always trying to lure the monogamous Joel McCrea into bed with her. It got to the point where Joel, "frightened to death," asked to be alerted if she so much as entered his dressing room, Morse recalls. [25] But on Sturges's set, she behaved like a professional. For all his gregariousness, Sturges, she felt, was as shy as she was, and he took great pains with her performance. He called her a child of the camera, born to be photographed. You could photograph her from any angle, in any type of lighting, and she'd look perfect. Early on, though, Sturges noticed a certain archness about Veronica's acting when she'd overprepared herself, and he finally told her, "Don't ever walk on my set knowing anything about your lines or scenes." [26] She followed his instructions and gave the most nuanced performance of her career.

There was one scare during the production. They were shooting a scene where Sully and the girl dunk each other in his swimming pool, and, following Veronica's doctor's orders, her double was hired for the day. But, when the shot was through, Veronica herself dove into the pool. Sturges began filming as Joel repeated the routines he'd just done with the double. Clearly, they were having fun. But after one playful dunk, Veronica at first did not resurface, and when she did come bobbing up, her petticoat was wound over her head. Joel quickly untwisted the slip and rushed her to the side of the pool while Preston summoned the studio doctor—who pronounced both her and the fetus fine. [27]

Preston, Holly Morse recalls, was always very concerned about Veronica's well-being. When they were shooting the scene where she runs to tell the studio chiefs that Sully is alive, Veronica slipped and fell. She was then seven months pregnant, and Preston was the first to leap from his chair, pick her up and make sure she wouldn't miscarry.[28]

Sturges's cinematographer this time was the gifted John Seitz. Paul Jones was again producing, assisted by Holly Morse. What impressed Morse was how Sturges managed both to pose as the all-knowing boss and to remain open to the ideas of creative people around him. One of their first mornings on the set, Morse suggested a possible shot, in front of the actors, and Preston drew himself up and scoffed, "I thought you were the *assistant* director." Morse got mad and walked off the set. That afternoon, he pulled Sturges aside and made another suggestion, now out of the cast's earshot. Preston shook his head. Morse's shot "absolutely wouldn't work, wouldn't work," Sturges declared. Then, he walked back on the set and called, "Joel, I've got a great idea"—it was verbatim what Morse had just suggested. Three minutes later Sturges walked by Morse and handed him a fifty cent piece. The incident was never mentioned, and Morse continued privately offering Sturges his thoughts.

Preston was less creative in his dealing with Paramount's front office. Buddy DeSylva was every bit as jealous of his power as Sturges, and after a brief period of reticence on both sides, they began testing each other. One incident particularly infuriated Sturges. They were shooting a long opening scene where Sully and his two studio chiefs move from the projection booth to an outer office, all the while arguing about Sully's commitment to making a socially meaningful film. The scene is nine pages long, and Sturges wanted to shoot it, like the love scene in *The Great McGinty*, seamlessly, in a single take. Joel was nervous. So Preston said, "Lets take a crack at it, kid." If it didn't work, he promised he'd break up the master shot with close-ups.

Since four pages a day was an average shooting schedule, they'd allotted two days for this scene. Filming began at nine, and the rule was you called the production man when you'd finished your first shot, usually five or ten minutes after the hour. But on this particular day, the boom had to be laid out and the three actors, who are constantly moving, regrouping, and circling each other while conversing nonstop, needed considerable rehearsal. When the production man called shortly after nine, Morse explained their strategy. Still, throughout the day, the front office continued pestering him for news of actual footage in the can. Buddy DeSylva had no interest in time-consuming artistic filmmaking. And the production man was clearly annoyed when, at five o'clock, there was still no first shot recorded. Then, shortly after five, they did four takes in a burst, sent them off to the lab, and arranged a screening at six o'clock the following morning. The shot looked great: the absence of cutaways gave it a compression that added to the script's humor and intensity. They chose the best of the takes and at nine o'clock were ready to move on to a new set—a day ahead of schedule.

So Morse complained when he saw on his assistant director's chart that night that the studio was marking them *behind* schedule. "When you don't get a shot by five, you're not a day ahead, you're a day behind," the front office insisted, common sense holding no weight with the bureaucrats.

A week passed, and one day Sturges confronted Morse. "Young man," he said, "you're counting me a day behind." And when Morse explained what had occurred, Sturges said, "Well, isn't that a little silly? We're a day ahead, aren't we?" And Morse said, yes, they were. "Then, the next day," Morse recalls,

> instead of being the first one on the set at eight o'clock, Sturges arrived about nine fifteen. He went to lunch, and instead of being right back in forty-five minutes, he took two hours. About a week went by, and he said, "Oh, I forgot to tell you, when we're really a day behind, will you let me know?" And I said, "By tonight we'll be really a day behind." So the next morning, eight o'clock he was there. He came right back after lunch. But we lost two days. The studio lost thousands of dollars.

In the long run, Sturges also lost, insisting on having the last word, rather than shrugging at the bureaucratic nonsense and getting on with his movie. One wonders where Paul Jones was during Sturges's late arrivals and long lunches. Surely Jones knew that, however untouchable Sturges seemed now, it was foolish to antagonize DeSylva. And maybe Jones, who makes a cameo appearance (as a portrait of a dead husband whose expressions change in reaction to his wife) in *Sullivan's Travels*, did in fact warn Sturges against his costly revenge—if so, Preston, increasingly obstinate, ignored him. The more famous he became, the less pressing it seemed to please the people he worked for.

Still, filming progressed smoothly. Thousands of dollars were spent on a set for the director's palatial house, but attention was also lavished on the train and prison scenes. Sturges researched precisely what prisoners wore, in what states they were still chained, under what circumstances their privileges could be removed, whether they went to church or worked on Sunday. Interestingly, Sturges's original plan was to use a Charlie Chaplin comedy in the church scene. The lighter Walt Disney cartoon was chosen when Chaplin turned him down.

Many scenes were shot on location. Sturges was filming fifty miles outside Los Angeles when he received word that Louise's water had burst, and she was being rushed to the hospital two months before her due date. Afterwards, Preston would tell Louise that, while he did not believe in God, he knew there must be some power who realized her womb was two inches too small to carry a full-term child and had her give birth prematurely. But, the early morning of June twenty-fifth was an anxious time for the Sturgeses. On the occasion of his son's eighteenth birthday, Preston recalled that day for Mon:

> Eighteen years . . . ago was a pretty wild night. The bag containing you had broken, although you weren't due to be born for another two months, and Dr. Alward said that hot or cold you were coming in very shortly. Everybody was scared to death except your mother who was certain all would be well. Then an X-ray was taken . . . and the old floor nurse who looked at it gave us re-newed hope. Although you were upside down you looked like a wrestler sitting in his corner with his arms resting on the ropes, impatient to spring out at his opponent. "He'll live," said the old nurse, "Look at the way he's sitting there . . . rarin' to go! You see some of them all crouched into their corner as if they were afraid of their shadow!" When very early in the morning you finally did make your appearance, you were so tiny you were damn near born in the hospital corridor while the nurses were galloping your mother down toward the delivery room. Leo Calibo and I came through Hollywood and Los Angeles at ninety miles an hour to be there for your arrival . . . but it had already occurred so I gave a seventy-five-cent cigar to the elevator man and shook him warmly by the hand. He is probably still wondering why.

Mon "looked like a hundred year old Chinaman who's had his head shrunk by those Central American Indians" when Preston first saw him. A week later he turned blue and had a transfusion, during which he "changed seventeen shades and came out of it pink and healthy."[29] He was named Solomon Sturges IV and called Mon, after his grandfather. He would soon be an exceptionally beautiful blonde child.

Once he saw his son safely in the world, Sturges rushed back to his film set. When Holly Morse had suggested they hold up shooting until his return, "No, young man, the show must go on," Preston had told him—and he said Morse himself should direct the scene they'd just worked out. So, around ten-thirty on the twenty-fifth, Morse was directing Joel McCrea when he thought he saw some stirring in the woods behind him. Morse went back to look, and sure enough, Preston was there. "I said, come on in," recalls Morse. "But he said no, no, go ahead and finish the scene. So I finished the scene and, at lunch time, when everybody was gathered, he drove in and passed out cigars. You see, if he'd come earlier, in the middle of a scene, it wouldn't have been so spectacular."[30]

Preston and the infant Mon.

Sturges finished *Sullivan's Travels* in early July—nine days late and about $70,000 over budget. Reactions at previews in Inglewood and Long Beach were, according to Gilletti's laugh meter, strongest in the slapstick scenes, though there was also a "four" (Gilletti's highest rating) for one line where a policeman asks Sully why, if he's really a famous movie director, he's dressed like a bum, and he answers, "I just paid my income tax."

DeSylva worried about the opening film-within-a-film being too long and the montage of flophouses and soup lines being both too long and too explicit. "Soft pedal misery," he, like Sully's production chief, advised Sturges after the first preview. He got Sturges to eliminate some "gruesome characters" and complained even about the scene in the black church. Here his suggestions for cutting—"Suggest shot of preacher, then panning shot of people; or drop the preacher altogether"—would not only have ruined the scene's rhythms, but undermined its tone, which the preacher sets when he urges his congregation to welcome the prisoners. Wisely, Sturges fought DeSylva on this point, and won.

The early trade paper reactions to *Sullivan's Travels* were mixed. Reviewers, while praising parts of the film, complained that ultimately Sturges fails to heed his own message: audiences want jokes, not preaching, and *Sullivan's Travels* preaches. But, when the film officially opened, January 28 at the New York Paramount, the response was overwhelmingly favorable. The *World-Telegram* said, "Preston Sturges, the current wunderkind of the Paramount Studios, has attacked a long-standing problem of the motion picture industry in his new film at the Paramount Theatre and has come up with one of his most entertaining and enlivening essays." The *Wall Street Journal* declared he'd "hit the jackpot." And while Howard Barnes in the *Herald Tribune* agreed with the trades that "parts of the picture, taken by themselves, are far better than the work as a whole," the *New York Mirror* gave "formal notice to Preston Sturges that this department considers him just about the most interesting artist now engaged in doing things with the motion picture."

Bosley Crowther, in the *Times*, called it "a beautifully trenchant satire" and, as usual, praised Sturges, though he expressed reservations about the film's happy ending, which he expounded on in a February 3 letter to Preston. "I feel you might have gotten more ironic punch into it," he writes. "Here was a man returning to a world and a life which he knew was phony but after a sobering experience. Could not the irony of that compromise have been pointed more sharply? Sullivan really had a reason for laughing, rather bitterly, at himself."

After the war, when *Sullivan's Travels* arrived in Paris, the French theorist André Bazin—while hailing Sturges as "sensational," America's "anti-Capra" and heir to the best comic tradition—would echo Crowther's reservations. Why does *Sullivan's Travels* leave us unsatisfied? asked Bazin. "It is because Sturges did not dare—or was not able—to play out the game that he had begun and that he owed us. . . . The tragedy should have dialectically abolished the comedy and reality should have overwhelmed the film. Only then would the final return to Hollywood have had the ironic character it needed and which would have made the viewer question Sullivan's final wisdom." [31]

But did Sturges really intend the viewer to question Sullivan's wisdom? What Crowther and Bazin, from their very different positions, seem to be demanding is some Hemingway-like rueful conclusion, by Sully or at least Sturges, that life is intolerable but must be endured anyway—and this was not Sturges's point. His point was that life is also wonderful, that suffering does not discredit joy. They coexist, as misfortune does with luck, poverty with wealth, defeat with triumph. And if the film's ending is unsatisfying this is not because it wants irony, but, on the contrary, because it paints life as unfair and implies there's very little Sully or anybody else can do about it. "The God of Hate seems infinitely greater than the God of Love and always much nearer and easier to get at," Preston had written to his Uncle Sidney Biden, about Nazism, five years earlier. Unlike Sullivan, Sturges had no dreams of changing the world.

Yet, what seems to have impressed neither Crowther nor Bazin is that the resolution of *Sullivan's Travels* is, on one level, an exuberant tribute to comedy. "But with a little sex in it," the studio head nervously qualifies Sully's depiction of his important film, in the beginning. Finally united with the girl and pledged to marry, sex is very much on Sully's own mind at the end. Walpole said life is a comedy to those who think, a tragedy to those who feel. *Sullivan's Travels* goes further to imply that, in a world where neither the thinking nor the feeling person has any choice but to perceive misery everywhere, it is a fine thing to celebrate sex, with its promise of fecundity, and success with its validation of desire and struggling.

Two months after Mon Sturges's birth, when he was eight pounds and finally able to leave the hospital, Sturges threw him and his mother a grand homecoming party. No one can remember if Jeannie La Vell was present, but most everyone else Sturges knew was there—and since most everyone knew about Jeannie, the occasion had its irony. It was a warm August night. Sturges had hired a full orchestra, which burst into "Louise" as Mrs. Sturges's Lincoln pulled into the driveway, then changed to Brahms's "Lullaby" as Mon was ushered forth in the arms of Mrs. Morrow, his baby nurse. Preston embraced his wife and son, then, overcome with emotion, called Bertie Woolfan to his side and proclaimed this was the man who'd made Solomon Sturges possible.[32] It was an evening full of splendor and high hopes.

19

Sullivan's Travels set a record during its first three days at the New York Paramount and remained a *Motion Picture Herald* box office champion for a month. Then, like *The Power and the Glory*, it suddenly lost steam. Still, wherever it was seen, it made an impact. The thirteen-year-old François Truffaut, discovering this, his first Sturges film, in a Paris movie theatre, was deeply affected; and a coming generation of American artists and intellectuals, now in high school or college, were astonished to find a Hollywood movie that spoke to *them*. The filmmaker Richard Leacock remembers how for months he and his Harvard friends regaled each other with dialogue they'd memorized from *Sullivan's Travels*.

Whether he liked it or not, Sturges was now taken seriously as an artist. In 1942, all sorts of newspaper pieces coupled him with the twenty-five-year-old *wunderkind*, Orson Welles, who had just made *Citizen Kane*. But, "Orson Welles isn't having everything his own way in establishing the coming age in Hollywood," observed a characteristic article, in the *New York Motion Picture*. "True, his *Citizen Kane* leaped out of the rut and showed something new in treatment and technique but then along came Preston Sturges to demonstrate a new angle of approach to plot, character and treatment. No flash in the pan, this Sturges." [1]

Like Cecil B. DeMille, Sturges had taken to spending hours every day personally replying to correspondence from his public. [2] He received scores of letters about *Sullivan's Travels*. An executive officer of the NAACP wrote congratulating him on the "decent treatment of Negroes" in the church scene: "I was in Hollywood recently and am to return there soon for conferences with production head writers, directors, and actors and actresses in an effort to induce broader and more decent picturization of the Negro instead of limiting him to menial or comic roles. The sequence in *Sullivan's Travels* is a step in that direction and I want you to know how grateful we are." [3] A fifteen-year-old would-be-writer requested a copy of the script, which Sturges sent along, advising him: "Copies are very difficult to obtain once the picture is completed, so a good plan might be to protect it in some kind of folder." Preston sent another script to a cartoonist, who wrote saying he loved the comedy and thought Sully's final speech was "a masterpiece," but he had mixed feelings about the rest of the film. "Opinions differ," Sturges told him. "Some people didn't care for the slapstick portions of the picture but liked the more dramatic scenes, including the chain gang sequence. It was no surprise, however, that different portions of the picture would appeal to different people and your letter is greatly appreciated." [4]

Vic Potel (the studio cameraman in *Sullivan's Travels*) wrote with special discernment. Sully, he felt, was the prototype of "everything that is sincere but muddling in Hollywood, he is believable to the nth degree as is every one of your characters, particularly little Veronica whom you have molded into the very essence of the heartbreak, the sophistication, the faith, the childlikeness that is also Hollywood." "For a while," Potel continued, "I was deathly afraid you were going commercial (but brilliantly) and that you would be persuaded to smother that bubbling originality that is Preston Sturges and [let them] put you in the groove—for God's sake don't let them! [*Sullivan*] has convinced me otherwise and I am grateful! Preston you have a soul as deep as the ocean and you've only *begun* to take the gold out that is there—there still remains tons and tons of it." [5]

At first, Sturges couldn't make up his own mind about *Sullivan's Travels*. Writing about it in an article for the *New York Times*, shortly after the film's opening, he was most interested in acquitting himself of pretension. "*Sullivan's Travels*," he wrote, "is the result of an urge, an urge to tell some of my fellow filmwrights that they were getting a little deep dish and to leave the preaching to the preachers." It was a movie, he said, nothing more. To Bosley Crowther, Preston wrote that he too was dissatisfied with the film's ending: "I know it wasn't right, but I didn't know how to solve the problem which was not only to show what Sullivan found out but also to tie up the love story. It would have been very easy to make a big finish either way, but one would have defeated the other." [6]

"I have taken a few on the chin already and will take more," he predicted. [7] Five years later, Preston was still complaining to Crowther that his director friends "loathed" his filmmaking picture. "But I saw it about a year ago and liked it. If allowed only one I would be willing to hang my hat on [*Sullivan's Travels*]." [8] Ultimately, Sturges would come to feel that he'd said everything he hoped to say in this film. [9]

By the time *Sullivan's Travels* was released, in January 1942, Pearl Harbor had been attacked, and America was at last at war. Chaplin and Lubitsch had already turned their comic gifts to making films attacking Hitler (*The Great Dictator* and *To Be or Not To Be*). Now, Sturges watched his close friends rush to join the army. And it was not just immigrant Jews like Willy Wyler and Billy Wilder who were anxious to fight. John Huston, who'd finally directed a first film, and Frank Capra, at the height of his glory, were just as passionate. Even the ailing author Dashiell Hammett, at forty-seven, enlisted. From 1917 Ivar, Gilletti was called up as was the houseboy whom Preston and Louise considered family, Leo Calibo.

Remembering this period in Hollywood, John Houseman would write: "For most of the people around me the shock of Pearl Harbor had been followed by a sense of relief that the long suspense of our uneasy neutrality had come to an end."[10] Yet, at forty, Houseman, who'd grown up in France and London, felt curiously detached from all this patriotic fervor. As did Sturges. The boy who'd gone to such lengths to join the Air Service in World War I was nowhere to be found in the successful Hollywood filmmaker. Mencken ironically dismissed the war as "the current crusade to save humanity,"[11] and Sturges may well have agreed, may well have thought this had all happened before and there was nothing especially urgent or noble about fighting Nazis. "I imagine I could still fly if necessary but then I always had a very strongly developed imagination," he wrote a friend from his old Air Service unit. "The peculiar thing is that I have absolutely no *desire* to get in. Either this war has not been as well advertised as the last one or else there is a great difference between eighteen and forty-four, or else you don't fall for the same guff twice or something."[12]

Still, the studio heads wholeheartedly supported the war effort (between 1942 and 1944, "Save Film And Win The War" was printed on every page of film script), and Sturges did his share as well: writing a cautionary script about military secrets called *Safeguarding Military Information*. He also played himself in Paramount's *Star Spangled Rhythm*, a patriotic all-star film whose sequences hang on an elaborate plot to convince G.I. Eddie Bracken, home on leave, that he's been made head of Paramount. Sturges, looking very virile, gets to throw a temper tantrum because his boss has walked out on a screening of his latest picture. "I'm going to Metro," he declares, throwing an ashtray.

This scene reflects Sturges's growing reputation for volatility. "Temperamental as some people have found Preston Sturges,"[13] Louella Parsons began one of her 1941 gossip columns. While Preston had been solicitous with everyone on his first few sets, he increasingly felt free to vent his anger on his worshipful stock company. This did not mean he had a low opinion of them.

Gilletti going off to war. (Photo courtesy of Nina Laemmle)

On the contrary, he placed whole-page ads extolling the gifts of his character actors and was as intensely involved with Al Bridge's performance as with Joel McCrea's. Much of the time, as with his wives, Sturges's temper tantrums with the stock company had nothing to do with them personally. It was just his mood.

There was more spleen, though, in Preston's attacks on Bill Demarest. Sturges believed he'd made Demarest's career, while Demarest was becoming more confident about his own talents and ability to do very well with or without Sturges. Some felt the raves Demarest got for *Christmas in July*, *The Lady Eve*, and *Sullivan's Travels* went to his head—he thought anything he did was hilarious.[14] And the cockier Demarest grew, the more relentlessly Sturges picked on him. "If something was being discussed that had the possibility of being not quite understood by the not quite literate set, somehow Preston would make Demarest the butt of it," Louise recalls. Louise had become close friends with Demarest's wife Lucille. "I know you're uncomfortable," she told Lucille, after one Sunday night party where Preston "verbally abused" Bill Demarest. "And I definitely am uncomfortable. So let's see each other when we don't have to be around Preston."[15]

To his new friend René Clair, on the other hand, Sturges could not have been more gracious. In Europe, Clair was king of comedy, but as an expatriate in Hollywood he had trouble getting work. When Preston urged Paramount to give Clair a film to direct, Buddy DeSylva argued that Clair's name meant little to the average American. So to placate DeSylva, Sturges himself agreed to produce Clair's film, which became *I Married a Witch*. Sturges got Veronica Lake for the lead and assigned *four* writers, including himself and Dalton Trumbo, to the screenplay. But soon Dalton Trumbo (sounding like Preston in his disputes with B. P. Schulberg) announced that he was resigning from the project because, "In looking back over whatever work of mine has been successful in the past, I find it was all accomplished under conditions which gave me the illusion of independence while I was writing."[16] Working with Clair and Sturges, however, "at no time have I had any idea what the next sequence would be." Chastened, Sturges accepted Trumbo's resignation and soon backed off himself, leaving all the creative decisions to Clair, who made an engaging off-beat comedy.

By now, it was the spring of 1942, and Sturges was deeply involved with his own next film, tentatively named *Is Marriage Necessary?* It would be released as *The Palm Beach Story*. "Premise," he wrote in early notes for the screenplay: "that a pretty woman can do anything she wants and go anywhere she wants without money. 2. That a pretty woman can use her appeal for the advancement of her husband." This would be his fifth film in two years and, the opposite of his last movie, it would be all about wealth and beauty. The settings were New York and Palm Beach, the tone was sophisticated. Narratively, it was Sturges's most autobiographical work since his 1930 play, *Recapture*.

As with *Sullivan's Travels*, the film opens at frenzied pitch. A maid faints. A woman, bound and gagged, desperately struggles to extricate herself from a closet. Another woman, her exact double, throws on a wedding dress and rushes off to embrace and marry an overwrought young man. "And They Lived Happily Ever After," read the titles over the receding bride and groom. " . . . Or Did They?"

With no explanation for this mystifying prologue, the film moves five years forward. The groom, Tom, is now a beleaguered inventor who has so far failed to get the necessary $99,000 for his current scheme, an airport for small planes in the center of a city. The bride, Gerry, is a beautiful woman who requires luxury. Tom and Gerry are so far behind on rent payments that their Park Avenue apartment is offered to an old Texas millionaire. But the millionaire, called the "Wienie King" because he invented the Texas "wienie," likes Gerry and, rather than grabbing her apartment, gives her money for the rent. He throws in more for a new dress and hat, figuring, why not? It makes him happy. And she accepts this windfall with the same largess.

But when Tom learns what's happened, he wonders how Gerry can behave so shamelessly. She in turn wonders how he can fail to see that what she's done is harmless. Being attractive to men is a gift, not something to be ashamed of. In the past, she's tried to use her wiles to attract customers for Tom, but always Tom has become foolishly jealous and lost his opportunity. Now she's leaving him. He'll do better without her—maybe he'll even find a wife who can cook. And she'll find a man who can fulfill her needs. When he protests that they love each other, she at first denies this and then says it's irrelevant. She takes off without money or baggage for Palm Beach.

Just as she's predicted, her beauty and resourcefulness work miracles. The "Ale and Quail Club," a brotherhood of raucous hunters, collectively buy her a train ticket. On the train, she meets one of the wealthiest men in America, John D. Hackensacker III, headed for his Mar-A-Lago-type mansion in Palm Beach. Though tight by nature, Hackensacker is so infatuated with Gerry that he buys her beautiful gowns and jewels, then invites her to journey from Jacksonville to Palm Beach on his private yacht. Meanwhile Tom, who's done everything he can to dissuade Gerry from leaving, receives a visit from the Wienie King, who gives him the money to fly to Florida.

When Hackensacker and Gerry pull into Palm Beach, Hackensacker's much-married sister, Maude, is there to greet them, as is an irate Tom. Thinking quickly, Gerry introduces Tom as her brother. Maude immediately latches onto him and invites brother and sister to stay at the Hackensacker mansion for as long as they like. When they're alone, Tom begs Gerry to come back to him, but she replies that she's sticking to her plan for finding a wealthy husband. Maybe she can even get Hackensacker to build Tom his airport. That night Hackensacker, deeply in love, tells Gerry he'd like nothing better than to underwrite Tom's airport, but Tom refuses to accept patronage under false pretenses. Besides, he hates Hackensacker for courting his wife.

At the end of the evening, Hackensacker hires an orchestra and serenades Gerry, singing "Good Night, Sweetheart," under her window. But now, as Tom helps her out of her dress, Gerry weakens and falls into his arms. The next morning they explain the whole situation to Hackensacker and Maude, who are sad but remarkably understanding. Hackensacker even agrees to go ahead with the plan for Tom's airport—brokenhearted as he is, he'll more than ever need a project. "I don't suppose you have a sister?" asks Hackensacker. "Oh, didn't you know about that? That's how we got married in the beginning, both being twins," Gerry replies.

"Of course that's another plot entirely," says Tom, as the film's last scene returns to the wedding chapel which was seen in the opening sequence. Tom and Gerry are joined by their identical twins, who marry Hackensacker and Maude. Again the titles read, "And They Lived Happily Ever After . . Or Did They?"

For anyone aware of Preston's history, *The Palm Beach Story* is a treasure trove of personal references. Gerry, after splitting with Tom, meets a millionaire on the train to Florida, much as Sturges, after splitting with Estelle, met Eleanor. Tom, like Preston in his twenties, is an inventor unable to turn his ideas into luxuries for his ambitious and beautiful wife. She, like Estelle, announces she doesn't love him anymore. Then he, in a twist on what Preston told his first wife, asks, "Do you object to spending the night under the same roof as me?"

Just as Preston, when he was first married, was embarrassed to even feel another woman's bosom against him while dancing, Tom, fox-trotting with Maude, holds her so far from his body that she complains he's letting her "flop around." Where Eleanor called Preston Wunkie, Gerry calls Hackensacker Snoodles. The Hackensacker mansion is filled with the sort of showy acquisitions that impressed Eleanor's mother. The couples dance in a frond-lined ballroom like the one at the Everglades Club. Tom's airport for small planes is a variation on Preston's ill-fated heliport.

As with *Recapture*, there's a wish fulfillment angle because the separated couple meet again as lovers. What's more, where Pat, in the play, is really finished with her ex-husband Harry, Gerry still adores Tom.

This is an intimate film, with a leisurely pace and, for all its nods to Preston's past, very little narrative tension. Unlike the Huttons, the Hackensackers are bemused and decidedly idle millionaires. Circumspection is John D.'s only real flaw, while Maude, for all her foibles, is well-meaning, and the Texas Wienie King is munificence personified. Nowhere to be found are the more troublesome rich—Paris Singer with his passion for control, Ed Hutton's crowd who laughed and laughed at Preston's love letters. Wealth confers not power but a sort of dazed good will on the characters in Sturges's story.

Again, the question of destiny versus free will is an issue. When Gerry berates Tom for putting pride before profit, he fatalistically informs her, "The way you are is the way you have to be, honey." And, "Nobody who's been married to me for five years is going to be a flop. You're going to get your airport if I have to build it for you myself," she, confident in her own powers, retorts.

Yet, more than ideas, ambience is crucial now. Edith Head's effulgent costumes and the vaguely decadent Park Avenue apartment and Palm Beach home set the tone for the worldly dialogues. Here, for instance, are Gerry and Tom discussing the divorce she's just proposed:

TOM: If you want a divorce, you're certainly entitled to it. I don't know where the money's coming from.

GERRY: Oh, the next husband always pays for that.

TOM: Oh, you have him all picked out, have you?

GERRY: Oh, you're such a child . . . I may not even get married again. I might become an adventuress.

TOM: I can just see you starting for China in a twenty-six-foot sail boat.

GERRY: You're thinking of an adventurer, dear. An adventuress never goes on anything under three hundred feet with a crew of eighty.

TOM: Well, you just let me catch you on a three-hundred-foot yacht or even a two-hundred-foot yacht.

GERRY: At least I wouldn't have to worry about the rent. Oh, I'm sorry. Let's go and have some dinner, hmm?

TOM: How can you think of food at a moment like this?

GERRY: Because I'm a woman maybe and a little more practical than you.

Are you going to put on your dinner jacket or shall I take off my new dress?

In *The Palm Beach Story*, women are altogether different from men. They're more practical, more fickle, wiser, and more sophisticated. They are also utterly dependent. Marriage, or at least a rich man, most certainly *is* necessary for Gerry, who, smart as she may be, no more dreams she could support herself in the style she desires than does Isabelle in *Strictly Dishonorable*. Unlike the girl in *Sullivan's Travels*, she has no wish for personal achievement, and unlike Jean in *The Lady Eve*, she's practical not for the sake of her heart, but to assure her material well-being. Still, Gerry's love of luxury is more than vulgar materialism. Just as her beauty is a gift and mark of favor, money, for her, means freedom from petty concerns, such as importuning landlords and grocers. Surely, she'd agree with the butler in *Sullivan's Travels* who claims poverty is a "positive plague," inimical to delight and passion. Mary Desti's quip, "There's nothing the matter with me that a little money won't cure," perfectly describes the heroine of *The Palm Beach Story*; though Gerry scarcely embodies the other side of Mary, the mother who at the end of her life told Preston that money had never been profoundly important to either of them, however much they'd enjoyed it.[17]

The Palm Beach Story is less cinematically audacious than *Sullivan's Travels*, though there are some striking moments. At the end of the prologue, for instance, the camera tracks back to watch the bride and groom through titles ("And They Lived Happily Ever After") framed in boxes which, as five years pass, transform into a plaque for Tom and Gerry's Park Avenue apartment. A long train scene in which members of the "Ale and Quail" hunting club grow increasingly drunk and obstreperous (winding up on a wild "posse" chase with their dogs through the sleepers) is Sturges's slapstick at its best. And the final trick shot of *two* Gerrys and *two* Toms at the altar is cleverly orchestrated. As always, there are superb minor characters. A porter, for instance, who when asked whether Gerry got off the train alone, replies: "Well, you might practically say she's alone. The gentleman who got off with her give me ten cents from New York to Jacksonville . . . She's alone, but she don't know it." There's also "Toto," Maude's current imbecilic foreign suitor and the Wienie King, with his good heart and arrogant deafness.

After the ambitious *Sullivan's Travels*, Sturges's fifth film has an air of wanting merely to give pleasure, but that air is deceptive. From its aggressive working title to the message of its "happy ending," *Is Marriage Necessary?* is not half so agreeable—or romantic—as it appears. Take, for instance, the young inventor Tom who, like Jimmy in *Christmas in July*, yearns to achieve success on his own merit. Not only is he deprived of the satisfaction of having his ideas truly appreciated—he gets his $99,000 for the humiliating reason that another man falls for his wife. Or take the way Maude preys upon Tom, who's clearly repulsed by her. (Tom's twin looks scarcely more infatuated as he marries Maude at the end.) Or consider Gerry's attitude toward marriage—"You can always find a good provider if you really want one." This sounds just like Jean in the beginning of *The Lady Eve*, only Jean changes when she falls in love, where Gerry does not. Her returning to Tom, like the revelation that her twin sister can marry Hackensacker, is a mere plot contrivance. If *The Lady Eve* is the last screwball comedy, *The Palm Beach Story* is a sort of mannerist recreation, with atmosphere and narrative ploys intact, but no real suffering or affirmation.

Where, one wonders, were the enforcers of the Production Code while Sturges was preparing this movie? True, the Breen Office did reject the initial title, which was changed to *The Palm Beach Story*, and at first balked at all the sexual innuendoes. The script's "present version," they had written Paramount in November 1941, "is unacceptable because of the sex-suggestive situations and the sex-suggestive dialogue that runs throughout the script. As you know the industry at all times has tried to avoid giving offense to the American public and particularly to recognized civic and religious groups, where these groups have made it manifest that certain themes or treatments thereof give them offense. Of late, they have let it be known that stories centering around the theme of a light treatment of marriage and divorce, in connection with detailed discussions thereof, has been a source of serious complaint." [18] When he received this letter, Paramount's "decency" expert, Luigi Luraschi, immediately set up a meeting where he and Sturges defended their film's harmlessness. They must have been quite persuasive, for just a week later the Breen Office was agreeing that lines like "You have no idea what a long-legged gal can do without doing anything" should be "perfectly acceptable if delivered straight." And even Maude's marital record could be made palatable to the American public if, rather than six divorces, she'd had "perhaps four or five at most"! [19] So *The Palm Beach Story* was shot essentially as Sturges had conceived it.

Joel McCrea, who'd gotten along so well with Sturges on *Sullivan's Travels*, was immediately cast as Tom, and Claudette Colbert became the worldly Gerry. The way this happened, Colbert recalls, is that when the lights came up after a screening of *Sullivan's Travels*, she turned to Preston and said, "I want you to write a picture for me." Preston had known Colbert since the thirties. At one point, they were even coupled in newspaper gossip. ("Among the cutest things on Claudette Colbert's bracelet was a diminutive gold enve-lope with a very minute letter from Preston Sturges," read one insinuating article, in a New York paper.)[20] And while it's doubtful they were ever lovers, Sturges knew Colbert more intimately than he did most Hollywood stars.

As Maude, Sturges cast Mary Astor, who'd just played the completely dif-ferent role of a femme fatale in John Huston's *Maltese Falcon*. The part of Hackensacker Preston wrote specifically for the radio singer, Rudy Vallee. Preston had first seen Vallee that August when Charley Abramson was visiting L.A., and the two friends set out to catch Ronald Colman's new film, *My Life with Caroline*. They arrived in time to see the other half of the double bill, a Three Stooges musical comedy, *Time Out for Rhythm*, which was not especially noteworthy except for Vallee's performance. Though Vallee was not playing a comic role, whenever he appeared on screen, the audience burst out laughing. "This guy's funny, and he doesn't realize it," Preston told Charley.[21]

"In seeing *Time Out for Rhythm*," Preston wrote Rudy Vallee, "I thought I perceived how you should be used and how you should not be used in pictures. It gave me the idea of showing a gentleman on the screen . . . with the qualities and some of the faults that the word might imply."[22] So Sturges began writing a character who would display Vallee's talents, including what Gerry calls his "nice little voice."

Buddy DeSylva and Frank Freeman were far from overjoyed when Pres-ton introduced Vallee to them as his latest discovery. They begged Charley Abramson to dissuade his friend from "this Rudy Vallee kick," sure he would ruin the picture. But Charley was so confident of Preston's instincts that he made a wager with DeSylva and Freeman that after *The Palm Beach Story*, Paramount would sign Rudy Vallee on as a Paramount actor—and they did.[23]

For the bawdy "Ale and Quail" Club, Sturges cast Bill Demarest (again named Billdocker), Jack Norton, Robert Greig, Roscoe Ates, Dewey Robin-son, Chester Conklin, and Sheldon Jett. Al Bridge plays the conductor with the impossible task of controlling this unruly flock, and, as in *Christmas in July*, Julius Tannen plays a Jewish store owner. Formerly a vaudevillian, Tan-nen was one of Sturges's favorite actors. Because he was an older man, some-times it took many takes to get his performance absolutely right. Once, when Sturges was praising Tannen's work, someone challenged him: "Yes, but it took so much effort to wring that scene out of him that you have to wonder if it was worth it." And Sturges replied that when you can draw something that fine from a once great actor, it is always worthwhile.[24]

The Palm Beach Story began shooting in late November 1941 before *Sul-*

Preston with the Ale and Quail Club and other stock company regulars. From left to right, back row: Dewey Robinson, Jack Norton, Preston, William Demarest, Robert Warwick; middle row: Robert Greig, Jimmy Conlin, Arthur Stuart Hull, Roscoe Ates, Chester Conklin, Al Bridge; front row: Sheldon Jett, Snowflake, Torben Meyer, unknown, Arthur Hoyt.

livan's Travels opened. Since Sturges's latest film (*The Lady Eve*) was a hit, DeSylva was still indulging him. He got a budget of just under a million dollars, nearly twice the cost of *McGinty*, and his sets for the Park Avenue apartment and Palm Beach house were as spectacular as Cecil B. DeMille's. Gerry's luxurious bedroom/bath/dressing room suite, Sturges told newspaper reporters, was modeled on the rooms of his former mother-in-law, Marjorie Hutton. Claudette Colbert was being paid $150,000. And while the stock company received nowhere near that sum, they were excited just to be making a new Sturges picture. Paul Jones was producing what would turn out to be his last film with Sturges. Victor Milner, from *The Lady Eve*, was cinematographer. All the ingredients were right. Yet, somehow the mood on Sturges's set was less ebullient than usual.

More and more, Sturges was insensitive to other people's feelings. There was an incident with character actor Vic Potel, for instance. Potel, who had a small role in *The Palm Beach Story*, dabbled in painting on the side. His speciality was Hollywood subjects sketched with Grandma Moses-type primitive enthusiasm, and Sturges liked his work enough to buy two of Potel's Keystone Kops scenes for The Players. At the time of *The Palm Beach Story*, Potel was working on a grand scale painting depicting an encounter between Pola Negri and Gloria Swanson. He planned to insinuate other actors, directors, and technicians as onlookers in the background. When Paramount publicist Teet Carle learned about the project, he convinced the *Los Angeles Times* to run a story on Potel and his painting. A good idea, Carle and Potel thought, would be to have a photo of Sturges and Potel standing in front of Potel's half-finished canvas on a set for *The Palm Beach Story*.

Sturges agreed. But when Carle and Potel arrived, one rainy afternoon, to take the photo, Preston was in no mood to help anyone. From Preston's petulant, sulky look Carle could immediately see he'd suffered some small disappointment, probably he'd been proven wrong in a creative decision, which always particularly irked him. So Carle urged Potel to forget the photo for that day, but Potel insisted on asking Preston to pose. Sturges said, no, he didn't have time. And when Potel began complaining about the time *he'd* taken, dragging the painting to the set, "Sturges really laid him low with some cruel words about the pip-squeak needs of Potel's compared to Sturges's problems," Carle recalls. "We never got the picture. I wonder if Potel ever finished the painting."[25]

Mary Astor also had problems with Sturges, whom she felt she could never please. "It was just not my thing," she said of playing man-crazy Maude. "I couldn't talk in a high, flutey voice and run my words together as he thought high-society women did, or at least *mad* high-society women who've had six husbands and six million dollars."[26] Between the lines, one can read Mary Astor's dissatisfaction with Sturges's interpretation of the society woman. She didn't perceive that, by exaggerating, Sturges aimed to suggest a more complicated reality, so her performance came off somewhat brittle. Mary Astor probably didn't try all that hard to please Sturges. Unlike Veronica Lake and Ellen Drew, she wasn't a newcomer nor was this film crucial to her image in the movie world. Like Louise Sturges, she must have wondered why Sturges was so consumed by his filmmaking.

Certainly, Claudette Colbert was not. A bona fide star, she'd work her eight hours, then, Joel McCrea recalls, "take off her false lashes and say, 'Good evening, gentlemen.'" While Sturges never wanted to quit work and McCrea was happy to stay with him until dinner (which they often ate, with Frances

Preston with Claudette Colbert on the set of The Palm Beach Story.

Dee, at The Players), Colbert was obdurate about not acting for a moment longer than she was required. And Sturges, who'd been so patient with Veronica Lake, felt wounded by Colbert's cool professionalism. Perhaps in retaliation, on an least one occasion he took pleasure in humiliating her. Colbert was now in her late thirties. One morning, in front of all the cast and crew,

275

Sturges told her: "You know, we've got to take your close-up shots as early as possible. You look great in the morning, but by five o'clock you're beginning to sag."[27]

Later, Colbert scored her own small triumph. Teet Carle recalls finding her "chuckling" one day, while Preston was "pouting." They had just come from the rushes, and Colbert confided in Carle that they were going to have to re-take a Palm Beach scene where, like Preston and Eleanor at Paris Singer's skylit Everglades Club, Gerry and Hackensacker dance the night away. The day before, Sturges had insisted on trying an unusual shot, which involved placing the camera and the dancers on a moving platform. Both Colbert and Victor Milner had argued the shot would never work, but Preston was adamant. Now the rushes had proven him wrong, and Colbert was gloating.[28]

Colbert remembers Sturges as not a very happy person. Working with him wasn't as much fun as working for Lubitsch or Mitchell Leisen. Still, they spoke French together on the set, which could be amusing since nobody else understood them, and Colbert greatly admired Sturges's creative gifts.[29]

So did Rudy Vallee, who couldn't believe his good luck at appearing in a Preston Sturges picture. And he did not just appear, he all but stole the show, with his curious mixture of pomp and sweetness. One of the film's loveliest moments comes when Claudette Colbert, climbing to her upper berth, squashes his pince-nez, then stoops and picks the pieces off his eyelids as he smiles, beatifically. Vallee felt he and Sturges had much in common, and they quickly became friends as well as colleagues. Sturges, Vallee recalls, used to ridicule the Jewish accents of many people in the industry, often read H. L. Mencken to the cast over lunch, and was always correcting everyone's grammar. Sturges could be a martinet, but essentially he was very kind.[30]

He was also forever bursting with enthusiasm, and while he was shooting *The Palm Beach Story*, told everyone he met that they absolutely had to read a new book called *Two Lifetimes in One: How Never To Be Tired: How To Have Energy To Burn*. The author was Marie Beynon Ray. She wrote in an exhorting, upbeat style, and Preston claimed she'd changed his life (but he also, later, claimed he'd never actually read the book—he didn't need to). Energy, she wrote, "is the invariable factor in all great success."[31] And she endorsed a recent Harvard University report on fatigue which concluded: "The phenomenon formerly called fatigue is better described as *boredom. It is boredom that causes a reduced rate of work.*"[32] Preston wholly agreed with Miss Ray, fatigue was in the mind, you had to constantly fire your imagination and apply yourself before it was too late and you'd missed out on life. Sturges had the "Wienie King" say as much in *The Palm Beach Story*. "You'll get over [being broke]," he tells Gerry. "You'll get over being young too. Some day you'll wake up and find everything behind you. Gives you quite a turn. Makes you sorry for a few of the things you didn't do while you still could."

And Sturges practiced what he preached. At forty-four, he was seizing the day. With the war on, his diesel engine was suddenly in demand, and, as Preston's fame grew, so did the popularity of The Players. He enlarged the terrace and kitchen, added a small dance room and made sure that, war or no war, the best foods were available. His restaurant made $394,934 in 1942, though what happened to most of that money was a mystery to Preston. In 1944, he would make only a $25,691 profit on a gross of $657,261.

Partly this was because he was determined to keep prices down. The Players's bartender Dominique remembers arguing with Preston over the sixty-five cents The Players charged for Black Label Scotch, Preston's own drink. Preston wanted Dominique to charge rates as low as the Brown Derby's, and it took Dominique and Monsieur Pillet nearly an hour to convince him that, since The Players offered not just a bar and food but entertainment, they *had* to charge more. Dominique also felt The Players's food was much too inexpensive. On the middle floor, overstuffed ham sandwiches cost just twenty-five cents. Why, you couldn't buy the ham itself for that price![33]

Even generous Monsieur Pillet was disturbed when waiters were left free to walk off with food from his kitchen. In the early forties, someone, probably practical Henry Henigson, listed thirteen problems and ideas for improving The Players. At the top of the list were:

1. The question of the number of exits. The advisability of closing some of them or rearranging the inner working for better physical control of property of the premises.
2. The advisability of changing the physical arrangements where waiters pass the checkers, eliminating so far as is practicable the possibility of waiters avoiding checkers.

But Sturges paid no attention. His aversion to taking even the simplest precautions fit well with his theory of living life fully. You don't waste energy closing off exits, you open doors.

In his sexual arrangements, Sturges was following a similar logic. Maybe he was in love with Jeannie La Vell, maybe not, but anyway the affair continued, while Preston became less concerned about concealing his infidelity from Louise. When she learned of it, she was not only hurt but deeply puzzled. However much she recognized intellectually that this was a familiar pattern for Preston, Louise couldn't help wondering what had changed about *her* to make him want another woman. The apparent answer was that she had become a mother. It was a bitter irony for Louise that Preston's turning from her coincided with her giving him the son he so wanted. And while she loved her son, Louise felt even more distanced from Preston by the demands for impeccable maternal behavior he now placed on her. Mon was to have the *real* mother Preston had been deprived of. Louise was to be the "purveyor of cookies and warm, tender maternal thoughts at all times."[34]

Still, she was committed to her marriage. Despite the fact that she'd divorced her first husband, Louise in her heart disapproved of divorce, especially where a child was concerned. She must have hoped Jeannie was a fleeting fancy, that if she waited patiently, Preston would come back or at least explain his infidelity to her. Perhaps it was with this thought in mind that Louise took off with Mon and his baby nurse for a holiday at Soboba Hot Springs while Preston threw himself into *The Palm Beach Story*. She wrote him affectionately, but quizzically at that time:

> *Dearest Puddin' Head,*
> . . . When do you want us home? Or do you? Have the domestic amenities or such as you've had time for palled by comparison to the care-free life? Just thought I'd ask, since, unless you are really champing, I haven't the slightest intention of setting you scot-free.[35]

How Preston felt, or was *trying* to feel about the situation, during the first year of his son's life, can be guessed at from a story idea he submitted to Paramount after he finished *The Palm Beach Story*. It was called *Love in the Afternoon*, and had themes in common with *Unfaithfully Yours*, the unproduced farce about adultery Preston wrote in New York when Eleanor was leaving him.

This is how he begins his outline for the story: "We see a happy man. He sings while he shaves and [goes] down the stairs to breakfast with his handsome wife and grown children . . . arrives happily at his office, which seems to be peopled by Ziegfeld Follies girls. He pinches the telephone girl's cheek and winks at another girl and hurries into his office where he kisses his secretary a fond good morning. Now he plunges into his work at which he is very successful. We leave him making a date for lunch with a little actress in a show he has backed. Presently one of his grown children discovers a few of her father's improprieties and with great difficulty father is reformed."

Now Sturges's "father" becomes virtuous, but miserable. Gone is the spring in his step; his business suffers. His wife becomes so unhappy she calls a conference of her children. Maybe, she tells them, their father is in love, and if so, it's not so terrible. She says, "Of course you don't really know this, children, but before your father married he was a very gay blade. We can only be grateful to him for having suppressed his natural penchant all these years, and now if it has caught up with him, we will just have to make the best of it."

She tells the children to give father a "hint" that it's all right with her if he loves someone else. Apprised of his family's tolerance, father returns to his former ways. "We see a happy man," Sturges concludes his treatment. "He sings as he shaves and descends to breakfast with a happy family."

Buddy DeSylva had no interest whatsoever in *Love in the Afternoon*. Why would a man in Preston's tax bracket want to sell a story idea anyway? DeSylva gracelessly asked Preston's agent. So that was the end of the project, though not of Sturges's speculations about infidelity in marriage. It had always been Preston's conviction that men and women are fundamentally different. Men, he told Louise, are smarter than women, and—life with Mary Desti notwithstanding—he insisted that it was man's "natural penchant" to be promiscuous, while women were faithful. *Love in the Afternoon* implies that a reasonable woman will learn to accept her husband's peccadilloes. Then, they can go on as before.

But of course Louise and Preston couldn't go on as before, because before they were passionately in love with each other. A year after he wrote *Love in the Afternoon* Preston, congratulating Gilletti on his new wife, sounded considerably more cynical about marriage. "The less times you marry," he wrote, "the more chances you have of being monogamous, which in the occident is considered to be an ideal condition and for all I know may be."[36]

As soon as he'd finished *The Palm Beach Story*, Preston moved on to his next project, a movie based on a book that he'd been assigned to adapt three years earlier. This was René Fülöp-Miller's *Triumph Over Pain*, a highly subjective history of anesthesia, whose most compelling chapters told the story of a nineteenth-century dentist, W. T. G. Morton. According to Fülöp-Miller, Morton was the first man to reveal the anesthetizing properties of sulphuric ether and therefore the father of painless medicine. But in the late thirties, when Paramount bought Fülöp-Miller's book for Gary Cooper, protests began pouring in from prominent dental societies that claimed that Morton was a mere appropriator of other people's ideas, not fit for a biographical tribute, not at all like, say, Louis Pasteur.

The real "discoverer" of anesthesia, according to the preponderance of Paramount's correspondence, was a shy Hartford dentist named Horace Wells; others credited a Dr. Jackson or a Dr. Long. Sturges was not put off by the controversy. Besides, it was perfectly clear from Fülöp-Miller's book that

Morton didn't "invent" ether, whose properties had been known for centuries, nor did Fülöp-Miller deny the importance of Horace Wells and Dr. Jackson. As Fülöp-Miller depicted Morton, he was neither a brilliant scientist nor an exemplary individual. He was "a little man with a little mind" who exemplified the Puritan ethic as it was understood in the mid-nineteenth century. His god was money, and when he set out to discover a painless way to extract teeth, he had no larger goal than attracting patients to his dental practice.

Yet, the implications of that discovery overwhelmed him. Where Tom in *The Power and the Glory* was an extraordinary man ruined by ambition, Morton was a petty man exalted by circumstances. He was not the first to discover ether, but he was the first to reveal its properties to the medical world so surgery patients would no longer suffer. Morton's was a true sacrifice. For when he disclosed the secret of painless surgery, he lost the edge he had over other dentists; his practice went downhill, and the world rewarded him not with prizes and fame, but with ignominy, overriding his patent, accusing him of greed and of stealing Horace Wells's or Dr. Jackson's discovery.

It's easy to see why Preston was drawn to this story, which argued his deepest convictions—that virtue is irrelevant to success, that mankind is ungrateful, that heroes are not pure. As with McGinty, Morton had no trouble when he merely sought personal profit; it was when he attempted to do good that he was defamed. Sturges may have been especially attracted to *Triumph Over Pain* because, after his tussle with Bianca, he'd had fourteen stitches in his arm *without* anesthesia. He could appreciate how excruciating surgery was before Morton. Like Tom in *The Palm Beach Story*, Morton was an inventor. He was also a lowly dentist, who saw his work as a business while the impeccably educated Dr. Jackson practiced the fine art of medicine. Fülöp-Miller's story even had a comic angle. One of the first patients Morton experimented on was a music teacher named Eben Frost. From the moment Morton painlessly extracted his tooth, Frost's "whole life was devoted to the new task of shadowing Morton and perpetually retelling the story of the painless extraction," Fülöp-Miller reports.[37]

Still, unlike the films that made Sturges famous, *Triumph Over Pain* was not essentially comic. It was a drama with comic interludes and, from Paramount's point of view, in the early forties, a risky venture. Never inclined toward biography, Paramount would have been happy to drop *Triumph Over Pain* when Gary Cooper left the studio and Sturges moved on to become a director. It was Sturges who remained committed to the project. After *The Palm Beach Story*, he pleaded with Frank Freeman to let him both produce and direct the Morton biography. And Freeman, while expressing strong reservations, gave the fair-haired boy his way.

Sturges's first cut of this film, which would be called *The Great Moment*, begins with a biting prologue. Over scenes of wreckage of war, we hear a cheerful voice:

"One of the most charming characteristics of Homo Sapiens, the wise guy on your right, is the consistency with which he has stoned, crucified, hanged . . . boiled in oil and otherwise rid himself of those who consecrated their lives to his future comfort and well-being, in order to preserve all of his strengths and cunning for the erection of ever larger monuments, funeral shafts, obelisks, triumphal arches, statues-on-horseback and further hocus-pocus to the eternal glory of tyrants, kings, dictators and other politicians who led him, from the rear, to dismemberment and death.

"This is the story of the Boston dentist who gave you ether: 'Before whom in all time surgery was agony, since whom science has control of pain.' It should be almost unnecessary then to tell you that this man, whose contribution to human mercy is unparalleled in the history of the world, was ridiculed, reviled, burned in effigy and eventually driven to despair and death by the beneficiaries of his revelation.

"Paramount Pictures Incorporated has the honor of bringing you at long last the true story of an American of supreme achievement: W. T. G. Morton of Boston, Massachusetts."[38]

This first version opens in the present and cuts back and forward in time, presenting events out of sequence to amplify their dramatic impact. William Morton has recently died. Eben Frost, Morton's assistant, redeems his cherished medal from a pawnshop and brings it to his grieving widow, Lizzie, at the Morton farmhouse. Together, they reminisce about Morton's rise and fall.

A flashback shows how the Boston dentist's greatest moment was also his undoing. Morton's Letheon enables Dr. Warren of the Massachusetts General Hospital to painlessly amputate a patient's leg. A parade of adoring fans hail Morton after the operation. That night, champagne flows freely at the Morton mansion. But when the well-wishers are gone Lizzie tells her husband she's had a horrible fear. What if someone were to learn that Letheon is just plain sulfuric ether, available in any drugstore? Then, Morton's "discovery" would be of little value to them. Well, as a matter of fact someone has learned, Morton confesses. The Massachusetts Medical Society refused to administer Letheon unless they knew its formula, so he told them. "You weren't such a fool as to tell them the most valuable secret in the world, just for the asking!" cries Lizzie.

MORTON: But Lizzie they were going to take her leg off without it— without anything! They were just going to strap her down and hack it off!

MRS. MORTON: Whose leg?

MORTON: I don't know—some servant girl!

FADE OUT.

In a following scene, Morton is receiving medals and tributes from doctors around the world, but at home his dental assistants have learned the secret of Letheon and are quitting and going into business for themselves, taking his patients with them. An unscrupulous designer replicates Morton's ether inhalers, and when Morton claims to have invented them, the man taunts him: "So you invented bottles, huh?" Meanwhile, colleagues like Horace Wells and Dr. Jackson are asserting that they, not Morton, "invented" ether. Morton grows ill from anger, and his doctor sends him to the country to rest with his family.

The film briefly turns to Lizzie and Frost in the farmhouse; then to a second flashback, where a somewhat older Morton tends his successful farm. A letter arrives from the United States Senate. After years of reviling and neglect, Morton is at last to be awarded $100,000 by Congress for his contribution to humanity. Setting off for Washington, Morton assures his wife, "The money's as good as in the bank." But the inevitable doubts about his importance arise, and Morton loses everything he's made fighting for recognition, which is never granted.

What sort of person attracted such gross ingratitude? For the answer, Sturges turns to Morton as a young man—from here on, the narrative moves chronologically.

We meet Morton as a medical student so poor he's forced to give up his studies and go into dentistry. Morton is in love with flighty, materialistic Lizzie. Over her father's disapproval, they marry and begin a family. Even more than Morton, Lizzie is determined that her husband should become rich and famous. He opens a nice new office, but then the patients yelp so when he extracts their teeth that they drive off other clients within earshot. Looking for a way to stop the patients' screaming, Morton visits his former professor, Dr. Jackson, who—remembering Morton as a "dull student"—offhandedly recommends chloric ether as a palliative. Morton experiments on himself and his animals with both chloric and sulfuric ether and finds the latter more effective.

While Morton is still in an early stage of experimenting, his former partner Horace Wells from Hartford confides in him that he's discovered a way to painlessly extract teeth—with nitrous oxide, or laughing gas. Wells demonstrates his method at Harvard Medical School where in his anxiety he administers too little anesthesia. His patient cries out in pain, and Wells trundles back to Hartford.

Morton, meanwhile, perfects his sulfuric ether, which he names Letheon, to the point at which he's ready to experiment on a first patient. Eben Frost is so impressed when Morton painlessly pulls his tooth that he offers himself as the dentist's assistant and tells everyone he meets of the miraculous extraction. Letheon makes Morton the most popular dentist in town. Lizzie is rich beyond her dreams, but Morton discovers he is no longer content with wealth for its own sake. He's seen that Letheon can transform dentistry. Now, he approaches Dr. Warren of the Massachusetts General Hospital and asks if he can administer his Letheon to one of Warren's surgical patients. Warren agrees and is so gratified by their initial success that he invites Morton to help him with a subsequent surgery. But the day of the next operation Morton is suddenly informed by a hospital committee that rules forbid him to administer any drug without revealing its formula. Morton protests that he can't do that because "it's the secret of my business." Rather, he offers to give Letheon to medical doctors for free. Warren thinks this a generous proposition, but the committee refuses, and Morton walks off. He's on his way out of the hospital when he comes upon Dr. Warren's patient—a young servant girl. Because he can't bear the thought of her needless suffering, Morton acquiesces to the committee and reveals his secret to the world.

Unlike *Diamond Jim, The Great Moment* is faithful to the biography it's based on. Conceptually, the film is quite audacious—both in this first cut, which Preston shot in the spring of 1942, and in the revised version released by the studio. In both versions, Morton is portrayed as far from the familiar movie good guy. He's intellectually second-rate, greedy, manipulative, insecure as Jimmy in *Christmas in July*, far from altruistic. A scene in which the exasperated dentist orders his screaming patient to keep his "clap shut" and not alarm customers in the waiting room shows Morton as the opposite of softhearted; as does a later scene in which he tries experimenting on his own dog, until Lizzie rescues it. And, though he loves his wife, Morton is a neglectful husband—like Preston, he misses dinner parties because he devotes all his energy to work.

Still, no matter how wanting Morton is in the conventional virtues, Horace Wells and Dr. Jackson are even less appealing. Wells is so pusillanimous that he gives up experimenting with laughing gas after a single embarrassment. And Jackson, for all his superior intellect, whiles his nights away in bars and displays not the slightest interest in ether's humanitarian possibilities until it seems Morton will profit from them. Nonetheless, Sturges makes it clear Morton would probably never have conceived Letheon without these forerunners. "Well, maybe they all did discover the use of ether before [Morton]," sighs Lizzie. "I guess they did all right—why should they lie about it? Only it seems so cruel to have let people go on suffering so long—after they knew

Dr. Jackson (Julius Tannen) receiving Morton (Joel McCrea, far right) and Dr. Horace Wells (Louis Jean Heydt) in his "greenhouse" of an office.

how to stop it. All I know is that three months after my husband discovered anesthesia the whole world was using it!" Whatever his life was before and after, Morton at a crucial moment behaved nobly and was punished for that.

Louise Sturges says Preston was attracted to the book *Triumph Over Pain* because of its ironies, which his film underscores. Particularly effective is the skewed chronology: Sturges shows Morton's sorrows before his triumph, thus stressing the ingratitude of his benefactors. The prologue bitterly derides a world that rewards men who kill while neglecting those who palliate suffering. Yet, Sturges offsets his sardonic message with farcical interludes, usually involving the goofy Eben Frost. In one scene Frost, having inhaled inferior ether, leaps from the dental chair, upsets a table, breaks his violin over Morton's head, and disappears out the window, screeching orders all the while, like a cavalry sergeant. Horace Wells's demonstration of laughing gas at Harvard Medical School also ends in slapstick. And the young Lizzie, with her chattering, easy tears, and petty concerns is very much in the comic mode.

There are a number of striking cinematic effects—when Morton's drill-fleeing patients appear as shadows on his glass door; when Dr. Jackson receives Morton in a window-encased office, the fitting "greenhouse" for ideas he has no inclination of sharing with mankind. Yet, in both its versions, *The Great Moment* is more stylistically conventional than Sturges's earlier films, with none of their breakneck speed or agitation. The ending—where, to strains of "Ave Maria," Morton walks a dark, vaulted hall into a pool of light in the servant girl's chamber—is pure melodrama. And with its stolid pacing and quaint nineteenth-century décor, it recalls *The Power and the Glory* more than *McGinty*. This was certainly a directorial departure for Sturges.

It was also his first time out as producer. From the day he began writing films, Preston had yearned for the triple honor, writer-director-producer, which would put him alone in charge of a movie. When Bill LeBaron left Paramount, there'd been some talk of making Preston head of production, and he'd have relished that distinction, but in a way this was better still. Preston had never forgotten how A. C. Blumenthal pulled the movie rights to his play out from under him when he was in Paris, how even the best producers, like Paul Jones and Brock Pemberton, interceded between his vision and the final work. Being allowed to produce *The Great Moment* must have been enormously gratifying for the boy in Preston, who'd suffered humiliations, who'd never be content with artistic success, like Isadora's, who wanted to be a powerful figure in the world. But the fact that Preston chose *The Great Moment* as his first production is also significant. Vic Potel's fears that Preston might be "going commercial" must have been forever allayed by his choice of such a difficult subject and his willingness to accept just $450,000, half the budget on *The Palm Beach Story*, for his first production.

The studio initially wanted Walter Huston for Morton, but Sturges insisted on Joel McCrea. Opposite him, as Lizzie, was Betty Field, who'd made a striking impact three years earlier in *Of Mice and Men*. As Horace Wells, Sturges cast Louis Jean Heydt, whose aging pretty looks were just right for the shy dentist and, as Dr. Jackson, Julius Tannen, whose performance Preston would describe as "magnificent." Harry Carey, the silent western star, made a dignified Dr. Warren, and, in the Washington scene, Porter Hall played a folksy but enigmatic President Pierce. Preston gave Bill Demarest his most important role so far as the doting Eben Frost, and the rest of the stock company filled in the minor roles—Jimmy Conlin played a pharmacist, Georgia Caine was Lizzie's mother, Vic Potel was the dental patient who suffered at Morton's hands *before* ether.

The Great Moment began shooting on April 8. The mood on the set was

285

sanguine, with everyone convinced they were making yet another first-rate Sturges film. But from the start, there were troubles with Buddy DeSylva, who Joel McCrea felt was just looking for a reason to put Preston down. DeSylva, who'd never understood *Sullivan's Travels*, had given up trying to empathize with Preston's creative goals; he saw Sturges as simply a difficult man ambitious for power.[39] It could not have helped that, without self-effacing Paul Jones as buffer, these two egoists had to deal directly with each other; and, despite Preston's new hyphenate title, Buddy was still boss.

On *The Great Moment*, DeSylva felt freer than usual to criticize Sturges because Frank Freeman too was skeptical about the subject matter. British censors forbade depictions of surgery, so Sturges had to shoot a separate version of crucial scenes for the United Kingdom. And there was also the matter of queasy Americans. "I have already spoken to you about the scene of the leg amputation being too brutal as written, for an audience to bear," DeSylva complained at the end of the first week of shooting.[40] A month later he was reminding Preston that he'd promised to catch up on some lost time: "Today's three shot which was played by capable actors and was certainly simple enough, required twenty-one takes. I am sure that at that rate you will not pick up much time—even perhaps *lose* some ground.

"I suspect your answer will be that you are doing your level best at present. I am sure that you sincerely feel that way. But even persons who are doing their best can put a little pressure on and do a little more than their best." And he couldn't resist needling Preston, "[As] Mr. Freeman point[s] out [this film is not] the best gamble in the world."[41]

The pressure did not let up when *The Great Moment* came in on budget and a day ahead of schedule. When he saw a first cut of the film, Frank Freeman was put off by the prologue's unflattering references to war heroes. Shouldn't the deflating references to obelisks erected "to the eternal glory of generals on horseback" be eliminated from what is otherwise "a great motion picture?" he asked DeSylva in a private memo, in which he makes it clear that he has no intention of confronting the film's volatile director—this will be Buddy's chore. So while Buddy made the fuss, he was not acting exclusively on his own authority when he instructed Preston to provisionally change his title to *Morton the Magnificent*, or when he wondered if the prologue couldn't say something to the effect of: "In these days of war, we think it an opportune time to reveal the life story of the Boston dentist who gave you ether." "The following is not an attempt at final phraseology—only a suggestion," he diplomatically prefaced this idea.[42]

Sturges told his last wife, Sandy Sturges, that "everything I ever wrote I

Preston (middle) between Joel McCrea (left) and William Demarest on the set of The Great Moment, *extolling the cure for pain.*

subsequently had to live out. . . . I [am] like a man with the gift or curse of writing his own future." [43] And some of the alternative prologues he conceived for *The Great Moment* underscore an uncanny affinity between Morton's later life and Sturges's own. One prologue blurted, "Morton died of anger." Another read: "It is sometimes quite difficult to distinguish [great men] from

287

men who are not great: they eat about the same things, they sleep the same number of hours, they work about the same length of time and their achievements are also quite average except during the few incandescent years, weeks or minutes during which they become immortal." Greatness, in other words, was not integral to a person's nature, like greed or intelligence, but imposed from the outside, arbitrary and ephemeral.

The prologue Paramount finally settled on was in equal parts ironic and celebratory: "Of all things in nature great men alone reverse the law of perspective and grow smaller as one approaches them. Dwarfed by the magnitude of his revelation, reviled, hated by his fellow man, forgotten before he was remembered, Morton seems very small indeed until one incandescent moment he ruined himself for a servant girl and gained immortality."

But the prologue was not Sturges's only worry. While there were those in the preview audiences who loved *The Great Moment*, others were confused by the unusual chronology—as some viewers had been ten years before by *The Power and the Glory*. Here, though, the issue was not clarity—*The Great Moment was* clear—but narrative structure. No matter how much *The Power and the Glory* skips back and forth in time, its last scene is also the end of the story. If you nod through the first half, you can still watch everything tied up in the final minutes. *The Great Moment*, however, finishes at the story's climax, which only makes sense in light of the dénouement, and that comes near the beginning. However conventional its style, *The Great Moment* is structurally complex and demands concentration.

Buddy DeSylva was all for putting less pressure on the audience, while Sturges clung to his flashbacks as not just the boldest but the *only* dramatic way of telling Morton's story. "I do not believe in presenting fiction as biography," he later explained his strategy. "I believe a biographer has two obligations: He must be true to his subject and he must not bore his public. Since then he cannot change the chronology of events, he can only change the order of their presentation. Dr. Morton's life, as lived, was a very bad piece of dramatic construction. He had a few months of excitement, ending in triumph and twenty years of disillusionment, boredom and, increasingly, bitterness. . . . To have a play you must have a climax, and it is better not to have the climax at the beginning." [44]

There was a further problem with *The Great Moment*, and that was the formal balance. Where *Sullivan's Travels* seamlessly integrates comedy and drama, in *The Great Moment* the comedy feels grafted on. William Demarest, leaping out of windows or fainting at the sight of blood, has little to do with the grim story that precedes and follows his antics. Indeed, the comedy seems so out of another film that one can't help suspecting calculation on Sturges's part—an attempt to appease the studio with a few crude belly laughs. Yet, both Louise Sturges and Joel McCrea say this was not the case—Sturges was committed to the slapstick, he would have been no more amenable to eliminating the comedy than to changing the time scheme.

As it happened, DeSylva did not want Sturges to eliminate the comedy, nor did he have a cohesive plan for improving the drama. Since he couldn't identify with the material, DeSylva had only his dissatisfactions to guide him—the film felt too long, too awkward, too downbeat. *Something* had to be done, but while he wanted a drastic reconception, all he could come up with were superficial touch-ups—like rewording the prologue and changing the title. Ultimately, he would undermine the impact of Morton's sacrifice by chopping off the first flashback. But for a long time, Sturges held his ground. His first four films had been at the very least succès d'estimes. He was among the most illustrious figures in the film industry. It must have seemed impossible to Preston that Paramount would so mishandle a Sturges film that they'd risk losing him. After all, *The Palm Beach Story* was due out in December, and from the warm preview responses everyone was anticipating another hit like *The Lady Eve*.

But when Sturges's fifth film opened in New York the critical reception was far cooler than usual. Archer Winsten in the *New York Post* found *The Palm Beach Story* slight, and concluded that even Preston Sturges "can stumble. You will discover him spinning out airy nothings of matrimonial contention to boring lengths."[45] Kate Cameron in the *News* called it "not as completely satisfying a film entertainment as other Sturges pictures,"[46] while Bosley Crowther was harsher. Though he praised Rudy Vallee's performance and loved the slapstick bits with the Ale and Quail Club, Crowther thought the film "generally slow and garrulous." And he either missed or was unconvinced by the sober undertones, for he ended his review with a cautionary word for Sturges: "Maybe that Mr. Sullivan of 'Sullivan's Travels' went back to making hey-hey films after rubbing against harsh reality. But Mr. Sturges shouldn't try it. He's too good."[47]

This was not the final word on *The Palm Beach Story*, which, with its wit, fluidity, and love of artifice, is more highly valued today than in the early war years. Yet, the tepid reviews, particularly from Sturges's great fan Bosley Crowther, must have disturbed Preston; they may even have shaken his absolute faith in his artistic instincts. At Paramount, these reviews seemed to validate DeSylva's doubts about Sturges's next film, which still had no release date. For the first time in his happy life as a film director, Sturges had made a movie that might well be reedited without his consent. For all his pretty titles, Sturges could see he was as powerless as he'd been twelve years before when Brock Pemberton decided to rewrite parts of *Strictly Dishonorable*. As then, he could not accept that his vulnerability was inevitable for an artist working in a commercial medium. He'd risen too high to be worrying, in his father's words, about always having everyone liking him. Rather, he felt it was time to treat DeSylva as just what he seemed—an enemy. "Each shameful thing that has happened to me has really been a proof of my own weakness," Sturges wrote a sympathetic reporter.[48] Whatever the consequences, he was determined to become strong.

There was an irony to Preston's chafing for power because, in Hollywood terms, he was already amazingly strong. In the early forties, he and Frank Capra were among the handful of American filmmakers writing, directing, and producing their own films for a major studio.[1] And in that commerce-minded world, he triumphed not because his films were hugely profitable—even *The Lady Eve* was only a modest hit by Hollywood standards—but because of his talent and personal charisma.

These two aspects of Sturges's success were inextricable. "Probably never before has a first picture made its director so well known," wrote Alva Johnston in his 1941 *Saturday Evening Post* profile of Sturges. This was not only because *McGinty* was an extraordinary movie, but also because Sturges captivated reporters. Here was a man who invented rowing machines and diesel engines, who owned his own restaurant, who was incredibly rich but made a point of living far from the showy Bel Air set, who had a wife that—according to one article—looked like a Vogue model and talked like Rebecca West.[2] Here was a prodigious creator who claimed he would never have written a word if he hadn't been stricken with appendicitis in his late twenties. Moreover, there was Sturges's intriguing childhood. Nearly a fourth of Alva Johnston's two-part piece is devoted to Mary Desti. And other reporters quickly followed suit, outdoing each other with tales of Sturges's art-happy mother and businessman father, of how when asked to choose between the two parents, young Preston "instantly" chose the businessman but was nonetheless whisked away by art. Sturges, ever the ham, embellished and mythologized his history for feature writers, whose articles drew interest to his films, which in turn began to be interpreted biographically. This last development did not especially please Sturges, though it must have seemed a small price to pay for fame.

Preston at work, about 1942. (Photo courtesy of Nina Laemmle)

And he was, beyond his mother's wildest dreams, famous. He was a household name. So much so that a *Vogue* article in the early forties said of Sturges: "Lubitsch and Hitchcock, each with the stamp of a great personality on his work, are names not half as familiar to the American public."[3]

"It all seems too good to be true. I suppose anything does that happens so quickly," Lizzie says of Morton's glory in Preston's first version of *The Great Moment*. And at the height of his fame, Joel McCrea's Morton looks more dazed than triumphant—fittingly, since he has no control over his success. Sturges, in the early forties, must have felt similarly vulnerable, must have known that the adulation could end as swiftly as it had started. Not only was celebrity fickle, but the mind that conceived *Child of Manhattan* was not the mind that conceived *McGinty*. Sturges's enthusiasm and wisdom were consistent, but his work was not.

There must have been melancholy days when Sturges brooded about the uncertain future. Yet, at other times he felt completely secure in his genius.

Preston told Bertie Woolfan that, even if he lost his entire fortune and was sitting at the side of the road without a dime, he would need only a pen and paper to write himself back to the top of the world again.[4] And Sturges admitted that he found fame addictive: "The more you stand in the limelight the more scarred you will become and the more you will love the limelight. It is shameful but that is how it is," he wrote in an unfinished memoir from this period.[5]

Mary Desti had said that art is "a jealous mistress," [6] and, for Preston, fame was even more so. There were weeks when Louise rarely spoke to her husband except at their Sunday night parties. Though she tried keeping her son up until the late hours when Preston arrived home, this became increasingly difficult and, she felt, awkward for everyone.

Photos taken of the Sturgeses at this time suggest not so much tension as crossed purposes. One magazine picture shows a magisterial Louise reclining on a canopy bed while Preston sits on the floor, surrounded by toys and constructing some gadget, apparently for his nearby son. They all look lost in their own worlds. In another photo, in the game room, Preston—one of his cigarette-sized cigars drooped from his lower lip—is intensely involved in a billiards maneuver. Several feet away is perched a little blonde boy, who holds himself absolutely still and watches his father reverently. The father, though, seems oblivious to Mon.

Home movies from the summer of 1942 show the family somewhat more relaxed—Louise, in a black knit suit, teases and coaxes her one-year-old to play in the kidney-shaped pool. Preston swims alongside them. An inflated ball appears. Preston watches to see how his son will react. Preston and Louise simultaneously reach for the boy—carefully avoiding physical contact with each other. Later on in the reel, there are shots of handsome Leo Calibo in his uniform, home on leave, playing with the baby; of Monsieur Pillet in his chef's cap warmly embracing Mon; of Mon back in the pool with his matronly nurse, and in a perky sailor's cap at his first birthday party. Never, in the twenty-odd minutes of film, does the boy smile. Never does Preston seem fully at ease. Yet, in his own way he was proud of Mon. Years later, Preston recalled for his son how during the shooting of the swimming pool footage Mon had disappeared into the bathhouse. He emerged hollering, "Fah! Fah!" Since no one understood what he meant, Mon dragged his nurse back into the bathhouse where he showed her how he'd opened a gas valve in the barbecue stove. The gas was escaping into the room, and he'd been trying to warn them of "fire." Preston thought that was "pretty fine." [7]

Preston could enjoy "the little boy," as he called Mon, immensely for short periods of time, and he loved the—for him—exotic idea of domesticity. But the reality was less fascinating. Work and fame seemed more compelling than trying to penetrate a one-year-old's mind. Still, Preston told Louise, when the child became older and more interesting, he fully expected to be a good father.

For the time being, however, he was preoccupied with a film he'd begun writing in the midst of the controversy over *The Great Moment*. While this was a comedy, its plot was far from benign. Once again hero worship was a target of satire. Now Sturges also spoofed virginity, motherhood, baby Jesus, and, more daringly in 1942, soldiers going off to fight fascism.

Preston got the idea for *The Miracle of Morgan's Creek* in the late thirties. His heroine—as he saw her then—was a small-town girl seduced by the local banker's son, who refuses to marry her when she becomes pregnant. Distraught, she tries to kill herself by jumping into Morgan's Creek, but is fished out by an old hermit, who cares for her during her pregnancy. Sturges envisioned "some very stirring scenes," where the girl plays harmonium for the solicitous old man. One stormy night, he drives her into town, and she gives birth to sextuplets. Now, everyone wants responsibility for fathering this miraculous brood, but she says even the banker's son is "just boasting." The credit is all hers, and the hermit's.

While he was shooting *The Great Moment*, Sturges approached Buddy DeSylva with his *Morgan's Creek* idea, suggesting Betty Hutton and Harry Carey for the lead parts. But DeSylva wanted nothing to do with Carey and felt Betty Hutton couldn't carry a film by herself. So Sturges eliminated the hermit and wrote in a character for Betty's current co-star, Eddie Bracken.

Though far less sentimental than Sturges's original idea, the film *The Miracle of Morgan's Creek* retains the crucial ingredients of a spouseless mother and miraculous births. Here too, the best families are unconventional, and the true husband is not the one who seduces but the one who protects.

Set in small-town America, *The Miracle of Morgan's Creek* is the story of Papa Kockenlocker, a village constable, and his two daughters: beautiful Trudy and her younger sister Emmy, a precocious fourteen-year-old. With his wife dead, Constable Kockenlocker imagines countless tragedies just waiting to befall his young girls. After reading a newspaper editorial, "Are Military Marriages a Menace?," he forbids Trudy to attend a soldiers' ball in the church basement. But Trudy is determined to "kiss the boys good-bye" and fools her father, telling him she's just going to the movies with harmless Norval Jones. Then, she gets Norval to loan her his car to drive to the dance, promising she'll pick him up after the last feature.

Norval is a sorry soul on many counts. He's an orphan with a funny face and a stutter and a tendency to get so unnerved in front of the draft board that his blood pressure mounts, he sees spots in front of his eyes, and his fondest wish—to enlist in the army—is dashed repeatedly. Similarly unsuccessful are his attempts to win Trudy, who likes him in a sisterly sort of way, but would much prefer to dance with the romantic soldiers. So Trudy leaves poor Norval at the cinema and takes off for a good time. When she returns, it's eight in the morning. Papa Kockenlocker explodes at Norval for keeping Trudy out all night. What he doesn't know is that while Norval fumed at the cinema, Trudy married a soldier with a name that sounds like Razkiwatski; he's going off to war—leaving her pregnant. (Trudy has only the dimmest recollection of her soldier and no memory of the crucial event.)

Since Trudy has no marriage certificate to dignify her pregnancy, the only way she can escape eternal shame, resourceful Emmy decides, is to forget the Razkiwatski episode and marry Norval. Norval eagerly agrees. Only now Trudy "can't do it" because when she realizes how sweet Norval is she falls in love—and you can't make someone you love a bigamist. Rather, they follow Norval's harebrained plan to stage a false wedding to get her a marriage certificate as Mrs. Razkiwatski, with the upshot that Norval lands in jail, and Trudy is forced to tell the truth to Papa.

Now, Constable Kockenlocker's paternal instincts come to the fore. Guarding Trudy's secret, he moves the family to a farmhouse outside town, where he tenderly cares for the expecting mother. On Christmas Eve, Trudy goes into labor. Rushing her to the hospital, Constable Kockenlocker anticipates a dishonorable birth, but then Trudy produces not one or two but *six* perfect baby boys. Morgan's Creek becomes the focus of international admiration. The governor, anxious to keep everything clean, orders Norval immediately released from jail, made an army officer, and retroactively married to Trudy. Though initially overwhelmed, Norval, the concluding titles reveal, "recovered and became increasingly happy for, as Shakespeare said: 'Some are *born* great, some *achieve* greatness, and some have greatness *thrust upon them.*' "

Clearly Norval, like McGinty, Jimmy MacDonald, and Morton, belongs in the last category. Nothing short of a miracle could win this clumsy stutterer his heart's desire. Structurally too, *Miracle of Morgan's Creek* is very much in the Sturges mold. It opens at breakneck speed, in the middle of the action. The plot is tortuous; the names—Kockenlocker, Razkiwatski—are tongue twisters of the first order. And beneath all the nonsense about Trudy's not remembering having sex, as with *The Lady Eve*, there's a pointed Biblical analogy—here the Virgin Birth, audaciously mocked by all the Christmas Eve antics.

Yet, *The Miracle of Morgan's Creek* is also a departure for Sturges, who in his first six films worked mostly with urban landscapes and urban types. Here, for the first time, he confronts small-town America—with a difference. Morgan's Creek is worlds from the popover-baking heartland of *Remember The Night*, farther still from Capra's small towns, with their solid virtues and homogeneity.

There's nothing homogeneous about Morgan's Creek. From the foreign doctor and shopkeeper to the lawyer anxious to "sue anyone anytime for anything," the inhabitants are as diverse and scrappy as city folk. And though perpetually thrown together, they certainly do not blend. Nor do they easily inhabit their landscape. For every genteel Mrs. Johnson (Norval's foster mother) rocking contentedly in front of her house, there's a Trudy snagging her sexy dress on the white picket gate and a Norval careening off the quaint front porch into the briars. Maladroits abound: a febrile, perpetually astonished newspaper editor; a vindictive, leering banker; Papa Kockenlocker. Belligerent and sentimental as *McGinty*'s Boss, Trudy's father is a man for whom assault is the ultimate expression of love. His perpetual discomfort mirrors the turmoil beneath the calm of rural American life—as does Norval's anxiety. Here, for instance, Norval, with growing agitation, relives the trauma of his draft exam:

> I'm perfectly calm. I'm as cool as ice. Then I start to figure that maybe they won't take me and some cold sweat runs down the middle of my back and my head begins to buzz and everything in the middle of the room begins to swim. And [he slaps his hands] I get black spots in the front of my eyes, and they say I've got high blood pressure again, and all the time I'm as cool as ice.

Norval's emotional universe is without gravity, his every raw nerve is exposed. Though he complains of being homely, the real problem with his face is that it's so terrifyingly guileless. And he can't contain his feelings which, like symptoms of some mysterious disorder, spew out in spots, tremors, stutters, and hysterical giggles, which seem to aggravate rather than relieve the problem.

Where *Easy Living* and *The Lady Eve* mix farce and comedy, *Miracle of Morgan's Creek* mixes farce and melodrama, maximizing the pain and violence inherent in both forms. Take an early scene in which Emmy beats her father up while Trudy sits on him. Or the way Papa swings down a fire pole to punch out a bank manager. Or the climactic moment when a judge, a sheriff, a federal marshal, and an army sergeant struggle for possession of quavering Norval. Or imagine the trauma of the "miracle"—six babes delivered from one small girl!

The Miracle of Morgan's Creek maximizes the pain and violence inherent in farce and melo-drama. On the set of Miracle, from left to right: Diana Lynn, Preston, William Demarest, and Eddie Bracken.

Sturges displays the town's benign face in long shots of Trudy and Norval or Trudy and Emmy wandering the spacious streets, past front lawns and pretty shop windows. By placing his protagonists in the foreground, Sturges stresses their narrative importance; yet, as in *The Great McGinty*, the crowd constantly threatens to consume the individual. Trudy, whose dearest wish is to quietly resolve her own problem, gets her crime announced by a siren-blaring police car. The Kockenlocker sisters can't talk in their own room without Papa intruding, and even the orphan Norval is constantly scrutinized by gossipy neighbors. For in Morgan's Creek, private and public space are indistinguishable. Crowds swell not only on the streets and in the meeting halls, but in homes and yards with gates around them. Crowds are America's majority. Myths to the contrary, they're not noble or kind or understanding—merely susceptible. The "miracle" itself is meaningless until it's announced in their newspapers.

Given its obsession with community, it's fitting that *Miracle of Morgan's*

Creek is less about individuals falling in love than about families. Mostly, it's about families as unconventional as Preston's own—Papa Kockenlocker is a widower, Norval is an orphan, Trudy can't remember the name of her spouse. Like Solomon Sturges, Norval will give not life but love to Trudy's offspring. And Sturges suggests that no one will be the worse for that. They'll all live happily ever after. Or will they? For Sturges also makes it clear that Trudy would never have married Norval but for her pregnancy. She doesn't give this ungainly clunk the time of day when her mind's on romance. It's as an expecting mother that she falls for him. The image of plaintive Norval and his beloved unified by their common cause is gratifying. Yet, the plot admits another interpretation. Trudy's brief fling with marriage—or, more to the point, sex— is disastrous. Afterwards, she rejects passion for protection and gets swallowed by the narrow ethos of the town.

The Breen office, which had found it hard to accept Maude's multiple marriages in *The Palm Beach Story*, was beside itself over Preston's latest project. It was not just the pregnant girl with no husband in sight, or the blasphemous miracle, or the mockery of a wedding that disturbed them, but that Sturges was actually making fun of the war effort. A soldier gets a girl pregnant and leaves the hard part of fathering to a draft reject. What an idea, at a time when Hollywood was desperately trying to solace the War Department because the chemicals used to create celluloid were precisely those used to create gun powder. Movies were, as one skittish Hollywood administrator put it, "liquid bullets."[8] If the studios wasted precious material on dubious ventures, the government might leap in with their own censors, might even drastically curtail the number of films that could be made.

Sturges got a violent reaction to the unfinished script of *Miracle* that he submitted to the Breen Office: "Much of this material in the present script . . . appears to us to be unacceptable, not only from the standpoint of the Production Code, but, likewise, from the viewpoint of political censorship."[9] They didn't approve the "joy-riding" in military jeeps, didn't want it noted that the trouble "started in a church basement," they even objected to Norval's stuttering (which Preston stubbornly refused to remove). Trudy's pregnancy had to be "drastically cut down and the matter entirely rewritten. . . . It is agreeable—and necessary for plot purposes—to establish the fact that Trudy is pregnant. The unacceptability of much that follows is due to the fact that the point is hit several times, and thus gives out a flavor and an atmosphere which, in our judgment, is unacceptable."[10] Yet, between the lines, one can read that the Breen Office (and indeed all the censors who became embroiled with

Miracle—including the Catholic Legion of Decency) both abhorred *Miracle* and found it "very funny . . . from a strictly entertainment standpoint."[11] That despite (or because of?) its audacity, they found it funny and timely and true.

Betty Hutton[12] was born in Battle Creek, Michigan, the town Eleanor Hutton's grandfather made famous, though there was no relationship between them. Buddy DeSylva gave Betty Hutton her start as an actress, writing a part for her in his Broadway musical, *Panama Hattie*, and then bringing her to Hollywood where she quickly became typed as a rambunctious singer. Like Dick Powell, Betty was eager to break out of musicals. Like Veronica Lake, she was fussy about the personalities she worked with and was convinced only the right director could appreciate her talents. She was awed by Preston's films and overjoyed when he picked her to play Trudy, opposite Eddie Bracken. But Eddie Bracken was not so happy.

Eddie, who had been a child actor in Hal Roach's *Our Gang* comedies, also came to Paramount from Broadway in the early forties. He made eight movies in two years—three (*The Fleet's In, Happy Go Lucky, Star Spangled Rhythm*) with Betty Hutton. Although he was billed over Betty, he felt she upstaged him because—while the directors always promised there'd be no music—inevitably someone wrote a song for Betty, and he was given no comparable opportunity to show off. So Eddie did not pretend that the prospect of another film with Betty Hutton pleased him. Preston called Eddie into his office and asked him what was wrong. Didn't he like the script? Eddie explained that he loved the script, but it seemed to him that Betty was the real star. Preston told him not to worry—this would be *his* film, and he promised there would be no songs.[13]

The other roles were easily filled. For Emmy, Preston (uncharacteristically) cast according to type the gifted pianist Diana Lynn, who'd recently made her acting debut in 1942 as Ginger Roger's spunky roommate in Billy Wilder's *The Major and the Minor*. The role of Papa Kockenlocker was written for Bill Demarest, who would give the performance of his career: catapulting from under a patchwork quilt when the alarm goes off, stalking Norval in a kitchen apron, murderously lunging at Emmy as she coolly wonders, "Papa, can't you learn to be a little more refined?" Where Eddie Bracken's Norval sluices dismay from every pore in his being, Demarest's Kockenlocker concentrates all his emotions in an individual cantankerous gesture. Where Norval is psychologically transparent, Kockenlocker's floridly suspicious mind is as impenetrable as Billdocker's in *Christmas in July* or Eben Frost's in *The Great Moment*. Physically too-angular Demarest makes an amusing contrast with doughy Bracken.

Preston (left) directing William Demarest on the set of The Miracle of Morgan's Creek.

There were wonderful parts for the stock company: an overwrought news-paper editor (Vic Potel), a justice of the peace (Porter Hall), and Mr. Johnson (Al Bridge), who declares that Trudy, with her dim recollection of events, "doesn't need a lawyer, she needs a medium." Brian Donlevy and Akim Tamiroff would make memorable cameo appearances in their *McGinty* per-sonas. John Seitz, having missed *The Palm Beach Story* and *The Great Moment*, returned as Sturges's cameraman, and Preston was again producing the film himself.

Because of the film's delicate subject matter and Sturges's reputation for volatility, *Miracle* was closely watched by Paramount executives. After seeing rushes of an early scene where Trudy drives Norval's car wildly up to the movie theatre, they sent Sturges a memo, demanding, "In view of the Government's rubber-conservation program, it will be necessary to eliminate [the screeching of tires] when dubbing." Sturges did. He also fit in some of the "subtle propaganda" the industry kept pleading for, by having Norval caution Trudy against driving ten miles to the swimming hole to drown herself: "You're not supposed to use your tires for anything like that." And by having the soldiers' ball conserve on sugar and serve sour "Victory Lemonade." To portray soldiers drinking liquor was, in Breen Office jargon, "undesirable." Because it was also undesirable to have soldiers soberly marrying women they'd known for an evening, Sturges had an impossible dilemma, which was exacerbated when the war department insisted that he insert a scene showing "three or four fresh and clean-cut" soldiers with no signs of a hangover the morning after the reckless marriage. Sturges did as he was told, but the morning after scene feels almost tongue-in-cheek, as does a dancing scene where Trudy bashes her head against a ceiling lamp, which purportedly triggers her subsequent rashness. For all the talk of lemonade and marriage licenses, Sturges's point—that Trudy got drunk and slept with a soldier—came across loud and clear.

So Sturges had no real quarrel with the Breen Office or the War Department. He also willingly accepted war regulations limiting to $5,000 what could be spent on material for new sets. *Miracle*'s town, including a bank, a movie theatre, a city hall, and a post office, was pieced together from the ten-year-old *Tom Sawyer* set and other streets on the Paramount ranch. The ranch was thirty-five miles from Hollywood. Every morning, a bus carrying Sturges's cast and crew left Paramount at seven A.M. and returned twelve hours later. Since shooting went into late December, the inland weather was often bitingly cold, the hours arduous.

And Sturges was moody. With constant provocation from the front office, he more than ever demanded total power on his set. Eddie Bracken recalls what a dictator Preston could be. After finishing a typical scene, Sturges would, in his most imperious voice ask, "Well, Eddie, did you like that?"

"Yes, Mr. Sturges."

"Betty, did you like it?"

"Yes, Mr. Sturges."

"John, how was it for camera?"

"Perfect."

"And how about the rest of you, everybody like it? . . . Well, we'll do it once more."

"That," says Eddie Bracken, "was to let everybody know he was God."

Sturges, Bracken recalls, could also be very cruel, not only with the stock company but with his principals—who were much younger and less famous than Barbara Stanwyck or Joel McCrea. When they were shooting the bedroom scene where Trudy tells Emmy she thinks she's married, Sturges had the two actresses "crying their eyes out," he was so insulting about their performances. And when Eddie was playing a very physically demanding scene with Bill Demarest on the Kockenlocker porch, he became so out of breath he literally could not get his last line out. So Bracken stopped. And Sturges began screaming, "Why did you stop? . . . It was perfect up to that time . . . What's the matter with you, why don't you get yourself another brain?" "He was out of his mind really," recalls Bracken. "He came over stamping his feet, he came right up to me." But Bracken, who'd been a champion amateur fighter, could take only so much. "I had a habit that, whenever I got mad I would look you straight in the eye and smile. The message was, one more word and you're gonna be flat on your back. So I smiled that way at Sturges, I had my right hand up. I said, 'I know you're angry with me, but I'm angry too. Mr. Sturges, if you're right about something you can step on my fingers, I don't care. But when I can't help it—and I can't talk if I can't get breath—you're gonna get hit right off the chair.' So he calmed down and started to laugh. Sturges and I never had any real problems."

Bracken believes Sturges's cruelty was for the most part calculated to deepen the performances. Once the actors gave him what he wanted, Sturges's anger would dissipate, and "he'd love everybody again and tell them how beautiful they were. All of a sudden Lucifer was gone, and Jesus Christ was back," says Bracken. The reason the actors revered him on good days and bad was that he was a superb director with an infallible instinct for honest performance. Sturges could immediately sense whenever Bracken was just playing for a laugh. "He would say, 'I don't want Eddie Bracken, I want Norval Jones.' All of a sudden he would bring me back to believability." Bracken also admired Sturges's inventiveness. When there was trouble with a long shot of Trudy and Emmy walking through town, because the microphones cast shadows everywhere, Sturges came up with the (then startling) idea of dubbing the sound first and shooting without mikes. He also conceived a kind of teleprompting so the actors could read their lines if they forgot them.

Sturges had a miraculous memory and loved to play games during camera set-ups. Bracken remembers one game in particular where the cast would read Sturges a list of objects numbered from one to a hundred. Sturges was allowed to hear the list just once. Then, the next day, they'd quiz him. They'd ask, for instance, what is number seventy-four? And invariably Preston would come up with the right answer. (Bracken later learned that Sturges's mnemonic device was to memorize beforehand his own list of associative objects—seven, for instance, might on his list be a pair of dice. So if the cast's number seven were mice on a matchbox, he'd imagine mice on a matchbox playing dice.)

Bracken, who says he came to love Sturges like an older brother, respected him from the start because he kept his word about not writing songs for Betty Hutton, and because the film really was Norval's. Weaving and stuttering and flailing his arms about, Eddie upstaged Betty every chance he got, and Preston knew just what he was doing and encouraged him—because this one-upmanship was fruitful. Sturges also loved it when Betty got the idea to contract Eddie's symptoms during the false wedding scene, and the two of them outdid each other stuttering. "That was a wonderful scene—we shot it twenty-two times," Bracken recalls. "Each time we had to stop because somebody was laughing. Betty was screaming, Porter Hall [the justice of the peace] couldn't keep a straight face. There'd be people on the side giggling and laughing, and it would kill the scene. So on the twenty-first take Sturges finally screamed at everybody. He got everybody so scared you could hear a pin drop. He said, 'Let the audience laugh, you don't laugh.' So everybody was very serious, and this time he broke up!"[14]

Such exuberant moments, while salutary for the film, did not ingratiate Sturges with a front office preoccupied with cutting costs and saving celluloid. Learning that Sturges had ordered fifty takes of a particular sequence, Buddy DeSylva excoriated him:

> I think it is absolutely disgraceful. You, along with every other director, have been warned that the Company must conserve film. [That you could] waste this much film when you had at least two takes that might have been used actually amounts to sabotage. . . . No other director on the lot needs fifty takes to get a scene. Either you do not properly explain to the actors what they are called on to do, or you engage inadequate actors, or perhaps the actors get so upset after take #15 or #20 that they are no longer capable of giving you what you desire.[15]

The animosity between Buddy DeSylva and Preston was obvious to everyone. "If Buddy had talked to Sturges like a friend and explained what he wanted, Sturges would have explained what he was doing, and they could have handled it in a very diplomatic way," says Bracken. "There were good parts of Sturges and good parts of Buddy DeSylva, I loved him, but they could not reach each other diplomatically."

During the production of *Miracle*, even Frank Freeman sent Sturges a

Frank Freeman visits Preston on the set of The Miracle of Morgan's Creek.

memo about his extravagance. Paramount directors were expected to shoot at least three pages a day, and Freeman calculated that Sturges was shooting an average of 2.8. Therefore, there was no hope of his finishing in the estimated thirty-six days. Was forty days possible? Freeman wondered.[16]

Preston was profoundly upset by this implied criticism from his staunchest ally. He composed three drafts of a reply, all of which overlooked the issue at hand to complain about Freeman's not trusting him. What Sturges expected from the head of Paramount was not just more autonomy than any other filmmaker on the lot, but the professional equivalent of unqualified love: an intense emotional commitment to his talent. Perfect trust. What artist, in his or her secret heart, hopes for less? And Sturges must have wondered why that was so much to ask from a patron. Isadora, after all, never justified herself to Paris Singer, who happened to be her lover as well as her benefactor. Indeed, for all his talk of being a businessman, Sturges's deepest model in his dealings with Paramount may well have been that nemesis of his childhood, the great dancer, with her idealism, quixotic demands, and entangling of family with work.

Yet, Sturges had also learned from both Isadora's history and his own experience of antagonizing Brock Pemberton. Perhaps remembering his break with Pemberton, Sturges filed away his complaints and, assuming a comradely tone, sent Freeman a brief note saying he hated letters—why not have breakfast or dinner and talk?[17] Freeman replied placatingly, and all seems to have gone well for a while. But a month later some new incident impelled Preston to draft another letter to Freeman:

> *My dear Frank*:
>   How many years and how many pictures does it take to win the confidence of Paramount? How many years before my fellow workers say: "I know he is doing his best?"[18]

This time he signed "Cordially Yours" and sent the letter off.

Perhaps because he believed it dishonorable to air family matters in public, or perhaps because he felt humiliated by his powerlessness, Sturges kept his problems with Paramount to himself. Even Louise, away with the baby at Soboba Hot Springs, had to ask him, "If something was wrong with your work, you'd tell me, wouldn't you?"[19]

When he finished *Miracle*, way behind schedule in late December 1942, there were still no plans for opening *The Great Moment*. At first it seemed *Miracle* would be released immediately. "Both the Company and Sturges feel that because of its contemporary theme—the problems facing young Americans in wartime—'Miracle' should hit the theatres as soon as possible. Studio and Sturges feel that 'Triumph Over Pain,' which deals with the discovery of anesthesia won't lose its interest by being deferred," announced a February issue of the *Hollywood Reporter*.[20] But then Sturges had to add and remove scenes in *Miracle* in order to appease the Catholic Legion of Decency and the War Department. Since Paramount had a policy of making more movies than they actually needed to fill their theatres, there was no pressure to release *any* Sturges film right now.

The Great McGinty, *Christmas in July*, and *The Lady Eve* had opened, four months apart, in August, November, and February 1940–41. Now, over a year had passed since *The Palm Beach Story*. How frustrated Preston must have felt when *Miracle's* release was postponed until after the summer. Yet, he pushed ahead. He'd made seven films in three years, his creativity had a pulse and desire of its own. And, despite Paramount politics, it was thriving.

During the Spring of 1943, Sturges began preparing a film based on Mark Twain's *A Connecticut Yankee in King Arthur's Court*, with Bing Crosby as the Yankee. The combination of Sturges and Twain would surely have proved fascinating, but Warner Brothers had the rights to the book and at the last moment decided to keep it for themselves.[21] So Sturges began conceiving an original film that would star Eddie Bracken. "As I wanted to do something with a wartime background," recalled Sturges, "I thought for a month or so along the lines of what I call Monsieur Beaucaire in modern clothes. By that I mean a hero who is believed by all to be a villain but who in the end is introduced as a man of great honor with a long list of decorations. I had some difficulty in finding a valid reason for the hero to pretend he was not a hero and while searching around for a reason it suddenly occurred to me that it would be very easy to find a reason for a man who was NOT a hero to pretend that he WAS a hero."[22]

The greed and self-satisfaction of Twain's medieval court pervade the film Sturges ultimately wrote that spring, *Hail the Conquering Hero*, which is as formally complex as *Sullivan's Travels* and as personal a work as Sturges ever made. Years later, he would say that of all his movies this had the least "wrong with it."[23] Even more than *McGinty* and *Christmas in July* and *Miracle*, it was a film about winning and losing in America, about what America values, about our selfishness and yearning to be good.

Like *McGinty*, *Hail the Conquering Hero* opens in a nightclub. Here Woodrow Truesmith sits, miserably nursing a drink, as a chorus stirringly croons the sentimental "Home to the Arms of Mother" (written by Preston). In walk six marines, back from Guadalcanal, who've gambled away their leave money. Woodrow stands them all to a round of beer and, when they come to thank him, explains that he too joined the marine corps, but was dismissed after a month because of chronic hay fever. For a year he's worked in a boat yard, while writing his beloved mother and his girlfriend, Libby, that he's fighting overseas. He's also told Libby he's in love with another girl so she won't wait for him. The reason he's so ashamed about being rejected by the marines is that his father was a marine hero who died in battle the day Woodrow was born; Woodrow's whole life has been dedicated to following in his father's footsteps.

Five of the marines sympathize with Woodrow's predicament. The sixth, Bugsy, was raised in an orphanage and has an exaggerated sense of filial duty. Bugsy sneaks off and places a call to Woodrow's mother, then insists that Woodrow speak with her. The marine sergeant, thinking quickly, tells Mrs.

Truesmith that her son's been honorably discharged. To help Woodrow out, the marines give him a uniform with medals and insist on accompanying him home to Oakridge, where the whole town turns out to greet them at the train station, welcoming their hero home.

Woodrow, who hates hypocrisy almost as much as he fears dishonor, grows increasingly distressed as the town proceeds to heap awards on him. They burn his mother's mortgage, plan to build him a statue, nominate him for mayor. This candidacy is difficult to worm out of since the incumbent Mayor Noble is a self-interested businessman, while his perennial adversary, the veterinarian Doc Bissel, has no charisma and loses to Noble every four years. Eager for change, the townspeople rally around Woodrow. Woodrow's modesty and protests that he doesn't want the job only make him more desirable. Many applaud his demurs as shrewd politics. "We Want Woodrow" becomes the town's battle cry. And the marines, catching the campaign fever, chime in with stories about Woodrow's heroic deeds to enhance his image.

The pressure on Woodrow is so great he plans to run away, but suddenly decides to tell the truth, whatever the consequences. He confesses that he's never fought a battle, then packs and prepares to leave home forever. Now that she realizes Woodrow has always loved her, Libby insists on coming with him. At the train station, they spot the townspeople striding toward them. "A lynching mob!" Woodrow cries. But it turns out the people have come to affirm that they still want Woodrow. They appreciate the courage it took for Woodrow to reveal his cowardice. Besides, as one character notes: "Politics is a very peculiar thing, Woodrow. If they want you, they want you. They don't need reasons anymore, they find their own reasons."

Hail the Conquering Hero's narrative has a *McGinty*-like satirical edge. There's the marine reject who becomes a war hero simply by donning a military outfit; the town that greets Woodrow with four bands just because his mother reports he's been honorably discharged; the election committee that presumes first that Woodrow is a war hero and then that war heroes naturally make the best mayors; and the worthy veterinarian who always loses elections because worthiness doesn't win votes. The masses are turbulent and myopic. Woodrow's zealous fans turn everything he says to their own purposes; the "Welcome Home Woodrow" committee forgets all about the hero as its members vie to display themselves. Mayor Noble greets Woodrow with self-aggrandizing clichés, which the musicians mistake for cues and burst into showy march tunes, stealing the limelight. The forgiving crowd that pursues Woodrow to the train station at the end of the film might as well be a lynch mob, purpose is so incidental to their emotional fervor.

But *Hail the Conquering Hero* goes beyond satire to probe the longings of loners and misfits for a "normal" life in America. Woodrow craves honor. Mother-deprived Bugsy desperately wants a conventional home. Mrs. Truesmith asks to be compensated for her martyred husband. While mocking the reality of American politics, Sturges—no less than Capra—validates the common man's yearning for his American birthright. It's fitting that the minister burns the Truesmiths' mortgage in church because, for Americans, land is sacred.

Set in fictitious "Oakridge," California, *Hail* is Sturges's only film about the West—the end of the trail, the dream fulfilled. Yet, *Hail* gives little sense of boundless time or wide open spaces. Frequently, Sturges grips his characters in tight close-ups, and even the medium and long shots are filled to the edges with faces of the marines, the election committee, the crowd. Faces are squeezed between faces. Space is so cramped, this California village might as well be *Christmas in July*'s Lower East Side; and what room there is overbrims not with trees, but with placards. Like the unblemished politician, the unfettered West is a fantasy. Here as elsewhere, there's no escape from human wants and human prejudices. And Norval's identity is even more precarious than Mary's in *Easy Living*, because, where both are judged by their new clothes, Norval has no sense of himself apart from his mother, his girl, his neighbors, people.

The people in Oakridge range from a fussy chairman of the welcoming committee to erudite Doc Bissell, who wonders if even his wife votes for him, to Mayor Noble, who's both utterly cynical and an embodiment of simple faith. It's never occurred to him that what's best for the Noble Chair Company might not be best for America, so he with a light heart looks out for himself. Most of the other characters, though, are more conflicted. They're the folks who honor General Zabriski because they happened to get his statue at a bargain, but they also need to believe Woodrow is truly heroic—whatever they imagine that means. Spokesman Judge Dennis in his high-pitched voice tells the "hero":

> Woodrow, there's something rotten in this town. Nothing you can put your finger on exactly, but a kind of something you can feel. It's like the town was selfish, everybody thinking about little profits and how *not* to pay the taxes and reasons for *not* buying bonds and not working too hard and not working at night because it's nicer in the daytime. Oh, things that are all right in peacetime, things you used to call thrift and relaxation that made many a fortune, but things that are plain dishonest in wartime.

Things that, the judge implies, can be changed—you don't have to settle for selfish leaders, or as Catherine reproved her powerful husband in *The Great McGinty*, it's a shame "never to do anything except to shake [the people] down."

Woodrow reiterates this message in his confession at the political rally:

> I came here this morning to say good-bye to you, to tell you that I had been called back into the Marine Corps for limited service and that for that reason I would be unable to run for Mayor. . . . Well, I'm not going to do it. . . . You'd better save your hoorays for somebody else . . . for somebody who deserves them . . . like Doc Bissel here . . . who's tried for so long to serve you . . . only you didn't know a good man when you saw one so you always elected a phony instead. . . . Until a still bigger phony came along, then you naturally wanted him. . . . This should have been the happiest day of my life. It could have been, instead it's the bitterest. It says in the Bible "my cup runneth over." Well my cup runneth over . . . with gall. This is the last act . . . the farce is over, the lying is finished, and the coward is at least cured of his fear.

Woodrow is not Sturges's first virtuous protagonist—even McGinty was good-hearted and true to his own code, while Jimmy MacDonald and Hopsie and Jean and Sully and Gerry and Tom and Morton and Norval were all upright and deserving folks. Sturges's two earlier "heroes"—Morton and Norval—were, like Woodrow, celebrated and willing to sacrifice. But the difference here is that Woodrow is not just celebrated, he's celebrated precisely *for* his sacrifice; his success is not a matter of luck but of virtue rewarded. And the film ends with the medal-laden marines waving a fond farewell to Oakridge. Sturges, who'd told his Uncle Sidney that "hatred seems to be the most natural, the most usual, and the most enthusiastic emotion in man," who espoused "very little hope"[24] for changing the status quo, and whose films up to now ended with miracles, not justice, seems here to be engaging the possibility of a benign American majority. There's no escaping the message that Oakridge is ennobled by its contact with the marines, real and would-be. And this in a film that started out scabrously mocking hero worship and from a director who claimed he had no enthusiasm for the war.[25]

For all the complaints about Sturges's extravagance, *Miracle* had cost only $754,000, and—since Preston was asking for no big stars—Paramount projected that *Hail*'s budget would be just slightly higher. They would save money by shooting on the *Miracle* set, changed only in detail—the music store would become a cafe, the bank a drugstore. Eddie Bracken got a $15,500 raise;

William Demarest, cast as the marine sergeant, and Franklin Pangborn, as the head of the welcoming committee, both made $1,000 a week, and there were larger roles for many others in the stock company. Jimmy Conlin was cast as Judge Dennis, who smells something rotten in Oakridge. Harry Hayden (formerly Mr. Waterbury) became Doc Bissel; Al Bridge the sardonic campaign manager; Raymond Walburn, in his first Sturges film since *Christmas in July*, Mayor Noble.[26] Esther Howard, a busybody in *Miracle*, was cast as Mrs. Noble, while Georgia Caine got the film's most dangerously sentimental role, Mrs. Truesmith. Sturges gave Chester Conklin, from the Keystone Kops, a cameo part as a messenger who thinks his pate is a fine spot to stick a telegram.

A more important role went to a man Preston had picked out among a crowd of extras in *Miracle*. "You know I saw you hit a guy the hardest punch I ever saw landed . . . the night you knocked out Lesnevich," Preston told Freddie Steele, and he asked the former middleweight champion of the world to come talk to him at lunch time.[27] The two struck up a friendship. Preston so liked Steele's intense looks and simple manner that he promised to write a part for him in his next film. The result was Bugsy, a shell-shocked marine, who was raised in an orphanage and (in a bit of self-mockery), like Preston, reveres motherhood. It was typical of Sturges's absolute faith in his instincts that he gave this untried actor such a crucial part. For Bugsy's mother complex becomes a metaphor for the town's more general malaise and sense of deprivation which make the urge for inclusion in the American Dream so poignant.

Like Bugsy, Woodrow's "girl" Libby has no parents; she was brought up by her aunt and always lived to marry Woodrow. When Woodrow, hoping to save Libby the shame of marrying a marine reject, lied and told her he loved another girl, she became engaged to Forrest, but she makes it clear she'll take Woodrow back if he wants her. Libby is both the most sensible person in the film, and, in Woodrow's words, "crazy," willing to throw over an appropriate match to follow a pariah—because he happens to be the man she loves. Since Libby's new fiancé is Mayor Noble's son, her character conveniently links the political plot with the love story. Still, Libby, always in Woodrow's shadow, is a rather thankless role. She's the sort of girl Mrs. Sargent in *Remember the Night* would have loved her district attorney son to marry: sweet, loyal, and unsurprising.

To play Libby, Sturges picked a dark-haired ingenue, Ella Raines, who'd just made her film debut at Universal. Sturges discovered her at a casting call. Looking a little like Ellen Drew, she had a wholesome, straightforward charm and could deliver Libby's wry lines in a pleasing deadpan. Buddy DeSylva from the start was wary about Ella Raines—but then he'd also been skeptical about Veronica Lake and had fought against casting Rudy Vallee, whose performance in *The Palm Beach Story* was now being praised by everybody. As Mayor Noble says about Woodrow's heroism, Sturges's instinct for talent was the one thing no one at Paramount could "challenge, question, or doubt," so DeSylva reluctantly let Preston cast this new actress.

Then, the early rushes came in and Ella Raines looked stiff and fearful. She herself realized she was not doing her best. It was her first leading role, her first time off the Universal lot. She wasn't long out of college and she "simply froze," she recalls. "The first scenes for me came out awful." [28]

This time, it was not Buddy DeSylva, but Henry Ginsburg, an executive known as Paramount's "Hatchet Man," who confronted Sturges. By the fourth day of shooting, Ginsberg was not only insisting that Ella Raines leave the cast, he had himself appointed a Paramount contract player to replace her. Sturges was furious. Just before lunch, he came up to Ella, explained Ginsberg's position, and promised that he would refuse under any conditions to capitulate. "Don't worry," he said, when Ella burst into tears. "I will not continue with this picture without you." He then went off to Ginsburg's office to talk. [29]

Whatever these two men said that day was so traumatic that it in effect ended Preston's career at Paramount. Surely, Preston in no uncertain terms defended Ella Raines, insisting that he could not stay on the film unless she did, because she'd already been announced for the role, and dropping her now would mean a public humiliation for her. Surely, Ginsberg disparaged Ella and maybe Preston as well. And then Preston lashed back. . . . Because more than Ella was at stake, a friend of Preston's recalls. Firing his star was a personal affront to Preston, one that he would not tolerate. [30] He won his point; Ella Raines stayed on. But the war? That "awful day about Ella Raines will be with me always," Preston would years later write Frank Freeman, acknowledging that he "erred" in holding on to his resentment against Paramount over this episode. [31]

Still, this "awful day about Ella Raines" was only the climax of a long struggle, an indication of Paramount's growing irritation with their fair-haired boy and of Preston's own intransigence and indifference to authority. Paramount, after all, was not the only place to make films. "There is a world elsewhere," Preston must have thought. Or maybe it wasn't a conscious decision at all. Maybe anger and fear of powerlessness and guilt and incredulity about his sudden fame all overwhelmed him, and he relinquished his careful professional discipline and simply let go.

Torben Meyer attributed Sturges's moods to "super sensitiveness. One might say that is the price you pay for being our most brilliant head and our greatest director in Hollywood," he told Preston. "It is the kind of similar feelings we, your actors, have every time we start rehearsing a scene for you, because we never know, when the storm will start."[32]

Preston, smarting from the Ella Raines incident and anticipating larger problems with Paramount, was now stormy much of the time. According to one reporter, he was "smoking like a chimney."[33] The weather was often unbearably hot at the Paramount ranch, where shooting for *Hail* began July 14, 1943 and continued into September. While Ella Raines grew more confident and was soon giving a perfectly respectable performance, there was always some new battle to be fought. There was, for instance, the eleven-page sequence between Woodrow and the marines in the bar, which—like the opening of *Sullivan's Travels*—Sturges intended to shoot in a single take, breaking only for a cut-away to Bugsy in the phone booth. He hoped Paramount had learned by now that, while this sort of shot took hours to rehearse and set up, it could ultimately *save* them time and money. But again the front office was obsessed with immediate results. Early in the day, they began complaining about Sturges's not having any actual footage in the can. At two o'clock, Buddy DeSylva arrived and started berating Preston. So when, by six o'clock, Sturges had all the eleven pages done and had saved Paramount nearly three days' shooting time—while creating a spectacular opening for their movie—he retaliated even more recklessly than he had two years earlier by reshooting this bar sequence what felt to Eddie Bracken like 101 times, and he added salt to the wound by printing his second take.

Sturges also vented his wounded dignity on the actors. One day, Bracken decided to try out his confession speech in front of the cast and crew and, when he was done, Sturges, in his most imperious voice inquired, *"Are you going to play it like that?"* with everyone listening. Bracken immediately recognized that his error was in attempting the speech without consulting Preston. And he managed to placate his boss, while also salvaging pride, by replying with exaggerated unction, "Of course, I'm not going to play it like that. Do you think for a minute I would try to do anything with this speech without hearing from you first?"

Yet, Bracken was perplexed about the way Sturges chose to edit this crucial sequence, where Woodrow confesses to the townspeople that he's never been in the marines. When they shot the speech in front of everyone on the lot, the audience was visibly moved, many were crying. So when Bracken first saw himself on screen, in a long establishing shot, he was disappointed: that emotion did not come across. But Sturges had also had John Seitz shoot close-ups.

These, Bracken felt, were more effective. The nearer the camera drew to Woodrow's face the more moving the scene became, and when the camera came right up to Woodrow's eyes, Bracken saw the speech could be as powerful on the screen as for the live audience. Nonetheless, Sturges chose to show all but the last minutes of the speech in a medium shot, holding Norval at precisely the distance he'd held the sergeant in an earlier scene where he lies to the crowd about Woodrow's heroism. When John Seitz asked Preston why he didn't immediately pull in and show Woodrow in the more compelling close-ups, Preston replied, "Because it's my movie, not Eddie Bracken's."

And Eddie interpreted that impulse as egoism. Perhaps on one level it was. But surely it was also the opposite, an aesthetic self-effacement, for in pulling back Sturges sacrifices emotional intensity for comic distance, both from Woodrow and the crowd. Indeed, those who later accused *Hail* of sentimentality should have looked more closely at this scene where, until he relents in the final close-ups, Sturges refuses to endorse Woodrow's importance, where he disparages melodramatic identification and demands that we scrutinize rather than feel.

Sturges finished shooting *Hail* in September. After *Miracle*, he must have been eager to avoid disputes with the censors for he gave them little cause to fret. There's no pregnancy, no untoward sex, even the kisses are awkward. When Woodrow gets tipsy, it's on cooking wine. And while mocking hero worship, Sturges was consistently respectful of the marines. He also anticipated demands for "subtle propaganda" and had Mrs. Truesmith gently lecture a guest who likes butter on his pancakes, "Maybe you haven't heard there's a war on, Sergeant." Except for some desultory warnings, the censors left Preston alone this time. And preview audiences were loving *Miracle*, which was now scheduled to open at the beginning of the new year. However, *The Great Moment* still had no release date, and then the previews for *Hail* got a mixed reception. Buddy DeSylva told Sturges he planned to reedit his latest film as well as *The Great Moment*.

It was now December. Sturges was scheduled to begin a new film called *The Inventor*, but his contract expired on the eleventh, and he'd been arguing with Paramount for over a year over renewal terms. The problem was not money or perks, which Frank Freeman had been more than generous about. The problem was power. Sturges wanted never again to be subjected to another Ella Raines incident, never to have a production head lecture him in front of his cast and crew or, worse still, destroy his work in the editing room. And while he knew these were impossible demands, Sturges had an idea about how he could at least make Buddy DeSylva think twice before antagonizing him. The idea was a clause in his contract permitting him, for two weeks after every film, to leave Paramount if he wasn't happy with their plans for editing. This would allow him, if not final cut, at least considerably more impact on the finished product.[34]

It was really not all that unreasonable a demand. (In practice, this sort of thing happened all the time.) But Sturges himself *was*—at least from Buddy DeSylva's and Henry Ginsberg's point of view—unreasonable. Even Frank Freeman saw Sturges as someone who had to be constantly reined in, and while Freeman pleaded with Sturges to stay on, it's hard to imagine DeSylva would have been sorry to lose this troublesome filmmaker.

On December 12, Sturges met with Frank Freeman, who rejected his two-week clause but with affection and urgency asked Sturges to accept a raise and go on making great films for Paramount. He would get no better deal at any other studio, Freeman was sure. And independent production, which so appealed to Sturges now, had its own pitfalls. Furthermore, Sturges was impatient, and independent filmmaking was a slow business. Only half-joking, Freeman bet Sturges $100 that if he formed his own company, in a year's time he'd still have no new film released to the public.[35] Sturges left Freeman's office undecided about signing the contract, but later that morning he went to speak with Buddy DeSylva, and whatever transpired between these two affirmed Sturges's instinct that he should leave.[36]

That afternoon, Frank Freeman sent him a handwritten letter:

Dear Preston,

Buddy has told me of your talk with him after our meeting this morning.

After the years of association a parting cannot take place without my telling you how deeply I regret the necessity of a separation. You have made the decision, and I can understand your reasons. Whether I agree with them or not is another question.

Wherever you go and whatever your work may be our best wishes will be with you always, and I assure you I will always be one of your admirers—
Sincerely,
Frank Freeman

It was four years almost to the day since Preston began shooting *The Great McGinty*, yet it must have felt like a lifetime. Leaving Paramount was such a trauma for Preston it took him weeks to tell even Louise that he hadn't renewed his contract. It was the end of an era. He would never be so fruitful again.

Though Sturges quit his job in December of 1943, he spent much of the following year at Paramount, pushing for *The Miracle of Morgan's Creek*, *Hail the Conquering Hero*, and *The Great Moment* to be released. These ironic films with exclamatory titles made a curious triumvirate. They were at once politically charged and in love with slapstick; morality tales which (except for *The Great Moment*) favored a comic happy ending over a satirical truth. Even *Miracle*, the most accessible, was so stylistically disjointed it couldn't help but disturb a thoughtful viewer. Yet, they were the reverse of didactic, refusing easy judgments.

Miracle opened at New York's Paramount Theatre on January 19, 1944, and became a hit instantly. Writing Preston his reactions, Charley Abramson signed off, "Ecstatically Charley," [1] and the daily reviewers were similarly euphoric. "If Preston Sturges's *Great McGinty* commanded the 1940 'original script' Academy Award, he should be elected next President of the United States for his originality in *The Miracle of Morgan's Creek*," wrote Wanda Hale in the *Daily News*. Archer Winsten, in the *Post*, declared that Sturges "has lifted the entire movie-going public several feet out of the morasses of wartime worries. For an hour and a half it's like having the war won, the income tax repealed and nothing to do but laugh." Bosley Crowther said, "a more audacious picture—a more delightfully irreverent one—than this new lot of nonsense at the Paramount has never come slithering down the path. Mr. Sturges, who is noted for his railleries of the sentimental, the pompous and the smug in his classics, *The Great McGinty*, *Sullivan's Travels* and *The Lady Eve*, has hauled off this time and tossed a satire which is more cheeky than all the rest." Everyone raved about the performances, singling out William Demarest and Eddie Bracken for special praise.

The weekly and monthly reviews were also laudatory, though James Agee, in *Time* and the *Nation*, and Manny Farber, in the *New Republic*, expressed reservations. Both were impressed by Sturges's satire and formal deftness, yet they found the film ultimately "hollow." Each used that word, and they accused Struges of condescending to his public, in effect, of compromising his art for success in Hollywood. "There is always in a Sturges film," wrote Farber, "the feeling that he is above most of his comedy effects and that he is stooping quite far to make use of a comedy of which he realizes the entertainment value, as well as the fact that he realizes that a more profound, devastating satire (of which he is more capable in movies than anyone I know) is impossible in Hollywood and slapstick is a formula to rest comfortably in." [2]

James Agee, intrigued by Sturges's newspaper profiles, attributed *Miracle*'s "hollowness" to Preston's own "bitter" childhood. Writing in *Time*, Agee declared, "Sturges's brilliant, successful yet always deeply self-sabotaging films suggest a warring blend of the things he picked up through respect for his solid stepfather, contact with his strange mother, and the intense need to enjoy himself and to succeed which came from thirty years of misery and failure. From his life with his mother he would seem to have gotten not only an abiding detestation for the beautiful *per se*, the noble emotion nobly expressed, but also his almost corybantic intelligence. From Solomon Sturges, on the other hand, Preston may have derived his exaggerated respect for plain success, which leaves him no patience towards artists of integrity who fail at the box office. The combination might explain his matchless skill in producing some of the most intoxicating bits of nihilism the screen has known, but always at the expense of a larger excellence." [3] In a longer review in the *Nation*, Agee, while comparing Sturges's "shiftiness of style" approvingly to Joyce's and Picasso's, complained that his "stylization of action" held the "characters, and the people they comically represent, and their predicament, and [Sturges's] audience, and the best potentialities of his own work, essentially in contempt." [4]

Agee's analysis is perplexing. Comparing Sturges to Joyce and Picasso is flattering enough. But one wonders why if "shiftiness of style" is good, "stylization of action" is contemptuous; and don't Joyce and Picasso stylize too? What seemed to bother Agee and Farber was Sturges's contradictoriness— that he was a satirist enamored of physical gags, a humanist who resisted fleshing out his characters, an observer always, always ambivalent, an artist of the world as well as his style was fragmented, who couldn't or cohesive vision. And he was working not in rarefied literature or the fine arts, but in cinema, where even intellectuals, it seemed, expected consistency.

Sturges's public response to arguments like Farber's and Agee's was to reiterate his famed dislike for art and insist that he was proud to be called the "Toscanini of the Pratfall." Yet, his correspondence from this time shows he was not without lofty ambitions. Replying to one irate viewer, who accused *Miracle* of "contributing to the delinquency of minors," Sturges declared that he was not interested in instructing youngsters: "It is my intention some day to bring you Ibsen, Shakespeare, Molière, yea even Sophocles, Aristophanes and others who did not write for children in a chain of adult theatres or at least theatres with adult hours."

Of course, *Miracle*'s passionate fans (including General Eisenhower) far outnumbered its detractors. Servicemen particularly loved this war bride film, which in two months made more money than *The Lady Eve* made altogether; it would go on to become the year's biggest hit.[5] Concluding a reply to one of *Miracle*'s admirers, Sturges said he would be interested to know this man's opinion of his coming film, *Hail the Conquering Hero*: "Although it is not quite as funny, it has some sentimental passages which I think make up for that."[6]

When Sturges left Paramount, Buddy DeSylva fulfilled his threat to recut *Hail the Conquering Hero*. But DeSylva's version of the film was poorly received at a February preview, and, with *Miracle* a hit, Freeman gave Sturges four more days' shooting time and permission to reedit DeSylva's cut. Everyone agreed that the end of the film needed tinkering. Sturges's original version had included a penultimate scene where the town elects Woodrow mayor by a landslide. Now Sturges saw he could predict Woodrow's victory in the previous scene where the mob follows him to the train station. So Sturges eliminated the elections and cut directly to the marines' taking off for war: heightening the emotional impact. Thus, in addition to restoring many of DeSylva's cuts, Sturges also tightened and intensified his own work.[7]

In early May, Sturges's new version of *Hail* was previewed in New York for Paramount executives. Freeman cabled DeSylva that everyone was very enthusiastic, adding, "WILL YOU CONVEY INFORMATION TO STURGES OR SHALL I WIRE HIM OPINION. WOULD MUCH PREFER YOUR HANDLING STURGES DIRECT UNLESS YOU WISH THAT I SHOULD WIRE HIM."

So it had come to the point where Freeman was reluctant to give Sturges even good news! Freeman must have been especially reluctant to relay the good news that Sturges's cut of the film was better liked than DeSylva's because this would give Sturges an opening to argue that DeSylva's version of *The Great Moment* was inferior as well. Indeed, Sturges, needing no cues from Freeman, sent a hand-delivered private letter, pleading his cause:

> *Dear Frank,*
>
> While there's life, there's Hope . . . at least in my breast. With the present postponement of *Hail the Conquering Hero* there should still be time to save *The Great Moment* from the mediocre and shameful career it is going to have in its present form and under its present title. The majority of reviews in the trade papers should be enough of a foretaste, the handwriting is on the wall, and I don't see what Paramount, its stockholders, you . . . and myself are going to gain by putting out a picture in the form of a guaranteed, gilt-edged disaster, when, by the expenditure of less than fifty thousand dollars and some of my time which I will give for nothing you are nearly certain to have a picture of dignity and merit which will reflect credit on all of us and do a great deal more business. Our recent adventures with *Hail the Conquering Hero* and its New York preview should, I believe, at least give me the benefit of the doubt. I don't think I came through the adventure as a complete idiot and when I tell you that *The Great Moment* should be called *Triumph Over Pain* and that it should not be cut in its present streamlined form, you ought to listen to me.[8]

But Freeman did not listen. The film would be released in DeSylva's version. DeSylva's editing did not substantially alter Sturges's conception. The final three quarters of the film is almost unchanged. And Sturges was exaggerating when he told friends that DeSylva edited for slapstick, because all the slapstick bits were in Sturges's own cut, although the balance with dramatic moments was subtly different since Sturges's version was longer. Essentially, what DeSylva did was to elimate the first long flashback and with that Morton's intriguing early confession to Lizzie that he'd sacrificed the secret of Letheon for "some servant girl." In DeSylva's version, there's no mention of the servant girl until she appears in the last scene, waiting to have her leg amputated. This makes Morton a far less interesting character throughout most of the film and also ruins the plot suspense surrounding this girl and Morton's sacrifice which Sturges so carefully set up.

The trade paper reviews Preston's letter alludes to were respectful but cool. William Demarest's wild comic interludes offended many critics. *Daily Variety*, for instance, commented, "The tale of W. T. G. Morton, discoverer of the anaesthesian [sic] properties of ether, is overloaded with slapstick humor that detracts considerably from the serious and worthy theme." A reporter named Harrison Carroll pointed out that Paramount executives cut *The Great Moment* after Sturges left the studio. Probably, Preston himself had leaked the news. Yet, when DeSylva confronted Preston with Carroll's accusation, Preston immediately called Carroll and claimed full responsibility for the movie. DeSylva (who, ironically, was himself now planning to leave Paramount to go into independent production) wrote Preston a friendly note, thanking him for making the call. "Perhaps I was a little touchy," he apologized. "The only time that Paramount was mentioned in one of your reviews was in this case, by Harrison Carroll. God knows Paramount (and I) have contributed little enough to your movies." Yet, he felt "a little bit burned" at being blamed for a less successful Sturges venture. "As I told you in the commissary we unit men must stick together. I shall always be rooting for your success." [9]

And in a similarly unrecriminatory tone, Preston wrote "Buddy": "My personal opinion of the film in its present form, after seeing it again, was stated with some clarity in a letter to Frank Freeman. . . . I will be very glad to send you a copy of the letter if you have not seen it but all this is water under the bridge and I say The Hell with it." [10]

Sturges also begged another reporter in whom he'd confided his frustrations over *The Great Moment* not to print anything concerning his quarrels with Paramount: "This because, although I have fought bitterly against stupidities in this particular branch of the theatre, and with some good results, I have kept the quarrels within the family walls and have never yelled out my accusations for the edification of the neighbors. Each shameful thing that has happened to me has really been a proof of my own weakness. I believe I will soon be strong enough to correct this matter. I would rather do that than yelp about it." [11]

It was no surprise when *The Great Moment* opened, in November 1944, to very mixed notices. While Wanda Hale in the *Daily News* called it "an entertaining as well as an enlightening picture," Archer Winsten found it "funny as a crutch" and Joel McCrea "about as full of vital character as a fish on a platter." Bosley Crowther, obviously baffled by what he found "a rather radical departure from [Sturges's] familiar satiric vein," mused, "Perhaps scientific inspiration is not conventionally reverenced in this film. But at least Mr. Sturges has triumphed over stiffness in screen biography." The monthly film critics ignored this film which apparently struck them as irrelevant to the Sturges *oeuvre*, and *The Great Moment* was a commercial failure.

Still, elsewhere Sturges's career was flourishing. *Miracle* was selling tickets like mad, Sturges had *two* scripts nominated for Oscars, in the *New York Times* Bosley Crowther was calling him director of the year, everyone was fighting about whether he was more like Molière or Chaplin. Because, three months before *The Great Moment*, *Hail the Conquering Hero* had opened. The trade and daily reviews were unanimously positive. And while James Agee had his usual reservations and Manny Farber complained that "when the hero unmasks himself to the townspeople as a phony, by showing the humiliation and lunacy of everyone concerned, Sturges evades the whole issue *revoltingly* and runs off to a happy ending," others saw this as Sturges's breakthrough film, the work where he managed to balance his impulses toward satire and sentiment. When *Hail the Conquering Hero* opened in Paris, André Bazin would ask, "Why should Sturges be reproached for his inhumanity when his true purpose is to proclaim collective determinism and the mechanics of society, proving their foolish independence from the human truth to which they refer?" And he called *Hail* "a work that restores to American film a sense of social satire that I find equalled only (due allowances being made) in Chaplin's films." [12]

"In this fast and noisy small-town comedy," wrote Bosley Crowther, "the smartest satirist in Hollywood has pulled himself tightly together and thrown all his weight at one point." Praising *Hail*'s "comprehensive maturity," he predicted, "A Hollywood Voltaire is budding. Or shall we just say that Mr. Sturges has arrived?" [13]

It would perhaps have been more accurate to say he was leaving. Yet, this film, in so many ways a consummation, does convey the promise of new achievement. And the most fitting tribute to its complexity is that critics would continue to argue about *Hail* well beyond the end of the decade and Sturges's Hollywood career. [14]

PART V

Good-bye to All That

I was never able to understand . . . why if one wanted to do a thing one should not do it. . . . For I have never waited to do as I wished. This has frequently brought me disaster and calamity, but at least I have had the satisfaction of getting my own way.

Isadora Duncan, *My Life*

In 1947, when Louise sued Preston for divorce, she would tell the judge that her husband had for several years been avoiding their home because his work required more stimulating company. And Preston would explain to Louise's attorney that he wanted "to experience all sensations."[1] All sensations—how lusty that sounds, and Preston was a lusty man, loving food and wine and sex. Yet, sensation for him was more than sensual pleasure. He had all his life been uncannily excited by beauty—in a performance, a person, an idea; now, in his mid-forties, he longed to live like a young man at fever pitch always—the more so as he grew increasingly aware of his mortality. Preston began telling reporters that he got his energy from "living in contemplation of death."[2] He had first explored this idea through the character of the Wienie King, in *The Palm Beach Story*, who warns Gerry that one day she'll wake up and find everything behind her: "Makes you sorry for a few of the things you didn't do while you still could."

Preston also liked to tell about how he found Ella Raines moping around the set, depressed because her dressing room had been painted green instead of blue. "I asked her," said Preston, "to picture herself on her death bed. She was eighty years old. She was just drawing her last breath. Now at that moment she recalled herself at twenty, on the threshold of her career, possessed of youth, health, beauty, fame, wealth and everything else she wanted. I asked whether she would want to remember, at that last moment, that she had allowed a whole day, or even one of those golden minutes, to be spoiled just because a painter had made the walls the wrong color." Ella Raines, said Preston, immediately perked up.[3]

Preston often said that the only things you regret in life are your economies. This had been his mother's philosophy. The older he got the more connected he felt to Mary Desti, the more he forgot about her willfulness and

Preston relaxing on his boat.

appreciated what an original person she had been. But he never forgave his mother for leaving his father. Preston had a white streak through his hair and was now a father himself as well as a husband and lover. And while he often complained that Louise bored him, he also said he needed his family.[4] However exceptional Preston Sturges was, he was also a middle-aged man with middle-aged needs and worries. He was deeply attached to his house and garden. He was plagued by never-ending intestinal problems, he was sure he had ulcers, though they never showed up in tests.

When Gilletti returned to Los Angeles, shortly after Preston left Paramount, he was amazed by the transformations in the Sturges household. Preston's attitude toward Louise had changed completely. And while Louise had always had a sly wit—ironic, but genial—now she had a bitter sense of humor. Gilletti's new wife couldn't believe it when she heard her husband or Ernst and Nina Laemmle talk about how in love Preston and Louise had been.[5]

One night the Gillettes invited the Sturgeses for dinner. Louise spent the whole evening wearing very dark glasses because she had a black eye. Preston had hit her. And she, a Midwesterner—who had never heard her parents so much as raise their voices in anger—was profoundly shocked and ashamed. As with Eleanor Hutton, it was no great issue that roused Preston's violence, but something "very trivial. He had a great deal of anger and a great deal of hatred and a great deal of loathing of humanity," she recalled, years later.[6] He also had a great deal of guilt, and no more than Bianca did Louise make it easier for Preston by walking out on him. Louise Sargent had not been the divorcing kind in the first place. Now she had a son to think about and was eager for more children. She would do everything she could to make the marriage endure.

The year he left Paramount, Preston must have been as anxious as Louise to maintain at least the fiction of their marriage, for so much else in his life was changing. He was declaring his independence from the Buddy DeSylvas and Henry Ginsbergs of the world. He was striking out on his own, as a filmmaker. Though the major studios offered him salaries as large as $6,000 a week, there was no price high enough to seduce Sturges back into dependency. Rather, he planned to become an independent director-producer like Orson Welles and, like Isadora Duncan, to accept a patron.

A partnership was actually what Howard Hughes had for months been proposing to Sturges. Preston had met Hughes casually in the thirties and liked what he knew of the reclusive millionaire. Sturges admired the fact that Hughes (unlike Paris Singer) had multiplied his father's fortune and that he considered himself an inventor as much as a businessman. When The Players opened, Hughes began showing up for late meals, sometimes keeping the orchestra playing until four in the morning while he danced with some ingenue, but often just dining alone or talking to Preston about their shared passion for engineering.[7]

Hughes and Sturges also had in common a pronounced iconoclasm and restlessness with the motion picture industry. As well as producing *The Front Page* and *Scarface*, Hughes, over the past decade, had grown obsessed with aviation, directing *Hell's Angels* (1930), about planes and fliers, founding Hughes Aircraft, and setting a record for flying around the world. Even now, as he and Preston began conceiving a joint production company, Hughes was rushing to deliver his and Henry J. Kaiser's "flying boat" (later nicknamed the Spruce Goose) to the War Department. Unlike Preston, Hughes actually got contracts for his wild inventions.

Also unlike Preston, Hughes was a daredevil, who though morbidly afraid of germs, constantly subjected himself and others to dangerous flying maneuvers. He was seven years younger than Sturges and even more inclined to fleeting passions. He recklessly hired and fired employees, would go to great pains to buy an aircraft, only to lose interest and sell it the same week, and he was always turning up with some new beautiful woman. Hughes was also secretive and suspicious and, though Preston didn't like to remember this, had himself directed a few movies. He also so interfered with the gifted Howard Hawks, whom he'd hired to direct *The Outlaw*, that Hawks walked off the set.

Howard Hawks and Willie Wyler were among many who warned Preston against going into business with such a volatile partner. *Time* magazine called Sturges and Hughes "two of the most combustible personalities in cinema."[8] Still, Preston followed his own instinct: with his tremendous financial resources, Hughes seemed to him an ideal partner—the more so because Hughes's current preoccupation with the Spruce Goose would deflect him from interfering with any day-to-day aspects of filmmaking. Indeed, when they officially announced the formation of California Pictures, Hughes called a press conference where he told reporters, "I want to make one thing clear—I can't devote any time whatsoever to the motion picture business until the war is over. Sturges is the one man in whom I have complete confidence. I am happy to turn over to him the full control and direction of all my motion picture activities."[9]

Preston spoke of Hughes as "a man of courage, vision, and capital."[10] There was nothing Preston hated worse than lawyers quibbling about semantics or anticipating unpleasantness, so he would have been happy to leave their partnership as a gentlemen's agreement—and later, in his memoirs, remembered it as just that. But in fact there were the myriad details of a power balance to be ironed out, and it was eight months before a mutually agreeable contract was devised. Hughes initially envisioned Preston as a salaried employee, which Preston found unacceptable, since he could be an employee anywhere. Preston wanted the right to direct what he liked and to approve any film California Pictures sent out into the world, and Hughes in turn demanded his own guarantees and privileges.

Louise remembers Hughes turning up around midnight for nightly conferences. He was always disheveled and shabbily dressed and he was nearly as deaf as Henry Henigson, though he refused to admit his hearing problem. Preston, she recalls, said Hughes "never ate anything but soda crackers and was definitely undernourished, and Preston thought he might die before he signed the contract." So she left "masses of milk and very nourishing oatmeal cookies" in the refrigerator behind the bar, and the men consumed them as they eagerly conversed—often not so much about the contract as about engineering feats or some new idea Preston had for a movie.[11]

It was Preston's shrewd friend Henry Henigson who in August 1944 finally presented Hughes with what seemed a workable contract. Out of one hundred shares of the company's "Class A" stock, Preston would own forty-nine shares and Hughes fifty-one—with the option to buy Preston's shares should he at any time want to end the partnership. Hughes would put up the money for everything, including Preston's $2,500-a-week salary, which was, Preston figured, $3,500 less than he could earn at MGM or Fox, so he too was making a financial investment. Preston would have complete creative freedom, the chance to direct his own films and to select other properties for the company. Henry Henigson (who received shares of "Class B" stock) would be business manager. California Pictures would have a bear in a field of poppies as its insignia, and everyone hoped it would open new frontiers.

Preston had many ideas for his new enterprise. One was to find a way to revive D. W. Griffith's career. Preston must have remembered what a sensation *Birth of a Nation* made when he was still a teenager, running the Maison Desti. Now Griffith was nearly seventy, impoverished and unemployed. Griffith's fragile romanticism was considered out of step with the times, and Griffith in return professed to scorn new movies. Sturges was one of the few contemporary filmmakers Griffith openly admired. He made a point of telling people *Miracle of Morgan's Creek* was the funniest film he'd ever seen.

Griffith's and Sturges's views on life were radically different. Yet, they shared the vision of film as an art form. And as with Jean Renoir and René Clair, Sturges was eager to ally himself with a man of stature whom Hollywood was neglecting. In the early forties, Herb Sterne, from the *Hollywood Reporter*, introduced the two filmmakers. Eddie Bracken remembers Griffith eating lunch at Sturges's table at Paramount every day for months—though Bracken found Griffith so unassuming he thought the great film pioneer was just a prop man.

"I am going to find out what the name David Wark Griffith means to people today and then try to see that his [new film] . . . fits the anticipation," Preston wrote a colleague in July 1944. Soon after, Preston conceived the idea of having Griffith direct *9 Pine Street* with Lillian Gish, who'd starred in the play on Broadway.[12] Griffith seemed willing, and Dudley Nichols was so eager to see the great director working again that he offered to write the screenplay for free. A meeting was arranged at the Roosevelt Hotel, where everyone turned up but Griffith. An hour late, Griffith finally staggered in, very drunk and not the least bit humbled by his circumstances. "Whatever gave you people the idea I wanted to direct another film?" he blustered.[13] Sturges was not amused, and that was the last said of the Griffith project. "The world," Herb Sterne concludes, "isn't big enough for two egos like Preston's and Griffith's."[14]

Another project Sturges flirted with was an adaptation of Joseph Herge-sheimer's 1917 novel *Three Black Pennies*, about three generations of a Penn-sylvania mining family. Hergesheimer was one of Preston's favorite authors, and Sturges must have been attracted to the book's thematic conflict between passionate individualism and romantic love. As they corresponded, Herge-sheimer became increasingly enthusiastic about a movie, but Preston began worrying that the material wasn't distinctive enough for his California Pic-tures debut, and put it off for the time being.

With both the Griffith and the Hergesheimer projects, Preston was turning to artists who had moved him in his youth. But he was also well aware of what was considered "Sturges material," and began outlining two ideas very like his latest films. The first he conceived for Freddie Steele, the mother-crazy ma-rine in *Hail the Conquering Hero*. It was about a man suffering from amnesia who drops off a freight train in a small American town. Preston described the story:

> Little by little [the man] discovers his past life and the audience discovers it at the same time. He finds that he was the bad boy of the town, that he got a girl in trouble, that he committed a crime to raise money, that he was arrested, possibly sent to the penitentiary and that he escaped. He is no longer bad and he now wishes to expiate his crimes. As he is on his way back to the penitentiary, he is seized by the envoys of the San Diego Naval Hos-pital and we now discover the end of his story. After escaping he had enlisted in the marines. He is a brave hero and the list of his decorations is very long. It is felt that his second adventure has wiped out his early record, and he is permitted to stay in the town with the girl and his son.[15]

While this reads like a cross between *Miracle of Morgan's Creek* and *Hail the Conquering Hero*, another of Sturges's ideas sounds like a farcical *Great Mo-ment*. Here the hero is a beleaguered small-town inventor who after much bungling finally devises a useful machine. His "electrical, high frequency bat sound" succeeds in terrifying mosquitoes. "Unfortunately, however, the sound it gives off is the mating call of the bats, and it attracts all the bats in the Western Hemisphere." Obviously still smarting from his own experience with both the patent office and *The Great Moment*, Sturges added a note at the end of his treatment: "I am quite sure that a little man who braves ridicule to improve the lot of his fellow men, and is thanked by their jibes, is an interesting character. The United States owes a great debt to its inventors. Far from being grateful to them, it places every obstruction in their way and makes it enormously difficult to secure a patent." [16] The prospective film was alliteratively titled *The Wizard of Whispering Falls*, and Eddie Bracken told reporters this would be his last film with Sturges.

The idea Preston finally settled on had attributes of all these abortive projects. It involved a figure from silent pictures, provided challenging roles for the Paramount stock company, and was about Sturges's favorite themes of heroism, luck, and the American Dream.

The silent film figure was comic Harold Lloyd whose movies Preston had discovered about five years after D. W. Griffith's. Lloyd's name was always linked with Chaplin's and Keaton's. But they were all very different, of course. Where Buster never smiled, Harold flashed his horsey white teeth constantly. Where Chaplin's films took pains to reveal the obduracy of the world, Lloyd's were more about one's self, about how you could do anything if you mustered up the will power.

Of the three great silent comics, Harold Lloyd is most like the boy next door. He wears glasses, is shy and laughs inappropriately, rather like Eddie Bracken.[17] Neither courage nor dexterity come easily to Harold who, in *Grandma's Boy*, needs Grandad's "lucky charm" to confront a neighborhood prowler and, in *Safety Last*, climbs the face of a building only when there's no other choice. In *The Freshman*, Sturges's favorite Lloyd film, Harold isn't even really on the college football team. He's merely the water boy. But when he's summoned to replace injured players, Harold makes the spectacular winning touchdown. Tom Dardis, Lloyd's biographer, notes that one of the "chief attractions" of Lloyd's films "is our delight in seeing something attained with difficulty."[18] Indeed, a significant difference between Sturges and Lloyd as filmmakers is that, while Sturges's characters are redeemed by good fortune, Lloyd's earn their success.

In the early twenties, Lloyd was more popular than either Chaplin or Keaton. But, by 1944, the silent films that made him famous were two decades old. Lloyd felt defeated by sound, unhappy with his talkie films like *Movie Crazy*. Though he was only fifty, Lloyd had not made a movie in six years when Sturges approached him with his idea for *The Sin of Harold Diddlebock*.

The two men had first met when Lloyd was working at Paramount in the mid-thirties. Later, Sturges got Lloyd a job as radio host. Sturges was obviously less troubled by the comic's raspy voice than he was impressed by his image on film and intrigued by *The Freshman*, with its mixture of satire, slapstick, and excitement in the football scenes. Sturges's idea, he told Lloyd, was to begin a film with the last reel of *The Freshman*, then to show what happened to Harold *after* he won that game.

Lloyd was hesitant at first. He'd been careful with his large earnings so he could now get by without working, and he much preferred to throw himself into hobbies—stereo photography, Shriner activities—than to make a film that might damage his reputation. So Sturges began courting Lloyd. He visited Lloyd's dilapidated Greenacres mansion and insisted on buying beautiful new living room curtains. He promised that Lloyd would not simply be an actor in a Sturges vehicle, he too would have a creative voice.

Then, just when Lloyd began getting interested, Howard Hughes, determined not to be financially exploited (he was paying Henry Henigson less than Sturges made on his first writing assignment), offered Lloyd an insultingly low salary. "The Harold Lloyd picture disappeared from our schedule the instant I mentioned what you were willing to pay him," Preston wrote his partner in October.[19] Reluctantly, Hughes raised his offer to $50,000 for Lloyd's performance and another $50,000 for the football scene in *The Freshman*, against a sum equal to 7.5 percent of the producer's gross.[20] Lloyd accepted, but insisted on adding a clause to the contract, stipulating that if he didn't like the way Sturges conceived a scene, he would play it anyway, but Sturges would also have to direct the scene *his* way. Afterwards, they'd watch the rushes and determine whose idea worked best.

For the first time in over a decade, Sturges had no boss hurrying him, and he took some time musing about the shape and tone of his new film. On one note page he scribbled:

> Harold Lloyd story:
> Unsuccessful worm.
> Drink and many difficulties.
> Difficulties force resourcefulness.
> Resourcefulness brings success.
> Success brings confidence.

Further down the page, he launched into oratory:

> I salute you, America! For your indomitable courage in the face of almost insurmountable obstacles and for your scorn of these overwhelming odds. . . . I salute your odd religions and your prairie schooners and your women who followed their men and brought forth peaceful homesteads in the shadow of the eagle and the echo of the thundering herd. I salute your welcome to the scum as well as the flower of the old world and your dream of equal opportunity. I salute your enormous success and your colossal blunders pursued with the same impatient energy.

This impatient energy Sturges recognized as his own, which was why it was foolish, he must have thought, that film critics and even other directors like his friend René Clair advised him to conserve his talents. Their idea was that if he did less his films would be deeper. Clair had said that Preston was "like a man from the Italian Renaissance: he wants to do everything at once. If he could slow down he would be great."[21]

But Preston knew he was great, or at least as good as he could be, because he did not conserve, because he refused to slow down and spent his energy and excitement unsparingly. And this he saw as not just peculiar to himself, but profoundly American, as what made him different from René Clair and Jean Renoir, the true heir to the pioneer spirit of his Sturges forebears. These ideas would work their way into his film with Harold Lloyd. *The Sin of Harold Diddlebock*, Sturges's most extravagant film, is a defense of all large endeavors.

The film opens with *The Freshman*'s last reel where Harold twice runs the length of the football field in the game's final minutes to score a winning touchdown. Between shots of Harold's feat, Sturges inserts images of E. J. Waggleberry, the president of an advertising agency, who is sweating out the plays on the sideline. After the game, Waggleberry races to hand Harold his card and promises he'll have a job waiting for this gifted boy when he graduates.

By the time Harold takes up the offer, the boss clearly has no idea who he is. Nonetheless, Waggleberry offers Harold the lowliest job in the firm, assuring him it's most satisfying to rise from the bottom. Harold tries to tell Waggleberry all his great advertising ideas, but Waggleberry warns him to "contain them, save them, don't squirt them all out at once." A great believer in rules and homilies, Harold holds his tongue. "Success," he reminds himself, "is just around the corner."

But success is not around the corner for Harold, who does precisely what he's told and gets nowhere. Twenty-two years pass. Now Waggleberry calls Harold into his office and fires him for not living up to his "great hopes." He's forty-four, with no job, or wife for that matter, since he's passed up the opportunity to propose to six increasingly beautiful Miss Otis sisters, waiting for the sensible moment to marry.

One sad Tuesday Harold for the last time walks through Waggleberry's revolving doors. On an impulse, he gives the corner beggar, Wormy, a handful of bills, and suddenly life picks up. Wormy escorts Harold for his first alcoholic drink. Emboldened by liquor, Harold buys himself a loud plaid suit and bets a thousand dollars on a horse with thirty-to-one odds against it. The horse wins. Harold bets again and wins again, all the while making friends and drinking up a storm. When he wakes up Thursday morning, he discovers he spent his winnings, plus his entire life's savings, on a circus he bought late Tuesday night, and he has no idea what he did all day Wednesday.

The rest of the film shows Harold scheming to get rid of the circus—which turns out to be a terrible investment since animals devour so much food—and in a single wild day winning the great job that eluded his years of diligence. What Harold did Wednesday remains a mystery until the very last scene when the seventh Miss Otis sister announces that *at last* he's married her.

Like *Christmas in July*, *The Sin of Harold Diddlebock* paints a grim picture of American business, where hard work and perseverance are given lip service, but in fact mean nothing, where paternalistic slogans mask executives' profound indifference to original minds. Like Mr. Baxter in the earlier film, Mr. Waggleberry, scion of the firm's founder, is himself utterly without imagination or self-confidence.[22] Though he's capable of childlike enthusiasm for winning athletes, he forgets them as soon as they're off the field—much as Hollywood forgot Griffith and Lloyd when they were out of the limelight. It's not that Harold's Horatio Alger-like ideal of diligence is inherently foolish. It's just foolish in America where the Mr. Waggleberrys rule: like it or not, you have to impress them.

The Sin of Harold Diddlebock is structured in two parts that cleverly mirror Harold's two long runs in the opening football sequence. In the first part of the film—as in Harold's initial run, where he brazenly cheats—Diddlebock is reckless and lucky. In the second part—as with Harold's winning run—Diddlebock goes beyond luck to use his brains and skill to achieve something important.

With its parody of American business and emphasis on chance, the first part of the film is typical Sturges material. Sturges satirizes the two-faced American businessman by showing Mr. Waggleberry so animated he tears his suit to shreds during the football game, while at the office he sits placidly wearing a bow tie. And Sturges spoofs the peculiarly American nature of Harold's plight by showing the passage of time through the succession of American presidents on his work calendar. From Harding to Coolidge, through four Roosevelt administrations to Truman. Twenty-two years pass for Harold at Waggleberry's, and he's as insignificant as when he began.

So it's an exhilarating moment when cautious Harold at last is fired from his steady job and descends into a bar filled with iniquitous gleaming liquor bottles. "You awake the artist in me," remarks the bartender, with a twinkle in his eye. The ensuing scene, in which the bartender invents a lethal Diddlebock cocktail, and the next one, where Harold insists on buying "Formfit Franklin's" loudest checkered suit, have the light-headedness of Mary's adventures in *Easy Living*. Harold buys the suit and cuts his hair and even gets the nerve to bet on a racehorse because under the influence of liquor he has for the first time in years really looked at himself in the mirror and seen a person he doesn't admire.

"An old scarecrow" is how Harold describes himself, and the operative word is "scare." "Look at our forefathers!" he exclaims. "Look at Washington! Look at Valley Forge! Look at the pioneers! Then look at me! . . . Men were men in those days. They mined the earth . . . and tamed the wilderness and brought forth peaceful homesteads in the shadow of the eagle and the echo of the thundering herd." [23]

Like Jimmy MacDonald's speech about the robber barons in *A Cup of Coffee*, Harold's outburst reveals horror of a life wasted in petty circumspections and nostalgia for the challenges that bred American heroes, even—maybe especially—tainted heroes. It takes losing his job to make Harold understand that his failure in business was a failure to dare. And Harold failed to dare, Sturges suggests, because he thought too small. He worried about putting away every cent he made rather than about making more money, about following orders rather than about astounding the world with his cleverness.

The second—and more problematic—part of the film shows Harold finally throwing caution to the wind. Since he can't possibly afford the circus he's rashly bought, he must sell it. To sell it he must find a rich buyer—a banker, he decides. To entice a banker, he must come up with an advertising scheme—something he's never done during his twenty-two years with Waggleberry. First, he gets a crowd-pleasing slant—this circus will be for poor children. Then he drags his growling lion Jackie into every bank president's office in town, figuring he'll get arrested and have his circus publicized for free in the news headlines. All goes according to plan: as terrified bankers cringe behind desks and dive into chandeliers, reporters leap on the story, making the poor children's circus a cause célèbre. Emerging from jail, Harold finds the bankers eager to be hailed as do-gooders, all vying to take the circus off his hands. (Only Ringling Brothers outbids them.) Mr. Waggleberry, calling Harold's campaign the best advertising idea he's ever heard, rehires and promotes Harold, who discovers he spent Wednesday marrying the last of the Miss Otis sisters and is headed for connubial bliss.

As always, there's an edge to Sturges's happy ending. The bankers who fall over themselves trying to buy the poor children's circus are the very men we've seen routinely snubbing poor people. Waggleberry appreciates Harold only when he's no longer an employee. In order to achieve social validation, Harold has to break the law.

As with Sturges's Paramount films, *The Sin of Harold Diddlebock* posits a seemingly impossible dilemma and devises a way out. Only here, rather than stressing ironies and the vulnerability of his protagonist, Sturges dwells on slapstick bits and on Harold's boldness. Because Harold is so bold, we don't fear for him as we do for Jimmy and Norval and Woodrow. Indeed, once Harold gets his courage *The Sin of Harold Diddlebock* becomes painless. It's as if Norval had made his confessional speech the day he arrived home in Oakridge. For all its frantic verbal confrontations and a lion chase where Harold (in *hommage* to *Safety Last*) pursues Jackie across a window ledge, *The Sin of Harold Diddlebock* lacks narrative tension. Then too, the pace is more languid here, there are many attenuated shots with little visual complexity. The cutting is oddly predictable, the message is more often spelled out than portrayed.

Ernst Laemmle, who'd sat up late nights acting as Preston's soundingboard when he wrote *The Lady Eve* and *Sullivan's Travels*, blamed *The Sin of Harold Diddlebock*'s flaws on the fact that Sturges no longer listened to even his most trusted advisers. On his earlier scripts, Ernst felt, Preston really wanted honest feedback. Now, it seemed, all the praise had gone to his head, and he was relying exclusively on his own judgment.[24]

Yet, Preston did bring Ernst along with him as story editor to California Pictures. He also brought Jeannie La Vell who—whether for purely personal reasons, or because Preston had also stopped listening to her advice—soon quit. "Dear Boss—This is it—I'm leaving," she wrote.[25] But others stayed on. Henry Henigson, who sternly reproved Sturges's extravagance and teased his friend mercilessly, as Preston teased Henry, stuck with Sturges no matter how difficult he became. Sturges's Paramount stock company was similarly loyal. Jimmy Conlin got the major role of Wormy this time, but Franklin Pangborn (cast as "Formfit Franklin") and Rudy Vallee (as a banker) and Torben Meyer (as a barber) happily played their smaller parts because this was a Sturges picture. Georgia Caine had a walk-on as a bearded lady in the circus. When someone asked how she could show her face in a beard, she replied that she would do *anything* Preston Sturges asked her to do.[26]

Sturges could be similarly noble. He made a point, for instance, of placing an ad in the *Hollywood Reporter*, after every film, thanking the stock company individually for their performances. But if an actor did not live up to Preston's standards of loyalty, Preston might well turn on him, as Bill Demarest discovered when Sturges ran his normal ad for the company after *Miracle of Mor-*

gan's Creek; beside Demarest's name Sturges quipped: "Magnificent as Constable Kockenlocker, but now has to be borrowed like a big star . . . the Hell with him."

The reason for this snide remark was that Sturges had very much wanted Demarest to play a role in his Harold Lloyd film. Since Paramount had signed Demarest to a long-term contract after *Miracle*, Preston had to get permission from Buddy DeSylva himself in order to borrow him. And DeSylva, then exasperated with Preston about *The Great Moment*, refused to release Demarest.

Preston was furious—partly because he felt proprietary about Demarest, as he did about all his stock company, partly because he hated losing any contest with DeSylva, but also because Demarest had been in all his films so far. Preston felt a superstitious anxiety about making a movie without Demarest. So he came up with the idea of having Demarest appear in just one scene disguised in a lion's costume. That way Demarest could bring the film good luck without jeopardizing his contract. Demarest agreed, and the plan might well have worked, only Sturges, piqued that Buddy DeSylva should never know he'd been one-upped, began talking about the joke. Soon the story became twisted so it was Demarest who felt compelled to appear in the picture rather than Sturges who wanted Demarest. When an item about the lion's costume appeared in the trade papers, Buddy DeSylva confronted Demarest, who at that point felt he had no choice but to back out of *Diddlebock*.[27]

Demarest felt so lastingly hurt by Sturges's retaliatory comments in the *Miracle* ad that he would later tell interviewers he and Sturges never spoke after this episode. If that were true, it would be unusual behavior for Sturges, who rarely carried a grudge. And indeed there's proof he and Demarest did make up, at least in the short run, because among Sturges's private correspondence is a very friendly telegram dated four years after the lion costume incident, in which Demarest wishes Preston luck on his new film (*Unfaithfully Yours*): "I KNOW IT WILL BE GREAT EVEN IF I AM NOT IN IT LOVE AND KISSES BILL DEMAREST."[28]

There was no talk of a role for Eddie Bracken in *Diddlebock*: not, presumably, because of any interdiction from Paramount but for the same reason Sturges stopped working with Joel McCrea—he was ready to experiment with new talent. He cast Margaret Hamilton as Harold's acerbic sister, Lionel Stander as the bookie who places Harold's winning bet, and Arline Judge as a manicurist whose nails Harold starts buffing in his drunken elation. It was because of this manicurist's scene that Preston, after twenty-five years, heard from Peggy Sage, former employee of the Maison Desti, who now had a cosmetics line of her own and wrote wondering if her old boss could show bottles of her "shimmer-sheen nail polish" in his new movie. Unfortunately, Preston had shot all the manicurist's scenes by the time Peggy's letter arrived.

Sturges defied the American unions by hiring an émigré cameraman, Curtis Courant, whom Charlie Chaplin recommended. Special effects expert John P. Fulton was engaged to do matte photography for the lion episodes. Werner Heymann began creating the musical score, while Harry Rosenthal wrote a romantic violin theme for the love sequences with Miss Otis.

The role of Miss Otis was smaller even than Ella Raines's in *Hail the Conquering Hero*, yet crucial. She had to personify youth. Sturges took a long time searching for the right actress. Then, he did something he'd never done before. He cast a woman he was in love with.

Frances Ramsden was a glamorous and sophisticated New York model. She was tall like Louise with long dark hair and bangs and a self-confident, but vulnerable nature. She was twenty-two years younger than Sturges. They first met, Francie says, in 1942 when she was visiting Hollywood, and her fiancé's friend, the playwright Jacques Thery, thought it would be fun to take her for lunch to the Paramount commissary. Francie remembers walking in the door and seeing "a man with a leonine head and a white streak through it" seated at the center of a large table. Preston Sturges. But she knew nothing about film. Was this the man who married the Hutton girl? she thought to herself. Preston insisted that Francie and Thery join the table, seating Francie next to himself. He remarked approvingly that she was unusual looking, not just the typical Hollywood brunette. She should have a screen test, he said, and insisted on setting the date for that Tuesday. When Sturges announced that he would personally supervise Francie's test, everyone at the table seemed to think this a tremendous honor. Francie, though, was headed back for New York and marriage. She never showed up for the test.[29]

After she got married, Francie and her husband moved out to Los Angeles. One day, Francie recalls, she bumped into Jacques Thery, who said they must have dinner that night at a restaurant that had the best French food in Los Angeles. It turned out to be The Players. "I was taking a sip of wine and cutting into the Duck Bigarde," Francie recalls, "and I heard this voice towering over me say, 'Ah-hah! The young lady that runs away from screen tests!' So that was the beginning."

It was the summer of 1945. The affair with Jeanie La Vell was finished, and Preston rarely went home anymore except to keep up a good face at Sunday night parties. He and Louise communicated by leaving cryptic notes for each other on the banister—in all but fact, their marriage was over. So Preston did

Frances Ramsden. (Photograph courtesy of Frances Ramsden)

not bother to disguise his attraction to Francie. Francie was also immediately infatuated with Preston. She remembers how, after only a few dates, they sat in his car, and he told her he'd fallen in love with her, and he wanted her to stay with him. "That's when he first announced that he was serious, and it would break his heart if I left," she recalls.

337

Preston honking for his secretary, Caroline Wedderburn.

So she stayed with him, filing suit to divorce her husband, and soon Preston again began talking to her about becoming an actress. He said she had all the attributes—she had style, grace, a good voice, she photographed beautifully. In fact, he said, he was thinking of making her Miss Otis in his Harold Lloyd film. And when she protested that she had no experience, he told her his theory that when you star in a picture you don't have to be a great actress because the director follows your every move and makes sure you're photographed at your best. Actresses in minor roles are on their own and have to know their craft. He said if she decided to stay in the business she too would know her craft, but for this first film she'd be handled like a baby.

Francie was not convinced. But one day Sturges took her by surprise. She was in his office with all his California Pictures associates: his secretary Caroline Wedderburn, a sort of a female Gilletti whom everyone loved and who wasn't the least bit impressed by celebrities; his PR man Steve Brooks, another good friend; and Henry Henigson. There was also a British actress named Eve in the room. Suddenly, Sturges pulled the *Diddlebock* script from his desk and said to Francie, why don't you read this scene? And he said Eve should play the part of Harold. The scene he chose came early in the film: Harold and Miss Otis, standing by the office filing cabinets, review Harold's sad history with the Otis sisters. Miss Otis's comments elicit Harold's confessions of gross misjudgment, but she addresses him with school girl politeness, as Mr. Diddlebock, and it's important that she never seem intentionally ironical.

When Francie finished reading the scene, Preston told her, "If you photograph as well as you read that script, you've got the part." He then rushed Francie, Eve, Caroline, Steve, and Henry into his station wagon, and down to a jewelry store next to the Brown Derby on Vine Street. Preston went into the jewelers and bought two enormous gold bracelets—one for Frances, one for Eve—to commemorate the occasion. "He made everything into a celebration," Francie recalls.

By now, the press was avid for news about the casting of *Diddlebock*. But Preston, remembering the Ella Raines incident, refused to announce Francie in the role before both Howard Hughes and Harold Lloyd approved of her. When Preston introduced Harold Lloyd to Francie, Lloyd commented, "You know she can eat beans off my head," because at five-foot-seven and three-quarters, she was taller than he was. He was teasing, of course, height wasn't the issue, nor was talent for that matter, the important thing was whether he and Francie could play well together. After viewing their first screen test, Lloyd, Howard Hughes, and everyone else who mattered agreed that they could.[30]

Like most independent production companies at the time, California Pictures set up offices at the Goldwyn Studios and arranged for United Artists to release their first two films. *Diddlebock* began production on September 12, 1945 with a projected finishing date of November 24 and a budget of just over a million dollars: Sturges's largest ever. In other ways too this was Sturges's most ambitious project. Without the safety net of Paramount's vast production staff, he was really on his own this time, having only Henry Henigson to help him cope with the hundred technical and administrative difficulties that arise daily on a film set. He had the appearance of total creative freedom, yet he'd given Harold Lloyd the contractual right to insist they shoot scenes *his* way. Then too, by casting Francie when he was so newly in love with her, Preston brought his romantic life, with its intensities and complications, to the set. And he was projecting a complex, in some ways contradictory, image of himself as he began his first independent production. He was a clever businessman, forging a partnership with millionaire Howard Hughes to make profitable entertainments. He was a maverick, hiring an émigré cameraman and experimenting with silent film footage and an aging comic. He was a Pygmalion, determined to make Francie a star.

There are conflicting impressions of Sturges's attitude toward his players on the *Diddlebock* set. Francie remembers that Preston was very scrupulous about never criticizing anyone in front of an audience. If he liked a performance, he would made a fuss over the actor publicly, but if he was displeased, he'd take the person aside and either blast him to hell, if the actor was being rude or recalcitrant, or just quietly tell him this is the way I want it and let's do it again over here, where nobody can see us. But others remember Sturges's public anger. Margaret Hamilton (who eventually thanked Preston for his astute direction) was at first frightened by his outbursts,[31] and Ernst Laemmle felt the mood on the *Diddlebock* set was not nearly as positive as it had been for the Paramount films.

The company records are, in any case, far more chaotic, for Preston had no Buddy DeSylva tracing his progress. And Sturges, always prone to extremes, was now particularly volatile. Sometimes four-year-old Mon visited his father's set, but for the most part Sturges was putting family life behind him and devoting himself totally to romance and work. Louise says someone told her he looked like a cobra at this time, that his eyes were half-closed, he'd thrown off all discipline.[32] But Francie remembers he was filled with enthusiasm and determined to enjoy himself. He seemed to want to be always in motion. He bought a boat smaller than the Destiny and began sailing again to Catalina on weekends. He had a Harley-Davidson motorcycle, which he told Francie (who'd had a single motorcycle lesson) she could drive, and they took off at forty miles an hour down Santa Monica Boulevard.[33] He got a little Austin convertible. Mornings, he put the windshield down, and had the prop man serve himself and Francie coffee on the hood. They'd drive around the sound stage, eating breakfast.

Orson Welles was shooting *The Stranger* on the set next door and sometimes joined them for coffee. Francie remembers one morning when Preston was up high checking on the arc lights, and as he began climbing down his trousers caught on a nail and split. While the wardrobe woman stitched up the seam, Orson Welles wandered in; he took one look at Preston and said, "Some sharp-toothed assistant director, I presume"—alluding to the conventional wisdom that assistant directors are "ass-lickers." And Preston laughed and laughed—still showing a sense of humor about himself.

Harold Lloyd poses with four-year-old Mon on the set of The Sin of Harold Diddlebock.

Francie enjoyed being with Preston on the set and working with Harold Lloyd, but was concerned about her own performance. What particularly intimidated her was the scene where Miss Otis comes to release Harold from his jail cell. She wasn't sure how her character would walk down the long prison hall or respond to the sight of the lion. They rehearsed the scene one afternoon, then Preston closed the set, intending to begin shooting first thing the next morning. He and Francie went off to The Players, but Francie was so worried that, after dinner, Preston took her back to the set, and they practised the short scene for hours until she felt confident. "The next morning I came on the set, and nobody knew that we'd rehearsed the night before," she recalls.

While Francie worried about her own work, Harold Lloyd was anxious about every aspect of the production. Lloyd had been called "The King of Daredevil Comedy," yet he did not enjoy stunts for their own sake and, whenever he could, avoided physical danger. He'd constructed elaborate sets for *Safety Last* and had no qualms about using a double when he could get away with it.[34]

Lloyd told Sturges he wanted nothing to do with the stunts planned for the emboldened Harold in the second half of *Diddlebock*. "I've gotten a little past that point," said Lloyd, who had lost twenty pounds so he could look forty-four years old, but was really fifty. And Sturges seemed amenable. He shot the first stunt with a double, but then, as Lloyd relates in his oral history:

> Sturges came around and said, "Harold, he doesn't look like you at all. You can do it. Your actions will be different from his and you'll get more out of it." . . . He said, "Won't you try?" And I did. . . . That's the way it went through the picture. Everything that these stuntmen would do, I would watch them—and when we finally got through, there wasn't one scene with the stuntman. He had finally talked me into doing everything they had done.[35]

Talking Lloyd into doing the stunts, not to mention first shooting them with a stuntman, took time and money. It was also costly working with Jackie the lion, particularly as Lloyd had it in his contract that he would never rehearse with the beast. Many precautions were taken. Jackie's trainer (who'd brought him up from a cub) was on the set at all times, Jackie's two front teeth were ground down, and he was eighteen years old, but . . . still a lion. And Lloyd's apprehensions were confirmed when they were shooting one of the bank scenes, and Jackie turned toward Harold and began growling. Harold got no fight from Preston this time. Shooting stopped, and they finished the scene with a stuffed lion's head.

The sequences where Harold runs after Jackie on the building ledge also demanded legerdemain. Sets were constructed only twenty-odd feet off the ground, then given the illusion of height through John Fulton's matte photography.

Sturges might have spent more time on the photography (which would prove unconvincingly flat) if he wasn't coping with Harold Lloyd's querulousness. Lloyd was uncomfortable with the sound of his own Nebraska accent, with the amount of dialogue Preston assigned him, with Sturges's direction, and finally with the plot itself. Time and again he disputed Sturges's decisions, which meant a scene had to be shot two ways—only a temporary solution, since, invariably, Lloyd and Sturges continued to disagree in the projection room. For two weeks, they actually made two versions of the film. Reading Lloyd's account of their dispute, one can imagine Sturges wearing himself out, tactfully evading the actor's suggestions:

> [Sturges] didn't want gags to come in it, he wanted his dialogue. But this called for business, it just cried for it. I came to him with business, and he said, "Hell, the business is too good for my dialogue." I said, "Preston, this

is terrible." He said, "It'll kill the dialogue." I said, "*Let* it kill the dialogue, what are we after? We're after entertainment, laughs." [Preston said], "Harold, I can't do it." So I stopped looking for business. There was the difficulty we had.[36]

The more profound difficulty was that Lloyd and Sturges disagreed about the nature of Harold Diddlebock. Lloyd was used to playing heroic underdogs, and Sturges had no patience with simple heroes. For Sturges, Harold Diddlebock was not a brave man who overcame his superficial cowardice, but equally cowardly and courageous. Thus, the wonderful scene in the bar where Harold brays like a horse under the influence of his first drink, and then—in his normal voice—inquires who's making all the racket.

Lloyd, though, felt uncomfortable with Harold's contradictoriness. "Preston wanted his character to be a schizophrenic, which I felt was an irritating character that the audience wouldn't like," he recalled. "They must like you, they must feel sorry for you, they must work with you. . . . Well, this character, this schizophrenic, they couldn't do that with him."[37]

Sturges never spoke openly against Harold Lloyd, but he reveals some of his irritation in a letter to a reporter who was planning an article about superstition on movie sets. Lloyd was superstitious about everything, wrote Preston: "Principally about going out of buildings, sets or anything else [any other than] the same way as he went in. If I didn't want him to come on a set to help me direct another actor, I merely placed a lamp in the entrance he had used the first time and he was blocked."[38]

Though Preston was scheduled to finish around Thanksgiving, production dragged into the new year, and *Diddlebock* came in more than $600,000 over budget. Henry Henigson pushed up the date for the opening, and Preston had to admit that more than the year Frank Freeman predicted had passed with no new Sturges film released. In retrospect, most people blamed the delays and extravagance on Sturges. Joel McCrea feels his friend lacked the self-discipline to perform without pressures from a studio. "Preston had a weakness because if he had a sizable income he'd dog it along," says McCrea.[39] Others fault Sturges's disorganization, though both Harold Lloyd and Francie Ramsden say Sturges always came to the set with his scenes fastidiously diagrammed. "Even down to the hat someone was going to wear," says Francie. And Lloyd remembers that Sturges showed infinite patience in the cutting room—probably because he was hoping to wear Lloyd down. Indeed, both the overtime and the extravagance on *Diddlebock* could be explained by Lloyd's constantly disputing Sturges's judgments, compounded by Sturges's determination to outwit Lloyd.

Yet, it's also true that Sturges was having a good time on *Diddlebock*. "He

Preston directing The Sin of Harold Diddlebock.

was a professional, but he did have fun doing what he did, and that might confuse people," says Francie. "Everything went like clockwork, but he took time off to laugh. He always had special shoes he'd buy for the extras if they had to stand a long time. He would bring Coca Cola for people to have if they were sitting around in the hot sun." In other words, he was as gallant with his movie company as with the guests at his restaurant. He may have seen Cal Pix as an extension of The Players, a sort of fiefdom where he could play lord of the manor, lover, friend, sometime father, and filmmaker at once. The boy who despaired of getting out from under his mother's shirttails had created his own dominion.

As usual, Preston anguished about editing his film. "I will endeavor to re-call those parts of the film during which I, as the author and director, felt a certain embarrassment and wished to Christ we would get to the next step sooner," [40] he began in a long critique after an early preview. Details worried him. Should a moment between Harold and Wormy be extended? How could he tighten the football passages? He solicited lists of suggestions from friends and had his assistant, Seymour Stern, analyze all the changes. "The whole picture as we saw it yesterday seems to me greatly improved," Stern wrote Sturges at one point. "It's closer to realizing its character and purpose of FAST COMEDY." [41]

In the fall of 1946, Howard Hughes came to a Westwood preview of *Did-dlebock* and didn't laugh once or stay a moment after the film finished. [42] Even at ninety-one minutes, *Diddlebock* was too long, Hughes said. But *Variety* called it "surefire box office," and when it officially opened, more than a year after Preston finished shooting, on February 18, 1947, in the Lincoln Theatre

in Miami, the reviews warmly praised both Lloyd and Sturges, though ticket sales were moderate. The same was true in Portland and San Francisco where *Diddlebock* also played briefly, but moderate sales would not defray the cost of a $1.7 million production. Hughes refused to open *Diddlebock* in New York or Los Angeles and in May withdrew it from all theatres. James Agee, who'd managed to catch it out of town, called *Diddlebock* an "exceptional picture,"[43] but most of the major critics never saw Sturges's version of the film.

Hughes did not so much change *Diddlebock* as nibble away at it. He eliminated a scene where Harold and Wormy approach a daydreamy banker, played by Rudy Vallee, hoping to sell him their circus, only to discover that Vallee is trying to unload an unprofitable circus of his own. Like the butler's exegesis on poverty in *Sullivan's Travels*, this scene has little narrative importance, yet it adds texture to the film. Since Vallee's banker is sufficiently imaginative to buy a circus, he balances the grotesque bankers seen later on. Hughes chopped moments from two long conversations between Harold and Wormy and Harold and Miss Otis, and—his one outrageous gesture—added a talking horse for the finale. Then he held onto *Diddlebock* for four years and finally released it through RKO. It was now nineteen minutes shorter and titled *Mad Wednesday*. The reviews this time were also mostly positive. "A zany film farce," said the *New York Herald Tribune*. The *Times* (where a T. M. P. rather than Bosley Crowther was reviewing) more accurately deemed it "a curious mélange of ingenious comic spirit and lethargy. When Mr. Sturges is sparkling on all cylinders, the show is hilarious and Mr. Lloyd responds with the remarkable comic zest that made him an idol way back in the hot jazz age. But in his twin capacity as author and director, Mr. Sturges flashes like a sputtering neon sign and as a consequence, *Mad Wednesday* runs an erratic course during which moments of wonderfully funny nonsense are overshadowed by stretches of painfully dull writing and imagery."[44]

Mad Wednesday closed as swiftly as *The Sin of Harold Diddlebock*. In a final irony, Harold Lloyd, whose career Sturges had set out to revive and honor, sued Howard Hughes, California Pictures, and RKO for damages to his reputation.[45] (The suit was settled out of court for $30,000.) Yet, with all its troubles, the film retains a certain fascination. And while many would perceive *The Sin of Harold Diddlebock* as the beginning of the end of Sturges's career as a filmmaker, it was in a strange way also his epiphany: the one time in his working life when he did exactly as he pleased.

Duҏ uring all the turmoil over *The Sin of Harold Diddlebock*, Sturges was also
working on his next project for California Pictures: a film based on *Colomba*, a nineenth-century novella by Prosper Mérimée, best known as the
author of *Carmen*. *Colomba* takes place after the battle of Waterloo and is both
a revenge tale and a comedy of manners, filled with wry observations about
war and the British upper class. Since the story involves an exotic beauty,
Colomba appealed to Hughes as a vehicle for his young "protégée," the actress
Faith Domergue.

Much in *Colomba* attracted Sturges, who was more than ever fascinated by
war and its aftermath. As he wrote the final draft of his script, in July 1946,
the soldiers had come marching home with the euphoria of victory. But there
were soldiers who didn't come home, or who came home, like Preston's friend
Willie Wyler, with a burst eardrum, wondering if they'd ever work in their old
jobs again. As Preston saw it, World War II had solved nothing; there was no
war to end all wars. Even the postwar boom digusted him. "Does not the
present tremendous prosperity, due to the war effort prove . . . that a similar
prosperity could have existed in peacetime?" Preston began a letter to a friend.
"Does it prove that we are willing to work harder to die than to live, or that
we are capable of a tremendous effort only during an emergency . . . like a
paralytic during a fire? If war is the solution why didn't Roosevelt declare war
on poverty?"[1]

Following Mérimée's book, Sturges's screenplay begins as two English
tourists, Colonel Nevil and his daughter Lydia, meet a handsome Corsican
lieutenant named Orso on a boat to Corsica. The Colonel and Orso fought
on opposite sides at Waterloo, yet there's no animus between them, since they
both love to hunt and kill and fiercely adhere to male codes of honor. Orso's
father, we learn, was recently murdered, and while the courts convicted a ban-

dit, Orso's sister Colomba insists the real villain is her family's ancestral enemy, the Barricini family. Orso doesn't know whom to believe. As in the novel, he is torn between his French respect for the law and a Corsican passion for vendettas. But Sturges changes the bored Lydia of the novel into a war widow, intensely opposed to any sort of violent conflict. "I have no interest in honor . . . I have seen too much of its results," she says. Sturges also gives Lydia a child named David, whose fascination with his grandfather's pistols, hunting and battle stories make him a natural heir to the male legacy of war.

The scenes with David have autobiographical resonance. Sturges refers to David, as to Mon, as the "little boy," and there's a fascinating inversion of the terrible night when Solomon Sturges woke Preston to tell him he was *not* his father in a scene where Orso wakes David to promise he will be his father from now on. Sturges's writing is full of nuance; his characters are intelligently drawn, and the last scenes have tragic scope. Sturges departs from Mérimée's happy ending to have Colomba killed and Orso badly wounded when he shoots the Barricini sons. And where Mérimée suggests that the Barricinis indeed plotted to kill Orso's father, Sturges has the death occur in a hunting accident, making Orso's revenge, spurred by a scheming Colomba, utterly meaningless. In a surreal finale, the Barricini grandchild chases David with a loaded pistol, and David narrowly escapes death when the elder Barricini stops this blood-thirsty boy. The film ends with old Barricini spanking *both* children for mimicking their elders. Thus Lydia's pacifist view seems validated. But the film also ends with Lydia vowing never to leave Orso, to love him "as you are," in other words, with his warrior instincts, so the future is uncertain.

Sturges called his script *Vendetta*. Since he was himself still preoccupied with *Diddlebock*, he hired Max Ophüls, a Jewish refugee from Hitler's Germany, to direct this antiwar film.

Ophüls, who would go on to make such celebrated films as *Letter from an Unknown Woman, Madame De*, and *Lola Montès*, had been well known abroad for his witty and stylish *Liebelei*. Dreading exile, he had stayed on in Europe far longer than Jean Renoir or René Clair. It was not until 1941 that he fled with his wife and son to Hollywood, where he was quickly embraced by the refugee crowd at The Players. But he found *Liebelei* meant nothing to Americans, and spent four years fruitlessly looking for work until Sturges in 1945 proposed his name to Hughes for *Vendetta*. And Hughes, preoccupied with his plane, made no protest, though he did capitalize on Ophüls's desperation to pay him a lamentable $750 a week.

Ophüls was full of ideas about *Vendetta*. His recent experiences in Europe

Preston on the set of Vendetta.

had confirmed an innate pessimism, and he wanted to make sure fear of com-
merical failure would not impel Sturges to lighten *Vendetta*'s bitter conclusion. "Dear Preston, dear Henry," he wrote in the spring of 1946: "I did some
research as to what American pictures with unhappy endings paid their way";
and he provided a long list, including *Broken Blossoms, The Scarlet Letter, Back
Street, A Star Is Born, Dark Victory, How Green Was My Valley,* and *The Power*

349

and the Glory. With it settled that Faith Domergue would play Colomba, Sturges and Ophüls offered the role of Lydia to Madeleine Carroll, but neither she nor James Mason—whom Sturges had wanted for Orso—were available; so they ultimately cast lesser knowns George Dolenz (as Orso), Nigel Bruce (as Lydia's father), and Hilary Brooke (as Lydia).

Production was set to begin in August. Then, the first week in July, Howard Hughes nearly died in an air crash.

The Spruce Goose, grounded because of one mechanical trouble or another throughout the war years, was at last ready for a test flight. The morning of July 7 Hughes took it up over Long Beach and headed toward Los Angeles. An hour later he crashed into a Beverly Hills mansion. (Fortunately, no one was home.) Badly hurt, he was rushed to the Good Samaritan Hospital, where the staff who met him said he'd never survive the night.[2]

Francie Ramsden recalls first hearing the news on her car radio, as she and Preston were preparing to load baskets of food onto Preston's sail boat in San Pedro. They put the food back in the car and rushed to the hospital.

Despite his third-degree burns, smashed ribs, and crushed chest, Hughes proved physically resilient. As he lay restlessly in bed recovering, he began taking an unwonted interest in Sturges's new film. Why, he wondered, did this unknown German director work so slowly? Did he enjoy wasting Hughes's money? And when Sturges sent Ophüls's dailies to the hospital to amuse his partner, Hughes didn't like what he saw. He particularly didn't like the way Ophüls handled Faith Domergue, and one day he peremptorily ordered Sturges to fire Ophüls.

This posed a real dilemma for Sturges. Though he sincerely liked and admired Ophüls, Sturges hadn't the contractual strength to override Hughes's order, nor could he bear to seem impotent. So he fired Ophüls as if it were his own idea. Ophüls, upset and confused, departed. Four months later, however, he was able to write Preston:

> I am sorry for the picture *Vendetta*—very sorry. But whatever your motive could have been, which prevented you from letting me direct it (and this hurt me very much), it did not change my friendly feelings toward you, and my gratitude for many things I owe you. Beautiful hours of creative understanding, many laughs, and last not least, shelter for two years.
>
> A wise President of the U.S. should make a law which would bring Christmas and Yom Kippur together on one day. Let me anticipate him and say to you: Froehliche Weihnachten![3]

And Preston, attempting a high-handed tone, replied:

My dear Max:

The whole *Vendetta* episode was regrettable, from beginning to end and should teach me never to do favors, since the whole thing was a favor to Mr. Hughes. . . .

Personally, I am bloodied but unbowed and will continue to do favors whenever I wish to.[4]

That Preston did not help his friend Max find other work in Hollywood says as much about Sturges's own diminishing credibility as about his loyalty to Ophüls. A decade after *Vendetta*, when their fortunes were reversed, these two men met again in Paris. After Ophüls's death, his widow replied to a condolence letter from Sturges:

Preston, dear Preston,

I am happy you both renewed your friendship here in Paris. Then I know—malgré tout—Max loved you very much.[5]

Though he managed to hide it from Ophüls, Preston must have been livid about Hughes's giving him orders. What deterred him from striking back was that *Diddlebock* was now going into previews: Preston wanted nothing to interfere with its smooth editing and release. So he tried to put on a good face and go about directing *Vendetta*.

It was not, however, in Preston's nature to be humble, so he couldn't help showing his irritation in little ways. He began taking long lunch hours. He rented horses and went riding into the hills. (Though Preston was led to believe no one would be charged for these excursions, Howard Hughes received a large bill, which did not help their relationship.)[6] Matters got worse as Faith Domergue, with Hughes as her ally, increasingly asserted herself, demanding more close-ups. Hughes too was full of suggestions, while Preston time and again reminded them that on the set, *he* was king.

But Hughes obviously wanted a more creative role than his contract permitted, and Sturges had no interest in collaborating. It all came to a head at eight in the morning on October 30. Hughes phoned Preston at Francie's house and announced that he'd closed the *Vendetta* set and was exercising his right to buy Sturges out of the partnership. Hughes's lawyers would meet Preston at The Players.

"Well, Preston is a very interesting man," says Francie, remembering that morning. "We sat at The Players having coffee, and, of course, Hollywood being what it is, everyone in town showed up . . . Willie Wyler, Bill Cagney, Steve Brooks, Henry Henigson. . . . It was eleven o'clock in the morning when

Francie Ramsden sailing, about 1946.

Hughes's lawyers finally arrived. They came in a big black shiny car and in their black suits, looking very grim, with portfolios under their arms. They put their papers in front of Preston, and Preston with a flourish signed the papers, and he handed me the pen, and he said, 'Come on, Frances, let's go sailing.' I stood up, and the two of us walked down to our car and drove to San Pedro and went sailing. He was a grand seigneur to the end. He wouldn't let anyone know how he felt." [7]

Hughes would have Sturges's script rewritten and go through two more directors before releasing a completely transformed *Vendetta* in 1950. By then, Sturges would have other woes, but in 1946 his mind was all on California Pictures. Publicly, Preston assumed a worldly tone. "Interruptions have been frequent in Mr. Hughes's productions," he told a reporter. "But he has never made a failure. Both he and I are doers, and neither of us is content to sit by and watch someone else work. I became an independent producer to get away from supervisions. When Mr. Hughes made suggestions with which I disagreed, as he has a perfect right to do, I rejected them. When I rejected the last one, he remembered that he had an option to take control of the company and he took over. So I left."[8]

But intimates saw Preston deeply shaken by the break-up of his film company, and what this said about his own powerlessness. Louise, then separated from Preston, was surprised when he turned up at her house one day, stretched out next to her on the bed and lay his head on her shoulder, like a disappointed child.[9] Joining California Pictures was Preston's first seriously bad career decision. He was too much the optimist not to believe everything would come right in the end, but he also knew his years as Hollywood's fair-haired boy had passed.

24

Preston's blatant affair with Francie Ramsden was the last straw for Louise Sturges, who in the spring of 1946 moved with Mon to a house on the beach. She hired a lawyer who on April 30 sued for divorce on grounds of "mental cruelty"—a popular charge at the time, and demanded that something be done to stop Sturges from sequestering his assets. Louise said she wanted "reasonable support" for herself and their child, and also the house with the old trees on Ivar Avenue.[1]

Louise believes that if she had not filed for divorce Preston would have been happy to go on as they were because he had no intention of marrying Francie Ramsden. Francie says she and Preston never discussed marriage until both of their divorces were finalized, but, in any case, Sturges was not inclined to remain in a loveless marriage. Years later, when both their lives were in shambles, Preston would write Louise that he should never have left her, that if he needed "some additional or younger female society" he should have taken it "outside as Catholic husbands do."[2] So he came to believe that he initiated the divorce, which, in all but the technical sense, was true.

Still, Sturges was determined to keep the only home he had ever owned, and Louise also wanted it. Ultimately, Louise gave in, and the divorce was finalized on November 7, 1947, nine years almost to the day after their marriage. Louise got $57,000, half of Sturges's interest in California Pictures, 20 percent of his "literary income" (not to exceed $350 a week), some property, and $45 a week child support for Solomon IV. She got sole custody of Mon, while Preston kept the house. The talk in Hollywood was that Louise had been too much a lady and should have demanded more. But in 1947 $57,000 was no small sum, and with Preston then earning over $8,000 a week, a percentage of his salary was substantial.

At least it seemed so to Louise, who was not acquisitive and was eager to be done with lawyers and documents. She was trying to efface everything about Preston from her life—tearing up her recipes from all those Sunday night dinners, shying away from many of their mutual friends. (Charley Abramson was an exception.) Sometimes she struck out in a blind rage—once accusing Preston of stealing her pearls, then almost immediately forgetting the accusation. With Louise in her current mood, Preston made a point of not introducing Francie to Priscilla Woolfan, so Louise would not retaliate by keeping the Woolfans from Mon.

Preston was pleased that the childless Woolfans treated Mon like a nephew. Mon was now visibly distressed by his parents' break-up, but Preston was not discouraged. "One of the reasons I have never worried the slightest about my divorce from Louise is because I have no fear whatever of being separated from my son," Preston wrote his wealthy New York friend John Hertz, Jr. "We would not be separated if she took him to live in China. I could not know this and be so sure of it except for the fact that I am a child of divorce myself." [3] But Preston, like Mary, was a distracted parent, often absent from his adoring child. One day the five-year-old boy disappeared, and after much frantic searching was discovered walking along Sunset Boulevard, looking for his father's house. [4]

Once her divorce was finalized, Louise took off for Europe, enrolling Mon in a Swiss school, while she traveled and made new friends and settled for a while in Italy. Louise was neither independently wealthy like Eleanor nor did she have Bianca's desire to work, yet she spent her money with abandon. Louise had been the sensible wife for so long, it must have been a great joy to seize the moment, and she began recovering her humor and interest in life. So far away from Preston she may have believed she was really through with him. But she was not, nor was he with her, for the fact of their son and the terms of the divorce contract bound Preston to Louise as he'd never been bound to anyone. And these were not the only remnants of their romance. In the mid-forties, Preston told Francie Ramsden that the great loves of his life were herself and his first wife Estelle. But there was also something singular about Preston's passion for Louise Sargent, whom he wooed from her husband and married just before *The Great McGinty* and *The Lady Eve*. As intensely as he counted on the endurance of his astonishing talent, she counted on the endurance of his love, and the disappointment would weigh on both of them.

"*The Sin of Harold Diddlebock* has been renamed *Mad Wednesday* or *Shrove Tuesday* or something equally appropriate," Preston wrote Bosley Crowther.

Henry Henigson (left) with Mon and Preston at Christmas, about 1947.

"In any case I am weary of it and have no more interest in it than the news about an old ex-wife. . . . I seem to have wasted the last three years horsing around with independent ventures and stock companies and various other efforts all to the accompaniment of gentle laughter from the collector of the

Internal Revenue, but as I also wasted the first thirty years of my life I don't suppose this matters very much."[5]

When California Pictures was dissolved, at the end of 1946, Preston was eager to return to the world of the big studios. Superficially, that world was much the same as when he left it three years before, yet there were signs that times were changing. The Depression was over, and with it the golden age of screwball comedy. This was the era of the "problem" film, the "quality" picture made at a relatively low cost and with no crowd scenes or spectacles because Hollywood could no longer count on its huge wartime grosses. Britain was imposing a seventy-five per cent sales tax on all foreign films, and television was beginning to lure away movie audiences. By 1948 there would be more than a million television sets in American homes; a year later the Supreme Court would order the studios to divest themselves of their theatre chains, drastically reducing revenues.

In the late forties, the intensifying Cold War caused the movie industry to be confronted by the House Committee on Un-American Activities. Many of Sturges's friends, including John Huston and Willie Wyler, openly crusaded against Hollywood blacklisting, while, as a *Life* reporter noted, "Sturges's politics are at present . . . unknown."[6] When friends told Sturges they were being called before HUAC, and that they would refuse to name names, and would understand if Preston in the future chose not to associate with them, he replied that this was ridiculous. Preston treated them no less warmly when their names appeared in the Hollywood papers under the headline "Hide Behind the Fifth" than he had earlier. They had behaved honorably by not exposing others, he felt. But he also said privately that he thought the HUAC hearings were a wonderful comedy.[7] He felt no more impelled to take sides than he had been driven to enlist in the war.

Ever the paradox, Sturges on a personal level perennially sided with underdogs. Besieged daily by people in trouble, he often responded generously—as to a Mrs. Exie West who wrote describing how she had been with Mary Desti the night Edmund Biden kidnapped, then returned, the infant Preston. Preston enclosed a small check with his affectionate reply to her note and continued sending Exie West money every month until she died four years later, like Mary, of leukemia.[8]

Still an avid fan of the fights, Preston was especially solicitous toward boxers like Larry Williams. Formerly Jack Dempsey's sparring partner, Larry was now punch-drunk, often wandering into some busy intersection to "direct" traffic. One day Preston learned that Larry was going to be put in an institution because he could no longer care for himself and had no one with whom to live. Perhaps thinking of his old photographer friend Arnold Shroeder, Preston invited Larry to move into the apartment attached to his own garage.[9]

Veterans also won Preston's sympathy. Moved by Bertie Woolfan's tales of mutilated young men, Preston visited the Veterans' Hospital in the San Fernando Valley, and invited a group of veterans to be his guests every Thursday night at The Players. So, having written *The Great Moment* and *Vendetta*, Sturges was not just preaching against war, he was in his small way helping its victims.[10]

He was also enjoying himself. Every weekend, summer or winter, he went sailing with Francie. Often Preston's secretary, Caroline Wedderburn, or Howard Hughes's uncle, the writer Rupert Hughes, or Priscilla and Bertie Woolfan would also come along. Preston had a rule that whenever you went out beyond the breakwater you had to bring two weeks' supply of food, water, and gasoline so you were prepared for an emergency. "That's the last frontier out there, you don't fool around with it," he said of the ocean, to Francie. He also taught her how to navigate and drop anchor in the bays—Fourth of July, Emerald Cove, and Cherry Cove were their favorites. Sometimes they swam off the boat. Often they just sat on the deck, talking, drinking Preston's favorite old fashioneds with scotch, and grilling steaks on a barbecue Preston invented, which hitched onto the side of the boat and had a special pipe to absorb ashes.

On and off the boat, everything had to be done Preston's way, he was king of the roost. Francie remembers Preston's showing José Iturbi how he should conduct, and lecturing Frank Lloyd Wright on the best way to restyle a house. Wright, says Francie, looked at Preston as if he was crazy, but Wright also respected and liked the unusual filmmaker.[11] Sturges's megalomania was so transparent that people who had strong egos themselves were often diverted by it. Others found it a small flaw to bear in such an amusing and talented man.

Certainly, the major studio executives, remembering *Miracle of Morgan's Creek* and *The Lady Eve*, were all eager to have Sturges working for them. Sturges's most spectacular job offer in the fall of 1946 came from his old nemesis, Samuel Goldwyn, who wanted to give Sturges his own building.[12] Sturges turned Goldwyn down: extravagant offers, he now knew, were no guarantee of creative freedom. What he wanted was a boss who was both intelligent enough to appreciate his talent, and reticent about interfering with his work.

Darryl Zanuck, head of production at Twentieth Century-Fox, was intelligent, if not reticent. The only non-Jewish mogul in Hollywood, Zanuck was also singular in valuing writers more than actors. Though intensely involved with every Fox project, Zanuck had a flair for working with strong-minded directors, like Elia Kazan, John Ford, and Otto Preminger. It was under Zanuck that Ford had made *The Grapes of Wrath* and *Young Mr. Lincoln*. Ford proclaimed Darryl Zanuck "head and shoulders above all other producers." [13] Many agreed with Ford—like Irving Thalberg in the thirties, Zanuck was considered Hollywood's most creative producer. And Zanuck greatly admired Sturges. When Zanuck lent Henry Fonda to Paramount for *The Lady Eve*, he asked, in lieu of money, for Sturges to make a film for Fox. Sturges immediately submitted *Song of Joy*, but Zanuck demurred, and they still hadn't settled on a project when Sturges left Paramount.

Then, while Preston was shooting *The Sin of Harold Diddlebock*, he discovered the abandoned offices of the old Fox studio on Western Avenue and prevailed on Joseph Schenck, the current president of Fox, to let him convert them for his film company. He put in French windows and a skylight, turned a former storeroom into a playroom with exercycles and muscle-builders, and transformed William Fox's large executive quarters into a Greenwich Village-type artist's studio, where he himself presided. "If ever I can repay your kindness in any way, please don't hesitate to call upon me," Preston wrote, thanking Schenck for the offices, and he added: "Incidentally, and along these lines, I owe Mr. Zanuck a picture for having lent me Henry Fonda for *The Lady Eve*. I acknowledge the indebtedness and I have for some years been ready and willing to pay off." [14]

No sooner had California Pictures disbanded than Zanuck took Preston up on his offer. It turned out that Spyros Skouras, long ago Preston's barracks mate in the Air Service and now president of Fox, was also a Sturges fan. "DELIGHTED TO LEARN YOU ARE OURS LEGALLY," Skouras cabled Preston on December 24, 1946, when their contract was finalized. That contract made Sturges a writer-director-producer with a salary of $8,825 a week. He would be the third highest-paid man in America.

Still, the real allure for Preston at Fox was the prospect of making films with Darryl Zanuck. Both men professed unbounded mutual respect, though it's worth noting that their contract was for just thirty weeks and was predicated on Preston's selling Fox one of his least characteristic screenplays, *Matrix*. This was the old fashioned melodrama about the woman who rejects a virile suitor to marry a ne'er-do-well who needs mothering. As story editor at Fox, Julian Johnson had turned down *Matrix* thirteen years earlier. *Matrix* may have attracted Zanuck and Johnson now simply because it could be made on a low budget; but it's also possible Zanuck was so eager to hire Sturges that he never bothered to read the script. "On the subject of *Matrix*, I frankly was not very enthusiastic and neither was Julian [Johnson]," Zanuck would write Preston two months later. "I sincerely do not believe it has the freshness or originality associated with your previous accomplishments, and frankly I don't think you are too crazy about it although I have never discussed it with you." [15] To this last, Preston retorted: "I am enormously fond of the story and will surely make it some day if my strength holds out." [16]

Preston signed his contract with Fox less than eight weeks after leaving California Pictures. Then, for the next two months, he sat around waiting for an assignment. Late in February, Zanuck wrote Sturges apologizing for "what may appear to be my negligence," and explaining how he'd been deflected by Fox's many new projects, including the controversial *Gentleman's Agreement*. Since Zanuck still had not conceived an idea truly worthy of Sturges's talents, he suggested a film for Fox's top-grossing star, Betty Grable. "More than anything else, I would like you to write and direct a picture with [Grable]," Zanuck wrote Sturges. "After *Mother Wore Tights* she cannot go backwards. She is one of the three biggest solo stars in our industry, and she must go forward. I know it is unreasonable for me to place an order with you for a project like this, yet I have the feeling you will come up with something that is fresh and original and will give her an opportunity to go on." [17]

As flatteringly as it was phrased, this was a request for a star vehicle, which—on his close to $9,000-a-week salary—Sturges could not refuse. For a month, Preston screened two Grable films a day and made a show of studying Grable's talents. But he knew he was being used and felt chagrined about it. "I am not overpoweringly enthused about the prospect [of the Grable film] as yet, but as all the young lady's pictures gross a minimum of four million dollars what I have to say will at least be heard by a great number of people," he consoled himself in a letter to his Turkish stepfather, Vely Bey, with whom he'd recently reestablished contact.[18]

The film was to be a comic western, loosely based on Earl Felton's "The Lady From Laredo." In Felton's story, a tough beauty arrives in a small western town and pretends she's the awaited school teacher so she can escape jail for some minor skullduggery. Because the beauty hates everything to do with the law, she rejects the overtures of the town's handsome sheriff, who is madly in love with her. But learning of her criminal record, the sheriff informs her that she has to marry him, because if she doesn't he'll turn her in. Sturges kept only the story's western setting and the idea of a woman of the world posing as a demure school teacher. He called his script *The Beautiful Blonde from Bashful Bend* and set it in a stylized Old West, full of gun-happy eccentrics. He made the beautiful crook a sharpshooting singer named Freddie. Freddie's trouble is she can't help pulling the trigger whenever her man looks at another female. The joke is that every time Freddie shoots, her bullet hits the town's judge in the rear.

As usual, Sturges thoroughly researched his subject. Since he'd invented a Mexican friend named Conchita for Freddie, he got a language expert to send him a long list of Spanish words, noting how they were pronounced at the turn of the century. He created roles for his character actors—an overbearing wife for Margaret Hamilton, a sheriff for Al Bridge, an irascible widower for Richard Hale—and continued watching Grable's movies, but the script progressed slowly. Zanuck prodded Sturges to hurry, then wrote him a tactfully critical letter at the end of August when the first ninety pages were in. Zanuck had three main objections. It "seemed to me that every time Conchita opened her mouth she was forcibly trying for laughs," Zanuck warned Preston. "Occasional overstressing for extraneous laughs" was, he felt, a problem throughout the script, which was furthermore too long.[19]

Sturges immediately wrote a defensive reply to Zanuck's suggestions, but thought better and never mailed it. Then, five days later, he received another memo from Zanuck who, blaming financial pressures caused by the British sales tax, announced that Fox could not afford to shoot *The Beautiful Blonde* in technicolor. Of course, no Sturges film had ever been shot in technicolor, but Betty Grable's films were. An early draft of Sturges's reply to Zanuck shows Preston's true feelings about Grable and the project, as well as his hurt pride:

> *My dear Darryl*:
> You can make a so-called Sturges picture in black-and-white and it might even have Miss Grable in it, but you can't make a Grable picture in black-and-white without losing your shirt, your drawers and your long winter underwear with the flap in the back. That is my opinion. Miss Grable is the child of color and without color and your brilliant idea of presenting her in it she would long since have vanished from the screen.

Preston was obviously sensitive about his high salary, for he proceeded to tell Zanuck:

> I have been extremely anxious for you and your stockholders to receive more than a fair exchange for the large amount of money you have contracted to pay me. I was vain enough at first to think you had hired me for a certain type

of picture I had made for Paramount which had been well-received throughout the world; but when I found that you had not but wanted me to help out
with Miss Grable's career, I swallowed some disappointment and then proceeded to do my sincere best to carry out your wishes.

As for the script he had written:

THE BEAUTIFUL BLONDE FROM BASHFUL BEND is not really a
screenplay at all, but only a vehicle disguised as a screenplay fashioned for the
sole purpose of representing the luscious Betty Grable to her customers in the
full color to which they are accustomed. Granted that I have thrown in as
many jokes as I can and that I have some facility along this line, and granted
that I will throw in some more jokes and tie it all up at the end in a very
workman-like way, the picture . . . will still be a very minor effort in both
your life and mine. For this waste of our lives the only excuse can be that
the picture was charmingly done and made a great deal of money which we
subsequently spent on better ventures. If this divertissement is not to be
made in color, I suggest that we immediately lay it aside to be picked up later
and that I instantly get to work on a story strong enough to succeed without
color.[20]

Sturges immediately crossed out his second paragraph, and allusions to the
"workman-like" way he was planning to tie up "this waste of our lives" project
were also eliminated from the far less unctuous letter he finally sent Zanuck.
But here too he (perhaps accurately) construed Zanuck's reluctance to shoot
in color as a function of his disappointment with the first ninety pages of the
screenplay, concluding "I feel a grave emergency exists." Thus, Sturges offered to make a black-and-white film for Fox, based on a script he had written
in the thirties, right after *McGinty*. It was called *Symphony Story* and was colorful enough without technicolor. Preston mentioned that Charles Boyer always wanted to play the lead role and suggested that Zanuck speak with Ernst
Lubitsch, who particularly admired this script.[21] (*Symphony Story* had also been
Bianca Gilchrist's favorite of Sturges's screenplays. She thought it far more
original than *The Great McGinty* and had wanted him to "bust out" with it for
his directorial debut.)[22]

   Preston would later tell reporters he'd been inspired to write *Symphony
Story* because of an experience back in the early thirties: a scene he was writing
for *The Power and the Glory* kept coming out differently than he'd planned.
Wondering why, Preston noticed some music was playing in the next room.
On a subconscious level, the tune had influenced his writing. *Symphony Story*
would now take precedence over the Grable project. The film that evolved
from it, retitled *Unfaithfully Yours*, would reflect Sturges's complex and volatile

nature, his deepest feelings about love, art, performance, and women, the conflict between his ironic intellect and the passions that stirred him—for evil and good. It would be judged, by common consensus, his last important film.

Unfaithfully Yours opens on the day of a concert. The symphony's famous British middle-aged conductor, Sir Alfred de Carter, is flying in from abroad. At the airport to greet him is his beautiful young wife Daphne, accompanied by his manager, Hugo, his secretary, Tony, and his wife's younger sister Barbara with her stodgy husband August. While every word out of Barbara's mouth is a sarcastic disparagement of August, Sir Alfred and Daphne behave like storybook romantics. They gaze deeply into each others' eyes, exclaim how miserable they've been on their own, and embrace passionately. Sir Alfred has plans to spend a festive day with his wife before the evening's concert, but then his brother-in-law asks for an audience. It seems that when Sir Alfred was leaving for England, he quite innocently asked August to "look after" his wife. August took him literally and hired a private detective to tail Daphne.

Sir Alfred's first response is outrage. He rips the detective's report to shreds and nearly strangles August for doubting Daphne's honor. Inevitably, though, the conductor seeks out the bad news. When he learns that late one night Daphne spent thirty-eight minutes in the room of his young secretary, Tony, Sir Alfred leaps to the conclusion that Daphne and Tony are lovers. He arrives at the concert hall greatly agitated. While conducting his first piece, Rossini's Overture to *Semiramide*, Sir Alfred imagines himself murdering Daphne and scheming to get Tony convicted for the crime. Then, during the second number, Wagner's reconciliation theme from *Tannhäuser*, Sir Alfred fantasizes about writing Daphne a large check and forgiving the young couple. While conducting his finale, Tchaikovsky's *Francesca da Rimini*, Sir Alfred envisions himself challenging Tony to a fatal game of Russian roulette.

So distraught is Sir Alfred by now that he leaves the concert without taking his bows and races home, where he decides to carry out his murder scenario. But what was so easy in his mind proves hopelessly complicated, as he wrestles with a recalcitrant recorder. Daphne returns to find Sir Alfred on the floor surrounded by broken chairs and other traces of his failed revenge. When he peremptorily asks if she's ever visited Tony's hotel room, Daphne says, yes. One night while Sir Alfred was gone, August called looking for Barbara. And Daphne, having suspicions about Barbara and Tony, ran to look for her in Tony's room:

Well the door was open a little so I marched right in, ready to give her a good piece of my mind, but there wasn't anybody there which certainly made me feel a lot better and I started to leave a lot happier than I had felt when I arrived and then I suddenly realized how terrible it would look if anybody saw me coming out of that room, you know, because Tony's about my age and well to anybody who didn't understand how you and I felt about each other it would look, well you know how dumb some people are. . . . So just before I opened the door I peeked through the keyhole and right there just by the freight elevator I saw this great big old jerk squinting around the corner.

Knowing that "the kind of a man who checks up on his wife is the kind of a man who hired detectives to help him do it," Daphne guessed this was a sleuth and waited and waited for him to depart. "For thirty-eight minutes! He kept you there himself!" cries Alfred, delirious that he has reason to believe his wife is innocent. He begs Daphne never to make him tell what "vulgar" and "contemptible" ideas made him so fiendish earlier that night. As they embrace, Sir Alfred murmurs: "A thousand poets dreamed a thousand years, then you were born, my love."

Unfaithfully Yours contains familiar Sturges motifs: the romantic foreigner (Sir Alfred) opposed to the dogged American (August); the lover who trusts what he's told rather than what he feels. Like *Diddlebock, Unfaithfully Yours* takes place in New York—but, with almost every scene set in a splendid interior, what a different New York it seems! And where *Diddlebock* favored dialogue at the expense of images, *Unfaithfully Yours* fully exploits all aspects of cinema. Sturges's dialogue, his emphatic camera movement, the characters' gestures, the visual detail and the music all deftly interact, like sections of an orchestra. Sometimes they press the same idea—as in the forgiveness fantasy, when Wagner's noble chords ring out as Alfred professes highmindedness while signing $100,000 over to Daphne. But they're more often counterpointed for comic effect—as when Sir Alfred, blinded by a sweater he's drawing over his head, tells August he's never seen him look better. Or in the final scene where Sir Alfred urges Daphne "by all means" to wear her sexy purple dress with the plumes at the hips (in which he's murdered her in his fantasy), but the camera pulls in on him wincing at the prospect.

This dark comedy is uncannily like *The Lady Eve*, but without its double heroines. Like Hopsie Pike, Sir Alfred de Carter is heir to a large business fortune. (In the film, Alfred discreetly tells August his family has "kept England regular since Waterloo"; but early drafts of the script make it clear that Sir Alfred is modeled on Sir Thomas Beecham, and the product that keeps England "on time" is Beecham's Carter's Little Liver Pills.) Daphne, like Jean, comes from humbler stock, and Sir Alfred's passion to spoil her is laced with some mistrust of her father and her past, compounded by his anxieties about all beautiful young women and love in the first place. Like Hopsie, Sir Alfred is made to suffer for doubting the woman he adores. But here the analogy ends because whereas we know Jean is "on the up and up" while Eve is a phony, Daphne's nature and motives are more mysterious.

Whoever the "real" Daphne is, the woman we see is a creation, defined by her dime-store novel professions of love, her youthful beauty and exquisite costumes. When she stomps her foot in exasperation at Alfred, she for a moment seems young and vulnerable, but most of the time she's as elusive as her husband's fog-bound plane in the film's opening. She has no confession scenes, no fantasies, no exposed inner life. For all we know, Daphne's love for Alfred is an elaborate sham, though lines like, "How could I fall in love with anyone else when you took my heart with you?" could also be guileless.

Beyond its fascination with guise and reality, *Unfaithfully Yours* is Sturges's most eloquent comment on what it is to be an artist. Both Sir Alfred and his brother-in-law August enjoy their millions, but August merely watches his money grow, while Alfred creates. "A little magic wand" is Daphne's pretty conceit for the conductor's baton; art is also real and joyous. "Nothing serious about music. Should be enjoyed flat on the back with a sandwich in one hand and a bucket of beer in the other," quips Sir Alfred, who is nonetheless appalled when he learns that Mr. Sweeney, the private detective, is an ardent music lover. "I'd always hoped music had a certain moral and antiseptic power," Sir Alfred bristles at Sweeney's enthusiasm. Ultimately, though, Sir Alfred honors human contradiction and offers Sweeney free tickets for his concert that night.

And a brilliant concert it is. As Rossini's overture triggers Sir Alfred's murder fantasy, the murder fantasy in turn affects the way Sir Alfred conducts. "What did you have in your head? What visions of eternity?" marvels Sir Alfred's manger, Hugo, of the performance. And though less ethereal than Hugo supposes, Sir Alfred's visions were certainly fruitful. If conducting compels Sir Alfred to suffer his demons, he in turn uses those demons to conduct.

A great pleasure of *Unfaithfully Yours* is its stylishness: the cryptic fantasy scenes with their slightly ghoulish light and heightened acting; the flamboyant camera movement, which echoes Sir Alfred's aggressive conducting. A scene where the camera focuses on Sweeney's advertisement-filled window from the inside, so all the writing is backwards and indecipherable, speaks volumes on confusing appearances. Sturges's pacing, while slower, is every bit as assured as in the Paramount films, and the minor characters are similarly memo-

Sir Alfred (Rex Harrison, right) confronts the tailor (Julius Tannen) in front of Sweeney's advertisement-filled window in Unfaithfully Yours.

rable—particularly Sweeney, who rushes to wash his hands before greeting the great conductor, and Sweeney's neighbor, a philosophical tailor, who is affronted by Sir Alfred's outrage while trying to digest his lunch. Though Daphne and her sister Barbara are intentionally one-dimensional, August manages to seem both offensively punctilious and endearingly daft.

But the center of the film is indisputably Sir Alfred. After seeing *Unfaithfully Yours*, Preston's friend John Hertz, Jr., would cable him, "IT IS MY OPINION THAT YOU NOT ONLY WROTE, DIRECTED, AND PRODUCED THE PICTURE BUT THAT YOU ALSO PLAYED THE LEAD."[23] Even down to his foreign upbringing, Alfred is, indeed, more like Preston than any other character he created. What August calls Alfred's "temperament" reflects Sturges's own excitability, and the way Alfred in a rage ignites the sleuth's report, then shoves the burning paper in the face of a hotel detective, recalls Sturges's tantrums. And with some grimness: Sturges never insists on his protagonist's virtue. He even has Alfred move as if to hit Daphne

Preston turns musician on the set of Unfaithfully Yours.

at one point, whereupon she taunts him, "That's right strike me, you brute. Oh, don't you dare?"

The difference between Sir Alfred's and Daphne's age is roughly the difference between Preston's and Francie's. And like Preston, who brooded all evening long when a stranger mistook him for Louise's first husband, Sir Alfred feels threatened by Daphne's past. He experiences pangs of jealousy more deeply than most people, but his relief is similarly immoderate. Alfred's euphoric final lines: "A thousand poets dreamed a thousand years, then you were born, my love," were written by Preston for Eleanor when he followed her to Paris. ("With every Prince, Lord, millionaire and fortune hunter over here pursuing [Eleanor], she has been completely fine, dear and honorable—I worship her,"[24] Preston wrote Charley Abramson at that time—which was also when he threw his wife down the staircase.)

In the first draft of *Unfaithfully Yours*, the connections between Preston and Sir Alfred are even more striking. Here Alfred was married and divorced four times before meeting Daphne, and there's a long monologue where he ruminates on romance "You see, Hugo," Sir Alfred tells his manager, "I have no faintest wish or desire to think of myself as the lord and master of that dream of loveliness reclining in the next room. . . . When I was very young and first married I tried out that role. . . . I just want to be the favorite man . . . the one she is fondest of . . . the lover not the proprietor . . . o-o-o-h . . . the lover-in-LAW, in all probability, since this is the twentieth century and it's always nicer for the children . . . but still: the lover."

This speech is lifted almost verbatim from a passage in a letter Sturges wrote his father the summer Eleanor left for Europe: "I've thought out a lot of things . . . and I'm going to be a much nicer husband than I was before. I used to think of myself as the proprietor . . . very foolish I know . . . but I'm all over that. From now on I ask only to be the Favorite Man . . . a sort of Lover-in-Law. If you figure this out, you'll see it has farreaching effects. It means that one cannot sit back and rest on one's laurels, but on the contrary [must] continue to put the best foot forward and be at least as gentle and nice to one's wife as one was to one's fiancée."

What's intriguing here is not so much the similarity between Alfred's words and Preston's, but Sturges's ability to stand back from his own emotions and ruefully laugh at them. Like Preston, Sir Alfred may with all his heart disavow jealousy and proprietorship, but he's condemned to go on suffering the one and perpetrating the other. Sir Alfred's elation at Daphne's seeming innocence will be transient, a calm before some new suspicion grips him. "I could imagine life with you being a series of ups and downs," Hopsie told Jean in *The*

Lady Eve, and Alfred's experience is more disturbingly cyclical. His nature dooms him to repeat his errors. But these errors, the film implies, are not altogether absurd because people *are* untrustworthy. Daphne's stagy airs and conversation drum home the opacity of all human nature, how we can never really distinguish the "true" feelings from the pose. The film's "happy" ending is also ambiguous, since Alfred's wild suspicions linger, with the chaos on the floor, despite Daphne's alibi. Indeed, just as Schopenhauer called walking "arrested falling," success in *Unfaithfully Yours* is disaster averted. *Unfaithfully Yours* is also far less sanguine than *Sullivan's Travels* about art's power to uplift the human spirit. Yet, at least in the Freudian sense, art *is* cleansing. Sir Alfred purges his basest instincts by conducting music; his fitful, imperfect life is redeemed by art.

Anticipating trouble from the Breen Office, Zanuck urged Sturges to eliminate Sir Alfred's four former wives and all the jokes about his family's laxative fortune. On the whole, though, Zanuck found the script "magnificent." "It is profound and at the same time it is brilliant," he wrote Preston, and his few substantive criticisms were astute. It was Zanuck, for instance, who suggested that Sir Alfred's first fantasy should be the revenge and not, as Sturges had originally planned it, the forgiveness sequence.

"I think your first two retrospects should be reversed," Zanuck noted. "The murder episode should come first and it should be played in such a way that the audience does not think that it is a retrospect but that he has really committed murder." It was also Zanuck who urged Sturges to have Sir Alfred doubt Daphne right up to the last minute and who prodded him to expand on a too abrupt ending while tightening some long early sequences where Sir Alfred meets his future wife at a charity concert in Michigan. (This entire scene is cut in the final version.) Except for the idea about making the murder seem real, Preston used all these suggestions, while he less willingly trimmed the Russian roulette fantasy to accommodate Zanuck's zeal for economy. Preston came up with the title *Unfaithfully Yours* (from his unproduced 1931 farce) to replace *Symphony Story*, which Zanuck found offputting.[25] Previously, Sturges had suggested the title *A Comedy of Murders*, Chaplin's original name for *Monsieur Verdoux*.

Besides following Zanuck's suggestions, Sturges initiated substantial revisions of his own during the two months before *Unfaithfully Yours* went into production: softening Daphne's sister Barbara, while eliminating some of Daphne's more humanizing dialogue. One crucial cut was Daphne's reaction to her sister's presumed infidelity: "Naturally those things don't mean as much to a woman as to a man . . . because none of us are quite as good as men imagine . . . or as bad either." Along with these lines (borrowed almost verbatim from *The Lady Eve*) went Daphne's worldly wisdom and the film's interest in a sympathetic female protagonist. Sturges was moving further and further from the screwball format. And with Sir Alfred a foil not only to chance, but to his own ruthless psyche, *Unfaithfully Yours* challenges the very premise of comedy—that the human will triumphs.

When preproduction began on *Unfaithfully Yours* in November 1947, music was a crucial concern. Sets were constructed to simulate Carnegie Hall, and, while he made a point of playing the Philistine in public (assuring reporters that his musical tastes were "low"[26] and he relied totally on his music director, Alfred Newman), Preston showed considerable expertise in selecting Sir Alfred's concert program. Together with Francie, a music lover, he compiled three pages of suggestions for the revenge and Russian roulette fantasies (including Debussy's *Danses sacrées et profanes* and César Franck's *Symphony in D Minor*). But from the start Preston was set on using the reconciliation theme from *Tannhäuser* for the forgiveness fantasy, which is recapitulated when Alfred embraces Daphne in the final scene. Consciously or not, he was choosing the very music he'd first heard that summer forty-three years ago when his mother dragged him from his father and Chicago to Bayreuth, Isadora, and the beginning of his life in the arts.

Casting proceeded slowly. Preston's first choice for Sir Alfred was James Mason, whom he'd also wanted for *Vendetta*. Like Preston, Mason was tall and dark, with a deep resonant voice and an air of intelligence. Soon Mason would come to Hollywood and become a close friend of Preston's and Francie's. But Mason was now embroiled in a law suit, and Zanuck, thinking ahead, worried that gossip about the trial might diminish Mason's appeal in an ad campaign. It was with the idea of maximizing publicity—ironically, as it turned out—that Zanuck and Sturges offered the part to a very different sort of British actor, Rex Harrison. Harrison was not a star, but he was a distinctive performer who'd attracted attention in *The Ghost and Mrs. Muir* and *The Foxes of Harrow*. Though under contract to Fox, he was very selective about his projects and told Zanuck that he would have to see the entire script of *Unfaithfully Yours* before accepting the role of Sir Alfred, because "in an idea of this nature it is not so much the 'what' as the 'how.'" At forty, he also worried about Sir Alfred's age. "One thing I do feel strongly is that it would be unwise, especially after [*The Foxes of Harrow*] and *Escape* to portray me in a role a little passé. . . . I should certainly not play anything over my own age, and my brother-in-law should be a contemporary. The wives could, of course, still look very much younger!!"[27]

Preston took it upon himself to write Harrison a long letter that not only reassured but captivated the actor, who in early December accepted the part of Sir Alfred, cabling Zanuck that he was "tremendously looking forward" to meeting Preston Sturges.[28] Harrison was not disappointed. The two men immediately hit it off. "Preston was a man I loved," Harrison said, in his autobiography.[29] The conductor Robin Sanders-Clark was hired to teach Harrison conducting. They worked nightly for seven weeks, sometimes staying up until two or three in the morning because Harrison was as much a perfectionist as Sturges himself. (Though Harrison was left-handed, he insisted on learning to conduct with his right hand.) Since Harrison couldn't read music, he memorized the score by beats, and his proficiency paid off, freeing him to throw himself into the conducting. Just to be safe, Sanders-Clark coached Harrison during his concert scenes. "I had an off-camera mike and I would prompt him, always a bar or two bars ahead," he recalls.[30]

Compared to Sir Alfred, Daphne was a minor character, and the way she comported herself and wore clothes were nearly as important as her acting. Sturges wanted Francie Ramsden for the part, and Zanuck tentatively acquiesced. "Just for your private ears there is a helluva race starting here Tuesday. Zanuck has told me I can pencil Francie in [for *Unfaithfully Yours*]," Sturges wrote Bosley Crowther, the fall of 1947.[31]

The race Sturges referred to involved Francie's health. Francie had fallen from a convent window when she was five years old and had, ever since, been prone to painful spinal disc attacks. Just a year ago she'd nearly drowned when she got a spasm swimming off Preston's boat. Now Fox's insurance company, Lloyds of London, refused to insure her in *Unfaithfully Yours* unless she had a major disc operation. So on November 5, 1947 Francie entered Hollywood Presbyterian Hospital. The surgery went well, and she began memorizing Daphne's lines while recovering.

But then Zanuck had second thoughts about casting an unknown actress opposite Harrison, who hadn't enough star appeal to draw a large audience on his own. Increasingly, Zanuck wanted a female star and one day suggested Gene Tierney, who'd played with Harrison in *The Ghost and Mrs. Muir*. While saddened about Francie, Sturges knew that, unlike Howard Hughes, Zanuck truly had the good of his film in mind, and agreed. Zanuck genuinely appreciated Sturges's large-mindedness. "I . . . am grateful for your acceptance of my sincere recommendation in connection with Gene Tierney. More than anything else I want your first picture for us to be both a critical and a box

Preston (left) and Rex Harrison conferring on the set of Unfaithfully Yours.

office success," he wrote Preston, in early December. "The combination of Harrison and Tierney is positive insurance and in these hazardous box office days it would be foolish if we did not take every possible advantage for ourselves." [32]

Ultimately, Gene Tierney rejected the role, complaining that it was too small compared to Harrison's, and was replaced by Linda Darnell, who considered it an honor simply to work with Sturges. "At last I have found a director!" Darnell exclaimed.[33] Barbara Lawrence, still a teenager, became Daphne's sister Barbara. Sturges told Zanuck that the role of August was "loosely tailored for Rudy Vallee," and Zanuck was happy to follow Sturges's instinct here.[34] Zanuck also gave Sturges a free hand with most of the minor players—Lionel Stander became Sir Alfred's manager, Hugo; Edgar Kennedy was cast as Sweeney;[35] and Al Bridge as a house detective who makes the mistake of piecing together the detective's report that Sir Alfred purposely destroys. Robert Greig, Georgia Caine, Julius Tannen, Frank Moran, and Torben Meyer also got character parts. Victor Milner, who'd shot *The Lady Eve* and *The Palm Beach Story*, was hired to direct photography.

Zanuck was adamant that, rather than waiting to tighten his film in the editing room, Sturges should make all his cuts *before* shooting began. Zanuck was also on the warpath about multiple retakes. Sturges drafted, but never sent, a reply to Zanuck's official memo on this subject:

> I sincerely hope . . . that I will be able to show you some other avenues of economy besides the rather dangerous one of discouraging the number of takes a responsible director considers necessary. Time and again I have heard it said of some director: "He took thirty takes and then used the second one" as if this were some proof of his lack of discernment. The fact that he was forced to accept the second take as the best of a bad lot has never indicated to me that he was wrong in trying to improve upon it, within the time limitations dictated by good sense and a proper evaluation of the importance of the scene. The fact that he lost does not prove he was wrong to gamble.[36]

In truth, both Sturges and Zanuck were gamblers, and neither intended to stint on *Unfaithfully Yours*. "It is my opinion that this picture must reek with brilliance. By this I do not mean that everything should be lit up but that it should have a plush and rich feeling,"[37] Zanuck told Sturges; and, between the elaborate clothes and hiring a full orchestra and paying Rex Harrison $100,000 and Linda Darnell $80,000, on top of Sturges's own prodigious salary, Zanuck was budgeting the film at just under two million dollars: not a modest sum for any filmmaker in the forties and Sturges's highest budget ever. Shooting was scheduled to last fifty-seven days, considerably longer than *The Lady Eve*, but about a third shorter than the average film of its day, according to *Newsweek*.[38] To minimize retakes, Sturges rehearsed actors off-camera between scenes. Yet he sacrificed none of his characteristic flair: donning a red fez on the set and serving everyone a free lunch from The Players.

Unfaithfully Yours was to be written, directed, and produced by Preston Sturges, but Zanuck made his presence known from the outset. February 20, the very first day of shooting, Zanuck complained to Preston that he didn't like the quality of the camera work. On day seven, Zanuck still found the photography "very spotty and uneven" and was also displeased with the pace of the master shot. "When the dialogue comes so rapidly it sounds more like a rapid recital than actually a scene between two people,"[39] Zanuck criticized the early scene in which August tells Sir Alfred that he's had Daphne tailed. The impression of two irascible instruments snapping at each other is precisely what makes this scene "Sturgesesque," and Preston managed to get around Zanuck here, though it was daunting, having to defend himself so early in the game. And even Sturges, always eager to have an audience for his dailies, was disconcerted when Zanuck showed up at all the rushes and began firing off memos full of strong advice.

"I sincerely hope the film will speak more convincingly than any arguments I could advance, that your confidence in me will be to some extent restored and that for the sake both of this film, and for my very necessary authority with the people I work with, if I am to be of any value to this company, that you will reconsider what sounded very much like a prejudgment and let me continue with an easy heart in the making of a film that should do us all a little good," Sturges, obviously smarting from a Zanuck memo, wrote his boss the second week of production.[40] And, alerted to Sturges's sensitivity, Zanuck made an effort to resume his old technique of flattering Sturges before exhorting him to better work.

"If this does not make a genuine star of Rex then we had better give up on him entirely . . . but more than this I think it puts you once again in the forefront as a creator of top flight entertainment," Zanuck pronounced, when *Unfaithfully Yours* was finished.[41] Still, even though Sturges had come in on time and on budget, Zanuck was dissatisfied. It now occurred to him that Sturges had been permitted "at least one full week" more than necessary, and in a memo addressed to all the Fox directors, Zanuck used *Unfaithfully Yours* as an example of extravagant filmmaking.[42]

Sturges could not sit by to see the rules changed retroactively. "I presume that part of the job of being the head of a great studio consists of telling the directors that they could have done it in half the time if they had really put their can to the grindstone, or however the metaphor goes, so I do not hold it against you," he wrote Zanuck. "I normally work seventeen hours a day but will try to do more in the future."[43]

Zanuck replied, "As for yourself, I have never known anyone to work any harder as an individual, and this report comes to me from . . . everyone who was closely associated with you." Yet, he persisted in his righteous tone about the budget: "If the picture is an enormous success it will make money. If it is a big success it will break even. If it is just successful it will lose money."[44]

However hurt he felt, Preston made an attempt to look on the bright side. Darryl Zanuck was not Buddy DeSylva. Preston respected Zanuck, and besides, with Spyros Skouras essentially a businessman, there was no one else to turn to at Fox. "I hope *Unfaithfully Yours* will be merely the first in a series of successes both commercial and pride-satisfying, for your excellent company," Preston wrote Zanuck, before the film's first preview.

Preston asked his old friend Gilletti to make a laugh meter for this Riverdale preview. There were lots of chuckles, but few "hearty laughs" and only five "yells" during the film's 126 minutes. Ninety-four people walked out before or after the concert numbers. "The only complaints," Zanuck reported, "were on the overall length of the picture and, of course, the musical numbers. These really seemed to stop the picture completely like an extraneous song in a musical"; and he added that the audience liked Harrison as a "character actor," but "when Harrison got romantic in a serious vein and became rather poetic," they found this "jarring with the humor." In other words, the audience rejected the most original aspects of Sturges's work, and Zanuck, who frequently took issue with the reactions of a preview audience, here seemed to take their side rather than Sturges's.[45]

He was in a rush to release *Unfaithfully Yours* and got Sturges to agree to eliminate twenty-one minutes from the print the day after the preview. When, at the end of that day, Zanuck discovered that Preston still had cut only twelve minutes, Zanuck lost patience, writing, in a "confidential" memo: "Because this has been primarily your undertaking I have allowed you to take more time in the editing of this film than on any other film in the history of Twentieth Century Fox—I would say more time by about 300%. . . . I intend to COMPLETE the cutting tonight."[46]

Zanuck was not behaving as if he had a hit on his hands, but neither had he lost faith in the movie. Three weeks after the confidential memo, Zanuck screened *Unfaithfully Yours* for Fox executives in New York. The response, he wrote Sturges, was "enthusiastic. Many of them said they thought it was the finest picture you have ever been associated with."[47] Preparations began for an advertising campaign that might have recouped all the production expenses which so distressed Zanuck.

Then at the beginning of July, Rex Harrison became the focus of an altogether different sort of publicity. Estranged from his wife, Lilli Palmer, Harrison for a year had been having an affair with the Hollywood actress Carole Landis. Harrison and Landis saw each other openly, but had no plans to marry. On July fourth, Harrison, coming from an appointment in Malibu, discovered Landis dead on her bathroom floor. She'd had a hard life and was emotionally fragile. An autopsy immediately established her death as suicide, from liquor and Seconal. There was no indication of any rift with Harrison. Still, the press pursued him, "swarming into the garden, up the trees, even, some of them, onto the roof" of his house, he wrote in his autobiography; and while they never actually accused Harrison of murdering Landis, there was an unstated suspicion.[48] People began comparing Harrison's implication in Landis's death to the Fatty Arbuckle scandal—perhaps, like Arbuckle, Harrison would never work again. In fact, the playwright Maxwell Anderson had just hired Harrison to play Henry VIII in his *Anne of the Thousand Days* on Broadway and was eager to go ahead with the project. But Harrison got not a word of support from Fox. No statement was made in his defense.

There was even, finally, a halt to Zanuck's memos to Sturges. With reporters climbing trees to get a glimpse of Rex Harrison, Fox was in no rush to release a film where he fantasizes about murdering his wife! The opening of the film was postponed, the advertising campaign canceled. A real death hung over Sturges's black comedy, and Zanuck—so intrepid on the set and in the editing room—had no courage to speak out in its defense.

Zanuck did, however, defend *Unfaithfully Yours* against Spyros Skouras's idea that subtitles should be used to explain that the murder and Russian roulette scenes were merely fantasies:

> IF YOU HAD SHAKESPEARE, ALEXANDRE DUMAS AND ERNEST HEMINGWAY COMBINED THEY COULD NOT WRITE A FOREWORD THAT WOULD IN ANY FASHION HELP THE DREAM SEQUENCES AS YOU CANNOT CURE THE SUBNORMAL INTELLIGENCE LEVEL OF SOME AUDIENCES WITH SUBTITLES. ANYBODY WITH A FOURTH GRADE EDUCATION CAN UNDERSTAND WHAT HARRISON IS TRYING TO DO AND I THINK THAT IF WE HAVE TO AIM AT THOSE FEW IMBECILES WITH A LOWER IQ RATING WE SHOULD GO OUT OF BUSINESS. UNFAITHFULLY YOURS ACCORDING TO ALL INDICATIONS MAY NOT BE A POPULAR BOX OFFICE PICTURE BUT YOU CANNOT SAVE IT WITH LAST MINUTE TITLES.[49]

When *Unfaithfully Yours* opened on November 5, 1948, at New York's Roxy, Zanuck wrote Sturges that "the opening day's business . . . was almost the worst in the entire history of the house and certainly the lowest we have had in many years."[50] And Sturges, then in the middle of another troubled project for Fox, exculpated himself as tactfully as possible, replying: "I am sorry UNFAITHFULLY YOURS had a bad first day's business. I have no idea what advertising preceded the opening at the Roxy or how much anticipatory excitement Mr. Harrison's and Miss Darnell's names caused in the hearts of the customers. . . . God grant that some of the . . . reviews will be good and that the picture will build to an enormous gross."[51]

The reviews praised *Unfaithfully Yours*, with qualifications.[52] The *New York Daily News* called it "an adroit, literate light piece that builds from a familiar base to highbrow farce comedy." *Newsweek* found it "sophisticated adult entertainment," obviously of the Sturges mold, though not as masterful as his Paramount movies. There was no mention of Carole Landis's death. Rex Harrison's performance was praised by everyone. But the *Herald Tribune* complained that the film's humor was "on the heavy side," and though he called *Unfaithfully Yours* "a dilly of a sardonic slapstick comedy," even Bosley Crowther had his reservations: "Four years have been permitted to go gurgling down the drain since the last release of a Sturges picture . . . —and that's too long. Also, a shade of something fatal to a champion may be perceived in his new picture at the Roxy. That's a slip in his timing and his speed. Like a boxer who takes too long a lay-off, Mr. Sturges has slowed up a bit. And this is something which his public will be first to note and deplore." Archer Winsten, writing a mixed review in the *New York Post*, struck the same note, observing: "[Sturges's] timing is off in the matter of comedy, and his sense of public taste is slightly awry both in what he chooses to do and in how he does it."

Certainly Crowther and Winsten were right that Sturges did not connect to the country's current mood—or at least to that mood as Hollywood perceived and reflected it. Nor was Preston inclined only and always to make ebullient comedies. Though there's no rule, often the comic mind grows darker and more inward with time. Charlie Chaplin had just a year before shocked Hollywood with *his* murder comedy, *Monsieur Verdoux*. Chaplin, always conscious of the world's injustice, used a social context, while *Unfaithfully Yours* was more explicitly psychological.

And still *Unfaithfully Yours* was and is a seductive movie, the last film Sturges approached with the illusion of invulnerability. No studio filmmaker is autonomous, but, for all Zanuck's memos, Sturges had a great deal of control. Moreover, there was an unspoken trust between himself and Zanuck, founded on Zanuck's respect not for Sturges's commercial record, which wasn't extraordinary, but for his genius. "To own a talent like singing is like to own maybe a trained bear that dances to make people laugh. . . . It is the bear, the talent, they want. For [the owner] . . . they care nothing," the opera singer Gus had complained to Isabelle in *Strictly Dishonorable*. And what would become of the owner if his bear stopped dancing?

All creators must find a way to sustain belief in their own powers, and Sturges, always superstitious, deeply needing approval, had come to rely on the good opinion of the world. For him, the mixed reviews and box office failure of *Unfaithfully Yours* were immeasurably destructive. He'd had career setbacks before, but not since the early thirties on Broadway had he found such reason to doubt his art.

CHAPTER 25

Bianca Gilchrist flew in from Paris just as Preston was finishing the script for *Unfaithfully Yours*. She came to have her teeth fixed by her Los Angeles dentist. Or maybe the dentist was really an excuse for her to return full of success and exotic stories to the city she'd left in a huff. Not only were Preston and Bianca delighted to see each other, but many of the people who'd found Bianca odd and abrasive before were now fascinated by her life as a war spy and then a businesswoman in the fashion world. After Bianca went back to France, she wrote Preston: "By the time you get this letter, you will have finished your *Symphony Story*. I know you don't need my prayers, but you've got them. Good luck, Preston. I hope they all think it's as wonderful as I do." [1]

Preston must have been gratified to have sustained a twenty-year relation-ship with the formerly stormy Bianca, and the past was with him in other ways as well. Sometimes unpleasantly. His old lung troubles came back. He had a persistent cough, and a Los Angeles specialist diagnosed cancer and said he'd have to have a lobe of a lung removed. But Gilletti convinced Preston to go to Chicago for a second opinion. Preston consulted with a Dr. Block, who discovered that there was no cancer, the lung stayed in.

Divorced, with a young son, Preston was of an age to be drawn back to his own childhood. An old friend came to lunch one day and couldn't get over how much Preston resembled Paris Singer. [2] Then, Preston's Turkish step-father, Vely Bey, reemerged, married again and living with teenage sons in Belgium. Having read of Preston's fame, Bey wrote, wondering if his stepson would even remember him, and Preston, eager to impress this large figure of his youth, wrote back describing their Avenue Charles Floquet apartment and "your sweet mother Grandmère" and "the time you and mother played a joke on me by serving my soup in a brand new chamber pot." [3]

A lively correspondence sprung up between them. Of his marriage to Mary,

Bey mused: "If financial conditions had been better perhaps things might have turned [out differently]. . . . At least that was her opinion and mine." [4] But the man who'd slapped Preston for laughing at Sacha Guitry had not altogether mellowed and soon was writing that he didn't like *The Miracle of Morgan's Creek*, no matter how highly people spoke of it, and since Preston was so rich, why didn't he send each of Bey's sons an American tie "in separate paquets." [5] Preston, meanwhile, was wondering whether Bey could send *him* a "finest grade billiard cloth" and a French waistcoat for his valet. At the end of the decade, Preston would give his stepfather no idea about his growing financial troubles: thus the ironic coincidence that when Preston received Bey's letter, saying he'd read in *Time* magazine that Preston was the third best-paid man in America, Preston was just then writing Bey, asking if he could arrange a desperately needed loan for him with a Belgian bank. [6]

The Biden family also reentered Preston's life when, on a trip to New York, Preston met and took a liking to his father's son by a second marriage, also named Edmund Biden. Thirty years old, Edmund lived on Riverside Drive with his wife Dorothy and their four-year-old daughter, and had a job at the counter at Walgreen's Drugstore. Because Preston believed so strongly in the importance of heredity, he was predisposed to like his half brother. "A fine young man" [7] he described him, after their brief meeting, and he invited Edmund to come west and apprentice at his restaurant, with the idea of one day managing it. Edmund wrote back saying New York was no place to raise a child and he'd gladly accept Preston's offer—at which point Preston found the Bidens an apartment and sent $300 in advance for their move; but it was over a year before Edmund got himself to Los Angeles. Sturges must have thought very highly of the blood tie, for he not only held the job for Edmund, but got rid of the apartment and invited the Bidens to live with him.

The restaurant Edmund went to work at was not the bustling nightspot it had been in the early forties. After the war, The Players's original troubles were compounded because the restaurant began losing customers. In 1948, the gross income was down $400,000 from three years before, a drop nearly as dramatic as the decline in the film industry.

Sturges blamed his restaurant's problems on the incident involving B. P. Schulberg, the producer who'd years before quarreled with him about the importance of screenwriters. One night, while Schulberg was dining at The Players, someone made an anti-Semitic comment to him. Schulberg summoned Monsieur Pillet and insisted he evict the man (who, to make matters more complicated, happened to be one of Schulberg's former screenwriters), but Pillet, while regretting the insult, said there was nothing he could do. So the following day Schulberg sent Preston a telegram, insisting that he fire Pillet. And when Sturges defended his manager, Schulberg concluded that Sturges himself was anti-Semitic.

No one who knew Preston could believe he was biased against all Jewish people. Henry Henigson, Willie Wyler, Charley Abramson, literally, his best friends were Jewish. Yet, it was true Preston made fun of the Jewish studio heads, and as business worsened, he began speculating that Hollywood Jews were boycotting The Players because he had antagonized Schulberg.[8]

More plausible explanations for The Players's demise were the changing times and the fickleness of customers. To survive these, a restaurant must be fortified with a large reserve of cash, and Sturges had never saved money. Still, it was not in his nature either to close for lack of capital, or to modestly cut back on costs; so he drew on his salary from Fox to redecorate, install a new bar on the ground floor in place of the drive-in, and to begin constructing what he felt sure would give The Players a whole new lease on life: a dinner theatre.

Preston may have gotten the idea for his theatre from the Writers' Club (which he'd joined when he first came to Hollywood) where dinner was served at seven, followed by a series of one-act plays. But Preston planned to offer dancing as well as food and drama. "The stepped pit of the auditorium has to turn into a dance floor complete with ringside tables in two minutes," he wrote John Hertz, Jr., adding: "I have also devised a new (I believe) method of shifting scenery by a sort of overhead switchyard composed of garage door tracks."[9] The cover charge would be a mere two dollars. People could smoke and drink while they watched the plays.

Preston told Louise he felt the theatre was "one of the soundest money-making ideas I have ever had in my life": but then what, besides writing and directing, had ever made him money? And if he calculated the costs, Preston must have known that to finance a dinner theatre he would go through all the money he made and run up credits with the butcher and the grocer—and Louise. Still, if the risk was foolish in financial terms, Preston's attitude toward The Players was very like Isadora Duncan's quixotic enthusiasm for her schools and tours and studios. More than Paris Singer's or Vely Bey's, Isadora's influence showed on fifty-year-old Preston.

While plans for the dinner theatre proceeded at The Players, at Fox Sturges resumed work on the Betty Grable project, now scheduled to be shot in Technicolor. There were mixed signals from Zanuck, who professed to find Sturges's revised script "great," but nonetheless changed some of his dialogue and added a new plot angle. Zanuck also made the unusual decision to submit

Sturges's work to a studio reader, who complained of "an inane number of slapstick pratfalls and beanings," and described the script as "patently overlong." [10]

"It goes without saying that in a picture like this, direction and acting make all the difference between an hilarious comedy and a silly bore," the reader concluded. But here he was wrong, for the problems with the film *The Beautiful Blonde from Bashful Bend* are very much the problems of its screenplay.

Set at the turn of the century in the American Southwest, *The Beautiful Blonde* is the tale of Freddie, a sharpshooting nightclub singer, and Blackie, her gambling man. When a new girl in town, Roulette, takes a shine to Blackie, Freddie twice sets out to shoot the duo, but by a wild coincidence, both times hits the judge in the rear.

Fleeing the law, Freddie, with her Mexican friend Conchita, heads for the train station where they discover the luggage of a Hilda Swandumper, who's died on the way to her new teaching job in Snake City. Conchita convinces Freddie she has no option but to pose as the awaited teacher.

So Freddie and Conchita proceed to Snake City, where they are welcomed by such bastions of the wild West as a gun-happy demented widower, Mr. Basserman; a native son, Charlie, who can't shoot; and a U.S. federal marshal with a Swedish accent. Freddie's schoolteaching consists of intimidating Mr. Basserman's delinquent sons, whom she subsequently hires to protect her from Blackie. Blackie says he's come to Snake City because he can't live without Freddie, while she suspects he's looking for the $1,000 reward on her head. Whichever, Blackie inadvertently sets off a gunfight that culminates with Basserman trying to hang both Charlie and Blackie. Freddie saves the day by expertly shooting them free.

Freddie's flair for shooting does not go unremarked by the federal marshall, who now realizes her true identity and feels compelled to turn her in. In court, Freddie and Blackie speak poignantly of their love for each other. The judge, moved, seems about to commute Freddie's sentence. Then, Roulette flirts with Blackie, and Freddie's trigger finger starts to itch. As Conchita struggles to wrest Freddie's pistol from her, a bullet flies off and homes, once again, in the judge's rear.

Just as *The Miracle of Morgan's Creek* and *The Lady Eve* parody Bible stories, *The Beautiful Blonde* satirizes the scarcely less sacred myths of the American West, sometimes with genuine humor, as when Basserman, having instigated a vicious gun battle, reveals that he's "plum forgot" what it was all about. Or when no one gets hurt for all the knife-waving and trigger-pulling. Sturges's conviction that people don't change is credibly argued through Freddie and

Blackie, who continue to love each other for, rather than despite, their evil ways. Yet, though there are appealing minor characters—the judge's overbearing wife, Elvira, the likable villain Basserman, always whining about being a social outcast—and some effective visual humor in the completed film, *The Beautiful Blonde* lacks subtlety. Its narrative, with the long gun battle, full of individual jokes rather than sustained satire, is predictable. The American small town, so distinctively evoked in Sturges's last two Paramount films, is here reduced to a series of gags, while characters like the ghoulish Basserman brothers lack the real strangeness of Sturges's earlier oddballs. Like the lion episodes in *The Sin of Harold Diddlebock*, large sections of *The Beautiful Blonde* feel forced because no serious ideas complicate the increasingly outrageous slapstick. Of all Sturges's work, *The Beautiful Blonde* most resembles his 1930 operetta *The Well of Romance*. Both revel in low jokes at the expense of their genres, and neither is a labor of love.

In the fall of 1948, both Sturges and Zanuck approached *The Beautiful Blonde* as a sensible commercial project. "I do not want this picture because of cost or a wrong calculation on our part to be the first and only Betty Grable film that has failed to make a profit," Zanuck prophetically warned Fox's production manager. Then, after seeing the wardrobe sketches for Grable's costumes, Zanuck approvingly wrote Preston: "I think they are wonderful, particularly the first red dress. The main reason I wanted to see them is that once when we made a picture called *The Shocking Miss Pilgrim* we did not show Grable's legs in the picture and in addition to receiving a million letters of protest the incident almost caused a national furor." He was glad to see Preston was giving Grable a split skirt in the opening and showing her in panties later on. "I know it perhaps sounds like a silly thing to worry about but from a commercial standpoint Betty's legs are no joking matter."[11]

Casting went quickly. Cesar Romero, Hollywood's perennial Latin lover, became Blackie, Rudy Vallee was cast as Charlie, and Porter Hall as the judge. Preston's old friend Richard Hale got his largest role in a Sturges film, as Mr. Basserman, with the look-alikes Sterling Holloway and Danny Jackson as his sons. Sturges proved he had not lost his fervor for unearthing old movie figures, picking the former Swedish dialect comic Ed Brendel (whom he'd met at the fights six months earlier) to play Snake City's federal marshall.

The production was allotted forty-six days, eleven days fewer than *Unfaithfully Yours*. Sturges agreed to the schedule under duress, perhaps believing he could later talk Zanuck into extra days, or maybe really thinking he could work as swiftly as he had at Paramount. Of course, there's no reason why he should not have worked that swiftly, if he'd been directing one of his Paramount scripts; or conversely, if he had come to terms with the fact that this was not a Sturges film and been content just to get it over with. But, though Sturges himself had dismissed *The Beautiful Blonde*'s screenplay as "workman-like," he was temperamentally incapable of setting out to direct a merely workman-like film. So he was in trouble from the outset: having neither the material to make a great movie nor the resignation to accept that he would not.

Shooting began at the end of September, with Sturges working in Technicolor for the first time. This process alone must have intrigued him, and Betty Grable, though no Sturges fan, was initially cooperative. The opening scenes are the script's strongest, and Zanuck approved of how Sturges directed these. "I am highly pleased," he said of the early rushes, particularly praising a production number where Betty Grable sings plaintively of love, while surreptitiously grabbing a gun and heading off to shoot her lover. Zanuck found the second shooting of the judge "hilarious," though by the time Freddie and Conchita got to the train station, Zanuck had the feeling "that many of the characters were . . . endeavoring to *reach* for laughs and thus they became strained, far-fetched and not too funny." Zanuck had little good to say for the rushes from here on.

Besides, Sturges soon was running behind schedule, and Zanuck responded with the familiar chiding memos. "Since writing you the note this morning I have just looked at our production reports and I see where you have now fallen three full days behind. . . . I don't know what the cause is but unless we can hold an even keel from here on this presents a very serious problem," he wrote in late October.[12] The next week *Unfaithfully Yours* opened to mixed reviews, and Zanuck assumed a harsher tone. He'd decided the success of *The Beautiful Blonde* depended on the hilarity of the bloodless gun battle, and when Sturges at first resisted piling on slapstick, Zanuck insisted they together draw up a long list of comic routines that Sturges would execute. No mention was made of the scene's real trouble—the absence of comic ideas—though Zanuck surely saw what was happening. "We have no story points at issue, therefore we are certainly out on a limb," he'd noted earlier.[13] Now, in the seventh week of production, with Sturges laboring over every shot, Zanuck wrote, "I hate to be cross or disturbed but I cannot conscientiously tell you anything except this—for what you are shooting and the type of scenes you are doing you are spending more time than they are worth."[14]

He was right, of course. But Zanuck's approach did not help Sturges, whose ability to direct was so tied to his self-confidence. This was further undermined when Betty Grable became hostile, according to Preston, because Ray Klune, Zanuck's production manager, poisoned her mind against the project.

One day Klune walked into Grable's dressing room, and after that her attitude changed completely. Like Sturges's theory about Jews boycotting The Players, the idea that Ray Klune brainwashed Grable was an oversimplification. Grable would later claim she'd never wanted to make the film in the first place because she objected to her character's bawdiness, which was precisely what Sturges, who envisioned Grable as a young Mae West, found intriguing in the role. "I always leave the selection of the story, direction, and cast to Darryl Zanuck, for whom I have great respect. . . . But if he ever gives me Preston Sturges again, you'll hear Grable's voice!" said Grable.[15]

However galled Sturges was by Grable and Zanuck, in public he maintained an accommodating air. An example of his deference to Zanuck is the way he cast the small role of Freddie's grandfather. Since the grandfather's only appearance is in a scene Preston had scheduled to shoot near the end of production, no actor was needed until late November. Then, Sturges's choice for the role was Tom Moore, a well-known silent film actor who'd fallen upon hard times and asked Priscilla Woolfan to recommend him to Preston. Sturges gave both Moore and Priscilla Woolfan the impression that Zanuck would make the final decision, but in fact, Zanuck was willing to leave the casting to Sturges; it was Sturges himself who insisted on Zanuck's having the last word. "Russell Simpson was kind enough to read the [grandfather] part for me this afternoon and read it beautifully, probably a little bit better than Tom [Moore], although I personally would prefer to use Tom," he told Zanuck, "I don't know whether sentiment should enter into these matters or not. Certainly, it is not up to me to be sentimental with other people's money. I would like some advice."[16] Zanuck advised to him use Russell Simpson, and he did.

As 1948 drew to a close, Sturges had good reason for ingratiating himself with Zanuck. Every day The Beautiful Blonde fell further behind. "It is quite true that I *did* venture the optimistic prediction that I would pick up some time after I got out of the fight sequence," Preston answered one indignant memo from Zanuck. "What I did *not* have in my head, however, and what I have since realized with horror, was the fact that the latter part of my script had been scheduled at six and seven pages a day . . . for the purpose, of course, of fitting it into the forty-six days originally. You know better than I do whether this amount of pages per day is possible. It does not seem to matter how hard I drive or how much I accomplish, each day the result is the same; we have slipped a little further into the red."[17] And he was now facing a financial crisis. Trying to keep The Players running at a loss, while constructing a dinner theatre and living life as he wanted, Preston had run up debts everywhere. When he tried to use his real estate as credit to borrow capital, he discovered his house was pledged for $13,000 in unpaid taxes, the restaurant's value was diminished by its unfinished theatre, and besides, no bank would allow him to spend a cent on himself before he paid off his lapsed mortgages and the $45,000 he currently owed Louise and Mon.[18] Meanwhile, his contract with Fox was up for renewal in December, which meant his enormous salary might any day evaporate.

While Zanuck was fretting about overtime, Sturges was contemplating bankruptcy. "My financial equilibrium has suddenly developed such a lack of balance, as the result of taxes, divorces, starting independent companies and other eccentricities, that I am going to have to holler for help in the shape of some cash, almost at once," Preston wrote Zanuck the day after they decided against casting Tom Moore as the grandfather. Preston added that he would need to know immediately if Fox wanted "my services after December 31."[19]

They did not. And Sturges, who'd indignantly marched out of Paramount five Christmases before, was now wiser and less optimistic about his future prospects. He had little interest in evening the score or apportioning blame this time, he wanted the chance to again make personal films in Hollywood. On December 17, with production on *The Beautiful Blonde* finally drawing to a close, he wrote Zanuck a long letter asking for another job at Fox. The by turns pleading and self-righteous tone may be calculated, but his points are heartfelt:

> I told you in my note the other day that I hated leaving Twentieth Century-Fox without trying even once that which I am temperamentally best suited for and what I have always done with the greatest success: the development and furthering of new and eager personalities in pictures that do not cost too much money. When I remember that I made *The Lady Eve* for $666,000 and *The Miracle of Morgan's Creek* for $775,000, I am outraged to see the slow, demoralizing, enthusiasm-sapping, absurdly expensive methods of film production that are growing like a cancer in the heart of this industry, making ruinously dangerous, as you said yourself a year ago, all the forms of interesting experimentation and removing all the long shots from a business that always has been and always will be a gamble. I sincerely believe that only an invention in shooting and production technique can shake us out of our lethargy and that is why I keep returning, with almost a rude insistence, to the idea of making some pictures for you in the old studio on Western Avenue. . . . I am certain that I can do at least two pictures in a year. I have done it before and you have heard of all of them. It means working sixteen hours a day but I like to work sixteen hours a day and when you are doing what you want to do, sixteen hours pass like sixteen minutes. All of this I am perfectly willing to do on any equitable basis whatsoever. It can be straight

salary plus originals, or drawing account against percentage of the gross, or a separate corporation. The more pictures you get out of me for a year's pay, the better I will like it. Give it some thought, my dear Darryl, before you chase me away from this excellent company.[20]

While Preston's methods for saving money may have been dubious, he was unquestionably eager to work hard and, more significantly, to experiment. The entertainer who had always resisted discussing his larger vision here finally sides with the underdogs and crazy dreamers his films champion. In his astute description of Hollywood—"a business that always has been and always will be a gamble"—he challenges the very idea of "sensible" filmmaking, of patching together movies like *The Beautiful Blonde*, rather than letting one person pursue an idea.

Preston's letter to Zanuck is a bit like Jimmy's last-ditch appeal to Mr. Baxter, in *Christmas in July*. But when Zanuck refused him, Sturges must have felt like McGinty, who'd climbed so high, only to land right back where he began.

Trying to reassure Louise about his financial viability, Sturges wrote: "My new picture, *The Beautiful Blonde from Bashful Bend*, was previewed in Riverside one week ago and the laughter nearly took the roof off. Darryl Zanuck says that it is not only the funniest picture he has ever been connected with but the funniest picture he has ever seen and that it will make millions for the company."[21] Zanuck, however, recalls walking around the block ten times after a Pomona preview, convinced Sturges had "crucified" the studio's most important star.[22] Zanuck reedited *The Beautiful Blonde* himself, then called in a studio director to add new footage. On May 28, 1949, the film opened to reviews which glanced over Grable's serviceable performance to concentrate on Sturges's writing and directing. "An eighth grade approach to sex and Betty Grable," declared *Variety*.[23] Even Bosley Crowther had to admit Sturges's "fine hand" had "slipped quite a little,"[24] while, in the *Post*, Archer Winsten saw *The Beautiful Blonde* as a portent. Calling the film "dull, flavorless and labored," he lamented the change that had come over Preston Sturges. "This is a dreadful loss to Hollywood production," wrote Winsten. "It comes at a time when the fresh satire and rowdy humor of Preston Sturges are most grievously missed. It comes without explanation, like darkness at noon."[25]

It's significant that, while he complained about Zanuck's reediting, Sturges did not absolve himself of his film's shortcomings, nor did he disparage his critics or his public, many of whom wrote him angry notes, deploring *The Beautiful Blonde*. From the time he wrote *The Guinea Pig*, Preston had accepted

Brander Matthew's view that a play should please its audience. After nearly two decades in Hollywood, he grudgingly respected reviewers as well. "I must confess that I approve heartily of a severe press," he wrote Rupert Hughes, three days after *The Beautiful Blonde* opened. "It is the only thing which has kept this art, which thinks of itself as an industry, from becoming an industry." [26]

C H A P T E R 26

In the winter of 1949, Preston's debts seemed endless. He owed the IRS and the chicken dealer and the butcher, who one day marched in demanding $10,000 on the spot: to no avail, since Sturges had nothing to give him. Preston had never incorporated because he thought it unmanly to distinguish between one's self and one's business.[1] Anyhow, remembering that his mother always regretted bankrupting the Maison Desti, Preston refused to give up on The Players, instead borrowing from his friends, his stock company, anyone, just to keep it going. "Sufficient unto the day is the evil thereof," Sturges had Norval tell Trudy in *Miracle*, and he too tried to live one day at a time. Still, his troubles took their toll. Preston felt dizzy. He felt pressure at his right ear and eye. Finally, he made an appointment with the Chicago physician, Dr. Block, who'd examined his lung. Dr. Block could find nothing specifically wrong with him, though there were mild symptoms of a heart disorder. "I hope the heart symptoms I showed in Chicago were induced by anxiety about the other matter [dizziness]," Preston wrote the doctor, when he got home.[2]

From Mon's Swiss school, Sturges got reports that his son thought life was a game and ignored his schoolwork. Louise, meanwhile, was living extravagantly in Italy, oblivious to her precarious situation. "As I dictate this letter I am what is called a ruined man," Preston enlightened her, and went on to warn of a future that promised "extremely modest alimony" for Louise while "at my not too distant death, I will not be able to leave [Mon] anything at all." There was, however, an alternative. If Louise would agree to accept the Ivar Avenue house as collateral and sign the $45,000 Preston still owed her back to him, then the banks would give him a loan so he could at last pay off his creditors. Soon, The Players theatre would open and make great sums of money for the whole family. His reputation redeemed, Preston would in no time be back on a studio payroll.[3]

"That you are at present swimming pool and yacht poor with a restaurant that *always* could have made money if given its head is a worrisome but not an insurmountable trouble. Over here, you see some real ones—I suspect over there too," Louise, moved by the poverty in postwar Europe, replied to his appeal.[4] But she also cabled that she was "NATURALLY DISPOSED TO HELP" and signed over her $45,000, thereby rendering herself and Mon completely dependent on Preston's future ability to earn.[5]

It was May before Sturges found a job, this time at MGM, writing a screenplay about an inventor-industrialist who suddenly loses his memory and is forced to reevaluate his life. Clark Gable was to play the lead, but producers Larry Weingarten and Kenneth MacKenna were hedging their bets on Sturges, offering him a flat $50,000 salary ($25,000 when he delivered the script and the remainder after he'd made the corrections they deemed necessary) and no promises that he would direct the film. To Henry Henigson, who was off in Europe, Preston wrote, "As always in such cases, I mean working with producers, there is not only the task of writing what I personally consider a good script but injecting into it also those elements which the studio considers necessary . . . sometimes more obstacles, more heavies and more plot than I personally consider necessary. Larry Weingarten and Kenneth MacKenna . . . are extremely intelligent, courteous and pleasant, and I assure you that I am bending over backwards to do what they wish." He went on to write at length about the new theatre, implying that his salvation lay here.[6]

Ever the wise friend, Henigson replied, "Why (and I dare say you have) not give some thought to doing what you once did and get out a script that can be done for reasonable money—then make up your mind to do it for that and that sum only. . . . You may need, at this time, to make an investment and that only of your time and talent—would that I had such a storehouse. . . . Your business is not a restaurant and you may get satisfaction out of owning one but you must, to be happy, be expressing yourself as you should with the money as a secondary problem—that must come based on effort to a man in your position. . . . I am not happy that you must write about the G. D. restaurant whether it becomes phenomenally successful or not."[7]

Essentially, Preston accepted Henry's strategy for reviving his film career. Deploring his reputation for extravagance, Preston contradicted it wherever he could—telling Harry Cohn, for instance, "All I hear about myself is extravagance. I have never been extravagant in my life, except with my own money": which, if California Pictures can be considered his "own money" was true. Preston also wrote letters to Henry Ginsberg and Frank Freeman at Paramount, assuring them he was able and willing to make the same sort of films he'd made half a decade before and describing elaborate methods he'd contrived for working cheaply. Preston likened his reputation for being difficult with the plight of a dentist who can't get work because he's known to be painful. He was determined to prove he was a reasonable man. "Healthy disagreement we must have, it is its aftermath which is sometimes dangerous and there, beyond question, is where I erred," Preston wrote Freeman, who bore his former protégé no animus, but did not want him back.[8]

On the issue of "the G. D. restaurant," however, Henigson had hit a sore point because, perverse though it seemed to so many who saw Sturges exclusively as a filmmaker, he did care deeply about his restaurant's success. Perhaps it was the childhood wish to be a businessman like his father, or the joy he took in playing the grand host. Then, too, Preston had never taken his identity from being a writer. He now said maybe he wasn't a writer at all, maybe writing was just a piece of luck that had come his way and could at any moment vanish. He had lost the wild confidence that he could create anytime, anywhere. Now his property seemed more reliable than his talent. And yet, on some level, Preston did realize that building The Players theatre was tilting at windmills. In the mid-fifties, he would regret that he had not "accepted my loss and wiped off the plate years sooner."[9] But even in October 1949, he told a reporter: "I am very much afraid that The Players is past helping at this point. The bulk of its customers has formed the habit of going elsewhere and nothing in the world is so difficult to change as a habit."[10] Still, Preston would not give up without a fight.

Nor did working on The Players theatre deter him from doing the best job he could on his MGM script. Entitled *Nothing Doing*, it is the story of industrialist Big Kim Kimble, who owns oil wells, builds dams and bridges, manufactures cars and airplanes but has never been happy in love. One day Big Kim's memory lapses: He sits down at a business conference on Tuesday, and the next thing he knows it's Friday night. So he consults famous Dr. Rothmuller who, explaining that Big Kim's subconscious is rebelling against his life-style, prescribes a six-month holiday, incognito, in a remote hamlet.

Thus, Big Kim reluctantly arrives in the small village, but, rather than relaxing, he spends his half year stirring up local business and falling in love (though he won't admit it) with a widow, Mrs. Jones. Big Kim's memory returns completely. When his six months are up, he tells Mrs. Jones his true identity and strides off to his old life. The catch is that once Big Kim leaves the hamlet his memory lapses return. Dr. Rothmuller concludes the only cure is marriage. Big Kim returns for Mrs. Jones.

Like the musical *Brigadoon*, whose plot it affectionately parodies, *Nothing*

Doing says all men need love and nurturing. But it also insists that some people don't need vacations at all, that, as Sturges told Henry Henigson during the time he was writing this screenplay: "Nothing is more demoralizing than *not* doing something."[11] Or, as Mrs. Jones puts it: "Isn't it wonderful to be active all the time!" Sturges refuses to sentimentalize rural living, showing its pre-eminent traits as leaking pipes and stultifying archaism. There's even a nice twist on *Remember the Night*'s perfect homemaker, Mrs. Sargent, in Mrs. Jones's mother, who's a dreadful cook. The script has some vintage Sturges satire, not to mention accent gags, in the scenes between Big Kim and Dr. Rothmuller. Here, for instance, Dr. Rothmuller uses the famous industrialist's illness as an occasion to flaunt his own superiority:

DR. ROTHMULLER: . . . now listen carefully: you probably won't understand but I will try to tell you anyway . . . your mind is divided into two parts . . . the prosence-phalon in the front, which we will call Mr. A . . . and the rhombencephalon in the back, which we will call Mr. B . . . Mr. A is your conscious, Mr. B is your subconscious. . . . Mr. A decides that you need a new car and buys it . . . but Mr. B drives it for you because he is in much closer contact with your nerves, your muscles, your glands and your whole body generally . . . a dog can wiggle his ears but Mr. A cannot . . . he has to ask Mr. B to do it for him.

BIG KIM: I can wiggle my ears . . .

DR. ROTHMULLER: Naturally . . . exactly what I'm talking about . . . you can probably hold onto a tree with your feet too . . . everything primitive comes very natural to you because you are more B than A.

BIG KIM: Like a dog.

DR. ROTHMULLER: Exactly . . . and to business conferences you react exactly like a dog . . . you look out the window . . . you chew your pencils . . . you scratch yourself . . . you wish you were chasing a chicken.

BIG KIM: Is that so . . .

DR. ROTHMULLER: Positively. Now: you understand, *Everybody* is made up of Mr. A and Mr. B, but in the high intellectual type . . .

BIG KIM: Is that in again?

DR. ROTHMULLER: Oh yes . . . in the high intellectual type, Mr. A learns to control Mr. B. . . . to hold him in check and use him to his advantage like a good partner. But in the low primitive type . . .

BIG KIM: Like me, I suppose . . .

DR. ROTHMULLER: Correct . . . Mr. B grows stronger than Mr. A . . . he can't stand what Mr. A is doing . . . he is bored to the point of insanity . . . he wants OUT. . . .[12]

With his signature airplanes and oil wells and car (named "the Kimble" and a bane to its namesake), Big Kim is clearly modeled after the auto tycoon Henry J. Kaiser, but also after Sturges himself. Even Big Kim's illness is a variation on Sturges's mysterious dizziness; and like Sir Alfred in *Unfaithfully Yours*, Big Kim is a powerful man, driven by subconscious urges. "I think anything you do will be lucky," Mrs. Jones tells Big Kim. The inventor, enslaved to his psyche but blessed by chance, makes an intriguing protagonist. The peripheral figures—a conventional Mrs. Jones, her son Butch, her suitor Lucas Stone, who thrives on accumulating mortgages—are less distinctive, particularly in the final draft, revised to please Sturges's MGM producers.[13]

Nothing Doing is also wordy, with little narrative urgency and an almost compulsively upbeat tone. It's as if the more troubled Sturges became personally, the more impelled he felt to efface pain from his writing: a gesture toward commerce-minded Hollywood, but a risky choice for the comic artist. Still, unlike *Beautiful Blonde*, *Nothing Doing* is unmistakably the work of Preston Sturges. He submitted a final draft of his script to MGM in September. But there seemed no rush to make the film, either with or without Sturges, and by early October Preston was complaining to Henry: "Again I am in a sort of miasma at MGM. I have always worked my damnedest to make a good impression there and nothing has ever come of it. First with Thalberg . . . this time with Dore Schary and Larry Weingarten."[14]

He was not doing much better in his private life. Preston was proud that his mother had never complained, and he didn't complain now either. "He took things silently," Priscilla Woolfan recalls.[15] But he was not an easy man to be around in bad times. Maxine Merlino, a mutual friend of Preston's and Francie's, remembers days when Preston took her and Francie and Caroline Wedderburn out on his boat. He'd dock in a cove and sit listlessly for hours, just staring into space. Occasionally, Preston might perk up and say something nice about her clothes or throw her quarters to dive for when she swam by the side of the boat. Still, it could be boring, particularly since Preston didn't want anyone else to do anything when he was moody.[16] She thought it all must have been very boring for Francie.

It was also exasperating for Francie that after both their divorces were finalized in 1948, Preston did not propose to her. When she broached the subject, he said he wouldn't marry her, and when anyone asked why, Preston enigmatically replied that love wasn't all you needed for a good marriage. Trust was just as important as love. "Keep your ledgers blank at the beginning of your relationship, and you won't have anything but happy hours to record in them later," he would write Francie two years later, congratulating her on her marriage to a young writer.[17] So perhaps there was some real or perceived betrayal early in their love affair, or maybe, as Francie speculates, Preston, so recently and expensively divorced, was just scared of marriage. Then too, their relationship was as volatile as Preston's and Bianca's, they were always fighting and making up. Gossip columns were filled with tales of their troubles. Francie remembers one time when she got especially mad at Preston and went off for a few days on her own, and she thinks he saw another woman during her absence. Otherwise, Francie says, he was faithful to her for the entire five years.

But Preston changed a lot during the time Francie knew him. When they first met, Preston was a big man, who enjoyed his old fashioneds. But then came the troubles with Darryl Zanuck and the endless bills. Preston's "black Irish moods" set in; he began drinking to obliterate his problems. Though he never got maudlin, he could be morose, Francie recalls. One night, at a black tie party given by the French consul general, Preston was still searching for more champagne as the rest of the guests were going home. When Francie finally coaxed him to leave, Preston wouldn't admit he was drunk and insisted on driving—two blocks from the consul's home, he crashed into a tree and collapsed over the steering wheel. Terrified, Francie called Caroline Wedderburn, who hurried over with loyal Sully, the bartender from The Players. Preston soon came to. Still, these incidents were becoming increasingly painful. Francie knew that if she wanted to keep her sanity, she would have to leave Preston.

So Francie booked a ticket to New York. The night before she was scheduled to leave, she sat up late with Preston and their close friends James Mason and his wife Pamela. Preston looked very crestfallen, and they all tried to talk her into staying on. "You can't leave Preston, that's ridiculous!" said James. But she'd made up her mind. The next morning Preston and Caroline Wedderburn and Priscilla and Bertie Woolfan drove Francie to the train station. She embraced Preston, and boarded the train east, while he went home in a black mood. He did not, however, change his mind about marrying Francie.[18]

Recapture

They tell me to rest on my laurels, but they don't know.
Laurels are very uncomfortable.
Preston Sturges before the opening of *Recapture*,
January 1, 1930

C H A P T E R **27**

What *did* change Sturges's mind about marriage was Sandy Nagle, a round-eyed nineteen-year-old, who looked a little like Veronica Lake with dark hair. Sandy lived up the hill from The Players. Walking home from her job at Blue Cross one day she noticed that the restaurant's sign was shooting sparks and ran to warn one of the men out back building the theatre—Preston. In his baggy work clothes, Sturges (like Sully when he meets the girl in *Sullivan's Travels*) looked like anything but a famous film director. Nor was Sandy much impressed a few days later when Preston came out and introduced himself by name, because she'd never seen a Sturges film. Every day after that Sturges made a point of happening to be outside at just the time Sandy passed by The Players. Once he ran out with a copy of *Who's Who* and showed her his long list of credits. "I don't want you to think I'm a total bum," he said.

Soon Sturges began inviting Sandy to dinner. Then, he told her his secretary could only work days; would she type for him at night, and make life easier by also moving into the house with him? He assured her, Sandy remembers, that his motives were pure, though he did begin mentioning he'd like to marry her.

"This beautiful plain lovely" girl is how an actor who knew Sandy at the time describes her.[1] A realtor's daughter, Sandy had grown up in Washington, D.C., and Boston, in a close-knit Irish Catholic family. She traveled west with a first husband who, Sandy says, she knew was all wrong the morning after the day she married him. They quickly separated and Sandy as quickly got a job, having no doubts she could take care of herself without a man's income. Yet, for all Sandy's maturity, many of Preston's friends saw her as a child because she was so open to life, so eager to learn. And she adored children: "Darling boy," she called Mon, not understanding how Preston could remain divorced

Sandy Nagle, five months before she met Preston.

from the mother of this beautiful son. So when Preston began talking to her about marriage, she thought he was kidding.

She began working for him, though. The first night Sandy typed for Preston she was amazed at how much physical energy he invested in his art, how he acted out all the parts and got very upset when he noticed that during quiet spells she began reading a book: he was creating even when he wasn't actually dictating words, Preston informed her. The script Preston was then writing, with no studio commitment and on just a few thousand dollars advance, was called *A Present for Uncle Popo*. Set in France, the plot follows a beautiful young chambermaid, Monique, who is sent to the Riviera as a "gift" from one old army pal to another, then winds up in love with a third friend, David, Marquess of Hereford. David also falls for Monique, but mistrusts her humble origins, and his snobbery must be punished before he wins Monique's hand. While *A Present for Uncle Popo* ultimately validates the poor but beautiful female, its condescension toward Monique's family recalls *Child of Manhattan*, and Sturges's writing here is similarly loose and undistinguished.

Asked about the deterioration of Sturges's writing in the late forties and fifties, Billy Wilder would speculate that to create a good movie you need "a good deal of luck, an enormous amount of talent, and total concentration: that is the thing that started to waver with Sturges. . . . You have to have the confidence as you step up to the plate that you're going to hit the home run. Unless you've got that enormous self-confidence that you're going to carry it through people sense it . . . things will go wrong."[2] Some historians have surmised that Sturges's later scripts are inferior because, desperate for money, he calculated to please not himself, but a wide commercial audience. Yet, for Sandy, who watched him nightly, Preston remained to the end an undauntable enthusiast, incapable of writing cynically for a particular audience, or of simply tossing off a piece of writing for a salary, because he threw all his being into his work. Every assignment was researched with great care, though sometimes, Sandy recalls, Preston would hit a bad point, and he'd say—not in a depressed way, but very matter-of-factly—that maybe he really wasn't a writer at all. He'd point out how he'd never been educated as a writer, he'd never even finished high school. Maybe the writing was something that had come his way. "His attitude was lady luck was here and now she's gone; it was very objective," remembers Sandy, but she also knew that, as much as he cared about his screenplays, Preston was very distracted at this time in his life.[3]

Though a little cash came in when Sturges convinced MGM to remake the film *Strictly Dishonorable* with Ezio Pinza, Preston's finances were in chaos. The new theatre was devouring what little money Preston made, while the restaurant continued losing customers. Nothing had been done about the exits, so waiters were still walking off with sides of beef. Moreover, rumor had it that Preston's half brother Edmund was taking home whisky by the crate.[4] Since Preston couldn't conceive of accusing a relative of stealing, he ignored the gossip. He also continued picking up checks for his friends' dinners, though the next day he might be asking these same friends for thousand dollar loans. He owed his lawyer and doctor and agent as well as perennial creditors; and he made no pretense of remorse, viewing reminders of his debts as personal insults. "During the course of a somewhat rocky though not uneventful career, I have found that people around me usually lost all confidence in me at the exact moment that I was about to pull out of my difficulties and come through with a rather high degree of success," Preston replied to a note reminding him of his debts from his long-suffering lawyer, Victor Ford Collins.[5]

Real estate and social security taxes, mortgage payments and staff wages were all long overdue. Struggling to make ends meet, Preston borrowed large sums from wealthy friends like Willie Wyler, but he also asked the less affluent for help, procuring $500 from Jimmy Conlin, $3,000 from Louise, even $1,350 from Francie, who was herself struggling to get by in New York.[6] Preston was grasping at straws but also, perhaps, testing his friends' loyalties. He would later tell Louise, "When I started getting into trouble I assumed that those people for whom I had done the most would fight their way to my door in order to repay my kindnesses. I was startlingly wrong. A 'taker' has always been a taker. He was grafting on his parents and brothers and sisters when he was three years old and he has been grafting on everybody he knew ever since. He would not know *how* to give, or repay, or do a generous thing. He is a highly trained specialist, and his specialty is getting things out of other people."[7]

Brian Donlevy, Akim Tamiroff, and Bill Demarest were among those Preston perceived as "takers," while Rudy Vallee, notoriously tight with his money, proved touchingly magnanimous. Learning that Vallee was performing in New York, Sturges asked Francie to go speak with him about an impending financial crisis. And Vallee simply asked how much Preston needed and handed her a check for $7,000 on the spot.

But for every wolf at the door sent running, there was another to take its place. In the summer of 1950, for instance, Preston was paid a large sum to vacate his land to make way for the Hollywood Freeway. Rather than finding a new house, however, he insisted on transporting the one he had, which resulted in two years worth of work adjusting the old house to its new grounds on Franklin Avenue, and yet another huge outlay of capital.

"We are still feeling pinched on money as it has been coming through only in dribbles from the *Strictly Dishonorable* deal," Caroline Wedderburn wrote Francie, at the end of 1950. "The Boss is designing sets for the theatre. The opening is postponed until the rush is over on the writing."[8] The writing she referred to was Preston's book for a stage musical based on *The Good Fairy*, which he'd been hired to write by producer Harry Rigby, a great fan of his films. Working with composer-lyricist Hugh Martin and choreographer Gower Champion, Sturges was updating his 1934 film script and tailoring it for Nanette Fabray in her first starring role.

Remembering his only other experience with a stage musical, *Well of Romance*, Sturges must have been hard-pressed, indeed, to take on this show. Besides, the composer-lyricist was working in New York, while Sturges was in Hollywood. Sturges changed *The Good Fairy*'s plot to make the orphan older and tired of being an orphan. She journeys to Paris with the other orphan girls, but leaves them at the Louvre and takes off on her own, winding up with a job dancing for a Folies Bergère-type nightclub. As with *Uncle Popo*, Sturges's book is overwritten, its humor forced.

Sturges came east for the Philadelphia opening. Here Nanette Fabray was praised, but the show, entitled *Make a Wish*, was found badly in need of rewriting. Sturges stayed on for a week, then, telling reporters he couldn't afford any more time away from Hollywood, returned home—leaving *Make A Wish* to Abe Burrows, the famous play doctor. When the show opened to slightly better notices on Broadway a month later, it was more Burrows's work than Sturges's.[9] (Burrows got no credit, however, because Sturges's contract guaranteed him sole authorship.) It was also one of a growing number of desultory projects that did little to enhance Preston's reputation in Hollywood.

Meanwhile, the dinner theatre was, for better or worse, a labor of love, and Preston oversaw the creation of its every feature: peach-tinted mirrors, maroon drapes, cupids, candles and two hundred velvet chairs that slipped under banquettes at dinner, then became theatre seats as the tables scudded off on tracks, and the paneled floor sank in tiers so that everyone in the room had a perfect view of the stage production. After the final curtain call, elevators raised the tiers to a single height, and the theatre turned into a ballroom. "It was like a French opera house, all red plush and gold gilt," recalls an actor in one of the plays.[10] Sandy thought it was like being at the Hollywood Bowl, with a ceiling on top.

But if the theatre's ambience was all nineteenth-century elegance, the dinner menu was devised for twentieth-century cost effectiveness. Preston had consulted with Ray Rand, who operated the Ray's Roundup, a popular L.A. restaurant dedicated to the principle that your costs should never be more than 50 percent of what you charge for food. Determined to follow Rand's example, Sturges sacrificed some quality and, at the theatre, limited the nightly menu to just one meat, one fowl, and one fish dish—which also made preparation and busing much simpler. To maximize liquor sales, drinks were served between the one-act plays as well as with dinner and dancing. The plays cost two dollars and forty cents, the dancing one dollar. They were the lure, while the real money would be made on the bar and restaurant.

Always conventional in his theatre tastes, Sturges planned to open with three popular one-act plays: *The Monkey's Paw*, a horror tale adaptation;

Saroyan's *Hello Out There*, about a lonely girl who falls for a prisoner; and Chekov's ironic comedy about a widow seduced out of mourning, *The Boor*. The plays were cast both with lesser-known movie actors—Leonard Mudie, Cathy O'Donnell—and newcomers. Costumes were by Edith Head and Frank Richardson, while Sturges directed the whole production, rewriting the plays as he went.

Preston named his theatre The Playroom. (He would later rename it The Ten O'Clock Theatre and finally The Players Theatre.) Its premier was set for April 24, 1951, with reservations held until six and curtain at ten. Sturges described the first night as "a grand scale soup and fish opening, complete with searchlights, stars, suckers and sables." [11] It was 11:30 by the time the plays got started, so there was not much enthusiasm for dancing when the curtain came down at 1:30 A.M. The following day's *Variety* declared "The show is fine," and praised the actors and Sturges's "thoroughly professional staging," while questioning whether it would all pay off. Would theatre lovers wait around for a ten o'clock curtain, and would Hollywood bistro types be converted to Saroyan and Chekov? [12] A short article in *Newsweek* also expressed doubts about mixing food with drama. "People seeing theater in the same building with a restaurant have their mouths shaped for cabaret," Preston acknowledged. "But tragedy isn't something you have to go into mourning for. Theater in which you eat is the oldest form of theater." [13]

The theatre's first audiences were enthusiastic, but small, and coordinating the dining and drinking with three one-act plays was more difficult than Preston had imagined. Often, Sandy recalls, the curtain went up late because people hadn't finished eating, and Preston wouldn't have the actors insulted by someone chewing in the second row. The plan for serving drinks during intermissions was a fiasco because there was no way waiters could both collect and fill orders before the next play began. Actors were under contract for an entire run, but still this was Hollywood. Soon after the opening, Cathy O'Donnell, cast as the girl who falls in love with the prisoner in *Hello Out There*, was offered a big role in a movie that was shooting in London. When she told Preston, he said, of course, she should go and assured her Sandy could easily take her part. Sandy's only acting up to then was in a play at her girl's academy. "Being in love with me he decided I was one of the world's most gifted natural actresses," she recalls. Being in love with *him*, she'd been to all the rehearsals and practically memorized all the lines in the plays.

Sandy went on to play the romantic lead in Sturges's second production, a full-length farce, John Murray's and Allen Boretz's 1937 *Room Service*. (It's not surprising that this tale of an ingenious theatre promoter who overcomes Herculean obstacles to get his show on the boards appealed to Sturges at this time.) To help his friend, Eddie Bracken played the lead role for no pay, and Al Bridge, Julius Tannen, and Frank Moran also joined the cast. They opened July 25 to high praise from *Variety* and proceeded to sell out.

During rehearsals for *Room Service*, Eddie Bracken got to know Sandy, whom he found not just pretty and amiable, but intelligent, strong-willed, and ironic like Preston. Preston told Eddie that he was going to experience life again through Sandy's eyes.[14] She had everything ahead of her, while, in his gloomiest moods, Preston thought everything was over for him. Yet, he was as passionate about Sandy as he'd been about Estelle thirty years earlier. Like Eleanor, Sandy was devoted to her mother and married Preston over her family's objections. She had to forego a church marriage because of Preston's divorce.[15]

They were married by a judge on the stage of The Players theatre, after the evening's performance of *Room Service*, on August 15, 1951, thirteen days before Preston's fifty-third birthday. Eddie Bracken gave Sandy away; Edmund Biden was Preston's best man. It was Sturges's fourth marriage, but the only one at which guests were present. As the curtain fell on *Room Service*, Preston told the audience there'd be no dancing that night, but they could stay if they liked and witness his wedding. Many did and later mingled with the 250 invited guests.

The beginning of Preston's fourth marriage was very like the early days with Estelle. Just as Preston and Estelle devoted themselves to the Maison Desti, Preston and Sandy spent day and night at The Players. José Iturbi had lent them his house in Beverly Hills (since their own house was still unfit for habitation), but the restaurant was their real home. Here they ate all their meals, and while Preston ran from restaurant to theatre, Sandy not only acted in the plays, but bartended during a three-day strike and kept a shrewd eye on the exit doors. A year and a half after their marriage, Sandy gave birth to a first son, Preston, whom she was soon tucking in a basket and carrying off to The Players.

Sturges may have seen The Players as a refuge, like the farm Morton retreats to in *The Great Moment* when the medical world betrays him. Also like Morton, Sturges was haunted by his drastic change of luck. He still drank heavily. Ronald Durling, who acted at the Playhouse thought Sturges seemed "a tired old man" who was drinking himself to death. But he was also "magnificent looking" and, for all his problems, deeply happy with Sandy. "They had a kind of closeness that didn't need words, that didn't need displays, that

Sandy Sturges on her wedding day.

didn't need actions of any kind," says Durling. "They were simply together, there was never any question. She was quietly *his*, and he was there for her in his manic, restless, moving way."[16]

As ever, Preston was the jealous lover. When actors approached Sandy, hoping she'd put in a good word for them with the boss, she warned them that if Preston caught them so much as speaking with her they'd have no chance of working in a Sturges play. And while Sandy never doubted Preston's fidelity, in her own way she too was intensely romantic. Once, when Preston was working out of town for a few weeks, Sandy forgot their anniversary. "Darling," she wrote:

I am stricken! August fifteenth came and went for me as torturously as have all the days since you've been gone . . . that it was the anniversary of my true birthday (because my life began really when I became your wife) escaped me entirely. I adore you for remembering and cover you with kisses. I miss you so much that I would leap at the chance to exchange a year of my life for one more night with you. Am I insane? [17]

Preston's relations with his first son were more complicated. Somehow, ten-year-old Mon always compared unfavorably to Preston's recollections of himself as a child, and Preston took no pains to hide his disappointment. On weekend visits, Mon was invariably devastated, Sandy recalls. [18] It could not have helped that Sturges showed far more attention to his new baby than he had to Mon. Little Preston, as they called him, saw his father all day long, for Sturges was not off making *Sullivan's Travels* or *The Miracle of Morgan's Creek* anymore. Indeed, in his mid-fifties, Preston was as close as he'd ever come to domestic happiness—yet, he was frustrated in his art and plagued by financial crises. *Room Service* had a solid eighteen-week run, and other successful productions followed—notably Sturges's version of one of his favorite twenties plays, Robert Sherwood's *The Road to Rome*. [19] Between July 28 and November 3, the theatre grossed $25,866.32, but Sturges figured that because of the restaurant's losses during that time, he was $20,000 poorer. [20]

One day Preston and Sandy went to the bank, hoping to get a first mortgage to finish reconstructing their house on Franklin Avenue, and an officer told them the government had put a lien on all their assets. No money could be touched. The Internal Revenue Service had discovered that The Players, besides being way behind on property taxes, was using money withheld from employees' salaries to pay bills rather than the IRS. A government agent soon arrived, demanding immediate restitution, but there were simply no funds to be had. A note to Preston from his distraught business manager, Milton Cashy, conveys the hopelessness of Preston's finances in the spring of 1952:

> Unpaid wages are behind some weeks. . . . Real estate taxes on the 8225 Sunset Boulevard property are unpaid and must be paid to keep [the] Hollywood State loan without their demanding payment in full. On your second, third and fourth mortgages no payments are being made so the loans are in default. . . . At the Harbor your boat is in sinking condition and the taxes are in arrears . . . creditors of The Players are calling me daily regarding unpaid bills. Waiters that have been unpaid stop me and ask for their money. [21]

It was not long before the government put a lien on the engineering company, the boat, and the house as well as Sturges's bank accounts. Now nothing could be mortgaged or used against loans until the IRS was paid off. Even the theatre's profits were immediately appropriated, and Sandy recalls months where they couldn't cash a personal check. The government suggested a deal whereby Sturges would pay them back in increments, over a period of time, but this could work only if Sturges commanded a regular salary.

The fact that everyone knew he was desperate to make money did not enhance Sturges's chances of getting a job at one of the studios, which were themselves undergoing hard times, with ticket sales down owing to the rise of television. Indeed, television was beginning to look like the logical spot for Sturges. "I am of this moment tremendously enthusiastic about television," Sturges had written Bosley Crowther in 1949.[22] By 1951, a decade before Marshall McLuhan's theory of hot and cool media, Sturges was perceptively analyzing this new technology: "I saw a hundred comedians' jokes burned up in half an hour by one [television] comedian," he wrote John Hertz, Jr. "I met a man who was reducing the world's masterpieces to thirteen minute shots. I told him television should be slow because it was aimed at small, leisurely groups, taking their ease, not large, rude, impatient crowds."[23]

Sturges drew up proposals for two possible television series. The first, which he called "The Sturges Stories," would broadcast one-act plays from the stage at The Players, with Sturges himself playing master of ceremonies. A second series he called "Station F.A.T.E.": "The trademark of this series looks something like the top of the Eiffel Tower popping out of a cloud," Preston began his proposal. "We see great sparks and hear, first, a lot of cracklings and sputterings, then the good-natured voice of the announcer: Good evening, ladies and gentlemen, this is Station F.A.T.E., pronounced fate, broadcasting on more wavelengths than you ever knew existed . . . for much, much longer than you realize. . . . [Station F.A.T.E.] is [not] . . . concerned with morality as you, dear listeners, have learned it in the various Sunday Schools or other well-intentioned classes set up by your various and most innumerable religious sects. Station F.A.T.E. concerns itself exclusively with the operation and smooth functioning of that difficult to isolate but very authentic external element, or force, known as fate." Sometimes, he says, its working will seem "immoral," sometimes "right and proper."

A Sturges series about the machinations of fate is an intriguing proposition. But no one bought either of his proposals. When Preston applied for directing jobs, television executives invariably replied that they hadn't the money or the material to tempt such a gifted man as Sturges. True or not, this closed the discussion. For now, Sturges's affiliation with television was limited to offers to emcee quiz shows (which he turned down) and make guest appearances. Once a local show called "City At Night" visited Sturges at The Players. Another time, Sturges agreed to judge a televised beauty contest. He appeared looking very gray, his cheeks creased like a man ten or fifteen years older, and was presented as a figure "associated with some of the greatest films ever made in Hollywood." [24]

Introductions of this sort confirmed Preston's suspicions that he was already a has-been. As he wrote an admiring friend, Peter Prince, in England:

> Picture-making, in Hollywood at least, has become so ponderous and fearsomely expensive, so many safeguards are taken and such desperate efforts have to be made to insure a box office return, that most of the lightness and the experimentation into new paths and even the insistence upon quality have become commercially dangerous and less and less possible of execution. In my own case I have run into a further complication, which is that my previous films are, for some reason, so well remembered that with each new effort I run into competition with myself and will presently either have to give up or dye my hair, change my name and start all over. [25]

Irony aside, the idea of jettisoning his fame and embracing a second chance must have appealed to this master of comic deliverance, who, for all his creased skin, was still yearning to accomplish and create. And if he drank heavily, even debilitatingly at times, he was, nonetheless, Louise Sturges recalls, able to pull himself back into shape if he got an assignment he wanted. Sturges did not find it easy writing "on his own time," after $6,000-a-week salaries, but he forced himself to resume work on *Matrix*, which had always been a favorite project, despite the low opinions of Harry Cohn and Darryl Zanuck. The story, as he'd written it in the thirties, was a synopsis; now, with Sandy typing, he revised and wrote dialogue.

The premise was the same: a woman turns down the strong, successful man who adores her and marries a mewling loser because he appeals to her mothering instincts. The difference, in the 1952 script, is that here Sturges focuses on the rich suitor, who is now named Steve Craig and is heir to a great family fortune. Alluding to the years before income taxes diminished the Craig coffers, Craig banters: "Once upon a time, rich men were rich." And, on the whole, the script is more revealing of Sturges's personal feelings on wealth and the maternal female than it is narratively engaging.

This was not, Sandy Sturges recalls, for lack of effort: Sturges threw himself wholeheartedly into *Matrix*, refashioning it time and again. He worked harder still when, in the summer of 1952, Frank Freeman finally called and asked him to adapt Jerome Robbins's 1948 musical, *Look Ma I'm Dancing* for a Gene Kelly-Betty Hutton film. "Papa Freeman came through for me again," Sturges cheerfully informed Paramount's publicist Teet Carle. Sturges did not, however, intend to be loyal to this tale about internecine tensions in a classical dance troupe. He first conceived a script about a dance diploma-by-mail course; and, when Paramount turned this down, created a triangular love story between a poor but gifted musical comedy writer, the small-town beauty who loves him, and her rich admirer. The reverse of *Matrix*, here the poor man is worthier, and the story ends well for everyone.

Sandy remembers Sturges reading everything he could get his hands on about ballet and working both diligently, night after night, and in impulsive bursts. Once they went three days and nights without sleeping. The script that emerged was full of slapstick bits, malapropisms, and physical business, but little real irony. Nor were Sturges's sentimentalized characters as credible as Jerome Robbins's more cynical troupe. And it was all futile in the end since, once the script was submitted, Betty Hutton suddenly insisted that her new husband should be hired to direct the movie. Paramount refused, and she broke her contract, so Frank Freeman canceled the film.

This was the summer of 1952. The following year, Willie Wyler hired Sturges to rewrite Ben Hecht's script for *Roman Holiday*, about a British princess who falls in love with an American reporter in Italy. In fact, Wyler was pleased with all but a few scenes in Hecht's script; he'd asked the studio for rewrites to give Preston work. Wyler recalls meeting with Preston after he'd appraised the Hecht script. "There's one good line in it," Preston told Willie, who, no stranger to his friend's ego, reminded Preston that his small salary justified only a few minor revisions. Wyler's warnings were to no avail. Sturges came back with a script substantively the same as Hecht's, but with every single line rewritten and elongated.

After reading Preston's revisions, Wyler inquired: "Preston, remember you said there was *one* good line? Where is it?"

"I decided not to use it," Preston replied.[26]

Wyler proceeded to shoot *Roman Holiday* from Ben Hecht's script, but this was the least of Sturges's worries. With no prospects for steady work in film *or* television and his restaurant falling deeper and deeper in debt, even Preston could see that he would not weather this storm: The Players would have to be sold. If it took him so much longer than everyone else to come to this conclusion, it was not only that Preston was the eternal optimist, but also because property had such symbolic importance for him. As a nomadic child, he'd adored watching his mother furnish their apartments with splendid furniture. When he and Louise separated, Preston would not give up his house. Even in the late forties, without a cent to pay his creditors, Sturges was imploring Vely Bey to buy him the best quality billiard table cloth, for he saw beautiful objects as avatars of well-being. Sturges's films were all about that, of course. His winners were rewarded with penthouses and medals and diamond rings. Now, like Jimmy in the middle of *Christmas in July*, when it's revealed that he *hasn't* won the coffee slogan contest, Preston was being ordered to return the fruits of his luck and inspiration. Preston told Sandy that he felt fate was trying to erase every trace that he was here on earth.[27]

In 1953 The Players was sold at auction to its main creditor, Joe DeBell, for $79,013.20, essentially the price of DeBell's first mortgage. Still unable to repay the IRS, Sturges went on to sell the engineering company and, a year later, his house. DeBell, who bought the house as well as the restaurant, said the Sturgeses and Bidens could always live there; he even promised to resell the house to Preston for no profit as soon as Preston could afford it. When, Preston must have wondered, would that be?

In the summer of 1953 Preston got a call about a Broadway-bound play named *Carnival in Flanders*. The play was based on Jacques Feyder's 1935 film, *La Kermesse héroïque*, set in the sixteenth century, about a Flemish town that throws a carnival to protect itself from invading Spaniards. Though the film had been a great success, the show was $80,000 in debt and embroiled in a law suit when its director quit and Sturges was asked to rewrite and direct the production. The play's prospects, given its poor out-of-town reviews, were unpromising. Yet, Sturges immediately accepted the job. He had two years before left *Make a Wish* in Philadelphia to rush back to Hollywood; now he couldn't wait to leave. Preston took off for San Francisco in August. A month later, entrusting the Bidens with the house on Franklin Street, he followed *Carnival in Flanders* to New York and sent for Sandy and the baby.

He would never see his home, California, or his eldest son again.

Sturges was leaving behind $250,000 worth of debts to creditors[1]—including the IRS and Louise, who'd received only a fraction of her alimony since 1949 and was now supporting herself and Mon by renting out apartments on some property she had acquired on Little Santa Monica Boulevard. This was a sad comedown for Sturges's child, born to a life of ease. And while the Woolfans had promised to pay for Mon's education, Sturges—remembering Solomon Sturges's constancy during his own youth—felt dishonored by his son's changed circumstances. He longed to be able to do right by Mon and Louise, as well as by his new family.

So, two decades after he left for Hollywood, Preston returned to New York in 1953, weighed down by responsibilities—but also a successful man. Whatever he did or did not accomplish in the future, Preston Sturges had made his mark on film history. Sturges's Paramount movies were being revived, taught in schools, and argued about by intellectuals. He was, as the young French critics were putting it, an *auteur*. Penguin Books's film journal had commissioned Preston's former story editor, Seymour Stern, to write an article on Sturges's "work." The critic Manny Farber was calling Preston "the most spectacular manipulator of sheer humor since Mark Twain."[2]

Only half-jokingly, Preston had begun saying that, like Twain, he'd probably wind up on the lecture circuit. He didn't like that idea. He didn't like people talking about his "work" as if it and he were finished. "The more you stand in the limelight the more scarred you will become and the more you will love the limelight," Preston had written in his unfinished 1944 memoir, and he yearned for the limelight still.

Sandy remembers a night in 1951 when Sturges was holding court with a crowd at The Players, and he pointed out that the famous novelist William Faulkner was sitting among them. Suddenly, all eyes turned to Faulkner, and

Preston, resenting the distraction, plangently whispered : "He may be a Nobel Prize winner, but he's only five feet tall."[3] Physically, Preston towered sixteen inches above Faulkner and, away from Los Angeles, he was eager to reestablish his stature in the world.

The Algonquin, with its small old rooms and literary ambience, was Preston's favorite hotel in Manhattan. He settled in and began revising *Carnival in Flanders*. The book Sturges inherited was, Sandy recalls, "awful." True to form, Sturges completely rewrote it, which unnerved the actors who now had less than a month to learn new lines and revamped staging. Lucinda Ballard, the costume designer, says Sturges "almost went insane" trying to get the show ready for a September 8 premiere.[4] When it opened, the reviews were devastating, with Sturges's book particularly singled out for disparagement. After six performances, the production closed.

"I was genuinely sorry to hear of the tragedy of *Flanders*," Sturges's friend John Parker wrote to him. "I feel . . . the cause [was not any] inconsistency attributed to the book, but . . . the psychological anxiety that must have hovered over the production from the beginning of the trouble. It's about time for your luck to change."[5]

In fact, there were already signs that Sturges's luck was improving. Lester Cowan, who'd produced *The Story of G.I. Joe* and *My Little Chickadee*, had asked him to write and direct a film version of Bernard Shaw's *The Millionairess*, starring Katharine Hepburn and José Ferrer. This was quite a step up from *Carnival in Flanders*.

The idea to revive Shaw's late play about an indomitable heiress had been Hepburn's. In 1952, she'd toured the play through England, to great acclaim. Her *Millionairess* was less successful when she brought it to Broadway; in the *New York Times*, Brooks Atkinson called the play "senile" and Hepburn's performance "one-note."[6] Undaunted, Hepburn was now eager to make a film of her performance, and delighted to be working with Sturges.

Their first problem was a blessing in disguise. Shaw had it in his will that none of his works could be modified for film adaptations. Lester Cowan won a dispensation from the estate, allowing Sturges to change twenty percent of the play, but this still precluded the rampant rewrites Sturges had done lately.[7] Indeed, Sturges's script is tight-knit and very faithful to Shaw with whom he had many ideas in common. Both are satirists fascinated by the relationship between power and money; they share an attraction to the heroic individual, and neither believes in a benign fate.

Shaw's "millionairess," Epifania, is a woman who has received from her now deceased father a single condition for marrying: the man of her choice

Preston's caricature of Sandy and William Faulkner, sketched on a Players menu, 1951.

should be handed 150 pounds, which he must within six months turn into 500,000. Ever on the lookout for a man who's her mental match, Epifania discovers a virtuous Egyptian doctor, who surprises her by insisting that, to marry *him*, she must fulfill his mother's condition: go out into the world with only thirty-five shillings and survive on her own. With her intelligence, force of character, and lack of moral scruples, Epifania easily fulfills her part of the bargain, meanwhile trampling over the sort of little people the doctor is committed to help. Though dismayed by Epifania's errant acquisitiveness, the doctor is seduced by her great beating heart. "I have never felt such a pulse," he exclaims, and so virtue marries power.

Sturges changed very little of Shaw's dialogue and maintained all the subtleties of the play while "opening it up" with montage shots, a few outdoor scenes, and glimpses of the doctor's Arab clinic. He adds a revealing moment, reminiscent of an early sequence in *Diamond Jim*, where Epifania manages to get ahead of nine women on line for a job by dropping sixpences on the floor to divert them. Sturges also expands the section where Epifania turns the doctor's thirty-five shillings into a fortune. His few original scenes are concise and vividly written. Gone are the aimless speeches and the forced jokes that so weighed down his late Hollywood scripts. He was writing in top form. And loyal Priscilla Woolfan seems to voice many of Sturges's own deepest feelings in her letter congratulating him on this new project:

> Preston dear, you know of course how happy we are over your good fortune! We knew of course that it would come eventually, but it was hard "to wait, and not be tired by waiting, and being lied about, not deal in lies, and being hated, not give way to hating—and yet not look too good, nor talk too wise." Read that wonderful poem [Rudyard Kipling's "If"] over some time. So much of it applies to you, and what you have gone through even to the line about walking with kings and yet not losing of the common touch.
>
> I know that working with a great artist like Katharine Hepburn is going to be a joy to you. It will be give and take and exchange of talent between two extraordinary people and that beautiful white light within you will glow again.
>
> Of course we miss you—we miss you terribly—there is a big empty space which no one else can fill, but we don't want you to come back. You are in the right place where you will be understood and appreciated. We wait with confidence the picture which you will bring forth.[8]

Katharine Hepburn proved not just a "great artist," but a sympathetic friend and collaborator. She worked daily with Preston on the script and, when it was finished, pronounced it "just wonderful."[9] Lester Cowan was pleased as well. His idea was to shoot the film in London, on independent American and British financing. With the American half of the film purportedly funded, Lester Cowan began taking off on weekends for London, looking for English backers, locations, and stars. Meanwhile, Sturges was bringing home a weekly salary.

The idea that Preston should be paid in weekly checks, rather than a lump sum when he was finished, was Charley Abramson's. Charley, now working for Famous Artists, was, after all these years, *officially* Preston's New York agent. Suspicious of independent productions, Charley arranged for Preston to be paid every Friday, which he was, from November until the beginning of January, though Cowan insisted on a bizarre pay scale, whereby Preston could be paid $1,600 one week and $350 the next.[10] Sometimes Charley had to badger Cowan all Friday to be sure he came up with the money.[11]

For while Cowan's track record and demeanor inspired confidence, there was something mysterious about his finances and future plans, Sandy recalls. One time, when he got back from a weekend in London, Lester announced that Alec Guinness had been hired to play the millionairess's first husband. By January, Cowan was saying that he had lined up Alistair Sims, a studio and all the English backers. At that point, Katharine Hepburn asked, "Well, Lester, why are we here?" And he said, "You're absolutely right, we should all be in London."[12]

Hepburn and Cowan flew to England, but since this was Sandy's first trip abroad, the Sturgeses took a boat. Sandy remembers rushing to get a passport. The officer inquired if she wanted her own or a joint passport with Preston. "If she has her own passport, then she doesn't need me to travel, does she?" asked Preston. "Of course not," said the officer. "We'll have a single passport," Preston replied.

The Sturgeses, arriving in a blizzard, were met by a limousine, which drove them to a luxurious suite at the Dorchester Hotel. Lining their mantlepiece were invitations to all sorts of parties, including a luncheon two weeks later at the House of Lords. At that luncheon, Preston met Alec Guinness. When Preston said how happy he was that Guinness would be acting in his movie, Guinness replied that he was delighted as well, but what film was this? He knew nothing about *The Millionairess*.

"You never got the feeling that Lester was trying to put one over on you," Sandy recalls. "It was just that he was so keyed up about what he wanted to happen that it all became true to him." And he always had reasons for disparities between what he was claiming and the apparent truth. The fact that Alec Guinness didn't know he'd been cast in the movie, for instance, Cowan blamed on misunderstandings between himself and Guinness's agent. Any minute, Cowan promised, everything would be settled, and they'd be ready to shoot. Cowan seems to have had no ulterior motives for his prevarications; like the theatre producer in *Room Service*, he felt sure his backers *would* materialize. But whatever money Cowan had was now quickly dwindling. A week after the Sturgeses arrived, Cowan stopped paying Preston's salary, saying he'd still pick up the hotel bill, and then (without informing Sturges) he stopped paying the Dorchester as well. Katharine Hepburn returned to commitments in America. Thirty years later she would tell her biographer that she still read Preston's script with pleasure and that *not* being able to film *The Millionairess* was "certainly the greatest disappointment" of her career.[13]

For his part, Lester Cowan could never admit that *The Millionairess* had fallen through and over the next two years frequently wrote Preston that he'd managed to get funding for this or some other project that Preston would be paid large sums to direct. "MILLIONAIRESS REINSTATED . . . SOME IMMEDIATE CASH AVAILABLE IF YOU NEED," he, misleadingly, cabled at one point.[14] Yet, while never admitting any guilt on his own part, Cowan seems to have been genuinely sorry about Sturges's predicament when the project collapsed. "I am very much aware of your current situation and hope that you will be successful in landing whatever you are after," he wrote Preston, the spring of 1954. He urged Preston to "please write me—as a friend,"[15] and would visit him in Paris, still unable to produce the approximately $9,000 he owed Preston for *The Millionairess*, but bearing one of Preston's favorite books by H. L. Mencken and lots of American baby shoes as peace offerings.

Preston stayed in London until March 1954, when even Lester Cowan could no longer pretend that production on *The Millionairess* was imminent. (A film of *The Millionairess*, starring Sophia Loren and Peter Sellers, was finally made in 1960, but no one from the Cowan production was involved.) Now, a vacation seemed in order. Preston had not been abroad since 1932 when he came hoping to win back Eleanor, and Sandy had never seen Europe. Little Preston was a year old, even younger than Preston had been when Mary Desti first "dragged" him across the Atlantic. Sturges decided to buy a car and, true to form, chose a 1922 Rolls Royce Shooting Break. Maybe he remembered his mother's automobile, with the polished brass trim, which Isadora Duncan's students sat on in the 1908 photograph. Mary Desti too had lived beyond her means because she adored beauty. "There is something remarkably satisfactory about driving a Rolls . . . even an old grandaddy likes ours," Preston wrote his friend John Weiler in America. "The purchase of so much pleasure is really quite inexpensive."[16] The Sturgeses piled their trunks and loads of Little Preston's toys in the back of the Rolls, and headed off.

Their first stop was in Belgium, to visit Vely Bey: a solid bourgeois now, married to the widow of a chocolate manufacturer. Bey so vividly remembered Mary Desti's feisty schoolboy that he had trouble recognizing Preston as a grown man. Bey told Sandy that he was stunned that Preston had led a useful life. And once, when his former stepson was out of earshot, Bey confided in Sandy that Mary Desti had been "really crazy—a likable woman, but crazy." Bey was whispering, he explained, because he didn't want "the young man" to hear.[17]

From Belgium the Sturgeses drove south to France, stopping in Le Touquet, then Fleurines, where Mary had once owned a house. Then, to Paris.

They moved into the Royal Malesherbes (not so luxurious as the Dorchester, but with a kitchen), in the eighth arrondissement, and began walking everywhere: to see Mary Desti's elegant apartments behind the Eiffel Tower, to 4 rue de la Paix where the Maison Desti was long gone, but otherwise the building looked very much as it had in Preston's childhood. Here was a world without the passion for change which transformed American cities year after year. The pace was slower, the mood less volatile. Careers were not made in a flash, but neither was fame so quickly dissipated as in New York or Los Angeles. Preston said he wouldn't mind staying in France for a while, if only to avoid the American taxmen.

Besides, five years before, Preston had written Louise: "If the worst comes to worst, I will probably go to France to live, where I seem to have some reputation, and try my hand at making French pictures. I have no intention of sweating it out in Hollywood, building, as they say, a new life."[18] After the war, when *Sullivan's Travels* and *Hail the Conquering Hero* opened in Paris, the influential critic André Bazin had praised Sturges as a genius of American satire. Now a younger generation of ardent French cinéastes, writing in Bazin's *Cahiers du Cinéma*, were constructing a "pantheon" of American film artists in which Sturges figured prominently. Like Sturges, most of these future New Wave directors—François Truffaut, Jean-Luc Godard, Claude Chabrol, Eric Rohmer—had no patience for "deep-dish" literary films. Cinema, they felt, demanded its own form and subject. They adored the Hollywood genres and spent whole days at Henri Langlois's Cinémathèque, studying John Ford and Howard Hawks the way American college students studied Molière and Shakespeare. Sturges's films were also favorites at the Cinémathèque. Preston was considered one of the few true American "auteurs" because he wrote as well as directed his movies. A particular fan of Sturges's was Truffaut, who'd been deeply impressed by *Sullivan's Travels* as a child and now wrote wanting to interview the visiting celebrity.[19]

As well as the *Cahiers du Cinéma* critics, there was an older generation of French and German directors now living in Paris. Preston and Sandy began seeing a lot of Jean Renoir, René Clair, Erich Von Stroheim, Max Ophüls, who was currently working on *Lola Montès*, and Marcel Pagnol. Often they gathered at a smart club off the Champs-Elysée called the Élysée Matignon, which was down a floor from the street, behind a heavy oak-paneled door, like a speakeasy, and catered to film and theatre people. One night, over dinner, Clair suddenly turned to Sturges and said, "Preston, there's something about your French that I find very puzzling."

"Is it my accent?" asked Preston.

"No, that's perfect," said Clair. The conversation went on for a while, then Clair announced, "I've got it. You speak the French of a schoolboy of sixteen."

"That's not extraordinary," replied Preston. "I was a sixteen-year-old schoolboy when I left France." [20]

The Sturgeses became especially friendly with Marcel Pagnol, whose country home they often visited on weekends. Once, Sandy remembers, in the midst of a champagne lunch on the beach, Pagnol—still charming and vibrant at sixty—excused himself to go to the bathroom. He came back looking "dreadful." He said he'd had a shocking experience. He looked in the mirror and saw, staring back at him, a very old man.

Preston, only three years younger than Pagnol, may have been similarly shocked at the physical signs of his own age—the now almost completely gray hair, the furrows and jowls. In a maudlin mood, he'd tell Sandy, "Youth belongs to youth" and marvel that she'd married him. He suffered painful indigestion. When it got especially bad, he'd moan, "I hope to God I don't croak tonight!" But then he'd been complaining about hemorrhoids and gas twenty years ago in letters to his father. And he could still work all night without sleep and sire a beautiful child! No, as with Pagnol, what must have been shocking for Preston was that he felt so much younger than his visage. Now fifty-six, he'd begun predicting that he'd live no longer than his mother's sixty years. Yet, unlike Mary Desti, who in her fifties stopped worrying about her makeup and resigned herself to old age, Preston was not going gently into that good night.

When it became clear they'd be staying a while in Paris, Preston and Sandy began looking for a place to rent. They found a small house on the Boulevard Berthier, built by a British painter. The landlady retained the first floor, and they had the spacious artist's studio, with its twenty-foot ceiling and loggia, and a small third floor, which had been servants' quarters. There was a pretty white-tiled basement, formerly a kitchen, which Preston made into his office and a tiny backyard where Little Preston could play when his parents weren't strolling him through the Jardin d'Acclimation in the Bois de Bologne or the Parc Monceau.

Preston grew increasingly devoted to his new son. He ordered him special toys—a ferryboat, a bridge, a turntable, and locomotive—from a store he'd discovered in London and described him, in a letter to Charley Abramson, as "a beautiful, lovable and extraordinarily intelligent child." [21] Sandy says Preston could never criticize either of their babies, where he was very objective about Mon, whom he'd never known so intimately. The summer of 1954, Mon wrote Preston:

Little Preston with his father when the Sturgeses first moved into their house on the Boulevard Berthier. Note the bust of "Big" Preston, age 11, on the mantle behind them.

Barbara Stanwyck was asking about you when Uncle Bert examined her. She thinks that you are one of the greatest. It made me very proud of you.

I miss you very much and wish you luck and I will love you always.

Much love to Sandy and my brother.[22]

Preston took a long time replying and then spent much of his letter lecturing Mon about grammar and avoiding clichés. Priscilla Woolfan, in her turn, lectured Preston about parenting: "Preston dear—write to [Mon]," she said. "All the other boys [at school] have fathers who write to them and come see them—can you not remember what your father meant to you?"[23] Priscilla wrote Preston frequently, telling about Mon's changing schools, then about his eighth-grade graduation, where Mon was ranked third in his class. Once, the Woolfans threw a badminton party for Mon's friends, and the week before, after a long consultation about the menu, Mon turned to Priscilla and said, "Aunt Priscilla—I want you to be glamorously casual."

"I tried. I tried hard," Priscilla reported.[24] Another time, she wrote Preston that *Christmas in July* had been adapted for television. James Mason introduced the show, saying, "*Christmas in July* was written by Preston Sturges, one of the greatest and most brilliant talents to come out of Hollywood."[25]

Willie Wyler also began corresponding. At the end of July 1954, Willie sent Preston a *Time* magazine piece, quoting Sturges ridiculing Hollywood:

Having settled down to the good expatriate life in Paris, veteran Movie Director-Playwright Preston (*Strictly Dishonorable*) Sturges, 55, figured the time was proper to burn behind him all the bridges leading back to Hollywood. His holocaust blazed merrily in the columns of France's weekly *Arts* Magazine. "We must never forget that the cinema is an art," warned he. "But it is an art so much more costly than the others . . . that the artist must tie himself to the businessmen. In that lies all the drama—rather the comic opera—of Hollywood: a group of fat businessmen—good fathers, not very funny, who amuse themselves, big cigars in hand, discussing stock-exchange quotations, the percentage of returns on their stocks, world tendencies . . . condemned to conjugal existence with this heap of drunkards, madmen . . . divorcees, sloths, epileptics, morphinomaniacs and assorted bastards, who are in the considered opinion of the management, artists."[26]

Wyler wrote, "I imagine that the story may have come out quite differently from the way you intended," and urged Preston to correct the misimpression. "Perhaps you know how stupidly oversensitive people in this picture business are, and how they consider it traitorous for anyone of their 'own' to criticize them publicly. I feel sure you had not intended to 'burn your bridges,' as *Time* put it."[27]

Preston had not, of course, intended to burn his bridges, but he must have been tired of playing the martyr's role and surely was cultivating this new image—as "Hollywood's Bad Boy" run off to Paris—to camouflage the more humiliating fact of his failure to get work. It was a way to salvage pride, saying he was fed up with crass American businessmen and announcing, as he now did to anyone who inquired about his expatriation, that in twenty years he'd managed to antagonize every studio boss in Hollywood. This did not speak well for Sturges, and it may have cost him jobs. However, where had four years of pleading with Darryl Zanuck and Frank Freeman gotten him? And it must have seemed the last straw that Willie Wyler should be preaching discretion to him, when the very papers that delighted in revealing Sturges's heresies were proclaiming Wyler's 1953 *Roman Holiday* a huge success. The most curious revelation of the *Time* article was that Preston, who had spent his whole public life in Hollywood posing as a Philistine, was now valorizing the artist. Years before, Preston had told Pagnol that he would probably not be able to duplicate his American success in French cinema "because at best, my efforts have been a French point of humor filtered through an American vocabulary." [28] He was no more inclined now than then to relinquish American filmmaking.

It was out of necessity that he began thinking along the lines of an international project. He wrote the English titles for Pagnol's *Les Lettres de mon Moulin*. (Later he asked Pagnol's manager to take his name off the credits, fearing people would think this was the only job he could get.) [29] Encouraged by his new friend Alec Guinness, Sturges also resumed work on an original script he'd begun in Hollywood, called *The Great Hugo*, about the last royal family in Europe. Sturges described *The Great Hugo* as "not only very funny but also very much *about* something . . . it has satire, a tender love story, some savage reality including an atom bomb, a lot of very big laughs." [30] Many pages are gone from Sturges's narrative treatment, but the atom bomb scenes (uncannily prescient of Stanley Kubrick's *Dr. Strangelove*) are powerful black comedy. Here, for instance, is a dialogue between the Baron and his scientist:

"What do you mean *something* has gone wrong," said the Baron frowning a little, "you asked permission to experiment with a little atom bomb like this . . . like a canary's egg . . . a sort of atomlet . . . if it is no good throw it away and forget about it."

"But that's not the situation, Your Excellency," said the miserable Doctor Von Dickle. "The reason it is *no* good is because it is *too* good. We can't stop it! . . . all of a sudden it started.

"What?"

"It," said Doctor Von Dickle in a voice full of horror. "It started to do it by *itself*! We can't stop it."

"You can't stop it from doing *what?*" said his Excellency palely.

"From subdividing itself," said the miserable Doctor. "From splitting itself over and over and over . . . and over. From each four comes eight . . . There is no mathematical end to it."

As with so many of the scripts Sturges tried peddling on his own in the fifties, nothing came of *The Great Hugo*. Instead, in the summer of 1954, Sturges got a call from the prestigious French Gaumont studio with a definite offer for *him*.

Gaumont's idea was to create a film based on a popular *Figaro* newspaper column, spoofing the eternal rivalry between England and France. The columnist was in real life a Frenchman, Pierre Daninos, but he wrote in the guise of a perfect English gentleman named Major William Marmaduke Thompson. The fictional Major Thompson had lived twenty-five years in Paris and was still baffled by the French mentality. He was forever complaining about some French quirk (such as mistrustfulness), while extolling British idiosyncrasies. Typical was a column called "Martine and Ursula," about the differences between Major Thompson's decorous, horse-loving British first wife, Ursula, and his current obstinate, sensual French wife, Martine. "The French devote to love the care we bring to making tea," observes Thompson, in a characteristic passage. It was familiar material, presented by an amiable curmudgeon. Sturges, with his expatriate childhood and perfect French, struck Gaumont as the ideal man to convey Daninos's stereotypes on both sides of the Channel.

Initially, Daninos himself was supposed to write the screenplay. Then, his columns were released as a book, *Les Carnets de Major Thompson*. Daninos, Preston wrote a friend, "turned out to be so busy with his success that he never got around to [writing the script] and the first thing you know I found myself writing in French . . . for the first time in forty years."

Sturges pronounced his composition "excellent"—except for "an occasional error of syntax or grammar."[31] The story was another matter. Preston often quoted Voltaire that the "success of a play depends almost entirely on the choice of its subject."[32] *Notebooks* was merely a skein of wry observations. Making a film from it was "like trying to make a film of the telephone directory," Preston would later tell a *Time* reporter. As with the stories for his Hollywood films, Sturges's first impulse had been to ignore *Notebooks* and write an original screenplay. He wrote a script, in his words, "about an author who creates a fictitious character . . . who subsequently appears."[33] But when *Notebooks* became a best-seller, Gaumont was determined to capitalize on its popularity and demanded a faithful adaptation.

So Sturges needed a means to convey comic ideas without the armature of a strong narrative, and also with as little dialogue as possible, since he was shooting both a French and an English language version and could not count on finding a thoroughly bilingual cast. Recently, Preston had been impressed by Jacques Tati's *Monsieur Hulot's Holiday*, a showcase for Tati's expressive face and gestures. Through mime, Tati managed to bring a character and his world to life, using minimal plot and no dialogue.

The strategy Sturges devised for his film gleaned both from Tati and from his own "narratage," created back in the thirties for *The Power and the Glory*. It intermeshed two very different types of sequences. The one type, employing mime and a voice-over narration (in French or English, respectively), shows the author Major Thompson observing various aspects of French life for his book called *The Notebooks of Major Thompson*. The other, conventional dialogue scenes show Thompson *living* French life with his very French wife Martine, their son Marc, and a maniacal British governess, Miss Ffyth, whose presence never fails to fuel cultural enmity.

The household scenes, taken from Daninos's single essay on Major Thompson's personal life, form a story of sorts. The Thompson family inhabits a large Parisian apartment festooned with the Major's animal trophies. Enter Miss Ffyth, hired by the Major over Martine's violent protests, who proceeds to subject young Marc to endless barbell exercises and lectures on French history from the English viewpoint. Martine implores the Major to fire this martinet, but he refuses to dismiss a British subject—even when the irate French cook walks out, leaving the Thompsons to Miss Ffyth's wretched English cooking. Tension reigns until Miss Ffyth conveniently inherits a fortune from a Maharaja and quits voluntarily. The same day Major Thompson learns his book is a success and, over a reconciliatory (French!) meal, Martine announces she's pregnant. "Vive la France!" exclaims the euphoric Major.

Such is the patently thin plot line. More appealing are the "narratage" scenes, interspersed between the Major's domestic crises. Here, on the soundtrack, the Major is heard composing "his" essays—on French bureaucrats, French motorists, French handshakes—which are silently enacted on screen. Monsieur Taupin—Major Thompson's friend and the film's epitome of Frenchness—does most of the miming. In the sequence demonstrating French mistrustfulness, for instance, Monsieur Taupin, dining in an obviously first-class Parisian restaurant, suspiciously eyes his sumptuous oysters, noisily wipes his pristine goblet with a floppy white handkerchief, and is delighted to have his first bona fide gripe when the bill arrives and he's been slightly overcharged.

One of the deftest sequences, in the finished film, is a "narratage" flashback of Major Thompson's courtship of Ursula, his very British first wife. Here the Major and Ursula circle round and round each other on horseback, all the while guzzling whiskey, until Ursula drifts onto the Major's steed, and the lovers collapse in a pond. Here the pacing is as sharp, the comic mood as swiftly defined as in *The Lady Eve*'s more famous horseback courtship. So, while by no means a Preston Sturges picture, *The French They Are a Funny Race*—as *Notebooks* would be called in its English language version—has a certain delicacy suggestive of Tati and shows far more directorial restraint than *The Beautiful Blonde* or even *The Sin of Harold Diddlebock*.

Sturges's main problem, besides the predictable material itself, was the casting. Noël-Noël, a cabaret star and farceur, was a logical choice for Monsieur Taupin, but the Thompsons were more difficult to find. Sturges first offered the Major's role to David Niven, who in January of 1955 eagerly cabled him, "MCI TELLS ME YOU INTERESTED IN ME FOR PICTURE. HOPE SO MUCH THIS IS TRUE AS HAVE ALWAYS WANTED WORK WITH YOU." [34] But Niven's enthusiasm waned after Preston sent him the English language screenplay, and by May Niven was writing that his plans had changed and, though Sturges offered to revise anything Niven disliked in *Notebooks*, he was unavailable. Preston then offered the role to Brian Ahearn, who also turned it down. In June, a month from production, the part was still not cast when someone suggested the British actor-vaudevillian Jack Buchanan. Buchanan, who'd played in Lubitsch's *Monte Carlo* (1930) and more recently in Minnelli's *The Band Wagon* (1953), was still best known in England. Preston rushed to Worthing to see Buchanan's show, liked it, and hired him on the spot.

"First of all I want to tell you how much I look forward to working with you, how much I believe you will bring to the role, and how much the picture will do for all of us," Sturges wrote Buchanan when he got home to Paris. "As I told you in Worthing, after seeing your remarkable performance, I believe bilingual pictures offer extraordinary possibilities to those of us who are slightly bilingual."

"Slightly" was the operative word, for Buchanan's French, Sturges soon learned, was extremely rudimentary, though better than Martine Carol's English. Martine Carol was to play the Major's wife Martine. Gaumont wanted Carol because of her fame as a sex goddess. She'd also that same year played the star role in Max Ophüls's *Lola Montès*. But Carol had no ear for language. Her English was all phonetic, Sandy recalls. She spoke with a heavy accent and elided her words, while Buchanan declaimed French with British cadences. Sturges, who since *The Guinea Pig* had been mocking unpronounce-able foreign names and patois, now had authentically incomprehensible stars. What's more, they couldn't understand each other in either language. Carol's English was especially befuddling. When they were shooting an opening breakfast scene for the English version, Martine said her lines, which were followed by perfect silence. Preston asked Buchanan whether he'd forgotten his reply. Of course not, he said, but he couldn't distinguish the cue. From then on, they tried to position Carol as close as possible to Buchanan so she could nudge him at the appropriate moment.[35]

Once production began, Sturges was eager to disprove his reputation for extravagance and made a great show of saving money. The dialogue scenes were shot consecutively in French and English. Wardrobe was kept to a mini-mum by borrowing clothes from Sandy, the cast, and the crew. Because the film had so many short scenes located throughout Paris, camera set-ups at first proved a problem, and Sturges began falling behind schedule until it occurred to him he could hire a second camera crew to shoot while the other was relo-cating. This was not the costly choice it would have been in Hollywood, Sturges assured reporters, since union rules and salaries were so much more reasonable in France. Sturges himself was unfailingly reasonable and good-natured, according to his colleagues. Pierre Kast, Sturges's assistant director, told the American reporter Alida Carey an anecdote that revealed both Pres-ton's resourcefulness and his ability to sacrifice perfection to a larger good:

> We were all in the Bois de Vincennes to shoot a fox-hunting scene. . . .
> All—actors, horses and the lot—except for a pack of hounds. Standing to
> one side, Sturges waited, then decided it was too late to find the dogs and
> useless to get angry about it. So he rewrote the script, making it read, "one
> day when we had *lost* the pack . . . ," and the sequence turned out funnier
> than before.[36]

Jack Buchanan was full of praise for Sturges's professionalism, calling Pres-ton the "smoothest" director he'd worked with since Lubitsch.[37] Everyone spoke of Preston's energy and good humor when coping with the drawbacks of French filmmaking: notably its inferior organization and technology. Sturges claimed to find even the absence of prop trucks and state of the art machinery a refreshing challenge. "In Hollywood they're used to being ba-bied, having every wish anticipated; here you must do more for yourself," he, approvingly, told Alida Carey.[38] And he described to a BBC interviewer how when he needed to lift a camera seven feet into the air for a shot in the Aus-terlitz station, his crew fortified a hopelessly primitive French boom with manhole covers.

"That's the sort of thing we do constantly," he went on. "You often pick up an actor in the middle of the street—if you want a cab, for instance, you just stop a passing cab and say, 'Do you think you could act?' to the driver. He generally says, 'Yes, I'd be delighted to,' and means it. In America, it would be an actor and a specially hired cab, but over here if you need a French taxicab for your scene, you just stop one and say to the driver, 'This is your role, would you go over there and get made up?' And the perfectly amiable old man does quite well." [39]

Sturges's determination to please continued in the editing room, where he allowed his executive producer, Alain Poire, to talk him out of scenes which varied the film's comfortable tone with flashes of violence: one episode with a chiropractor and another involving French and English schoolboys remained on the cutting room floor. In the end, both versions of the film, together, cost $540,000—only slightly more than *The Great McGinty*. The French, who'd loved the book, were pleased to see it faithfully adapted. The International *Herald Tribune* singled out two of Sturges's scenes as "among the funniest seen on the screen this year," [40] and in 1956 *Les Cahiers de Major Thompson* ranked as the ninth most popular film in France. It went on to make profits throughout Europe.

Sturges, however, was far more interested in the American opening—scheduled for May 1957. Walter Reade had bought the film's United States rights and intended to release it as *The Notebooks of Major Thompson*, but Sturges was not happy with that name. "Insofar as America is concerned, the book title means nothing," Preston wrote Walter Reade, "Noël-Noël means nothing . . . Jack Buchanan as the star is a hindrance . . . Martine Carol means very little . . . and everybody thinks I am dead! I'm not kidding! They teach my scripts in the public schools, and some kid who had been studying me nearly fainted when he was introduced to me one day. He thought he was talking to a ghost." [41] With such a plethora of unrecognizable talent, a catchy title—Preston argued—was crucial. His choice was *The French They Are a Funny Race* (the genteel half of a lewd couplet from "Mademoiselle from Armentières").[42] Walter Reade disagreed. Letters went back and forth on the subject until Preston got so worked up he contacted Bosley Crowther, who supported him.

"Well, Sir! We put it over!" Preston wrote Crowther. "That is to say that after a few persuasive arguments from me, formidably backed by a photostat of your letter agreeing with me, the American distributors . . . are going to call it *The French They Are a Funny Race*." [43] Preston was trying to summon his old enthusiasm, but he was also hedging his bets by making clear the film's story was not his idea. "The subject matter guarantees that the picture cannot be a great popular smash, but I hope parts of it will amuse you," Preston wrote the *New York Post*'s Archer Winsten. "Noël-Noël is extraordinarily good, and on the whole, the picture is worth anybody's seventy-nine cents or whatever they are getting these days." [44]

Walter Reade offered Sturges a mere $2,000 to come to New York for the opening. Preston accepted and wrote Charley Abramson to book him the Algonquin's "smallest, least expensive room"; he arrived on May 5 for two weeks of publicity. [45] Over lunches at Sardi's and the St. Regis, Sturges himself rather than his new film was the main topic. Sturges spent a lot of time explaining how he was both overjoyed to be in Paris and anxious to return to Hollywood, should the opportunity arise. He told one reporter he felt like a "barber with scissors in pocket," working wherever work appeared, [46] and belatedly refuted the reports about his excoriation of the American studio system. He'd been misquoted, he said, and he told the film critic Andrew Sarris that he was no martyrlike Orson Welles or Erich Von Stroheim. He really did belong in Hollywood.

It could not have been easy to watch the filmmaker Manny Farber had called "an extreme embodiment of the American success dream" come home with only a small French film to show for his years away from Hollywood. [47] Sarris thought Sturges seemed "like an exiled king holding court for his last remaining supporters." [48] And when *The French They Are a Funny Race* opened at New York's Baronet theatre, on May 20, 1957, the influential reviewers were obviously sorry not to have better news. The *Herald Tribune* said: "Half of [the vignettes] are quite funny in the old Sturges manner; half are labored and flat." *Newsweek* called *The French* "quite a funny picture." *Time* admired the silent film strategies, while summing up the material as "old jokes, but as Sturges tells them they get a fresh and hearty laugh—especially when the director puts his best foot forward and doesn't put all his weight on the arch." The most disheartening review was Bosley Crowther's. Speculating that Sturges must have "mellowed" during his expatriation, Crowther wrote "It grieves me to tell you that, for the most part, *The French They Are a Funny Race* is a generally listless little picture, without wit, electricity or even plot. . . . The French they must be funnier than this."

"It's too damned bad that in my overanxiety to be cooperative I allowed Poire to persuade me to take out the more violent scenes I had shot . . . so Bosley could say I had mellowed," Preston wrote a business acquaintance, the day *The French* opened. "Years ago, when I started directing, William Wyler gave me one piece of advice—he said the hardest thing about directing was 'resisting the impulse to be a good fellow.' If you fight for what you believe in they say you are 'hard to handle' and you don't get any work. If, through a desire to be 'easy to handle,' you give in about things you know are wrong— and there are no previews to find out who is right—the critics say you have 'mellowed' and don't know your business—it's a hard world!" [49]

Though his twelfth film didn't do as badly as he'd feared (making a modest profit even in America), it did nothing to revive Sturges's reputation in the film world. Preston was profoundly disappointed. Yet, he had never fooled himself about this venture. Writing to Priscilla Woolfan, Preston said: *The Notebooks of Major Thompson* "wasn't a very cinematic subject in the first place, and I told that to the French company that made the film, but they were so awed by the success of the book in France that they would not listen to me . . . so I made it . . . and I think it was better to do that than not to do any-thing . . . the alternative." [50] Refusing to give in to self-pity, he was playing the hand he was dealt.

In June of 1956, Sandy gave birth to a second son. They called him Thomas, "after Sandy's father, my mother's brother, the central character in my picture *The Power and the Glory*, and the speakeasy proprietor in whose joint I laid the play *Strictly Dishonorable*," Preston wrote a friend. As if that weren't enough, "for good luck," they threw in Preston. So now there were three Prestons in the household.[1] They nicknamed Thomas Preston Tom-Tom. His godfather was José Iturbi and his godmother Madame de Massieux, the Sturges's landlady. He was baptized in the Cathedral of Notre-Dame. When she heard about Tom-Tom's baptism, Priscilla Woolfan—knowing Sturges's aversion to religious rituals—saw it as a sign of Preston's great devotion to Sandy. Doubtless, that was true. But Preston, who'd started signing off letters to his friend Charley Abramson "God bless you," (much as his mother had closed letters to him) and who spoke so often these days of providence, had grown more indulgent of the religious impulse.

"The real American is not a gold chaser or money lover, as the legend classes him, but an idealist and a mystic," Isadora Duncan had written in her autobiography.[2] More than ever now Preston felt drawn to mystical explanations. "The funny thing about success is that either everyone wants you or nobody wants you and you yourself never know exactly why," Preston wrote Jimmy Conlin and his wife Dorothy in Los Angeles. "There is also the element of luck. I had so very much of it for so many years that it is quite natural for the dice to roll differently for a while."

Yet, unlike Isadora, Preston never was nor would be an idealist. Nor was he attracted to American transcendentalist authors like Emerson and Thoreau. Rather, it was the skeptical pragmatists Ben Franklin and Mark Twain he was quoting in letters home. Now, for instance, Preston was rereading Franklin's autobiography, and highly recommending it to Mon, along with some pretty cynical advice about power. Mon had written Preston that the boys in his new

Tom-Tom.

school were nice, "but the whole place has an air of snobs, where the rich rule and all that." [3]

"Don't worry about the rich appearing to rule," Preston answered him. "The rich always rule . . . not because they are rich but because they were bright enough to become rich. A government of the rich is called a plutocracy. A government of the poor is called a democracy. In both cases, the rich rule, and you aren't going to change it, so don't try. Just get rich yourself." [4]

There were no signs of this happening imminently. Preston could spare little of the modest salary Gaumont had paid him to fortify Louise and Mon. Louise's apartment house was hard to fill and even harder to supervise and keep up. Her letters told of a daily routine of grouting bathtubs and sinks, removing layers of rancid grease from broilers, and patching a crumbled garage wall with broken wood. Once, she complained about having to turn away an Asian man, when there were apartments to spare and he was better dressed and educated than the rest of her motley tenants, because of the pervasive racial prejudice. She never in word or tone blamed Preston for her reduced circumstances, and she always thanked him for whatever money he could send, but her letters were filled with gloom.

Priscilla Woolfan was more cheerful. "We have a new organ—a big one," she wrote Preston. "It is *so* beautiful. It has become the joy of my life. Sometimes we dream that you are here with Sandy—the children are playing on the floor—Mon is with us and I am playing the organ and of course you are admiring me extravagantly—I mean my playing—Isn't it a nice dream?"[5]

For Preston, 1956 was a trying year. The summer before, Sandy's mother had come to visit, and—with fresh air prescribed for Little Preston—the two women, the baby, and Bianca (now Sandy's good friend too) took off for Deauville, where Preston joined them on weekends. While Sandy was away, Sturges began an affair with a bisexual, thirty-five-year-old actress named Gaby Sylvia. Partly, Sandy now feels, it was that Sylvia was a gifted performer Sturges hoped would star in a play he was writing; her admiration was both professionally useful and gratifying to his wounded pride. Partly, it was the double standard Preston had been touting since his 1931 play *Unfaithfully Yours*: a loving *pater familias* can have affairs on the side without hurting anyone, so long as his faithful wife remains in the dark. Indeed, that fall, when Sandy came upon a letter from Sylvia, revealing that she and Preston were lovers, Sturges's response was: "There's only one thing disturbing you—I got caught." But Sandy was sincerely shocked and heartbroken about the affair. She still feels sure this was the first time Sturges betrayed her; and, with Tom on the way, it must have seemed all too like the affair Sturges began with Jean La Vell when Louise was pregnant. It was not. Preston was still in love with Sandy and broke off his affair before Tom was born (though Sturges still hoped to work with Sylvia), but the damage was done—there was now a new tension in the house, beyond the habitual worries over work and money.[6]

Recently, another independent project had fallen through. The producers were Halsey Raines (formally at MGM and a Sturges admirer) and John Shelton, working with putative backers in Sweden. The plan was for Preston to direct a script called *Long Live the King*, about a monarch who hates his job and arranges to be paid *not* to rule. Correspondence flowed back and forth, and they settled on a deal, whereby Sturges would be paid $50,000 before and during production and $50,000 after the film's release, when he would also receive a percentage of the producer's profits. Shelton came to Paris, supposedly bringing Preston his first check, but it became clear that he'd arrived empty-handed. And when the Swedish backers were called, at Preston's insistence, they first claimed they couldn't pay in dollars, then that they couldn't pay at all without obtaining certain arcane permissions. "I gave [Shelton] back his script and his contract and called Howard Hawks in Monaco to ask if he still wanted me to work for him. He said he did—asked me to dine with him in Paris on Thursday," Preston reported to Charley Abramson.[7]

Sturges met with Hawks in Paris and then spent five days at his villa in St. Jean-Cap-Ferrat. But all Hawks wanted, as it turned out, was for Preston to write the script for a film called *Cat Business* for $10,000 without any financial interest in the film's success. "I have never done anything but my very best work for anyone, and to do this and retain my first fine enthusiasm over a period of thirty years has required a rather special set of working conditions," Preston wrote Hawks, rejecting the deal, as soon as he returned to Paris. "I have been a happy writer, and this happiness came from hope. . . . I have always insisted on good odds."

Sturges could see that, like Lester Cowan, Hawks and Shelton were not villains, but well-meaning people; the problem was always lack of capital, yet Preston couldn't help reading some comment on himself in the collapse of the projects. If these people *really* wanted him, they'd find a solution, he suspected. Preston articulated his suspicions in a reply to yet another impecunious producer who'd expressed reservations about a Sturges script: "The sad part about your nice letter of the twentieth was that no one out your way fell 'madly in love' with my story, which is a nice way of saying it stinks. The terms can always be arranged between two people who want to work together."[8]

The script they were discussing was called *The Gentleman from Chicago*. This comic gangster film, as Preston described it to Priscilla and Bertie Woolfan:

[is] about an Italian-American gangster deported to Italy and there condemned by the government to live in the village of his birth and not to stray from it. Nobody wants to have anything to do with him, but he is a world famous character, and you don't get to be a world famous *anything* without some brains or energy or both. So he gets along. Then a strange thing starts to happen: The village, made famous by his presence, now starts to become prosperous. Tourists come by the thousands, and while there they spend money. Pretty soon this character is considered the town benefactor. When he is removed to an island (for having attracted too much attention to himself) the village, in despair, raises *hell*. At their request he is eventually allowed

to go back, but during his absence an Italian gang has moved in to prey upon the little town's prosperity. This makes for a fine blood and thunder finish because if ever there was a man indicated to rid a town of a rival gang, it is our friend. Twenty-nine men are exterminated and much fun is had by all.[9]

Sturges frequently compared *The Gentleman from Chicago* to *The Great McGinty* (though the writing is far more broadly comic). Eddie Constantine, a popular expatriate actor, was signed up to play the gangster, inspired, Preston said, by Lucky Luciano. Sturges was on the verge of signing a contract with a small company called Grey Films when Columbia Pictures announced *they* were producing a deported gangster movie, from Art Buchwald's book *A Gift from the Boys*.[10] The Sturges film was, in Preston's words, "dropped like a hot brick."[11] And so it went, from one possibility to another, with Preston always struggling to keep his spirits up.

For all his native optimism, Preston, Sandy says, "had lost his absolute unassailable belief that everything would work out all right in the end." He told her he felt like a person at a fire. There are certain people passing the bucket along, and if you're not in the line of bucket-passers, it doesn't matter how much desire you have to help put the fire out. You just can't. Sandy remembers how depressed Preston could get when deals fell through. "He'd be very down," she says. "But then he'd snap out of it and say, 'Well, let's go to work.' I don't mean to say he was joyful, but he'd pick up the phone, call somebody else, make an appointment to have somebody new read his script."[12]

Like Eleanor and Louise, Sandy speaks of Preston's "vicious temper," which came and went in a flash. What did not go was the duller pain of creative frustration. The ability to create at the height of his talent—the "beautiful white light,"[13] as Priscilla Woolfan described his creativity—was gone. However well he understood the vagaries of luck and success, he missed his old powers. Yet, in many ways, this was not a bad life. He was still a celebrity. Hollywood people coming to Paris always wanted to see Preston Sturges. He had dinners with Darryl Zanuck and Akim Tamiroff and Jackie Gleason; the Club Élysée Matignon became, like The Players in Hollywood, his regular haunt. Then too, domesticity gave Preston a new outlet for his energies. Mornings, he would wake up, Sandy recalls, to little boys climbing up, over, and around him. He and Sandy would have their breakfasts of coffee and cigarettes, talking, she recalls, about everything under the sun, before Preston went down to his office and Sandy took the kids to a park.[14]

But the small studio on the Boulevard Berthier was not built to contain two children. Sandy longed for a lawn where her boys could run and, like so many travelers abroad, missed not any particular place or even her family per se, but *being* in America—"seeing the American flag . . . hearing English in the streets." They had a little money, since in early July Preston had played a cameo part in Bob Hope's film *Paris Holiday*. His character (shades of Sullivan) was a famous French comic playwright who writes a serious play and is promptly assassinated. Preston, looking very gray and conveying dignified bemusement, appeared in a single scene and received $1,000 for the day.

So when a producer expressed interest in *Matrix*, the very script which a decade before had won Sturges his $8,825-a-week deal with Fox and was now buried somewhere in the basement of Preston's Los Angeles house, Sandy proposed going home to find it since the Bidens would never be able to unearth it. "I persuaded Preston that I might be able to," she recalls, "and, as a bonus, the boys could get a big dose of California sunshine for a couple of weeks."

At the end of July, Preston and Sandy went to the bank and withdrew $1,000, ostensibly for her to take to America. But in the end Preston gave Sandy only a hundred.[15] As with the issue of Sandy's passport when they were leaving for London, Preston could not bear to think of his wife as self-sufficient. He had never trusted that the women he loved would not, like his mother, be seduced by new romance. After all the strains of the previous year, this voyage, now that it was really happening, must have seemed less like an errand than a departure.

Preston put his family on the plane on the morning of July 29, 1957, went home and wrote them a long passionate letter signed "Papa Bear," and continued writing daily like a young lover. "You are the love—the joy—and the companion of my life,"[16] he told Sandy, who spent a few hours in New York with Charley Abramson and arrived in Los Angeles on July 30. The next night she mailed *Matrix*, but she'd found the house in chaos, and it was ten days before she could write Preston a balanced and affectionate letter. By then, Preston was beside himself. The note he wrote upon receiving Sandy's first letter from Los Angeles could have been written by Sir Alfred in *Unfaithfully Yours*:

> *My sweetest, dearest, beloved, adorable little darling,*
>   Listen you dirtie little bitch, it's lucky for you that you're not within hitting distance or I would take your antipays down and give you such a swatting it would be a long time before you would again plunge your husband in the condition I have been staggering around in for the past two weeks . . . unable to concentrate . . . unable to work . . . just plain unable. You arrived in Holly-

wood on Tuesday afternoon July 30th. You mailed me *Matrix* . . . Wednesday night. So far, so good. Excellent even. It would have taken *one minute longer* to include a message in pencil saying: It's dirty . . . but we have a house . . . we'll be all right! I would have received this message on Saturday afternoon August 3rd, along with the manuscript . . . SIXTEEN DAYS SOONER than your sweet letter that arrived, you stupid little jerk, at ten to five this afternoon. Have you any idea what goes on in the mind of a man who makes his living with his imagination? Visions of the house sold and the new owners allowing you to get *Matrix* out of the cellar: visions of the upper floor having been rented out to bring in a little dough . . . visions of you getting on a bus and going East . . . to your mother and a Blue Cross job.[17]

"Dearest darling," Sandy replied to this overwrought outburst. "You are a total idiot and you know how much I love you and miss you and just ache to put my face against yours." But the news she had sent from Hollywood was mixed. The house was standing all right, but was in execrable condition. The Bidens, she told Preston, had been living in filth, and Sandy spent her first weeks just trying to get out from under the squalor. All of their property had been sold to pay debts, they had no assets in Hollywood, and she desperately needed money for food and clothes for the boys. Still, California had no shortage of space or sunshine. Sandy was energetic and resourceful, and the Woolfans embraced her like their own daughter. "I am sure you know what a happy time we are having with Sandy and your two little angels," Priscilla wrote Preston. "Sandy has grown up. She isn't a little girl any more—she is a lovely charming interesting woman. We are enjoying her visit to the utmost and we speak of you every day and miss you."[18]

Sandy also visited Mon and Louise. "Louise looks very well, healthy, strong and alive. And of course pretty," she reported to Preston. "Her real estate and money problems you already know but nevertheless she seems happy."[19] Sandy, for all her discipline and strength, was lonely, and many of her letters pleaded with Preston to "come home."[20]

"We'll see how things shape up a little bit before deciding whether you join me (I'll hug you to death) or I join you (I'll also hug you to death)," he wrote in September.[21] With Sandy gone, he'd reverted to some of his old habits—staying up all night, drinking heavily.

Having no regular income, Preston was currently getting by on his mother's resourcefulness and letting other people invite *him* for meals rather than always playing the *grand seigneur*. Sometimes he would forget about eating and just drink for hours in the Café Alexandre, down the block from the Georges V Hotel, a haven for American movie people. Preston would lean out the window and call for visiting Hollywood friends to join him when they walked by. Or he'd arrange to drink and eat his meals at parties. When Billy Wilder's *Love in the Afternoon* opened, Wilder invited Preston to a lavish company party, replete with caviar and champagne, on the set of the Ritz Hotel. That may have been Preston's only meal that day. He'd been poor before and was not above scrounging.

Nothing came of the *Matrix* deal, however, and sometimes Preston got maudlin. "Old guys with troubles, myself included, bore me to death . . . so I would not hold it against you if you felt likewise," Preston wrote his friend John Hertz, Jr., in a letter asking for money. (Over the next two years, Hertz would send a substantial sum not only to Preston, but also to Sandy in Los Angeles.) "Young bohemians are fun, but the old ones are really depressing. We have not the romance of the bewhiskered sourdough with pick axe and gold pan, following the burro toward the sunset . . . and gold." [22]

When Francie Ramsden and her husband came to Paris, they spent a whole day with Preston—lunch, followed by drinks at the Café de Paris and cocktails at the Georges V. That night they went to the Club Élysée Matignon. Francie remembers how the Hollywood people in the room, who had known them as a couple, gasped when she and Preston walked together through the door. Later, Francie, her husband, and Preston went to Montparnasse where Preston commandeered a piano and began singing his songs. When Francie and her husband headed toward les Halles for onion soup, Preston asked them to drop him off at a bistro. "I remember how sweet he was, he was very kind, we embraced and then he turned to my husband and said, 'You take care of this young lady, she means a lot to me.' He disappeared into the caverns of this little bistro." Preston was still full of spirit, but he was no longer the great Preston Sturges, Francie recalls. [23]

Willie Wyler's wife Tally, visiting Paris with her teenage daughters, also saw a sea change in Preston. "Basically he still had all the mannerisms, all the Prestonness that he'd always had. Except he was sadder. I just found it heartbreaking to see him unemployed, drifting around Paris," she says. [24] Others, who hadn't known him in Hollywood, saw less of the pathos and just enjoyed his company. Bika de Reisner, Jean Renoir's assistant director who became Sandy's best friend in Paris, was extremely fond of the smart, funny American filmmaker. They were forever joking with each other. "I am sorry you are in bed with a fever, but anything is better than being in bed alone," Preston wrote her at one point. [25]

Another new friend was Alida Carey, who'd written an article in the *New*

York Times about the making of *The French They Are a Funny Race*. Preston always described Alida as "the second prettiest girl reporter in the world"—a joke, she recalls, since he never named the prettier one. Alida remembers Preston as "vibrant and gregarious," and sometimes touchingly generous. "Friendship to him meant kindness," she later wrote. "Once I had a temperature of 103 degrees and what appeared to be a bad grippe. Unexpectedly, someone knocked at my door, and a French doctor unknown to me announced that he'd come at the request of Sturges, who wanted to be sure that I had a proper diagnosis and that I'd be all right. After examining me, he said, 'I'm not worried,' and only later did I discover that he was . . . probably the top internist in Paris—and that there would be no bill for me." [26]

On another occasion, when Alida was moving from Paris to London, Preston spent a half hour charming the French railroad officials into loading her many crates and suitcases onto a crowded train. Herb Sterne, Preston's Hollywood friend, who'd long ago tried to arrange a collaboration between Sturges and D. W. Griffith, also remembers Preston's generosity at this time. No sooner had Sterne, now a publicist, moved into his apartment in Paris than Sturges turned up bearing a great assortment of bourbon and American canned goods.

The deaths of Max Ophüls and Jack Buchanan saddened Sturges in 1957. "Max was cremated last week and Howard [Hughes] got married. There must be a moral in there somewhere," Preston wrote John Hertz, Jr.[27] At fifty-nine, Preston himself was feeling well, though he complained that he was "getting to look too much like Dr. Schweitzer." [28] Still trying to sell *The Gentleman from Chicago*, he was again revising *Matrix* and also working on the play he hoped Gaby Sylvia would star in, *I Belong to Zozo*. He got the idea for this play, Preston told Mon, ten years before "when you were a small boy and I considered at one time assigning it to you and having whatever profits it made put into a trust fund for you." [29] Sturges composed both French and English versions of *Zozo*. The story focuses on romantic traumas in the life of fabulously wealthy Zoroaster Zanizli Zazzaroff. Zozo's mother arranges for him to marry a Greek heiress, but Zozo adores Gina, a hot-blooded hotel switchboard operator. Predictable intrigues ensue.

Sturges was completing a draft of *Zozo* when he received a letter from a man named Peter Lawrence. Lawrence, yet another Sturges admirer, had recently produced the Broadway musical *Shinbone Alley* and now was eager to make motion pictures. He'd optioned three properties. "One, I believe, is a story which you could do to great effect," he told Preston, though, predictably, money was scarce, and at first glance Lawrence appeared suspiciously like Halsey Raines and Arthur Cowan. There was more promise, though, both in the sophistication of his letter—Lawrence spoke shrewdly about the difficulties of satire and drew intelligent comparisons between Sturges and Chaplin—and in the property he had in mind: a *New Yorker* profile by the author Robert Shaplen.[30]

The scoundrel Philip Musica was Shaplen's subject. An eldest son of poor Italian immigrants, Musica began his career, in the early 1900s, bribing customs officials to boost the family grocery business. Inevitably, he moved on to scams and extortions, then suddenly went respectable. Assuming the name Frank Donald Coster, Musica bought out a failing pharmaceutical company named McKesson & Robbins, brought it around, and meanwhile became a noted philanthropist and yachtsman, living a sedate life in Fairfield, Connecticut. But Musica/Coster could not resist creating a sideline "crude drug department" which in 1938 was exposed as a fraud. Musica's real identity was now discovered, creating a scandal on Wall Street. With the United States Marshall literally at his door, Coster shot himself, leaving a note which insisted he was a victim of Wall Street plunder. In between criminal escapades, Musica had married and remained a devoted Italian son. The irony of his demise was that, as president of McKesson & Robbins, he'd finally achieved honest success and might have lived to quiet old age, but for his compulsion to dabble in crime.

There was much to attract Preston in Shaplen's profile of Musica: the great man with the tragic flaw (like Tom in *The Power and the Glory*); the crook who disdains an honest living (like Jean's father in *The Lady Eve*); the low-born who yearns to rise above his appointed station (like Jimmy in *Christmas in July*). There was the perfectly ordinary Musica family which, like Mary Desti's parents, produced a single remarkable child, and the comment on how one can't escape one's past in Musica's perpetual fear of exposure. By Musica's Fairfield bed table, Shaplen notes, there hung a framed Harriet Beecher Stowe aphorism: "When you get in a tight place and everything goes against you till it seems as if you just couldn't hold on a minute longer—never give up then, for that is just the place and the time when the tide will turn." This exhortation to steadfastness and hope in the face of terrible odds reflects Preston's own fierce optimism. Like Sturges, Musica achieved astonishing success in his forties and was humbled in the following decade.

It is obvious from Sturges's letter to Lawrence that he was excited not just by the prospect of work, but by the project itself. "I really think you've latched on to something," he began, and compared Musica's life to *The Great McGinty*, then continued:

I'm beginning to get the kind of idea I think you need: It has something to do with a crook getting hold of an enterprise for the purpose of looting it . . . then turning it unintentionally into a great success (which bores him . . . you notice he was not very gay in his prosperous years). It gets bigger and bigger . . . and he gets more and more depressed . . . BECAUSE THERE IS NO GETAWAY FROM AN HONEST VENTURE!

When his associates come around he ruins himself at first to pay them off . . . then is forced to loot the company a little . . . which only makes it more prosperous . . . like pruning a tree. When finally he kills himself it is more from irritation and to punish himself for his stupidity . . . than because he fears prison or being mugged again. He has never enjoyed respectability . . . and he has committed the unpardonable sin of crookdom: To give a sucker an even break.[31]

Charley Abramson told Preston he knew Lawrence to be "very creative, very able and, which is quite important, very honorable." Charley's only worry was that Lawrence had no film credits with which to attract backers. Still, sensitive to Sturges's enthusiasm, Charley urged him to proceed. On October 27, 1957, Preston flew to New York to confer with Lawrence. All went well, and contracts were to be finalized and sent off in three weeks. It seems not to have daunted Preston that he would be paid just $15,000, in three installments, for writing the screenplay. But, by December 16, when he still had not received the contracts, Preston confided in Charley, "If I sound irritated, it is much more at my own stupidity and carelessness for allowing myself to slip into a position where, to survive, I have to deal with fools, liars and shaky amateurs, rather than against these latter. You warned me twenty-five years ago against intolerance toward the schnooks one has to meet in this life, and I have succeeded reasonably well in following your advice—I have now expressed my private feelings and am again in excellent humor."[32]

Peter Lawrence was not a fool or a schnook, but he *was* an amateur in the film business. On December 30, Preston's contract went out, followed by a first check for $5,000, which promptly bounced. "I have no doubt that their intentions are good," Preston wrote Charley of Lawrence and his associates, on January 13, after he finally received his money, "but they fill me with as much confidence as a three dollar bill." Yet, his enthusiasm about the screenplay was undiminished.

On February 26, Sturges wrote Charley that he'd finished seventy-five pages which he considered "very good," and so they were. There was no gratuitous sentiment or overwriting. While skewing chronology, Sturges for the most part stuck to the facts as set out in Shaplen's profile, merely changing the emphasis and adding some characters here and there. Three figures besides

Musica/Coster himself become important in Sturges's screenplay. The first two are McKesson & Robbins executives—McGloon, a comptroller, and Thompson, the treasurer. Thompson, the more erudite, engages in philosophical discussions with Coster/Musica. Here, for instance, is a first dialogue between the two men as Thompson is inspecting Coster's shrewdly doctored finances.

> THOMPSON: (beaming) Splendid! Really splendid, Mr. Coster . . . this jump in business from 336,000 gross in '23 to nearly two million in less than two years is really remarkable! . . .
>
> COSTER: (pleased) Thank you very much, Mr. Thompson . . . we've worked hard, of course . . .
>
> THOMPSON: (indicating the accountants' statement) . . . And you say this was prepared by Price, Waterhouse? (then answering himself) Obviously, since it says so clearly enough across the top . . . rather unusual, as a matter of fact, that such a . . . still modest firm, if you will forgive me, should avail itself of such celebrated AND expensive accountants . . . but I must say that I approve HIGHLY of the procedure!
>
> COSTER: I don't think you can spend too much money on a first-class audit. There's no use fooling yourself, Mr. Thompson . . . you have to know the exact truth . . . down to the last penny!
>
> THOMPSON: (approvingly) How right you are! How VERY right you are! "Dreams lift up fools!"
>
> COSTER: What's that from?
>
> THOMPSON: The Bible . . .
>
> COSTER: Lot of truth in it!
>
> THOMPSON: Yes, isn't there? Or you can have: "Dreams are the children of an idle brain, Begot of nothing but vain fantasy, Which is as thin of substance as the air, And more inconstant than the wind."

Sturges told Charley Abramson he was writing the role of Thompson for Rudy Vallee and McGloon for Al Bridge. Akim Tamiroff, he felt, might play Musica/Coster. Preston mentioned no actor for the fourth major character—a gangster named Brandino, formerly Musica's business partner and one of the few who knows Coster's real identity. Brandino, who bears a grudge against Musica for an old business betrayal, is not a crucial figure in Shaplen's article. But Sturges expands his importance, creating a meeting between Coster and Brandino in a Little Italy restaurant, which signals a turning point in Coster's fortunes. At the restaurant, Coster offers Brandino $50,000 in cash to destroy the incriminating fingerprints Brandino has unearthed from police archives. Brandino accepts, and Coster heads back to Connecticut, relieved but also saddened. For his time in Little Italy reminds Coster how much he's lost, denying his Italian heritage. And Sturges invents a highly ironic upshot to the $50,000 payoff. Brandino has warned Coster against murdering him, saying he's written a letter exposing Coster's identity which will be automatically delivered to the police should he be discovered dead. Coster assures Brandino he won't touch him. But when Brandino leaves the restaurant, he is killed by a common thief for his money: setting Brandino's revenge on Musica/Coster in motion.

Sturges's screenplay *The Metamorphosis of Philip Musica* stops on page 106, with the announcement of Brandino's death. The script feels about three-quarters finished, but it is far more than a rough draft. The pacing is swift, the motivations complex, the story is consistently gripping. It has its lighter interludes, but is comic only in the blackest sense—like *Vendetta* and *The Power and the Glory*. Particularly interesting here is the development of Philip Musica—from a sharp young boy learning to bribe his first policeman to a "haggard man of sixty," fleeing his fate. Coster/Musica was in fact fifty-four when he killed himself; it is significant that Sturges, now fifty-nine, made him closer to his own age, and there are other connections between author and subject: both are men of action, both are more gifted than most everyone around them and not inclined to suffer fools. Like all Sturges's best scripts, *The Metamorphosis of Philip Musica* is filled with visual detail: of Coster's Italian-style villa in Connecticut, his yacht, his family's arrival at Ellis Island. There are some particularly well-drawn scenes of the older Musica boating from Connecticut by night, like a doomed general, to meet Brandino. Thompson's growing disillusionment with Coster is well-delineated in scenes where Thompson does some private sleuthing, hoping that he won't have to challenge his friend.

Sturges was to have received his second $5,000 check in February, but it never came. Lawrence, who'd grown so desperate he had importuned even Sturges's personal friend John Hertz, Jr., for funding (and was rebuked), was out of money. He'd underestimated the difficulties of independent film production. Now his company was dissolving. He was very contrite, very anxious that Sturges should feel free to sell his screenplay elsewhere. Sturges approached Walter Reade when he came to Paris and sent the script to Laurence Weingarten on the coast. He also sent it to Charley, just to get his opinion of the writing. (Charley, more the friend than the discerning admirer, blandly encouraged Preston: "I do think when you get it finished it should be very exciting.")[33]

It should come as no surprise that few appreciated *The Metamorphosis of Philip Musica*. After all, it took Sturges nearly a decade to sell *The Great*

McGinty, and buying a Sturges screenplay in 1958 was distinctly out of fashion. Whether Preston himself recognized the truly superior quality of his script is difficult to say, because he was always most enthusiastic about whatever he was working on at the moment. Still, his letters about this script are slightly different—less boasting, more gratified at discovering some answering intelligence to his own in the Musica character, the Shaplen profile, even in poor Lawrence himself. It was the last original script Sturges would write.

On the open market, *The Metamorphosis of Philip Musica* attracted even less enthusiasm than Sturges's other late fifties projects. By the spring he'd given up on it and gone back to *Zozo, The Gentleman from Chicago*, and a third project he'd had in mind for some time—a production of Robert Sherwood's 1927 *The Road to Rome* for French audiences.

Sturges, who'd rewritten and directed *The Road to Rome* for The Players, had always liked Sherwood's romantic reading of the Hannibal saga. The play's main characters are a priggish Roman dictator Fabius, his beautiful half-Greek wife Amytis, and the dashing conqueror Hannibal. The night before Hannibal is to advance on Rome, Amytis steals into his camp, makes love to him, and convinces him not to attack. Sturges must have responded to the many jibes at the self-righteous Romans, as well as to the "love is best" moral of Sherwood's tale. He may also have been attracted by the antiwar statement articulated by Amytis, who urges Hannibal not to retreat from the gates of Rome for her sake, but for a higher principle: "I want you to believe that every sacrifice made in the name of war is wasted," she tells him: "When you believe that, you'll be a great man."

Still, *The Road to Rome* is essentially a conventional play of the late twenties, and the fact that Sturges fastened on this rather than a more contemporary work is telling. He was out of sympathy with the theatre of his times—certainly with the recent American and English productions he'd seen in Paris. He dismissed Arthur Miller's *View from the Bridge*: "No poetry and no tenderness . . . only breast beatings about the terrible conditions of workers in America";[34] and called young Peter Brook's productions "pretentious crap."[35] Convinced that there were others like himself who preferred good old-fashioned entertainment, during the spring and summer of 1958, he adapted *The Road to Rome* and translated it into French. Ingrid Bergman became interested in starring as Amytis, with her future husband Lars Schmidt producing, but then she announced she wanted not Sturges, but Luchino Visconti to direct her. Sturges was hurt and immediately pulled out, so another possibility vanished.

Increasingly desperate, Preston began thinking of recycling his old material. Learning of Paramount's plans for a musical based on *The Great McGinty*, he contacted Frank Freeman, hoping to write the book. But Freeman replied that they were using contract writers. Then, over a friendly dinner, Preston convinced Darryl Zanuck (now living in Paris) to ask Spyros Skouras about the possibility of remaking *The Power and the Glory*. The saddest part of Skouras's refusal was that he misspelled Sturges's name, calling him Sturgess.

Not everyone in the movie business had forgotten Sturges, of course. Rudy Vallee and Caroline Wedderburn got together to phone Preston on his birthday; Jimmy Conlin and his wife Dorothy wrote regularly. William Demarest's wife Lucille, the feud over the lion's costume forgotten at least for the moment, looked him up when she came to Paris, and the Wylers spoke of him regularly. In 1958 Willie sent a check with his letter, reading:

> We were having a family . . . dinner and were speaking of old friends, among which you figure prominently. One doesn't have too many. I was sorry to hear that your business-luck had not been the best recently, so I thought perhaps the enclosed might be welcome. In any case I hope you won't think it presumptuous.
>
> On the other hand, Bob [Wyler's brother] and Tally reported you as being in good form and good spirits, full of health and charm and good humor. As ever. This, of course, I was delighted to hear, since it is still first in importance.
>
> We've been out of contact much too long, you and I. Let's keep in touch, Preston!

It was a warm gesture on Wyler's part. Still, Preston (who did not pursue the overture) must have been more depressed than cheered by this reminder of how different his fortunes had been from Willie's during the past decade. "I am beginning to feel like D. W. Griffith toward the end of his life . . . although he was about fifteen years older than I," Preston confided in Jimmy Conlin.[36]

He was lonesome for his family. After they left, he found a pair of Tom-Tom's socks behind the radiator and tacked them to the wall as a remembrance. To Sandy, he wrote constantly, in all his wide range of moods, and she replied that they must find a way to be together: either in Paris or L.A. "I would not ask you to come back to this address unless I had been able to afford the completion of the bathroom and the construction of a really beautiful balcony room . . . where the little boys could sleep at night," he told her.[37] She, the more practical, found these details ridiculous in light of the larger good of sustaining a relationship. But he was resolute. He also insisted that she write more often when letters were clearly not the solace for her that they were for him. "It's getting a little difficult for me to write to you," she told him at one point. "It almost, but not quite, seems like writing to someone I knew and loved a long time ago.[38]

In bitter moods, he threatened Sandy and also Louise and Mon that he'd cut off their money if they didn't write more often. Mon (doubtless coached by Louise) came up with a spirited response: "I have not replied to your last letter because I think that it was a foolish thing to say . . . I mean I do not write for money. If that was my chosen vocation I would tell you so. I am always happy to hear from you . . . and happy to write to you . . . but I don't think it should be a monetary affair."[39] It was all academic since Preston had so little money to offer.

By the summer of 1958, Preston was physically, as well as financially and emotionally, debilitated. Beyond his familiar indigestion, he'd developed trouble breathing. Sometimes he had to gasp for air. He wrote Bertie Woolfan about his asthmatic symptoms, and Bertie wrote back that it might be an emphysema related to allergy and suggested the high acid diet and acid tablets that he'd successfully prescribed for Mon's allergies. Preston's friend Bika, commenting on how infrequently the house had been cleaned since Sandy left, only half-jokingly blamed the dusty curtains for Preston's condition. He'd just given up smoking because of a racking cough, but was still drinking heavily. When Louise Brooks was given a tribute by the Paris Cinémathèque, Henri Langois insisted that she stop asking Preston to her parties because he was devouring all their liquor.[40] Others told similar tales. "I know—and not just from hearsay—of two prospective deals that went no further than a talk with you at 'the club,'" Sandy wrote him.[41] "It will never do you any harm to have someone say you drink like an ex-minister, but it can, has, and will do you much damage for just one more person to say you're a drunk or . . . 'if only he didn't drink so much,'" she, on another occasion, warned.[42]

One day Preston's secretary arrived to find him "wide-eyed and drained of color." He'd been up all night with chest pains. At the American Hospital, he was diagnosed as having suffered a transitory heart spasm brought on by stress.[43] In August, Preston turned sixty. His mother was dead at this age. On maudlin days he'd said he'd live no longer than she had, and he composed a "suggestion for an epitaph" that year:

> Now I've laid me down to die
> I pray my neighbors not to pry
> Too deeply into sins that I
> Not only cannot here deny
> But much enjoyed as life flew by.

He was not, however, so resigned to imminent death that he made out a will, as his L.A. lawyer had for years been urging him. More refused to buy life insurance, which he called "death insurance."[44] Maybe the pain of being excluded from his own father's bequests had made him bitter about all inheritance. Maybe it was the idea of being more valuable to his family in death than in life that he couldn't bear. Preston must also have hated to consider the possibility of his loved ones going on without him, and for this egoism they would all pay dearly. But probably the strongest reason why Preston did not insure for the future of Sandy and Preston and Tom-Tom and Louise and Mon is that, for all his morbidness, he could not really believe he'd die unredeemed for his sufferings. Luck and his own wits would yet win the day. Insurance policies, like union contracts, were for the lesser man.

In early December, Sturges wrote asking for help to Eleanor Hutton, who was now married to the musician Leon Barzin, and living very close to the Boulevard Berthier on rue de Monceau. At the time of their divorce, Preston had told Eleanor's uncle she owed him $90,000, apparently for his investments in their townhouse, though he'd promised never to ask her for anything unless he was "ill or desperate." Now, he was certainly both, but it was also nearly thirty years since he'd last spoken to Eleanor, and the handwritten letter Preston wrote speaks to his own embittered state of mind rather than any real hope of obtaining money. Indeed, his tone was guaranteed to put off his ex-wife, whom he still could not help needling about her privileged childhood. The former third highest-paid man in America unabashedly informed her: "So far as I know nothing has ever happened between the only wealthy person I ever knew well, and myself, which would prevent my turning to you finding myself, suddenly, in a gruesome situation."[45] Needless to say, she did not reply.

But, two weeks before Christmas, he did receive what at the time seemed a great stroke of good fortune: a cable asking him to come immediately to New York to direct a new Broadway comedy called *The Golden Fleecing*, set on a U.S. Navy ship docked in Venice. This was about all Preston knew of the script when he said yes to the offer. It was enough, he must have thought, that the producers, Elliott Nugent and Courtney Burr, who'd also produced *The Seven Year Itch*, had money to spend. They immediately sent him a check, which didn't bounce, and he arrived at the Algonquin Hotel on Christmas Eve, grateful for the cash, grateful for the work, grateful to be invited to America.

The man who'd insisted on summoning Preston from Paris was the author of *The Golden Fleecing*, Lorenzo Semple, Jr. Like Peter Lawrence, Semple was an admirer of Sturges's Paramount comedies, and like *Carnival in Flanders*, his play was in trouble. The director, Elliott Nugent, who was also one of the two producers, had been hospitalized for a nervous breakdown. No one could say when he'd be well and, with large investments riding on the production, a replacement was needed at once. The second producer, Courtney Burr, bowed to Semple's enthusiasm for Sturges. "We are all so happy you are arriving and I am looking forward to lots of fun, to say nothing of money," Courtney wrote Preston at the Algonquin.[1]

But from the start their collaboration was joyless. Sturges promptly fired most of Nugent's cast, then began arguing with Semple. "Sturges had not staged a play in a very long time, but he was a man accustomed to dominance, and his own unsureness was making him testy," Chris Chase, whom Preston cast as the ingenue, wrote in her memoir. "He would turn his irritability on the playwright, rejecting lines and scenes—'I've been around a lot longer than you, and I know about comedy and this isn't funny.' The writer would go home and rewrite, but he couldn't please the director. Sturges picked at him until he succeeded in alienating the person who'd been his most fervent admirer."[2] Furthermore, Sturges alienated the cast, Chase says, by assuming a superior attitude and tending to dwell on single words when entire scenes weren't working.

Preston was also difficult after rehearsals. He asked Chris Chase to dinner at "21," but insisted on leaving when the man at the door didn't recognize him. They proceeded on to a small Spanish restaurant in the Village, where Preston made a great fuss about the inferior brandy—obviously the best they had. But after dinner, when she and Preston walked leisurely through the

Village, and he showed her where the Maison Desti had been on Ninth Street and told stories about his youth, she saw another side to this proud man and felt sorry for his humiliations.[3] She felt sorrier still when Elliott Nugent returned a few weeks into Sturges's rehearsal and fired Sturges and his entire cast on the spot. (When *The Golden Fleecing* opened on Broadway, ten months later, Abe Burrows—who'd also replaced Sturges on *Make a Wish*—was directing. It got mixed reviews and closed after eighty-four performances.)

Preston, who had not given up his Paris apartment, could now have returned to France. But he stayed on in New York, accepting a $7,500 advance to write an autobiography he was entitling *The Events Leading Up to My Death*[4] for a young editor, Robert Lescher, at Henry Holt Publishers. The Algonquin gave him an office for free. He hired a secretary and threw himself into the project. "This book is in no sense, as its title might lead mine enemies to hope, a farewell letter to the world," he began. "I happen merely to have noticed that everyone I was privileged to observe behaved as if life were going to continue forever. Unfortunately this does not gibe with statistics. Looking around me I discover sadly that practically everyone I knew fifty-five, fifty, or even a measly forty-five years ago, is gone from this earth, usually without a trace. . . . These regretted persons, or most of them at least, did not quit this gloomy globe because of untoward accidents or by the contraction of tularemia, psittacosis or some other exotic disease, but simply because they had reached the end of their lives . . . like butterflies . . . or snakes . . . or orchids."[5]

When he began telling his own history, Preston found that his childhood was what most compelled him. He wrote about his father and Aunt Kate and Chicago and, of course, Mary Desti. She was the one he returned to time and again. He told of her silliness and obsession that he should become an artist and her unpredictability; about her leaving his beloved father and her marriage to the horrid Turk and all the chaos surrounding her determination to follow Isadora everywhere and always. He spoke too of "the remarkable advantages my remarkable mother managed to wring from a reluctant world and shower upon the head of her unappreciative son."[6]

Preston wrote thirty pages in a month and told John Hertz, Jr., he thought he was learning the art of book writing.[7] His breathing problems were gone, yet Muriel Angelus, visiting him around this time, says he was like a helium balloon when the air runs out.[8] Writing a book about one's past was not real work so far as Sturges was concerned. With the constant demands from Los Angeles, he was desperately low on cash. If he got to the theatre or had a great meal, it was—as in his early days in New York—because some wealthy friend paid for him. Much of the time he just roamed around town. Sometimes he'd knock on the door of a friend as late as one A.M. and say, "You have to let me in because I have a lot to talk about."[9] He got in the habit of saving rolls off lunch trays for his next morning's breakfast. Often, when he had an appointment for cocktails with Robert Lescher, he'd suggest they go to a Blarney Stone because there you got free nuts and crackers and dips along with the drinks.

The news from home was saddening. Edmund Biden's daughter, for whose safety the family had moved from New York to Los Angeles in the first place, had died tragically in a car accident. Sandy could no longer depend on Preston's erratic checks and had started working for Bertie Woolfan—which had Preston convinced she'd soon run off with some young doctor Bertie knew. Mon's grades were so bad he couldn't get into college and was planning to enlist in the navy.

"I wish to God dear old Solomon Sturges were alive," Preston, feeling responsible for his son's plight, wrote Mon from the Algonquin, "because there was a port to go to in a storm—*there* was a man one could depend on *never* to let you down. When *Strictly Dishonorable* was first published I sent him the first copy dedicated as follows—'In sickness or in health—in poverty or wealth—your strength was there for me to lean upon. I wonder where I'd be—if in adversity—I had not had your strength to lean upon.' He was a fine man, the gentleman for whom you are named. I regret bitterly that *your* father is not the oak tree that mine was."[10]

But then, in the spring of 1959, suddenly things began happening. David Sarnoff at NBC hired Sturges to write, direct, and produce a pilot for a television series.[11] A Canadian theatre producer expressed interest in both *I Belong to Zozo* and a musical based on *The Gentleman from Chicago*. "CONTRACT SIGNED EVERYTHING LOOKS MARVELOUS ALL MY LOVE POPSIE," Sturges cabled Sandy on June 26, when the theatre deal was finalized. Eddie Bracken saw a lot of Sturges during this period and remembers a marked change in his demeanor as work began materializing.[12] The writer Judy Feiffer, who'd met Preston that winter, when everything was going wrong, also sensed a rejuvenation. He was very hopeful, she says, very confident he'd have a comeback. "He was like an old bohemian—buoyant, with great positive feelings." There were happy times that summer: one night a friend showed *The Palm Beach Story* on the roof of his house on Waverly Place.[13] Another time, Billy Rose took Preston to see Jimmy Conlin in *Anatomy of a Murder*. Charley Abramson lived across the street from the Algonquin at the Royalton Hotel, and he and Preston saw each other constantly, as they had when they were in their twenties.

It was not Christmas in July, of course. The upfront money Preston received was modest, and there lingered a residual sadness from all those disappointments in the past decade, including a now nearly two-year separation from his wife and family. Still, he'd recovered his optimism. Indeed, it had never *really* been lost. Even in early April, when he was at his lowest, Sturges had replied to a despondent letter from Louise:

> *My dear old friend,*
> I address you thus because, however life may have pushed us around, eventually to the distant ends of the earth, there is no doubt that we were very close friends at one time, that we went through much together, and that we had pretty much the same hopes and aspirations. You must have felt as saddened by Bill LeBaron's death the other day, for instance, as I did.
> Your letter is hopelessly depressing and wrong from every standpoint, Louise. *Of course* it is awful to have made a poor investment in real estate and to be chained to it without any apparent way out (the one hope for all of us, incidentally, is that I may come up with a hit play . . . or book . . . or movie . . . and as one who has done it before I am probably the one, despite my age, most apt to do it again) and at this point I have no useful suggestions to make. You'll just have to grin and bear it . . . and hope for a turn in luck . . . because *luck does turn*, and the dice *will* come up the right way sooner or later. *That* you can be certain of. The silly people who take an overdose of sleeping tablets or turn on the gas, or jump in the canal usually do it on the eve of their change in fortune. It *is* possible to be cheerful just because one is alive and breathing.[14]

It was, in any case, possible for Preston Sturges. And by Mon's eighteenth birthday, at the end of June, he was more than cheerful—he was his old effusive self. "Please felicitate your mother for having brought you into this world so safely eighteen years ago, and in such trying circumstances," he wrote his son. And he ended the letter: "I took a complete physical check-up the other day and to my horror the doctor told me I was good for another twenty-five years."[15]

He was not, however. He died a month and a half later, in his room at the Algonquin: in the small hours of the morning, working on his book. He'd had a quart of cole slaw and a couple of beers. He felt his indigestion coming on and said to his secretary, as he'd said a hundred times to Sandy, "I hope to God I don't croak tonight." Then, he became contorted with pain: a heart attack they later speculated. The secretary called the front desk. A doctor was rushed up to administer a shot of adrenaline. But nothing worked. He died almost immediately. Charley Abramson was notified and insisted there be no autopsy. It was Charley who had the sad task of cabling Sandy in L.A.[16]

What went through Sturges's mind in those minutes before he finally lost consciousness? Maybe what a bad joke this was—death turning up just when things were improving—defying all those truisms about the darkest hour. Or maybe this was somehow what he'd had in mind all the past year, what he hinted about in the opening of his autobiography—that he was simply reaching the end of his life, like Max Ophüls and Jack Buchanan and the butterflies. But it's nice to imagine that in the throes of inconvenient death, Sturges's mind might have turned at least briefly to thoughts of his mother, and been comforted by those fierce words of hers which, glorying at intemperance, refused to valorize pain or sorrow. There's no tragedy, she had said, in dying. The tragedy is never to have lived.

POSTSCRIPT

Shortly after Preston died, Louise sold her real estate and moved to Mexico, where she remained for fourteen years, until 1974 when she returned to rent a small cottage house in Ventura, California. She now lives in Pasadena. Mon became an actor for a while, appearing with Eartha Kitt in the movie *Synanon* and with Elvis Presley in *Charro!* But when his wife died, he dropped out of sight, leaving his eight-year-old daughter Shannon in his mother's care. Mon has since reemerged and is working as a carpenter in the Los Angeles area. Louise raised Shannon alone. Shannon put herself through college, first at Northridge and then UCLA. She possesses the Sturges love of drama and, at twenty-four, has a part in a soap opera (*Days Of Our Lives*) and dreams of grander things.

Sandy raised her two boys in the old house transplanted from Ivar Avenue. Little Preston, now thirty-nine, is a lyricist and screenwriter. Tom-Tom, thirty-six, is president of Chrysalis Music Publishing Company and has generated two books of Preston Sturges's screenplays, productions of *A Cup of Coffee*, and other projects commemorating his famous father. Preston and Tom are married; each has a young son. When her children left home, Sandy went back to school and got a law degree. Then, nearly three decades after that fatal night at the Algonquin, Simon & Schuster asked Sandy to edit Sturges's unfinished autobiography. The result, *Preston Sturges By Preston Sturges*, was published in 1990, gleaning critical acclaim and some profit too.

NOTES

Except in the very few cited cases, all the letters and screenplays and plays (or drafts thereof) mentioned in these notes can be found in the 125-odd boxes of the UCLA Special Collections Library in Los Angeles. Donated by Sandy Sturges, this voluminous material has been skillfully arranged by Lilace Hatayama who, with the aid of the enormously helpful collections staff, will steer researchers to the appropriate box and folder. Sturges's unfinished 1959 autobiography, "The Events Leading Up To My Death," which resides in Sandy Sturges's private collection, is identified as, simply, Autobiography. Sturges is referred to as PS throughout the notes.

Introduction
1. André Bazin, *Cinema of Cruelty*, p. 35.
2. James Agee, *Agee on Film*, Volume One, p. 76.
3. Manny Farber and W. S. Poster, *Negative Space: Manny Farber on the Movies*, pp. 91 and 104.

Chapter 1
1. Mary Desti, *The Untold Story*, pp. 22–26.
2. Autobiography, p. 19. Much of the ensuing information is also from that manuscript and from Mary Desti's book about her life with Isadora Duncan, *The Untold Story*.
3. Roger Shattuck, *The Banquet Years*, p. 26.
4. Desti, *The Untold Story*, pp. 30–31.
5. Autobiography, p. 81.
6. Desti, *The Untold Story*, p. 22.
7. Author's interview with Louise Sturges, 6 June 1984.
8. Autobiography, p. 28.
9. Letter from PS to Louise Sturges, 31 July 1959.
10. The book is called *Solomon Sturges And His Descendents*, by Ebenezer Buckingham.

11. Buckingham, *Solomon Sturges And His Descendents*.
12. Ibid.
13. *Laneville Courier*, 21 October 1864.
14. Autobiography, p. xxv.
15. Autobiography, p. 25.
16. Ibid.
17. Letter from PS to Darryl Zanuck, 11 May 1948.
18. Barbara C. Schaaf, *Mr. Dooley's Chicago*.
19. Autobiography, p. 231.
20. Ibid., p. 197.
21. Letter from PS to Mon Sturges, 25 January 1958.
22. Undated letter from Estelle Beer to Solomon Sturges.
23. Mary Desti wrote this to Preston in a letter from Woodstock on 13 January 1931, after she heard about the critical and box office failure of *A Well of Romance*, his only operetta.
24. Isadora Duncan, *My Life*, p. 57.
25. Lucretia M. Davison, "Bayreuth Revisited," *Theatre Magazine*, 2 October 1904.
26. Fredrika Blair, *Isadora*, p. 84.
27. Temple was the daughter of Isadora's brother, Augustin.
28. It is telling of Preston's peculiarly romantic nature that in a 28 July 1944 letter, he wrote Temple, "Although I have never been a very good letter writer, I have never stopped loving you."
29. Letter from PS to Temple Duncan, 6 February 1959.
30. Desti, *The Untold Story*, p. 47.

Chapter 2
1. Autobiography, p. 167.
2. Desti, *The Untold Story*, p. 47.
3. There's no record of this play which seems to have had a brief run in the summer of 1905 or 1906.
4. Autobiography, p. 78.
5. Letter from Solomon Sturges to PS, 1930.
6. Autobiography, pp. 25–26.
7. Autobiography, p. 81.
8. Autobiography, pp. 79–80.
9. Isadora encouraged her pupils to take her last name, and many, like Irma, did.
10. Irma Duncan, *Duncan Dancer*, p. 90.
11. Duncan, *Duncan Dancer*, p. 88.
12. Author's interview with Sandy Sturges.
13. Autobiography, pp. 81–98A.
14. Letter from Dorothy Hunt to PS, during the run of *The Guinea Pig*.
15. Letter from Isadora Duncan to Mary Fanton Roberts. This letter is quoted in Fredrika Blair's *Isadora*, p. 206.
16. Autobiography, p. 81A. Preston recalls his mother writing "The Vendor of Dreams" with her "suitor" José Velasquez, who was a serious composer from the Yucatan.

17. Letter from PS to Louise Sturges, 31 July 1959.
18. Isadora Duncan, *My Life*, p. 233.
19. Blair, *Isadora*, pp. 207–208. Much of this information on Paris Singer is gleaned from her chapter 19.
20. Letter from Paris Singer to PS, 5 July 1927.
21. Cable from Paris Singer to PS, 15 September 1927.
22. Blair, *Isadora*, pp. 207–208. Blair quotes from Georges Maurevert's account of the occasion.
23. Autobiography, p. 109.
24. Letter from PS to Vely Bey, 25 October 1946.
25. Autobiography, pp. 156–157.
26. Desti, *The Untold Story*, p. 61.
27. Autobiography, p. 167.
28. Autobiography, p. 2.
29. Autobiography, pp. 160–161.
30. Letter from PS to Vely Bey, 25 April 1946.

Chapter 3
1. Autobiography, p. 198.
2. Autobiography, p. 199.
3. Autobiography, p. 202.
4. Autobiogoraphy, p. 204.
5. Autobiography, p. 206.
6. Author's interview with Sandy Sturges.
7. Autobiography, pp. 209–210.
8. Autobiography, p. 214.
9. Desti, *The Untold Story*, p. 68; Duncan, *My Life*, p. 318.
10. Autobiography, pp. 219, 220.
11. Autobiography, p. 224.
12. Richard Schickel, *D. W. Griffith: An American Life*, p. 267.
13. Autobiography, p. 229.
14. Joseph Wood Krutch, *American Drama Since 1918*, p. 10.
15. Autobiography, p. 262.
16. Autobiography, p. 270.
17. Autobiography, pp. 306–307.

Chapter 4
1. Leslie Fiedler, *An End to Innocence: Essays on Culture and Politics*, p. 124.
2. Frederick J. Hoffman, *The 20's*, p. 43. Gertrude Stein is quoted.
3. Letter from PS to Marcel Pagnol, 25 March 1947.
4. Walter Lippmann, review of Mencken's *Notes on Democracy, Saturday Review of Literature*, 11 December 1926.
5. *Smart Set*, January 1921.
6. Letter from PS to Ward Morehouse, 20 May 1948.
7. Author's interview with John Huston.
8. Autobiography, pp. 315–316.
9. Author's interview with Sandy Sturges.

10. Donald Spoto, *Madcap: The Life of Preston Sturges*, p. 47.
11. Letter from Isadora Duncan to Mary Desti, 29 August 1924.
12. Letter from Mary Desti to PS, 16 June 1927.
13. Autobiography, pp. 331–332.
14. Undated letter from Estelle Godfrey to PS.
15. Autobiography, p. 333.
16. Autobiography, p. 336.
17. Autobiography, p. 351.
18. Autobiography, pp. 353–354.
19. Autobiography, p. 355.
20. Undated letter from Estelle Godfrey to PS (seemingly written in 1922).
21. Undated letter from PS to Estelle Godfrey.
22. Undated letter from PS to Estelle Godfrey.
23. Undated letter from PS to Estelle Godfrey.
24. Undated letter from PS to Estelle Godfrey.
25. Autobiography, pp. 338–339.
26. Autobiography, p. 258.
27. Undated letter from PS to Estelle Godfrey.
28. Autobiography, p. 361.
29. Author's interview with Sandy Sturges.
30. Desti, *The Untold Story*, p. 168.
31. Autobiography, p. 373.
32. Autobiography, p. 259.
33. Letter from the former Estelle Sturges to PS, 17 March 1930.
34. Letter from PS to Sandy Sturges, 22 July 1958.
35. Letter from PS to General Sarnoff, 20 April 1959.
36. Autobiography, p. 370.
37. Author's interview with Sandy Sturges.
38. Autobiography, pp. 373–374.
39. Author's interview with Louise Sturges, whose feelings on this subject are corroborated by others as well.

Chapter 5
1. Autobiography, p. 375.
2. Autobiography, p. 376.
3. Letter from PS to Louise Sturges, 6 April 1959.
4. Letter from Solomon Sturges to Mary Desti, 11 April 1927.
5. Letter from PS to Solomon Sturges, 29 May 1927.
6. Letter from Paris Singer to PS, 5 July 1927.
7. Krutch, *American Drama Since 1918*, p. 155.
8. Letter from PS to Ward Morehouse, 20 May 1948.
9. In a 28 June 1929 letter to Pemberton, Preston describes Gandolphi as a "great character"; in his Autobiography, p. 378, Preston says the set of *Strictly Dishonorable* was an exact replica of Tomaso's.
10. Both of these stories are in Sandy Sturges's private collection.
11. Autobiography, p. 383.

12. Jim Curtis, *Between Flops*, p. 36.
13. Blair, *Isadora*, p. 391.
14. Letter from Mary Desti to PS, 20 July 1927.
15. Letter from Mary Desti to PS, 16 September 1927.
16. Autobiography, p. 386.
17. Brander Matthews, *A Study of the Drama*, pp. 79–175.
18. Letter from PS to "Judy," 29 December 1931.
19. *New York Herald Tribune*, 24 February 1929.
20. Curtis, *Between Flops*, p. 37.
21. Letter from PS to Bianca Gilchrist, 13 February 1939.
22. Curtis, *Between Flops*, p. 42.
23. Sturges wrote this in an early (unfinished) memoir, also entitled "The Events Leading Up To My Death," which he began in 1944.
24. Letter from PS to Ward Morehouse, 20 February 1948.
25. *New York Times*, 29 September 1929.
26. "The Events Leading Up To My Death," 1944.
27. Author's interview with Louise Sturges.
28. Letter from Charley Abramson to PS, February 1933.
29. Letter from Charley Abramson to Bianca Gilchrist, 1932.
30. Letter from Charley Abramson to Bianca Gilchrist, 13 April 1933.
31. Curtis, *Between Flops*, p. 44.
32. Ibid., pp. 44–45.
33. Ibid., p. 45.
34. Alva Johnston, "How To Become A Playwright," *Saturday Evening Post*, 15 March 1941, p. 86.
35. Ibid., p. 83.
36. Curtis, *Between Flops*, p. 46.
37. Johnston, "How To Become A Playwright," p. 84.
38. Preston Sturges, "Zero Hour Approacheth," 4 January 1930, written on the eve of the opening of *Recapture*.
39. Johnston, "How To Become A Playwright," p. 84.
40. Letter from PS to Ward Morehouse, 21 June 1948.
41. Johnston, "How To Become A Playwright," pp. 84, 86.

Chapter 6
1. Cable from Brock Pemberton to PS, 2 July 1929.
2. Letter from PS to Brock Pemberton, 12 July 1929.
3. Undated letter from PS to Brock Pemberton.
4. Undated letter from Brock Pemberton to PS.
5. Brock Pemberton, "This Business of Getting a Hit," *New York Times*, 27 September 1929.
6. Ibid.
7. Ward Morehouse, *Matinee Tomorrow*.
8. Letter from the Dramatists Guild to PS, 25 June 1930.
9. Letter from PS to the Dramatists Guild, 25 June 1930.
10. Letter from Solomon Sturges to PS, 6 October 1929.

11. It is conceivable that Preston got the idea for these, as for some of the characters in *The Great McGinty*, from the Tammany tales Andrew J. McCreery told him in Westchester.

12. Letter from PS to Solomon Sturges, 20 November 1929. The fact that Preston invested in the stock market, even after the Crash, suggests that he shared his father's faith that the economy would soon recover.

13. Letter from PS to Solomon Sturges, 20 November 1929.

14. Letter from PS to Henry Henigson, 29 June 1949.

15. Letter from PS to John Hertz, Jr., 16 November 1947.

16. No official copy of the play remains. Preston's draft, clearly still provisional, favors the interpretation of suicide, but every review of the play alludes to the ending as an accident. The difference is important since suicide addresses the conflict while killing Pat off avoids it entirely.

17. Brian Henderson, *Five Screenplays by Prestons Sturges*, p. 25

18. Letter from PS to Solomon Sturges, 30 January 1930.

19. Letter from PS to Solomon Sturges, 30 January 1930.

Chapter 7

1. Much of the information in this and the following chapter comes from an interview with Eleanor Barzin, the former Eleanor Hutton, at her Paris home on 8 December 1986.

2. Cable from Paris Singer to PS, 7 February 1930.

3. Undated cable from PS to Paris Singer.

4. I presume, from the correspondence with Singer, that Jacquet accompanied Preston to Palm Beach, though no mention is made of his presence during Preston's visit.

5. Undated letter from PS to Eleanor Hutton, March 1930. The italics are mine.

6. Undated letter from PS to Eleanor Hutton, March 1930.

7. This letter from Edmund Biden to the Huttons is dated 25 June, but it seems likely it was sent earlier in 1930.

8. Letter from PS to Eleanor Hutton, 10 March 1930.

9. Letter from PS to Eleanor Hutton, 6 March 1930.

10. Undated letter from Eleanor Hutton to PS, March 1930.

11. Letter from PS to Eleanor Hutton, 17 March 1930.

12. Undated letter from PS to Eleanor Hutton, March 1930.

13. Letter from PS to Paris Singer, 10 March 1930.

14. What Jacquet specifically objected to here was the campy "marriage stuff" in the chorus.

15. Undated letter from PS to Eleanor Hutton, March 1930.

16. Author's interview with Sandy Sturges.

17. Curtis, *Between Flops*, p. 64.

18. PS wrote Solomon Sturges about the yacht club and his "cruiser" on 7 April 1930. Solomon wrote back, "You say you bought a cruiser. Just what is that. A steamship or a sail-boat? I will not make any date with you yet."

19. Author's interview with Eleanor Barzin, 8 December 1986. Eleanor recalls of this episode: "Mother kept eyeing the bracelet. She said, 'Where did you get

that?' And I told her, my husband gave it to me. And she said, 'I want to look at this.' And you know what she wanted? She went to Paris, and she wanted a bracelet as big as mine."

20. Letter from PS to Billy Rose, 1 March 1945.
21. Letter from Solomon Sturges to PS, 5 February 1945. This letter, specifically addressing the box office failure of *Recapture*, is consistent with Solomon's attitude toward Preston's writing.
22. Letter from Mary Desti to PS, 13 January 1931.
23. Preston told his father in a letter (23 May 1931) that Mary instructed him "to make a little opening in the turf of her mother's grave and mix the ashes in."
24. Cable from the Singers to PS, 14 April 1931.
25. PS to the former Eleanor Struges, 1937.

Chapter 8

1. Eleanor says she went into debt paying off the bills for both the house and Preston's expensive decoration.
2. Undated letter from Marion Whitely to PS.
3. Preston's first letter to Eleanor after her departure, summer of 1931.
4. Letter from PS to Solomon Sturges, 24 August 1931.
5. In an early draft of *Unfaithfully Yours*, Sir Alfred, obviously deceiving himself, professes: "I have no faintest wish or desire to think of myself as the lord and master of that dream of loveliness reclining in the next room. . . . When I was very young and first married I tried out that role. . . . I just want to be the favorite man . . . the one she is fondest of . . . the lover not the proprietor . . . o-o-oh . . . the lover-in-*law*, in all probability, since this is the twentieth century and it's always nicer for the children . . . but still: the lover."
6. Letter from PS to Solomon Sturges, 6 January 1932.
7. *New York Times*, 5 June 1932.
8. Letter from PS to Henry Henigson, 23 May 1955.
9. Like so many of Sturges's black characters, Julius is a happy-go-lucky stereotype.
10. Letter from Pemberton to PS, 3 August 1931.
11. Letter from PS to Pemberton, 31 August 1931.
12. Letter from PS to Jimmy and Dorothy Conlin, 5 September 1958.
13. Letter from PS to Eleanor Sturges, 11 September 1931.
14. Curtis, *Between Flops*, p. 68.
15. Letter from PS to Solomon Sturges, 9 September 1931.
16. Ibid.
17. Letter from PS to Eleanor Sturges, 11 September 1931.
18. Curtis, *Between Flops*, pp. 69–70.
19. Author's interview with Eleanor Barzin, 8 December 1986.
20. Letter from PS to Eleanor Sturges, 8 March 1932.
21. Letter from Brock Pemberton to PS, 28 November 1931.
22. Author's interview with Mary Orr, fall 1985. An interesting footnote to Ms. Orr's story is that she was the author of the original story upon which Joseph Mankiewicz based *All About Eve*.
23. Letter from PS to Solomon, 8 March 1932.

24. Undated letter from Solomon Sturges to PS around May 1932.
25. Undated letter from Eleanor to PS.
26. Agreement between PS and A. C. Blumenthal, 1 April 1932.
27. Letter from Bianca Gilchrist to Solomon Sturges, 24 May 1932.
28. Cable from PS to Mr. Bickerton, 19 May 1932.
29. This is mentioned in Eleanor's undated correspondence with PS, 1931–1932.
30. Author's interview with Louise Sturges.
31. Letter from PS to the former Estelle Sturges, 6 July 1932.
32. Letter from PS to Harry Close, 4 May 1933.
33. Letter from PS to the former Estelle Sturges, 6 July 1932.

Chapter 9
1. Letter from PS to Solomon Sturges, 6 January 1932.
2. William Cole and George Plimpton, "S. J. Perelman," *Writers At Work: The Paris Review Interviews*, p. 252.
3. Cable from Walter Wanger to PS, 12 May 1930.
4. "The Events Leading Up to My Death," 1944.
5. Author's interview with Sandy Sturges.
6. Elmer Thompson's well-being was a central issue of Preston's and Charley's correspondence in the early thirties, and Eleanor came to visit Elmer when she was in New York.
7. Charley Abramson wrote Bianca, when she first arrived in Hollywood (undated letter 1932): "You can't imagine how much these months at 125 meant to me; these profitable talks with you and Preston and how much I do miss them."
8. Letter from PS to John Hertz, Jr., 16 November 1947.
9. Interviews with Edwin Gillette, Louise Sturges, and Priscilla Woolfan. Solomon Sturges's correspondence during this period shows an increasing affection and admiration for Bianca.
10. Letter from PS to Solomon Sturges, 29 September 1932.
11. Letter from PS to Charley Abramson, 23 September 1932.
12. Letter from Charley Abramson to Bianca Gilchrist, 26 November 1932.
13. Letter from PS to Charley Abramson, 23 September 1932.
14. The Laemmles and James Whale ultimately settled on a script very like the Wells story; their 1933 *The Invisible Man* is set in England and stars Claude Rains.
15. Memo from PS to Carl Laemmle, Jr., 11 October 1932.
16. Letter from PS to Charley Abramson, 22 November 1932.
17. Solomon Sturges's letter to PS on 13 May 1934 states explicitly a philosphy Preston's father had often urged before.
18. Letter from PS to Charley Abramson, 28 December 1932.
19. Letter from PS to Charley Abramson.
20. Letter from Solomon Sturges to PS around September 1937.
21. Letter from PS to Solomon Sturges, 23 March 1933.
22. Letter from PS to Mr. Geller of William Morris, 8 August 1932.
23. Letter from PS to Harry Close, 4 May 1933.
24. William Wright, *Heiress*, pp. 13–60.

25. Letter from PS to Carol Lorraine Noble.
26. Letter from PS to Solomon Sturges, 15 April 1933.
27. Letter from PS to Charley Abramson, 28 December 1932.
28. Interview with Jesse Lasky in the *Hollywood Reporter*, 22 February 1933.
29. *Hollywood Reporter*, 22 February 1933.
30. B. P. Schulberg, *Hollywood Reporter*, 27 February 1933.
31. *Hollywood Reporter*, 22 March 1933.
32. Letter from PS to Solomon Sturges, 15 April 1933.
33. Curtis, *Between Flops*, p. 86.
34. Letter from PS to Solomon Sturges, 24 June 1933.
35. And yet, in the surviving print I saw, Sturges's name remains at least as large as Lasky's and Howard's.
36. This oft-repeated story cannot be verified.
37. Letter from Charley Abramson to PS, 19 August 1933.
38. Letter from Solomon Sturges to PS, 27 August 1933.
39. This is part of a letter from PS to Solomon Sturges, IV, 2 January 1957. Interestingly, Preston concludes his point: "This did not change the relative merits of directors and writers (who are actually vastly more important) but it changed my salary and the way people treated me."
40. "The Events Leading Up To My Death," 1944.

Chapter 10
1. Letter from Charley Abramson to Bianca Gilchrist, 13 April 1933.
2. "The Events Leading Up To My Death," a rough draft for a 1944 memoir.
3. Letter from PS to Temple Duncan, 28 July 1944.
4. Undated letter from the former Eleanor Sturges to PS, 1933.
5. Letter from PS to the former Estelle Sturges, 8 March 1930.
6. Letter from the former Estelle Sturges to PS, 17 March 1930.
7. Letter from Solomon Sturges to PS, 8 November 1933.
8. Letter from Solomon Sturges to PS, 8 November 1933.
9. Letter from Solomon Sturges to PS, 16 October 1932.
10. Letter from Solomon Sturges to PS, 1 April 1937.
11. Letter from Solomon Sturges to PS, 13 March 1938.
12. Both Bianca and Preston professed this break a blessing in disguise, since the nose had always been crooked, and she was now impelled to have it fixed.
13. Interview with Nina Laemmle. This story was told to her.
14. Interview with Herb Sterne at the Motion Picture Home, 21 May 1986.
15. Bianca Gilchrist wrote Eleanor's Uncle Harry Close (in an undated letter) about the 1933 earthquake: "Although the earthquake didn't do any damage, we were all pretty much shaken up by it. Do you know that we still feel tremors occasionally? I was on the sixth floor of an apartment house at the time of the first quake and saw the building bend down and almost crack in two. The walls (interior) split in places and the light fixtures were bent askew."
16. Jim Curtis's unpublished interview with Rouben Mamoulian, 3 August 1977.
17. Undated letter from PS to Sidney Biden.
18. Author's interview with Louise Sturges, 6 June 1984.
19. Letter from PS to Solomon Sturges, 9 September 1933.

20. Letter from PS to Solomon Sturges, 27 September 1933.
21. Jim Curtis's unpublished interview with Rouben Mamoulian, 3 August 1977.
22. Author's interview with John Huston, 9 July 1984.
23. Undated letter from Bianca Gilchrist to Harry Close.
24. Letter from PS to Marcel Pagnol, 27 January 1949.
25. Letter from Solomon Sturges to PS, 1 August 1938.
26. Author's interview with Louise Sturges, 6 June 1984.
27. Undated letter from Charley Abramson to Bianca Gilchrist, 1932.
28. Letter from PS to Charley Abramson, 4 May 1933.
29. Letter from PS to Charley Abramson, 4 May 1933.
30. Letter from Charley Abramson to PS, 8 May 1933.
31. Cable from Charley Abramson to PS, 26 May 1933.
32. Cable from PS to Charley Abramson, 16 June 1933.
33. Letter from PS to Arnold Shroeder, 17 May 1939.
34. Letter from PS to Solomon Sturges, 24 June 1933.
35. Letter from PS to Sidney Love, 5 March 1939.
36. Letter from PS to Solomon Sturges, 10 July 1933.
37. Letter from PS to Arnold Shroeder, 17 May 1933. Arnold Shroeder never fully recovered from his brain injuries, and Preston would support him for the rest of his short life.
38. The information on Sturges's relationship with the Woolfans comes mostly from my two interviews with Priscilla Woolfan on 20 July 1984 and 7 January 1988, but also from my conversations with Louise Sturges and Sandy Sturges.
39. Letter from PS to Sidney Love, 30 August 1933.
40. Memo from PS to Carl Laemmle, Jr., 11 October 1932.
41. Memo from PS to Darryl Zanuck, July 1947.
42. Letter from PS to Jack Gilchrist, 10 July 1934.

Chapter 11
1. Letter from PS to Solomon Sturges, 9 September 1933.
2. Author's interview with Sandy Sturges.
3. Letter from PS to Solomon Sturges, 9 September 1933.
4. Letter from PS to Fred Meyer at Universal, 14 August 1935.
5. In a 5 May 1938 letter, Merritt Hulbert of the *Saturday Evening Post* rejected Preston's proposal, telling him, "The 'Biography of A Bum' strikes me—to be perfectly frank about it—as the outline of a pretty good story, but the little sides issues, the apparent irrelevancies which make a story like this come to life, are missing. Anyway, greatly to my regret, the boys do not feel that it would be worth your time to work this up as a serial for us."
6. Letter from PS to Sol Siegel, 22 September 1958.
7. Author's interview with Sandy Sturges.
8. Memo from Thalberg to PS, in Sandy Sturges's private collection.
9. It's interesting to note that in the movie version of *Child of Manhattan*, Madeleine and Vanderkill marry in the end.
10. Letter from PS to Solomon Sturges, 3 January 1934.
11. Letter from PS to Leonard Louis Levinson, 18 July 1938.

12. Letter from PS to Harry Cohn, 4 December 1933.
13. Letter from Julian Johnson to PS, 5 December 1933.
14. Letter from PS to Solomon Sturges, 3 January 1934.
15. Letter from B. P. Schulberg to PS, February 1934.
16. Letter from PS to B. P. Schulberg, February 1934.
17. Letter from PS to Solomon Sturges, 11 April 1934.
18. Jim Curtis's unpublished interview with Rouben Mamoulian, 3 August 1977.
19. *Hollywood Reporter*, 28 February 1934 and 6 June 1934.
20. Letter from PS to Solomon Sturges, 29 October 1934.
21. Letter from PS to Albert Deane, 2 March 1941.
22. Axel Madsen, *William Wyler*, p. 104.
23. Curtis, *Between Flops*, p. 98.
24. *Universal Weekly*, 16 June 1934.
25. Molly Haskell, *From Reverence To Rape*, p. 118.
26. Sturges's *Fanny* script was ultimately adapted for an MGM film called *Port of Seven Seas*, directed by James Whale and released in 1938. The film starred a disconcertingly aristocratic Maureen O'Sullivan as "Madelon" ("Fanny" seemed too risqué to the American producers) and hammy Wallace Beery in the pivotal role of César, played so movingly by Raimu in the Pagnol film. Still, Frank Morgan gave a superb performance as Panisse, the older husband, and the film is lovingly faithful both in spirit and word to the original. Though at the time it failed completely at the box office, this adaptation holds up well.
27. Madsen, *William Wyler*, p. 109.
28. Undated letter from PS to Solomon Sturges.
29. Madsen, *William Wyler*, pp. 109–110.
30. Cable from William Wyler to Henry Henigson, 1 February 1935.

Chapter 12
1. Preston amplified this point in a letter to his friend, John Hertz, Jr., telling him, "The only trouble with my writing articles is that if it took me as long proportionately as it does to write you a letter I would die of starvation between publications. The only thing I can write fast and with great ease is dialogue. In prose, which Le Bourgeois Gentilhomme I think it was, discovered he had been talking all his life, I am constantly looking for Le Mot Just," 17 December 1947.
2. Letter from Solomon Sturges to PS, 24 March 1935.
3. Though Preston, a great self-publicist, throughout the thirties frequently placed his own newspaper ads and "leaked" apocryphal stories about his imminently becoming a director, this agreement with Universal seems to have been authentic, for it's cited in the company's newsletter.
4. Letter from PS to Solomon Sturges, 16 March 1935.
5. Autobiography, p. 229.
6. Letter from PS to Captain Jud Allen, 25 August 1944.
7. Information for this paragraph comes mostly from an article in the *New York World Telegram*, 17 August 1935.

8. Curtis, *Between Flops*, pp. 102–103.
9. Letter from PS to Solomon Sturges, 20 June 1935.
10. Letter from PS to Solomon Sturges, 16 March 1935.
11. Letter from PS to Fred Meyer, 14 August 1935.
12. Letter from Fred Meyer to PS, 31 October 1935.
13. Letter from Edward Sutherland to Carl Laemmle, Sr., 7 November 1935.
14. Letter from PS to Carl Laemmle, Sr., 8 November 1935.
15. Letter from PS to William LeBaron, 26 April 1939.

Chapter 13
1. Many of the facts in this paragraph came from Douglas Gomery, *The Hollywood Studio System.*
2. John Houseman, *Front & Center*, p. 112.
3. Letter from Cecil E. ("Teet") Carle to author, February 1986. Information for this paragraph also comes from an article in the *New York Herald Tribune*, 13 June 1943, and from Gomery, *The Hollywood Studio System.*
4. Letter from Teet Carle to author, February 1986.
5. Author's interview with Edwin Gillette, 1 August 1984.
6. Budd Schulberg, *Moving Pictures*, p. 380.
7. Albert Bermel, *Farce*, p. 45
8. Author's interview with Edwin Gillette, 5 June 1984.
9. Author's interview with Edwin Gillette, 5 June 1984.
10. Letter from PS to Solomon Sturges, 15 July 1937.
11. The information in this and the following paragraphs comes mostly from two interviews with Edwin Gillette on 5 June 1984 and 1 August 1984.
12. Undated letter from Bianca to PS.
13. Interview with Edwin Gillette, 5 June 1984.
14. Letter from PS to Sidney Love, 27 July 1937.
15. Letter from Henry Henigson to PS, June 1937.
16. Undated letter from Marcel Pagnol to PS.
17. Curtis, *Between Flops*, p. 118.
18. Correspondence between PS and Joseph Copp, Jr., 10 November 1937.
19. Letter from PS to Solomon Sturges, 28 August 1937.
20. Letter from PS to Solomon Sturges, 9 August 1937.
21. The New York reviews appeared on 8 July 1937.
22. Author's interview with Edwin Gillette, 5 June 1984.
23. Letter from PS to Solomon Sturges, 3 May 1938.
24. *Los Angeles Times*, 14 September 1938.
25. *New York Daily News*, 29 September 1938.
26. *Variety*, 30 September 1938.
27. Cover article in *Redbook*, October 1938.
28. Letter from Solomon Sturges to PS, undated but from around September 1937.
29. Letter from PS to Solomon Sturges, 5 November 1937.
30. Letter from PS to Sidney Biden, 23 July 1937.
31. Memo from A. M. Botsford, 18 July 1938, in the Paramount Film Archives.

32. Paramount memo, 29 July 1938, in the Paramount Film Archives.
33. Paramount memo sent off with official contract, 1 September 1938, in the Paramount Film Archives.

Chapter 14

1. The project was never completed.
2. Undated letter from Bianca to PS.
3. Letter from Joseph Cobb, Jr., to PS, 26 November 1937.
4. Curtis, *Between Flops*, p. 119.
5. Author's interview with Louise Sturges, 6 June 1984.
6. Author's interview with Tally Wyler, August 1984.
7. Author's interview with Louise Sturges, 7 August 1984.
8. Curtis, *Between Flops*, p. 121.
9. Cable from Louise Tevis to PS, 26 September 1938.
10. Letter from Bianca Gilchrist to PS, 27 November 1938.
11. Letter from Bianca Gilchrist to PS, 16 November 1938.
12. Interview with Priscilla Woolfan, 7 January 1988, and Curtis, *Between Flops*, pp. 122–123.
13. Letter from Bianca Gilchrist to PS, 21 November 1938.
14. Letter from Bianca Gilchrist to PS, 16 November 1938.
15. Letters from Bianca Gilchrist to PS, 13 July 1939, 22 August 1939, 29 August 1939, 4 September 1939, and 23 January 1940.
16. Letters from Bianca Gilchrist to PS, 8 May 1940 and 20 February 1940.
17. Cable from Bianca Gilchrist to PS, 30 September 1945.
18. Cable from PS to Bianca Gilchrist, 19 January 1946.
19. Material in the above paragraphs was gleaned from interviews with Louise Sturges on 6 June 1984 and 7 August 1984 and from an interview with Edwin Gillette on 5 June 1984.
20. Preston retrieved this bar from a nightclub he bought, and immediately sold, so he could get Snyder's a liquor license.
21. Author's visit to the house, as well as interviews with Sandy Sturges, June 1984, and Louise Sturges, 7 August 1984.
22. Letters from PS to Bianca Gilchrist, 4 January 1939 and to Sidney Love, 23 January 1939.
23. Letter from PS to Albert Lewin, 6 February 1939.
24. Memo from Albert Lewin to William LeBaron, 27 April 1939.
25. William Boehnel, *New York World Telegram*, 18 January 1940.
26. Frank Nugent, *New York Times*, 18 January 1940.
27. Letter from Mitchell Leisen to PS, 10 January 1940.

Chapter 15

1. Johnston, *Saturday Evening Post*, 15 March 1941, p. 91.
2. Author's interview with Muriel Angelus, 16 November 1988.
3. Curtis, *Between Flops*, pp. 127–128.
4. Interviews with Edwin Gillette, 1 August 1984, Joel McCrea, 1 August 1984, and Nina Laemmle, August 1984.

5. Interview with Louise Sturges, 6 June 1984.
6. Interview with Eddie Bracken, 24 October 1988.
7. Curtis, *Between Flops*, p. 130.
8. Johnston, *Saturday Evening Post*, 15 March 1941, p. 91.
9. Johnston, *Saturday Evening Post*, p. 93.
10. Author's interview with Holly Morse, summer 1984.
11. Curtis, *Between Flops*, p. 132.
12. Author's interview with Muriel Angelus, 16 November 1988.
13. Johnston, *Saturday Evening Post*, 8 March 1941.
14. Letter from PS to Albert Deane at Paramount, 2 March 1941.
15. Author's interview with Muriel Angelus, 16 November 1988.
16. Author's interview with Muriel Angelus, 16 November 1988.
17. Letter from PS to Jack Gilchrist, 20 February 1940.
18. Seymour Stern, program notes for a subsequent release of *The Great McGinty*.
19. Author's interview with Edwin Gillette, 5 June 1984.
20. *New York Times*, 15 August 1940.
21. Profile of PS in the *New York Times*, 4 August 1940.
22. Johnston, *Saturday Evening Post*, 8 March 1941, p. 5.
23. Manny Farber, and W. S. Poster, "Preston Sturges," 1954 (from the essay collection *Negative Space: Manny Farber on the Movies*).
24. Curtis, *Between Flops*, p. 135.

Chapter 16
1. Letter from Charley Abramson to PS, 28 September 1939.
2. Letter from Robert Gessner to PS, 3 September 1940.
3. Letter from Henry Henigson to PS, 28 February 1941.
4. Solomon Sturges's will, dated 2 December 1939. Preston told Sandy Sturges that Solomon discussed the provisions of the will with him before having the attorney prepare the final draft. Preston told Solomon he was in full accord with Solomon's decisions. Later he said that he should have suggested to Solomon that Marie be the sole beneficiary during her lifetime, but that on her death, the principal should revert to the family (himself).
5. Letter from PS to E. B. Sturges, 14 January 1949.
6. Ibid.
7. Letter from Alexis Pillet to PS, 20 December 1940.
8. Letter from PS to Alexis Pillet, 18 January 1941.
9. Letter from PS to Sidney Love, 5 November 1937.
10. Author's interview with Mel Epstein, summer 1984.
11. Author's interview with Louise Sturges, 7 August 1984.
12. Ibid.
13. Sturges's patents and inventions, enumerated in box 52 of the UCLA Special Collections Library.
14. Author's interview with Holly Morse, summer 1984.
15. Paramount promotion material for *Christmas in July*.
16. Cable from Frank Freeman to PS, 11 September 1940.
17. Howard Barnes, *New York Herald Tribune*, 6 November 1940.

18. Archer Winsten, *New York Post*, 6 November 1940.
19. Bosley Crowther, *New York Times*, 6 November 1940.
20. Ibid.

Chapter 17
 1. Letter from Albert Lewin to PS, 17 January 1939.
 2. One of Temple Duncan's husbands was also named Angus.
 3. Author's interview with Sandy Sturges.
 4. Author's interview with Mel Epstein, summer 1984.
 5. Barbara Stanwyck, "The Most Fun I Ever Had," *Woman Magazine*, 12 May 1941.
 6. Letter from Cecil Teet Carle, 10 February 1986, pp. 6–7.
 7. Stanwyck, "The Most Fun I Ever Had."
 8. Telegram from Al Lewin to PS, 19 March 1941.
 9. Cable from John Huston to PS, 26 March 1941.
10. Bosley Crowther, *New York Times*, 27 February 1941.
11. Bosley Crowther, *New York Times*, 12 March 1941.

Chapter 18
 1. Author's interview with Sandy Sturges.
 2. Letter from Leo Calibo to Louise Sturges, 3 November 1942.
 3. Author's interview with Herb Sterne, 21 May 1986.
 4. Curtis, *Between Flops*, pp. 144–145.
 5. Much of the information about these parties comes from a letter sent to me by Nina Laemmle, June 1986.
 6. Jean Renoir, *Renoir—My Life And My Films*.
 7. Author's interview with Louise Sturges, 6 June 1984.
 8. Author's interview with John Huston, 9 July 1984.
 9. Author's interview with Billy Wilder, 31 July 1984.
10. Letter from PS to Sidney Love, 25 October 1939.
11. Letter from PS to Sidney Love, 6 October 1944.
12. Author's interview with Louise Sturges, 7 August 1984.
13. Letter from Nina Laemmle to author, 29 June 1986.
14. Letter from PS to the Screen Directors Guild, 30 August 1940.
15. Cable from PS to Buddy DeSylva, 1 May 1941.
16. Spoto, *Madcap*, p. 171.
17. Author's interview with Eddie Bracken, 24 October 1987.
18. Author's interview with Louise Sturges, 6 June 1984.
19. Author's interview with Sandy Sturges.
20. Author's interview with Holly Morse, summer 1984.
21. Many of my ideas on *Sullivan's Travels* were inspired by Robert M. Polhemus's book on the comic novel, *Comic Faith: The Great Tradition from Austen to Joyce*.
22. *New York Motion Picture*, October 1942.
23. Author's interview with Joel McCrea, summer 1984.
24. Curtis, *Between Flops*, p. 154.
25. Author's interview with Holly Morse, summer 1984.

26. Jeff Lenburg, *Peekaboo: The Story of Veronica Lake*.
27. Ibid.
28. Letter from Teet Carle to author, 1986.
29. Letter from PS to Solomon Sturges, IV, 18 June 1959. This was Preston's last letter to his son.
30. Interview with Holly Morse, summer 1984.
31. Bazin, *The Cinema of Cruelty*, p. 37.
32. Curtis, *Between Flops*, p. 158.

Chapter 19
1. Larry Reid, *New York Motion Picture*, April 1942.
2. Author's interview with Mel Epstein, summer 1984.
3. Letter from Walter White to PS, 22 April 1942. Yet, like so many filmmakers of his era, Sturges frequently played the black servant for laughs—note, for instance, the black chef's superciliousness in the early land yacht scene in *Sullivan's Travels*.
4. Letter from PS to J. Graham Hunter, 7 April 1942.
5. Letter from Vic Potel to PS, 12 February 1942.
6. Letter from PS to Bosley Crowther, 27 February 1942.
7. Letter from PS to the *New York Times*.
8. Letter from PS to Bosley Crowther, 22 July 1947.
9. Letter from Teet Carle to author, 1986.
10. John Houseman, *Front and Center*, pp. 21–22.
11. Carl Bode quotes from Mencken's letter to Dreiser on p. 358 of his critical biography, *Mencken*.
12. Letter from PS to "Jay," 29 April 1943.
13. Louella Parsons, 29 April 1941.
14. Author's interview with Joel McCrea, summer 1984.
15. Author's interviews with Louise Sturges, summer 1984.
16. Undated letter from Dalton Trumbo to PS.
17. Letter from Mary Desti to PS, 13 January 1931.
18. Letter from the Production Code Administration to Luigi Luraschi, 8 November 1941.
19. Letter from the Production Code Administration, 17 November 1941.
20. In Solomon Sturges's 14 April 1935 letter to PS, he quotes this article, saying only that it comes from a New York paper.
21. Curtis, *Between Flops*, p. 160.
22. Letter from PS to Rudy Vallee, 15 September 1941.
23. Curtis, *Between Flops*, pp. 160–161.
24. Letter from Teet Carle to author, 4 March 1986.
25. Letter from Teet Carle to author, 1986.
26. Mary Astor, *A Life on Film*, p. 170.
27. Author's interview with Nina Laemmle, August 1984.
28. Letter from Teet Carle to author, 1986.
29. Author's interview with Claudette Colbert, 4 November 1988.
30. Author's interview with Rudy Vallee, summer 1984.

31. Marie Beynon Ray, *Two Lifetimes In One: How Never To Be Tired: How To Have Energy To Burn*, 1940.
32. Ray, *Two Lifetimes In One*, p. 75.
33. Curtis, *Between Flops*, p. 165.
34. Author's interview with Louise Sturges, 7 August 1984.
35. Letter from Louise Sturges to PS, 1942.
36. Letter from PS to Edwin Gillette, 15 April 1943.
37. René Fulop-Miller, *Triumph over Pain*, p. 140.
38. Letter from PS to Ben DeCasseres, 16 July 1944. Here Sturges describes the film's opening scene, which was subsequently eliminated by the studio.
39. Author's interview with Joel McCrea, 1 August 1984.
40. Memo from Buddy DeSylva to PS, 14 April 1942.
41. Memo from Buddy DeSylva to PS, 14 May 1942.
42. Memo from Buddy DeSylva to PS, 17 August 1942.
43. Letter from PS to Sandy Sturges, 20 December 1957.
44. Letter from PS to Captain Jud Allen, 25 August 1944.
45. Archer Winsten, *New York Post*, 11 December 1942.
46. Kate Cameron, *New York News*, 11 December 1942.
47. Bosley Crowther, *New York Times*, 11 December 1942.
48. Letter from PS to Ben DeCasseres, 15 August 1944.

Chapter 20
1. Charlie Chaplin and Orson Welles were writing, directing, producing, and also acting in their films, but they had their own production companies, as for a brief while did Ernst Lubitsch (who had once had his own production unit at Paramount).
2. Alexander King, *Vogue*, 15 August 1944.
3. Ibid.
4. Author's interview with Priscilla Woolfan.
5. "The Events Leading Up To My Death," an unfinished memoir, dated 2 April 1944.
6. Letter from Mary Desti to PS, 13 January 1931.
7. Letter from PS to Mon, 18 June 1959.
8. Letter from Joseph H. Hazen to Paramount officials about his meeting with government officials.
9. Memo from the Breen Office, 21 October 1942.
10. The real "miracle" is that the Breen Office overlooked Trudy's highly suggestive name—Kockenlocker!
11. A "confidential" letter from Russell Holman to Paramount's Luigi Luraschi.
12. She was born Betty June Thornburg.
13. Author's interview with Eddie Bracken, 24 October 1988.
14. The information in this section comes mostly from my interview with Eddie Bracken, 24 October 1988.
15. Letter from Buddy DeSylva to PS, 16 December 1942.
16. Letter from Frank Freeman to PS, 6 November 1942.
17. Note from PS to Frank Freeman, 8 November 1942.

18. Letter from PS to Frank Freeman around 8 December 1942.
19. This letter from Louise Sturges to Preston is only dated "Friday," but it's clearly written in early November, probably 1942.
20. *Hollywood Reporter*, 12 February 1943.
21. Ultimately, Warners must have relented, for *A Connecticut Yankee in King Arthur's Court*, starring Bing Crosby, was made by Tay Garnett for Paramount in 1949.
22. Letter from PS to a Mr. Frank (explaining that he did not plagiarize Mr. Frank's idea in *Hail the Conquering Hero*), 23 October 1944.
23. Andrew Sarris, *Hollywood Voices: Interviews with Film Directors*.
24. Letter from PS to Sidney Biden, 23 July 1937.
25. Letter from PS to "Jay," 29 April 1943.
26. Sturges did some research on Marine Corps language and found that "Charlie Noble" is slang for the smoke pipe from the ship board galley and, according to the marine glossary, "a good thing to stay away from."
27. Paramount publicity notice.
28. These quotes are from a letter from Teet Carle (who discussed the incident with Ella Raines) to me, winter 1986.
29. Ibid.
30. Ibid.
31. Letter from PS to Frank Freeman, 14 July 1950.
32. Letter from Torben Meyer to PS, 26 March 1948.
33. Harold Hefferman, *Detroit News*, 25 August 1943.
34. Letter from PS to John Hertz, Jr., 18 July 1950.
35. A number of successful filmmakers, including Frank Capra and Orson Welles, formed their own (often short-lived) production companies at this time.
36. My information about Sturges's leaving Paramount comes from his own correspondence with John Hertz, Jr., and Frank Freeman and from a letter from Teet Carle to myself, winter 1986.

Chapter 21
1. Undated letter from Charley Abramson to PS.
2. Manny Farber, *New Republic*, 7 February 1944.
3. James Agee, *Time*, 14 February 1944.
4. James Agee, *Nation*, 5 February 1944.
5. Curtis, *Between Flops*, p. 190.
6. Undated letter from PS to Mr. Westhaver.
7. Brain Henderson, *Five Screenplays by Preston Sturges*, p. 685.
8. Letter from PS to Frank Freeman, 22 June 1944.
9. Letter from Buddy DeSylva to PS, 26 August 1944.
10. Letter from PS to Buddy DeSylva, 25 August 1944.
11. Letter from PS to Ben DeCasseres, 15 August 1944.
12. Bazin, *The Cinema of Cruelty*, pp. 41–44.
13. Bosley Crowther, *New York Times*, follow-up to his film review, 13 August 1944.
14. Especially insightful thoughts on *Hail the Conquering Hero* can be found in James Agee's reviews in *Agee on Film*, Volume One, André Bazin's review in

Cinema of Cruelty, Manny Farbers (and W. S. Poster's) 1954 "Preston Sturges" essay reprinted in *Negative Space: Manny Farber on The Movies*, Jim Harvey's Sturges section in *Romantic Comedy*, and Brian Henderson's introduction to the film in *Five Screenplays by Preston Sturges*.

Chapter 22

1. Curtis, *Between Flops*, p. 214.
2. Noel F. Busch, *Life*, 7 January 1946.
3. Ibid.
4. Curtis, *Between Flops*, p. 214.
5. Author's interview with Edwin Gillette, 5 June 1984.
6. Author's interview with Louise Sturges, 6 June 1984.
7. Curtis, *Between Flops*, p. 198.
8. *Time*, 1944.
9. Tony Thomas, *Howard Hughes in Hollywood*, p. 93.
10. Letter from PS to Howard Hughes, 9 May 1944.
11. Author's interview with Louise Sturges, 6 June 1984.
12. Letter from PS to Dudley Nichols, 1 July 1944.
13. Author's interview with Herb Sterne, 21 May 1986.
14. Richard Schickel, *D. W. Griffith: An American Life*, p. 596.
15. Letter from PS to Elizabeth Dickinson, 2 September 1944.
16. Sturges's proposal for *The Wizard of Whispering Falls*, 22 June 1945.
17. Critics reviewing *Miracle of Morgan's Creek* and *Hail the Conquering Hero* frequently compared Eddie Bracken to Harold Lloyd.
18. Tom Dardis, *Harold Lloyd: The Man on the Clock*, p. 160.
19. Letter from PS to Howard Hughes, 30 October 1944.
20. Letter from Henry Henigson to George Cohen, 22 June 1945.
21. James Agee, *Time*, 14 February 1944.
22. Mr. Waggleberry is a name play on *Christmas in July*'s Mr. Waterbury.
23. It's interesting to see how Sturges adapted this speech from his earlier notes on America.
24. Author's interview with Nina Laemmle, August 1984.
25. Letter from Jean La Vell to PS, 28 April 1945.
26. Letter from Torben Meyer to PS, 15 November 1948.
27. Curtis, *Between Flops*, pp. 204–205.
28. Cable from Bill Demarest to PS, 7 February 1948.
29. Much of the information in this chapter comes from an interview with Frances Ramsden, 21 May 1989.
30. Author's interview with Frances Ramsden, 21 May 1989.
31. Letter from PS to Margaret Hamilton, 23 October 1945.
32. Author's interview with Louise Sturges, 7 August 1984.
33. Curtis, *Between Flops*, p. 213.
34. Dardis, *Harold Lloyd*, pp. 119–121.
35. Harold Lloyd's Oral History, Elliott Nugent Collection, January 1959, housed at Columbia University.
36. Ibid.
37. Ibid.

38. Letter from PS to Iles Brody, 12 February 1946.
39. Author's interview with Joel McCrea, summer 1984.
40. Sturges's notes to himself after the Huntington Park Preview, 2 December 1946.
41. Memo from Seymour Stern to PS, 12 November 1946.
42. Curtis, *Between Flops*, p. 219.
43. Agee, *Agee on Film*, Volume One, p. 17.
44. The New York reviews appeared on 25 January 1951.
45. Dardis, *Harold Lloyd*, pp. 283–284.

Chapter 23
1. Notes for a letter from PS to Rollin Brown, 3 December 1945.
2. Donald L. Bartlett and James B. Steele, *Empire: the Life, Legend and Madness of Howard Hughes*.
3. Letter from Max Ophüls to PS, 23 December 1946.
4. Letter from PS to Max Ophüls, 27 March 1947.
5. Letter from Hilde Ophüls to PS, 1957.
6. Author's interview with Sandy Sturges.
7. Author's interview with Frances Ramsden, 21 May 1989.
8. Tony Thomas, *Howard Hughes in Hollywood*, p. 98.
9. Author's interview with Louise Sturges, 7 August 1984.

Chapter 24
1. *L.A. Examiner*, 30 April 1946.
2. Letter from PS to Louise Sturges, 31 July 1959. This letter was written a week before Sturges died.
3. Letter from PS to John Hertz, Jr., 4 November 1947.
4. Author's interview with Sandy Sturges.
5. Letter from PS to Bosley Crowther, 22 July 1947.
6. Noel F. Busch, *Life*, 7 January 1946.
7. Author's interview with Sandy Sturges.
8. Letter from PS to Mrs. Exie West, 19 February 1946.
9. Author's interview with Sandy Sturges, 18 July 1984.
10. Author's interview with Frances Ramsden, 21 May 1989, and letter from the Veterans' Administration to PS, 8 June 1948.
11. Much of this information comes from author's interview with Frances Ramsden, 21 May 1989.
12. Autobiography, p. 182.
13. Mel Gussow, *Don't Say Yes Until I Finish Talking*.
14. Letter from PS to Joseph M. Schenck, 16 April 1946.
15. Letter from Darryl Zanuck to PS, 20 February 1947.
16. Letter from PS to Darryl Zanuck, 24 February 1947.
17. Letter from Darryl Zanuck to PS, 20 February 1947.
18. Letter from PS to Vely Bey, 9 July 1947.
19. Letter from Darryl Zanuck to PS, 20 August 1947.
20. Draft of letter from PS to Darryl Zanuck, 25 August 1947.

21. Letter from PS to Darryl Zanuck, 25 August 1947.
22. Letter from Bianca Gilchrist to PS, 8 May 1940. It is a nice coincidence that Bianca made a brief trip to California just as Sturges was preparing to shoot *Unfaithfully Yours*.
23. Cable from John Hertz, Jr., to PS, 24 November 1948.
24. Letter from PS to Charley Abramson quoted by Curtis in *Between Flops*, pp. 69–70.
25. In Sturges's 1931 play there is also a character named Daphne, who—the seeming opposite of Sir Afred's wife in the film—is a bawdy, straightforward, call girl.
26. Louise Sturges says Preston's taste was "low," indeed. He was very distressed when she one year received a subscription to the symphony: "I had to sneak around him to go."
27. Letter from Rex Harrison to Darryl Zanuck, 19 November 1947.
28. Cable from Rex Harrison to Darryl Zanuck, 4 December 1947.
29. Rex Harrison, *Rex*, p. 87.
30. Curtis, *Between Flops*, p. 230.
31. Letter from PS to Bosley Crowther, 1 November 1947.
32. Letter from Darryl Zanuck to PS, 11 December 1947.
33. Seymour Stern, quoted in the *New York Times*, 11 July 1948.
34. Letter from PS to Darryl Zanuck, 3 November 1947.
35. In a nice reference to his part in *The Sin of Harold Diddlebock*, one of Kennedy's first gestures as Sweeney is to offer Sir Alfred a drink.
36. Draft of a letter from PS to Darryl Zanuck, 8 July 1947.
37. Memo from Darryl Zanuck to PS, 20 February 1948.
38. "Hollywood, The Panic Is Over," *Newsweek*, 10 May 1948.
39. Memo from Darryl Zanuck to PS, 27 February 1948.
40. Memo from PS to Darryl Zanuck, 3 March 1947.
41. Memo from Darryl Zanuck to PS, 6 May 1948.
42. Memo from Darryl Zanuck to his directors, 27 April 1948.
43. Letter from PS to Darryl Zanuck, 8 May 1948.
44. Letter from Darryl Zanuck to PS, 10 May 1948.
45. "Confidential" letter from Darryl Zanuck to PS, 11 June 1948.
46. "Confidential" memo from Darryl Zanuck to PS, 11 June 1948.
47. Letter from Darryl Zanuck to PS, 29 June 1948.
48. Harrison, *Rex*, pp. 92–93.
49. Cable from Darryl Zanuck to Spryos Skouras, 26 October 1948.
50. Memo from Darryl Zanuck to PS, 6 November 1948.
51. Letter from PS to Zanuck, 8 November 1948.
52. The New York reviews appeared on 6 November 1948.

Chapter 25
1. Letter from Bianca Gilchrist to PS, 26 April 1948.
2. Letter from Marguerita Dun to PS, 23 January 1947.
3. Letter from PS to Vely Bey, 25 October 1946.
4. Letter from Vely Bey to PS, 18 June 1946.

5. Letter from Vely Bey to PS, 14 June 1949.
6. Vely Bey's letter to PS is dated 14 June 1949. There is only a draft of Sturges's letter about the bank loan to Bey, dated 19 June 1949. It seems he decided not to proceed with it after receiving his stepfather's letter.
7. Letter from PS to Vely Bey, 11 June 1947.
8. Schulberg, hearing how Sturges felt about their disagreement, later wrote him (on 2 June 1949) a warm note, saying the incident had been "generated by wartime emotion" and was "on my part at least, entirely erased."
9. Letter from PS to John Hertz, Jr., 10 August 1948.
10. A reader's report on *The Beautiful Blonde from Bashful Bend*, 14 September 1948.
11. Letter from Darryl Zanuck to PS, 20 September 1948.
12. Letter from Darryl Zanuck to PS, 29 October 1948.
13. Letter from Darryl Zanuck to PS, 29 October 1948.
14. Letter from Darryl Zanuck to PS, 17 November 1948.
15. Louella Parson's interview with Betty Grable, 10 October 1949.
16. Letter from PS to Darryl Zanuck, 23 November 1948.
17. Letter from PS to Darryl Zanuck, 17 November 1948.
18. Letter from PS to Louise Sturges, 19 March 1949.
19. Letter from PS to Darryl Zanuck, 24 November 1948.
20. Letter from PS to Darryl Zanuck, 17 December 1948.
21. Letter from PS to Louise Sturges, 19 March 1949.
22. Gussow, *Don't Say Yes Until I Finish Talking*, p. 144.
23. *Variety*, 25 May 1949.
24. Bosley Crowther, *New York Times*, 29 May 1949.
25. Archer Winsten, *New York Post*, 29 May 1949.
26. Letter from PS to Rupert Hughes, 31 May 1949.

Chapter 26
1. Author's interview with Sandy Sturges.
2. Letter from PS to Dr. Block, 13 July 1949.
3. Letter from PS to Louise Sturges, 19 March 1949.
4. Letter from Louise Sturges to PS, 22 March 1949.
5. Cable from Louise Sturges to PS, 25 March 1949.
6. Letter from PS to Henry Henigson, 12 August 1949.
7. Letter from Henry Henigson to PS, 16 October 1949.
8. Letter from PS to Frank Freeman, 14 July 1950.
9. Letter from PS to J. J. Parker, 21 June 1955.
10. Letter from PS to Paul V. Coates of the *Mirror*, 18 October 1949.
11. Letter from PS to Henry Henigson, 29 June 1949.
12. Sturges's final script for *Nothing Doing*, 23 August 1949.
13. With mercenary Lucas Stone, who owns all three mortgages on Mrs. Jones's hotel, Sturges gets in a few digs at Joe DeBell who owned three mortages on The Players.
14. Letter from PS to Henry Henigson, 11 October 1949.
15. Author's interview with Priscilla Woolfan, 20 July 1983.
16. Curtis, *Between Flops*, pp. 236–237.

17. Letter from PS to Frances Ramsden, 8 July 1950.
18. All of the information about Frances Ramsden's impressions come from an interview on 21 May 1989.

Chapter 27
1. Author's interview with Ronald Durling, 15 November 1984.
2. Author's interview with Billy Wilder, 31 July 1984.
3. Most of the information for this section of the chapter comes from many interviews with Sandy Sturges.
4. Author's interviews with Sandy Sturges and Priscilla Woolfan.
5. Letter from PS to Victor Collins, 1952.
6. Letter from PS to Jimmy Conlin, 12 April 1950.
7. Letter from PS to Louise Sturges, 7 November 1956.
8. Letter from Caroline Wedderburn to Francis Ramsden, 1950.
9. Curtis, *Between Flops*, p. 254.
10. Author's interview with Ronald Durling, 1984.
11. *Newsweek*, 7 May 1951.
12. *Variety*, 26 April 1951.
13. *Newsweek*, 7 May 1951.
14. Author's interview with Eddie Bracken.
15. Sandy's first marriage had been annulled.
16. Author's interview with Ronald Durling, 15 November 1984.
17. Letter from Sandy Sturges to PS, 2 September 1953.
18. Author's interview with Sandy Sturges; and Spoto, *Madcap*, p. 223.
19. Samuel French, Sherwood's publisher, cabled Sturges that Sherwood was dismayed to learn his dialogue had been rewritten.
20. Letter from PS to Samuel French, 4 November 1951.
21. Letter from Milton Cashy to PS, 1 April 1952.
22. Letter from PS to Bosley Crowther, 16 November 1949.
23. Letter from PS to John Hertz, Jr., 14 November 1951.
24. Jack Roark's Beauty Pageant, KECA-TV.
25. Letter from PS to Peter Prince, 16 January 1949.
26. Curtis, *Between Flops*, pp. 262–263.
27. Author's interview with Sandy Sturges.

Chapter 28
1. Author's interview with Alida Carey, 5 October 1989.
2. Manny Farber, with W. S. Poster, *Negative Space*, pp. 89–104.
3. Author's interview with Sandy Sturges.
4. Curtis, *Between Flops*, p. 265.
5. Letter from John Parker to PS, 17 September 1953.
6. Brooks Atkinson, *New York Times*, 18 October 1952.
7. Curtis, *Between Flops*, p. 266.
8. Undated letter from Priscilla Woolfan to PS.
9. James Spada, *Hepburn: Her Life in Pictures*, p. 131.
10. A contract was signed 14 November 1953.

11. Author's interview with Sandy Sturges.
12. Author's interview with Sandy Sturges.
13. Spada, *Hepburn: Her Life in Pictures*, p. 131.
14. Cable from Lester Cowan to PS, 2 June 1954.
15. Letter from Lester Cowan to PS, 1 June 1954.
16. Letter from PS to John Weiler, 3 September 1956.
17. Author's interview with Sandy Sturges.
18. Letter from PS to Louise Sturges, 19 March 1949.
19. Because of a series of misunderstandings, the interview never took place.
20. Interview with Sandy Sturges.
21. Letter from PS to Charley Abramson, 19 January 1957.
22. Letter from Mon Sturges to PS, 2 July 1954.
23. Undated 1954 letter from Priscilla Woolfan to PS.
24. Letter from Priscilla Woolfan to PS, 4 December 1955.
25. Undated 1954 letter from Priscilla Woolfan to PS.
26. *Time*, 19 July 1954.
27. Undated letter from William Wyler to PS.
28. Letter from PS to Marcel Pagnol, 25 March 1947.
29. Alida Carey, "This Cockeyed Caravan: A Preston Sturges Memoir," *North American Review*, December 1988.
30. Letter from PS to Dink Templeton, 6 April 1954.
31. Letter from PS to John Parker, 21 June 1955.
32. Letter from PS to a woman identified as "Judy," 29 December 1931.
33. Letter from PS to Walter Reade, 12 August 1957.
34. Cable from David Niven to PS, 18 January 1955.
35. My information about the shooting of *The French They Are a Funny Race* comes from an interview with Sandy Sturges and remarks Sturges made to reporters.
36. Alida Carey, *New York Times Magazine*, 2 December 1956.
37. Ibid.
38. Ibid.
39. Curtis, *Between Flops*, p. 293. He discusses a BBC radio interview with Sturges.
40. Carey, *New York Times*, 2 December 1956, quoting the *International Herald Tribune*.
41. Letter from PS to Walter Reade, 16 February 1957.
42. The line in "Mademoiselle from Armentières" goes, "The French they are a funny race—they fight with their feet, and fuck with their face."
43. Letter from PS to Bosley Crowther, 2 February 1957.
44. Letter from PS to Archer Winsten, 26 April 1957.
45. Letter from PS to Charley Abramson, 19 January 1957.
46. Archer Winsten, *New York Post*, 28 May 1957.
47. Manny Farber (with W. S. Poster), *Negative Space: Manny Farber on the Movies*, pp. 89–90.
48. Andrew Sarris, "Hail The Conquering Sturges," *Village Voice*, 10 September 1979.
49. Letter from PS to Frank Kassler, 20 May 1957.
50. Letter from PS to Priscilla Woolfan, 15 March 1958.

Chapter 29

1. Letter from PS to Grace Barnett, 3 September 1956.
2. Isadora Duncan, *My Life*, p. 79.
3. Undated letter from Mon Sturges to PS.
4. Letter from PS to Mon Sturges, 2 January 1957.
5. Letter from Priscilla Woolfan to PS, 5 May 1947.
6. Author's interview with Sandy Sturges; and Spoto, *Madcap*, pp. 241–244.
7. Letter from PS to Charley Abramson, 15 July 1956.
8. Letter from PS to Jim Henaghan, 20 May 1957.
9. Letter from PS to Priscilla and Bertie Woolfan, 27 March 1957.
10. The film was released in 1960 as *Surprise Package*.
11. Letter from PS to Stanley Donen, 7 December 1958.
12. Author's interview with Sandy Sturges.
13. Undated letter from Priscilla Woolfan to PS.
14. Author's interview with Sandy Sturges.
15. Letter from Sandy Sturges to PS, 17 February 1958.
16. Letter from PS to Sandy Sturges, 29 July 1957.
17. Letter from PS to Sandy Sturges, 19 August 1957.
18. Letter from Priscilla Woolfan to PS, 16 August 1957.
19. Letter from Sandy Sturges to PS, 14 August 1957.
20. Letter from Sandy Sturges to PS, 14 March 1958.
21. Letter from PS to Sandy Sturges, 7 September 1957.
22. Letter from PS to John Hertz, Jr., 2 April 1957.
23. Author's interview with Frances Ramsden, 21 May 1989.
24. Author's interview with Tally Wyler, August 1984.
25. Letter from PS to Bika de Reisner, 28 July 1959.
26. Carey, "This Cockeyed Caravan: A Preston Sturges Memoir," pp. 60–64.
27. Letter from PS to John Hertz, Jr., 2 April 1957.
28. Letter from PS to Alida Carey, 1 September 1957.
29. Letter from PS to Mon Sturges, 1 October 1956.
30. Robert Shaplen's *New Yorker* profile was entitled "The Metamorphosis of Philip Musica" and ran in two parts, on 22 October 1955 and 29 October 1955.
31. Letter from PS to Peter Lawrence, 8 August 1957.
32. Letter from PS to Charley Abramson, 16 December 1957.
33. Letter from Charley Abramson to PS, 2 April 1958.
34. Letter from PS to Sandy Sturges, 25 March 1958.
35. Ibid.
36. Letter from PS to Jimmy Conlin, 5 September 1958.
37. Letter from PS to Sandy Sturges, 7 September 1957.
38. Letter from Sandy Sturges to PS, 24 April 1958.
39. Letter from Mon Sturges to PS, 28 November 1958.
40. Author's interview with Richard Leacock, 6 December 1988.
41. Letter from Sandy Sturges to PS, 29 April 1958.
42. Letter from Sandy Sturges to PS, 24 October 1957.
43. Spoto, *Madcap*, p. 247.

44. Curtis, *Between Flops*, p. 279.
45. Letter from PS to Eleanor Barzin, 7 December 1958.

Chapter 30
1. Undated letter from Courtney Burr to PS.
2. Chris Chase, *How to Be a Movie Star or a Terrible Beauty Is Born*, pp. 195–196.
3. Ibid., p. 197.
4. Sturges's memoirs, initially rejected by his publisher, were revised and edited by Sandy Sturges and published by Simon and Schuster as *Preston Sturges By Preston Sturges*.
5. Autobiography, p. 1.
6. Ibid., p. 21.
7. Letter from PS to John Hertz, Jr., 16 March 1959.
8. Author's interview with Muriel Angelus, 10 November 1988.
9. Carey, "This Cockeyed Caravan: A Preston Sturges Memoir," p. 64.
10. Letter from PS to Mon Sturges, 25 November 1958.
11. Curtis, *Between Flops*, p. 286. The series was to be called *It Happened Exactly Here*. Sturges's idea was to show some historically important spot—such as the theatre where Lincoln was assassinated—as it exists today. "A small amount of research will pinpoint not only the location of the theatre but the exact location of the box where The Great Emancipator sat. It may be the shelves of a grocery store today or the bathroom of a colored family's apartment or a place in the air over the roof of the garage," Sturges wrote Sarnoff.
12. Author's interview with Eddie Bracken, 24 October 1988.
13. Author's interview with Judy Feiffer, 23 January 1989.
14. Letter from PS to Louise Sturges, 6 April 1959.
15. Letter from PS to Mon Sturges, 18 June 1959.
16. Author's interview with Sandy Sturges.

WORKS OF PRESTON STURGES

The Guinea Pig (1929, play)

Author: Preston Sturges. Producer: Preston Sturges. Director: Walter Greenough. Settings: William Bradley Studio. Theatre: President, New York. Opening: January 7, 1929. Number of Performances: 64.

Miss Snitkin	Rhoda Cross
Seth Fellows	Robert Robson
Sam Small	Alexander Carr
Wilton Smith	John Ferguson
Helen Reading	Ruth Thomas
Robert Fleming	John Vosburgh
Catherine Howard	Mary Carroll
Natalie	Audree Corday

Strictly Dishonorable (1929, play)

Author: Preston Sturges. Producer: Brock Pemberton. Director: Brock Pemberton, Antoinette Perry. Settings: Raymond Sovey. Costumes: Margaret Pemberton. Theatre: Avon, New York. Opening: September 18, 1929. Number of Performances: 557.

Giovanni	John Altieri
Mario	Marius Rogati
Tomaso Antiovi	William Ricciardi
Judge Dempsey	Carl Anthony
Henry Greene	Louis Jean Heydt
Isabelle Parry	Muriel Kirkland
Count Di Ruvo	Tullio Carminati
Patrolman Mulligan	Edward J. McNamara

Recapture (1930, play)

Author: Preston Sturges. Producer: A. H. Woods. Director: Don Mullally. Settings: P. Dodd Ackerman. Theatre: Eltinge, New York. Opening: January 29, 1930. Number of Performances: 24.

Mrs. Stuart Romney	Cecilia Loftus
Rev. Outerbridge Smole	Hugh Sinclair
Monsieur Remy	Gustave Rolland
Gwendoliere Williams	Glenda Farrell
Monsieur Edelweiss	Joseph Roeder
Auguste	Meyer Berenson
Henry C. Martin	Melvyn Douglas
Patricia Tulliver Browne	Ann Andrews
Capt. Hubert Reynolds, D.S.O.	Stuart Casey
Madame Pistache	Louza Riane

The Big Pond (1930, film)

Producer: Monta Bell. Director: Hobart Henley. Dialogue Director: Bertram Harrison. Based upon the play by George Middleton, A. E. Thomas. Scenario: Robert Presnell, Garrett Fort. Dialogue: Preston Sturges. Photography: George Folsey. Editor: Emma Hill. Sound: Ernest Zatorsky. Musical Arranger: John W. Green. Studio: Paramount Long Island Studio. Production and Distribution: Paramount. Release Date: May 1930. Running Time: 72 minutes.

Pierre Mirande	Maurice Chevalier
Barbara Billings	Claudette Colbert
Mr. Billings	George Barbier
Mrs. Billings	Marion Ballou
Toinette	Andree Corday
Ronnie	Frank Lyon
Pat O'Day	Nat Pendleton
Jennie	Elaine Koch

Fast and Loose (1930, film)

Director: Fred Newmeyer. Dialogue Director: Bertram Harrison. Based upon the play *The Best People* by David Gray, Avery Hopwood. Screenplay: Doris Anderson, Jack Kirkland. Dialogue: Preston Sturges. Photography: William Steiner. Sound: C. A. Tuthill. Studio: Paramount Long Island Studio. Production and Distribution: Paramount. Release Date: November 1930. Running Time: 70 minutes.

Bronson Lenox	Frank Morgan
Marion Lenox	Miriam Hopkins
Alice O'Neil	Carole Lombard
Henry Morgan	Charles Starrett
Bertie Lenox	Henry Wadsworth
Carrie Lenox	Winifred Harris
George Grafton	Herbert Yost
Lord Rockingham	David Hutcheson
Millie Montgomery	Ilka Chase
Judge Summers	Herschel Mayall

The Well of Romance (1930, play)

Libretto and Lyrics: Preston Sturges. Music: H. Maurice Jacquet. Producer: G. W. McGregor. Director: J. Harry Benrimo. Settings: Gates and Morange. Costumes: Eaves, Schneider & Blythe. Theatre: Craig, New York. Opening: November 7, 1930. Number of Performances: 8.

Ann Schlitzl	Laine Blaire
Wenzel	Tommy Monroe
Frau Schlitzl	Lina Abarbanell
Gertrude	Elsa Paul
Mildred	Mildred Newman
Louise	Louise Joyce
The Grand Chancellor	Louis Sorin
The Princess	Norma Terris
Poet	Howard March
Lieutenant Schpitzelberger	Louis Rupp
Second Lieutenant	Syuleen Krasnoff
Third Lieutenant	Eugene Racine
General Otto	Max Figman
A Gypsy	Edis Phillips
Joseph	Joseph Roeder
A Waiter	Pat Walters
First Guardsman	Rowan Tudor
Second Guardsman	James Libby
Butterfly (the Cow)	Lo Ivan (Front) Ruth Flynn (Rear)

Child of Manhattan (1932, play)

Author: Preston Sturges. Producer: Peggy Fears. Director: Howard Lindsay. Settings: Jonel Jorgulesco. Theatre: Fulton, New York. Opening: March 1, 1932. Number of Performances: 87.

Miss Sophie Vanderkill	Helen Strickland
Eggleston	Joseph Roeder
Otto Paul Vanderkill	Reginald Owen
Spyrene	Ralph Sanford
Clifford	Charles Cromer
Flo	Judy Abbot
Madeleine McGonegal	Dorothy Hall
Gertie	Mitzi Miller
Buddy McGonegal	Jackson Halliday
Mrs. McGonegal	Maude Odell
Martha	Jacqueline Winston
Lucinda, Limited	Franz Bendtsen
Constance	Joan Hamilton
Myrtle	Eileen Bach
A Girl	Elizabeth Young
Yvette	Louise Sheldon
Lilly	Peggy Fish
Gladys	Mary Orr
Jewel	Geraldine Wall
Aunt Minnie	Jessie Ralph
Lucy McGonegal	Harriet Russell
Nurse	Florence John
Doctor	Alexander Campbell
John Tarantino	John Altieri
Charley	Alexander Campbell
Panama C. Kelly	Douglas Dumbrille
A Waiter	Charles Hubert Brown

They Just Had to Get Married (1932, film)

Director: Edward Ludwig. Assistant Director: Eddie Snyder. Based upon a play by Cyril Harcourt. Screenplay: Gladys Lehman, H. M. Walker (Uncredited: Preston Sturges). Additional Dialogue: Clarence Marks. Photography: Edward Snyder. Editor: Ted Kent. Sound: Gilbert Kurland. Make-up: Jack P. Pierce. Production and Distribution: Universal. Release Date: January 1933. Running Time: 69 minutes.

Sam Sutton	Slim Summerville
Molly	ZaSu Pitts
Hume	Roland Young
Lola Montrose	Verree Teasdale
Marie	Fifi D'Orsay
Hampton	C. Aubrey Smith
Radcliff	Robert Greig
Montrose	David Landau

Lizzie	Elizabeth Patterson
Fairchilds	Wallis Clark
Mrs. Fairchilds	Vivian Oakland
Rosalie Fairchilds	Cora Sue Collins
Wilmont Fairchilds	David Leo Tollotson
Bradford	William Burress
Mrs. Bradford	Louise Mackintosh
Langley	Bertram Marburgh
Clerk	James Donlan
Tony	Henry Armetta
Mrs. Langley	Virginia Howell

The Power and the Glory (1933, film)

Producer: Jesse L. Lasky. Director: William K. Howard. Assistant Director: Horace Haugh. Screenplay: Preston Sturges. Photography: James Wong Howe. Editor: Paul Weatherwax. Art Director: Max Parker. Sound: A. W. Protzman. Musical Direction: Louis De Francesco. Musical Score: J. S. Zamencik, Peter Brunelli. Costumes: Rita Kaufman. Production and Distribution: Fox. Release Date: August 1933. Running Time: 76 minutes.

Tom Garner	Spencer Tracy
Sally	Colleen Moore
Henry	Ralph Morgan
Eve	Helen Vinson
Tom Garner, Jr.	Clifford Jones
Mr. Borden	Henry Kolker
Henry's Wife	Sarah Padden
Tom (the Boy)	Billy O'Brien
Henry (the Boy)	Cullen Johnston
Mulligan	J. Farrell MacDonald
Edward	Robert Warwick

Imitation of Life (1934, film)

Producer: Carl Laemmle, Jr. Director: John M. Stahl. Assistant Director: Scotty Beal. Based upon the novel by Fannie Hurst. Adaptation: Preston Sturges. Screenplay: William Hurlbut. Photography: Merritt Gerstad. Editors: Phil Cahn, Maurice Wright. Art Director: Charles D. Hall. Sound: Gilbert Kurland. Make-up: Jack P. Pierce. Production and Distribution: Universal. Release Date: November 1934. Running Time: 106 minutes.

Beatrice Pullman	Claudette Colbert
Stephen Archer	Warren William

Elmer	Ned Sparks
Aunt Delilah	Louise Beavers
Jessie Pullman (Age 3)	Baby Jane
Jessie Pullman (Age 8)	Marilyn Knoylden
Jessie Pullman (Age 18)	Rochelle Hudson
Peola Johnson (Age 4)	Seble Hendricks
Peola Johnson (Age 9)	Dorothy Black
Peola Johnson (Age 19)	Fredi Washington
Martin	Alan Hale
Landlord	Clarence Hummel Wilson
Painter	Henry Armetta
Doctor Preston	Henry Kolker
Butler	Wyndham Standing
French Maid	Alice Ardell
Mr. Carven	Franklin Pangborn
Restaurant Manager	Paul Porcasi
Hugh	Walter Walker
Mrs. Eden	Noel Frances
Tipsy Man	Tyler Brooke

Thirty Day Princess (1934, film)

Producer: B. P. Schulberg. Director: Marion Gering. Assistant Director: Art Jacobson. Based upon the story by Clarence Budington Kelland. Adaptation: Sam Hellman, Edwin Justus Mayer. Screenplay: Preston Sturges, Frank Partos. Photography: Leon Shamroy. Editor: June Loring. Art Director: Hans Dreier. Associate: Bill Inhen. Sound: J. A. Goodrich. Production and Distribution: Paramount. Release Date: May 1934. Running Time: 74 minutes.

Princess Catterina	Sylvia Sidney
Nancy Lane	Sylvia Sidney
Porter Madison III	Cary Grant
Richard Gresham	Edward Arnold
King Anatol	Henry Stephenson
Count	Vince Barnet
Baron	Edgar Norton
Managing Editor	Robert McWade
Spottswood	George Baxter
Mr. Kirk	Ray Walker
Parker	Lucien Littlefield
Lady-in-Waiting	Marguerite Namara
Mrs. Schmidt	Eleanor Wesselhoeft
Doctor at Gresham's	Frederick Sullivan
First Detective	Robert E. Homans

484

Second Detective	William Augustin
Policeman	Ed Dearing
Spottswood's Friend	Bruce Warren
City Editor	William Arnold
Sergeant of Police	Dick Rush
Radio Man	J. Merrill Holmes
Gresham's Butler	Thomas Monk

We Live Again (1934, film)

Producer: Samuel Goldwyn. Director: Rouben Mamoulian. Assistant Director: Robert Lee. Based upon the novel *Resurrection* by Leo Tolstoy. Adaptation: Maxwell Anderson, Leonard Praskins. Screenplay: Preston Sturges (Uncredited: Thornton Wilder). Photography: Gregg Toland. Editor: Otho Lovering. Art Director: Richard Day. Production Designer: Sergei Sudeikin. Sound: Frank Maher. Musical Director: Alfred Newman. Costumes: Omar Kiam. Studio: United Artists. Production: Samuel Goldwyn. Distribution: United Artists. Release Date: October 1934. Running Time: 85 minutes.

Katusha Maslova	Anna Sten
Prince Dmitri Nekhlyudov	Fredric March
Missy Kortchagin	Jane Baxter
Prince Kortchagin	C. Aubrey Smith
Aunt Marie	Ethel Griffies
Aunt Sophia	Gwendolyn Logan
Matrona Pavlovna	Jessie Ralph
Simonson	Sam Jaffe
Theodosia	Cecil Cunningham
Korablova	Jessie Arnold
The Red Head	Fritzi Ridgeway
The Colonel	Morgan Wallace
Tikhon	Davison Clark
Kartinkin	Leonid Kinskey
Botchkova	Dale Fuller
Judge	Michael Visaroff
Judge	Edgar Norton

The Good Fairy (1934, film)

Associate Producer: Henry Henigson. Director: William Wyler. Assistant Director: Archie Buchanan. Based upon the play by Ferenc Molnár. Screenplay: Preston Sturges. Photography: Norbert Bodine. Editor: Daniel Mandell. Art Director: Charles D. Hall. Sound: Joe Lapin. Gowns: Vera West. Make-up: Jack P. Pierce.

Production and Distribution: Universal. Release Date: January 1935. Running Time: 98 minutes.

Luisa Ginglebusher	Margaret Sullavan
Dr. Max Sporum	Herbert Marshall
Konrad	Frank Morgan
Detlaff	Reginald Owen
Schlapkohl	Alan Hale
Dr. Schultz	Beulah Bondi
Dr. Motz	Eric Blore
Telephone Man	Hugh O'Connell
Joe	Cesar Romero
The Barber	Luis Alberni
Head Waiter	Torben Meyer
Doorman	Al Bridge
Moving Man	Frank Moran
Moving Man	Matt McHugh

Diamond Jim (1935, film)

Producer: Edmund Grainger. Director: A. Edward Sutherland. Assistant Director: Joseph McDonough. Based upon the book by Parker Morell. Adaptation: Harry Clork, Doris Malloy. Screenplay: Preston Sturges. Photography: George Robinson. Editor: Daniel Mandell. Art Director: Charles D. Hall. Sound: Gilbert Kurland. Musical Direction: C. Bakaleinikoff. Musical Score: Franz Waxman, Ferdinand Grofé. Gowns: Vera West. Make-up: Jack P. Pierce. Production and Distribution: Universal. Release Date: August 1935. Running Time: 90 minutes.

Diamond Jim Brady	Edward Arnold
Lillian Russell	Binnie Barnes
Jane Matthews/Emma	Jean Arthur
Jerry Richardson	Cesar Romero
Sampson Fox	Eric Blore
Horsley	Hugh O'Connell
Pawnbroker	George Sidney
Harry Hill	William Demarest
A. E. Moore	Robert McWade
John L. Sullivan	Bill Hoolahahn
Bartender	Lew Kelly
Brady (the Child)	Baby Wyman
Brady (the Boy)	George Ernest
Brady's Father	Robert Emmett O'Connor
Brady's Mother	Helen Brown
Brady's Aunt	Mabel Colcord
Secretary	Fred Kelsey

Station Agent	Charles Sellon
Physician	Purnell Pratt
Minister	Tully Marshall
Poker Player	Al Bridge

Next Time We Love (1935, film)

Producer: Paul Kohner. Director: Edward H. Griffith. Assistant Director: Ralph Slosser. Based upon the story "Say Goodbye Again" by Ursula Parrott. Screenplay: Melville Baker (Uncredited: Preston Sturges). Photography: Joseph Valentine. Editor: Ted Kent. Art Director: Charles D. Hall. Sound: Gilbert Kurland. Musical Score: Franz Waxman. Gowns: Vera West. Make-up: Jack P. Pierce. Production and Distribution: Universal. Release Date: January 1936. Running Time: 87 minutes.

Cicely Tyler	Margaret Sullavan
Christopher Tyler	James Stewart
Tommy Abbott	Ray Milland
Michael Jennings	Grant Mitchell
Madame Donato	Anna Demetrio
Frank Carteret	Robert McWade
Kit	Ronnie Cosbey
Mrs. Talbor	Florence Roberts
Otto	Christian Rub
Professor Dindet	Charles Fallon
Asst. Stage Manager	Nat Carr
Swiss Porter	Gottlieb Huber
Hanna	Hattie McDaniel
Designer	Leonid Kinskey
Juvenile	John King
Ingenue	Nan Grey

Love Before Breakfast (1935, film)

Producer: Edmund Grainger. Director: Walter Lang. Assistant Director: Phil Karlstein. Based upon the novel *Spinster Dinner* by Faith Baldwin. Screenplay: Herbert Fields (Uncredited: Preston Sturges). Additional Dialogue: Gertrude Purcell. Photography: Ted Tetzlaff. Editor: Maurice Wright. Art Director: Albert D'Agostino. Sound: Charles Carroll. Musical Score: Franz Waxman. Make-up: Jack P. Pierce. Production and Distribution: Universal. Release Date: March 1936. Running Time: 90 minutes.

Kay Colby	Carole Lombard
Scott Miller	Preston Foster

Mrs. Colby	Janet Beecher
Bill Wadsworth	Cesar Romero
Contessa Campanella	Betty Lawford
College Boy	Douglas Blackley
Stuart Farnum	Don Briggs
Fat Man	Bert Roach
Charles	André Beranger
Brinkerhoff	Richard Carle
Steward	Forrester Harvey
Southern Girl	Joyce Compton
Friend	John King
Telephone Girl	Nan Grey
Captain	E. E. Clive

Hotel Haywire (1937, film)

Producer: Paul Jones (Uncredited: Henry Henigson). Director: George Archain-baud. Assistant Director: Stanley Goldsmith. Screenplay: Preston Sturges (Uncredited: Lillie Hayward). Photography: Henry Sharp. Editor: Arthur Schmidt. Art Director: Hans Dreier. Associate: Robert Odell. Set Decoration: A. E. Freudeman. Musical Direction: Boris Morros. Make-up: Wally Westmore. Production and Distribution: Paramount. Release Date: June 1937. Running Time: 66 minutes.

Dr. Zodiac Z. Zippe	Leo Carrillo
Dr. Parkhouse	Lynne Overman
Phyllis	Mary Carlisle
Bertie Sterns	Benny Baker
Mrs. Parkhouse	Spring Byington
I. Ketts	George Barbier
Judge Newhall	Porter Hall
Genevieve Stern	Collette Lyons
Frank Ketts	John Patterson
Elmer	Lucien Littlefield
O'Shea	Chester Conklin
Switchboard Operator	Terry Ray
Reception Clerk	Nick Lukats
Mrs. Newhall	Josephine Whittell
Reilly	Guy Usher
O. Levy	Teddy Hart
Fuller Brush Salesman	Franklin Pangborn

Easy Living (1937, film)

Producer: Arthur Hornblow, Jr. Director: Mitchell Leisen. Assistant Director: Edgar Anderson. Based upon a story by Vera Caspary. Screenplay: Preston

Sturges. Photography: Ted Tetzlaff. Special Effects Photography: Farciot Edouart. Editor: Doane Harrison. Art Director: Hans Dreier. Associate: Ernst Fegte. Musical Direction: Boris Morros. Costumes: Travis Banton. Make-up: Wally Westmore. Production and Distribution: Paramount. Release Date: July 1937. Running Time: 88 minutes.

Mary Smith	Jean Arthur
J. B. Ball	Edward Arnold
John Ball, Jr.	Ray Milland
Mr. Louis Louis	Luis Alberni
Mrs. Ball	Mary Nash
Van Buren	Franklin Pangborn
Mr. Gurney	Barlowe Borland
Wallace Whistling	William Demarest
E. F. Hulgar	Andrew Tombes
Lillian	Esther Dale
Office Manager	Harlan Briggs
Mr. Hyde	William B. Davidson
Miss Swerf	Nora Cecil
Butler	Robert Greig
1st Partner	Vernon Dent
2nd Partner	Edwin Stanley
3rd Partner	Richard Barbee
Jeweler	Arthur Hoyt
Saleswoman	Gertrude Astor

Port of Seven Seas (1937, film)

Producer: Henry Henigson (Uncredited: Carl Laemmle, Jr.). Director: James Whale. Assistant Director: Joseph McDonough. Based upon the *Fanny* trilogy by Marcel Pagnol. Screenplay: Preston Sturges (Uncredited: Ernest Vajda). Photography: Karl Freund. Montage: Slavko Vorkapich. Editor: Frederick Y. Smith. Art Director: Cedric Gibbons. Associates: Gabriel Scognamillo, Edwin B. Willis. Sound Recording: Douglas Shearer. Musical Score: Franz Waxman. Costumes: Dolly Tree. Make-up: Jack Dawn. Production and Distribution: Metro-Goldwyn-Mayer. Release Date: July 1938. Running Time: 81 minutes.

César	Wallace Berry
Panisse	Frank Morgan
Madelon	Maureen O'Sullivan
Marius	John Beal
Honorine	Jessie Ralph
Claudine	Cora Witherspoon
Brueneau	Etienne Girardot
Captain Escartefigue	E. Allyn Warren

Boy	Robert Spindola
Customer	Doris Lloyd

College Swing (1937, film)

Associate Producer: Lewis Gensler. Director: Raoul Walsh. Assistant Director: Rollie Asher. Dance Director: LeRoy Prinz. Based upon an idea by Ted Lesser. Adaptation: Frederick Hazlitt Brennan. Screenplay: Walter DeLeon, Francis Martin (Uncredited: Preston Sturges). Photography: Victor Milner. Editor: LeRoy Stone. Art Director: Hans Dreier. Associate: Ernst Fegte. Sound: Harold Lewis, Howard Wilson. Musical Direction: Boris Morros. Costumes: Edith Head. Make-up: Wally Westmore. Production and Distribution: Paramount. Release Date: April 1938. Running Time: 86 minutes.

George Jonas	George Burns
Gracie Alden	Gracie Allen
Mable	Martha Raye
Bud Brady	Bob Hope
Hubert Dash	Edward Everett Horton
Ginna Ashburn	Florence George
Ben Volt	Ben Blue
Betty	Betty Grable
Jackie	Jackie Coogan
Martin Bates	John Payne
Dean Sleet	Cecil Cunningham
Radio Announcer	Robert Cummings
Skinnay	Skinnay Ennis
Slate Brothers	Themselves
Prof. Yascha Koloski	Jerry Colonna
Prof. Jasper Chinn	Jerry Bergen
Grandpa Alden	Tully Marshall
Dr. Storm	Edward J. Le Saint

With Bob Mitchell and St. Brandan's Choristers

Never Say Die (1938, film)

Producer: Paul Jones. Director: Elliott Nugent. Assistant Director: Harold Schwartz. Based upon the play by William H. Post. Screenplay: Don Hartman, Frank Butler, Preston Sturges. Photography: Leo Tover. Special Effects Photography: Farciot Edouart. Editor: James Smith. Art Director: Hans Dreier. Associate: Ernst Fegte. Set Decoration: A. E. Freudeman. Sound: William Wisdom, Walter Oberst. Musical Direction: Boris Morros. Costumes: Edith Head. Make-up: Wally Westmore. Production and Distribution: Paramount. Release Date: April 1939. Running Time: 82 minutes.

Mickey Hawkins	Martha Raye
John Kidley	Bob Hope
Jeepers	Ernest Cossart
Jasper Hawkins	Paul Harvey
Henry Munch	Andy Devine
Poppa Ingleborg	Siegfried Rumann
Prince Smirnow	Alan Mowbray
Juno	Gale Sondergaard
Mama Ingleborg	Frances Arms
Kretsky	Ivan Simpson
Dr. Schmidt	Monty Woolley
Kretsky's Bodyguard	Foy Van Dolson
Julius	Donald Haines
Chemist	Gustav von Seyffertitz

If I Were King (1938, film)

Producer: Frank Lloyd. Associate Producer: Lou Smith. Director: Frank Lloyd. Assistant Director: William Tummel. Based upon the play by Justin Huntly McCarthy. Screenplay: Preston Sturges. Photography: Theodore Sparkuhl. Special Effects Photography: Gordon Jennings. Editor: Hugh Bennett. Art Director: Hans Dreier. Associate: John Goodman. Set Decoration: A. E. Freudeman. Sound: Harold C. Lewis, John Cope. Musical Direction: Boris Morros. Musical Score: Richard Hageman. Costumes: Edith Head. Make-up: Wally Westmore. Production and Distribution: Paramount. Release Date: November 1938. Running Time: 100 minutes.

François Villon	Ronald Colman
Louis XI	Basil Rathbone
Katherine de Vaucelles	Frances Dee
Huguette	Ellen Drew
Father Villon	C. V. France
Captain of the Watch	Henry Wilcoxon
The Queen	Heather Thatcher
René de Montigny	Stanley Ridges
Noel le Jolys	Bruce Lester
Tristan l'Hermite	Walter Kingsford
Colette	Alma Lloyd
Robin Turgis	Sidney Toler
Jehan le Loup	Colin Tapley
Oliver le Dain	Ralph Forbes
Thibaut d'Aussigny	John Miljan
Guy Tabarie	William Haade
Colin de Cayeuix	Adrian Morris
General Dudon	Montagu Love

491

General Saliere	Lester Matthews
General Barbezier	William Farnum
Burgundian Herald	Paul Harvey
Watchman	Barry McCollum

Remember the Night (1939, film)

Producer: Mitchell Leisen (Uncredited: Albert Lewin). Director: Mitchell Leisen. Assistant Director: Hal Walker. Screenplay: Preston Sturges. Photography: Ted Tetzlaff. Editor: Doane Harrison. Art Director: Hans Dreier. Associate: Roland Anderson. Set Decoration: A. E. Freudeman. Sound: Earl Hayman, Walter Oberst. Musical Score: Frederick Hollander. Costumes: Edith Head. Make-up: Wally Westmore. Production and Distribution: Paramount. Release Date: January 1940. Running Time: 94 minutes.

Lee Leander	Barbara Stanwyck
John Sargent	Fred MacMurray
Mrs. Sargent	Beulah Bondi
Aunt Emma	Elizabeth Patterson
Frances X. O'Leary	Willard Roberston
Willie	Sterling Holloway
Judge (New York)	Charles Waldron
District Attorney	Paul Guilfoyle
Tom	Charley Arnt
Hank	John Wray
Mr. Emory	Thomas W. Ross
Rufus	Snowflake
"Fat" Mike	Tom Kennedy
Lee's Mother	Georgia Caine
Mrs. Emory	Virginia Brissac
Judge (Rummage Sale)	Spencer Charters

The Great McGinty (1940, film)

Associate Producer: Paul Jones. Director: Preston Sturges. Assistant Director: George Templeton. Screenplay: Preston Sturges. Photography: William Mellor. Editor: Hugh Bennett. Art Director: Hans Dreier. Associate: Earl Hedrick. Set Decoration: A. E. Freudeman. Sound: Earl Hayman, Richard Olson. Musical Score: Frederick Hollander. Costumes: Edith Head. Make-up: Wally Westmore. Production and Distribution: Paramount. Release Date: August 1940. Running Time: 81 minutes.

Dan McGinty	Brian Donlevy
Catherine McGinty	Muriel Angelus
The Boss	Akim Tamiroff

George	Allyn Joslyn
The Politician	William Demarest
Thompson	Louis Jean Heydt
Louie	Harry Rosenthal
Mayor Tillinghast	Arthur Hoyt
Bessie	Libby Taylor
Mr. Maxwell	Thurston Hall
The Girl	Steffi Duna
Madame LaJolla	Esther Howard
Chauffeur	Frank Moran
Catherine's Girl	Mary Thomas
Catherine's Boy	Donnie Kerr
The Lookout	Jimmy Conlin
Benny Felgman	Dewey Robinson
Manicurist	Jean Phillips
Cop	Lee Shumway
Pappia	Pat West
Secretary	Byron Foulger
Dr. Jarvis	Richard Carle
McGinty's Valet	Charles Moore
Policeman	Emory Parnell
Cook	Vic Potel
Watcher	Harry Hayden
Opposition Speaker	Robert Warwick

Christmas in July (1940, film)

Associate Producer: Paul Jones. Director: Preston Sturges. Assistant Director: George Templeton. Screenplay: Preston Sturges. Photography: Victor Milner. Editor: Ellsworth Hoagland. Art Director: Hans Dreier. Associate: Earl Hedrick. Sound: Harry Lindgren, Walter Oberst. Musical Direction: Sigmund Krumgold. Make-up: Wally Westmore. Production and Distribution: Paramount. Release Date: November 1940. Running Time: 70 minutes.

Jimmy MacDonald	Dick Powell
Betty Casey	Ellen Drew
Dr. Maxford	Raymond Walburn
Mr. Baxter	Ernest Truex
Bildocker	William Demarest
Schindel	Alexander Carr
The Announcer	Franklin Pangborn
Tom	Michael Morris
Dick	Rod Cameron
Harry	Harry Rosenthal
Mrs. MacDonald	Georgia Caine
Mr. Schmidt	Torben Meyer

Mr. Hillbeiner	Al Bridge
Mr. Jenkins	Byron Foulger
Mrs. Casey	Lucille Ward
Mr. Zimmerman	Julius Tannen
Mrs. Schwartz	Ferike Boros
Mr. Waterbury	Harry Hayden
Furniture Salesman	Vic Potel
Mild Gentleman	Arthur Hoyt
Large Gentleman	Robert Warwick
Thin, Sour Gentleman	Jimmy Conlin
Large, Rough Gentleman	Dewey Robinson
Cashier	Arthur Stuart Hull
Sophie's Mother	Esther Michelson
Patrolman Murphy	Frank Moran
Sign Painter	Georges Renevant
Porter	Snowflake
Man (Shoeshine Stand)	Preston Sturges
Secretary	Kay Stewart
Man with Telephone	Pat West
Secretary	Jan Buckingham
Porter	Charles Moore

The Lady Eve (1940, film)

Associate Producer: Paul Jones (Uncredited: Albert Lewin). Director: Preston Sturges. Assistant Director: Mel Epstein. Based upon the story "Two Bad Hats" by Monckton Hoffe. Screenplay: Preston Sturges. Photography: Victor Milner. Editor: Stuart Gilmore. Art Director: Hans Dreier. Associate: Ernst Fegte. Sound: Harry Lindgren, Don Johnson. Musical Direction: Sigmund Krumgold. Costumes: Edith Head. Make-up: Wally Westmore. Production and Distribution: Paramount. Release Date: February 1941. Running Time: 97 minutes.

Jean	Barbara Stanwyck
Charles Pike	Henry Fonda
"Colonel" Harrington	Charles Coburn
Mr. Pike	Eugene Pallette
Muggsy (Ambrose Murgatroyd)	William Demarest
Sir Alfred McGlennan-Keith	Eric Blore
Gerald	Melville Cooper
Martha	Martha O'Driscoll
Mrs. Pike	Janet Beecher
Burrows	Robert Greig
Gertrude	Dora Clement
Pike's Chef	Luis Alberni
Bartender	Frank Moran

Guest at Party	Evelyn Beresford
Guest at Party	Arthur Stuart Hull
Piano Tuner	Harry Rosenthal
Lawyer	Julius Tannen
Lawyer at Telephone	Arthur Hoyt
Steward	Jimmy Conlin
Steward	Al Bridge
Steward	Vic Potel
Wife	Esther Michelson
Husband	Robert Dudley
Purser	Torben Meyer
Passenger	Robert Warwick

New York Town (1941, film)

Producer: Anthony Veiller. Director: Charles Vidor (Uncredited: Preston Sturges). Assistant Director: Stanley Goldsmith. Based upon a story by Jo Swerling. Screenplay: Lewis Meltzer (Uncredited: Preston Sturges). Photography: Charles Schoenbaum. Editor: Doane Harrison. Art Director: Hans Dreier. Associate: William Pereira. Sound: Hugo Grenzbach. Musical Direction: Sigmund Krumgold. Musical Score: Leo Shuken. Costumes: Edith Head. Make-up: Wally Westmore. Production and Distribution: Paramount. Release Date: November 1941. Running Time: 94 minutes.

Victor Ballard	Fred MacMurray
Alexandra Curtis	Mary Martin
Paul Bryson, Jr.	Robert Preston
Stefan Janowski	Akim Tamiroff
Sam	Lynne Overman
Vivian	Eric Blore
Shipboard Host	Cecil Kellaway
Gus Nelson	Fuzzy Knight
Bender	Oliver Prickett
Master of Ceremonies	Ken Carpenter
Toots O'Day	Iris Adrian
Brody	Edward J. McNamara
Henry	Sam McDaniel
Peddler	Philip Van Zandt

Sullivan's Travels (1941, film)

Associate Producer: Paul Jones. Director: Preston Sturges. Assistant Director: Holly Morse. Screenplay: Preston Sturges. Photography: John F. Seitz. Special Effects Photography: Farciot Edouart. Editor: Stuart Gilmore. Art Director: Hans Dreier. Associate: Earl Hedrick. Cartoon Clip: "Playful Pluto" (1934), Walt Disney Productions. Sound: Harry Mills, Walter Oberst. Musical Direction: Sigmund Krumgold. Musical Score: Leo Shuken, Charles Bradshaw. Costumes: Edith Head. Make-up: Wally Westmore. Production and Distribution: Paramount. Release Date: January 1942. Running Time: 90 minutes.

John L. Sullivan	Joel McCrea
The Girl	Veronica Lake
Mr. LeBrand	Robert Warwick
Mr. Jones	William Demarest
Mr. Casalsis	Franklin Pangborn
Mr. Hadrian	Porter Hall
Mr. Valdelle	Bryon Foulger
Secretary	Margaret Hayes
Butler	Robert Greig
Valet	Eric Blore
Doctor	Torben Meyer
The Mister	Al Bridge
Miz Zeffie	Esther Howard
Ursula	Almira Sessions
Chauffeur	Frank Moran
Bum	Georges Renevant
Cameraman	Vic Potel
Radioman	Richard Webb
Chef	Charles Moore
Trustee	Jimmy Conlin
Labor	Jimmie Dundee
Capital	Chick Collins
Mr. Carson	Harry Hayden
Counterman (Owl Wagon)	Roscoe Ates
Preacher	Arthur Hoyt
One-Legged Man	Robert Dudley
Sheriff	Dewey Robinson
Colored Preacher	Jess Lee Brooks
Public Defender	Julius Tannen
Man at Railroad Shack	Emory Parnell
Cop	Edgar Dearing
Woman (Poor Street)	Esther Michelson
Old Bum	Chester Conklin
Railroad Clerk	Howard Mitchell
The Trombenick	Harry Rosenthal
Mrs. Sullivan	Jan Buckingham
Counterman (Roadside)	Pat West
Desk Sergeant	J. Farrell MacDonald
Yard Man	Perc Launders
Dear Joseph	Paul Jones
Director	Preston Sturges

Safeguarding Military Information (1941, film)

Produced by the Research Council of the Academy of Motion Picture Arts and Sciences; Darryl F. Zanuck, Chairman. Screenplay: Preston Sturges. Studio: Paramount. Release Date: August 1942. Running Time: 9 minutes.

The Palm Beach Story (1942, film)

Associate Producer: Paul Jones. Director: Preston Sturges. Assistant Director: Hal Walker. Screenplay: Preston Sturges. Photography: Victor Milner. Editor: Stuart Gilmore. Art Director: Hans Dreier. Associate: Ernst Fegte. Sound: Harry Lindgren, Walter Oberst. Musical Score: Victor Young. Gowns: Irene. Make-up: Wally Westmore. Production and Distribution: Paramount. Release Date: December 1942. Running Time: 88 minutes.

Gerry Jeffers	Claudette Colbert
Tom Jeffers	Joel McCrea
Princess	Mary Astor
John D. Hackensacker III	Rudy Vallee
Toto	Sig Arno
Mr. Hinch	Robert Warwick
Mr. Osmond	Arthur Stuart Hull
Dr. Kluck	Torben Meyer
Mr. Asweld	Jimmy Conlin
Mr. McKeewie	Vic Potel
Wienie King	Robert Dudley
Manager	Franklin Pangborn·
Pullman Conductor	Arthur Hoyt
Conductor	Al Bridge
Colored Bartender	Snowflake
Colored Porter	Charles Moore
Brakeman	Frank Moran
Orchestra Leader	Harry Rosenthal
Wife of Wienie King	Esther Howard
Ale & Quail Club	William Demarest, Jack Norton, Robert Greig, Roscoe Ates, Dewey Robinson, Chester Conklin, Sheldon Jett
Prospect	Harry Hayden
Nearsighted Woman	Esther Michelson
Officer in Penn Station	Edward J. McNamara
Waiter in Diner	Mantan Moreland
Proprietor of Store	Julius Tannen
Jewlery Salesman	Byron Foulger
Taxi Driver	Frank Faylen
O'Donnell	J. Farrell MacDonald

The Great Moment (1942, film)

Producer and Director: Preston Sturges. Assistant Director: Edmund Bernoudy. Based upon the book *Triumph over Pain* by René Fülöp-Miller. Screenplay: Preston Sturges. Photography: Victor Milner. Editor: Stuart Gilmore. Art Director: Hans Dreier. Associate: Ernst Fegte. Set Decoration: Stephen Seymour. Sound: Harry Lindgren, Walter Oberst. Musical Score: Victor Young. Make-up: Wally Westmore. Production and Distribution: Paramount. Release Date: November 1944. Running Time: 83 minutes.

W. T. G. Morton	Joel McCrea
Elizabeth Morton	Betty Field
Professor Warren	Harry Carey
Eben Frost	William Demarest
Dr. Horace Wells	Louis Jean Heydt
Dr. Jackson	Julius Tannen
Vice-President of Medical Society	Edwin Maxwell
President Pierce	Porter Hall
Dr. Heywood	Franklin Pangborn
Homer Quinby	Grady Sutton
Betty Morton	Donivee Lee
Judge Shipman	Harry Hayden
Dr. Dahlmeyer	Torben Meyer
Dental Patient	Vic Potel
Senator Borland	Thurston Hall
Priest	J. Farrell MacDonald
Mr. Abbot	Robert Frandsen
Morton's Butler	Robert Greig
Mr. Chamberlain	Harry Rosenthal
Porter	Frank Moran
Cashier	Robert Dudley
Colonel Lawson	Dewey Robinson
Mr. Stone	Al Bridge
Mrs. Whitman	Georgia Caine
Sign Painter	Roscoe Ates
Mr. Gruber	Emory Parnell
Mr. Whitman	Arthur Stuart Hull
Frightened Patient	Chester Conklin
Streetwalker	Esther Howard
Receptionist	Byron Foulger
Patient	Esther Michelson
Mr. Burnett	Jimmy Conlin
Presidential Secretary	Arthur Hoyt
Whackpot	Sig Arno
Little Boy	Donnie Kerr
Morton's Little Boy	Billy Sheffield

Morton's Little Girl	Janet Chapman
Morton's Little Girl (Older)	Tricia Moore

I Married a Witch (1942, film)

Producer: Preston Sturges. Director: René Clair. Assistant Director: Art Black. Based upon the novel *The Passionate Witch* by Thorne Smith, completed by Norman Matson. Screenplay: Robert Pirosh, Marc Connelly (Uncredited: Dalton Trumbo). Photography: Ted Tetzlaff. Special Effects Photography: Gordon Jennings. Editor: Eda Warren. Art Director: Hans Dreier. Associate: Ernst Fegte. Set Decoration: George Sawley. Sound: Harry Mills, Richard Olson. Musical Score: Roy Webb. Costumes: Edith Head. Make-up: Wally Westmore. Studio: Paramount. Production: Paramount. Distribution: United Artists. Release Date: November 1942. Running Time: 76 minutes.

Wallace Wooley	Fredric March
Jennifer	Veronica Lake
Dr. Dudley White	Robert Benchley
Estelle Masterson	Susan Hayward
Daniel	Cecil Kellaway
Margaret	Elizabeth Patterson
J. B. Masterson	Robert Warwick
Tabitha	Eily Malyon
Town Crier	Robert Greig
Vocalist	Helen St. Rayner
Justice of the Peace	Aldrich Bowker
Wife	Emma Dunn
Martha	Viola Moore
Nancy	Mary Field
Harriet	Nora Cecil
Allen	Emory Parnell
Rufus	Charles Moore
Prison Guard	Al Bridge
Guest	Arthur Stuart Hull
Bartender	Chester Conklin
Young Man	Reed Hadley

Star Spangled Rhythm (1942, film)

Associate Producer: Joe Sistrom. Director: George Marshall. Assistant Director: Art Black. Screenplay: Harry Tugend (Uncredited: Arthur Phillips). Sketches: George Kaufman, Arthur Ross and Fred Saidy, Melvin Frank and Norman Panama. Photography: Leo Tover, Theodore Sparkuhl. Editor: Paul Weatherwax. Art Director: Hans Dreier. Associate: Ernst Fegte. Musical Direction: Robert Emmet

Dolan. Make-up: Wally Westmore. Production and Distribution: Paramount. Release Date: December 1942. Running Time: 99 minutes.

Pop Webster	Victor Moore
Polly Judson	Betty Hutton
Jimmy Webster	Eddie Bracken
B. G. DeSoto	Walter Abel
Sarah	Anne Revere
Mimi	Cass Daley
Hi-Pockets	Gil Lamb
Mr. Freemont	Edward Fielding
Mac	Edgar Dearing
Duffy	William Haade
Sailor	Maynard Holmes
Sailor	James Millican
Tommy	Eddie Johnson

with Bing Crosby, Bob Hope, Fred MacMurray, Franchot Tone, Ray Milland, Dorothy Lamour, Paulette Goddard, Vera Zorina, Mary Martin, Dick Powell, Veronica Lake, Alan Ladd, Eddie "Rochester" Anderson, William Bendix, Susan Hayward, Jerry Colonna, Macdonald Carey, Marjorie Reynolds, Betty Rhodes, Dona Drake, Lynne Overman, Gary Crosby, Johnnie Johnston, Ernest Truex, Arthur Treacher, Sterling Holloway, Cecil B. DeMille, Preston Sturges, Ralph Murphy, Walter Catlett, Katherine Dunham, Walter Dare Wahl and Company, the Golden Gate Quartette, Slim and Sam.

The Miracle of Morgan's Creek (1942, film)

Producer and Director: Preston Sturges. Assistant Director: Edmund Bernoudy. Screenplay: Preston Sturges. Photography: John F. Seitz. Editor: Stuart Gilmore. Art Director: Hans Dreier. Associate: Ernst Fegte. Set Decoration: Stephen Seymour. Sound: Hugo Grenzbach, Walter Oberst. Musical Score: Leo Shuken, Charles Bradshaw. Song: "The Bell in the Bay" by Preston Sturges. Costumes: Edith Head. Make-up: Wally Westmore. Production and Distribution: Paramount. Release Date: January 1944. Running Time: 99 minutes.

Norval Jones	Eddie Bracken
Trudy Kockenlocker	Betty Hutton
Emmy Kockenlocker	Diana Lynn
Constable Kockenlocker	William Demarest
Justice of the Peace	Porter Hall
Mr. Tuerck	Emory Parnell
Mr. Johnson	Al Bridge
Mr. Rafferty	Julius Tannen
Newspaper Editor	Vic Potel

Governor McGinty	Brian Donlevy
The Boss	Akim Tamiroff
Wife of Justice of the Peace	Almira Sessions
Sally	Esther Howard
Sheriff	J. Farrell MacDonald
First MP	Frank Moran
Cecilia	Connie Tompkins
Mrs. Johnson	Georgia Caine
Doctor	Torben Meyer
U.S. Marshall	George Melford
The Mayor	Jimmy Conlin
Mr. Schwartz	Harry Rosenthal
Pete	Chester Conklin
McGinty's Secretary	Byron Foulger
McGinty's Secretary	Arthur Hoyt
Man	Robert Dudley
Man Opening Champagne	Jack Norton
Hitler	Bobby Watson
Mussolini	Joe Devlin
Nurse	Jan Buckingham
Head Nurse	Nora Cecil
Nurse	Judith Lowry
Soldier	Freddie Steele

Hail the Conquering Hero (1943, film)

Producer and Director: Preston Sturges. Assistant Director: Harvey Foster. Screenplay: Preston Sturges. Photography: John F. Seitz. Editor: Stuart Gilmore. Art Director: Hans Dreier. Associate: Haldane Douglas. Set Decoration: Stephen Seymour. Sound: Wallace Nogle. Musical Direction: Sigmund Krumgold. Musical Score: Werner Heymann. Song: "Home to the Arms of Mother" by Preston Sturges. Make-up: Wally Westmore. Production and Distribution: Paramount. Release Date: August 1944. Running Time: 101 minutes.

Woodrow Truesmith	Eddie Bracken
Libby	Ella Raines
Sergeant	William Demarest
Forrest Noble	Bill Edwards
Mayor Noble	Raymond Walburn
Corporal	Jimmy Dundee
Mrs. Truesmith	Georgia Caine
Political Boss	Al Bridge
Jonesy	James Damore
Bugsy	Freddie Steele
Bill	Stephen Gregory

Juke	Len Hendry
Mrs. Noble	Esther Howard
Libby's Aunt	Elizabeth Patterson
Judge Dennis	Jimmy Conlin
Reverend Upperman	Arthur Hoyt
Dr. Bissell	Harry Hayden
Chairman of Committee	Franklin Pangborn
Progressive Band Leader	Vic Potel
Mr. Schultz	Torben Meyer
Regular Band Leader	Jack Norton
Western Union Man	Chester Conklin
Officer	Robert Warwick
Conductor	Dewey Robinson
Porter	Charles Moore

With Julie Gibson and the Guardsmen

The Sin of Harold Diddlebock (1946, film)

Producer and Director: Preston Sturges. Assistant Director: Barton Adams. Screenplay: Preston Sturges. Technical Director: Curtis Courant. Photography: Robert Pittack. Special Effects Photography: John P. Fulton. Editor: Thomas Neff. Art Director: Robert Usher. Set Decoration: Victor A. Gangelin. Film Clip: *The Freshman* (1925), Pathé. Sound: Fred Lau. Musical Score: Werner Heymann. Love Theme by Harry Rosenthal. Make-up: Ted Larsen (Uncredited: Wally Westmore). Studio: Samuel Goldwyn. Production: California Pictures. Distribution: United Artists. Release Date: February 1947. Running Time: 91 minutes.

Harold Diddlebock	Harold Lloyd
Miss Otis	Frances Ramsden
Wormy	Jimmy Conlin
E. J. Waggleberry	Raymond Walburn
Bartender	Edgar Kennedy
Manicurist	Arline Judge
Formfit Franklin	Franklin Pangborn
Banker	Rudy Vallee
Max	Lionel Stander
Barber	Torben Meyer
Harold's Sister	Margaret Hamilton
Circus Manager	Al Bridge
Mike	Frank Moran
Coachman	Robert Greig
Professor Potelle	Vic Potel
Bearded Lady	Georgia Caine
Banker	Robert Dudley
James Smoke	Jack Norton

Banker Blackston   Arthur Hoyt
Snake Charmer   Gladys Forrest
Doorman   Max Wagner
With Jackie, the lion

Vendetta (1946, film)

Producer: Howard Hughes (Uncredited: Preston Sturges). Director: Mel Ferrer (Uncredited: Max Ophüls, Preston Sturges, Stuart Heisler, Howard Hughes). Assistant Director: Edward Mull. Based upon the novel *Colomba* by Prosper Mérimée. Adaptation: Peter O'Crotty. Screenplay: W. R. Burnett (Uncredited: Preston Sturges). Photography: Franz Planer, Al Gilks. Editor: Stuart Gilmore. Art Director: Robert Usher. Sound: William Fox, Vinton Vernon. Musical Direction: C. Bakaleinikoff. Musical Score: Roy Webb. Including selections from *Tosca* and *La Bohème* by Puccini, and "Torna a Sorrento" by Di Curtis. Aria from *Tosca* sung by Richard Tucker. Make-up: Norbert Miles. Studio: Samuel Goldwyn. Production: California Pictures/Hughes Productions. Distribution: RKO-Radio. Release Date: December 1950. Running Time: 84 minutes.

Colomba Della Rabbia   Faith Domergue
Orso Della Rabbia   George Dolenz
Lydia Nevil   Hillary Brooke
Sir Thomas Nevil   Nigel Bruce
Padrino   Donald Buka
Mayor Barracini   Joseph Calleia
Brando   Hugh Haas
Prefect   Robert Warwick

Unfaithfully Yours (1948, film)

Producer and Director: Preston Sturges. Assistant Director: Gaston Glass. Screenplay: Preston Sturges. Photography: Victor Milner. Special Effects Photography: Fred Sersen. Editor: Robert Fritch. Art Director: Lyle Wheeler. Associate: Joseph C. Wright. Set Decoration: Thomas Little, Paul S. Fox. Sound: Arthur L. Kirbach, Roger Heman. Musical Direction: Alfred Newman. Music: Gioacchino Rossini, Richard Wagner, Peter Ilyitch Tchaikovsky. Costumes: Bonnie Cashin. Make-up: Ben Nye. Production and Distribution: 20th Century-Fox. Release Date: November 1948. Running Time: 105 minutes.

Sir Alfred de Carter   Rex Harrison
Daphne de Carter   Linda Darnell
Barbara   Barbara Lawrence
August   Rudy Vallee
Anthony   Kurt Kreuger
Hugo   Lionel Stander

Sweeney	Edgar Kennedy
House Detective	Al Bridge
Tailor	Julius Tannen
Dr. Schultz	Torben Meyer
Jules	Robert Greig
Dowager	Georgia Caine
Telephone Operator	Isabel Jewell
Telephone Operator	Marion Marshall
Doorman	J. Farrell MacDonald
Fire Chief	Frank Moran

The Beautiful Blonde from Bashful Bend (1948, film)

Producer and Director: Preston Sturges. Assistant Director: William Eckhardt. Based upon a story by Earl Felton. Screenplay: Preston Sturges. Photography: Harry Jackson (Technicolor). Technicolor Consultants: Natalie Kalmus, Leonard Doss. Special Effects Photography: Fred Sersen. Editor: Robert Fritch. Art Director: Lyle Wheeler. Associate: George W. Davis. Set Decoration: Thomas Little, Stuart Reiss. Sound: Eugene Grossman, Harry M. Leonard. Musical Direction: Alfred Newman. Musical Score: Cyril Mockridge. Costumes: Rene Hubert. Make-up: Ben Nye. Production and Distribution: 20th Century-Fox. Release Date: May 1949. Running Time: 79 minutes.

Freddie	Betty Grable
Blackie	Cesar Romero
Charles Hingleman	Rudy Vallee
Conchita	Olga San Juan
Basserman Boy	Sterling Holloway
Doctor	Hugh Herbert
Mr. Jorgensen	El Brendel
Judge O'Toole	Porter Hall
Roulette	Pati Behrs
Mrs. O'Toole	Margaret Hamilton
Basserman Boy	Danny Jackson
Mr. Hingleman	Emory Parnell
Sheriff	Al Bridge
Joe	Chris-Pin Martin
Sheriff Sweetzer	J. Farrell MacDonald
Mr. Basserman	Richard Hale
Mrs. Hingleman	Georgia Caine
Mrs. Smidlap	Esther Howard
Conductor	Harry Hayden
Messenger Boy	Chester Conklin
Freddie (Age 6)	Mary Monica MacDonald

504

Dr. Schultz	Torben Meyer
Bartender	Dewey Robinson
Dr. Smidlap	Richard Kean
Grandpa	Russell Simpson
French Floozy	Marie Windsor

Make A Wish (1951, play)

Book: Preston Sturges (Uncredited: Abe Burrows). Based upon the play *The Good Fairy* by Ferenc Molnar. Music and Lyrics: Hugh Martin. Producers: Harry Rigby, Jule Styne, Alexander H. Cohen. Director: John C. Wilson. Dances and Musical Ensembles: Gower Champion. Settings and Costumes: Raoul Pene Du Bois. Theatre: Winter Garden, New York. Opening: April 18, 1951. Number of Performances: 103.

Dr. Didier	Eda Heinemann
Dr. Francel	Phil Leeds
Janette	Nanette Fabray
Ricky	Harold Lang
Poupette	Helen Gallagher
Policeman	Howard Wendell
Marius Frigo	Melville Cooper
Paul Dumont	Stephen Douglass
The Madam	Mary Finney
Felix Labiche	Le Roi Operti
Sales Manager	Howard Wendell

Carnival in Flanders (1953, play)

Book: Preston Sturges (Uncredited: George Oppenheimer, Herbert Fields). Based upon the screenplay *La Kermesse héroïque* by Charles Spaak, Jacques Feyder, Bernard Zimmer. Music: James Van Heusen. Lyrics: Johnny Burke. Producers: Paula Stone, Mike Sloane, Johnny Burke, James Van Heusen. Director: Preston Sturges (Uncredited: Bretaigne Windust). Special Ballet and Musical Numbers: Helen Tamiris (Uncredited: Jack Cole). Settings: Oliver Smith. Costumes: Lucinda Ballard. Theatre: Century, New York. Opening: September 8, 1953. Number of Performances: 6.

Siska	Pat Stanley
Jan Breughel	Kevin Scott
Tailor	Paul Reed
Butcher	Paul Lipson
Barber	Bobby Vail
Innkeeper	Lee Goodman

Mayor	Roy Roberts
Cornelia	Dolores Gray
Martha	Dolores Kempner
Courier	Matt Mattox
Three Mourning Women	Sandra Devlin
	Julie Marlow
	Lorna Del Maestro
1st Officer	Ray Mason
2nd Officer	George Martin
3rd Officer	Jimmy Alex
Duke	John Raitt
1st Citizen	Wesley Swails
2nd Citizen	Norman Weise
Lisa	Jean Bradley
Katherine	Undine Forrest
Orderly	William Noble

Letters from My Windmill (1954, film)

Producer: Jean Martinelli. Director: Marcel Pagnol. Based upon the stories "The Three Low Masses," "The Elixir of Father Gaucher," and "The Secret of Master Cornille" by Alphonse Daudet. Screenplay: Marcel Pagnol. English Subtitles: Preston Sturges. Photography: Willy Faktorovitch. Editor: Monique Lacombe. Art Director: Robert Giordani. Associate: Jean Mandaroux. Sound: Marcel Royné. Musical Score: Henri Tomasi. Make-up: Paul Ralph. Studio: Marseille Studio. Production: Mediterranean Film Company. Distribution: Tohan Pictures. Release Date: December 1955. Running Time: 120 minutes.

"The Three Low Masses"
Dom Balaguere	Henri Vilbert
Garrigou/The Devil	Daxely
The Old Woman	Yvonne Gamy
The Marquis	Keller
The Chef	René Sarvil

"The Elixir of Father Gaucher"
Father Gaucher	Rellys
The Abbot	Robert Vattier
Father Sylvestre	Christian Lude
M. Charnigue, apothecary	Fernand Sardou

"The Secret of Master Cornille"
Master Cornille	Edouard Delmont
Alphonse Daudet	Roger Crouset
Vivette	Pierrette Bruno

Les Carnets du Major Thompson;
The French They Are a Funny Race (1955, film)

Producers: Alain Poire, Paul Wagner. Director: Preston Sturges. Assistant Directors: Pierre Kast, Francis Caillaud. Based upon the book *The Notebooks of Major Thompson* by Pierre Daninos. Screenplay: Preston Sturges. Photography: Maurice Barry, Christian Matras, Jean Lallier. Editor: Raymond Lanny. Art Director: Serge Pimenoff. Associates: Robert André, Robert Guisgand, Claude Moesching. Sound: Jene Rieul. Musical Score: Georges Van Parys. Costumes: Suzanne Revillard (Pinoteau). Make-up: Jean-Jacques Chanteau, Alexandre S. Ranesky, Maguy Vernadet. Studio: Paris-Studios-Cinéma Billancourt. Production: S. N. E. Gaumont-Paul Wagner. Distribution: Gaumont (France); Continental Distributing (U.S.A.). Release Date: December 1955 (France); May 1957 (U.S.A.). Running Time: 105 minutes (France); 82 minutes (U.S.A.).

Major Thompson	Jack Buchanan
Martine Thompson	Martine Carol
M. Taupin	Noël-Noël
Miss Ffyth	Totti Truman Taylor
Ursula	Catherine Boyl
M. Fusillard	André Luguet
Mlle. Sylvette	Genevieve Brunet

Paris Holiday (1957, film)

Producer: Bob Hope. Associate Producer: Cecil Foster Kemp. Director: Gerd Oswald. Assistant Director: Paul Feyder. Based upon a story by Bob Hope. Screenplay: Edmund Beloin, Dean Riesner. Photography: Roger Hubert (Technicolor, Technirama). Editor: Ellsworth Hoagland. Sound: Frances Scheid, Robert Biart. Musical Score: Joseph J. Lilley. Costumes: Pierre Balmain. Production: Tolda Productions. Distribution: United Artists. Release Date: May 1958. Running Time: 100 minutes.

Robert Leslie Hunter	Bob Hope
Fernydel	Fernandel
Zara	Anita Ekberg
Ann McCall	Martha Hyer
American Ambassador	Andre Morell
Serge Vitry	Preston Sturges
Judge	Jean Murat
Doctor Bernais	Maurice Teynac
Shipboard Lovely	Irene Tunc
Golfer Patient	Roger Treville
Inspector Dupont	Yves Brainville

A Cup of Coffee (1988, play)

Author: Preston Sturges. Producer: SoHo Rep. Director: Larry Carpenter. Settings: Mark Wendland. Costumes: Martha Hally. Theatre: Greenwich House, New York. Opening: March 25, 1988. Number of Performances: 16.

Julius Smith	Willie Carpenter
Lomax Whortleberry	Robin Chadwick
J. Bloodgood Baxter	Nesbitt Blaisdell
Oliver Baxter	Richard L. Browne
Tulip Jones	Ellen Mareneck
Ephraim Baxter	Gwyllum Evans
James MacDonald	Michael Heintzman
Postman, sign painter	
and Mr. Raskkmussen	Tom Bloom
Youth	George A. Tyger

SELECT BIBLIOGRAPHY

Agee, James. *Agee on Film: Volume 1.* New York: Grosset & Dunlap, 1941.

Astor, Mary. *A Life on Film.* New York: Dell Publishing Company, 1967.

Axel, Madsem. *William Wyler: The Authorized Biography.* New York: Crowell, 1973.

Bartlett, Donald, and James B. Steele. *Empire: The Life, Legend, and Madness of Howard Hughes.* New York: Norton, 1979.

Bazin, André. *The Cinema of Cruelty: From Buñuel to Hitchcock.* New York: Seaver Books, 1982.

Bergman, Andrew. *We're in the Money: Depression America and Its Films.* New York: New York University, 1971.

Bermel, Albert. *Farce.* New York: Simon and Schuster, 1982.

Blair, Fredrika. *Isadora.* New York: McGraw-Hill Book Company, 1986.

Bode, Carl. *Mencken.* Carbondale: Southern Illinois University Press, 1969.

Busch, Noel. "Preston Sturges." *Life,* 1 January 1946.

Capra, Frank. *The Name above the Title: An Autobiography.* New York: The Macmillan Company, 1971.

Chase, Chris. *How to Be a Movie Star or a Terrible Beauty Is Born.* New York: Harper and Row, 1968.

Cook, Pam, ed. *The Cinema Book.* New York: Pantheon, 1985.

Curtis, James. *Between Flops.* New York: Harcourt Brace Jovanovich, 1982.

Dardis, Tom. *Harold Lloyd: The Man on the Clock.* New York: Viking Press, 1983.

Desti, Mary. *The Untold Story: The Life of Isadora Duncan, 1921–1927.* New York: Horace Liveright, 1929.

Duncan, Irma. *Duncan Dancer.* Salem, N.H.: Arno Press, 1980.

Duncan, Isadora. *My Life.* New York: Horace Liveright, 1927.

Farber, Manny (with W.S. Poster). "Preston Sturges: Success in the Movies" (1954 essay). In *Negative Space: Manny Farber on the Movies.* New York: Praeger, 1971.

Fiedler, Leslie. *An End to Innocence.* Boston: The Beacon Press, 1948.

Franklin, Benjamin. *The Autobiography and Other Writings.* New York: New American Library, 1961.

Friedrich, Otto. *City of Nets.* New York: Harper & Row Publishers, 1987.

Gomery, Douglas. *The Hollywood Studio System*. New York: St. Martin's Press, 1986.

Graham, Sheila. *The Garden of Allah*. New York: Crown Publishers, 1970.

Gussow, Mel. *Don't Say Yes Until I Finish Talking: A Biography of Darryl F. Zanuck*. Garden City, N.Y.: Doubleday and Company, 1971.

Harrison, Rex. *Rex*. New York: Dell Publishing Company, 1974.

Harvey, James. *Romantic Comedy*. New York: Alfred A. Knopf, 1987.

Haskell, Molly. *From Reverence to Rape*. New York: Holt, Rinehart, and Winston, 1973.

Hecht, Ben. *A Child of the Century*. New York: The New American Library, 1954.

Henderson, Brian, ed. *Five Screenplays by Preston Sturges*. Berkeley: University of California Press, 1985.

Hoffman, Frederick J. *The 20's*. New York: Collier Books, 1962.

Holbrook, Stewart H. *The Age of the Moguls: The Story of the Robber Barons and the Great Tycoons*. Garden City, N.Y.: Doubleday, 1953.

Houseman, John. *Front and Center*. New York: Simon and Schuster, 1979.

———. *Run-through*. New York: Curtis Books, 1972.

Huston, John. *An Open Book*. New York: Alfred A. Knopf, 1980.

Johnston, Alva. "How to Become a Playwright." *Saturday Evening Post*, 8 March 1941 and 15 March 1941.

Krutch, Joseph Wood. *American Drama since 1918*. New York: George Braziller, Inc., 1957.

Lasky, Jesse L. *Whatever Happened to Hollywood?* New York: Funk and Wagnalls, 1973.

Lenburg, Jeff. *Peekaboo: The Story of Veronica Lake*. New York: St. Martin's Press, 1983.

Mast, Gerald. *The Comic Mind*. Chicago: University of Chicago Press, 1979.

Matthews, Brander. *A Study of the Drama*. Boston: Houghton Mifflin Co., 1910.

Mencken, H.L. *The Vintage Mencken*. New York: Vintage Books, 1955.

Morehouse, Ward. *Matinee Tomorrow: Fifty Years of Our Theater*. New York: Whittlesey House, 1949.

Polhemus, Robert M. *Comic Faith: The Great Tradition from Austen to Joyce*. Chicago: The University of Chicago Press, 1980.

Renoir, Jean. *My Life and My Films*. New York: Atheneum, 1974.

Rey, Marie Beynon. *Two Lifetimes in One: How Never To Be Tired: How How To Have Energy To Burn*. New York: The Bobbs-Merrill Company, 1940.

Sarris, Andrew. *Interviews with Film Directors*. New York: Avon, 1967.

Schickel, Richard. *D. W. Griffith: An American Life*. New York: Simon and Schuster, 1984.

Schulberg, Budd. *Moving Pictures: Memoirs of a Hollywood Prince*. New York: Stein and Day Publishers, 1982.

Schwartz, Nancy Lynn (completed by Sheila Schwartz). *The Hollywood Writers' Wars*. New York: Alfred A. Knopf, 1982.

Shattuck, Roger. *The Banquet Years*. New York: Vintage Books, 1955.

Spada, James. *Hepburn: Her Life in Pictures*. New York: Doubleday, 1984.

Spoto, Donald. *Madcap: The Life of Preston Sturges*. Boston: Little, Brown and Company, 1990.

Sturges, Sandy, ed. *Preston Sturges by Preston Sturges*. New York: Simon and Schuster, 1990.

Thomas, Tony. *Howard Hughes in Hollywood*. New York: Citadel Press, 1985.

Ursini, James. *Preston Sturges: An American Dreamer*. New York: Curtis Books, 1973.

Weinberg, Herman G. *The Lubitsch Touch*. New York: E. P. Dutton, 1968.

Wright, William. *Heiress: Marjorie Merriweather Post*. Washington D.C.: New Republic Books, 1978.

INDEX

Designer:	David Bullen
Compositor:	G & S Typesetters, Inc.
Text:	Janson Text
Display:	Walbaum
Printer:	Edwards Brothers, Inc.
Binder:	Edwards Brothers, Inc.